FRANK McLYNN

The Road Not Taken

How Britain Narrowly Missed a Revolution, 1381-1926

VINTAGE BOOKS
London

Published by Vintage 2013

2 4 6 8 10 9 7 5 3 1

First published in Great Britain in 2012 by The Bodley Head

Vintage
Random House, 20 Vauxhall Bridge Road,
London SW1V 2SA

www.vintage-books.co.uk

Addresses for companies within The Random House Group Limited can be found at: www.randomhouse.co.uk/offices.htm

The Random House Group Limited Reg. No. 954009

A CIP catalogue record for this book is available from the British Library

ISBN 9781844135240

The Random House Group Limited supports the Forest Stewardship Council® (FSC®), the leading international forest-certification organisation. Our books carrying the FSC label are printed on FSC®-certified paper. FSC is the only forest-certification scheme supported by the leading environmental organisations, including Greenpeace. Our paper procurement policy can be found at: www.randomhouse.co.uk/environment

Typeset in Dante MT by
Palimpsest Book Production Ltd, Falkirk, Scotland
Printed and bound by Clays Ltd, St Ives plc

To Lucy, with love

Contents

Illustrations

PREFACE

This is not a book aiming to provide a synoptic view of all rebellions in Britain, like David Hospool's *The English Rebel* (2009), or even one that sets out to identify the progressive or left-wing thread running through certain insurrections, as for instance in Edward Vallance's *A Radical History of Britain* (2009). The objective, rather, is to identify and zero in on those comparatively rare genuine 'revolutionary moments' in British (and especially English) history, defined as occasions when the possibility for overthrow of a regime and a drastic change of direction, politically, economically, socially, was present. These were the occasions when an anarchist's bomb, a bloody pogrom, or a volley fired from the gun of a frightened and panicky soldier might have ignited a general conflagration. For my purposes a revolution need not necessarily be in a leftward direction, provided it satisfies the criteria for monumental change. The book is primarily a work of synthesis and interpretation, with no claims to definitive solutions. If anyone is stimulated to provide more cogent reasons why this nation-state has avoided real revolution, I shall be delighted. Though based on a range of primary sources, *archival* research has been limited to the material in Chapters Eight and Nine, where I am a recognised authority. Perhaps I should add a word about 'where I am coming from', as our American cousins say. I am not a Marxist nor even a socialist, but I do have an instinctive sympathy for the underdog and this has informed my work; the villains tend to be members of the elite or their minions. I have tried to achieve empathy with those seeking to change things while sceptical long-term about the human capacity for far-reaching social amelioration. In the eras I am describing, the wretched of the earth genuinely were struggling for bread-and-butter survival. British society today with its generous welfare provisions, is very different, though inequality persists, and even hardship. There is relative deprivation, of course, but no one could seriously claim that today's citizens face the spectre of starvation and therefore have no choice but to pick up the cudgels or raise the barricades.

As with all my recent books, I must particularly acknowledge the invaluable help given me by my wife Pauline and my editor Will Sulkin.

Frank McLynn, Farnham, December 2011

INTRODUCTION

Revolution

The riots in England in 2011, perhaps even more than the Poll Tax riots of 1990 or the miners' strike of 1984, provoked much loose talk about the dangers of revolution and with some reason, for on this occasion civil disorder was accompanied by the near collapse of the world financial system. Nevertheless, unless any of the 'Big Four' banks were to collapse, which would mean that the apocalypse really was at hand, revolution in Great Britain remains a distant chimera. It is a matter of historical record that Britain has never experienced a true revolution, in the sense that the French Revolution of 1789–94 was 'true', with all the convulsions, confusions, chaos, terror and bloodshed that the term connotes. This proposition of 'no revolution' may surprise those who think of riots, rebellions, coups d'état or simply transfers of power within the elite as revolutionary acts. But real revolution is a very different animal (see Appendix). Political scientists would probably say that all the above phenomena represent struggle *within* the regime whereas revolution, properly so called, means struggle *about* the regime – the idea is to change the *whole* system not just irritating or irksome parts. Unfortunately the concept of 'regime change' has been sullied by recent attempts to rationalise US foreign policy, where 'change' usually means no more than the ousting of a hostile despot and his replacement with a friendly, pro-US one, paying lip-service to 'democracy'. Changing a regime should, in short, refer to root-and-branch transformation of the social structure, the economy and the political system. Astonishingly, such a process has never happened in British history.

True revolution is bound to involve violence for the very simple reason that no entrenched elite ever voluntarily surrenders its power. As President J. F. Kennedy, seeking reasons for the Cuban Revolution, said in 1962: 'Those who make peaceful revolution impossible will make violent revolution inevitable.' Revolutions also typically precipitate several waves of change and the French Revolution, involving five years of anarchy, upheaval and blood-letting, is probably the best-known such process, although all the 'great' revolutions – Russian, Chinese, Mexican, Cuban – have this feature. It hardly needs to be said, perhaps, that revolutions do not occur spontaneously, that they need leaders, ideologies and mass mobilisation. As Che Guevara memorably remarked: 'The revolution is not an apple that falls when it is ripe. You have to make it fall.' Essential preconditions are smugness, complacency, incompetence and resistance to change by an elite. Meanwhile the 'have nots' or the deprived (even if only relatively so) have to crack under the strain of enduring the unendurable. There has long been a debate in revolutionary theory between advocates of 'subjective conditions' (Lenin, Mao, Guevara) and 'objective conditions' (Marx, Engels, Stalin). The former, in a modern version of the old adage that faith can move mountains, assert that willpower is the prime factor in triggering revolution (this is usually referred to as voluntarism). The latter stress that premature revolution leads only to disaster, that the time must be right, the conditions propitious and the timing of the revolutionaries perfect; for such people the so-called 'revolutionary moment' is everything. Of course, and this is the point made repeatedly in the study that follows, the presence of these 'objective conditions' does not mean that a revolution will succeed. As Lenin stated, some would say in the teeth of his own experience: 'A revolution is impossible without a revolutionary situation; furthermore, not every revolutionary situation leads to revolution.' In our narrative we will present seven clear revolutionary situations which did not, in the end, lead to revolution. Whether this was because of inept revolutionary leadership, misperception of the conditions, sheer bad luck or contingency or whether, in some profound sense, there is something in the very nature of Britain that precludes revolution – all this it will be our task to discover.

Some who have written about revolutions, especially in the 1960s, have tended to romanticise revolution, but this is a serious error. Everyone who has studied revolutions must surely be depressed by the disappointing outcomes. Overwhelmingly, what is revealed is the collision between a priori ideologies, belief in the perfectibility of Man or at least the emergence of a 'new Man' and basic, stubborn and irreducible human nature. The other obvious point is that revolution is necessarily a voyage into the unknown and as such will throw up unintended consequences. This is what the short-lived German dramatist Georg Büchner had in mind when he said that revolutions, like Saturn (in Roman mythology), devour their own children and what Simon Bolivar meant when, after a lifetime of armed struggle, he remarked cynically at the end of his life: 'He who makes a revolution ploughs the sea.' The dispassionate observer is bound to conclude that the human sacrifice involved is not worth the small gains usually made. Marxists have sometimes been heard to say that one generation of the proletariat should sacrifice its short-term interests for the sake of future generations, but this seems self-evidently absurd. If we start from human nature, we are bound to pose the question posed by the cynic (exact identity and provenance disputed): 'What has posterity ever done for me?' And if the creation of the 'new Man' means killing millions of recalcitrants who refuse to adapt and to give up the old sins of venality, corruption, greed and selfishness, is not the revolution thereby confusing means and ends? One is reminded of the notorious American war criminal in the Vietman War who remarked: 'We had to destroy the village in order to save it.' All sober observers have been appalled by the huge loss of life occasioned by revolutions and the scant results achieved by so much bloodshed. Oddly enough, one of the most trenchant observations on this point comes in a movie. In Sergio Leone's *A Fistful of Dynamite*, set in the Mexican Revolution, the bandit Juan Miranda (played by Rod Steiger) is urged to join the Mexican Revolution and responds indignantly: 'The people who read the books go to the people who can't read the books, the poor people, and say, "We have to have a change." So the poor people make the change. And then the people who read the books, they all sit around the big polished tables, and they talk and talk and talk and eat and eat and eat. But what has happened to the poor people? THEY ARE DEAD!' Nevertheless, and this is the point made by Mark Twain (cited at the end of Chapter Three), elites cannot be absolved of blame for crass stupidity and blinkered resistance to change, for it is the sheer hopelessness of their position that leads the dispossessed to conclude that anything is preferable to the status quo and to launch into the unknown, regardless of consequences. Far worse than the myopia of revolutionaries and their disregard of human nature is the obscene complacency of elites in history when faced by grotesque inequality, the starvation of the wretched of the earth, and even the despised aspirations of the middle sectors of society. 'Let them eat cake' – the words attributed to Marie Antoinette – are apocryphal, yet the mind-set they connote has been depressingly evident throughout history.

I

The Origins of the Revolt of 1381

The Peasants' Revolt is the name usually given to the seismic events of 1381 but is actually a misnomer, since craftsmen, tradesmen and urban workers played a greater role in the rebellion than peasants properly so called. Nonetheless it was the first large-scale revolt from below against the feudal system and its overlords and beneficiaries. Contemporary witnesses and chroniclers of the event were all hostile to the rising and recoiled in horror as from satanic forces of chaos. For the learned monks of the time, the only historians available, the revolt was a monstrous attempt to subvert the principles of order which governed the universe; for them such an outburst of 'insanity' was like trying to reverse the fundamental laws of physics, such as gravitation. The chronicler Jean Froissart described it as like Lucifer rebelling against God, and it was he who first introduced the notion of 'envy' as the motivator of social discontent and rebellion, ushering in a mindset which is still with us, whereby a cant word is used to explain away all ills in society, and the responsibility for sin is taken away from the sinner and dumped instead on those who react to it.[1] The serious historian cannot be content with such simple-mindedness and must probe deeper in the quest for causality. It is customary nowadays to return in effect to Aristotle's hierarchy of causes[2] and to identify a trio of factors operating as the motors behind any significant historical event: preconditions, precipitants and triggers. Although this approach can be overdone and result in a rigid schematisation, the troika works particularly well in explicating the causes of the Peasants' Revolt. Accordingly, we can identify the Black Death as a precondition, the Hundred Years War as a precipitant and the Poll Tax of 1381 as a trigger.

The Black Death, described in hideous detail in Boccaccio's *Decameron*, was a pandemic that swept across the 'world-island' of Asia, Africa and Europe in the 1340s. Everything about it is still the subject of scholarly debate. Some say that it started in central Asia as a bacterium associated with the *bobak* species of marmot, was a species of bubonic plague, and reached the Crimea by 1346, whence it was carried by fleas nesting in black rats on merchant ships and spread to Europe.[3] It was devastating Western Europe by 1348 and invaded England in 1348–9. Yet there is increasing scepticism about bubonic plague as the referend of the Black Death, with some opting for Africa as the original starting point, and central Asia as the secondary host; the 'Africa first' view tends to identify the plague as a species of ebola.[4] From the unsatisfactory 'fit' between the historical evidence and the usual symptoms of bubonic plague, scholars have been tempted into speculation about other possible causes: N. F. Cantor, for instance, thought the Death might have been a combination of anthrax and other epidemics.[5] Still others opt for a 'perfect storm' – a bizarre one-off congruence of typhus, smallpox and pneumonic and bubonic plagues.[6] There is also a neo-Malthusian view entertained in some quarters, based on 'homeostasis' whereby Nature obeys a 'Malthusian limit', so that when population outstrips resources it finds ways to cut down on the surplus mouths.[7] However, there seems to be general agreement that central Asia was a major vector of the disease, with another of history's notorious unintended consequences manifesting itself. The Mongol conquests of the thirteenth century had created a 'Pax Mongolica' in Asia, from which developed a burgeoning silk trade, and it was the Silk Route that was the original vector of the Black Death as far as the Crimea.[8]

There is a closer consensus too about the mortality from the pandemic. All told, it reduced the world's population from an estimated 450 million in 1300 to 350–375 million in 1400. Between 25 and 50 million of the total 75 million deaths were in Europe, which bore the major impact of the Death. Europe lost 30–60 per cent of its people (most experts opt for a figure in the 45–50 per cent range) and it took 150 years to regain the lost ground. Mortality was particularly heavy in the Mediterranean countries (an estimated 75–80 per cent) and relatively low in Germany (20 per cent). 100,000 people died in Paris, while the population of Florence declined from 110–120,000 in 1338 to

50,000 in 1351.[9] The impact in England seems to have been about halfway between the experience of Germany and Italy. The generally agreed mortality rate is around 50 per cent, with urban areas predictably suffering more grievously than the countryside. England's population may have declined from around 4 million to little more than 2 million. Local studies confirm the picture: no more than one-third of the taxable population survived the pandemic, with Rochester in Kent, for example, losing half its inhabitants, while Essex lost at least 50 per cent.[10] Perhaps even worse, the disease became endemic, and there were further outbreaks in 1361–2, 1369, 1375, 1379–83 and 1389–93.[11] The rapid demographic change resulting from the plague was just one of the reasons why 'Peasants' Revolt' is a misnomer, for both town and countryside were hit by post-Black Death stresses, with the further implication that there can be no simple cut-off point between town and countryside or dichotomy between town and country.[12]

A catastrophically declining population produced a shortage of labour and thus, if the normal laws of supply and demand were allowed to work, rising costs of labour (wages). It was precisely this situation that the feudal elite of England was determined to prevent and the immediate result of the Black Death was the notorious Statute of Labourers of 1351. Work was made compulsory for all persons, male and female, under the age of sixty. All those who could be construed in any sense as 'labour' – i.e. not just peasants and agricultural labourers – were forbidden by law to charge pre-plague prices for their work or goods. This applied to a wide range of occupations: farmers, saddlers, tailors, fishmongers, brewers, bakers, carters, servants, carpenters, masons, roofers, thatchers, shoemakers, goldsmiths, blacksmiths, spurriers, tanners, plasterers, riverboatmen, as well as shepherds, ploughmen and swineherds.[13] The punishments ordained for evasion of the law were tough: three days in the stocks for first offenders and 300 per cent fines of the 'added value' or mark-up applied by shopkeepers; at the limit there was imprisonment for repeat offenders or recidivists.

Some authorities claim that by 1370 70 per cent of the business of the king's courts was tied up with trying to enforce this equivalent of the famous papal bull against the comet. 671 justices of the peace worked to enforce this statute alone.[14] Ever since the Emperor Diocletian attempted price-fixing in AD 303 it had been obvious that certain market forces simply could not be overcome, but the feudal lords persisted. Alarmed by the 'drift' in costs and prices even in the teeth of such a draconian law, the elite tried to hit back at the lower orders in other ways, such as the reissue of the sumptuary laws in 1363, forbidding the masses to wear clothing associated with aristocratic privilege. Villages hit back by claiming exemptions from feudal levies and duties, claiming Domesday Book as their authority. In 1376–7 more than 100 villages asked for a copy of this book so that they could formulate their demands – this was the so-called 'Great Rumour'.[15] Meanwhile in the economic sphere a dual system began to operate. Alongside the statutory prices and incomes policy there rose up a black economy, adding another dualism to the many divisions already existing in English society.[16]

Alongside the profound long-term causes of the 1381 revolt were political precipitants caused by the Hundred Years War (1337–1453) between England and France. The early years of the war, with the glorious victories at Crécy and Poitiers and the martial fame of the Black Prince, saw England carrying all before her. But by the end of the 1360s, and for twenty years thereafter, the advantage switched to France.

The Black Prince was a devotee of *chevauchée* – a scorched-earth policy designed to bring the enemy to a rapid battle, both to save its citizens and restore its credibility. *Chevauchée* had been the tactic used by William the Conqueror to lure Harold of England to a premature battle at Hastings in 1066 and was a staple tactic of the Spaniards in the wars of reconquest (*Reconquista*) from the Moors from the eleventh century on. The Black Prince was an expert in Spanish affairs – his last great victory was at Najera in the Iberian Peninsula in 1367 – so he knew all about *chevauchée*, and it recommended itself to him also as a way round the manpower shortages in his armies caused by the Black Death. But from 1369 until his death in 1376 the prince was in decline, crippled by the mysterious illness (cancer or multiple sclerosis?) that would carry him off at the age of forty-five.[17] The initiative shifted to France, where King Charles V found a warrior just as able as the Black Prince in the form of Bertrand du Guesclin, the so-called Eagle of Brittany. Trusting to Fabian tactics, Guesclin refused to be drawn by *chevauchée*. The only thing that prevented him from being a figure as famous as Joan of Arc was that he was not of noble birth. When the fastidious French aristocrats refused to serve under him, he recruited his own retinue.[18] His death in 1380 should have helped the English, but at that very moment a new menace appeared in the form of marauding Scots. In the 1380s Scotland was a permanent thorn in England's flesh, and this period of Caledonian dominance would culminate in victory at the Battle of Otterburn in 1388.

The 1370s saw many signal failures in France, especially the fiasco of an expedition commanded by Sir Robert Knolles in 1370.[19] The lamentable showing of English arms on the continent severely disillusioned the 'middling sectors' in society – the knights, merchants and townsmen whose alienation would have significant effects since they were represented in the House of Commons. Such was the military advantage held by France from 1369 on that the decade of the 1370s was one of constant invasion fears in England – fears which did not abate until around 1386. As if the military debacle was not enough, Parliament also had to deal with an onslaught from John of Gaunt. Scion of the house of Lancaster and third surviving son of Edward III, Gaunt was effectively *the* power in the land even before Edward's death in 1377, and even more thereafter when the ten-year-old Richard II succeeded to the throne. In an uncanny parallel with the Black Prince's malady, Edward III was from the early 1370s in the grip of dementia.[20] Both during these years and during Richard II's minority there was no effective king in England; the realm was ruled by a series of councils with full executive authority, but controlled by the most powerful man in the kingdom, and this meant John of Gaunt.

Tyrannical, capricious, corrupt, venal, devious, Gaunt was sworn to loyalty to Richard by the Black Prince on his deathbed and kept his word, even though there were many dark suspicions that he hankered for the crown himself. Already associated with military failure in France, Gaunt further increased his massive unpopularity by despotic dealings with Parliament and the City of London. The famous Good Parliament of April–July 1376, held while Edward III was still alive, seemed at first to be a check to his powers as it denounced corruption at court, secured the dismissal of many key Gaunt henchmen and imposed a new set of councillors ready to change policies when the infant Richard II succeeded.[21] But by intimidation and packing Parliament with his cronies, Gaunt struck back the next year. First he refused to admit the new councillors appointed by the Good Parliament and, in the Bad Parliament of 1377, revoked all the reforms of the year before.[22]

Next Gaunt proceeded to tighten the screws on the City of London, which had defied him by asserting its traditional rights and prerogatives. To show the burghers what they were dealing with, he unleashed one of his aristocratic thugs, Sir Ralph Ferrers. In 1378 this bravo burst into Westminster Abbey during Mass, violated sanctuary and killed a squire named Robert Hawley, who had taken refuge there. In the ensuing uproar Gaunt defiantly defended the indefensible and threw an armed guard around his protégé. Now in control of Parliament after the 'packing' in the Bad Parliament, at the parliamentary session in Gloucester in 1378 he forced the members to strip London fishmongers of their monopolies and had all rich merchants who opposed him ejected from their places and positions.[23] Paranoid rumours of a most lurid kind arose in London, to the effect that Gaunt was planning to move all international trade away from London and set up Southampton as a commercial rival. Londoners were already uneasy about the growing importance of Southampton in Italian, and particularly Genoese, trade.[24] When it was learned that the Genoese ambassaor in London, Janus Imperiali, was negotiating with Gaunt, supposedly over this very transfer of power, two assassins stabbed him to death in a London street (August 1378). The outraged Gaunt demanded that the two thugs (who were soon apprehended) should be arraigned for treason and that their trial should be held in Northampton, away from the influence of the London merchants who opposed him. The trial was delayed while Gaunt patched up an uneasy peace with the Scots, but in November 1380 he came south for the hearings. The two assassins pleaded guilty but conveniently implicated the three most powerful merchants who opposed Gaunt; consequently they lived with the shadow of treason over them.[25] It became clear that one of the two thugs, John Algor, had framed the merchants at Gaunt's bidding to save his own life. His accomplice John Kirkby was not so lucky. Condemned to a traitor's end, he suffered the awful barbarity of being hanged, drawn and quartered. Gaunt had shown the political elite in London, by naked aggression and blatant power, what they might expect from him.[26]

Socio-economic factors, the war in France and Gaunt's machinations were now to coalesce in spectacular fashion. The English military crisis in France reached an apogee in 1377, as French warships raided with impunity up and down the island coastline, further diminishing the credibility of Gaunt and his clique; some would even claim the impotence of England when faced with French privateers was one of the hidden triggers for the great revolt of 1381.[27] Tired of the fiscal burden of the Hundred Years War, the parliamentary classes decided to decant it onto the lower classes. Before 1377, in the so-called 'Lay Subsidy', the English Crown took one-fifteenth of each household's movable property in tax; land and capital were not subject to a levy. The catastrophic population decline as a result of the Black Death meant that the Lay Subsidy could no longer raise the huge sums necessary to pay for the war in France. It is significant and symptomatic of the mentality of the ruling elite that at no time did they consider simply cutting their losses and ending their war. Feudal notions of honour, to say nothing of the loss of the mouth-watering amounts of loot to be uplifted on French campaigns, ruled this out. With feudal lords still basking in the memory of Crécy, Poitiers, Sluys, Espagnols-sur-Mer and other 'glorious' exploits, they threw good money after bad and ordained heavier and heavier taxes to finance a losing game. Accordingly, for the first time ever in English history taxation was made universal. By the terms of the First Poll Tax of 1377 a levy of four pennies was taken from every man and woman over the age of fourteen, in an era when fourpence represented three days' wages for an agricultural labourer.[28] In this way the sum of £22,000 was raised, though it was not made clear whether the Poll Tax was to be a 'one-off' or whether it was to replace the Lay Subsidy permanently. There was violent antipathy to the new tax, not least because the worse-off members of society were being mulcted to support a war which benefited only the aristocrats, had produced no worthwhile results and was being waged incompetently. But at first there were only murmurings of protest. Encouraged by the lack of overt resistance, the Crown proposed a Second Poll Tax in 1379. This was an altogether more serious matter. Evidently poll taxes were here to stay. Although the explosion did not occur yet, it was clear to the perceptive that such a tax burden, added to the many existing grievances of the lower orders, heralded serious trouble. As Sir Charles Oman justly remarked of the Second Poll Tax: 'Its relation to the rebellion is merely the same as that of the greased cartridges to the Indian Mutiny of 1857.'[29]

The Second Poll Tax was supposed to raise far more than the first, as it replaced the former flat rate with a sliding scale in which seven classes were identified: landowners from dukes to esquires; knights of the crusading orders; lawyers; townsmen and merchants; notaries, legal apprentices, pardoners and 'common married men and women'; foreign merchants; and all religious. Despite the apparent hierarchy of status thus implied, the differential tax imposed outraged nearly everyone by its unfairness. It repeated the tax of fourpence for the humble layman and levied £6 13s 4d on dukes and archbishops, £4 on earls, £2 on barons and knights, £5 on judges and rich lawyers, £1 on merchants and 3s 4d on monks and priests.[30] Despite all this, the Second Poll Tax raised less than the First, bringing in just £18,600. It became apparent that opposition to the tax was stiffening, mainly taking the form of evasion or getting officials (by threats or bribery) to depress and undervalue assessments. The sum raised was soon gobbled up by the cost of the *chevauchée* still being mindlessly operated in France. Just how inadequate the tax was to finance the army can be gauged from one simple statistic: the bill for the army in France for the *first six months* of 1379 was over £50,000.[31] Further calamity came with the failure of a major expedition to France in 1380 under the 25-year-old Earl of Buckingham. Even while John of Gaunt was absent in Scotland, he had his agents call a new Parliament, which met in Northampton in November 1380. Simon Sudbury, Archbishop of Canterbury and Chancellor of England, addressed the assembly in an atmosphere of urgency, tension and crisis.[32] All were agreed that affairs had reached a dangerous pass. Sudbury told Parliament that the Crown was determined to rescue Buckingham by a new subvention, and to this end Richard II had already pledged most of the royal jewels as security for loans from merchants in the City of London. Further loans pledged against government funds were out of the question – it is not clear whether Sudbury told Parliament this was because Gaunt had reneged on a previous deal with the merchants. But Sudbury stressed that something had to be done quickly. The army needed reinforcement, the English coast was wide open to incursions by the Franco-Spanish fleets, and the wages of the English troops in Calais, Brest and Cherbourg were nine months in arrears. At this very juncture a revolt in the manufacturing towns of Flanders had cut off the main destination for the export of English wool. The wool industry collapsed, as did the revenues.[33] Sudbury ended his peroration by asking Parliament for the unprecedented sum of £160,000 – eight times the uplift on the 1379 tax.

The Commons initially responded that Sudbury's demands were preposterous and outrageous. Their exasperation would have been fuller had the disingenuous Sudbury revealed to them that he was working as Gaunt's agent, that part of the huge sum demanded was to finance an entirely new, but as yet clandestine expedition to Portugal. Ferocious lobbying scaled down Sudbury's demands and he agreed to a sum of £100,000. When it became clear that the government was in earnest about raising huge sums, the members immediately thought how they could best protect their own interests. The Northampton experience of November 1380 revealed a House of Lords cynically protecting the interests of the wealthy and a House of Commons cravenly buckpassing.[34] It was a low point in English history and one that deserves to be studied closely by those who parrot mindless bromides about the glories of the British constitution. The Parliament at Northampton proved spineless, self-serving and cowardly. Alternative taxes would have alleviated at least part of the crippling burden which the Commons now proposed to lay on the common man and woman. On the other hand, poundage would have hit the mercantile interest and tenths and fifteenths would have impacted on landowners, everyone from the great feudal lords to the merest householder. It was therefore decided to dun the masses and the clergy.[35] One-third of the £100,000 tax agreed would be raised from the clergy and two-thirds from the common people. Parliament resolved to impose another flat rate per capita tax of 1s 4d–1s 8d, i.e. four or five times the burden of the previous tax, and a sum representing two weeks of arduous toil for an agricultural labourer. The government appointed collectors for each county and sub-collectors for villages and towns, backed by the power of mayors, constables and bailiffs.[36] The complacent Parliamentarians seemed blithely unaware that they were on the edge of a precipice, and the only elite member to spot the obvious danger was England's treasurer Thomas Brantingham, Bishop of Exeter, who abruptly and prudently resigned. In an evil hour the ambitious Sir Robert Hales took his place, unaware that he was accepting a poisoned chalice. Sudbury, exulting in the power he had enjoyed only since February of that year, seemed to feel that Gaunt's patronage gave him all the protection he needed.[37]

The predictable response of the masses was tax evasion on a vast scale. The main tactic was for villages and rural communities to make false returns to the commissioners of taxes, largely through under-reporting the numbers of adults eligible to pay. A principal wheeze was not to count unmarried women (widows, aunts, sisters, young daughters, etc) on the grounds that, since they did not work for money, it was monstrously unjust to make them taxable. Roughly one-third of those liable to pay disappeared from the census rolls; it was as if a calamity as great as the Black Death had suddenly overtaken England. 458,720 men and women disappeared from sight. Whereas the First Poll Tax of 1377 had registered 1,355,201 souls, that of 1381 uncovered only 896,481. In general, the further away from London the locality, the greater the discrepancy between the 1377 and 1381 figures. In Bedfordshire numbers dropped by 27 per cent, in Norfolk by 25 per cent, in Kent by 22 per cent and in Berkshire by 31 per cent. Yet this was restraint itself alongside the figures recorded in the south-west and north-west of the country. Cornwall, for example, which had recorded 34,274 adult inhabitants in 1377, contained only 12,056 in 1381. Cumberland's figures declined from 11,481 to 4,748, Westmoreland's from 7,839 to 3,859 and Lancashire's from 23,880 to 8,371.[38] What had happened was that the tax collectors were bribed or coerced by, or in some cases simply colluded with, the communities they were investigating. Sir Robert Hales, who became treasurer on 1 February 1381, reacted with fury to the civil disobedience. Entirely new commissions of inquisition wielding draconian powers were sent into the countryside, backed by the armed force of royal serjeants-at-arms – little more than licensed thugs. They were told to concentrate initially on the counties of the south-east, on Somerset, Devon, Cornwall, Gloucestershire and Yorkshire. The rumour ran that these new commissioners could levy amounts in excess of the taxes due, as 'compensation' for people's previous mendacity, and that they could keep these sums for themselves.[39] The new commissioners were given secret instructions to use all means necessary to force the nation to comply with the tax demands. This was something of an 'open sesame' to the licentious militiamen, who immediately turned to sexual molestation as their preferred method of enforcement. In each village the young unmarried girls were lined up, publicly groped and threatened with 'virginity examinations' if their fathers did not pay the full amount due. The notorious collector John Legge and his henchmen were fond of lifting up girls' skirts in public (in an era when women wore no underwear), shaming the fuming parents into making a proper return and paying the appropriate taxes.[40]

It should not have been a surprise when the tolerance of the common people finally snapped. After all, peasants and artisans who had already been bullied by the general rules of feudal lordship, by the Statute of Labourers and the sumptuary laws, had first had an unjust and unprecedented tax imposed on them to promote an unpopular and pointless war and then, when they tried to evade the exactions, were visited by the likes of John Legge and his locusts. Yet the government was taken completely unawares. The fuse was lit in the village of Brentwood, Essex, on 30 May 1381. The royal commissioner Sir John Bampton was confronted by sullen villagers, who told him flatly that he would get no more money from them. When he ordered the 'malefactors' arrested, a hostile crowd forced his serjeants-at-arms to back off. Bampton's party fled to London in disarray, leaving the villagers slightly appalled at the easy victory they had won and apprehensive about the consequences.[41] At first they hid in the woods, fearing reprisals, but word soon reached them that other Essex villages had declared solidarity with them. Soon the royal commissioners were in full flight from the villages of Fobbing, Corringham and Stanford-le-Hope, and the trouble spread in the early days of June to Bocking, Coggeshall and Temple Cressing. Braintree, Dunmore, Ashen, Dedham, Little Henny and Gesingthorpe were other villages who supplied able-bodied men for a campaign of resistance. Although there is no evidence of a prior conspiracy, the Essex rebels acted with admirable speed and efficiency, both now and later.[42] All males who could bear arms were summoned to a rendezvous, where they organised themselves into military companies and took an oath to hunt down and target those royal officials, well known to them, who were a byword for corruption and injustice. The first leader of the Essex rebels to be clearly identified was one Thomas Baker of Fobbing, whose daughter was said to have been sexually molested by the tax inspectors.[43] Yet in retrospect it was perhaps no surprise that Essex took the lead in the rebellion. The spirit of disaffection was clearly there in the county's response to the Third Poll Tax. Despite their proximity to London, the inhabitants defiantly declared a head count everyone knew to be risible: their taxable population of more than 48,000 in 1377 had apparently shrunk in three years to 30,748.[44]

Within days six government men were dead, executed in the manner that would become the norm during the rising: beheading. The government was powerless to raise a posse and order it into Essex, for its normal source of manpower for such an expedition, Kent, was sucked into the rebellion within days. One version of the origins of the 1381 revolt was that in Essex the trigger was the royal commissions, while in Kent it was the corrupt officialdom of the royal courts that was to blame. A local magnate named Sir Simon Burley claimed a man named Robert Belling as his serf, but the claim was resisted by Belling and his associates. When the royal sergeants were called in where the local bailiffs feared to tread, the result was a general explosion.[45] Here the early ringleader was Abel Ker from the village of Erith, near Dartford. After summoning the villagers of Kent to a grand rendezvous, he sent his newly formed levies at first against the local abbot, who ruled the abbey of Lesnes and with whom Erith had a long-standing conflict; the luckless prelate was forced at axe-point to sign up to the rebellion.[46] Next Ker crossed the Thames to confer with the Essex rebels. He brought back with him a sizeable force of Essex men thirsting for action. Their first objective was confrontation with Sir Robert Belknap, Chief Justice of the Court of Common Pleas, a widely hated John of Gaunt protégé. Belknap arrived in Dartford on assize duty on 4 June, confident he could quell all disturbances, but the town rose against him, took him captive, and made him swear on the Bible that he would never appear in Kent again as a law-giver before releasing him. Before doing so, however, they forced him to divulge the names of the people who had informed him about the Brentwood incident on 30 May. Once he revealed the names, the rebels mercilessly tracked down three of them, beheaded them and stuck their heads on poles.[47] Almost overnight, and it seemed by magic, the Kent and Essex rebels seemed to have the south-east of England at their mercy. Whether by luck or judgement, they had times their rebellion brilliantly, when the government had little force with which to oppose them. The only army within the borders of England was on the frontier with Scotland under Gaunt, as he sought to hammer out an agreement with the turbulent Scots. Most of the king's best troops had already embarked (or were at Portsmouth waiting to do so) on yet another quixotic foreign campaign, this time to help the King of Portugal fight Spain.[48] In any case the military gap between so-called regular troops and the rebels was not large, since many of the insurgents had had fighting experience in France; this was yet another way in which the Hundred Years War interconnected with the Great Revolt of 1381.

For a while the rebellions in Essex and Kent followed different courses. In Essex Thomas Baker led his host in pursuit of the sheriffs, constables, royal manor stewards, justices of the peace and even retired commissioners on their 'most wanted' list: prominent names were those of Sir John Bampton, Walter Fitzwalter, Thomas Mandeville, William Berland, Geoffrey Dersham, Thomas Tyrell, Clement Spicer, Robert Rikeden and Sheriffs Sewale and Gildesburgh. It is said that most of these, and certainly Sewale, made little attempt to escape, but sat at home paralysed by fear, as if unable to comprehend the catastrophe that had overwhelmed them.[49] All these men were prominent Essex landowners. In Kent Abel Ker took his men to Rochester Castle to force the issue against Sir Simon Burley. This worthy had declared he was willing to recognise Belling's claim to be a free man rather than a villein provided he was given a 'severance payment' of £300 in silver – a demand way beyond Belling's means as Burley knew. The royal serjeants rode roughshod over the bailiffs at Gravesend, arrested Belling and confined him in Rochester Castle. This was accordingly a prime target for the Kent rebels. On paper this should have been an impossibly tough nut to crack for men who knew nothing of siege warfare; the fortress's walls were twelve inches thick and it had been the scene of ferocious resistance to King John in 1215, when he took it only after using trebuchets and Greek fire against the defenders.[50] Yet in a crisis the moral element is often more important than the material, and so it proved here. Worn down by remorseless psychological warfare, the constable of the castle, Sir John Newton, finally threw in his hand when the castle guards abandoned their posts. He surrendered the citadel and the rebels freed all prisoners. Froissart claims that Newton saved his life only by agreeing to join the rebels. The town of Rochester, maybe comprising around 3,500 souls at the time, joined the insurrection with avidity.[51]

Around the time of the 'siege' of Rochester, the rebels also swept through Maidstone and it was from this town that there hailed the greatest figure associated with the 1381 rising: Wat Tyler. Little is known about Tyler and virtually everything that is known is controversial. Around forty at the time of the revolt (a birth date of 4 January 1341 has been assigned to him), Tyler seems to have been a veteran of the French wars. Some say that on his return he had turned highwayman and emerged from a life of outlawry to be a leader of the wretched of the earth. All the evidence suggests both that he had the gift of oratory and considerable military experience. Certainly after the taking of Rochester Castle he emerges as the clear leader of both the Kent and Essex rebels.[52] Directing operations methodically, Tyler decided to 'mop up' in Kent before considering his next move. On 10 June parties of rebels converged on Cressing Temple, seat of the wealthy Knights Hospitallers, whose prior was the detested treasurer, Sir Robert Hales. The invaders sacked the manor, looted it, then pulled it to the ground and gutted it. They also broke into Sheriff Sewale's house, destroyed all the documents they could lay hands on and beat the sheriff up. The pattern was repeated in Essex, where John Ewall, escheator of the county, was captured in Coggeshall and murdered. Next day the Essex rebels were at Chelmsford, where more official records were burned.[53] The hostility to lawyers, government officials and their archives and records was noteworthy. Although much private settling of scores inevitably went on during the rebellion, it was never a simply mindless explosion of fury but visited its wrath on rational targets. There was a particular loathing of justices of the peace and commissioners of trailbaston, showing that the rebels' hatred was both locally and centrally directed: locally against the corruption of local justice by the power of feudal landowners, and centrally against the king's judges, who rode roughshod over the traditions and rights of local communities. Trailbaston – the quasi-judicial royal commission charged with seeking out high crimes such as homicide, rape, arson, extortion and conspiracy – was a particular grievance. Wat Tyler asserted, with reason, that much of the work of the trailbaston commissioners was simply a revenue-raising scam. As a penalty for 'conspiracy' they could order seizures of goods, but the said treason was defined in a most elastic way, essentially being whatever the commissioners said it was.[54]

Tyler's seizure of Canterbury on 10 June marked the point where the authority of central government effectively collapsed – it would not be restored until the end of the month. The rebels burst into the cathedral but, disciplined by Tyler, waited until Mass was over before forcing the monks to elect a new Archbishop of Canterbury. They declared Sudbury a traitor and announced that he would be beheaded when caught. Tyler made it clear that Sudbury was the target, not the Church in general, by sacking the archbishop's palace but leaving the monastic property alone. Mayors, bailiffs, officials and oligarchs were all forced to take an oath to 'King Richard and the true commons'. There was no resistance, and it was later alleged that the feudal aristocracy had uniformly displayed arrant cowardice during the crisis in early June.[55] Canterbury, a 'city' of about 7,000 inhabitants, was convulsed as the rebels went in search of further malefactors. Three 'traitors' were dragged out and beheaded and further victims were murdered at their posts, including John Tebbe, a former bailiff and member of parliament, who had served on one of the hated royal commissions, and John Tece, a manorial official and former bailiff. Another target on the rebels' list, William Medmenham, could not be traced, so they had to content themselves with vandalising his extensive properties. Houses of other 'villains' who had made themselves scarce were plundered and destroyed, notably those of Sir Richard de Hoo, Thomas Garmwenton and Sir Thomas Fog. As in Rochester, the townsfolk collaborated avidly with the rebels.[56] The day's triumph was crowned with the surrender of Canterbury Castle after an assault led by Tyler and Abel Ker. The Sheriff William Septvanz, a prime mover in the enforcement commission of May 1381 that sought to recover the unpaid Poll Tax, was forced to release all prisoners and handed over all documents and records, which were predictably consumed in a bonfire. Tyler then proceeded to ransack Septvanz's manor at Milton, again destroying all paperwork. Other unpopular oligarchs also suffered. Sir Nicolas Heryng's estate at Sheppey saw major depredations, with the loss of 2 oxen, 27 sheep, 482 wool hides and goods and chattels worth £24.[57] Late in the day royal heralds arrived to express the king's astonishment at such contumacy. Tyler replied with aplomb that the men of Kent and Essex had risen to save the king from the traitors who surrounded him. After an exchange of messages it was finally announced that Richard II had agreed to meet the rebels at Blackheath.[58]

Tyler now had to decide whether to march on London. The decision had to be based on numbers and the chances of success. How great were the rebel numbers and what was the number of 'loyalists' opposing them? Medieval chroniclers, as prone to exaggeration as ancient historians, claimed 50,000 rebels in Kent and 50,000 in Essex, making at least 100,000 in all. A more judicious estimate is around 10,000 men in arms – still a huge number for this era and certainly greater than anything the authorities could summon – of whom some 3,000 accompanied Tyler on his march to London.[59] Meanwhile the response of the Crown had been astonishingly tepid. Neither the gentry of the Home Counties nor the militia in London had been called up, and it has been pointed out that there was no competent military leader on the king's council at the time: John of Gaunt was in Scotland, Thomas Woodstock was in the Welsh marches and Edmund, Earl of Cambridge was on the high seas en route to Portugal, the recall of his expedition having arrived in Portsmouth just too late. There was therefore little military force Richard II could employ against the rebels in the short term, for Froissart's claim that there were 8,000 loyal armed men in London at the time was merest fantasy.[60] Tyler had his spies in London and was remarkably well informed about the situation in the capital; indeed, right at the start of the revolt two London butchers, Adam Atewell and Roger Harry, rode out to tell the rebels that they had thousands of sympathisers in the metropolis. The long feud between the City of London and John of Gaunt was fundamental, with the common people hating Gaunt as a tyrant and the City merchants detesting him as much for his meddling in London affairs as for his disastrous foreign policy. Within London there was further conflict, for only one-quarter of the population were full citizens with the right to vote, hold office or sit on juries. Lower-class Londoners had every reason to detest even the elite opposed to Gaunt, since these people in turn were guilty of corporate corruption, guild protectionism, monopolies and cartels.[61] There was thus a turbid stew in London that a clever politican could stir and, in the early stages of the revolt, Tyler was certainly that. The report that the king was willing to meet the rebels at Blackheath may have been one of Tyler's 'expedient exaggerations', but it certainly worked to convince the rank and file to follow their leader. Besides, if they were not to press on to London, what had been the point of the rising in the first place?

The rebels trekked out of Canterbury on the morning of Tuesday, 11 June and began arriving at Blackheath on the evening of the 12th. They passed through Maidstone (the earlier visit appears to have been a mere raid), releasing all prisoners from the jail. It is in the period 11–12 June that two other rebel leaders appear clearly at the side of Wat Tyler.[62] Released from Maidstone Jail was the well-known hell-fire preacher and rabble-rouser John Ball, an old enemy of Archbishop Sudbury. Ball and Sudbury had crossed swords many years before in York and Ball had been a thorn in the archbishop's side for twenty years and more. In the parlance of the time he was a 'hedge priest', that is, he was an itinerant preacher with no parish or living, hardly surprising since he had been excommunicated for his heresy. Froissart described him as 'crack brained', but to Froissart and the other chroniclers anyone who questioned the system of entrenched feudal privilege was by definition insane.[63] Ball's message was simple: Jesus Christ himself had told his followers to practise communism, which is why communal living and sharing wealth were the form of social organisation noted in the early chapters of the Acts of the Apostles before St Paul gained the upper hand and perverted the message of Jesus. St Francis and the early Franciscans were the only true inheritors of Christ's mantle but, sadly, the Franciscan order had also been transmogrified so as to accommodate man's sinfulness. In a word, Ball denounced the entire history of the Church, including such 'accretions' as the papacy, to say nothing of political bishops. As with Mussolini and the Italian Marxist Antonio Gramsci 550 years later, Sudbury decided that this was a voice that had to be permanently silenced and he prescribed a similar remedy: imprisonment for life. Ball has always fascinated historians, for his speeches and letters survive, enabling us to see into his mind in a way we cannot with Wat Tyler.[64] The other emergent leader in these days was Jack Straw, an altogether shadowy figure. It was at one time fashionable to argue that Straw and Tyler were one and the same, but this view has now been decisively refuted; the basis for the view was always highly circumstantial, resting as it did heavily on the unarguable fact that Chaucer, who lived through the Peasants' Revolt, mentioned Straw but not Tyler.[65] Since no reliable records were left by the rebels, we cannot know how the chain of command operated: whether Tyler, Straw and Ball formed a genuine triumvirate, whether Tyler was primus inter pares or indeed whether the decisions of the leaders had to be ratified by a rebel council or open meeting.

By the evening of 12 June Tyler's main force was at Blackheath, with vanguard patrols thrown out as far as Southwark and Lambeth. There were two very encouraging signs. From London came a host of sympathisers in boats, while the Essex contingents collaborated beautifully. After capturing Colchester, the Essex men performed the by now almost ritualistic ceremony of destroying court rolls and legal documents, adding a new refinement by coercing any landlords they could lay their hands on into signing new leases and charters. It was noticed that there was a higher level of general anti-religious feeling in Essex than in Kent, particularly evinced by the sack of Waltham Abbey and the consigning of all its records to the flames. From Colchester the Essex men moved on to London to effect a junction with Tyler. By the evening of 12 June they were at Blackheath, with the vanguard strung out in the fields around Mile End.[66] The paralysis at central government level in face of the rebels was matched by that in London. The mayor and his colleagues seem to have been frightened to call out the loyalists in the city, fearful that this would trigger a general uprising of the London proletariat in retaliation and even apprehensive of the reactions of the 'better sort'; the ruling clique on the council knew that there was a 'bitter and unscrupulous minority',[67] just waiting for a chance to unseat the incumbents. Three of the London aldermen indeed openly declared for Tyler and the rebels. One of them, John Horne, had an interview with Tyler that night and gave him secret encouragement.[68] That evening the rebels gave London a taste of what it might expect if it did not quickly come to heel. The Southwark houses of all jurors and questmongers (professional legal informers) who had done City marshal Richard Imworth's dirty work were raided. Imworth himself, also governor of Marshalsea Prison, fled at the approach of the rebels, who at once threw open the prison doors and released all the captives. The rebels then moved further along the south bank, stormed the Archbishop of Canterbury's palace at Lambeth, destroyed records and visited devastation on all his vestments, portable property and wine cellar, carrying off vast quantities of wine.[69] The raiders returned to Blackheath to receive Tyler's congratulations: true to his orders, they had not looted indiscriminately or at random but had plundered specific targets. He was also delighted to hear that the people of Southwark had welcomed the insurgents as deliverers. As the heath was lit up by hundreds of campfires that night of 12–13 June, Tyler had every reason to be satisfied. The feelings of euphoria were topped off by the arrival of Sir John Newton, still the hapless go-between, who told Tyler that the king would meet the insurgents next day.[70] The only slight worry for the rebel leaders was that food supplies at Blackheath did not suffice for such a host; it was feared that hungry men would go on the rampage the following day and abandon the careful discipline inculcated by Tyler.

While the rebels awaited the morning in a state of euphoria, feelings in the royal household were very different. The fourteen-year-old Richard II had moved his court from Windsor to the Tower of London, the better to deal with the crisis, but now the courtiers were feeling beleaguered. Crammed into the Tower confines were 600 soldiers, officials and servants. Among those present were William Walworth (Mayor of London), Treasurer Hales and his half-brother Thomas Holland, leading courtiers Nicholas Brembre, John Philipot and Robert Launde and the Earls of Kent, Arundel, Warwick and Salisbury – the last a veteran of the wars in France. Robert de Vere, Earl of Oxford and Richard's cousin Henry of Derby were no more than callow teenagers.[71] Most of all, Richard lamented the absence of any first-division military talents. The Earl of Buckingham was in France, Edmund Langley, Earl of Cambridge, was on the high seas bound for Portugal and John of Gaunt was at that very moment in Edinburgh. Richard did not even have as consolation the company of his old tutor Sir Simon Burley, the senior knight of the royal household. Having passed a gloomy and anxious night, Richard was not encouraged next morning by the arrival of Sudbury, whose solution to the crisis was to surrender his seals of office. Richard insisted the archbishop stay in his post and ordered him, Hales, Warwick and Salisbury to accompany him on his parley with the rebels. Richard had been reluctant to meet them face to face, but finally yielded to the agonised pleas of Sir John Newton, whose children were being held hostage by Tyler.[72] Richard set out on a barge with his four worthies, leaving the Tower by the Water Gate; four other barges accompanied him. They sailed first to Greenwich, then on to Rotherhithe, where the rebels were assembled on the river bank. As the barges approached, the ululations of the triumphant rebels could be heard and, also, if some of the more fanciful chronicles can be believed, the whizzing of arrows shot into the air in excitement by rebel bowmen. Alarmed by all this, Richard took the advice of his four counsellors. Salisbury argued that it would be madness to land: not only could the rebels seize the king and hold him hostage but they, his courtiers, had no guarantee they would not be butchered on the spot.[73] Richard therefore sent word that he would not be stepping ashore. Instead he received a deputation on board but was alarmed to find that his insurgent subjects were in no mood for negotiations. They presented *demands*. As an earnest of the king's good faith, they required him to surrender at once the five 'most wanted' men on their list: John of Gaunt, Chancellor Sudbury, Treasurer Hales, John Fordham, the Keeper of the Privy Seal and Sir John Plevington, Chief Baron of the Exchequer.[74] Later they would require the delivery of other 'traitors' named as John Bampton, John Legge, Sir Robert Belknap and Sir Ralph Ferrers. The king adamantly refused to surrender a single one of those named and ordered the barges to put about for the Tower. In great fear of being assailed by a shower of arrows, the boatmen did so, leaving the rebels fuming about the abortive outcome. Yet even after this overt demonstration of where Richard's true loyalties lay, they continued to profess loyalty to him and to draw a distinction between a 'good' king and the 'evil' courtiers who had misled him, the absent Gaunt above all.[75]

The disappointment over the king was soon forgotten as the rebels made 13 June a day to remember. It was the Feast of Corpus Christi, which in medieval England was not just a religious festival but an occasion for processions, organised games, revelry and misrule. Some say that the impressive organisation of the rebels was because they used the proximity of the religious festivals of Whitsun, Trinity and Corpus Christi as cover for their activities, including mass rallies and the bearing of arms, sanctioned by the traditional ceremony, the 'view of arms'.[76] If the absence of four major armies (respectively in France, Portugal, Scotland and Wales) may have been chance rather than calculation by the rebels, the congruence of these festivals was certainly not. The fiesta-like resonance of Corpus Christi explains the frequent cries of 'A revel! A revel!' noted by the chroniclers as the rebels went about their destruction of Lambeth Palace.[77] This particular Corpus Christi became a byword for a spree of systematic looting and an orgy of mayhem and violence. The key to the day's events was the securing of London Bridge. In those days the bridge resembled the modern Ponte Vecchio in Florence, as it was a commercial street with shops along its entire length and a stone chapel in the centre; a drawbridge at the Southwark end controlled access to London from the south bank of the Thames.[78] Mayor Walworth, a pro-government hard liner, sent Alderman John Horne to Southwark with a stern warning not to enter the City of London, but he chose an inapt envoy for Horne was one of the three aldermen who supported the rebels. Instead of delivering the warning, Horne told the insurgents that they had plenty of latent support in London and that hatred of Gaunt particularly disposed Londoners in their favour.[79] He found the rebels in Southwark, devastating the approaches to the Thames. The latent thread of xenophobia in the revolt was in evidence as the plunderers pulled down a Southwark brothel and tipped the Flemish prostitutes inside into the street. The rebels sent word into London that they would not loot or plunder any property except that of the 'traitors'. With many a wink and nod, Horne got London Bridge's gatekeeper to let down the drawbridge. The men of Kent poured into London.[80]

London was now torn apart by a three-pronged assault. A mob of sympathisers from within the City attacked Ludgate, the stone entrance to the City on London Wall. Many private grudges were settled that day, a frequent feature being the beheading of their masters by apprentices.[81] Meanwhile the men of Essex, encamped overnight at Smithfield outside the city walls, began a systematic destruction of the property of the hated Hospitallers, associated particularly with Sir John Hales. At first the Kentish contingents proceeded slowly, opening all jails and releasing the prisoners. But the pace of occupation became hectic with the securing of Ludgate. The next obvious target was Fleet Street and then the Strand, the most affluent, upmarket part of London, seat of the wealthiest men in the kingdom. By this time the three previously distinct groups were beginning to merge, with the men of Kent moving up from London Bridge, the Essex levies pouring in through Aldgate, having browbeaten and coerced the gatekeepers there, and the homegrown London rebels pointing out to their allies the most obvious targets.[82] The first objective for the fused forces was the Fleet Prison, which was broken into with ease; the disgorged prisoners swelled the throng of excited rioters.

Fleet Street was also the location of a number of houses owned by Richard Imworth, all of which had their roofs stripped before being gutted.[83] Moving along Fleet Steet, the rebel army next attacked the New Temple, headquarters of the Knights Hospitaller, of which Treasurer Hales was the prior. The enraged crowd burst into the seven-acre grounds on the riverside, looting and despoiling, with special destructive attention given to official documents. They ripped the tiles off the roofs of all houses, torched them, pillaged the treasure house of the Temple's round church and again destroyed all the rolls and parchments they could find. Next to be destroyed were the quest-mongers' houses and any property remotely associated with lawyers, for whom the rebels always entertained a particular animus.[84] By about 4 p.m. Fleet Street was an inferno, with fires blazing the length of it. Finally it was time for the pièce de résistance, John of Gaunt's glittering Savoy Palace on the Strand.

The Savoy Palace was the showpiece of the age. Built with the proceeds of plunder seized during the Crécy–Poitiers golden age of the Hundred Years War, it cost £35,000 to build – a third of the estimated annual wage bill for the *entire* English army.[85] Huge walls protected the palace from the hurly-burly of the Strand, while within those walls were state apartments, the great hall, cloisters, a chapel and fishponds, stables and thatched cottages for Gaunt's servants. Gates on the north allowed access to the Strand and opened on the south onto the Thames. The elated men of Essex and Kent found that London's rebels had already beaten them to the punch and had begun the work of wholesale desecration, but there was still plenty for the latecomers to do.[86] All the emphasis was on pure destruction. Precious furniture, glittering tapestries, sparkling linen joined beds, coverlets, chairs and tables in a massive bonfire; the palace itself was then set alight. There was no attempt to carry off the masses of gold, jewellery and silver plate; most of it was ground into small pieces to prevent its being melted down and reconstituted. One of Gaunt's jerkins or padded jackets was brought out and used for target practice.[87] Anything that the bonfires would not consume was hurled into the sewers. The luckless few who tried to loot were put to death at once on Tyler's orders, in one case by being thrown into the bonfire. Altogether Gaunt's losses on this one day of mayhem were estimated at £10,000 apart from the loss of the palace itself.[88] There was no proscription on making free with Gaunt's wine cellar, and soon a breakaway group of some forty men was enjoying a massive binge below stairs. Suddenly there was a huge explosion. The rioters had thrown three barrels onto the bonfire. Thought to contain gold and silver, they turned out to general horror to be gunpowder. The palace's structure had already been weakened by the fires, but the explosion provided the coup de grâce. The entire building began to crash down around the rebels' ears. Timber and stonemasonry crashed down and blocked the entrance to the wine cellar, trapping the revellers inside. With the Savoy crumbling, those above ground rapidly decamped. The entombed drinkers were abandoned to their self-inflicted Tartarus. Londoners later related that the cries for help from the unfortunates walled up alive went on for seven days, but in vain. Thirty-two corpses were later counted.[89] In the wild *sauve qui peut* scramble for safety no one gave any thought to their bibulous comrades. The survivors went in search of fresh prey. After liberating Westminster Jail, the rebels doubled back on their tracks to free Newgate Jail near Ludgate. As night fell, the raging fires and hugc plumes of smoke from the Savoy lit up the city in a hellish tableau.[90]

The next prominent victim of the rioters was Roger Legett, lawyer and professional questmaster, who even the partisan chroniclers admit was a dubious character. He fled for sanctuary to the chapel of St Martin-le-Grand but was dragged from the altar, manhandled all the way to Cheapside and there beheaded. The mob clearly cared little for the rights of sanctuary, but ingenious propagandists made the point that Gaunt and his ilk were now being treated to a dose of their own medicine; the memory of the outrages by Sir Ralph Ferrers and others of Gaunt's henchmen still rankled. The fury of the crowd was all the greater, for in their eyes the absent Gaunt was 'the one who got away'.[91] That evening the rebels carried out eighteen more documented executions and probably many more. Their next target was the Priory of St John of Jerusalem in the suburban fields of present-day Clerkenwell, the headquarters of the Knights Hospitaller. The insurgents destroyed all the priory buildings, gutted the main structure and started an inferno that took a week to burn itself out.[92] Then there were more beheadings, some of masters by apprentices, others of foreigners who were deeply loathed by the Londoners. At this juncture it becomes possible to discern two elements in the revolt unique to London. One was the struggle of a nascent proletariat against wealthy merchants *within* the guilds. This was distinct and different from the Gaunt–City struggle. Masters operating a closed shop had created many artificial barriers so that their apprentices could never become masters themselves. In response the dispossessed or journeymen apprentices had formed primitive unions; the outbreak of an initially rural revolt gave them a golden opportunity to avenge themselves on their exploiters. The complexity of the struggle in London becomes clear when we appreciate that the Gaunt–City conflict and the master–apprentice contest went on alongside quite separate faction-fighting *between* the various guilds. Finally, in what one observer has called 'playing Peisistratus'[93] (after the Athenian demagogue-tyrant of old), certain wealthy individuals took the side of the rioters against their own class, either out of jealousy or ambition or to settle private scores. The other special element in the London revolt was xenophobia. Alien merchants, particularly the Flemings and Lombards, were alleged to be sucking the wealth out of England and remitting it abroad. Flemings were particularly hated as they were thought to use cheap labour in Flanders and thus put English employees out of work.[94] The deep cause behind the hatred was that Flemings had filled the entrepreneurial gap left by the Jews after Edward I expelled them in 1290. Moreover, after 1370 greedy governments had sold them export-duty exemptions, allowing them to undercut domestic merchants. At least seven Flemings were murdered on the night of 13 June, but in the entire course of the revolt thirty-five were caught and beheaded; some authorities think the true figure for men of Flanders killed in London on 12–15 June to be of the order of 140–160.[95]

13 June was also notable for the fiery rhetoric of John Ball. The Feast of Corpus Christi was an appropriate moment for Ball to set out his theological wares, since the masses were traditionally summoned on this date by the 'hue and cry' and the ringing of church bells. Whether Ball used the imagery of the bell in his sermon this day is unknown, but a quatrain attributed to him by the chroniclers is the following:

John Ball greeteth you all
And doth to understand he has rung your bell
Now with might and right, will and skill
God speed every dell.[96]

We do know for certain that he preached on one of his favourite motifs:

When Adam delved and Eve span
Who was then the gentleman?

He developed a primitive form of what would be later known as the labour theory of value: the feudal lords had sumptuous raiment, fine wines and the choicest food, but the source of all this was the surplus extracted from the serfs. He argued, as Rousseau would 400 years later, that the origin of social inequality was Man's sinfulness; God had created us all equal but evil men had enslaved and oppressed others, creating something known as private property that was supposed to be sacrosanct. Another strand in his thought was apocalyptic or eschatological. Ball believed that as punishment for this sinfulness, mankind would eventually reap a divine come-uppance; like many millenarians and chiliasts, Ball seemed to think that social revolution might precipitate the coming of divine vengeance.[97] Ball had to be careful how far to push this line of argument, for the vast majority of the insurgents simply wanted to be freeholders, not to share everything in common. Much debate has centred on whether Ball or the rebels in general were influenced by the thought of the Lollard sect, led by John Wycliff.[98] Wycliff, sometimes thought of as Martin Luther *avant la lettre*, denied the doctrine of transubstantiation and so subverted the supremacy and thaumaturgy of the entire priestly caste. Moreover, by holding that the clergy was irrelevant and that all authority depended on whether the holder enjoyed God's grace, he implicitly threatened secular lordship as well.[99] Some of the chroniclers held Wycliff responsible for the 1381 rebellion,[100] but two factors decisively rebut the allegation. In the first place, the great nobles did not necessarily view Wycliff's views as *socially* seditious and were indifferent to theological niceties. At one time, for his own reasons, John of Gaunt publicly supported Wycliff when he was being tried for heresy. At his trial in 1377, Gaunt made a dramatic intervention, lost his temper with the Bishop of London, who was acting as president of the court, and threatened to drag him out of St Paul's Cathedral by his hair. This gave the London crowd the excuse to riot, which they did, driving Gaunt out of the capital at great speed.[101] Secondly, Wycliff was no social egalitarian. His radical stance, like Luther's, was confined to Church matters alone. Just as Luther vehemently denounced the peasants' revolt in Germany in the 1520s, so Wycliff held aloof from the 1381 explosion in England. The true religious supporters of the Peasants' Revolt of 1381 were the mendicant orders, themselves bitter enemies of Wycliff. As William Langland pointed out, it was the friars, not the Lollards, who preached communism most fervently.[102]

2

Failure and Consequences of the Peasants' Revolt

By around 10 p.m. on the night of 13 June the rebels had spent most of their destructive energy and massed around the Tower, where Richard and his courtiers huddled fearfully, flinching at the cacophony outside and the cries that the 'malefactors' be delivered up to justice. Scholars debate whether the true number of armed men defending the king was 1,200 or 600 (the latter is more likely) but on paper, with regular troops in a good defensive position, the loyalists should have been well placed. That was an assessment, however, based purely on military strength on paper. Once again the issue of morale was crucial. The assembled oligarchs seemed broken in spirit and mostly defeatist in outlook. This had all along been the problem. If the king's men had had the courage and ingenuity to keep the rebels at bay and prevent them irrupting into London for just twenty-four hours after their arrival at Blackheath, they would probably have dispersed because of food shortages, for food supply was always Tyler's major headache.[1] Even when the rebels entered London, the problem did not entirely abate, for medieval cities always lived on a knife edge of subsistence and could not accommodate the sudden appearance of an extra 3,000–10,000 mouths. Yet the oligarchs continued listless and seemingly paralysed until the night of 13 June. Only then, when disaster stared them in the face, did hard-line opinion start to emerge. Mayor William Walworth argued vociferously that the king should use all the force at his disposal. Richard, though, inclined to pacific methods and now thought that his earlier refusal to negotiate had been a mistake.[2] He sent out two of his knights to parley with the chanting rebels outside, offering a full pardon if they would all disperse at once; this message was laughed out of court. When the guffaws ceased, the rioters told the envoys that they would leave only when the 'traitors' were surrendered. Richard then sent a second message, asking the rebels to put their demands in writing; this was regarded as merely insulting. Walworth took his chance and argued for an immediate offensive against the rebels. He saw no future in negotiations, especially as the young king was known to be hot-tempered and lost control of his emotions easily.[3] He argued for a four-part sortie, coordinating with Sir Robert Knolles (who would attack the rear) to catch the drunken and slumbering rebels unawares. Walworth received the enthusiastic support of John Philipot and Nicholas Brembre, two other wealthy merchants who were hawkish hard liners and feared the mob more than they hated Gaunt. Yet Salisbury, a veteran of Crécy and the one man in the Tower with campaign experience, overruled them. His opinion was that a sortie would soon bog down in inconclusive street fighting. In this he was probably right, for in the small hours of the 14th another rebel force from St Albans under Jack Straw began entering London from the north. Salisbury thought it better to lull the rebels by making concessions and backed the king in advocating negotiations.[4]

Richard therefore decided on a general muster of loyalists and announced a rendezvous at Mile End at 7 a.m. on the 14th, to which he also invited the rebels, asking them to put their grievances to him in person. It was agreed that the earlier fears of calling out anti-rebel elements in the City had been overtaken by events, and in inviting lobbying from the rebels Richard had the ulterior purpose of coaxing them away from the Tower so that their intended victims within could escape. Moreover, since Mile End was outside the city gates, if the rebels flocked to hear his words, this would give the loyalists the chance to close the gates against them once more. Some think the entire idea and the initiative at Mile End was a purely personal project by the juvenile Richard.[5] The young king left the Tower with an impressive entourage – Thomas and John Holland, the Earls of Oxford and Warwick, Sir Aubrey de Vere, Thomas Percy, William Walworth and Queen Joan, his mother; significantly none of the 'most wanted' personalities were in the party. With great difficulty the royal cavalcade forced its way through the throng outside. One of Tyler's chief lieutenants, Thomas Farringdon, got close enough to the king to cry out a demand for 'that false traitor the Prior'.[6] When Richard gave the ambiguous and enigmatic answer that he would have all that was just, Farringdon seemed satisfied and went back to the Tower to supervise operations there. But the incident seriously unnerved Sir John Holland and the Earl of Kent, who abandoned Richard and galloped off across Whitechapel fields. Once arrived at Mile End, Richard sent his mother back to the Tower with the tip-off for Hales, Sudbury and the other execrated ones to make good their escape. He was encouraged by the crowd of rebels waiting for him to believe that they had lifted the siege of the Tower but may have been disappointed that none of the rebellion's ringleaders (Tyler, Straw, Ball) was there to meet him. He asked the rebel representatives what they wanted. To his relief there was no mention of a purge of government or the execution of the guilty. Instead there was a very lawyerly manifesto calling for a charter of rights in the countryside, the abolition of fiefs, the setting of a rent limit of 4d an acre and an end to financial oppression through manorial courts, royal courts and the tax system.[7] Richard's presence at such a parley was profoundly disingenuous. His main aim was to lure the enemy away from the Tower, and to do so he would have agreed to almost anything. Warming to his theme, he promised the rebels liberties ensured by royal charters guaranteed with the king's seal. Then he overplayed his hand. He told them that in return for getting these charters, the rebels must now scour the land and deliver all traitors to him.[8] He seems to have been carried away by the euphoria of the moment and granted the rebels something they had not asked him for. But it was a classic non-meeting of minds. By traitors Richard evidently meant the 'wicked men' who had seduced and misled his subjects (i.e. Tayler, Straw, Ball et al.). The rebels interpreted his words as carte blanche to execute the traitors in the Tower. Maybe Richard counted on just such a misunderstanding of the ambiguity, hoping that the wanted men at the Tower had meanwhile flown the coop. Yet it could be said that by his unwary remarks he had brought many subsequent murders within the compass of the law.[9]

Richard may not have noticed that what he had agreed to was in essence the abolition of feudalism in all but name. The manifesto presented at Mile End, and even more that promulgated next day at Smithfield, alerts us to some of the profound issues at play in the rebellion. Apart from the complex situation in urban areas, and especially London, as already mentioned, three main elements may be discerned. Towns and cities were involved in a struggle to get charters of incorporation as boroughs from feudal overlords, usually churchmen. At St Albans, Dunstable, King's Lynn and Bury St Edmunds we can detect an obvious and open conflict between the towns and the local abbeys, where the abbots were the overlords.[10] Despite their role as supposed representatives of Christian charity, abbots and bishops were invariably more recalcitrant than the lay proprietors or the king. Often the town–Church conflict was confused with and overlaid by another kind of urban conflict – that between the 'have nots' who were free men and the wealthy merchants who formed the town oligarchy. It might be said that the situation in Winchester, Beverley and Scarborough was of this type.[11] This is why local government was often as unpopular as central government, albeit for different reasons. Mayors and other officials were theoretically constrained by votes and elections, but massive corruption meant they often coopted and re-elected themselves, before levying unmandated taxes and running up debts with consummate arrogance; the town of Beverley in Yorkshire provided almost a textbook example of this.[12] The second element was the more pervasive and bitterly contested. Basically, feudal lords were trying to put the clock back to the era before the Black Death and their villeins were trying to resist this. From the villeins the lord of the manor wanted compulsory labour, and from landless labourers he wanted their labour at the lowest possible rate – not the market price of 3d or 4d a day but the rate of 2d a day set artificially low by the infamous Statute of Labourers. The villein on the other hand wanted to be a tenant at a fixed rate, while the landless labourer wanted to be paid at the market rate.[13]

This struggle between capital (if we may so term the feudal lords) and labour took many forms. Sometimes lords of the manor tried to rescind the custom, which was becoming the norm in the fourteenth century, whereby villeins commuted their days of compulsory labour (*corvée*) on the manorial demesne for a money payment. Sometimes the struggle was not so much about the principle of a money payment in lieu of *corvée* but the amount considered reasonable for 'commutation' with 4d an acre being widely regarded as the just price.[14] At other times certain hawkish lords directed an out-and-out onslaught on the post-Black Death peasantry by levying charges to prevent migration, stopping the acquisition of free land by serfs and charging extra rents. At local level seigneurial courts were the instruments of social control used by the lords, for these enforced all the tenants' obligations, reinforced the *corvée* system and demanded the repair of buildings on short-term leases. All the pre-1381 evidence from the seigneurial courts shows the lords defending their prerogatives with vigour.[15] Their main problem was that it was difficult to find officials for these courts since the 'middle sectors' who manned the courts were the men in the middle in more ways than one, paid by and owing loyalty to the lords but under extreme pressure from their neighbours, the free peasants. Because of the general reluctance to serve as henchmen of the manorial lords as rent collectors, constables, ale tasters, etc, those refusing service were visited by heavy fines. At the limit the feudal lords had the royal tribunals and commissioners as back-up, which was why 1381 was not just about the parlous state of landlord–tenant relations but also about hatred of royal officialdom, as much through distaste at having to pay taxes for the pointless wars in France as about knee-jerk support for local exploiters.[16] The interlinking of all the elements in the social system explains why 1381 was not just an aggregate of personal vendettas of villeins against lords but was a *general* rebellion, in which the rebels made the link between lordship and Plantagenet government in general. The rebels wanted an end to local corruption, where the courts were bullied and manipulated by the feudal lords, *and* genuinely local courts free from central government interference.[17]

All these complexities and nuances were swept away by Richard II when he appeared to have conceded to the rebels unconditional surrender by the ruling class. Yet his initiative may be accounted a partial success, since the prospect of getting charters of freedom took the steam out of many rebels, who broke away from the main body, lured by Richard's promise that they could collect their documents later that day at St Paul's when his clerks had completed the laborious job of copying out each one by hand.[18] Yet the wider aim of inveigling the rebels away from the Tower was not secured. The trembling worthies who had put their trust in the king and the Tower rather than decamp from London soon realised that they had in effect been offered up as sacrificial victims. Richard had left them behind with the assurance that he could draw the rebels away and allow them to escape, but mature reflection prompted the conclusion that they had been left behind to guarantee *his* safety, as any party containing them was bound to be attacked.[19] When Queen Joan returned from Mile End with the depressing news that the crowd outside had not dispersed, Hales and Sudbury at least must have known that their last hour had come. Having persecuted Ball for so many years, the archbishop surely knew what to expect from a mob led by him. Sudbury said two Masses that morning and then confessed Hales and some others. Soon the crowd started taunting the guards, whose morale was already at rock bottom, with the news that food supplies in the Tower were running low.[20] Suddenly the shouting and haranguing ceased and the gates were flung open; the rebels entered without resistance. It seems clear from all the circumstantial evidence that a plot had already been hatched to suborn the guards, and any lingering notion of resistance would have been dispelled by the news being brought back excitedly from Mile End, that the king had in effect caved in and admitted defeat. So appalled was the Knighton chronicler by this abject surrender (the result either of treachery or collusion) that he pretended only 180 men-at-arms had been left behind, when all other sources mention the figure of 600.[21] The rebels were in grim and determined mood. Sudbury was plucked from his morning devotions in the chapel, haled outside to Tower Hill and beheaded. He did not die well: first he begged, pleaded and wept for his life, then, when the axe descended on his neck, it took no less than eight strokes to finish him off. Whether this was calculated cruelty by the executioners or simple incompetence does not appear. Also executed with Sudbury were Hales, Legge, Wiliam Appleton (Gaunt's physician) and a gentleman named as Richard Somenor of Stepney.[22] The future Henry IV was saved only because a guard hid him from the invaders. Queen Joan was roughly treated. Whereas on 12 June, as the rebels made their way to London, they had behaved respectfully when they overtook her coach on the way into London, this time they meted out insults and overfamiliarity, asking for kisses and embraces. When the terrified queen fainted, her servants bustled her out of the room and onto a waiting barge.[23]

The depredations and executions at the Tower were a signal for another day of destruction, arson and murder. By now Tyler's tight discipline was becoming unglued and the rebellion was in serious danger of collapsing into anarchy as an enraged mob sought to settle private scores under the rubric of finding 'traitors'. Unscrupulous merchants settled old feuds by inciting the crowd against business rivals whom they fingered as 'recreants'. Sir Robert Allen got a group of Kent rebels to evict Hugh Ware, a rival claimant to a piece of real estate, on his mere say-so that the property was his. A brewer, William Trenman, started expropriating the houses of Walworth's ally Nicholas Brembre on similar grounds. John Butterwick, under sheriff of Middlesex, had his property despoiled by the Essex rebels at three separate locations outside the city walls, in Knightsbridge, Westminster and Ebury.[24] But for more prominent rebel targets, death, not despoliation was the prescription. The immensely rich merchant Richard Lyons had already suffered at rebel hands in Suffolk as they searched for 'Public Enemy Number Three' (after Hales and Sudbury), Sir John Cavendish, the chief justice. Now the enraged mob found Lyons himself, dragged him out to Cheapside and beheaded him.[25] Next on their list was Richard Imworth, notorious as the brutal jailer of the King's Bench Prison in Southwark which the rebels had sacked on the night of the 12th. Imworth seems to have thought that the rebels would draw the line at breaching sanctuary in the hallowed Westminster Abbey so sat down at the altar there. He was dragged out without scruple or ceremony, manhandled along to Cheapside and beheaded.[26] Another to suffer mob fury was an unfortunate valet named John of Greenfield, who made the mistake of saying some kind words about William Appleton, Gaunt's physician, who had perished in the Tower. He too suffered the headsman's axe. Yet the murderous anger of the crowd on 14 June particularly settled on foreign entrepreneurs, and this time Scandinavians and Genoese, as well as Flemings and Lombards, were swept up in the maw of the rebellion's Moloch.[27] As on the day before, Flemings were a favourite target; to the crowd they were no more than brothel-keepers, pimps and ponces who had grown fat on human weakness. Once again the victims had no other thought than seeking sanctuary, but once again their hopes were forlorn. About forty Flemings holed up in the church of St Martin in the Vintry. They were dragged out and beheaded. All day long the murder toll rose. Several hundred died that day, their heads set on pikes, borne round the city in triumph and then mounted on the gate of London Bridge.[28]

Debtors had a gala day at the expense of creditors, forcing them to give up documentary evidence of their debts which were then destroyed. Insofar as there was direction to the actions of the crowd on 14 June, the ringmasters appear to have been Alderman John Horne and Thomas Farringdon; Horne was reported as acting as judge and jury in any case brought to his notice, invariably finding for debtors against creditors. Meanwhile Wat Tyler was pondering his next step. The wildest rumours circulated: he was going to burn London to the ground; he would take the king hostage; he would execute all nobles and bishops; he would make John Ball supreme and sole bishop in England, abolishing the clerical hierarchy. What Tyler actually did was to repudiate the deal negotiated by the rebels at Mile End in favour of a manifesto mark two.[29] The second manifesto included the demand for punishment against 'traitors to the crown' which the rebel negotiators at Mile End had unaccountably omitted. In addition to the abolition of lordship, which the first manifesto had asked for, Tyler now additionally demanded the abolition of the episcopacy and the game laws, the redistribution of Church property as a windfall for the suffering classes, the common ownership of property, and a federalism of county 'kingdoms' with Wat Tyler as 'king of Kent'.[30] There was also a puzzling call for 'no law but the law of Winchester', which has had commentators baffled. It could refer to the 1285 Statute of Winchester, whose provisions were supplanted by the Statute of Labourers or, more likely, it referred to Domesday Book, already acknowledged as the rebels' bible in the 'Great Rumour' of 1377. As against those who would make Wat Tyler a forerunner of the seventeenth-century Diggers in denouncing the 'Norman yoke',[31] the emphasis on Domesday Book as the core of peasant ideology means that Tyler and his followers were neither campaigning for the old Anglo-Saxon constitution nor appealing to Magna Carta of 1215, usually regarded as the fount of English liberty. Domesday Book still had great talismanic power (the impact of Magna Carta had already faded), reinforcing as it did (or at least as it seemed to) the supremacy of local traditions and ancient rights against the despotism of central government.[32] The second manifesto underlines two key aspects of the 1381 rebellion. Tyler and his clique of advisers mounted a sophisticated critique of the prevailing socio-economic structure. The hostile chroniclers ascribed to him genuinely revolutionary aims – and this is usually dismissed as elite paranoia – but at the very least it shows that revolutionary ideas cannot be considered 'anachronistic', even if the consciousness of the rebels was limited. The second facet of the manifesto underlines the essential weakness of Tyler's movement. He continued to make a distinction between a 'good' king and 'evil' courtiers, not realising that in this sense the interests of the elite were unitary. The rebels had thrown away their best card by not taking him prisoner at Mile End and holding him hostage as surety for the fulfilment of the promises he had made there. The direct appeal to the king as putative saviour of his poor people was trusting and ingenuous and has rightly been described as 'naive monarchism'.[33]

Envoys flitted between Tyler and Richard II, now at St Paul's, where his thirty or so clerks were acting as a kind of document factory, churning out copies of the charter of liberties granted by the king that morning at Mile End. Large numbers of the rebels began returning home, secure in their naive belief that they had now got all they fought for; this was particularly a characteristic of the Essex men. Led by Tyler, the Kent rebels were made of sterner stuff; they were determined to nail the king down to the specific commitments of the second manifesto in such a way that he could not later rescind them.[34] It may have been when he finally decided that the rebels could not simply be tricked into unilateral surrender that Richard II decided to use force. Walworth, always the hard liner, had hitherto been marginalised but now he came to the fore as the king's prime adviser. The old argument by Salisbury and others that force would precipitate a general rising in London had already been overtaken by events: London was in flames anyway. If Tyler was not stopped now, Walworth and the king reasoned, they might just as well ride away to Windsor, skulk there and await the tide of events.[35] The famous cunning of the Plantagenets now came to the fore. Walworth laid secret plans for Knolles to have his London-based levies at the ready, waiting for a signal. Richard meanwhile would take 200 men-at-arms to meet the rebels at Smithfield Square, where they would all be wearing concealed weapons while pretending to be attending a peaceful parley. It was clear that the royal party had a premeditated plan to assassinate Tyler, doubtless anticipating the nineteteenth-century colonial cliché, whereby if you want to panic the natives you should first kill their leader. Smithfield, on the other hand, was an artfully chosen location. It was a big open space, which would allow large numbers of rebels to assemble there, allaying all fears of treachery. On the other hand, if fighting broke out, the fact that Smithfield was a contained space, with St Bartholomew's hospital, the walls of Charterhouse and the waters of the river Holborn and Faggleswell Brook forming natural boundaries, made it possible for a numerically inferior force to prevail. It has been well said that Richard II and Walworth were supremely cunning and that bold, ruthless and calculating strategic planning lay behind the choice of Smithfield'.[36]

On the morning of the 15th Richard II went to pray in Westminster Abbey at the shrine of Edward the Confessor, doubtless to implore the saint-king to give celestial endorsement for the egregious treachery he and Walworth planned. If Froissart is to be believed, he appeared to dither, as if uncertain what to do next, presumably to allay any suspicions from Tyler's spies who might be watching him. He then followed an indirect and zigzag path from Westminster to Smithfield, already a meat market and a place of slaughter in general, infamous for the hanging, drawing and quartering of William Wallace nearly a hundred years earlier.[37] Ostensibly meeting the rebels for peaceful negotiations, all Richard's 200 men were secretly carrying weapons under their cloaks; Walworth and others wore armour under their finery. An overconfident Tyler approached the rendezvous with aplomb, apparently unaware that the leaders of the *jacquerie* had been lured to a similar parley and then slaughtered. If we, again, use Froissart as a guide, we find Tyler blithe and joking, warning his men that if there was any fighting they must take the king alive.[38] He and his men were drawn up on the western side of Smithfield Square, with the king and his men on the eastern side and the middle space clear. Walworth himself acted as the royal herald and in a loud voice summoned 'Wat Tyler of Maidstone' to come forward. What followed is decribed only in the chronicles, all of which were violently hostile to the rebels; the verbatim dialogue sometimes quoted has therefore to be taken with a pinch of salt, but none of the reported exchanges strain credibility. Tyler rode forward with just one companion. Displaying his horsemanship, he dismounted one-handed from his charger, made a perfunctory obeisance to the king, then lunged forward and shook his hand as if he were a comrade. It seems that he half regretted the initial gesture of deference and remedied it by overfamiliarity. He then attempted to patronise the monarch, pointing out the serried ranks of his host and saying they owed him absolute obedience, all the time playing with his dagger and tossing it from one hand to the other. 'Brother, be of good comfort, for you shall have, in a fortnight that is to come, forty thousand more commons than you have at present, and we shall be good companions.'[39]

Richard ignored the boast and asked why, now that the rebels had their charters, they did not go back to their homes. Tyler replied that he had not received a satisfactory answer to the demands contained in the second manifesto. Richard answered that the rebels could have all they desired, 'saving only the regalities of the crown'.[40] Rightly reading this as an evasion, a kind of Jesuitical reservation *avant la lettre*, Tyler may have acted foolishly. We have to remember that the chroniclers were determined to present the events of 15 June as pure accident and not the results of a carefully laid conspiracy. At any rate, it is said that Tyler then asked for a jug of water, which he swilled around his mouth and then spat out in front of the king. He then called for a jug of ale and took a huge swig, before climbing on his horse without being dismissed by his sovereign.[41] If this is what really happened, then it provided Walworth with exactly the pretext he needed. He rode forward to the king and announced that he was arresting Tyler for contumacious behaviour in the presence of his king and lord. Just to make sure Tyler took the bait, he had one of his squires cry out that Tyler was the greatest highway robber in the land, little more than a common thief.[42] One version is that the squire was an old enemy of Tyler's who had crossed swords with him before. In any event the accusation was rich coming from Walworth, who had made much of his money from brothel-keeping. Yet the provocation worked perfectly. Tyler ordered his valet to arrest the insulting miscreant. The valet pushed his horse into the royal retinue, whereat Walworth cried out that he was arresting the valet also. Infuriated, Tyler lashed out at Walworth, but his dagger was blunted by the chainmail worn by the mayor under his robe. Walworth in turn drew his sword and smote Tyler twice, on the head and shoulders.[43] A royal valet, Sir Ralph Standish, presumably primed for the occasion, rode forward and finished Tyler off with a mortal blow.[44] The dying Tyler wheeled his horse and galloped back towards the rebel lines but fell from his steed when just eighty yards from their ranks and collapsed in a heap in the empty space in the middle of the square. Walworth's grand stratagem had worked perfectly.[45]

This was the moment when the rebels should have taken immediate revenge and loosed a shower of arrows. Displaying genuine courage, Richard II rode forward up to the rebels and defied them to kill their king. All Tyler's preaching about the innocence of the king as against the guilt of his counsellors now worked against his men. They hesitated, put up their bows, and seemed at a loss what to do next. Seizing the moment, Richard cried out that if they wanted justice they should follow him at once to Clerkenwell Fields, a few hundred yards to the north.[46] Instead of shooting him down and then massacring his men-at-arms, the rebels acted like sheep and trooped meekly behind him. In vain the aldermen Sibley and Horne tried to dissuade them from throwing in the towel. For about an hour Richard stalled valiantly, pretending to discuss the exact wording of the charters, claiming not to understand certain clauses. Meanwhile Walworth put into action the second part of his grand plan. First he sought out the comatose Tyler, who had been carried, half-dead, into the hospital of St Bartholomew. Walworth and his men dragged the rebel leader from his deathbed and beheaded him; Tyler may already have been dead when the axe fell.[47] Then Walworth raced back to London to link up with Sir Robert Knolles and the loyalist battalion he had been raising. Suddenly, as Richard continued his charade with the rebel negotiators, the insurgents were alarmed to see a large force of the king's men approaching. Walworth completed their demoralisation by unwrapping Tyler's severed head and rolling it in front of them. Their spirits broken and their nerves cracked as if by sorcery, the benighted rebels fell to their knees and begged for mercy from the king.[48] Walworth and the hawks wanted an immediate bloodbath but Richard refused, saying that his subjects, bamboozled by evil men, had acted towards him in good faith. He announced that the rebels should depart immediately to their homes. Bowed and crestfallen, they began to drift away from the scenes where they had been the masters just hours before. Soon there was a mass exodus in the direction of Kent.[49] Walworth retrieved Tyler's head and brought it to the king, who ordered that it should be set up on London Bridge to replace Sudbury's. To show his gratitude for the day's work, he knighted Walworth on the spot, then bestowed the same honour on the other hard liners; Brembre, Philipot and Robert Launde.[50]

The collapse of the 1381 rebellion in London as though by magic was an astonishing phenomenon, to which historians have paid insufficient attention. Many questions remain without answers. Why was Tyler so over-confident and why did he go to the face-to-face meeting with the king without an adequate bodyguard? Why did he allow the king to ride just a few yards ahead of his troops while Tyler galloped across the width of Smithfield? Why did he not suspect treachery? Even if the rebels did not know about the dismal precedent for such talks in the French *jacquerie*, mere prudence and common sense indicated that they should have been on their guard. Most of all, why did the rebels apparently have no contingency plans in the event of Tyler's demise, through accident or treachery? Was rebel intelligence and staffwork so bad that no one picked up on the ominous developments in London, where Knolles was rallying a large force of loyalists? We know little about rebel dispositions for dealing with a counter-attack, other than that Tyler at one point sent 200 men north to apprehend John of Gaunt. Since Gaunt commanded an entire army on the Scottish borders, this initiative seems ludicrous.[51] Had the ease with which the rebels took London engendered a fatal sense that the Plantagenet regime was in general a paper tiger? Had the drift homeward of the Essex rebels on the 14th been a more serious drain on rebel manpower than usually supposed, so that the loyalists calculated they might be able to get away with their treachery? If this was the case, what can we deduce about rebel behaviour? That food shortages were much more serious than anyone has imagined, so that Tyler was left with a minimal force on the 15th? Or had there been dissension in the rebel councils, possibly over the mishandling of the first manifesto? Does the absence of any mention of Jack Straw or John Ball on the 15th mean that the rebels had already splintered into rival factions?[52]

Whatever answer we give to these questions, the immediate sequel shows clearly enough the deep character of Richard II. Reacting with the viciousness that always characterises elites that have had a narrow squeak in a revolutionary situation, he gave Walworth and his acolytes (Knolles, Brembre, Philipot and Launde) quasi-dictatorial powers to seek out and punish all rebels within a seventy-mile radius of London, giving them carte blanche to behead, mutilate and torture as they saw fit. Doubtless, Richard's anger increased as he reflected on the risks he had run, for it is observable in human beings that the true emotional reaction to brushes with death comes some time afterwards. Certainly, the king's orders breathe cold vengeance and smack of what one observer has called 'innate Plantagenet vindictiveness'.[53] Walworth acted with notable brutality in London. Fleming survivors of the anti-foreigner pogroms, including women, were given the privilege of personally executing rebels who had beheaded their kinfolk (turning 'an eye for an eye' into 'a head for a head' as decapitation was the preferred method).[54] It is reported that some rebels in London, unaware of the dramatic events in Smithfield, were still pillaging and looting when Walworth's death squads came upon them.[55] On 20 June Richard issued commissions for the punishment of rebels nationwide, and appointed Robert Tresilian, a hanging judge, as chief justice.[56] The other rebel leaders were of course marked men. Jack Straw was caught and beheaded without trial while trying to escape to the north. In the case of John Ball, it was decided that a show trial would be efficacious for lancing the boil of lingering rebellion. Ball was confronted with 'evidence' supposedly taken from Straw just before his execution, which accused Tyler of wanting to keep the king as a captive, a tame puppet he would tote around England and use to issue decrees that would legitimate Tyler's wishes; also on the charge sheet were Tyler's alleged plans to seize all Church property, abolish all clergy save mendicant orders, execute all magnates and finally, when all the oligarchic dross had been cleared out, kill the king himself.[57] These 'true confessions' were of course a tissue of nonsense, the most obvious black propaganda by the victors. Yet the elite went through the forms of law. Ball was tried before Tresilian in St Albans and condemned, but William Courtenay, Bishop of London, secured a stay of execution to see if Ball would repent of his 'sins'. To his great credit, he refused. When Ball had been teased and tormented enough he too was executed, but this time there was no 'merciful' beheading such as had been visited on Straw. He was consigned to the full horrors of a traitor's death, being hanged, drawn and quartered on 15 July.[58] The two most amazing survivors of the king's purge were Farringdon and Horne, who were imprisoned for eighteen months and then released.[59]

Richard based himself on the Herts/Essex border to oversee the work of pacification. Within a week of the drama of Smithfield the Earl of Buckingham landed with his army, having been recalled urgently from Portugal; had Tyler prevailed at Smithfield, a genuine civil war would have been the result. Much of the repression in the early days of the Walworth despotism was directed against the Kent rebels (and Richard sent Thomas Holland into Kent itself for mopping-up operations), but the men of Essex soon came to repent of their hasty departure on 14 July and tried to regroup. They began by sending envoys to Richard, then at Waltham, to claim the liberties promised at Mile End and apparently confirmed at Smithfield. Richard utterly repudiated all his promises on the grounds that they had been made under duress. So hard line was the mood that his councillors wanted him to execute the envoys, but he decided to grant them the traditional rights of safe conduct granted to heralds and emissaries.[60] But he did send them back with a chilling message, showing clearly that he had never meant a word of his previous pledges:

> Give this message to your colleagues from the king. Villeins you are and villeins you will remain; in permanent bondage, not as it was before, but incomparably harsher . . . While by God's grace we rule over this kingdom, we shall strive . . . to keep you in subjection, to such a degree that the suffering of your servitude may serve as an example to posterity, and that now and in future men like you may ever have before your eyes your present misery as something to contemplate, a reason for cursing you and for fearing to perpetuate crimes like yours.[61]

In despair the Essex rebels resolved to make a stand against Buckingham at Rettenden near Billericay. But this time they were up against the heavy cavalry originally destined to tear the heart out of the King of Spain. Buckingham, joined by the northern magnate Lord Thomas Percy, sent his heavy cavalry against entrenched rebel positions and breached them easily. A colossal slaughter ensued, with more than 100 rebel corpses counted after the brief battle.[62]

That was effectively the end of the rising in London and the Home Counties. Meanwhile the virus of rebellion had spread elsewhere in the nation. There were insurrections also in the north-east of England, at York, Beverley and Scarborough, and in East Anglia and neighbouring counties, with Norwich, Ely, Peterborough, Cambridge, Bury St Edmunds, Yarmouth, Northampton, Dunstable and St Albans particularly to the fore. As in the English Civil War 260 years later, the nation seemed split between a pro-rebel east and a pro-loyalist west, though it is true that there were serious enough risings at Winchester and Bridgwater, albeit isolated from the rebel mainstream. These urban risings can in turn be subdivided in various ways: some being struggles of would-be boroughs against abbots who were feudal superiors, some more properly class warfare between oligarchs and have-nots; others being exclusively urban phenomena (York, Winchester, Beverley, Scarborough) contrasted with the 'mixed' rebellions in St Albans, Bury St Edmunds and Cambridge, where townsmen made common cause with peasants and villagers.[63] There has always been a prevailing belief that in the fourteenth century the agrarian society of northern England was stable, immune to the 'contagion' of rebellion. Dubious as this proposition is, it is in any case irrelevant, for the great conflicts in Yorkshire were urban. York, Beverley and Scarborough were regarded by Richard II's advisers as three of the five most dangerous hotspots in the north (Hull and Newcastle were the others).[64] Here urban discontent was a function of populousness, size and wealth – particularly the wealth created by overseas trade. In York and Beverley much of the conflict was 'horizontal' – the 'in' members of a mercantile elite against the 'outs'. Craft guilds played no significant part in the turbulence in these towns in 1381. Scarborough was the most interesting case, for here we can discern the few with vast fortunes pitted against the craftsmen and retailers who had not fared so well from the burgeoning foreign trade.[65] Additionally, Scarborough exhibited the extreme volatility associated with a town that felt itself to be vulnerable and isolated militarily. Dominated by a royal castle, it was an obvious target for invading Scots, especially as it was the only port between the Humber and the Tyne. Laid waste by the Scots in 1378, Scarborough fused the anger it felt at lack of protection from the Plantagenet elite with a concomitant fury against illegal extortions by bailiffs and royal officials.[66] Though easily enough suppressed in the aftermath of Tyler's failure in London, the rising in Scarborough in June 1381 brought 500 men out onto the streets. It was both a very serious rising and a genuine mass movement.[67]

North of London and into East Anglia the rebellion was suppressed less easily. It is true that the outbreak in Ipswich collapsed ignominiously when John Preston, the rebel leader there, misread the situation after 15 June and had the temerity to approach Buckingham with a list of demands to be put to the king; he was arrested and executed on the spot.[68] St Albans, another hotspot, was the scene of a tremendous struggle between the abbot and the townspeople, with the added peculiarity that the St Albans burghers appealed for their validation, not to Domesday Book but to the Anglo-Saxon charter of Offa; here, as in Bury St Edmunds, where the appeal was to the laws of King Cnut (Canute), there were glimmerings of the protest against the 'Norman yoke' that became so popular in the seventeenth century.[69] The conflict in St Albans was so sulphurous that the abbey was just on the point of being burned to the ground when word came in that Tyler had been assassinated and the London rebels dispersed; even so, it took until the end of June for royal authority, and with it the hegemony of the abbot, to be restored. On 16 June Abbot de la Mare recognised the town as a borough, then confirmed Richard II's general charter of manumission and was forced to pay £1,000 as compensation and 'quitclaim'. News of this climbdown spread to neighbouring areas, forcing the abbot also to recognise Barnet, Rickmansworth, Redburn and Watford as boroughs. Only on 29 June with the arrival of Sir Walter Lee and a large body of cavalry and archers was the status quo ante restored.[70] The rebels in Suffolk at first achieved greater things. Here the dominant personality was John Wrawe, a priest but sadly, as would later transpire, a coward. Raising men in Sudbury, he took his band first to Liston-on-Stour and Long Melford, recruiting as he went, and entered Bury St Edmunds to a rapturous welcome, not surprisingly, as this town, in its struggle with the local abbot for borough status, was another St Albans.[71] The Suffolk rebels scored a great success by capturing and beheading Sir John Cavendish, Chief Justice of the King's Bench, in the village of Lakenheath. Next they plundered the home of their deadly enemy, the priory of St Edmunds at Bury and beheaded the prior, John Cambridge. A breakaway group rampaged in Thetford. Wrawe and his men occupied Bury St Edmunds for eight days, and this time looting and plundering distinguished the rebels as Wrawe, the 'king' of Suffolk, was too weak to restrain them. Anarchy continued until the Earl of Suffolk arrived in the county on 23 June with 500 men-at-arms.[72] The Suffolk rebellion was interesting as a social phenomenon. Quite apart from the distinctive situation in Bury St Edmunds, it exhibited both private score-settling by the prosperous against the even more wealthy and bitter class conflict between landlords and prosperous tenants trying to throw off their villein status. Needless to say, Wrawe was soon identified by the royal party as a 'monster' of the ilk of Tyler, Straw and Ball. Even though he turned king's evidence after the failure of the rising, this did not save him and he suffered the traitor's fate of being hanged drawn and quartered.[73]

There are strong grounds for saying that the rebellion in East Anglia was an offshoot of the original Essex rising, which spread from Essex to Suffolk and then to Norfolk and Cambridgeshire. Without question the insurrection in Norfolk was the most violent and turbulent outside London and, ominously, for the first time one can discern members of the gentry joining upper peasants and the urban proletariat. In Norfolk the Tyler of the piece was a dyer named Geoffrey Litster, but his second-in-command was Sir Roger Bacon, a gentleman. Other scions of the gentry serving with Litster, either voluntarily or under duress (naturally after the rebellion all claimed it was the latter) were Sir Roger Scales, Sir Thomas Morley, Sir John de Brewes and Sir Stephen Hales.[74] The last two, who seem to have been initially very able, went straight for the jugular by raising men and besieging Norwich on 18 June. Their future nemesis, Henry Despenser, a 38-year-old warrior prelate and Bishop of Norwich, made good his escape as the pillaging hordes swept into the city with minimal resistance.[75] Litster gave the town over to wholesale sack and rapine, targeting justices of the peace and tax collectors for decapitation. Reginald Eccles, a prominent JP, was one of the first to go to the executioner's block. Litster devised a scam that seems to have been unique to him, whereby he extorted hefty ransoms from the most wealthy citizens in exchange for leaving their properties unscathed. One such burgher, Henry Lominor, had to pay £666 to secure freedom from pillage.[76] The success he had secured in Norwich seemed to go to Litster's head. He styled himself the 'king of the Commons', held court in Thorpe market and feasted lavishly in the great hall of Norwich Castle. He also insisted that Morley, Scales, Brewes and Hales act as his personal servants, performing such tasks as tasting his food to make sure it was not poisoned and generally working as lackeys.[77] Meanwhile his men were laying waste the rest of north Norfolk, and sacked Yarmouth and other places. There seems to have been no attempt to coordinate action with Wrawe in Suffolk, and by the third week of June even Bacon was having second thoughts about his 'king'. Yet there could be no doubt about the seriousness of the situation in East Anglia. Soon the rebellion was spiralling into Cambridgeshire, and on 15 June Wrawe's men stormed into Cambridge, where the university was an object of particular detestation.[78] In a classic manifestation of 'town versus gown' the citizens of Cambridge joined them in gutting the university library and sacking Corpus Christi College. The townsmen did not regard the university as an august seat of learning but rather as a bloodsucking leech that enjoyed privileges at their expense and practised 'academic freedom' while colluding in local constraints on liberty.[79]

Despenser meanwhile made his base of operations at Burleigh, two days' ride from Norwich and planned his counteroffensive. He was one of those warrior-bishops, like Odo of Bayeux under William the Conqueror, who relished the battlefield more than the pulpit.[80] His first task was to construct a 'heartland' or defensive perimeter triangular in shape, bounded by Peterborough, Ely and Huntingdon. Once he had gathered a credible force, Despenser moved out against Peterborough, then under siege by the rebels. He achieved complete surprise, took the besiegers in the rear, and slaughtered large numbers of them. The survivors took sanctuary in the abbey church, but Despenser showed how much he really believed in God by violating sanctuary and butchering them.[81] Elated by his easy triumph, Despenser recruited more men for his ultimate target: recapturing Norwich. First he relieved Cambridge on 19 June, angered and dismayed by the devastation he witnessed, with St Mary's Church and Corpus Christi smoking ruins and dreadful tales of rebel mulcting and 'fines': £2,000 uplifted from Barnwell Priory outside the town and £3,000 from Cambridge University itself. Despenser now advanced cautiously on Norwich and immediately encountered serendipity. Finally rousing himself from his fantasies of kingship, Litster had decided to send envoys to the real king to ask for a pardon; he wanted it both ways, both the fruits of pillage and extortion *and* amnesty. The five envoys he selected were Morley and Brewes plus three commoners. Unfortunately for them, the travellers, pursuing a south-westerly track from Norwich to London, ran smack into Despenser's advancing army on 22 June.[82] Morley and Brewes dithered about how to comport themselves but finally betrayed the three commoner envoys to Despenser, who immediately beheaded them, though he had no licence or authority whatsoever to do so.[83] The bloodthirsty bishop pressed on to Norwich on the 24th, but found it abandoned by Litster and the rebels. Pursuing them implacably, he ran them to earth on 26 June. Litster was forced to make a stand at North Walsham, but Despenser's cavalry, led by the bishop himself, broke through the rebel lines with contemptuous ease. Despenser took no prisoners and executed all who surrendered. Litster he reserved for a traitor's death by hanging, drawing and quartering, though again it must be emphasised that the bishop had no authority to declare anyone traitor, much less carry out the sentence.[84] His draconian actions did the trick, however, and the rising in Norfolk collapsed as miraculously as the one in London after Tyler's death. Knowing that Sir Roger Bacon had friends in high places, he spared him, and Bacon was later, predictably, pardoned. Whereas the elite were merciless and bloodthirsty against the lower orders, they were prepared to take a 'boys will be boys' approach to their own rebellious kind.

Richard II and his government had regained their grip on the nation by the end of June. By mid-July the country was pacified and the principal rebel leaders had been executed. Unfortunately between July and November, when he was finally forced to call a halt, Richard positively wallowed in the reign of terror he had unleashed, becoming an addict of martial law and a devotee of cruel and unusual punishment.[85] Historians differ on the death toll during and after the Peasants' Revolt (as they do about the toll in most conflicts), but no one opts for a figure lower than 1,500, with some going as high as 7,000. A climate of fear descended on the nation and the mantle of repression and terror was dense, with a single word out of place sufficing to consign one to the gallows. The plethora of severed heads stuck on gates and gibbeted corpses added to the ambience of chaos. Neighbours 'fingered' each other as rebels, and servants informed against masters; the atmosphere was perfect for the settling of old grudges and private scores.[86] By November, when Parliament met, the reprisals were themselves becoming a threat to political stability. Different special commissioners were operating in the same county, and all of them were cutting across the work of judges in the regular judicial system. An entire new set of escheators had to be appointed to deal with forfeited property, and malicious litigants had begun to clog up the work of the courts by inserting charges of treason and rebellion into pre-existing lawsuits.[87] The November Parliament was determined to assert itself against the king and his officials. A titanic struggle ensued. Deeply unhappy about Richard's blatant perfidy in so flagrantly repudiating the pledges he had made at Mile End and Smithfield, the Commons were forced to back down on this issue when the king used overt menaces to force the ratification of his repeal through Parliament.[88] Yet the Commons extracted a price. They insisted that the king do something about the coterie of worthless cronies who surrounded him in his household and hinted that in their view the rebels had had more than a ghost of a case. The king was forced to agree to a general pardon for the rebels, excepting only around 100 named prominent leaders who had not yet been run to earth and who were expressly excluded from the amnesty. This conciliatory gesture by Richard, so at odds with his bloodthirsty antics over the previous five months, is sometimes set down to the influence of his future wife Anne of Bohemia (whom he married in June 1382). Even so, Richard wanted to exclude the citizens of Cambridge, Canterbury and Bury St Edmunds from the pardon. He got his way only with Bury St Edmunds, which had to pay a fine of 2,000 marks to have the sentence of outlawry lifted.[89]

The skeleton at the feast at the convocation of the London Parliament in November 1381 was John of Gaunt, one of the prime causes of the revolt. Whether through military calculation or a more devious political Machiavellianism – possibly reckoning that whoever won between Tyler and Richard II he could emerge as *tertius gaudens* – Gaunt made no attempt to march towards the scenes of murder and conflagration in London that June but remained in Scotland, justifying his inaction by negotiating what seemed a favourable treaty with the Scots. When he did finally march south, the wildest rumours circulated. One was that he was advancing on London with 20,000 men to make himself king; another was that he had freed all his serfs and was going to assume power at the head of a peasant army.[90] Meanwhile Gaunt's long-standing rivalry with Henry Percy, Earl of Northumberland, burst into the open. Northumberland shut the castle of Bambrugh against Gaunt, saying he could not receive him without explicit approval from the king. A loose cannon, whom the juvenile Richard II could not control, Gaunt came to Westminster for the Parliament in November with a huge retinue of men. Northumberland did likewise and, since London backed him against their hated Lancastrian enemy, there were even fears that the City would arise again and the erstwhile pro-Tyler levies make common cause with Percy's troops. In the end Richard II had to intervene to patch up the quarrel.[91] There are grounds for thinking that Richard remained suspicious of Gaunt. Although he had modelled himself on Gaunt – to the point where the king's critics said that he had all the vices of 'time-honour'd Lancaster' without any of his virtues – Gaunt had never mentored him properly or given him any significant guidance; Richard essentially had a disastrous childhood with no worthwhile male role-models.[92] Richard used Tresilian and his other acolytes to rain terror on the ex-rebels, using charges of treason, especially those of the swearing of oaths of confederacy against the institution of lordship and waging war against the king – ironically the one thing the rebels had *not* done. Gaunt and the other freelance dispensers of justice – including the aptly named Despenser – had to make do with private prosecutions through the Court of Common Pleas, which invariably had less successful outcomes than the king's terror.[93]

The Peasants' Revolt was a seismic event in English history. The lower orders rose up with a vengeance, killing 'traitors', beheading or manhandling royal officials, justices of the peace, escheators and tax collectors, murdering foreigners in the rage of xenophobia, attacking property, burning court records and manorial documents, stealing landlords' cattle, timber, hay and other goods, practising petty theft, grand larceny and blackmail, taking back enclosed land into common use, forcing servants to leave their lords, withdrawing rents, tithes, *corvée* and other services by tenants, refusing to recognise courts and tribunals, to say nothing of the many acts of private grudge-settling and personal vendetta. There could be no disguising the scale, scope or extent of the rebellion: 105 villages in Essex went on the warpath, 118 in Kent, 72 in Suffolk and 35 in Hertfordshire, apart from the many town risings already mentioned.[94] Although the conflict setting the rebels against the king and his officials was savage and bloody, one surprising aspect of 1381 is the low level of violence by and against feudal lords. Most landowners offered no resistance to the rebels until after 15 July when the king began his suppression of the rising. Most of the great nobles and magnates avoided arbitrary force in their dealings with the angry insurrectionists, perhaps tacitly conceding that the rebels had a point and there had been significant abuses of power by officialdom.[95] Although there were peasants in the rising, the rebellion was no more a rural *jacquerie* than the Pacific Ocean is pacific. The key social elements taking part were craftsmen and tradesmen, and the key to the initial success of the rising was the support for it by these elements in London.[96] There are two main perspectives in the theory of revolutionary causation, one stressing the Marxist notion of increasing immiseration, the other popularised by Alexis de Tocqueville that stresses the increasing expectations generated by rising prosperity (see Appendix). All the evidence suggests that 1381 was a Tocquevillian revolution. Not only were many of the key rebel players middle-aged, they were artisans and skilled workers, with a sophisticated understanding of law and government; insofar as peasants were to the fore in the rising they were 'upper' peasants, the most wealthy species of the genus.[97] The focus of rebellion was London and the south-east, then as now the most prosperous part of the country. Surprise had sometimes been expressed that in East Anglia the leadership seems almost to have devolved on the 'middle sectors' – clergymen, squires, knights – and it has been suggested that East Anglia exhibited anomie at its most glaring in the contrast between villages where free men had never disappeared and neighbouring ones which saw the manorial system at its most extreme.[98]

What were the consequences of the rebellion of 1381? Some commentators have expressed scepticism that anything at all was achieved after so much bloodshed, but this is an exaggeration. It is true that Richard II at once declared his abolition of serfdom null and void and that it would take two centuries of socio-economic change, not a sudden decree, to extirpate villeinage. Yet some indices of change were visible even in the near aftermath of the rising. 'Copyhold' tenure was increasingly set down in the manorial court rolls, while many landlords abandoned demesne cultivation and farmed out parcels of land to contractors at a set fee.[99] If these were gradual and long-term changes, some of the results of 1381 were immediate and even dramatic. In November 1381 Parliament gave up on the Poll Tax and opted to levy taxes on trade; no one ever again attempted to introduce this ill-starred venture until the disastrous events of 1990. Parliament too found a new lease of confidence and dug in against royal excesses. It refused to allow general alarm at the recent social unrest to be used as an excuse to increase the power of prelates.[100] Indeed, the Peasants' Revolt made Parliament reluctant to vote taxes at all, which in turn stymied English initiatives in the Hundred Years War. It may therefore not be an exaggeration to say that the events in England in 1381 were actually a turning point in the conflict with France, and that thereafter, until final defeat in 1453, England was always on the back foot.[101] Moreover, England remained uneasy and restive for the rest of the decade, with conspiracies and rumours of conspiracies, especially in Norfolk, Sussex and Kent, rife for the rest of the 1380s, some of which were blamed on the continuing problem of Lollardism.[102] At the level of personalities one can discern a varied impact of 1381. It is likely that Richard II's great success at Smithfield on 15 June gave him both an exaggerated idea of his own abilities and a false idea of the scope of kingly power, thus leading to the absolutist tendencies that would bring him to disaster and death in 1399.[103] In this connection it is interesting that the three aristocrats who were the principal suppressors of the rebels in 1381 – the Earls of Buckingham, Arundel and Warwick – were the three leaders of the 1388 oligarchic purge against the king. Richard had already made it clear that he preferred the company of toadies to aristocrats and, paranoid and vindictive as he was, distrusted both his subjects and his nobles.[104] Those who loathed and despised the most avid agents of Richard's thirst for blood in 1381 enjoyed mixed consolation. Despenser died in his bed after narrowly avoiding being dubbed traitor for opposing Henry IV in 1399. But Nicholas Brembre and Chief Justice Tresilian were executed for high treason on the say-so of the 'Merciless Parliament' of 1387.[105] John of Gaunt continued in the same old way, always the despot, always the trimmer. The revolt would not have changed his attitudes as he was always a man who preferred compromise, manipulation and 'transformation' of an opponent over confrontation, rebellion or ambitions for the throne.[106] If there was one clear winner of the Peasants' Revolt it was Gaunt, ironically the one man who had done more than any other to trigger it.

Finally, we must examine the impact of the rising on literature, and its reputation down the centuries, for otherwise the revolt would be of purely antiquarian interest. It is a commonplace that the great English poets of the late fourteenth century – Chaucer, Langland and John Gower – viewed the rebellion with loathing and detestation and, indeed, how could it be otherwise, for their careers depended on the favour of great lords. Gower makes it quite clear that, however corrupt English society is – and he gives many examples of this – any alternative, such as the Peasants' Revolt is even worse; at least fraudsters and embezzlers are examples of the 'banality of evil' and are not manifestations of Satan himself.[107] Gower tacked on what is now Book One of his *Vox Clamantis* as an afterthought following the events of 1381, having written what are now Books Two–Six in 1378–81. Gower is not in the class of Langland and Chaucer and *Vox Clamantis* is usually thought deficient in structure, architecture and resolution, not helped by the poet's notorious habit of plagiarising large chunks of Ovid's *Metamorphoses*. In Book One of *Vox* Gower clumsily changes tack several times in an attempt to make his dream allegory fit the facts of the rebellion. First he portrays the rebels as (literally) wild animals; his point is that in rebelling the peasants have abandoned their humanity. Wat Tyler himself is portrayed as a jay, persuading the other animals to devilry in a manner familiar from medieval beast fables.[108] Then Gower confusingly drops the wild-beasts motif and shifts to the tale of Troy as an allegory of London in 1381 (both admitted invaders). After the poet has told us how he flees Troy to escape death at the hands of the Greeks/rebels and skulks in a wood, he proceeds to make good his escape in a ship (the ship of state?). The ship, which at times seems to double as the ill-fated Tower of London, is almost engulfed by a hurricane/cyclone before coming to safe haven. Presumably the lack of any naturalistic sequence in the poem is meant to suggest the dimensions of a nightmare, for Gower, in common with all the chroniclers, thought that 1381 represented the unleashing of forces that were literally satanic. This is made explicit in his portrait of Wat Tyler: 'Just as this Devil was placed in command over the army of the lower world, so this scoundrel was in charge of the wicked mob. A harsh voice, a wicked expression, a very faithful likeness to a death's head – these things gave token of his appearance.'[109]

William Langland was also deeply influenced by the events of 1381. It is now the consensus among Langland scholars that the famous three rescensions of his *Piers Plowman* are all the work of a single author, that they were composed in the chronological order denoted by the A-B-C sequence and that the 'C' version represents Langland's 'cleaning up' his social criticism in the light of the events of 1381, so that the blame for that 'unnatural' event falls largely on the peasantry and so that he is completely dissociated from Lollardism or any hint of sympathy for the rebels.[110] This was all the more necessary, since some Langland experts view *Piers Plowman* as a classic manifestation of the 'divided self', with Langland's conscious impulses conservative and in favour of hierarchy and authority and his unconscious ones working in the opposite direction.[111] Yet another 'dream allegory', *Piers Plowman* is an ambitious attempt to investigate the true meaning of Christianity in both a practical and contemplative sense. It has been likened to Blake's *Prophetic Works*, Wordsworth's *The Prelude* and T. S. Eliot's *Four Quartets* but, with its multiple narrators and consciousnesses, overlapping voices (both of the author and the characters), its frequent digressions and its confusing tacking between naturalistic analysis and religious mysticism, it often brings Laurence Sterne to mind; certainly the shorthand tag 'surrealist' seems the most appropriate brief description.[112] Langland is a far more valuable source for 1381 than Gower, as he provides a deep, albeit idiosyncratic, description of the forces at play instead of lapsing into the most fantastical type of allegory. However, Langland's chief deficiency as a social critic is that he can never transcend the medieval mindset whereby rebellion among the lower orders in society must always be perceived as *contra naturam* and against natural order, being a literally diabolical manifestation of the underworld or Hell, with Wat Tyler, Jack Straw and John Ball as minions of Satan.[113]

Only in the seventeenth century, in the Cromwellian era of radical thought, was the true significance of 1381 apprehended. Whereas official Roundhead propaganda tried to make Wat Tyler and Jack Straw forerunners of Cromwell as fighters against royal tyranny, the Levellers saw Tyler as the first man to try to throw off the detested 'Norman yoke'. Yet it was not until the late eighteenth century that the high tide of pro-Tylerism was manifested. Whereas William Morris in *The Dream of John Ball* would see his hero as an egalitarian outlaw in the tradition of Robin Hood (who had himself been rescued from his medieval 'placing' as a merely thuggish outlaw),[114] Robert Southey concentrated on the martyr of Smithfield. After writing a play on Tyler in 1794, Southey composed a poem to mark the place in Smithfield where he was assassinated:

This is the place where England's injur'd sons
Rebell'd against their sovereign, for they found
His yoke was grievous. Pass not lightly on!
This is a place may well invite thy mind
To serious musings. Monarchs here may learn
If they oppress their people, if they waste
Their blood, and rob from the poor labourer
His hard earn'd mite, that there may come a day
Of vengeance. Here the citizens should think
That not by tumult and mad violence
Can peace be forc'd, and Order and Reform
But by the calm, collected public voice –
Marking our father's errors, be we wise![115]

Another great radical, Tom Paine, made an even more trenchant attack on the conservatism of Edmund Burke, whose anti-revolutionary thinking in many ways showed scant improvement on Gower and Langland. After describing Tyler as 'an intrepid, disinterested man', Paine continued to a withering evisceration of the views of Burke, of whom it was once well said that his ideology commits us to blaming the sailors if a ship encounters a storm at sea: 'All his [Tyler's] proposals made to Richard were on a more just and public ground than those which had been made to John by the barons, and notwithstanding the sycophancy of men like Mr Burke who seek to gloss over a base action of the Court by traducing Tyler, his fame will outlive that falsehood. If the barons merited a monument to be erected in Runnymede, Tyler merits one in Smithfield.'[116]

3
Jack Cade

Entire books have been written about the events of 1381 and, in a single chapter devoted to the general theme of revolution, it is not possible to do justice to every sub-theme or to explore down every byway: for instance, we have said nothing about the role of women in the revolt or the possible involvement of freemasonry.[1] The Peasants' Revolt was a unique event, triggered by particular events, which could have followed a very different course; in particular the denouement could have turned out otherwise. There was nothing predetermined or fated about it, and historical inevitability cannot explain it. Yet an overemphasis on its uniqueness risks making it a 'one-off' one-dimensional phenomemon.[2] All worthwhile historical analysis involves a combination of the particular, the specific, the contingent and the aleatory with the more general features of society in a given historical epoch. Marx's famous statement: 'Men make history but they do not make it in circumstances of their own choosing' has become a historian's cliché, but it is true. To set the revolt in a proper context, it is worth examining the thesis that the fourteenth century in Europe was an era of general crisis. Any suggestion of 'general crisis', however tentative, usually has the devotees of absolute historical uniqueness on their hind legs, yet it cannot be denied that in certain historical periods social and economic turbulence is observable over a wide range of roughly comparable societies. The famous examples are the 1640s and the explosion of Europe into general revolution in the late 1840s.[3] There are strong grounds for asserting that fourteenth-century Europe was another such era, exhibiting as it did signs of malaise and crisis in a number of spheres: climatic, demographic, cultural, religious, financial, socio-economic. Indeed, some historians are prepared to go even further and claim that there are grounds for postulating a worldwide crisis, most obviously in relation to the Black Death but also embracing calamitous events in Japan, China, Korea, India, south-east Asia and the rise of Tamerlane in central Asia.[4] It will therefore be useful to place the Peasants' Revolt in context, working inwards from the most general to the most specific factors, especially as the 1450 rising under Jack Cade is often considered the Mark Two version of the peasants' rebellion.

The deep structure of 1381 was that the peasantry had suffered almost a century of instability in living standards, had often hovered on the brink of starvation, and were determined that the great lords should not arrest their improved economic position and thrust them back to the breadline. Those who stress the 'hidden hand' of Malthusian pandemics like to argue that Europe, overpopulated at the end of the thirteenth century, then suffered a violent reaction, mainly caused by the Black Death, which saw Europe's population halved. On worst-case estimates France may have lost two-thirds of its population in the fourteenth century to plague, epidemics of disease, crop failure and the Hundred Years War. Naturally, the worst era was that of 1350–1420, immediately after the Black Death. The more temperate zones seem to have fared best, with a mortality of 40 per cent in Germany, 50 per cent in Provence and 70 per cent in Tuscany.[5] Not all of this can be attributed to the Black Death. Earlier in the century there were two other great disasters. The great cattle plague of 1315–21 (murrain and rinderpest) coincided with what has been called the 'Great Famine' of 1315–22, characterised by quasi-biblical flooding in northern Europe from late 1314 to late 1316 and again in the winter and spring of 1321, accompanied by failed grain harvests, mainly of winter crops. In 1316 the price of wheat soared to 325 per cent of the price the year before; wheat harvests in 1315–22 produced only 40–60 per cent of the normal yield, and some 15–20 per cent of the population of Europe perished from famine.[6] Some say the consequences of 1315–22 lasted two years and the peasantry was just revovering when it was engulfed by the Black Death. One of the reasons the Peasants' Revolt of 1381 was largely a middle-aged rising was that disproportionate numbers of the young had been carried off by the Black Death.[7] The situation was at its worst in England, where the first three Edwards were warlike and expansionist and plunged the nation into the disastrous and costly wars of Scottish independence.

Heavy taxation after the disaster of Bannockburn in 1314 coincided with the worst famine period. Moreover these taxes were directed not at landed income, which would have hit the feudal lords, but at movable goods – seed corn, ploughs, agricultural tools and implements, etc – which impacted most grievously on the peasantry.[8]

At the most basic level, then, the crisis of the fourteenth century involved catastrophic population losses, especially in the period 1350–1420, largely though not wholly attributable to the Black Death.[9] Fear of famine ranked second only to plague as a perennial terror, since crop failure was a recurrent reality and bad harvests bore mainly on the poor, thus accentuating the pre-existing social inequality. Langland's poem *Piers Plowman* repeatedly refers to this issue, as also the wafer-thin margin of subsistence for the peasantry, who endured scarcity of food before every harvest and a short-lived abundance thereafter, provided the harvests did not fail.[10] Some scholars refer the uncertainties of the weather, especially the great rains of 1315–17, to a distinct climate change. On this view, the so-called Medieval Warm Period, lasting from about 950 to 1250, then gradually morphed into the ferocious Little Ice Age, which lasted from the beginning of the seventeenth century to the end of the nineteenth; the fourteenth century would therefore have been a transition period, with the associated climatic uncertainties and warm summers no longer dependable.[11] Millenarians and eschatologists were always on the lookout for distinctive features of the weather which they could interpret as the wrath of God or the coming of the end of times. There *was* an apocalyptic element in the Peasants' Revolt, fed by the great storm of May 1381, which seemed to presage disaster; there had been a similar reaction to a ferocious gale in 1362.[12] Population losses and the uncertainties of the rural life paradoxically led to a 'population implosion' in English towns, and this was particularly noticeable in Kent. This phenomenon played its part in the revolt of 1381 since the new urban immigrants resented the power of the old, entrenched families who had survived the Black Death, making them form common cause with their countryside brethren. This was yet another reason why a rigid distinction between the revolt in the towns and the countryside in 1381 will not work. Demographic changes in the 1360s and 1370s prepared the way for violent conflict by underlining the gap between the new urban immigrants and their aspirations and the old methods of government and social control in towns and cities.[13]

Contributing to the sense of chaos in the fourteenth century was a general financial collapse of a kind that would not be seen again until the twenty-first century. The disastrously poor calibre of English leadership and elite savoir faire can be gauged by the decision of Edward III to add to Europe's woes and diminish its population still further by launching into the Hundred Years War. Just as Bannockburn had been followed by the Great Hunger and the cattle plague, so the 'glories' of Crécy were followed almost immediately, as if by some malign pre-established harmony, by the Black Death. Edward III has had a good press from historians and has certainly been overrated. His martial skills were not of the order of Richard I the Lionheart's, his judgement was poor and his main domestic legacy was the attempt to defy the laws of economics in the Statute of Labourers.[14] It may be an exaggeration to say, as one historian has, that he was 'an avaricious and sadistic thug . . . a destructive and merciless force', but this is closer to the truth than the 'Perfect King' hagiography accorded him by the mainstream academic establishment today.[15] Yet the obvious social instability caused by battle deaths and post-battle wounds, the plunder and pillage of the French countryside and the rape and mayhem visited on the French peasantry with the subsequent production of banditry, had even worse unintended consequences. Europe's financial system depended heavily for lubrication on the three great banking houses of Florence – Bardi, Peruzzi and Acciavioli. Edward III borrowed 1,365,000 gold florins to finance his campaigns in France and, after early reverses, suspended payment on the debt in May 1339, still owing 800,000 florins to the Bardi and Peruzzi houses. This is said to have been the first of only a few such defaults in English history.[16] The Bardi bank was particularly badly hit, for in 1340 Robert of Naples added to their woes by defaulting on his debts with them. The Bardis tried at first to escape their predicament by leading a revolt against the Florentine government in November 1340, but this failed; their banking house limped on until finally collapsing in 1346.[17]

As if all this was not enough, the years immediately before the Peasants' Revolt saw the medieval world embroiled in a religious crisis, often termed the Great Schism or (to differentiate it from the earlier one of 1054) the Western Schism, when two rival popes battled for supremacy. Religion was supposed to be the ultimate social cement in the so-called Age of Belief, the solid backbone of society that provided eternal and unshakeable truth, yet here was the Church itself in chaos and disarray. The situation was one memorably summed up by Herman Melville in *Moby-Dick*: 'Who's to doom when the judge himself is dragged before the bar?'[18] The college of cardinals elected a Neapolitan as Pope Urban VI in 1378, mainly, they claimed, to appease the mob, but immediately regretted what they had done when Urban proved despotic, paranoid and given to violent outbursts of temper. They then elected another pope to replace him (Clement VII). But Urban refused to abdicate, so Clement set up a rival court at Avignon. There had been rival popes before, but the novelty of the 1378 imbroglio was that this time a single group of princes of the Church had created both the pope and the 'antipope'.[19] What might have been thought a collective act of temporary madness by the cardinals quickly spiralled out of control, as the two popes became the focus for rivalries between the European powers. France, Spain, Burgundy, Savoy, Naples and Scotland opted for the Avignon pope, while England, Flanders, the Holy Roman Empire, northern Italy, Hungary and Scandinavia recognised the incumbent at Rome.[20] The schism continued after the death of the principals. Boniface IX was crowned in Rome in 1389 while Benedict XIII became the new Avignon pope in 1394. The rivalry created fanatical hatreds among religious zealots. After complex and tortuous negotiations the situation was finally resolved in 1417 with the election of Martin V, though a diehard Avignon faction held out until 1429.[21]

Incredibly, the schism took place when the Church was in danger from a variety of breakaway creeds that would finally burgeon with the sixteenth-century Reformation. In England this threat came mainly from the Lollards, with their dangerous heresy of viewing the pope as Antichrist and denying the 'real presence' in the eucharist. Although the Lollards were confusingly Janus-faced, opposed to official religion yet resolutely hostile to other religious 'dissidents' such as the friars, they benefited from complacency in the hierarchy of the cardinalate. It has been well said that the Church 'by the fourteenth century was a gigantic multinational corporation devoted to the perpetuation of its own power, privilege and wealth'.[22] Lollards apart, in England Catholicism manifested itself in an unseemly and bitter rivalry between the secular and regular clergy. Since Langland's *Piers Plowman* was designed as a master study of Christianity, it is a mirror in which we can view a wide spectrum of religious attitudes and understand the roots of this antagonism. Langland's detestation of friars is notorious, especially the Franciscans, whom he regards as having strayed from the path of St Francis into mere money grubbing. Particularly reprehensible was their habit of making confession easy in return for cash. By edging parish priests out of the principal role in hearing confession, the friars, thought Langland, were undermining its efficacy and sacramental status, as also the penitence that was supposed to go with it.[23] Yet Langland emphatically did not believe that 'my enemy's enemy is my friend', since, if anything, he regarded the anti-friar Lollards with even more abhorrence. Regarding all forms of communism or communalism as the mere enthronement of envy, Langland accused the friars of not really wanting to possess everything in common; what they coveted were the wealth and privileges of the elite. Langland's hatred of friars merged with his equal detestation of beggars. He characterised as humbug the regular clergy's selling point – that they rather than the secular clergy were the true Christians since Christ and his apostles had been beggars.[24] Of course Langland can himself be criticised for his strictures on the mendicant orders: while excoriating them for begging and taking money, he seemed to forget that they were forbidden by their own rules to own land.

Yet another concern for Langland was the growth of religious institutions and accretions that seemed to have nothing whatever to do with the teachings of Christ. Here he had the pardoners principally in mind. Pardoners were freelance religious functionaries who frequently overstepped their bounds by claiming falsely that they could grant absolution from sin. Pardoners carried a papal bull, which contained a formal statement of indulgence fixed with the seal of the bishops in whose sees they were licensed to preach. They were allowed to grant remission of the penalties for sin but *not* forgiveness from the sin itself. Needless to say, this distinction was too nice for simple peasants and artisans, and pardoners did nothing to enlighten their 'marks'. Moreover, pardoners were not supposed to *sell* indulgences, merely ask for alms, yet many of them 'sold' absolute forgiveness of sins at a premium rate.[25] The supposed regulation by bishops was usually a non-starter, for pardoners could bribe episcopal officials or bypass the bishop and go to the office of the local archdeacon for the necessary permission. Chaucer's pardoner in the *Canterbury Tales* is a virtual compendium of the corruption habitually alleged against his *confrères*.[26] Yet even without the problems of Lollards, friars and pardoners, the Church itself was riven with doubt and indecision, for it could not give a clear answer to the question: what is Jesus Christ's essential teaching on poverty and inequality? Langland's 'solution' to this was highly unsatisfactory. Attempting to square economic 'realism' with the clear teaching of Christ to give to the poor, he took refuge in the obfuscatory nature of original sin. Following the example of many senior churchmen he argued that 'in Christ there is neither bond nor free' was a prescription sub specie aeternitatis and applied to the heavenly world not the vale of tears, where serfdom was a consequence of original sin.[27] Neither Langland nor his mentors in the hierarchy seemed able to see the glaring holes in this argument. Not only was the Crucifixion in direct contradiction to any such casuistry, as it was meant to guarantee the brotherhood of Man, but on the 'original sin' scenario no explanation was offered for the privileged position of the lords. Were they somehow exempt from the consequences of the fall of Adam? One of the reasons *Piers Plowman* is so obviously a poem of crisis is that it shows, albeit unwittingly, the Church floundering in its own recondite theology, unable to give a clear lead to the peasantry.[28] It was not surprising that a contempt for clergy, churches and sanctuary was such a marked feature of the Peasants' Revolt.

The economic crisis in the fourteenth century was manifold but, simplifying, we can reduce it to three main headings. The central fact was the Black Death and its catastrophic impact on population levels. Since the plague caused an obvious labour shortage, those who survived should, by the normal laws of supply and demand, have seen a significant rise in real wages and living standards. But the feudal lords were determined to hang on to their privileges and struggled frantically to escape the implications of the Black Death through measures like the Statute of Labourers.[29] By enforcing to the letter feudal privileges and using royal officialdom as their executives, the great magnates tried to stem the tide of inevitability. Labour legislation to curb rising wages, the attempt to retain servile villeinage, and the attempt by landowners to recoup rent income in a period when the overall trend of rents was downwards were all efforts to swim against the flow of history. Yet none of this made armed insurrection inevitable. It was only the government's attempted introduction of discriminatory taxation to finance a futile and unpopular war that did that.[30] At the same time the feudal lords could, in the main, enjoy the support of organised religion, since the medieval mind saw any form of 'levelling' as the road to a world without order, a chaos world or, in theological terms, Hell itself. The Church faced the difficulty that its doctrines required it to regard poverty as a supreme evil; in this sense it was grateful for the (unwitting) support of St Francis and his followers, who stressed poverty as the greatest Christian virtue.[31] Unfortunately the seigneurial backlash was unleashed at the very time the peasants' aspirations were rising, as their favourable position in the labour market became clear. They perceived the vast Pacific Ocean of inequality that separated them from their 'betters' and were not prepared to tolerate it. Inequality and the seigneurial system were, then, two main pieces in the complicated mosaic of class conflict. A third was the fact that urbanisation and the market economy obviously collided with the requirements of the seigneurial system. This was clearly a factor in the greater militancy of Kent and Essex in the Peasants' Revolt, for there the market economy was more important. Beyond that, there was an obvious 'contradiction' between the need to expand production – implying greater freedom both for trades and the peasants – and the requirements of traditional aristocratic power. In this sense it is quite correct for Marxists to emphasise the fourteenth century as a key moment in the transition from feudalism to capitalism.[32]

A few more words about the three main factors in the economic crisis are appropriate. At the time of the Peasants' Revolt about 80 per cent of England's population still lived in the countryside and three-fifths of the peasantry were unfree, i.e. serfs. Their life was, in Hobbes's classic formulation, 'nasty, brutish and short'. A typical peasant eked out a living on a 'messuage' – a rectangle of land about thirty acres in extent surrounded by dwelling houses and outhouses for animals and tools. The peasant's one-storey house would contain two or at most three rooms, and was no larger than forty-five feet in length and fifteen feet wide. Additionally he would have access to strips of arable land within common fields and grazing rights on common pasture.[33] All the time the feudal lords were pressing for maximum profits, with rising rents and fines the norm. When an unfree tenant died, the serf who took over his plot had to pay a 'fine' in the manorial court to continue the tenancy. Fines, to obtain the lord's formal permission, were also payable if you wished to move from your village or give your daughter in marriage. Additionally, the lord levied forced labour or *corvée*, typically four days' work every two weeks. If any peasant dared to show entrepreneurial ability, for example by selling ale, he would have to pay a tax to the lord on any profits he made. Moreover, when a peasant died, the lord could take the family's best beast as a 'heriot'; the second-best animal was then taken by the parson as a 'mortuary' fee.[34] From 1250 to 1350 the lot of the peasantry was especially dire. Wages fell sharply relative to prices, increasing only by 5 per cent while prices rose by 25 per cent. Price inflation was so marked because of a booming export trade and the consequent import of bullion. Because of the basic overpopulation before the Black Death, opportunities for freelance labour outside one's own holding were rare.

Until about 1350 the climatic change damaged arable crops and further increased the pressure of a rising population on food supplies. The Black Death thus appeared initially to be a godsend to the survivors, as it gave them leverage. One of the first aspirations of the peasantry flexing their muscles in the changed labour market was an improved diet. Until about 1350 there was a de facto dietary law every bit as restrictive as the sumptuary laws. The rich dined on beef, lamb, pork, geese, sucking pig, cod, hake, whiting, haddock, herring and oysters, and also had access to fresh fruit and vegetables. A notorious feast held to celebrate the installation of George Neville as archbishop of York involved 3,000 people, not just the diners (clerics, knights, gentry, franklins, yeomen), but those who served them (servants, cooks, waiters, ushers, etc). In a dazzling display of conspicuous consumption the organisers of the feast provided 300 quarters of wheat, 104 oxen, 1,000 sheep, 304 boars and 2,000 pigs, plus thousands of geese, capons, mallards, cranes, chickens and other birds, to say nothing of pasties, tarts and custards.[35] The poorest peasants by contrast lived mainly on onions, leeks and cabbages. Hunting and trapping were scarcely possible in a culture where most game was considered a royal preserve and where poaching – of deer, boar, swans and even rabbits – attracted the most draconian penalties.[36] Yet after 1350 employers often evaded the letter of the Statute of Labourers by topping up the legal wage with free meals, some of them quite lavish. Gradually the peasants came to demand a better diet and for this 'wickedness' were excoriated by William Langland as follows:

> The labourers that have no land and work with their hands deign no longer to dine on the stale vegetables of yesteryear; penny-ale will not suit them, nor bacon, but they must have fresh meat or fish, fried or baked, and that hotter and hotter for the chill of their maw. Unless he be highly paid he will chide, and bewail the time he was made a workman . . . Then he curses the king and all the king's justices, for making such laws that grieve the labourer.[37]

The resentment towards the king and his officials was not surprising in a context where the only 'interface' between the monarch and the peasantry was in the form of taxation and judicial control. The previously mentioned grievances over trailbaston were compounded by the medieval system of 'purveyance' used to finance royal visits and tours through the countryside. Meant to allow royal households to obtain victuals at low prices (below their market value), the system was little more than legalised theft. Sometimes those subjected to purveyance were not paid but given chits which later proved almost worthless, redeemable for only a fraction of the value of the victuals provided.[38] The king and the great lords were less than happy when free labourers and even bonded serfs (in defiance of the law) took to the roads after the Black Death, taking advantage of the labour shortage and wandering around the country in search of higher wages. By the time of the Peasants' Revolt two different economic impulses were seriously weakening the fabric of the seigneurial system. The bullion-import-led inflation made it advantageous for the lords to pay for services in cash rather than kind, so that both the commutation of feudal services to money or rents produced what has been called 'bastard feudalism' at the very time the demands of the market were exposing the contradictions in the system.[39] The other impulse was the break-up of the tight village community as wage labourers and even ex-bond labourers cut loose in search of lucrative opportunities elsewhere. Beggars became a common sight on the highways of England, making vagrancy for the first time in English history a matter of acute concern. Langland, in his discussion of the proper Christian stance vis-à-vis poverty, liked to distinguish the 'deserving poor' from the undeserving, principally beggars. This was part of a general syndrome whereby he evinced almost pathological dislike of 'marginal' types who did not work for a living in a traditional, recognisable way. Langland's three bêtes noires (apart from friars) were beggars, hermits and minstrels, all of whom he identified as 'getting away with it'.[40] The phenomenon of beggary was at an all time high because of four main factors: the consequences of the Great Famine of 1315–16; the population implosion in towns following the Black Death; the consequent breakdown of village traditions of communal charity; and the 'bad example' of the mendicant friars.[41]

Further evidence of a late-fourteenth-century general crisis, in the form of a conflict between the forces of production and the political organisation of the state, comes from the French *jacquerie* of 1358 and the Ciompi revolt in Florence in 1378. Devotees of historical uniqueness like to say that these two and the Peasants' Revolt in England in 1381 were utterly different in character,[42] and it is true that if one concentrates solely on the *content* of the rebellions rather than their form this case can easily be made out. Yet all three were triggered by consequences of the Black Death, all three saw forces of production outrunning the capacities of the state, and all three featured an absence of increasing immiseration, famine or rising food prices.[43] In Florence the revolt of the Ciompi did not involve the peasantry and did not have the urban/rural mix of 1381 or the French *jacquerie*. Since the price of food was not an issue, there was no significant participation by women. Thus far one could assert a significant difference from 1381. Yet the features of general crisis were as observable on the banks of the Arno as in France or England. Florence was highly unstable in the period 1342–85, reeling as it did under the successive blows of the Bardi fiasco and the Black Death.[44] In the case of the French *jacquerie* we see a particularly close convergence with the Peasants' Revolt, with rural artisans spearheading the rising, an insurrection breaking out in early summer (May) in the French case and lasting about two weeks. As in England, the rebels claimed that their target was corrupt royal officials and advisers, not the king himself. The rebel profile – artisans, petty officials, well-to-do proprietors and some country clergy were ranged against the great nobility – uncannily pre-echoes 1381 in England.[45] And the Hundred Years War, again as in England, played a significant part, with the peasantry contemptuous of the nobility, who had failed so signally in the Battle of Poitiers. Once again new taxes and *corvées* designed to pay for unpopular war were the trigger; for the French peasants, having to defend the chateaux that were the very symbol of their misery, was simply the last straw.[46] As in the Peasants' Revolt one can see the rising as a reaction to both short-term and long-term causes, some going back to the grain crisis and famine of 1315. Where the *jacquerie* was different was in the bitterness of class hatred, the level of violence engendered, and the sheer loss of life. What is remarkable about England in 1381 is the relative lack of bitterness towards the great feudal lords as a whole, as opposed to particularly identified exploiters. Moreover, the revolt in France precipitated an epidemic of unrelated banditry, where English mercenaries, Gascon adventurers and Spanish and German *routiers* plundered and ravished at will throughout northern France; in contrast to England, levels of rape were significantly high.[47] Guillaume Cale, the French peasant leader, was something of a Wat Tyler equivalent, since he too was invited to talks and then treacherously seized before being tortured and beheaded. The architect of this atrocity, Charles the Bad, dared to put into words what Richard II had presumably only thought: that safe conducts and all the other aspects of the code of chivalry did not apply to low-lives of the base born.[48]

The Jack Cade revolt of 1450 is sometimes viewed as a rerun of 1381, but an awareness of chronology is important. Significant changes took place over those seventy years. These were years of violence – Henry IV's overthrow of Richard II and the wars of succession that followed, Henry V's famous campaigns in France, especially Agincourt, the drama of Joan of Arc in 1429–31 and the many domestic risings, most notably those of Archbishop Richard Scrope in 1405 and Sir John Oldcastle in 1415–17.[49] Yet the only real stirring of *radical* revolt in this period was the Lollard-inspired rising in southern England in 1431. As previously mentioned, the Lollards wanted a simpler Christianity, purged of all accretions. The Bible was regarded as the be-all and end-all, priestcraft was held to be nonsense and flummery, as were the cult of the saints and all images and statues, to say nothing of the sacramental nature of the eucharist. Anticlericalism and hatred of the Church were the hallmarks of a creed popular with literate craftsmen and artisans, which is conveniently summed up as an early version of Protestantism.[50] Centred mainly on Abingdon and Oxford, the 1431 outbreaks failed lamentably and were followed by bloody retribution and cynical vindictiveness by the authorities, especially Henry VI's acolyte Duke Humphrey of Gloucester. On pain of death Lollards were forced to recant their beliefs and perform heavy penances for their heresy. This concession was not even allowed to the ringleaders, who were summarily beheaded or hanged; Tyburn became known as 'the Lollard gallows'.[51] Lollardism seemed broken and the cause of reformist Christianity everywhere in retreat across Europe, perhaps most graphically illustrated by the burning at the stake of Jan Hus in Constanz in 1415. Yet severe repression often merely drives the opposition underground, ready to resurface at the first favourable moment. Such was the experience of the vanquished Lollards who, nineteen years after their great revolt, found a new saviour in Jack Cade. It is significant that prominent among those documented as Cade supporters in 1450 were the very people who had to make public recantation of their 'errors' in the 1430s.[52]

More importantly, significant socio-economic changes occurred in English society in the years 1381–1450. Villeinage was in significant retreat, Richard II's threats notwithstanding, as the inroads of market forces and the cash economy made themselves felt. Increasingly, labourers were released from serfdom into land tenure at fixed rents. A switch from customary to leasehold and copyhold tenure was increasingly noted on the manorial court roll. Many landlords abandoned demesne cultivation and farmed out parcels of land to contractors at a set fee. A prosperous peasantry came to the fore, with numerous families nudging up into husbandman and even yeoman status. By 1450 the yeomanry were the dominant class in the English countryside, and some former yeomen were even breaking through into the ranks of the gentry: the Paston family of Norfolk is the best-known case.[53] Wages rose steadily, despite the Canute-like efforts of the authorities to prevent this; there was a further statute in 1389 allowing justices of the peace to set official pay rates. The defiance of all the variants on the original Statute of Labourers was partly a function of economic laws which no royal decree could alter, and partly reflected caution on the part of the authorities. For the sake of credibility they had to insist on the spirit of wage freeze but ignored the letter of reality, largely because they were afraid of provoking another mass outburst like the Peasants' Revolt.[54] The south-east, scene of the most vicious atrocities on both sides in 1381, was, if not yet the garden of England, a prosperous and tranquil oasis of hedged and wooded landscapes, home of myriad flocks of sheep and an abundance of agricultural produce: wheat, barley, oats, rye and beans. There was a thriving timber trade and even a new woollen cloth industry, almost more important than wool production itself. The diet of the common man had improved, with meat and fish now sometimes present on peasant dining tables and, as a result, life expectancy climbed to thirty-five by 1450.[55] The authorities were also more inclined to turn a blind eye to minor infractions of the poaching laws, as long as general elite credibility was not impugned.[56] In pure socio-economic terms, with the pressures of the seigneurial system no longer so important, no glaring fiscal demands as in 1381, and the government concentrating its repressive powers mostly on religious heresy, the approach to the mid-century of the 1400s should have been peaceful enough, had there not been countervailing political currents. Yet even at the socio-economic level two trends might have worried the more thoughtful observer. Rising prosperity and rising expectations were precisely what underlay the 1381 rebellion, and here was the same pattern being repeated in the identical counties: Middlesex, Essex and Kent. Moreover, the status of urban craftsmen and artisans had not significantly changed since 1381, yet the irritant of a failing judicial system, corrupt ministers and incompetent misgovernment was particularly irksome to them.[57]

Furthermore, by 1450 there were uncanny parallels with the situation seventy years earlier. Discontent against government by cliques and favourites ran in tandem with anger over the incompetent prosecution of the endless wars in France. By the 1440s Henry VI was widely regarded as a disastrous monarch – a feeble-minded idiot, incompetent in government, an incubus in finance and a pawn in the hands of royal favourites. Henry VI wanted peace with France and favoured the peace party of Cardinal Beaufort and William de la Pole, Earl of Suffolk. Beaufort and Suffolk engineered Henry's controversial marriage with the domineering Margaret of Anjou. Charles VII agreed to this marriage provided Maine and Anjou were ceded to him; this shameful sacrifice was at first concealed from Parliament.[58] The marriage of Henry and Margaret in 1445 was widely unpopular, and to the long list of Henry's other faults and crimes was added that of suspected murder in 1447. In that year the Duke of Gloucester was arraigned for treason, at the behest of Suffolk, Beaufort and the third important favourite, the Earl of Somerset. Gloucester died in custody, the victim of either an assassin or starvation, neglect and prison-associated disease. Henry then promoted Suffolk and Somerset to dukedoms. The heir presumptive, Richard, Duke of York, was packed off to Ireland as governor, while Somerset departed to pursue a half-hearted conduct of the war in France.[59] Beaufort died in 1450 but another powerful prelate, William Ayscough, Bishop of Salisbury, proved another Henry VI stalwart, spearheading the Church's assault on Lollardism. Just below the level of Suffolk, Beaufort and Somerset was another trio of widely detested royal favourites: James Fiennes, 1st baron Saye and Sele, who acted as lord chamberlain and lord treasurer, and Thomas Daniel and John Tresilian. Saye had his power bases in Hertfordshire, Huntingdonshire and Cambridgeshire, Tresilian in Cornwall, and Daniel in Norfolk and Suffolk.[60] This motley congeries of royal favourites, all ultimately under the thumb of Suffolk, were bywords for corruption. Gangs of their thugs terrorised the countryside, burning, looting and murdering; the courts, directed at every turn by Suffolk, gave no redress. Officeholders appointed by the favourites were past masters of corruption; extorting and levying fines and taxes but not passing them on to the Exchequer. Goods such as cattle and cereals were routinely seized as 'royal purveyance' but never paid for. Intimidation, cattle rustling, threats, blackmail, pay-offs, shake-downs and extortion were just some of the crimes perpetrated by men above the law, who further outraged parliamentary opinion by elevating to the Privy Council men below the customary rank of hereditary peer. The instances of corruption and injustice were particularly marked in East Anglia and the Home Counties, above all Kent.[61]

Anger caused by chaos and incompetence at home was raised to a new pitch when Suffolk and Somerset displayed their sublime ineptitude abroad. The extent of the gathering debacle in France was masked by the marriage with Margaret of Anjou and the pause in the Hundred Years War which resulted, yet Suffolk and Somerset suddenly offered gratuitous provocation by launching a surprise attack on Fougères in Brittany in defiance of the existing truce. The French claimed the British were trying to detach the Duke of Burgundy from allegiance to his overlord, the King of France, and resumed hostilities.[62] The English then showed that treachery had virtually become a reflex action in the miasma of Suffolk-inspired corruption by making an unprovoked attack with privateers on an annual salt convoy leaving the Bay of Bourgneuf (23 May 1449). 110 ships were taken, 50 from Hanseatic merchants and 60 from the Flemings and the Dutch. The exploit was an unprovoked attack on peacetime trade, cold-blooded piracy in anyone's terms; not surprisingly, the masterminds proved to be the redoubtable trio of Daniel, Tresilian and Saye. The raid pointed up the low moral stature to which the Lancastrians had fallen by mid-century.[63] This unsavoury event occurred just when Somerset and Suffolk, by their attack on Fougères, had made Normandy super-vulnerable to a French counter-attack. In July 1449 Charles VII repudiated the truce and sent his armies into Normandy. His troops swept in and quickly took Coutances and Saint-Lô: Rouen itself surrendered in October 1449.[64] Suffolk was forced to go cap in hand to Parliament to request emergency war taxation, but the Commons was unmoved by the emotive stories about how Normandy was being lost. They had had enough of Suffolk. There was a financial and economic crisis in 1449–50 with declining yields from taxation and adverse terms of trade at the very time the inept Suffolk had reopened the war in France. Parliament flatly refused any increase in taxation, and its motivation seems to have been threefold. In the first place the declining tax yields were largely caused by the many exemptions Henry VI had granted to his stable of favourites. Moreover, the Commons did not trust the cronies and sycophants around the king to spend the money properly or wisely. Thirdly, the Commons tended to view Normandy as a separate entity from Lancastrian England and took the view that it was essentially nothing to do with them.[65]

January 1450 saw a number of dramatic events. One of Suffolk's acolytes, Bishop Adam Moleyns was sent to Portsmouth with money to pay the expeditionary force being fitted out for the relief of Normandy. Foolishly, the bishop decided to siphon off some of the money for his own use, was found out and executed by an angry crowd of some 300 soldiers and sailors. Before his death a confession was extracted from him which implicated Suffolk and his coterie in the defalcation.[66] Learning of this, the Commons moved to impeach Suffolk for treason, on the grounds that he was in effect plotting with the French for the downfall of England. At this very juncture, on 24 January, Thomas Cheyne raised the standard of revolt in Kent.

Gathering together the burghers of Dover and Sandwich, he published a list of traitors to be beheaded: on the list were Suffolk, James Fiennes (Lord Saye), William Ayscough, Bishop of Salisbury and Lord Dudley. Cheyne and his men marched on Canterbury, but on 31 January Cheyne himself was captured by the royalist forces, taken back to Westminster, charged with treason and hanged. A yeoman named Nicholas Jake also tried to head a rebellion in London and was likewise executed.[67] The Portsmouth rebels, however, continued defiant and took to flying the French red battle flag as their rebel emblem. Finding that the defeat of Cheyne did nothing to quell the rising clamour for his favourites' punishment, Henry VI bowed to the Commons and banished Suffolk for five years. To the enraged rebels this was tantamount to letting him off scot-free, and his exile did nothing to defuse the tense atmosphere in London. Suffolk made good his escape from the country on his way to continental exile, but as the ship taking him to Europe was sailing south from Ipswich it was intercepted somewhere in the Channel by a 'pirate'. Suffolk was taken aboard the pirate vessel, given a mock trial and executed.[68] As if that was not a dramatic enough event, news of it was received in London at the precise moment tidings came in of a terrible English defeat at Formigny near Bayeux, which definitively delivered Normandy to the French for all time. Suddenly, in addition to insurrection at home, Henry VI faced the very real possibility of a French invasion. It was a classic case of 'malice domestic, foreign levy'.[69]

Meanwhile in Kent the spirit of Thomas Cheyne was far from extinguished. Temporarily subdued rebels, furious at his execution, coordinated plans for a general rising. The main medium used was the series of annual fairs held at places like Rochester, Sevenoaks and Heathfield in Sussex; it is likely that the rebels swore oaths to support each other. Some say fiery preaching by itinerant preachers was another important conduit of rebellion.[70] The rebel profile was more interestingly nuanced than in 1381, largely because the traditional tripartite model of clergy, nobility and peasantry was beginning to break down. This time there were far more artisans, guild members, merchants, yeomen and even members of an inchoate middle class than under Wat Tyler's banner. Masons, stone-roofers, dyers, tailors, thatchers, carpenters, smiths, cobblers, weavers, tanners, butchers and bakers are frequently mentioned in the chronicles – what one historian uncharitably calls 'the rabble without a cause'.[71] In contrast to 1381, the rebels tended to be young and unmarried, with no marital or family responsibilities. Forty-shilling freeholders were particularly prominent. Their significance is that they can almost be described as part of a 'middle sector', for a minimum net revenue of forty shillings a year made one eligible to vote in local elections and to serve on juries. The forty-shilling men particularly resented the incursion of the central government and its corrupt placemen into local affairs and their meddling in counties where *they* (the forty-shilling men) were supposed to hold sway.[72] Insofar as the peasantry took part in the 1450 rising, it was the rich variety – the 'upper peasants' – who came to the fore. Henry VI was faced, then, with a knowledgeable and articulate foe when the rebels mustered at Rochester. Their grievances were lucidly set out. In the first place they wanted reassurance on the wildest of all rumours, which was that Henry VI intended to lay waste Kent and turn it into a wild forest in revenge for the Cheyne rising and the Suffolk murder. They called on the king to resume his lost demesnes, to claw back the Crown revenues he had given away and hence his power and dignity; to banish all the kinsmen and progeny of Suffolk and to extirpate all pro-French traitors (i.e. the peace party); to punish all involved in the death of the Duke of Gloucester and the loss of territories in France; to remove all the abuses of law imposed by the royal household and corrupt officialdom; to end the rigging of elections, the arbitrary procedures of justices of the peace and other court officials, and the depredations of tax collectors.[73]

The assembled rebels soon elected Jack Cade as their leader, and here the problems of interpretation of the 1450 rising begin. The profile of Jack Cade is no clearer than that of Wat Tyler seventy years earlier. Almost nothing reliable is known about him. Some say that Cade was his real name, that he had been in the employment of Sir Thomas Dacre of Sussex but had fled the country after murdering a pregnant servant girl. This would align him with a documented John Cade, yeoman, who went into exile in 1449 and had his effects confiscated.[74] Others claim that he was a disgraced physician named John Aylmer, who had married a squire's daughter but then lost his reputation by dabbling in the black arts. On 8 July 1450 Cade would famously declare that his real name was John Mortimer, implying thereby that he was a scion of the high-born Mortimer family. The Mortimers were the descendants of Lionel, Duke of Clarence, second son of Edward III. Part of the anti-Henry IV coalition in the early 1400s, the Mortimers insinuated that they had a superior claim to the throne over Henry VI. What Cade's objective was in claiming to be a Mortimer is uncertain; he cannot have been a genuine 'pretender' since all the famous Mortimers were both well known and the wrong age. He was probably claiming to be an 'obscure cousin' – that is an illegitimate son but one with royal blood.[75] Another theory is that the Mortimers were linked to Richard, Duke of York (Mortimer was the family name of York's mother), and that Cade was hoping to inveigle York into the rebellion or at least to 'bounce' Henry VI into assuming York's collusion. It is known that there were Cades in the Kent of 1450, but the entire issue of pseudonyms and *noms de guerre* in this rising is immensely complicated, with the rebels further muddying the waters by using titles such as 'King of the Fairies' 'Queen of the Fairies' and, more predictably, 'Robin Hood'.[76] Cade's deeds are clearer than his names. It is quite evident from the way he organised his army that he had a military background and had a high degree of martial skill, and the obvious presumption is that, like Tyler, he had fought in the wars in France. Some of his lieutenants seem to have been gentlemen, though in general the gentry properly so-called opposed the rebellion. Robert Poynings, a Sussex gentleman, was appointed as Cade's second-in-command. Another senior lieutenant, Richard Lovelace, appears to have been an aged veteran of the French wars.[77]

On 8 June Cade led his host in an advance on Canterbury. Quite how large his army was is disputed. Some of the chroniclers claimed that his effectives at the grand muster at Blackheath a little later were 50,000, but one has to take the way of the medieval writers with numbers with a large pinch of salt. More sober and reliable authorities put the total figure at 10,000–20,000, of whom maybe 4,000 marched with Cade to Canterbury.[78] This was not a case of a poorly armed rabble pitted against professional troops but rather one set of yeomen and other groups against others similarly situated. The late medieval state had no significant standing army but called out forces when needed, largely the military retainers of noblemen or the levies of the 'county array'. One of the factors that made it so easy for England to slip into the abyss of the Wars of the Roses in the mid-1450s is that the battles were waged between two sets of aristocratic retinues, not a standing army against ill-trained levies. There was little difference in 1450 England between the soldier and the yeoman farmer in terms of training and equipment; this meant of course that the State was extremely brittle – almost anyone could organise a force to overthrow it.[79] The central government could not depend on the county militia to support it, for the composition and background of such a body made it most likely to be sympathetic to rebels. The county array, based on the 'hundred' and its constables, was always more likely to incline to rebels as it was a community force, not one commanded by the king. This is why some historians favour the formula that the pre-existing militia structure provided Cade with a pre-existing rebel structure.[80] Moreover, most ordinary Englishmen were familiar with archery and bowmanship. One student of the period has graphically summed up the situation as follows:

> Far from being unarmed and placid rustics, a large portion of the English population owned and regularly trained with the most modern and effective weapons which existed in fifteenth-century Europe. Translated into twenty-first century terms, it was as if a flak jacket, helmet and assault rifle were household items as common as the family car, and the principal national recreations were the rifle range and the assault-training course.[81]

Cade was less successful at Canterbury than Tyler had been. He drew up his army in the western suburbs, expecting to receive the joyful acclamation of the city, but after three hours nothing had happened. The lukewarm response of Canterbury to the rebels was part of a general ambivalence in Kent that had not been in evidence in 1381. The difference was that this time there was fear of a French invasion, and some of the Kentish folk felt that England should not be divided in face of such a threat. Whereas the effects of the Hundred Years War in Kent generally favoured Cade, as people were tired of being attacked in their person or property by hordes of ill-disciplined troops marching to and from the Channel ports, in some locales there was a countervailing view that this was the lesser of two evils. Rye and Winchelsea in particular had borne the brunt of French raids in 1448–50.[82] After waiting in vain for three hours Cade took his forces onto the road to London.

Many more bands joined him: large numbers of men had been mustered for the defence of the coast but had now concluded that the real enemy lay within the kingdom not outside.[83] By this time Henry VI was alerted to the scale of the rebellion. Parliament, in session at Leicester, was prorogued while the king sent orders to crush the rebellion to four of his lieutenants: the Duke of Buckingham, and the Earls of Devon, Oxford and Arundel. The king then headed south and on 13 June reached his quarters at St John's Priory in Clerkenwell. Meanwhile on 11 June Cade reached Blackheath and pitched camp at the very place Tyler had chosen in 1381. Similarly, London began to prepare for a rerun of 1381; the City gates were fortified and a strong guard set on them. An embargo was placed on arms sales to those placing orders outside the City, passwords devised and the armed bands of the elite and nobles admitted inside the City only with special warrants specifying their business.[84] The mood in London was generally unhappy, for Londoners stood to suffer from double jeopardy: looting and high-handed behaviour both from royalist nobles and their armed retainers, and from Cade's men. Nonetheless, as in 1381, there were sections of the population pleased to welcome the rebels, if only because their presence gave the opportunity to settle private scores, grudges and vendettas.[85]

There was an eerie stand-off between Cade and the king until on 15 June Henry broke the logjam by sending a delegation by river to Blackheath, ordering the rebels to disband. In the delegation were the Archbishops of Canterbury and York, the Duke of Buckingham, the Bishop of Winchester and Viscount Beaumont. That Henry had no real intention of negotiating or offering terms became clear when he simultaneously sent out a scouting expedition under the Earl of Northumberland to ascertain the enemy's military strength.[86] Northumberland and his comrades Lord Scales and Lord Lisle seem to have set out with a secret hope that they could disperse the rebels by a mounted charge and then return to royal plaudits, but they took one look at the strength of Cade's encampment and beat a hasty retreat. The delegation meanwhile returned with a predictable answer from Cade: there could be no question of dispersing until the king had made good on the original rebel manifesto, whose conditions and terms were now widely known. The ensuing two-day silence was a message Cade could read with his eyes closed: the king was preparing for a military solution. Wisely Cade decided not to engage the royal forces in a pitched battle but to retreat before them and save his strength for a more favourable moment. Foolishly, the royalists construed this as weakness or panic. Sir Humphrey Stafford and Sir William Stafford recklessly set out after Cade with a fifty-strong vanguard.[87] They ran straight into a rebel ambush at Sevenoaks on 18 June and were massacred; the Staffords and forty men were left dead on the battleground. Cade's victory showed that he was a highly talented captain, and the exploit brought many waverers to his banner, as well as depressing the royalists.[88] Further recruits were added by the general alienation of the Kent populace in the days that followed. On 18 June – in what was presumably devised as a two-pronged assault in concert with the Staffords – Lords Dudley and Rivers, Sir Thomas Stanley and the detested Thomas Daniel burst into north-western Kent with a force of 2,000 desperadoes. There followed a three-day orgy of looting, plunder and mayhem as the forces of 'law and order' rampaged through Otford, Chipstead, Sevenoaks and Tonbridge. All this raid did was to alienate the people of Kent and bring in more recruits for Cade's army.[89]

There was an ominous development on 19 June when some of the royalist lords were heard to remark that Cade had a point and his rebels a case, that Henry really should weed out the traitors in his realm, whom – echoing the insurgents – they identified as Tresilian, Daniel, Saye, Lord Dudley and the Bishop of Salisbury. There were fears that some of the nobility and the gentry en masse might go over to Cade if something was not done. Realising that concessions would have to be made if he had any hope of suppressing the rising, Henry VI proclaimed that all 'traitors' should be taken into custody.[90] He ordered Henry Holland, constable of the Tower of London, to detain Lord Saye in the Tower, while privately assuring him that the arrest was a mere charade. A little later he tried to engineer Saye's escape, but Holland refused to play ball and hung on to his prisoner. Cast down by this 'contumacious' behaviour by his constable, Henry quit London on 25 June, heedless of all pleas that he should stay, whether from the lord mayor or his own wife Margaret. After a stopover at Berkhamsted Castle in Hertfordshire, Henry set up his court in Kenilworth Castle, Warwickshire, generally considered the most impregnable fortress in the realm.[91] The contrast with Richard II's decision to confront the rebels was glaring. Hugely buoyed by the king's flight, Cade reformed his army and marched back to Blackheath. The rebels' demands were now framed in the form of a petition, which was widely divulged. There was good news for the rebels from the West Country. The detested Bishop Ayscough of Salisbury had been captured in Wiltshire while he said Mass, dragged out of church, hacked to death and his remains defiled.[92] The hope now was that all the rest of the traitors would meet a similar fate. On 1–2 July Cade's men spread out and occupied Southwark, once again in a close replay of the events of 1381. It was at this stage that Cade first began to display delusions of grandeur. He began to dress in sumptuous, gaudy and colourful clothes, instituting his own version of the sumptuary laws by insisting that he alone could dress like that.[93] Although an elected leader, he was showing signs of authoritarianism. He executed an under-captain named Parys for indiscipline on 29 June and gave himself regal, or at least viceregal graces. The town of Lydd sent him a porpoise, traditionally the exclusive food of the high aristocracy, and Cade accepted it as his due.[94]

The occupation of Southwark can be seen as the turning of the tide of the rebellion, for the rebels cut loose and began looting, robbing and extorting. It was almost as though Cade's real problems began once he left his heartland in the Kent countryside and ventured into the 'great wen', England's capital and the traditional heart of darkness.[95] Although Cade had ordained capital punishment for anyone found looting, his men seemed to disregard the prescription and Cade seemed powerless to prevent them. The situation got worse when the rebels entered London proper.[96] Some say this was simply a repeat of the situation Wat Tyler had faced, others that Cade's soldiers alienated Londoners much more severely than the men of 1381 had done. Yet others pin the blame on Cade himself and say that he failed to make clear the boundaries between carnival and serious assaults on State power, and that he compounded this confusion by his folly in donning exotic dress and his burlesquing of the ceremonial robes of London's aldermen and dignitaries.[97] 3 July was another red-letter day in the rebellion, for on that day the rebels managed to cut the ropes on London Bridge (which had been drawn up) so as to bring the bridge down. Cade's men then poured across into London, their leader at their head, dressed in a blue velvet coat trimmed with sable fur. In another histrionic gesture, which again suggested carnival rather than a serious uprising, Cade had a sword carried in front of him on a pillow. Where an ancient Roman enjoying a triumph would have a slave at his shoulder whispering into his ear to remind him that he was mortal, Cade seemed to be moving in the opposite direction, progressively losing touch with reality as the revolt waxed. Even less attention than in Southwark was paid to the ban on looting, for the rebels immediately began a systematic plundering of the house of the wealthy alderman Philip Malpas.[98] Such was the hatred of the chroniclers for the rebels of 1450 that they turned the sack of the Malpas house into a kind of locus classicus, illustrating all that was wicked and depraved about the insurrectionists; in the process Malpas himself was rewritten as a hero. Cade's attempt to co-opt the (real or legendary) shades of King Arthur and Robin Hood were treated with contempt.[99]

For two days the rebels enjoyed a halcyon period of looting and execution. Cade turned a blind eye to the indiscipline and claimed to be restoring the rule of law by scrapping the hated system of *oyer and terminer* – widely considered a fig leaf behind which royal officialdom did precisely as it wished – and replacing it with a special commission to hear and condemn all who were considered traitors, exploiters or extortionists. The ambivalence felt even by elite members towards the Cade revolt is clear from the smooth transition in the machinery of justice: many of the original judges in the scrapped system, including Thomas, Lord Scales, the Lord Mayor Thomas Charlton and half a dozen others, remained to give legitimacy to the new commission.[100] Warrants were issued for the arrest of Tresilian, Daniel and others, while the prize catch, Lord Saye, was taken from the Tower to the commission's headquarters in the Guildhall. He was charged with treason, particularly for complicity in the death of the Duke of Gloucester, given a summary trial and then beheaded. Cade presided over the public degradation of Saye's corpse, which was dragged through the streets by horses. William Crowmer, Saye's son-in-law and sheriff of Kent, and five other elite members were also executed. For reasons of credibility (justice for all) Cade made a point of executing a notorious cut-throat and footpad named Richard Hawarden, who had previously skulked in sanctuary in St Martin-le-Grand.[101] Yet Cade's dispassionate meting out of justice and his regal airs did not impress London. Even in 1381, when the majority of the City had welcomed the rebels, there was a significant undertow of opposition, and the evidence is that even in the early stages of his occupation Cade did not enjoy the popularity that Tyler had done. Cade must be faulted for not accurately gauging the temper of the citizens, and for wasting his chances by conniving at the mass plundering of London.[102] By 5 July the patience of the London elite had snapped. We cannot trace all the stages whereby they were able to make common cause with the royalist troops who still lurked in the City's environs, but a plot was quickly hatched. The main thrust of the backlash was a scheme to retake the bridge from Cade's guard while the bulk of the rebel army was back in its billets at Southwark. The speed and efficiency with which the counter-strike was organised underlines the egregious cowardice and lack of leadership evinced by Henry VI; his presence near the capital would have tipped the balance decisively without the need for hard fighting.[103]

Just in time Cade got wind of the plan and ordered all his men back to London. This time they faced a hard fight to retake the City, and helped their cause by opening the Marshalsea Prison and encouraging the inmates to join them. The passage of London Bridge was contested, with the rebels massing on the south side of the river and the loyalists, partly troops from the Tower led by Lord Scales and Matthew Gough, and partly Londoners disillusioned with Cade, on the north bank. Ferocious fighting began around 9 p.m. on 5 July and went on all night, in Bosch-like scenes of darkness, fire and horror.[104] Much of the hand-to-hand fighting took place on the bridge itself, which in the grey light of dawn looked like a charnel house, the struts and gantries on the bridge charred and blackened with smoke and the Thames choked with floating corpses beneath, like a horrific Sargasso Sea of human bodies and body parts. The battle was a close-run thing: the loyalists had the advantage of the arms and materiel from the arsenal at the Tower, but Cade's men were superior in elan and fighting spirit. By sheer weight of numbers the loyalists eventually forced the rebels back from the northern shore and closed the City gates, but they could make no impression on Cade's position on the south side of the bridge. In pique and frustration Cade ordered the drawbridge section of the bridge torched.[105] By daybreak both sides were exhausted and agreed a truce; no exact count of the casualties was possible but the toll seems to have run into hundreds on both sides; among the fallen was Gough.[106] A truce, initially for two hours, was agreed, and in this time the rebellion seems to have fallen apart with amazing suddenness, just as in 1381. The few ministers of the Crown still in London seized the opportunity to offer a general pardon and conveyed the terms to Cade and his council, using priests as go-betweens. It must have been obvious that this was a mere stalling ploy to buy time and that the ministers were not sincere; for one thing they were binding an absent king to terms which he could easily repudiate. It seems that Cade saw all this clearly enough, but the majority of his supporters were against him. Having run out of steam and uncertain of the next step, they grasped eagerly at straws. Pardons were then issued to named individuals over the course of 6–7 July for all transgressions committed before 8 July. Whether through Machiavellianism by the ministers or foolishness on Cade's part, his supposed pardon was issued in the name of John Mortimer, which allowed the royalists to claim that 'Jack Cade' had never been pardoned.[107]

While his men drifted away to Kent, apparently satisfied with the government's worthless promises, Cade led a rump of diehards in an attack on Queensborough Castle near Dartford, but the advantage of numbers had now shifted to the defenders. Cade was now declared a traitor in his own name and a bounty of 1,000 marks (approx. £667) put on his head, with 500 marks reward for the capture of his chief lieutenants. Some of the Kentish men rallied at this manifest sign of government bad faith. A Faversham soapmaker named Robert Spenser tried to head a revival of the revolt, aiming to link up with Cade's outlaw band; he was quickly caught and was hanged, drawn and quartered. Realising that the game was up, Cade fled in disguise towards Sussex. On 12 July he was intercepted by the new sheriff of Kent, Alexander Iden. In a scrimmage at Heathfield in Sussex, Cade was badly wounded. Captured and due to be conveyed to London for a traitor's death, Cade evaded the executioner by dying of his wounds on 13 June while on the way back to the capital. His corpse was nonetheless subjected to the usual grisly ritual. He was beheaded at Newgate, his head raised aloft over London Bridge, and the quarters of his body sent to Blackheath, Norwich, Salisbury and Gloucester.[108] That was not quite the end of the story. Although the Cade rebellion was largely an affair of London and the Home Counties, there had been sympathetic uprisings in Hampshire, Dorset, Somerset and Wiltshire, which was particularly badly hit by the crisis in the cloth industry and was the domain of the hated Bishop of Salisbury. Kent and Sussex were not truly pacified until the summer of 1451. There was another rising in Kent in August 1450 under William Parmynter, a blacksmith from Kent who took the title 'Second Captain of Kent' (Cade had been the first). Parmynter was caught and executed but then, in hydra fashion, a third captain appeared. The third man, John Smyth, who raised his banner in October, was likewise captured and executed.[109] There was another five-day rebellion in Kent in April 1456 under a tailor, John Percy, who styled himself John Mortimer in imitation and memory of Cade. Unlike the Cade rising, these later insurrections featured very few rebels of gentry and yeoman rank but were overwhelmingly disturbances by skilled craftsmen and artisans: carpenters, thatchers, smiths, wheelwrights, fletchers, bakers, cloth workers.[110]

The parallels between 1381 and 1450 are sometimes almost uncanny both in general features and particular details. Both revolts took place after military humiliation by the French, both were triggered by grievances over taxation and both were centred mainly in south-east England, especially Kent and Essex, though the subsidiary roles played by Yorkshire and East Anglia in 1381 were assumed by the 'near West Country' (Hampshire, Dorset, Somerset and Wiltshire) in 1450. In both the treasurer of England lost his head, royal favourites were dragged from the Tower, prisoners released from the Marshalsea. On both occasions the rebel hosts camped on Blackheath and on both occasions the risings collapsed suddenly and mysteriously after seeming unstoppable. On both occasions a distinction was drawn between loyalty to the king himself and an angry attack on his corrupt advisers. On both occasions we can see clearly that the State was not yet the 'monopolist of violence' and was indeed amazingly fragile, brittle and vulnerable. Finally, it is not without significance that both risings began in the late spring, during the Whitsun holidays, and coopted the carnival mentality abroad at that season.[111] A treacherous monarch was in evidence on both occasions, for Henry VI, while lacking the courage of Richard II, proved just as capable of going back on formal promises made. Although in the immediate aftermath of the rebellion Henry began by making conciliatory noises – on 1 August he ordered a commission of *oyer and terminer* into Kent to investigate the grievances that had triggered the troubles – as soon as calm returned, he wound up this commission and sent the Duke of York to head a punitive expedition into the county. York was supposed to be heading a new commission, but what he mainly did was to hang and burn; significantly he made no distinction between rebels, and it mattered not to him whether those he seized had the worthless general pardon of 7–8 July or not.[112] Almost none of those named as exploiters and extortionists in the rebel manifesto received any more than a slap on the wrist. As if to show that the spirit of corruption was still alive and well, the government visited double jeopardy on those who had originally suffered at the hands of Cade and his men. Vast amounts of gold, silver, sapphires, pearls and other precious stones and trinkets had been uplifted by the rebels. Government forces took the recovered property back to the Exchequer in London, but those who had had their property stolen had to pay a premium or 'handling fee' to the Exchequer to get it back. One obvious result both of government cynicism and the brutal crushing of the revolt was that when the Yorkist earls rose in 1460 in the Wars of the Roses, south-east England was with them, not as supporters of the White Rose but as helpers in a crusade for good government.[113]

It has been the almost universal consensus of historians that the Cade rebellion was overwhelmingly political in nature, lacking in socio-economic content, and that the battles fought in London and Kent represented conflict *within* the regime rather than about the regime. The orthodox view, then, is that the 1450 revolt was political in motivation, triggered by resentment at corruption and the failure of the campaigns in France, that Cade was more politically conscious than Tyler, and that this manifested itself in a coherent, written programme for moderate political change.[114] However, there are two other competing theories in the field, one concerning the politics of conspiracy, the other a revisionist view of 1450, stressing its social and economic roots. The conspiracy theory – that Jack Cade was, as it were, a *prodromos* or John the Baptist to the Wars of Roses – receives its classical expression in Shakespeare's *Henry VI, Part Two*, where Cade is portrayed as a political agent of the Duke of York. This is how York explains it:

> YORK: And for a minister of mine intent
> I have seduc'd a headstrong Kentishman
> John Cade of Ashford,

To make commotion, as full well he can,
Under the title of John Mortimer.
In Ireland I have seen this stubborn Cade
Oppose himself against a troop of kerns,
And fought so long till that his thighs with darts
Were almost like a sharp-quill'd porpentine;
And in the end being rescued, I have seen
Him caper upright like a wild Morisco,
Shaking the bloody darts as he his bells.
Full often, like a shag-hair'd crafty kern,
Hath he conversed with the enemy,
And undiscover'd come to me again
And given me notice of their villainies.
This devil here shall be my substitute
For that John Mortimer, which now is dead,
In face, in gait, in speech he doth resemble.
By this I shall perceive the common's mind
How they affect the house and claim of York.
Say that he be taken, rack'd and tortured;
I know no pain they can inflict upon him
Will make him say that I mov'd him to those arms.
Say that he thrive, as 'tis great like he will
Why, then from Ireland come I with my strength
And reap the harvest which that rascal sow'd.[115]

In Act Four Shakespeare, notoriously conservative and anti-radical, goes way over the top in his portrayal of the insensate, mindless, destructive rage of Cade and his acolytes. Cade announces that there will be no more money, that everyone will wear the same clothes. Anyone who can read and write will be put to death as an enemy of the people, parchment, wax and documents are especially anathema, and all archives will be burned. Cade toys with offering Henry VI a deal, whereby the king will reign as a figurehead while Cade has the real power as lord protector. All prisoners will be released as by definition they are 'politicals'. All great lords will have to pay Cade tribute and all women will have to sleep with him before they are given permission to marry. A form of communism is announced: 'There shall be in England seven halfpenny loaves sold for a penny; the three-hoop'd pot shall have ten hoops; and I will make it a felony to drink small beer. All the realm shall be in common.'[116] The hatred of learning and intellectuals is just one of the many ways in which Shakespeare's Cade is a pre-echo of Mao in the Cultural Revolution or of Pol Pot in Cambodia. Lord Saye excites particular contempt for speaking Latin, while Dick the Butcher declares: 'The first thing we do, let's kill all the lawyers.' The mob is shown to be completely moronic, agreeing with whoever has just spoken and capable of being swayed by Cade with a facile reference to Henry V. Eventually Shakespeare tires of Cade and dispatches him from the plot quickly. Cade flees, has no food for five days, climbs into the garden of Alexander Iden (portrayed as a harmless oligarch full of integrity instead of the bounty-hunter he was) and is killed by him in a sword-fight – Cade is too weak with hunger to fence effectively. In this version Cade is even more radical than Tyler, leading Shakespearean scholars to say that the Bard confused his rebels, that his portrait of Cade is really one of Tyler.[117] The Cade–York nexus makes for good drama and good conspiracy theory, but few historians have been willing to subscribe to it. The obvious objection is that York showed himself a hard liner when carrying out his commission in Kent and harried Cade's men mercilessly. Nonetheless there are still those who take seriously the idea of Cade as York's stalking horse.[118]

The Cade–York link may be described as the 'right-wing' version of the 1450 revolt, but there is a more plausible leftist one to combat the orthodoxy described above. In brief, this states that Cade's rebellion was not as different from Tyler's as is usually thought, and that the roots of the revolt centred around the government's inability to solve the socio-economic problems of the time. The emphasis of historians has usually been placed on the Kent rebels, but if the men of Sussex are put under the microscope, a more nuanced, less purely political picture emerges. Once again some inchoate notion of general crisis in Europe is helpful. Europe in the 1440s suffered severe deflation because of a general European bullion famine. The main factors in this were the drain of gold and silver to the Near East and the closure and contraction of many European mints and mines.[119] The shortage of specie and credit and the general deflation had several consequences in England. More grain, wool and stock were being produced than the market could absorb, while rising rents and falling prices meant that peasants were unable to sell their surplus produce to offset the rent increases. A sudden dip into recession after years of rising prosperity produced all the symptoms of anomie which traditionally triggered rebellion in the late Middle Ages.[120] All of these *general* economic factors merged with the particular issue of economic warfare in the 1440s. Duke Philippe of Burgundy imposed protectionist embargoes on English cloth coming into the Low Countries for the benefit of the cloth-makers of Flanders, Brabant, Holland and Zeeland. In 1448–9 English exports of cloth fell by 32 per cent and other exports fell by 35 per cent, while imports of wine were halved in 1450. The town of Sandwich in Kent suffered a catastrophic slump, with wool exports down by two-thirds and woollen cloth at just one-tenth of the previous figure; wine imports plummeted by 75 per cent. The notorious privateering raid of 23 May 1449 can be seen as England's riposte to protectionism in the Low Countries. It may be that Sussex was worse affected than anywhere else in England by all these chill winds. Even as the county dealt with the adverse international trade situation, it was still struggling with the burden of villeinage and seigneurial exactions, for Sussex was more backward than Kent in this regard. The crisis of 1449–50 did at least see many tenants negotiate their rents downwards, and there was some successful resistance to customary taxes and fines.[121]

Controversy is bound to continue about the revolutionary implications of the Cade rebellion. It is interesting that both the approach stressing international economic recession *and* the Shakespearean Cade–York conspiracy thesis effectively 'place' the 1450 rising as rather more than a mere political disturbance. Naturally it can be interpreted at a more simple political level, with the stress placed on the Hundred Years War. If the Wars of the Roses were essentially an internalisation of impulses thwarted by defeat by France in the continental wars, then the Cade rising can be read as the first of a series of convulsions that would terminate only at Bosworth Field in 1485. Part of the difficulty in providing an accurate reading of both the Tyler and the Cade rebellions is that a study of contemporary turmoil elsewhere in Europe is not as helpful as it might be. For example, it has been persuasively argued that the best analogy for 1381 is not the *jacquerie* of 1358 or the Ciompi rising in Florence but the German Peasants' War of 1524–6.[122] It is likely, however, that the revolutionary thrust of the Cade rebellion has been underrated by concentration on the men of Kent. The Sussex rebels were more radical and egalitarian than those in Kent, and some even seem to have transcended the limitations of consciousness implied by the distinction between a 'good' king and 'bad' courtiers and advisers.[123] This simple-minded dichotomy continued to addle the mentality of rebels and confuse their objectives until the regicide of Charles I in 1649 provided the great breakthrough. The idea of a 'loyal rebellion' was a priori implausible, since it seemed to assume by definition that a monarch must be an ignoramus and could not possibly know what was being done in his name.[124] Both the Tyler and Cade revolts followed the classic pattern of pre-industrial popular revolts and suffered from obvious limitations. In many instances it would simply be anachronistic to expect a higher level of consciousness. As Engels would later point out, the peasantry of the Middle Ages were capable only of 'communism nourished by fantasy'; they could point to the future but not reach it.[125] Yet limited consciousness was not just the prerogative of peasants and primitive rebels. The obtuseness of the chroniclers in viewing all rebellion as wickedness and Satan's work is palpable. The chroniclers loved to concentrate on the violence and mayhem in all such risings, but always ignored its legitimate causes. As Mark Twain said of the French Revolution:

> There were two 'Reigns of Terror' if we would but remember it and consider it; one wrought murder in hot passion, the other in heartless cold blood; the one lasted mere months, the other had lasted a thousand years; the one inflicted death upon 10,000 persons, the other upon a hundred million; but our shudders are all for the 'horrors' of the minor Terror, the momentary terror, so to speak; whereas, what is the horror of swift death by the axe, compared with life-long death from hunger, cold, insult, cruelty and heartbreak? What is swift death by lightning compared with death by slow fire at the stake? A city cemetery could contain the coffins filled by that brief Terror which we have all been so diligently taught to shiver at and mourn over; but all France could hardly contain the coffins filled by that older and real Terror – that unspeakably bitter and awful terror which none of us has been taught to see in its vastness or pity as it deserves.[126]

4

The Pilgrimage of Grace

Although on several occasions in English history rebels and revolutionaries have virtually prostrated the State yet failed to deliver the knock-out blow, the element of 'near-miss' should never be discounted. Even if it could be argued that Wat Tyler and Jack Cade caught the government unawares and would not have prevailed in a contest where the elite could bring all its resources to bear, this emphatically cannot be said about the Pilgrimage of Grace of 1536–7. This was by far the most serious rebellion in England in the entire period between the Peasants' Revolt and the Civil War of the 1640s. On this occasion the rebels had the authorities on the ropes with no chance of a comeback, yet unaccountably failed to follow through and deal the coup de grâce. The main problem was the old one of limited consciousness and lack of imagination. It could be argued that the clearest sign of modernity in government was the ability to think outside the 'box' of kingship. All societies until about 1640 suffered from this. There were many coups, assassinations of emperors and rebellions by the legions in the Roman world, but no one ever thought of radical change in society; actual and would-be usurpers never considered any possibility other than replacing a deposed emperor with a new one. Similarly, in the medieval world, it was taken almost as an axiom that the removal of a king would but imply the succession of another. Where there was no obvious candidate to succeed a reigning monarch, any rebellion, however formidable, was almost bound to fall at that fence. The rebels of 1536 were particularly at fault in not thinking through the implications of this, for they were dealing with the most bloodthirsty and vengeful sovereign imaginable. Those who claim that the vilest dictators are those who begin as intellectuals (Lenin, Stalin, Hitler, Mao, etc) are on safe ground with Henry VIII. This was a man who began as a scholar and would-be enlightened ruler but ended life as the most horrendous of psychopaths.[1] Historians have always been kind to the absurdly named 'bluff King Hal'. On some indices, he was the most despicable human being who ever lived. Where even Lenin, Stalin, Hitler and Mao performed their egregious evil in pursuit of social dreams and goals, however misguided, Henry VIII performed his purely out of hypertrophied egotism, out of a sociopathic rage that any other human being could dare oppose their will to his. The sixteenth century was certainly not an era of bleeding-heart liberals, but even the Europe of the Borgias, Machiavelli and the conquistadores were appalled by the spectre of the English Nero, who is estimated to have executed 72,000 people during his reign.[2]

As is well known, the key event in the reign of Henry VIII (1509–47) was the failure of his first wife Catherine of Aragon to provide a male heir. This led the king to petition the pope to have his marriage annulled. Whether Pope Clement VII would have granted this in normal circumstances is unclear, but when Henry approached him in 1527 Clement was the prisoner of Holy Roman Emperor Charles V of Spain, following the notorious sack of Rome by Spanish troops that year. The failure to obtain the divorce led Henry to declare himself divorced anyway and also to announce that the pope no longer had religious jurisdiction in England. His principal adviser Cardinal Wolsey was arrested, charged with high treason on the grounds that his sympathies were primarily with the pope rather than his sovereign, and died in captivity, thus probably escaping the headsman's axe.[3] Thomas Cromwell became the king's principal adviser, but then the reasonably clear outline of the reign grows turbid. Everything about Henry VIII and his incumbency continues to be controversial. Was Thomas Cromwell the evil genius behind the English Reformation and the dissolution of the monasteries or was this Henry's personal policy?[4] Did Thomas Cromwell fall because of Henry's fury about the ugliness of his fourth wife Anne of Cleves – a marriage Cromwell arranged – or were more subtle, diplomatic factors involved?[5] Was Anne Boleyn a fanatical Protestant or a moderate Catholic? Was it she, rather than Henry or Cromwell, who really pushed the Reformation in England? Was she really guilty of adultery, as in the official treason charge that brought her to the executioner's block, or was this an absurd charge trumped up by Cromwell to curry favour with Henry?[6] While all these matters continue to be the subject of impassioned scholarly debate, it seems absurd to deny that Henry's determination to recognise no superior in eccesiastical as well as secular matters was the prime mover in the English Reformation. There has long been a tradition that Henry was merely 'responding' to a popular desire for religious change, evinced the century before by the popularity of Lollardism, and that he was a reluctant religious revolutionary.[7] However, the evidence for a widespread 'bottom-up' desire to break with the papacy and the Catholic Church is thin; the most that can be adduced is an untypical Protestant tendency in the larger towns and cities. Insofar as there was a decline in Catholicism, it was replaced not by an avid Protestantism but by religious indifference.[8] The Reformation had no other source than the king and his courtiers, especially Cromwell and Archbishop Thomas Cranmer.

It must be remarked straight away that if Henry was reactive rather than proactive in the matter of Protestantism, with the implication that there was a massive groundswell in favour of religious change, the great convulsion of the Pilgrimage of Grace becomes inexplicable. The Pilgrimage of Grace, in short, was a massive groundswell in favour of Catholicism and the old ways, and makes sense only with Henry as the proactive agent.[9] To get round this insuperable difficulty, advocates of a uniquely 'organic' English Protestantism have been forced to maintain that the motives for the Pilgrimage were overwhelmingly social and economic.[10] There *were* socio-economic factors in the rising of 1536–7, but these were both localised and ad hoc; the only overall binding glue in the rebellion was a desire to undo the Reformation and to return to the situation as it was in 1529. Furthermore, it is clear that Henry himself was the agency actuating the revolt, possibly because he was trying to go too fast. A glance at the legislation of the famous Reformation Parliament of 1529–36 brings this home clearly. In 1530 the charge of *praemunire* (alleging that the accused was primarily loyal to a person outside the realm, i.e. the pope) was reinstated. In 1532 the First Act of Annates deprived the Vatican of all but 5 per cent of its normal revenues from England. The 1533 Act in Restraint of Appeals forbade *all* appeals whatsoever to Rome. The 1534 Act of Supremacy made Henry the head of the Church and in the supplementary Act of First Fruits and Tenths transferred the taxes on ecclesiastical income from the pope to the

Crown. The Treason Act of 1534 made it high treason to deny the Royal Supremacy. Finally in 1536 came the Dissolution of the Lesser Monasteries Act.[11] The calendar is also eloquent on Henry's insensate speed in 1536. His marriage with Anne Boleyn was annulled on 19 May 1536, she was executed on 19 May and Henry's marriage to Jane Seymour was celebrated on 30 May. All of this was hard on the heels of the execution of John Fisher and Thomas More for opposing the Act of Supremacy (by which Henry made himself sole and supreme head of the Church in England), and simultaneous with the promulgation of Henry's famous Ten Articles in June 1536 (which introduced Protestant doctrines on baptism, confession, holy communion and purgatory) and the beginning of the dissolution of the monasteries.[12] Henry had alienated many of his subjects by his treatment of Catherine of Aragon, his breach with Rome, his proposal to dissolve the monasteries and even by his treacherous execution of Anne Boleyn. He proceeded to alienate many more powerful members of the clergy and aristocracy by two new statutes introduced during the flurry of new laws in 1534–6. The Statute on First Fruits and Tenths in 1534 introduced a perpetual tax on the clergy, allowing the king's government a one-tenth tithe on all clerical incomes, plus a first fruits tax equivalent to one year's revenue on each new clerical incumbent. The Statute of Uses of 1536 closed a legal loophole for those who had hitherto escaped feudal payments by setting up a trust. The new statute ordained that any benefits from such trusts had to be paid to the legal owner of the fiefs anyway, which made it pointless to set up a trust.[13] All these different streams fed into the mighty river of what was to become the Pilgrimage of Grace.

The feelings of anomie and perceptions of chaos resulting from Henry's over-rapid offensives on a number of simultaneous fronts can be clearly discerned in the outbreak of unrest at Louth in Lincolnshire on 1 October 1536. It has even been suggested that this accounts for the element of 'premature revolution' in Lincolnshire and for the fact that the vicar of Louth, Thomas Kendall, 'fired the gun too soon'.[14] The abbey at Louth Park had been dissolved on 8 September after Henry's first Act of Suppression (his idea was to dissolve the small abbeys and monasteries first and the large ones later). The wildest rumours began flying around the county: the coinage was going to be debased; sheep and cattle would be taxed; Church jewels would be seized; three parish churches would be amalgamated into one. There was particular animus towards John Longland, Bishop of Lincoln and his chancellor Dr Raynes, who seemed to be ardent advocates of Henry's policies. The traditional tocsin call to rebellion was heard when church bells were rung at Louth and Horncastle. In Horncastle a crowd of 500 people quickly gathered and forced local aristocrats and gentry to take an oath of fidelity to God and the king; anyone who refused or tried to equivocate was put in the stocks.[15] Gradually rebellion spread through the county, but with Louth and Horncastle always in the forefront. On 4 October the first clear indication of rebel demands emerged with a call for the death of Thomas Cromwell and the 'heretic' bishops of Lincoln and Canterbury. Other clerics put on a 'most wanted' list were Cranmer, Latimer, Thomas Goodrich (Bishop of Ely), George Browne (Bishop of Dublin) and John Hilsey (Bishop of Rochester).[16] The Lincolnshire gentry quickly became sucked into the rebellion, but from the very earliest days there was tension between the 'gentlemen' and the common people. Paradoxically, at this stage the commoners were the most ideological and the gentry were more concerned with economic grievances. Quite apart from the internal strains between old and 'new' gentry (roughly the traditional minor nobility and a new moneyed class grown rich from commerce), the gentlemen evinced the latent tensions in the rebellion by distancing themselves from the objectives of the masses. The gentry were concerned to wring concessions from the king while appealing to him as loyal subjects, but the more hard-nosed commons had no compunction about presenting *demands*. The gentry rebels were particularly furious about the Statute of Uses, which cut into traditional rights to dispose of assets after death and introduced the novel principle of a royal tithe on bequests.[17]

From Louth, Caistor and Horncastle the rebels converged on Lincoln, where they mustered on 6 October, about 30,000 strong. The townspeople received them joyously, for Lincoln itself was in decline because of falling wool exports. Here the rebels formalised their demands and couched them in the form of Six Articles – a quite obvious rebuke to the author of the more famous Protestant Ten Articles. The repeal of the Statute of Uses was an obvious item, as were the insistence on the dismissal of Cromwell and the ousting of heretic bishops from their sees. But the insurgents made further demands: no extra taxation should be levied except in time of war, and the Church must have all its ancient rights restored, with no tithes taken by the Crown. This implied both the repeal of the Statutes of Annates and that on First Fruits and Tenths. Moreover, further names were added to the list of those to be purged: Sir Richard Rich, Thomas Legh and Richard Layton, commissioners for the dissolution of the monasteries. Finally, the rebels required the issue of a full pardon once these concessions had been made.[18] A series of letters was sent to the king in London, but their 'impossibilism' must have been clear to anyone with any knowledge of the psychopathic Henry. The gentry made the elementary mistake of assuming that they could negotiate with the monarch, but Henry regarded the mildest suggestion that he moderate the pace of change as arrant treason. Whereas after a severe military defeat he might have been prepared, under duress, to dismiss unpopular ministers and bishops and repeal the Statute of Uses, he saw his own identity as bound up in the statutes passed by the Reform Parliament and would *never* concede on these.[19] The rebels had made the elementary mistake of not thinking through all the stages of their rebellion and asking themselves what they intended to do if the king defied them. Incidentally, the scope of rebel demands surely knocks on the head the idea that the Lincolnshire rising, as opposed to the later risings in Yorkshire, was a purely local affair involving the peasantry and the Duke of Suffolk.[20] The high profile of the clergy in Lincolnshire and the prominence of religious issues, particularly the dissolution of the monasteries, shows clearly enough that events in the county from 1 to 12 October were the opening shots in a would-be English Counter-Reformation.[21]

When Henry received the first letter from the Lincolnshire rebels he was, predictably, incandescent with rage. His first instinct was to summon Thomas Howard, 3rd Duke of Norfolk, a veteran of Flodden in 1513 where he had acted as deputy commander to his father, the Earl of Surrey, in the decisive victory against the Scots. Now in his early sixties, he might well have been the king's right-hand man but for his furious opposition to, first, Wolsey and later, Cromwell.[22] Another out-of-favour magnate Henry decided to call to court was the 68-year old George Talbot, 4th Earl of Shrewsbury, a natural hard liner and one who would presumably give Henry the sabre-rattling advice he wanted to hear. Among Shrewsbury's achievements was the defeat of the pretender Lambert Simnel at Stoke during Henry VII's reign.[23] But after mulling over his options Henry decided to pass them both over for the supreme command and give it to Charles Brandon, Duke of Suffolk. Now aged fifty-one, and a veteran of the French wars and the Field of Cloth of Gold, Suffolk had given serious offence thirty years earlier when he contracted a secret marriage with Henry's sister Mary, widow of Louis XII of France. Only the strenuous representations of Wolsey had saved him from the inevitable consequences of the royal wrath; always venal, Henry had finally been placated by a massive 'financial settlement' (i.e. bribe).[24] With that shrewdness and insight into other human beings' dark sides that so often characterises psychopaths, the king had correctly intuited that for this particular operation he needed a person of dubious morality, and Suffolk seemed to fit the bill admirably. It was agreed that Suffolk would be commander-in-chief of the king's expedition, but it was thought necessary, if only on prudential grounds, to coopt Norfolk and Shrewsbury as well, so they were given subsidiary commands. Together Henry and Suffolk decided on a massive bluff. Although they had no more than 3,000 combat-ready troops with which to oppose the rebels – and in this era so-called regulars were rarely of higher military calibre than rebels – Henry announced that he was sending 100,000 soldiers to Lincolnshire, threatening terrible retribution if the insurrectionists did not instantly submit. His written reply to the rebels' first letter was scarcely more conciliatory: 'How presumptuous you are, the rude commons of one shire, and that one of the most brute and beastly of the whole realm and of least experience.'[25]

Whether or not Henry's spies had told him of the division among the rebels between hard-line commoners and doveish gentry, this was the gap he exploited. On receipt of Henry's reply to their first letter, the gentlemen watered down their demands, avoiding specifics and referring merely to some vague 'grievances' that they hoped the king would address. But Henry, sensing weakness, would have none of it.[26] The gentry started to get cold feet. This was now a matter of serious rebellion and even to save face they would have to give battle to the king's forces. All the indications were that, with their numerical superiority, they would be successful, but the gentry wanted cast-iron certainties, not the hazards of battle. After all, if they lost, at best their fate would be loss of their estates and exile, and at worst they faced traitors' deaths. Faced with the king's intransigence, they panicked, tried to dump the commons and petitioned to secure pardons for themselves. Once again Henry proved utterly uncompromising, and in reply demanded that 100 'ringleaders' be handed over to the Duke of Suffolk with halters round their necks.[27] Their last hope was that Lord John Hussey, one-time chamberlain to Henry's daughter Mary, would prove a stout leader and reliable rallying point. But, at seventy-one, the aged Hussey turned out to be a ditherer, undecided about which way to jump. While Suffolk organised the royal forces, Shrewsbury acted quickly to arrest Hussey and issue a proclamation ordering the rebels to disperse or face death by battle or execution. Hussey paid the penalty for ambivalence, which to Henry was merely treachery by another name, and was executed the following year.[28] The robust response by king and authorities utterly demoralised the rebels. By 12 October only about a third of their original muster remained. The more obscure souls drifted away and kept their heads down, while the identifiable leaders fled north to Yorkshire. The Lincolnshire rebels had made every mistake in the book: they had not thought through the consequences of their actions, had underestimated and misread Henry, had backed the wrong horse in the form of Lord Hussey, and had effectively double-crossed their colleagues among the masses by stalling, delaying while Henry answered the petitions and preventing the commoners from striking south to secure a military solution. By 12 October Henry seemed to have won an easy victory against the opponents of his English Reformation.[29]

Some interim conclusions are in order. Henry's uncompromising stand made a military solution in Lincolnshire inevitable unless the rebels backed down. The king's rash bravado was a huge gamble, but it paid off, and his paranoia and bloodlust trumped reason again, as they so often had. But this was emphatically not a case of a cool gambler calculating the odds; above all he was lucky.[30] The Lincolnshire gentry should have sensed that they were dealing with a psychopath and pressed on south, but they seemed mesmerised by the mystique of royalty and bought the 'noble lie' that Henry was basically a good king who was being led astray by his courtiers. Suffolk displayed more political skill. He realised that to quell the Lincolnshire uprising he had to proceed with caution, for a bloodbath would have diminished the chances of a peaceful outcome in Yorkshire, where a fresh insurrection broke out on 8 October. The Yorkshire rebels, incidentally, had nothing but contempt for their Lincolnshire brethren. 'After so much talk it seemed ridiculous that the earlier rising should be so ignominiously ended and that without other agency than the threats of a blazon-coated herald and the blare of his trumpet: surely there had never been such a fall since the days of Jericho.'[31] The more thoughtful rebels in Yorkshire always thought that the rising in Lincolnshire was premature and should have been exactly coordinated with that further north. Lord Darcy (see p. 97), one of the leaders of what became known as the Pilgrimage of Grace, was said to have commented: 'Ah, they are up in Lincolnshire. God speed them well. I would they had done this three years ago, for the world should have been the better for it.'[32] The fact that the main rebellion broke out in Yorkshire *after* the Lincolnshire rising instead of simultaneously has usually been attributed to the overall leader of the Pilgrimage, Robert Aske, who was in Lincolnshire during the early days of October. Aske, it seems, wanted to see how Henry VIII would respond to rebel demands before committing himself in Yorkshire, for it was his cardinal weakness that he always regarded armed rebellion as a last resort. Certainly his 'wait and see' strategy was wrongheaded and disastrous, for the sudden collapse of the rebels in Lincolnshire undoubtedly harmed the cause of the Pilgrimage of Grace. It gave confidence to the government, confirmed Henry in his 'hawkish' attitude to rebellion and probably convinced many waverers that, with such poor rebel leadership, the king was bound to win in the end.[33]

It is a favourite pastime of Tudor scholars to distinguish between the fiasco of the Lincolnshire rising of October 1536 – ten days that certainly failed to shake the world – and the later and more serious insurrection in Yorkshire, which is considered the Pilgrimage of Grace proper.[34] There are certainly points of difference – more violence in Lincolnshire, for one thing – but the contrast between a non-existent leadership in the more southerly county and the more vigorous variety in Yorkshire will scarcely wash. It might have been better for the Yorkshire rebels if they had no distinctive leaders, for the ones they had were weak and lacklustre. No account of the Pilgrimage of Grace is adequate that does not give due weight to the poor leadership provided by Robert Aske, but there are many pieces missing in this particular jigsaw puzzle. Little is known of Aske or his early life except that he was a Gray's Inn lawyer in his early thirties and had only one eye. He was the third son of Sir Robert Aske of Aughton near Selby and Elizabeth Clifford, and was thus the privileged scion of an old Yorkshire gentry family long associated with Swaledale. On his mother's side he was well connected, for the Clifford family provided the first two earls of Cumberland, both Henrys; the first earl lived from 1493 to 1542 and the second from 1517 to 1570.[35] In the 1520s Aske had also been secretary to the 6th Earl of Northumberland. There are two main views on Aske. One was that he was a reluctant revolutionary who stumbled into revolt, tried to avoid it but finally concluded he could not. The other was that he was a prime mover from the beginning: deeply involved in events in Lincolnshire, where he promised the rebels support from Yorkshire, and a committed rebel from the earliest days (certainly 4–5 October at the latest), and already recognised as the de facto leader of the entire revolt by 6 October.[36] There is more agreement on his motivation and ideology. There are hints in the official archives that Aske was already regarded as a pro-Catholic political activist.[37] Aske was angry that the House of Commons had been dragooned into the acts of the Reformation: the Act of Suppression, the Act of Supremacy, the various acts declaring Mary illegitimate and allowing the king to will the succession, the Statute of Uses, the Statute for First Fruits and Tenths and the legislation that made words a treasonable offence. Aske declared the easy passage of these bills to be the merest corruption, since most members of parliament were pension-holders or officers of the Crown.[38] Most of all he was profoundly disturbed by the dissolution of the monasteries in the north of England. Some say that Aske was alarmed by the inclusion of socio-economic grievances in the petitions sent from Lincolnshire to the king. In his mind that made the rebellion a catch-all, not a Catholic crusade. Others say that he joined wholeheartedly in the rising only when he was sure the Pilgrimage would have primarily political objectives, that he moved the dissolution of the monasteries higher up on the Pilgrims' agenda than his colleagues really wanted, and that he was primarily an opportunist with ambitions to displace Thomas Cromwell as the king's first minister.[39]

8 October was a red-letter day in the history of the Pilgrimage of Grace, for on that day a serious revolt broke out in Beverley under Aske's leadership. The onset of the Pilgrimage proper once again finds

historians divided. Some say a rebellion in the north of England had become inevitable by the mid-1530s, for there was an over-determined causation of multiple causes; actually, using Occam's razor, we can say that the dissolution of the monasteries on its own would have been enough to trigger rebellion.[40] An implausible minority view is that the rebellion was no more than a conspiracy, that its timing was relatively adventitious, and that some factor other than Catholicism was paramount. For some writers that something was the ambitions of the House of York, still vigorous despite the defeat at Bosworth in 1485. Still others locate the conspiracy at court and see it as the outer manifestation of the struggles between the pro- and anti-Cromwell factions; the timing would thus be intimately connected with the sudden and unexpected fall of Anne Boleyn and Cromwell's virtually overnight hegemony.[41] Naturally, there are always radical empiricists in historical interpretation, those who deny any deep-seated causes and motivations in rebellion. On this view, the Pilgrimage of Grace began as a local demand for the redressing of grievances in Lincoln which quickly got out of hand, spiralled out of control and spread to Yorkshire, triggering a general rising in the north of England.[42] Yet the study of the evidence makes it clear enough that this was primarily a *Catholic* revolt. Aske and his entourage were actuated overwhelmingly by religious grievances: dissolution, the plans for Cromwell to proceed against parish churches, the exaction of first fruits, and so on. It is no exaggeration to say that the Pilgrimage of Grace was just as massive an indictment of Henry VIII and all his works as Magna Carta had been of King John and the Grand Remonstrance would be of Charles I.[43] Naturally, despite Aske's efforts, economic grievances loomed large also: the Fifteenths and Tenths due in 1537, the Subsidy tax, the rumoured new taxes on food, livestock and the sacraments and the new powers the government had claimed under the Statute of Uses. Particular indignation was aroused by the Subsidy, and Fifteenth and Tenth taxes for these imposts, usually raised only in wartime, were now being levied in times of peace, with no rebate allowed for poverty.[44] There were also economic issues peculiar to the north. The wool and cloth manufacturing industries had declined in the 1530s because of the 'cold war' between Henry VIII and Emperor Charles V, beginning in 1528–9, which cut off England from its traditional markets in Spain and the Netherlands. Additionally, the towns of the north-east were victims of a pincer movement, suffering through, in effect, being converted into 'clients' of the Hanseatic League in the Baltic, even as Cromwell blatantly favoured London's seaborne trade at the expense of other maritime towns.[45]

Once begun, the rebellion in Yorkshire spread rapidly as if by spontaneous combustion, astonishing everyone by the rapidity of its diaspora through the Ridings and beyond. Lord Darcy, commander of Pontefract Castle, already ambivalent about the rebellion, took out an insurance policy by warning Henry VIII that a rising in Yorkshire was imminent and asking for arms and reinforcements. Henry thanked him for the warning but sent no weapons or soldiers, already suspicious of Darcy and dubious about his true loyalties.[46] The initial focus of the insurrection was Beverley, appropriately for a town famous for its veneration of the Virgin Mary. The Beverley rebels at first stressed the spoliation of Holy Mother Church and the ruin of the commonweath by corrupt ministers in their manifesto of grievances; a particular fear was that parish churches were about to be expropriated in the same ways as the monasteries. Later they took a leaf out of the Lincolnshire book and added discontents about tax, especially the exaction of the Fifteenth and Tenths, feudal dues, and taxes on beasts, ploughs and the sacraments. The Beverley manifestos underlined the connection between the despoiling of the Church, the subversion of Christianity and the exploitation of the House of Commons – all of which were laid at the door of Cromwell.[47] The men and women of Beverley were particularly upset that the central government had intervened – via subpoenas, decrees and injunctions by the Court of Star Chamber – in the town's struggle with the Archbishop of York, who was their lord of the manor.[48] Moreover, they linked religious and economic grievances by underlining how the dissolution of the monasteries automatically reduced the amount of poor relief available. The Beverley rising was initially led by a lawyer named William Stapulton and was essentially a commons rising directed by the gentry. Alarmed at the incursion of socio-economic issues, which he felt muddied the waters, Aske moved quickly to take over the helm from Stapulton. He saw at once that he commanded a formidable movement, all the more fearsome in that the entire loyalist section of the gentry made itself scarce virtually from day one. Aske's abiding aim was for the gentry to control the rebellion, to prevent the radical element among the common people from becoming too influential and to play down economic issues while highlighting the religious ones; his view was that only then could he persuade the Yorkshire gentry to join the Pilgrimage en masse.[49]

Once in control of Beverley, Aske and Stapulton identified York and Hull as their next targets. The rebel armies began to move out on 12 October but the final decision to attempt a twin-track advance against Hull and York was taken on the 15th.[50] Aske issued a manifesto making it clear that his quarrel was with Cromwell, Cranmer and the rest of the 'corrupt' advisers, not the king himself. On the way to Hull Aske's forces swarmed into the great Cistercian abbey of Jervaulx and forced the abbot, Adam Sedbergh, to take the oath of loyalty to the Pilgrimage; although forced to do so, he was later executed for treason. Henry VIII, with his obsession with the power of words, would never accept duress as an excuse for any form of defiance, disloyalty or dissent.[51] The grandees of Hull were loyal to Henry, but he had not reciprocated their loyalty and had left them undefended and short of provisions. It was decided that Stapulton would advance on Hull while Aske aimed at the even more important target, York. Stapulton managed his part of the rebel strategy well and conducted a five-day siege, at the end of which Hull surrendered on 19 October, largely because the people had run out of food and there was no chance of reinforcement; additionally the rebels spread the rumour that Hull was trying their patience and they might have to resort to flame and arson, bombarding the town with Greek fire while their supporters within torched key buildings.[52] Stapulton sensibly ordered the rebel army to refrain from looting; his main concern was to get the burghers to sign up for the Pilgrimage. But the surrender terms contained a disappointing clause that the loyalist gentlemen were submitting on the strict condition that they did not have to take the oath of the Pilgrimage or serve as its captains. Aske meanwhile enjoyed a similar success at York, then the sixth city of England with a population of 8,000. York was more ambivalent in its sympathies than Hull, and the mayor soon agreed to open the city gates provided Aske pledged that there would be no violence and looting and everything would be paid for.[53] Aske entered in triumph on 16 October and set his men to administering the oath. Edward Lee, the Archbishop of York, a supporter of Cranmer and the Reformation but most of all a man in mortal dread of Henry, decided not to tarry, especially as he was likely to come face to face with the men of Beverley, who hated him for his manorial exactions – not to mention his endorsement of Henry's detested statute, ordaining that all who took the sacraments had to pay the king a fee.[54] He fled for safety to Pontefract Castle.

By now Aske had popularised the term 'Pilgrimage of Grace' for the rebellion he headed. The nomenclature served two purposes. It made the Pilgrims representatives of Holy Mother Church and thus gave their movement the sanctity of a crusade. And it gave a collective brand-name and identity to the insurrection, transforming what was originally a commons' rising in essence into a trans-class coalition which was dissociated and distinct from the failed Lincolnshire rising and clearly an altogether more serious matter.[55] In line with his policy of always foregrounding religious issues, Aske devised a form of oath, to be sworn on the Bible, which he insisted all recruits, willing or unwilling, should take. It ran as follows:

> Ye shall not enter into this our Pilgrimage of Grace for the Commonwealth, but only for the love that ye do bear unto Almighty God, His faith and holy church militant and the maintenance thereof, to the preservation of the king's person and his issue, to the purifying of the nobility, and to expulse all villein blood and evil councillors against the commonwealth from his Grace and his Privy Council of the same. And ye shall not enter into our said Pilgrimage for no particular profit to your self nor to do any displeasure to any private persons, but by counsel of the commonwealth, nor slay or murder for no envy, but in your hearts put away all fear and dread, and take afore you the Cross of Christ, and in your hearts His faith, the restitution of the Church, the suppression of these heretics and their opinions, by all the holy contents of this book.[56]

This seemed a fairly anodyne declaration – there was not even any mention of the hated Cromwell, which Aske felt might seem as though the main impetus for the Pilgrimage was political directed to factional ends. He aimed at solidarity in the north by persuading his fellow Pilgrims that there was universal enthusiasm there for the cause, though the truth was that, as in the German Peasants' Revolt eleven years earlier, many of the gentry signed up willy-nilly under threat of death.[57] Aske was also insistent that the clergy had to be in the forefront of the movement. As it was supposed to be a pilgrimage, he thought it best that high-ranking monks carrying crosses should be prominent. This would send a message to the king not only that his religious policy was wrong, but that its erroneous nature was perceived as such by all sections of the social order – for the clergy were not supposed to represent any one class.[58]

After taking York and Hull, Aske moved his host against Pontefract Castle. The castellan Thomas, Lord Darcy, was destined to be one of the key leaders of the Pilgrimage, but in the early days of the rising in Yorkshire he evinced a distinct lack of enthusiasm for it. Aged sixty-eight, Darcy had been a great favourite of Henry VII, but he had never cared for his son. Doubtless depressed and made circumspect by the poor showing of the Lincolnshire rebels, he nonetheless began by making fervent protestations of loyalty to Henry VIII. Yet the king never trusted him, unable to understand why Darcy could not deal as firmly with the rebels in his bailiwick as Suffolk and Shrewsbury had done in Lincolnshire. Darcy's position was actually intolerable: the king had sent him no reinforcements; he felt that he could not command the loyalties of his own tenants, who were sympathetic to the rebellion; and he was impressed by the many instances where a minatory declaration, such as Shrewsbury's in Lincolnshire, had brought insurgents to heel.[59] On the other hand, in his secret heart Darcy sympathised with the Pilgims. He disapproved of the dissolution of the monasteries and loathed Thomas Cromwell.[60] Moreover, his record of loyalty to Henry VIII was poor, he had often posited scenarios whereby the king could be removed by coup d'état, and in 1534–5 he had actively intrigued against him. On that occasion he had plotted with Eustace Chapuys, imperial ambassador to England, to get Emperor Charles V to invade the sceptred isle. Despite the emperor's lack of interest on that occasion, Darcy absurdly claimed that at a nod from him Charles V would have invaded.[61] Although Darcy always stated that he was forced into rebellion in 1536, no one took him seriously; his treachery towards Henry VIII was palpable. Some say he was the Yorkshire equivalent of his friend Sir John Hussey in Lincolnshire but, whereas Hussey never went beyond ambivalence (but was still executed), Darcy really was systematically disaffected.[62] Even so, he dithered for a long time. Once he realised there was no chance of armed support from the king, he surrendered Pontefract Castle to Aske after a token resistance and took the Pilgrims' oath. Darcy's adherence to the rebels convinced many waverers. One of the most important was Sir Robert Constable, at fifty-eight a veteran of Flodden and, like Darcy, a devotee of the old religion. His hatred of Henry's counsellors was notorious: on many occasions he was heard to wish that Cromwell was dead.[63] Perhaps the shrewdest of all the Pilgrims, Constable was probably actuated more by personal pique than hatred of heresy. Locked in feuds with other prominent Pilgrim families, notably the Percys and the Ellerkers, he was always something of a loose cannon. Nonetheless, he quickly took his place as the third man in a governing Pilgrim triumvirate, ranking just below Aske and Darcy.[64]

The fall of Pontefract Castle marked a decisive moment in the Pilgrimage of Grace. Almost simultaneously with the rising at Beverley headed by Aske, in Richmondshire Robert Bowes added another wheel, as it were, to the wagon of revolt by raising the Yorkshire dales in a much more clearly popular rebellion. The ancient county of Richmondshire took in the country between Ripon and Richmond, embracing the dales of Nidderdale, Wensleydale and Swaledale. In his famous 'Captain Poverty' letter, Bowes outlined a series of economic grievances, including the raising of rents on demesne households, deliberate depopulation through the destruction of townships and farmsteads, the enclosure of commons and the nefarious policies of the gentry, both depriving the peasantry of land through leasing farms and the ubiquitous nepotism and presence of placemen in the lower reaches of local government.[65] The 'Captain Poverty' letter created a sensation in the north and triggered risings in the Upper Eden Valley, the Durham Palatinate, the North Riding and northern parts of the West Riding, Penrith, Cumberland and Westmorland, north and east Lancashire and Northumberland. Although a popular element had always been present in the Aske revolt – as witness the number of drapers, glovers and innkeepers who can be identified in his ranks – and even predominated until he took control, the 'Captain Poverty' ideology threatened to split the rebel movement, underlining issues of taxation and landlordism rather than the religious grievances Aske wanted to be at the core.[66] Yorkshire, then, was divided in its motivation and heterogeneous impulses were always thereafter a divisive force. Cumberland and Westmorland, which joined the revolt with gusto, were even more out on a limb. There the rebel leaders did not speak of government exploitation, the robbery of the Church or fiscal reform but concentrated on the inadequacies of tenant rights, the raising of entry fines and officialdom's incompetence in not proving adequate defence against raiding Scots or patrolling the no-man's land on the frontier – as well as alleged breaches of the system of border service tenant right; the dissolution of the monasteries scarcely featured, except in the utterances of the devoutly Catholic leader John Atkinson.[67] This is why some writers underline the parallels between Cumberland in 1536 and the German Peasants' Revolt eleven years earlier.[68] Even within Yorkshire there were marked contrasts. Beverley was preoccupied with its battle over manorial rights with Archbishop Lee and paid little attention to taxation, but in Richmondshire that was the burning issue – and why the rebels there constantly harped on the necessity of having a national parliament somewhere more accessible than London. The heterogeneity of the 1536 rebellion has provided academic historians with a field day. Some say that only Aske's movement should be regarded as the Pilgrimage of Grace, with the Cumberland/Westmorland risings and Bowes's 'Captain Poverty' movement as things apart. Cherrypicking the evidence, some claim that the Pilgrimage was always essentially an aristocratic rebellion, but the overwhelming weight of the evidence reveals it as a genuinely popular affair.[69]

Anxious always to retain control of the rebellion by the gentry and aristocracy, Aske called a general muster and council at Pontefract. The convocation of various hosts in the town on 22 October brought together between 28,000 and 35,000 armed men, in no way militarily inferior to any army Henry VIII could bring against them as most were veterans of wars against the Scots. In addition there were 15,000 armed rebels in Cumberland, another 12,000–20,000 besieging the Earl of Cumberland in Skipton Castle and another 6,000 operating against the Earl of Derby in Lancashire.[70] The two last operations call for some explanation. In a telling instance of local grievances trumping the general cause of the Pilgrimage, a sizeable body of rebels attacked Skipton Castle without bothering to inform Aske. This caused a rift in the Aske family, for Cumberland's eldest son Henry was Aske's cousin and Aske's brother Christopher put loyalty to the earl before solidarity with his brother. The Earl of Cumberland was loyal to the king but in no position to put down the rebellion and was hard pressed. Although the rebels did not take Skipton Castle, they eliminated Cumberland as a military threat in the rear, despoiled his parks and uplifted his cattle, sacked his houses at Barden and Carleton and destroyed some of his estate records.[71] Apart from him, the only significant opposition to the Pilgrims in the entire north came from the Earl of Derby. An unimpressive figure, Edward Stanley, 3rd Earl of Derby, was Cromwell's creature and had been made Henry's plenipotentiary in the north-west and ordered out against the rebels. Even while Aske held his grand muster in Pontefract, Derby was making significant progress against the rebels in south Lancashire, mainly because the pro-Pilgrimage gentry there had lost their nerve. The power of the Pilgrimage can be gauged from one simple fact: although Derby owed everything to Cromwell, he still wavered before coming down on the king's side. Cynics have commented that this was just as well since, without any great talent himself, in his overweening pride he would still have insisted on being the Pilgrims' captain-general.[72]

With most of his army and most of the significant Pilgrims present, Aske hoped to form the movement into a cohesive whole. Among the luminaries at the conclave were Sir Robert Constable, Sir Thomas Percy, Sir Ralph Ellerker, Robert Bowes, Sir John Dawnye, Sir William Fairfax, Sir Oswald Wilstrop, Sir Marmaduke Neville, Robert Challoner, Thomas Grice, William Babthorpe and Roger Cassels – most of the great names of the Catholic north of England.[73] Altogether Aske could count on the support of at least 50,000 commoners, six nobles, twenty knights and thirty-five scions of the lesser gentry. Perhaps the most significant new recruit was Sir Thomas Percy, for the Percys were the great territorial magnates of Northumberland – an ancestral house that had made kings tremble as far back as Henry IV. Virtually an independent power in the north-east of England, the Percys posed a perennial problem for English monarchs: they were needed as a bulwark against invasion by the Scots, but were dangerous since they could turn against the Crown. Henry Algernon Percy, 6th Earl of Northumberland (1502–37), was famous as an admirer of Anne Boleyn, though he was married (without issue) to the daughter of George Talbot, Earl of Shrewsbury. Chapuys regarded him as disaffected, and there were frequent rumours that he had joined the rebellion. As Lord President of the Council of the North (he had been given the post earlier in the year), his adherence to the rebels would have been catastrophic for Henry VIII. Over his head in debt, he refused to join Aske on the grounds that he was ill – he actually did suffer acutely from ague – which so infuriated some of the commoner Pilgrims that they wanted to behead him.[74] His brothers Sir Thomas and Sir Ingram were made of sterner stuff. They had particular grievances, for Henry VIII had denied them the succession to the Northumberland earldom in the event of their brother's death; in exchange for liquidating Henry Algernon's debts, Henry VIII had been named as Northumberland's heir.[75] When Sir Thomas Percy arrived at Pontefract on 22 October with 10,000 stalwarts from the north-east and the promise of 20,000 more, this was very bad news for the king. As has been well remarked: 'The Pilgrimage generally took on the appearance of a Percy uprising because so many of its captains were attached to the family by present or former services, e.g. Aske, Monkton, Stapleton, Lascelles, Hamerton, Robert Constable, Norton and Gilbert Wedell.'[76] The gentry of Northumberland resented both the Statute of Uses and Henry's imminent annexation of the Percy lands, since both seemed to condemn Northumberland to poverty or at least to the status of appanage. Sir Thomas and Sir Ingram Percy were hawks where Aske was a dove, and were particularly sympathetic to Robert Bowes and his men.[77]

At the council at Pontefract Aske was ratified as the overall leader of the Pilgrimage. At first sight this seems surprising, as several of the Pilgrims would have been deemed superior in rank. Aske was initially reluctant to assume supreme command and did so only when no other option seemed possible. It seems two main factors were in play. The Pilgrims needed a personage of gravitas to treat with the king and possibly meet him in tête-à-tête conclave. The obvious choice was Archbishop Lee, but he continued to evade commitment and found reason after reason not to take the oath.[78] Darcy was an obvious choice, but he could not satisfy the commons that he was 100 per cent committed to their aims. Darcy indeed continued to agonise privately about whether he had made the right decision, whether he was not simply a soldier who had deserted his post or even a traitor who had failed his king. He rationalised his position in a twofold way: the king had sent him no ammunition or reinforcements and therefore had left him no choice; and he was not actually rebelling against the king but merely against his evil counsellors. After all, had not Henry VIII done well in the first twenty years of his reign, only to fall under the malign influence of Cromwell? Darcy still hoped that he would be the great peacemaker and that he could act as go-between to the king. When Aske asked him to head the Pilgrimage, Darcy replied that if he was to fulfil the role of intermediary, he could not also head the rebellion; it had to be one or the other.[79] So Aske was the leader of the Pilgrimage. He was the only member of the gentry the commoners would trust, and his supposed position as tribune of the people made him hated by some of the aristocratic Pilgrims, most unfairly, since his aim was always to channel the grievances of the commoners into purely religious objectives. At the same time, some of the Richmondshire host suspected, rightly, that at a pinch Aske would sell them out. He was thus the classic man in the middle, but to play this role successfully, he needed to be far more talented than he was. It would be a mistake to discount Aske as totally negligible. As has been well said: 'He, singlehandedly, was responsible for transforming a revolt of the commons over fears of confiscation into a rebellion against the king and the Cromwellian ascendancy.'[80] Ambitious certainly, charismatic and energetic, and in his own mind a man of destiny, Aske suffered from the crippling disability that he was not actually very bright, was a poor politician, a lacklustre leader and an unimaginative chess player. Boastful and blustering, he was also naive and credulous. Many commentators have seen his duplicitous brother Christopher as the more intelligent and impressive figure. 'It was he (Christopher), rather than the timid and colourless John (Aske), rather than Robert, who was too ardent and too honourable for success, who seems to embody the very spirit of the age.'[81] Robert Aske's naivety is nowhere more evident than in his bizarre decision to allow Christopher to attend Pilgrim councils, even though Christopher had already shown his hand by his backing of the Duke of Northumberland. Hardly able to believe his luck, Christopher sent detailed reports of Pilgrim thinking and strategy to the king; in a real sense Henry had his very own 'spy in the cab'.

A surprise development at the Pontefract meeting was the sudden arrival of the royal messenger, codenamed Lancaster Herald, to plead the king's case. It seems that he did not address the full council, but conferred with Darcy and Aske and assured them that the king would certainly grant their demands.[82] This was a rash promise: not only did it commit Henry to something he would never have consented to, but he especially hated it if any of his underlings took any action without clearing it with him first. The eventual upshot was predictable: Lancaster Herald was executed. At the full council Aske was able to report generally very satisfactory progress, with most of the north of England under the Pilgrims' heel. Particularly vehement in their animus against Cromwell were the Ellerkers, one of the great Yorkshire land-owning families.[83] Money was no problem, since there were many different sources of finance available to the Pilgrims: individual subscriptions from the nobles and gentry; money raised from the sale of the estates of the loyalist gentry who had fled; the public moneys and local taxes, especially the cess; and the lavish contributions made by the clergy to preserve the Church in danger.[84] Here again Aske was being naive. He always intended the Pilgrimage to be a mildly reformist movement which would get the king to reverse the deeds of the Reformation Parliament since 1529, but levying the public moneys was regarded in early modern England as an express act of treason and thus a truly revolutionary act. The council then voted for a general advance on London with 30,000 men. Despite the assurances of Lancaster Herald, it was generally expected that the Pilgrims would have to fight a battle on the way, but they were confident of prevailing. The battle plan was that Sir Thomas Percy would command the vanguard, with Sir Ralph Ellerker, Sir Robert Constable, Bowes and Stapleton as his lieutenants, in command of contingents mostly from Northumberland and the East Riding. The middle section of the army, comprising mainly troops from the West Riding, would be under Darcy and Sir Richard Tempest, while Aske himself would bring up the rear.[85] The Richmondshire men still labouring ineffectually at Skipton Castle were ordered to break off the siege and proceed south. To ease the strain on victualling, each division of the army would be taken to a different bivouac at night.

The Pilgrims set off in good heart, chanting hymns specially composed for the occasion. One of them ran as follows:

Christ crucified
For thy wounds wide
Us commons guide
That pilgrims be.

Another had these words:

God that rights all
Redress now shall
And what is thrall
Again make free
By this voyage
And Pilgrimage
Of young and sage
In this country
Whom grant grace.[86]

Meanwhile the royal forces were in disarray. Despite Henry VIII's knee-jerk reflex to solve all problems by violence or force of arms, his troops were in no condition to face the rebels, being outnumbered underpaid or unpaid, demoralised and scattered around the kingdom. Henry's problem was that of all English kings: there was no standing army and most troops had to be raised by individual noblemen and gentry. A standing army would have been too expensive for the English State, even if the notorious stinginess of the Tudors had not also been in play. It was another of Henry's reflex actions that when asked to pay an account of £x he would automatically offer £x-y. So, in this instance, he was reluctant to pay his soldiers anything at all – he seemed to think that they should be happy to risk their lives for his 'glory' – and certainly not the 8d a day the Pilgrims paid their levies.[87] The royal commanders were currently sited in different locations, sitting ducks for a skilful enemy commander, who could have picked them off one by one. They were lucky that Aske was as inept a captain as a politician. Shrewsbury had 6,000 men under his command, Norfolk 3,000, Suffolk 4,000 and Exeter 2,000. Nationwide the royalists were outnumbered four to one and in the battle zone five to one.[88] Shrewsbury, commanding the king's vanguard, had initially made his dispositions to deal with the Lincolnshire rebellion and had been caught offbalance by the outbreak of the Pilgrimage of Grace proper. The dreadful autumnal torrential rains made it impossible for Henry's forces to unite at short notice, and the weather and poor state of the roads meant they could not march more than twenty miles a day, and even that was a tiresome labour through thick mud.[89] Shrewsbury assured Norfolk that he would not give battle before he and Suffolk joined him, but Norfolk was fearful that the impetuous, glory-hunting Talbot would seek to engage the rebels before that. Norfolk thought that once he arrived on the scene, his reputation as the victor of Flodden (which had won him great renown in the north) would give him a psychological advantage; he even suspected, rightly, that the reason he had not been given supreme command was that Henry was jealous of his martial prowess.[90] Norfolk was right to fear Shrewsbury's impulsiveness. On 22–3 October Shrewsbury seized the bridges over the Don at Doncaster, but the following day his troops were sucked into a skirmish with the Pilgrim vanguard under Stapleton. After scattering the royal troops, Stapleton in a state of high euphoria requested permission to press his advantage and take Doncaster, which he might well have been able to achieve. Aske said no.[91] Stalling desperately until Norfolk could arrive, Shrewsbury sent a message to the enemy suggesting that, to avoid bloodshed, the Pilgrims should send four plenipotentiaries to discuss a truce; hostages would be given as pledges for their safety. The Pilgrims immediately countered by suggesting a conference of gentlemen on either side, to be held on neutral ground.[92]

Norfolk arrived on 26 October, but the combination of his forces and Shrewsbury's still left the royalists outnumbered five to one. The Pilgrims meanwhile arrived in force, occupied Doncaster and forced the leading citizens to swear the oath. Norfolk's scouts told him the Don was fordable and this, combined with the Pilgrims' placing of their most formidable troops in their van, alerted him that his situation was desperate.[93] Short of horsemen, he could neither harry the enemy nor prevent the Pilgrims from harrying him. Morale and motivation in his army were rock bottom, with men grumbling about being underpaid and many of them sympathetic to the Pilgrims. He decided on an outrageous bluff. He demanded that the Pilgrims surrender or accept the immediate ordeal of battle.[94] When this message was received in the Pilgrim camp, it caused indignation. Aske called a council of war and an impassioned debate ensued. The commoners and the Richmondshire men were adamant that Norfolk's preposterous demand was an obvious bluff, but Aske urged caution. He made several points. First, the result of a battle could never be predicted with certainty, and the odds against Norfolk were no greater than those faced by Henry V at Agincourt. If the Pilgrims lost the battle, their cause would be destroyed forever. Secondly, even a victory would certainly plunge the nation into civil war. The only conceivable beneficiaries of this would be the Scots, who would pour across the border to pillage, or the emperor, who would seize his chance to invade.[95] In these circumstances, surely it would be best to see if negotiation could secure their ends. Darcy weighed in with the argument that the heavy rain around Doncaster Bridge on the night of the 25th and the obvious onset of winter made this an inopportune moment to campaign; even if victorious, they would be advancing on London in the snow.[96] To which the obvious answer – the sources do not reveal if it was given – was that Aske and Darcy should have thought of this obvious fact at Pontefract when they gave the order to march south. The truth, of course, was that both Aske and Darcy feared that a victory would make the commons the dominant force in the Pilgrimage and they would no longer be able to control the movement in the way they desired, nudging it towards purely religious and conservative ends. Aske's failure of leadership at this point was egregious. For all the reasons mentioned, the Pilgrimage of Grace was already a revolutionary movement, and revolutions cannot be resolved by talks and negotiation.[97] The Pilgrims should have struck decisively while they held all the cards. A Caesar or a Cromwell would have done so, but there was no one remotely of that calibre among the rebels. There was always in their ranks a fatal division between a peace party and a war party, roughly though not invariably following the gentry/commoner divide. It was the misfortune of the peace party that many of their most vocal and vociferous members were absent, still at Skipton Castle or making their way slowly southwards from there.[98]

It was at this point that Norfolk played his trump card. He offered the rebels a truce. This was yet another bluff, since he later admitted that he doubted his troops would have fought the Pilgrims even if ordered to do so. When he had later to justify his pacific actions at

Doncaster to the king (who hated any form of compromise, even temporary), he pointed out that three factors made a military defeat of the rebels impossible: the enemy numbers, the foul, rainy weather and an outbreak of plague in his camp.[99] His main concern, once he had decided on the futility of battle, was to stall and sow dissension in the Pilgrim ranks, but he was under pressure for this 'softly, softly' approach from Shrewsbury, who always played the hawk to Norfolk's dove. There were effectively a war party and a peace party in the royalist camp as well as among the Pilgrims, and during the tense days at Doncaster it was Norfolk's abiding fear that the impetuous Shrewsbury might ruin everything.[100] His twofold strategy – stalling and sowing divisions – was based both on intelligence from his spies, including Christopher Aske, and his conviction that the coming of winter and shortage of victuals would force the Pilgrims to disperse if only he could blunt their triumphant momentum. In his letter to the Pilgrims he suggested the exchange of 'gentlemen', with proper securities given and hostages taken, so that a lucid account of rebel grievances could be hammered out and sent to the king. It is worth emphasising that Norfolk was being totally duplicitous. He knew Henry well and did not expect him to be bound by *anything* he might promise. He himself was prepared to say anything, do anything, even at the limit take the Pilgrims' oath – anything to buy time. But he was careful to put the king in the picture at every stage of his devious and Machiavellian plotting, so that the monarch would not think he was 'soft on rebellion'.[101] With his known hatred of Cromwell and his reputation as a devout Catholic, Norfolk posed to the Pilgrims as a man who understood their actions and motivations, who was secretly sympathetic to them and thus would be an invaluable intermediary to the king or an honest broker. He was also gambling that the aristocratic leaders of the Pilgrimage would draw back once they became apprehensive about the growing power of the commons. After all, if the Pilgrims won a great battle and swept on to London, causing the king to abdicate or flee abroad, what was to prevent them from becoming the masters of England, for then they would have no need of the 'gentlemen'. Norfolk shrewdly saw that the split between the commons and the aristocracy among the Pilgrims was their Achilles heel, and that he could appeal to class solidarity across the seemingly insuperable barrier of Catholicism ranged against the Reformation.[102]

He was right. Aske, Darcy, Constable and the other 'gentlemen' jumped at the chance of gaining their ends peacefully. But first they had to weather the storm of another acrimonious debate. On the council there was virtually a straight split between the leaders of the vanguard, who wanted to give battle at once, and Aske and the middle section of the Pilgrim army. Bowes and his followers argued that they had the royalists by the jugular and that it was madness not to press their advantage. They also alleged that Aske was trying to 'bounce' them, taking advantage of the temporary majority of the peace party on the council – because about one-third of the war party was still absent, on its way down from Skipton Castle. For the first time the overt fear was expressed by the commoners that the 'gentlemen' might try to sell them out.[103] Aske, however, insisted the council had to make an immediate response to Norfolk. He ingeniously turned one of the war party's arguments on its head by declaring that it would be folly to join battle when one-third of their own troops were still absent. Once again he mentioned the heavy casualties likely from the royalist artillery, the problems caused by the advent of winter and the fact that the heavy rains were making the Don unfordable. He also introduced a novel argument: that victory for *either* side in battle would destroy the realm, but did not explain how this would occur if Norfolk was triumphant; as with so many of Aske's utterances, it was a mere assertion.[104] Eventually Aske and Darcy won the argument more by attrition than logic; it was decided to accept Norfolk's offer of four gentleman envoys. The four pilgrims chosen to treat with Norfolk were Robert Bowes, Robert Challoner, Sir Ralph Ellerker and Sir Thomas Hilton.[105] Some have expressed surprise that Aske was not one of them, but three considerations seem salient. Since Aske was regarded as the fountainhead of the rebellion, Norfolk might be tempted to seize him even if this meant consigning the hostages to their original fate. From Aske's point of view, he wanted Norfolk to see that the Pilgrimage was no mere 'one man band', but had support in depth among gentry and noblemen. He also wanted to keep a low profile in case things went wrong at the conclave and he then incurred the wrath of the disgruntled war party.[106] The hostages were delivered, and the four envoys sat down with Norfolk and his council, including the Lords Shrewsbury, Rutland, Huntingdon and Surrey. Norfolk asked the envoys to write down their demands. They replied with a rough sketch of their grievances, setting out their basic and minimum demands: the restoration of Catholicism and the rights of the Church, the repeal of the statutes of the Reform Parliament, and the expulsion of all traitors, especially Cromwell and Sir Richard Rich. The lack of fine detail was deliberate: the initial articles were couched in general terms to which both the war and peace party among the Pilgrims could agree. The upshot of this meeting was another classic bit of committee fudge: an agreement that 'further talks' and a meeting of thirty representatives on either side were needed. No evasive lawyer with talk of 'further and better particulars' could have improved on Norfolk's doubletalk.[107]

The meeting at Doncaster Bridge with the thirty Pilgrim representatives, all gentlemen, at first dragged on inconclusively, increasing the suspicion of the commons that the gentry were stitching up a deal that would, in effect, sell them out to the king. Their suspicions were well justified. Norfolk told the envoys that he was quite aware they had all been dragooned into joining the rising and urged them to desert now en masse, thus winning them the king's mercy. When this ploy failed, Norfolk changed tack and pretended to be on the Pilgrims' side.[108] This naked duplicity should have convinced all present that Norfolk was not to be trusted and that the entire offer of meaningful talks was an elaborate charade. But he coaxed the Pilgrims into setting down their grievances in five articles, to be couched in general terms with the details to be settled later. The articles proposed a threefold remedy for the realm's ailments: a return to the situation at 1529, severe (preferably capital) punishment for Cromwell and Cranmer, and a general pardon by acts of Parliament or letters patent. Norfolk assured his interlocutors that there would be no difficulty in granting any of this and additionally promised a parliament in York to thrash out the grievances in detail. Finally, it was agreed that Bowes and Ellerker would go south with Norfolk and Shrewsbury's son to meet the king and present the articles as a united front.[109] Norfolk wrote immediately to the king to say that he had not committed him to anything that he could not revoke, but it was quite clear to any impartial observer that he had made binding concessions.[110] The hapless thirty envoys went back to Aske and Darcy and sold their useless and inconclusive talks with Norfolk as a great victory. A handful of the Pilgrims demanded stronger and more solid assurances, but the leadership accepted the Norfolk/Aske argument that the royalist lords could not bind the king to promises he had not consented to. Besides, Aske argued, stalling cuts both ways: the truce gave the Pilgrims the opportunity to explore other avenues, such as enlisting the help of the pope and the emperor.[111] Once again the Pilgrims' council accepted Norfolk's word and agreed a truce to last until their envoys returned from London. When the men of the Yorkshire dales arrived after their trek from Skipton Castle, they were stupefied to learn that a truce had been agreed in their absence. Aske called on them to disperse, in effect telling them to go home empty-handed after talks at a conference at which they had not been represented. Sullenly, the 'Captain Poverty' men set off home.[112] It needs to be stressed what a calamitous error the Pilgrims made with this decision. The truce was a disaster for the Pilgrims, who were unlikely ever again to have such a great chance to deliver Henry a crushing blow. They had been handed all the best cards and simply thrown them away. Henry, when he heard of the truce, was predictably angry yet shrewd enough to see that this was the beginning of the end for his enemies. With his cynical understanding of human nature, he knew that men will always band together for a great cause but that, if stalled, they will gradually lose heart and lack the impetus to reform for a second attempt. The behaviour of the Pilgrim leaders can be regarded either as arrant betrayal of their commoner allies or the most fatuous and egregious misguided optimism. Aske and his entourage seem genuinely to have believed that they could trust Henry and get him to dismiss Cromwell and the other hated agents of the Reformation.[113]

It seemed almost an omen for the Bowes/Ellerker mission's slim chances of success that on 29 October Latimer preached a sermon comparing the Pilgrims to Satan; both were deceivers. Cranmer meanwhile in his preachings portrayed the Pilgrimage as the result of northern barbarism and ignorance.[114] It was the familiar either/or used by propagandists against foes in all eras: either the opposition is stupid or it is evil. On arrival in Windsor on 2 November Norfolk had a 'debriefing' session with the king. Still thirsting for blood, Henry raged at Norfolk that he had not provided a military solution. Calmly Norfolk explained that this was impossible: more time would be needed to concentrate the scattered royal forces, they would need to be paid properly, and it would be best to wait until the rebel forces began to disperse. The most judicious course was still to stall. Henry was particularly incandescent at the demand the Pilgrims had made (and Norfolk granted) for a neutral venue for the talks at Doncaster, the safe conducts and hostages and the truce itself – all things, he averred, which could be granted only in a war between princes, not in a detestable rebellion of subjects against their sovereign.[115] Finally Norfolk calmed the king down, and the Pilgrim envoys were introduced. Henry glowered at Bowes and Ellerker and treated them to one of his spectacular bursts of temper, before finally stating that he would answer the grievances in his own hand.[116] He had further meetings with Bowes and Ellerker over the next couple of days, during which he appeared to soften his stance. He made no overt concessions but said he was willing to listen, subtly trying to throw the ball back into the rebels' court by asking them to 'prove' their allegations against Cromwell, Cranmer and Latimer. While Cromwell himself wisely kept his head down during the entire rebellion, Henry was at pains to defend his favourite. To the Pilgrims' taunts that Cromwell was a low-bred commoner, he claimed in response that Aske was no more than a serf; could the gentry not see that it was dishonourable to follow such a man?[117] As a refined stalling tactic he told the envoys to return north with the promise that he would do all he could to compose the quarrel, assuring them that Norfolk would follow in a few days with his written answer. Bowes and Ellerker accordingly set off north on 5 November but had not travelled many hours before they were arrested and brought back to court. Henry raged at them that Aske had already broken the truce, but all that had happened was that Aske had publicised it so that it would be harder for the king to renege or double-cross. Henry's instinct was now to detain the envoys indefinitely, but Norfolk talked him out of it. Norfolk stressed that Henry's actions would themselves be seen as a flagrant breach of the truce so that the enemy would have gained the propaganda advantage. He also plugged away at the theme that the gentry had all been coerced into the rebellion, but that detaining Bowes and Ellerker would harden their attitudes. The most likely upshot was the reappearance in the field of a powerful Pilgrim army, and this time it would be impossible to work the same confidence trick on them.[118]

Henry took the force of the argument and grudgingly released Bowes and Ellerker on 14 November to resume their journey north.[119]

He discharged his homicidal energies in an epic memorandum which Norfolk was to take back to the rebels. He always fancied himself as a great lawyer manqué and master theologian – he came close to executing his sixth wife Catherine Parr for disagreeing with him on theological minutiae – so set about demonstrating his contempt for the intellectual level of the Pilgrims. Basically the long document he composed was dedicated to the proposition that he was always right and his enemies always wrong, but it was enlivened by the captious point-scoring Henry so relished. This had been apparent in the early days of the Lincolnshire rising when he rebuked the rebels for daring to raise the issue of the Statute of Uses: 'As touching the Act of Uses, we marvel what madness is in your brain, or upon what ground ye take authority upon you, to cause us to break those laws and statutes, which, by all the nobles, knights and gentlemen of this realm, whom the same chiefly toucheth, hath been granted and assented to; seeing in no manner of thing it toucheth you, the base commons of our realm.'[120] The same mentality was evinced in the declaration to the Pilgrimage of Grace proper. Typical was his remark that it was 'a double iniquity to fall into rebellion and also after to procure matters to be set forth to justify that rebellion'.[121] Henry conceded nothing and demanded unconditional surrender before he would discuss the Pilgrims' demands. He reiterated the message he had given orally to Bowes and Ellerker that the rebels' grievances were 'too vague . . . general, dark and obscure' and would have to be fleshed out (another obvious stalling tactic). He even had the gall to sign off with 'Now note the benignity of your prince'.[122] This was clearly a declaration of war but the king muddied it with the kind of confusion he liked to poke fun at when (allegedly) detected in the writings of the Pilgrims. On the one hand he claimed the Pilgrims' demands were vague and obscure, but on the other he said he would send a full answer via Norfolk which would give entire satisfaction. How was this possible? It was not. It was a flat contradiction. He showed the real contents of his hand by attempting, *pari passu* to detach important Pilgrims from the leadership by promising rich rewards and lavish grants of land if they would defect.[123] In public he continued to claim that the entire rebellion was just an unfortunate chain of events caused by a handful of troublemakers, principally Aske, but his secret military preparations showed that he knew it was far more than this and was a genuine mass rebellion. The verbal message passed on to the Pilgrims' council when Bowes and Ellerker arrived back in the north on 18 November spoke merely of 'obscurity' in the demands, but the troika of Aske, Darcy and Constable should have been able to read the runes from this alone. Instead, they continued to place faith in the coming meeting with Norfolk at Doncaster.[124]

5

Treachery and Debacle

There were clear signs in early November that Henry's strategy of prevarication and dissimulation was paying off. Once again the Pilgrim triumvirate provided weak or non-existent leadership. Aske was preoccupied with trying to nail down the slippery Edward Lee, Archbishop of York, whose dispute with Beverley over his manorial transactions had been one of the triggers for the revolt in Yorkshire.[1] Lee had still not taken the Pilgrims' oath or signed up to the rebellion, and the tolerance of the Pilgrims' leaders towards him was singular. One of the factors staying their hand was that they had heard nothing from the pope. The rebellion was now into its second month and still there had been no words of commendation from Rome nor any other form of official encouragement by the Holy See. It was therefore important to line up a solid Catholic Church in England against Henry and the Reformation. Lee, however, continued slippery and evasive, not surprisingly in light of his career hitherto. Aged fifty-four when the rebellion broke out, he had always been fawning and sycophantic towards the king, who, however, suspected him of ambivalence towards the Reformation. Nonetheless Henry had a high opinion of his abilities and used him on many foreign missions in the 1520s.[2] The king had smiled tolerantly when Lee conducted a famous (and rancorous) theological dispute with Erasmus in the same era. This was why Aske wanted his help in the coming debate with the king on fine points of theology, but the prelate continued evasive and obfuscatory.[3] In the end Lee threw off the mask by preaching against the Pilgrimage, which confirmed the commoners in their view that the coming terms would be simply an aristocratic 'stitch-up' in which Aske and Darcy would do a deal with Norfolk to sell them out. Aske had to hurry Lee away to a safe house so that the divine could escape the fury of the commons.[4] The incorrigible Lee even then concocted a plan for collecting the treasonable opinions of the Pilgrims under the guise of doing theological 'research', but Darcy, another clever politician albeit no leader, spotted the dodge and prevented him.[5] Darcy and Constable were always disgusted with the archbishop but Aske, incredibly, continued to hope he could be won round. When the prospect of another council at Pontefract loomed, to which Lee was summoned, the archbishop asked Constable if he could stay at home. Constable replied that in that case he must send his opinions in writing. Lee spotted the trap and went to Pontefract; he reasoned, correctly, that it was easy to obfuscate later about an oral opinion, but there was no escape from tenets set down in writing. In this, as in so many other ways, Constable revealed himself as the most able of the triumvirate.[6]

While Bowes and Ellerker were at court with the king, Darcy seems to have decided to take out an insurance policy and, to an extent, to backpedal. He began with friendly correspondence with Shrewsbury and Norfolk, testing the water, as it were. Appealing to Shrewsbury as an old friend, he asked him frankly on 12 November whether Norfolk could be trusted, or whether the Pilgrims should be on their guard against sudden surprise attacks or assassination attempts.[7] There had already been some worrying incidents that did not exactly underline the king's good faith. Shrewsbury sent an emollient reply, expressing confidence that the crisis would soon be resolved and that the Pilgrims' grievances rested on misunderstandings.[8] Encouraged by this, Darcy opened a correspondence with Norfolk and other royalist grandees.[9] Correctly construing this as a sign that Darcy was wavering, Norfolk answered in a way that made Henry's bad faith and treachery obvious and undeniable. The king had decided that the best way forward was to assassinate Aske: this would provoke another rising which he was confident he could put down. Norfolk accordingly contacted Darcy, making it clear that his restoration to royal favour depended on his delivering up Aske, dead or alive. The devious psychopath on the throne wanted no paper trail that could later establish his treachery, so this message was conveyed to Darcy by Percival Creswell, a servant of Lord Hussey's. Darcy refused the proposition indignantly, on the grounds that it was inconsistent with his honour.[10] Norfolk followed up with a letter, hinting at the Creswell proposition and asking Darcy to comment on the widespread canard at court that the Pilgrimage was really an elaborate form of aristocratic conspiracy, aimed at unseating Cromwell. Darcy replied with a dignified apologia. He denied that there was any conspiracy, rehearsed the events since the beginning of October and asserted that he had been placed in an impossible position when the rebellion broke out and the king would not support him. He reiterated his refusal to betray Aske and declared that he would happily live and work as a kitchen porter if the entire Pilgrimage could be resolved peacefully and satisfactorily. But he stressed that this would be possible only when Bowes and Ellerker returned safely with firm commitments from the king, including a pledge to hold a parliament in the north.[11] Some see this letter as Darcy's death warrant for, as has been said: 'No past service, no future pardon, could protect a man who so boldly exalted his own honour above the king's pleasure.'[12] Darcy was justifiably indignant at Norfolk's intrigue, regarding it (rightly) as a de facto breach of the truce. The (temporary) detention of Bowes and Ellerker was another manifest infraction of the truce, and Darcy denounced it vociferously to the Pilgrims' council.[13] Opinions about Darcy and his real motivations continue to be divided to this day. Those dubious of his status as an honourable man are apt to emphasise that in any case Darcy had no one he could trust to kidnap or murder Aske, even if he had been so minded.[14]

Aske meanwhile laid contingency plans to guard against any surprise attack. Hull was put in readinesss to repel a seaborne assault. The Pilgrims' front line at the Trent was heavily fortified, and a second line of defence, thought impregnable, was prepared on the Humber in case the royalists managed to breach the first position on the Trent.[15] But in the period of 'phoney war' during the first three weeks of November, the Pilgrims' main efforts were concerned with securing foreign assistance. There were two main obstacles to this. In the first place putative foreign invaders were confused and bewildered as between the grandiose claims of the Pilgrims and the complacent aplomb of Henry VIII, who habitually referred to the rebellion as a flea bite and claimed that the rebels were merely beggars, callow apprentices and journeymen or peevish, unemployed youths.[16] Secondly, the general policies of powers potentially hostile to Henry militated against intervention. Francis I of France would dearly have liked to strike against Henry but was constrained in a threefold way.

He feared that the only result of an invasion attempt was that his other great enemy, the emperor, would then make common cause with Henry; he realised that for an effective invasion of England he would have to collaborate with the Scots, whom he found tiresome and unreliable; and he still vaguely hankered after making a dynastic match between Mary Tudor and the Duc d'Orléans.[17] Emperor Charles V, likewise, with no cause to love Henry, was not keen to intervene, even though his ambassador in England, Chapuys, told him that most of the country was disaffected. He feared that to do so would precipitate the Orléans/Mary Tudor dynastic match he wished to avoid and he also had to face the fact that his best troops were exhausted after the disastrous campaign in Italy.[18] Henry, always a lucky tyrant, was fortunate on this occasion that the two putative champions of Catholicism and the papacy were at each other's throats. Neither Charles V nor Francis I could grasp that England was potentially a greater prize than any of the picayune issues that detained them on the continent. Had they concerted plans or had one of them been given a free hand, Henry would have faced the nightmare scenario later faced by the British government in 1745, caught between a threatened invasion on the south coast and a victorious rebel army in the north. It was the abiding ambition of so many insurgents to repeat the doomsday script of 1066, when Harold Godwinsson faced Harald Hardrada in the north *and* William of Normandy in the south.[19]

With Francis and the emperor out of the reckoning, that left only the papacy. Pope Paul III wanted a genuine crusade against the heretic Henry, but he was hobbled by his own weakness and that of his chief lieutenant. The pope prepared a bull of deposition and excommunication against Henry but then seemed to lack the courage to publish it. Moreover, he placed too much confidence in Reginald Pole, the greatest English theologian of the age but emphatically not a man of action. In exile and in fear of his life from Henry's secret agents after he refused to back the king over the divorce of Catherine of Aragon, Pole skulked in Rome awaiting developments, hoping that he would be invited back as the new Archbishop of Canterbury once the Pilgrims unseated Henry.[20] Paul III constantly pressed Pole to accept a cardinal's hat, but Pole was unwilling. His mother and the rest of his family were in Henry's power, under close guard, and he did not want to provoke the tyrant further. Having expressly declined the pope's offer of a cardinalate, Pole was astonished to learn that he had been elevated to the purple anyway.[21] Henry predictably took his revenge and executed Pole's entire family for no other crime than that they were his kin, but they were doomed anyway, whatever happened about the cardinal's hat. The magma of the king's volcanic wrath had already been stirred by Pole's 'treason' in refusing to fall into line with Henry's dubious theological arguments.[22] Henry placed an enormous bounty on Pole's head – 100,000 crowns (£66,000), dead or alive. The last gasp of the movement to foment a foreign invasion came when Pole was sent to the Netherlands, ready to cross over into England if the emperor ventured an invasion. Charles V's regent in the Netherlands was the target for frenzied lobbying, but in the end he decided to aid Henry VIII instead. The Pilgrims' cause was not helped by Aske's half-heartedness. An envoy was equipped for the journey to the Low Countries and instructed to ask the regent for money, 2,000 arquebuses and 2,000 horsemen, pending the arrival of the main imperial invasion force. This overture was endorsed by the full Pilgrim council, but Aske foolishly countermanded it behind their back, so the envoy never even set out.[23]

On 21 November the Great Council of the Pilgrims met in York to hear the verbal report from Bowes and Ellerker and to decide future tactics. Aske was not present, though the other leaders were.[24] Once again, unaccountably, Christopher Aske was present. Not only was he thus privy to all the Pilgrims' thinking but he even had access to his brother's papers, enabling him to report to the king all the rebels' secret plans and strategies. How any rebellion with extensive aims could hope to succeed when a spy was reporting its every twist, turn and nuance was inconceivable, but it was just one of the many ways the aristocrats on the Pilgrim council flouted reason.[25] Bowes and Ellerker seemed to have been mesmerised (or were they traumatised?) by their time at court and gave the most vehement assurances that Henry VIII was sincere and could be trusted. At this Constable asked them to leave the room to allow the council to go into secret session. He then stunned his colleagues by producing an intercepted letter from Cromwell to the keeper of Scarborough Castle.[26] This missive let the cat out of the bag in a major way. It revealed that Henry was determined on a military solution to the rebellion, but had been persuaded by his advisers that he would have to bide his time before slaking his thirst for bloody vengeance. It made it very clear that the negotiations with the Pilgrims were simply a convoluted stalling device, designed to obfuscate and camouflage. There could be no clearer evidence of the king's perfidy and treachery. Yet, incredibly, the Pilgrim leadership chose to ignore it and to construe the letter as a personal interpretation by Cromwell; the myth of a gulf between king and chief minister was as vigorous as ever.[27] Darcy indeed ventured the bizarre judgement that all the points pointed to Norfolk's imminent displacement of Cromwell as the king's favourite. In vain did Constable and his advisers urge the council to accept the evidence of their senses and resume the march on London; in the circumstances, they urged, there was no point in meeting Norfolk. Darcy and the peace party outnumbered them and by this stage seemed a priori determined to accept the king's word, whatever damning evidence appeared. Never has there been a clearer example of a 'will to believe'. They clung for consolation to the offer Henry had made on 11 November that all but ten Pilgrims (one of them Aske) would receive a full pardon. They did not know that this offer had been made only after Suffolk advised the king that his forces were too weak to defeat the rebels at present and that all hopes of kidnapping Aske and Constable were vain.[28] Henry might disregard the very similar advice from Norfolk, whom he still did not trust, but he could not ignore it when it came from Suffolk, in whom he had full confidence.[29]

The Pilgrims continued their deliberations at York until 24 November. Their next task was to make a detailed reply to Norfolk, who had requested a meeting with 300 Pilgrim delegates at Doncaster in December to settle all outstanding issues. It was agreed that the 300 delegates, carefully selected to represent the peace party, would confer with Norfolk on the banks of the Don, on neutral ground, that safe conducts for all the delegates would be demanded, plus hostages to guard against any attempted seizure of Aske. The council members salved what in their own hearts they must have known was a humiliating climbdown by some routine and formal protests against breaches of the truth by the royalists.[30] Norfolk meanwhile had a tightrope act to perform, not committing his master to anything or infuriating him by overt conciliation but holding out tempting inducements to the Pilgrims to make peace. In his correspondence to Norfolk Henry had bellowed that he would offer no terms at all until the rebels handed over their 'traitorous' leaders and that the pardon was conditional on this; moreover he wanted unconditional surrender before he answered the detailed articles.[31] Norfolk suppressed this and consistently made encouraging noises to Aske and Darcy. He realised, as the king did not, that even a cherry-picked delegation of 300 nobles and gentlemen could not control or dictate terms to an angry host of 30,000 men. Henry's strategy was entirely directed to making over the 300, but he did not realise, as Norfolk did, that their agreement to a de facto surrender was not the end of the matter, that there would still have to be a 'hard sell' to the commoners.[32] But at least the king finally realised that there was a rift between the commons and the aristocracy that he could exploit; his apparent 'concessions' were solely aimed at widening this. To maintain the fiction that he was not dealing with rebels, Henry wrote about his wishes on 27 November not to the full Pilgrim council but to Bowes and Ellerker; even then he upbraided them for not having influenced the council to unconditional surrender.[33] The one mistake Norfolk did make was to let the enemy see the king's full reply to their grievances, which should have alerted all but the most purblind and obtuse to his real state of mind. The utterances were so bombastic and suffused with infallibility that they would have come better from a god than a king. It has been well remarked that his long letter 'displayed amazement, deeply injured innocence, self-justification, vanity, reproachfulness, truculence and contempt before a final spasm of anger against "your shameful insurrection and unnatural rebellion" and a pompous gesture of regal paternity'.[34]

Under massive strain from his precarious balancing act and the necessity permanently to employ doubletalk, by the beginning of December Norfolk was showing signs of cracking. His correspondence evinces signs of a despairing realisation that his task was sisyphean. It was clear to him that if Henry raised troops for a punitive expedition, the north would certainly rise again; moreover, there was no guarantee that the newly raised troops would not go over to the rebels.[35] He wrote to Cromwell that he had the worst of cards to play, that the Pilgrims were not content merely to be ranted at by Henry; they wanted a genuine settlement and, if they did not get it, they would continue with their military campaign; moreover, they would not surrender Aske, whatever threats or inducements were offered.

There must be a limit to how often the rebels could be bluffed or how long they could be stalled; and what then? Norfolk decided that the only way to blunt the king's intransigence was to scare him. In early December he told him that he would have to throw the rebels a sop or rather several juicy bones, for it was idle to think they could be defeated militarily. The real danger, according to Norfolk – and he was probably right – was that the longer inconclusive negotiations dragged on, the more the aggressive and belligerent commoners would wrest control of the rebel movement from the gentry – not surprisingly, since the king's intransigence left the gentry nothing with which to buy off the commons.[36] To make matters worse and complete Norfolk's despair, in an unwonted spurt of energy and elan the Pilgrims suddenly informed him they wanted a free pardon *before* they sat down to write out their detailed demands, they wanted the pardon confirmed by Parliament and they wanted the said Parliament to meet in the north.[37] Norfolk decided to break the logjam by daringly utilising his discretionary powers (though still subject to the king's overall instructions). He went out on a limb by offering a general pardon and the promise of a parliament, to be convened at York. This was advancing considerably beyond what the king wanted or had authorised. Henry was still insisting on the pardon with ten exceptions (six named persons and four unnamed) and a total rejection of the original five articles submitted by the Pilgrims. He had explicitly stated that if the rebels asked for a general pardon or a parliament, Norfolk was to stall.[38] Once the Pilgrims received Norfolk's 'generous' proposals, they announced that they would meet him at Doncaster on 5 December; on 2–4 December, immediately beforehand, they would hold a separate conference at Pontefract to hammer out their demands in a shape lucid enough even for Henry's fastidious sensibilities.

Henry VIII continued to insist that he would make no concessions and that if his 'generous' offer of a conditional pardon was not taken up, he would revert to military action. Norfolk as consistently warned him that this policy would lead to disaster, which elicited the predictable gibe of 'cowardice' from the king. But Henry welcomed the interlude while the Pilgrims prepared a more detailed statement of their demands. All the time he was hoping for a breathing space in which he could assemble a new army, so he instructed Norfolk to use the Pontefract articles as a further excuse to stall. When the detailed articles were prepared, Norfolk was to ask for a further twenty-day truce while king and nobles considered the demands. Meanwhile Henry wrote to Shrewsbury, asking him to try to suborn Darcy and Aske. The new wheeze would be to offer them a pardon on a document bearing Shrewsbury's signature; if the pair were gullible enough to fall for this, Henry intended later to repudiate the document as a unilateral and unauthorised venture by Shrewsbury.[39] With attitudes like this in play, it is not surprising that relations between Pilgrims and royalists continued tense. Darcy felt it necessary to reassure Shrewsbury that the Pontefract meeting was a genuine policy-making convention, not a war council held as a prelude to an armed attack.[40] And so at last the Great Council convened from 2 to 4 December. Aske, Darcy and Constable were there, with 5 lords, 22 knights, 25 members of the gentry and 16 representatives of the commons. The main business was to refine and elucidate the original five articles presented to the king, which he had found too vague. A separate, much smaller committee of the council was to prepare for the meeting with Norfolk at Doncaster on 5 December.[41] This committee at once voted to exclude Cromwell's relation Richard from attending the Doncaster meeting; this was to be an overt sign that the Pilgrims' real enemy was Cromwell. The committee further decided it would not accept *any* exceptions to a general amnesty and royal pardon. The clergy also came into its own with the Pilgrims' decision that they should review the Act of Supremacy in a mass meeting. Once again Archbishop Lee caused consternation. Finally flushed out and unable to equivocate any longer, he caused uproar by preaching a sermon arguing that no man could ever take up arms without his sovereign's permission. Again he was nearly lynched, but the fact that Aske once more intervened to save him made the commons even more suspicious that the ruling classes were simply closing ranks against them and that a deal was about to be stitched together to betray them. It seemed to the commons that from the very earliest days Aske had shown no sensitivity to the commons' anger towards Lee, and the intense animus between him and the people of Beverley over manorial rights.[42]

The Pontefract conference dealt with three main issues: religious, legal and constitutional, and economic. It was universally agreed that there could be no compromise on the dissolution of the monasteries, for the cause of the Church had to be upheld. Yet even here Aske and Darcy were prepared to sugar the pill by offering the king an annual rent from abbeys and monasteries. On the other hand, the Pilgrims insisted on a death sentence ('condign punishment') for Thomas Legh and Richard Layton for their role as commissioners in the dissolutions achieved so far. The issue of the Royal Supremacy was more thorny. In the form accepted and advocated by Cranmer and Latimer this was mere heresy, but Aske proposed a diplomatic settlement, whereby Henry would be allowed what he called 'temporal supremacy' over the Church, but with the papacy still having the supreme authority over the care of souls.[43] Ecclesiastical legislation was to be decided in future by the nation's chosen representatives, not by royal whim. The Act of Annates, whereby Henry VIII took the first fruits whenever a benefice changed hands, was to be rescinded on the grounds that no English king had received these tithes before or, at the very least, an annual fixed charge was to be agreed.[44] The legal and constitutional articles began with a demand for the execution of Cromwell; curiously, those other two hate figures, Sir Richard Rich, Speaker of the House of Commons, and Chancellor Audley were barely discussed, possibly because they were considered mere creatures of Cromwell.[45] The delegates to the conference expressed their suspicion that the Act of Succession, allowing the king to nominate his successor, was simply a device to allow Cromwell to inherit the succession. Then the articles proceeded with a demand for the legitimation of Mary Tudor by special act of Parliament.[46] The twelfth article of the long manifesto required the king to refrain from interfering in parliamentary elections or in the transactions of the Houses of Commons and Lords. There was to be complete freedom of speech in Parliament, more parliamentary representation for the north of England, especially Yorkshire, and a parliament to be summoned early in 1537 either at Nottingham or York. The powers of the lord chancellor were to be curbed, and anyone issued with a subpoena north of the Trent had to be tried in York.[47] Two points are salient about the Pilgrims' religious and political demands. First, there was the insistence that all issues between the king and the rebels, including the pardon, had to be secured by an act of Parliament, not a royal fiat which could be withdrawn at any time. Second, the demand for greater parliamentary representation for the north and for a parliament accessible to northcountrymen, preferably at York, is a clear sign of the historical division between north and south that has always bedevilled English society, and is also a primitive version of the Court versus Country political struggle that was to be so marked a feature of the seventeenth and eighteenth centuries. Yet, overall, it is quite clear that the dissolution of the monasteries rather than the Royal Supremacy was the core issue.[48]

In some ways the most interesting part of the detailed manifesto drawn up by the Pilgrims was the list of economic grievances, for this gives us a singular insight into social structure at the time. We can also discern the fissiparous forces at work in the rebel ranks. Whereas there was close to unanimity on the religious and political issues, the financial and economic grievances tend to underline local concerns most of all. The Percys and their host were most concerned with the Statute of Uses and the laws on inheritance, whereas Halifax and the West Riding concentrated on government attempts to eradicate 'flocking' – adulterating cloth with other fibres – which the rebels considered part of traditional Yorkshire folkways.[49] Wensleydale and Swaledale, the Richmondshire host, were most exercised by gressoms – the tithes payable to a feudal lord when a tenant first took possession of holdings. Gressoms, indeed, were the most widespread of all the economic grievances, affecting Lancashire and Cumberland as well.[50] In Westmorland the focus of grievance was on enclosure, which restricted grazing on common land. In the early sixteenth century more and more common land was being taken over by big farmers to maximise profits from sheep and the wool industry, and there arose the new levy of agistement – a charge exacted by the landlord to graze cattle and sheep on enclosed land.[51] Then there was the major irritant of nutgeld – a cash payment to the Crown imposed on freeholders; in Westmorland insult was added to injury because nutgeld could be transferred from the Crown to a feudal lord. Yet another incubus was sergeant corn, a payment in kind, usually oats, made to the sheriff by the tenantry for feeding the horses of his staff when he was on tour.[52] In Cumberland the issue of tenant right was paramount. This involved a form of tenure found there, in the palatinate of Durham, north Lancashire and the North and West Ridings of Yorkshire. It meant that tenants had to provide free military service when called upon by the warden of the marches. In law it was a customary tenancy held at the will of the lord but, in fact and by custom, it was a hereditary tenancy thought by the peasantry to deserve lenient landlordship, which it rarely received. Tenants in Cumberland and Northumberland were particularly affected because of the frequent wars with the Scots. In some areas there was a refinement known as cornage, where the tenant of a freehold owed military service specifically for the defence of the northern border; this was a tax based on the number of horned cattle owned.[53]

In addition to these particular taxes there was the permanent burden of the Fifteenth and Tenth, a direct government tax with a fixed yield, assessed by a community's own officials rather than Crown commissioners and thus distinguished from Subsidy, an open yield directly assessed by government officials who assessed the wealth of subjects each time the tax was granted; a variable rate of tax was set by Parliament. Both Subsidy and Fifteenth and Tenth were supposed to be levied only in wartime and were expressly not to finance everyday government, though this stipulation was widely disregarded. Henry VIII was a prime offender: he breached the custom here and elsewhere that taxes should not fall primarily on the poor and also the convention that if there was use of these taxes in peacetime, there should be exemptions for poverty.[54] A particularly iniquitous recent tax was that imposed on those whose chattels were worth less than £20. In a classic illustration of punishing the poor for being poor, the government mulcted all such people if they had the 'impertinence' to eat wheaten bread, goose or pork.[55] In addition to anger at the levies imposed on them, the commons deeply resented the perks and privileges granted to the already well-off classes. There were the tithe-farmers – leaseholders who paid a fixed rent to a patron, usually the Church, in return for being allowed to profiteer – and their habit of requiring payment in kind. There were the rapacious 'escheators' – men who administered forfeited property. There were the benefices held by absentees, laymen and even some who had been condemned by the Church as heretics. And there was the ubiquitous corruption of officialdom.[56] All this was compounded by particular nuances in the socio-economic byways of the north, such as the complaints about lazy and corrupt priests in Lancashire or the complication introduced by the great feud between the two leading aristocratic families in Cumberland, those of Lord Dacre and the Earl of Cumberland.[57] The dizzying complexity of England's taxation system and the turgid bouillabaisse it produced were all set against a background of general economic crisis in the 1530s, caused by a series of crop failures ever since 1527, with wheat prices 80 per cent higher in 1535–6 than they had been twelve months before.[58] Furthermore, the general perception among commoners was that the high levels of tax, both direct and indirect, were mainly to finance unnecessary and extravagant nonsense: Henry's taste for luxury, his palace building, the meaningless ostentation of the Field of Cloth of Gold, and much else. Every single one of the above issues received incisive treatment in the twenty-five articles the Pilgrims produced at Pontefract. Henry had disingenuously complained about the vagueness and obscurity of the original five articles. He would not be able to complain about lack of clarity in the Pontefract manifesto.

Norfolk and the peace party were now in the ascendancy among the royalists, but this very fact infuriated Henry. Never one to compromise even over the smallest detail and with a conditioned reflex towards solving any and all questioning of his authority or will with violence, Henry muttered to his confidants that Norfolk's pessimistic reports were simply a trick to get him to come to terms. Whereas Henry suspected secret sympathies for the rebels, the more likely reason for Norfolk's dovelike stance (quite apart from his judgement that he could not win a pitched battle) was his feeling that the upshot of any victory he won would simply be to enhance the power of the hated Cromwell.[59] To assuage his anger Henry indulged in one of his favourite pastimes: lawyerlike nitpicking, this time designed to show that Norfolk's 'defeatism' was self-contradictory. Like an inveterate pedant, the king quoted some of Norfolk's letters against others, juxtaposing them to show they had no intellectual coherence. Besides, he declared, Norfolk's estimates did not accord with the intelligence received from his spies.[60] Whoever these spies were, at this juncture (early December) they must have been mere sycophants, willing to tell Henry what he wanted to hear, at the expense of the facts. To any judicious observer it was clear that the Pilgrims held all the cards. Blustering profusely, the king partially backtracked and instructed Norfolk that, at the limit, he could offer a full and unqualified pardon and the promise of a parliament, provided he did it on his own recognisance and did not commit the monarch irrevocably. He made it clear that Constable was now the 'most wanted' of his enemies, probably because Constable had openly (and rightly) accused the king of breaking the truce.[61] Henry's antennae for his enemies was as sharp as Stalin's would later be, for Constable was by this time the leading light in the war party among the Pilgrims. It is not possible to trace his activities or influence day by day, but he seems to have been the driving force behind the gentry at the first of two meetings with Norfolk in Doncaster. Aske was not present, since the royalists refused to give hostages as a pledge of his safety.[62] At this first meeting Norfolk coaxed the rebels into considering a draft plan for disbanding the Pilgrim army. Possibly because of Constable's presence and Aske's absence this offer was not taken up, and the meeting broke up with both sides conceding failure. Looking for scapegoats, the angry Pilgrims once more targeted Lee, whose survival after the amount of provocation he offered was well-nigh miraculous. Possibly because Norfolk saw that there no point in making a national issue over Aske's security, this point was cleared up and the way cleared for a second meeting.[63]

The 300 delegates, including Aske, Darcy and Lords Scrope and Latimer, readied themselves for the vital second meeting with Norfolk. They rendezvoused at the house of the Grey Friars in Doncaster, whence the 40 members of the subcommittee proceeded to the house of the White Friars, where Norfolk awaited them; 10 knights, 10 esquires and 20 commoners made up the party, deliberately weighted so that the commons could not afterwards complain about a 'sell-out'. At the last minute on 6 December, a letter from Henry arrived, permitting Norfolk to offer a parliament in the north and an unconditional pardon.[64] Norfolk at last thought he saw the glimmerings of a realistic chance of an accord. He was originally supposed to have revealed to the rebels Henry's interim reply to the original five articles before considering their expanded form in the twenty-four articles now produced as a result of the Pontefract conference. He took the prudent decision to suppress this uncompromising and fire-eating document. His hope now was that he could bluff and talk his way round the amended articles, using the promise of the parliament as bait. His performance at the second Doncaster conference in December 1536 was a tour de force of diplomacy. He made the most soothing and emollient noises, assuring the delegates that he hated Cromwell as much as they did; at least there was nothing mendacious about this part of his package. When the names of Audley and Rich were mentioned he likewise revealed his contempt. He then offered a full and unconditional pardon and a parliament in the north. When the issue of the abbeys was raised, he suggested in the most conciliatory way that everything be frozen on an 'as is' basis until the convening of the parliament. Whenever 'dangerous' topics such as the treason laws of Mary Tudor's illegitimacy were touched on, he waved them away airily, saying all this too would be settled at the parliament.[65] All in all, Norfolk was long on bromides and hot air but very short on concrete proposals concerning the abbeys and the larger religious questions. At no time did he reveal the essence of Henry VIII's thinking: that the monarch was still bent on bloody revenge and had marked all the leading Pilgrims down for eventual destruction, nor that he would *never* rescind the policy of abolishing the abbeys and stealing their wealth. Norfolk brilliantly exemplified the old adage that the best way to tell a lie is to tell the truth. He truthfully conveyed to the rebels all Henry's honeyed words, but did not divulge, as he knew full well, that Henry had encouraged him to promise *anything* both to gain a breathing space and to exploit the gap between commons and gentry; still less did he drop any hint that Henry intended to repudiate all his promises later.[66]

The jubilant forty envoys returned to their 260 colleagues with news that they had gained all they wanted: a free pardon, promise of a parliament and a blanket assurance on the monasteries. The entire company returned to Pontefract to spread the good tidings, but their reception was not what they had hoped for. The commoners were not satisfied with the deal and demanded, as a minimum, that any pardon must be issued under the king's seal and that absolute and irreversible *guarantees* be given by the king concerning the abbeys and the parliament in York. In this they were vociferously supported by Constable, who stressed that Henry was treacherous and not to be trusted. Four days of acrimonious wrangling ensued. Aske tried to 'bounce' the commons once he realised the vast majority of the gentry were in favour of accepting the deal, and rode off blithely to agree the terms formally with Norfolk. But such was the uproar that he was recalled on the road and asked to return to Pontefract to sell the accord. Amazingly, he managed to do so, possibly because the commons still regarded Aske as essentially 'their' man, unlike Darcy, who was suspected of ambivalence.[67] To cut loose from Aske as leader was probably a bridge too far for the commoners, whatever their general misgivings. And so, to Norfolk's unconcealed delight, Aske was able to tell him that he had sold the deal to the Pilgrims.[68] What the rebels had agreed to was so astonishing that at this remove it seems incredible. In return for some vague promises, the Pilgrims had agreed to dissolve their army, return home, and maintain a truce until Norfolk returned from London with more details about the promised parliament and the abrogation of the theft of the abbeys. They had thrown away the only card that gave Henry pause: their armed forces. All it meant was that the bloodthirsty monarch had to wait patiently before taking his vengeance. Nothing significant (except the pardon) had been put in writing, nothing had been issued under the royal seal, nothing had been ratified by Parliament. It was utter folly for people who had already 'insulted' Henry by raising the banner of revolt (and if they knew anything of his mentality, they would have known that that was how he would perceive it) to put themselves at his mercy and to trust the word of a professional politician like Norfolk. On a cold analysis, all Henry had done was to announce that a pardon was in principle available. In their euphoria and relief that they would not have to fight a battle, the gentry did not even notice Norfolk's ominous wording: that each individual rebel would have to sue for the supposed pardon.[69] The Pilgrims seem to have believed that, far from revolution, a mere demonstration could change government policy and decide mighty events, even though throughout history it is axiomatic that governments always ignore peaceful manifestations and sit up only when armed force is on offer. A distinguished historian of these events sums up the Pilgrims' basic error: 'They had allowed the issue to be changed from a trial of strength to a trial of diplomacy, and though Henry might have been overcome by force, he had not his match as a diplomat.'[70]

What was in the minds of these 'rebels without tears' when they made this calamitous mistake? Many answers are possible but none seems entirely satisfactory. Was there a collective failure of nerve by the leaders when they were on the brink of success? Did they really trust Henry VIII and Norfolk or, alarmed by the growing power of their own commoners, did they cynically detach themselves and seek to make peace over their heads? Certainly the leadership in the

Pilgrimage of Grace was probably the worst in the entire history of major English rebellions. Both Wat Tyler and Jack Cade had made mistakes, but they never shrank from armed conflict as the Pilgrims did. Aske was a singularly bad leader. He was a poor politician – at this level almost a naive idiot – he dithered and vacillated and seemed almost to make it a point of principle to hand the initiative to Shrewsbury and Norfolk. He consistently allowed himself to be gulled, bluffed and out-thought. In retrospect it can seem that Henry out-thought the Pilgrims at every turn, but he was far from infallible and made some bad mistakes. Darcy and Aske were poles apart initially, but when Henry delayed returning Ellerker and Bowes in November 1536, he drove them together.[71] In common with other Pilgrim leaders, Aske made much of his gifts of compromise and patriotism and his unwillingness to plunge the country into civil war. Yet if the choice was civil war or execution – as it was – why would anyone have shrunk from warfare? The supine attitude of the Church – both in England and abroad – scarcely helped the cause.[72] The Pilgrims were also hopelessly split, not just on strategy and tactics but on basic ideology; on one view the Richmondshire rebels and the Cumbrian insurgents had very little in common with the Pilgrimage proper.[73] Worst of all was the divergence of commoners and gentry, each pursuing a separate agenda. Economic issues were paramount with the commons, religious and political ones with the gentry. Essentially, the gentry joined a popular rising so as to be able to control it, and it often seems as though fear of their own proletariat weighed more with the leadership than fear of a tyrant. Normally a rising on the basis of the socio-economic grievances outlined above would have seen aristocracy and gentry make common cause with the Court. On this occasion, taken by surprise, they had hurried to join in in order to contain events.[74] Aske, supposedly the friend of the commoners, had often pointed out to his gentry friends that, in the wake of a military victory over Norfolk, the commons might decide that their 'betters' were dispensable and move the country towards genuine revolution. There can be little serious doubt but that the gentry sold the commons down the river at Doncaster. Even within the gentry there were profound differences of viewpoint. Some saw the dissolution of the monasteries as a step too far, but could stomach the Royal Supremacy. Others again could have tolerated even these had not

Henry enacted the Statute of Uses. Perhaps the most egregious failure of the leadership was to think through their demands and construct a doomsday scenario. Did it really make sense to call for the removal and execution of Cromwell, Latimer, Cranmer, Rich and Audley and the others and see the king as a mere dupe of ambititious grandees?[75] Extirpating these men did not go to the root of the problem: the problem was Henry VIII himself. While the Pilgrims were mired in confusion, turbidity, lack of focus, internal dissension and even treachery, they were faced by a ruthless, single-minded, vengeful and terrifying tyrant who regarded any objection to his will as a perversion of the laws of the universe. Such was the king's egomania that he was angry with Norfolk for having been evasive with the rebels about his evasions concerning the monasteries and also, irrationally, about the pardon and parliament he had authorised Norfolk to allow.[76]

Now that the gentry had made their disastrous decision to trust the king and throw away all the advantages they had accumulated, the only sensible course was for the erstwhile rebel leaders to make their peace with the sovereign. From mid-December a stream of gentlemen – Sir Ralph Ellerker, Robert Bowes, Sir George Darcy, Sir Oswald Wilstrop, Marmaduke Neville, the Earl of Westmorland and many others trooped south to London and Windsor to make obeisance. They found that there was still a surprising measure of latent support for the Pilgrims in southern England, though inevitably there was some surliness. The gentlemen took to adopting what was virtually a catch phrase when anyone shouted, 'Traitor!' at them: 'No traitors, for if ye call us traitors we will call you heretics.'[77] The pell-mell scurrying to court to kowtow to Henry seemed particularly despicable since the Pilgrims overtly abandoned their colleagues under sentence of death in Lincolnshire. It will be remembered that Henry had not dared carry out these capital sentences while a powerful rebel army was still in the field lest it trigger a nationwide uprising. Now that the Pilgrims had unilaterally disarmed, he proceeded to implement the first stage of his bloody revenge. The Yorkshire men had not pressed to have their Lincolnshire *confrères* included in the general pardon possibly, it has been suggested, out of pique that these 'cowards' had surrendered prematurely to Shrewsbury.[78] Possibly most cynical of all – or was it simply stupendous naivety? – was Aske. After formally resigning as the leader of the Pilgrimage, he accepted with alacrity an offer from Henry to be his guest at Christmas court; the king also sent a safe-conduct, valid until Twelfth Night. Aske set off at once, notifying Darcy once he was on the road so that any discouraging answer would be meaningless.[79] Henry VIII was being supremely Machiavellian. By now he had got the measure of the gentry, and aimed to win them over by charm and cajolery, hoping thereby to trigger a rising by the commons alone, which he was confident he could suppress. It might be thought that for Aske to enter the lion's den was dangerous folly, since Henry could repudiate the safe-conduct and execute his arch-tormentor. Other invited gentlemen had turned down the invitation as they did not find the king to be trustworthy.[80] Yet on this occasion Aske had nothing to fear. Henry was prepared to be patient. He would not reveal his bloody hand until the rebel arms had completely dispersed and could not be reconvened at short notice. To this end he was prepared to connive at Aske's lavish treatment as his guest; it would make the eventual retribution he planned all the more piquant. Meanwhile he pursued a threefold trajectory. First, he sent his officials north to collect taxes, though all tax-collecting was supposed to be in abeyance until the promised parliament met. Then he spread disinformation, insinuating that the Pilgrims had surrendered unconditionally.[81] Finally he massaged northern sensibilities by announcing that not only would there be a parliament in York, but he would be touring the area in person and his new queen would be crowned there; this of course would give him the pretext of moving a large body of men north without arousing suspicion. If push came to shove, he was even prepared to hold a parliament, confident that he could bully it to do his will.

In London Henry received Aske in a friendly and even effusive way. The Spanish ambassador was an eyewitness to this odd meeting and reported Henry cajoling Aske with 'my good Aske' and other expressions of friendship.[82] The ingenuous lawyer could not penetrate the depth of Henry's serpentine wiles. The king meanwhile was bruiting it about that Aske had gone south to turn king's evidence, thus further widening the split between gentry and commoners, who, seeing the mass exodus south of the nobility who were supposed to be their protectors, naturally concluded that this was the coda to the Doncaster sell-out.[83] As the pièce de résistance of his systematic duplicity, during the Christmas festivities Henry asked Aske to compose a narrative of the Pilgrimage from day one, so that he might better understand the grievances that had convulsed his subjects. Aske set to work with gusto and pulled no punches. He tightened the noose around his own neck by a splenetic attack on Cromwell, which revealed his naivety at its apogee. As Geoffrey Moorhouse has remarked, 'Aske could not have been more offensive without bluntly calling Henry a heretic too.'[84] Grimly satisfied with Aske's self-indictment, Henry bade an affable farewell to Aske when he departed on the morning of 6 January 1537 (the safe-conduct expired at midnight that evening). The king's parting message was that he relied on 'my good Aske' to pacify the disturbances increasingly reported to him from the north: in other words, he was asking him to pacify the tumult among the commons he himself (the king) had caused. Aske made all speed to Yorkshire, where he found that the reports of disaffection were not exaggerated. He found the commoners restive, bitter, cynical and angry. Trying to pour oil on troubled waters, he found that his star no longer shone brightly among the common people. At a meeting in Beverley, when he was trying to reassure the crowd that Henry would keep his word, John Hallam pointedly asked why, if everything was so satisfactory, the king's commissioners were even then scouring the county, collecting the Tenth, when it had been expressly agreed at Doncaster that there would be no more tax collection until the parliament met; surely this revealed the true, contemptuous attitude of the king (Hallam was right – it did).[85] Other radicals and Hallam sympathisers weighed in with further points: it was clear that the opening of the new parliament would be delayed, for Henry was using the excuse of his new queen's coronation to stall; all the leading gentry had decamped to London; Hull, which had been handed over to the royalists after the truce, was now being fortified; Cromwell was still in favour; and by now the king's uncompromising answer to the original five articles was widely known. Moreover, so far from conciliating the Catholic north, Henry had sent up ultra-Protestant preachers to plug the Henrician orthodoxy.[86] All that remained was a rather touching faith that Norfolk would do something for them. Yet even he looked likely to disappoint. He was supposed to have returned north with official documentation ratifying the Doncaster accord once he had debriefed the king, but here it was, now already mid-January, and there was no sign of him.

In something like desperation, Darcy wrote to the king that unless Norfolk came north immediately with some concrete offers, he and the gentry would not be able to hold the line against the commons, and the rebellion would break out again. The grievances he instanced were the collection of taxes in defiance of the Doncaster truce, the execution of the Lincolnshire rebels, the fact that nothing had been done to rescind the dissolution of the monasteries thus far expropriated, and the provocative fortification of Hull and Scarborough.[87] Henry had delayed sending Norfolk back deliberately, hoping both to rack up class tensions among the Pilgrims and to gain further time while the rebel armies dispersed around the north. The ominous delay alarmed Darcy, one of the few leaders left who had not abandoned all hope in a *sauve qui peut* scramble. When Norfolk came, would it be as a benefactor and conciliator or with avenging fire and sword? The portents from Lincolnshire did not seem propitious. The only sign of conciliation there was that Henry had executed 'only' forty-six rebels instead of the 100 he had originally demanded.[88] At last, on 16 January, Henry sent Norfolk back north but in such a way as to make clear that the worst forebodings of all the Pilgrim pessimists were justified. Norfolk's instructions were to proceed through rebel territory methodically, administering a new oath of loyalty. Before taking this, subjects had to submit themselves to the king's mercy, reveal all they knew about the rebels including the naming of names, surrender all arms, renounce all previous oaths and bind themselves to be true and loyal vassals of Henry thereafter. All who refused to take the oath were to be summarily executed. This made clear that Henry wanted revenge on all who had ever been Pilgrims no matter how faithfully they had abided by the Doncaster truce. The oath-taking was also quite clearly an opportunity for private score settling, since anyone could denounce anyone else as a Pilgrim and the assertion would not be tested in a court of law. What was flabbergasting about the new oath was that it insisted those swearing it accept explicitly the Acts of Succession, Dissolution and Supremacy – precisely the issues on which the campaign of the Pilgrimage had been waged.[89] While all leading rebels were to be executed, their very movement, it seemed, was to be airbrushed out of history. Henry intended his revenge to be so total that, by the time he had finished, future historians would be uncertain whether there had ever been a Pilgrimage of Grace. Even as all this was going on, the king continued to smooth-talk the leading rebels. A pardon for Darcy was made out on 18 January and Henry wrote to him to thank him for his services and ordered him to victual Pontefract Castle secretly. On 24 January the monarch continued his charm offensive against Aske by thanking him for his services.[90] It took until the end of the month for Aske and Darcy to realise that Henry had completely duped them but by then it was too late for the luckless duo to do anything about it. The commons had utterly lost confidence in them. Once he had driven a wedge between commons and gentry that could not be taken out, Henry moved on to phase two of his operation, which was to get the aristocratic Pilgrims to denounce each other. One who took up the invitation avidly was Sir Ralph Ellerker, who spent January and February assiduously trying to trap into self-incrimination both Aske and Constable, especially the latter, with whom he had an ancient feud.[91]

Meanwhile John Hallam had taken over leadership of the marginalised and disgruntled commoners. He enlisted Sir Francis Bigod as partner in an attempt to revive the Pilgrimage and restore the position as it was before the ill-fated Doncaster agreement. The two planned to assemble another army of 30,000 men, this time cutting the treacherous gentlemen out of the loop, and then marching on London; they saw clearly enough what Henry's game was. Bigod was a member of an ancient gentry family from Mulgrave near Whitby, and his later plea that he had been forced into the rebellion – the usual defence against treason charges – was actually true in his case. When the rebellion broke out, he fled to the east coast and took ship for London, only to be driven back into Hartlepool by contrary winds.[92] Bigod was something of a religious fanatic of a conservative stripe, and once he realised the Pilgrimage would give him the scope actually to undertake his fantasy ambition – reforming the monasteries in a more traditional manner – he joined in with gusto. He and Hallam enjoyed lording it over underlings and putting abbots and priors to rights and to this extent might appear risible characters, but they saw more clearly into the mind of a tyrant than Darcy, Aske or Constable did. Bigod rightly pointed out that even the draft pardon they had seen evinced Henry VIII's bad faith, since a king would not couch a genuine pardon in the third person, nor would a genuinely conciliatory ruler continue to insist that he had absolute charge of his subjects, both body and soul.[93] The irony of Bigod's position in the Pilgrim movement was that he had a rough time at the Pontefract conference on 2–4 December, with the commons suspecting him of being Cromwell's agent and wanting to kill him.[94] Yet if they were sound political analysts, Bigod and Hallam were woeful strategists and planners. They aimed first to knock out Henry's two key strongholds in the north-east, Hull and Scarborough. Hull, which had capitulated once before, was considered the softer target and assigned to Hallam; Bigod meanwhile was to assail Scarborough, which had remained loyal to the king throughout the rebellion.[95] However, things went badly wrong almost from the beginning of the new revolt. Hallam underestimated the depth of opposition he was likely to meet in Hull. The burghers there had been forgiven by Henry for not opposing the rebels more strenuously, and in gratitude they petitioned him to fortify the town. When Hallam entered the town with a small band of followers, the townsmen quickly disarmed him and made him prisoner.[96] Bigod meanwhile proceeded to Beverley, hoping to raise Aske's stronghold as a prelude to the march on Scarborough. He did not make Hallam's mistake, and entered with a force estimated at between 400 and 800. He too was rebuffed and found no support, so fled in alarm. He was not to know that his correspondence with Hallam had been found on the person of that unfortunate Yorkshireman, so that his plans to attack Scarborough were known. His forces soon dispersed and he found himself a fugitive sought by two distinct parties: by the royalists as a traitor and by the Yorkshire commons, who had never overcome their distrust of Bigod and construed the fiasco at Beverley as a 'set-up' staged to allow the king to say that the truce had been broken. After three weeks on the run he was apprehended and sent south to Henry's tender mercies.[97]

The Hallam–Bigod conspiracy and the renewed violence placed Aske and Constable in a quandary. If they disowned the new rising, they would lose any remaining influence over the commons, but if they condoned it, Henry would use their compliance as proof that they were traitors and had broken the truce – exactly as ultimately transpired, since the king was far too cunning to let such an opportunity slip.[98] Bigod and Hallam appealed to Constable and Aske to join them, but they were rebuffed; their erstwhile leaders assured them that the king could be trusted and that precipitate action now could ruin everything. They were correct in that, unless the entire Pilgrimage was revived, the new outbreak was counterproductive and played into Henry's hands. As has been well said, 'The king was determined to have his executions, even if they provoked a new rising; but he was to be more fortunate than he as yet dared to hope.'[99] The only useful thing Aske did on behalf of the failed rebels was to ask his gentleman colleagues not to execute Hallam lest it provoke all Northumberland to rise, but they did not heed him and dispatched Hallam even before Norfolk came on the scene. Darcy seems to have kept the entire Hallam–Bigod fiasco at arm's length, but his ostentatious loyalty to the king did not stop Henry identifying the quondam keeper of Pontefract Castle as his main target. He sent Darcy orders to provision Pontefract Castle against the prospective royal visit to the north for the queen's coronation. His aim was to catch Darcy in a fork. If Darcy provisioned the castle, Henry could use that as evidence that he was preparing for a fresh rebellion. If he did nothing, he could then be accused of lukewarm action in the king's service, an obvious sign of treason.[100] As the days wore on, Darcy and his *confrères* became more and more concerned that they had been foolish to trust the king. They 'felt that, like the knight of the legend, they had blown the horn without drawing the sword, and they were now at the mercy of an opponent whose next move was incalculable'.[101] Henry, meanwhile, like a master chess player or gifted conductor of an orchestra, planned all his moves to perfection. He instructed Norfolk to proceed north slowly, taking care that he did not arrive at Doncaster before Candlemas Eve, and providing detailed notes on who was to be summoned to his presence, when and where. The main body of the gentry were to join him at Doncaster, Darcy at Pontefract, but Aske and Constable were not to be admitted to his presence until York. As a parallel operation the Earl of Sussex was sent to the north-west to link up with his brother-in-law Lord Derby and complete the pacification of Lancashire.[102]

True to his precise instructions, Norfolk arrived in Doncaster on 1 February. He found a very different atmosphere from the one that had obtained when he faced the Pilgrims there two months before. The gentry raised no objections to taking the new oath and seemed prepared to forget all those grievances that had loomed so large just eight weeks before. Fear of the commons, paranoia about the mob and concern for possible loss of their property were now uppermost. On 4 February Norfolk proceeded to York. Once again following Henry's devious instructions, he tried to ensnare Darcy. When Darcy attempted to underline his loyalty by pointing out that the countryside all around Pontefract was now peaceful not rebellious, Norfolk pointedly enquired why Dacre had not managed to encompass a similar situation in October.[103] Yorkshire still had fearful collective memories of the dreadful 'harrying of the north' by William the Conqueror after his victory at Hastings, and now Norfolk began to play on those ancient fears, acting with marked harshness and brutality. He repossessed the abbeys, turned out the monks and executed abbots with gusto. Henry VIII, always a master manipulator, had pressed the right buttons with Norfolk by jibing that he was too good a papist to deal firmly with the monasteries, and Norfolk was determined to prove him wrong.[104] Henry was not now content with the mere dissolution of the monasteries and took an exquisite delight in executing priors and abbots: 'he wanted blood above all things, and monastic blood would be an important and satisfying part of the ritual sacrifice he required'.[105] If ever Norfolk and his furies were inclined to show mercy, the king would immediately overrule them. The only thing to be said in Norfolk's defence was that the behaviour of Sussex and Derby in Lancashire was even more brutal and barbaric.[106] After meeting Aske, Norfolk commanded him to accompany his forces to the north-east; the two remaining trouble spots were Northumberland and Cumbria. Even as Norfolk departed for Northumberland, news came in of a great triumph by the royal forces at Carlisle. In the only significant hard fighting of the entire Pilgrimage, 6,000 rebels attempted to take Carlisle but were heavily defeated by Sir Christopher Dacre and Sir Thomas Clifford;[107] 700 rebels were said to have been slaughtered in a one-sided battle that turned into a slaughter, and seventy-four rebel prisoners were executed afterwards. Norfolk mopped up the remaining rebels in Northumberland by the end of February, again ordering mass executions. By the beginning of March the whole of the north of England once more lay under the harsh Henrician yoke. Norfolk rode in triumph through Newcastle and Durham.[108]

Only one thing marred an almost total triumph for Henry. Sixty-two of the rebels taken in Beverley after Bigod's botched rising were marked down for execution but found not guilty by local magistrates. On hearing this Henry flew into one of his spectacular rages, overruled the 'not guilty' verdict by royal warrant and had the men rearrested. When a new, handpicked jury at a second trial still found one of the men, William Levening, not guilty, Henry exploded in a fresh spasm of rage and demanded to know the names of the jurors, doubtless intending to execute them also.[109] For once Norfolk did not accede to his royal master's whims. Rightly fearing that such a grotesque travesty of justice finally would reignite the painfully reconquered north, Norfolk released Levening and found other victims to hang in chains. Obfuscating his action while dwelling on the torments of those he had executed, Norfolk managed to divert the king's attention. Henry could now move on to the final stage of his vengeance: dealing with the ruling troika of the Pilgrimage of Grace and all its other leaders. A long list of nobility and gentry was invited to come south to the king's presence.[110] The invitees had three choices: to comply, which meant putting themselves in the king's power; to flee abroad if they could find the shipping and they were prepared to forfeit their property and face a life of poverty; or to raise the standard of revolt. Their own folly and incompetence meant that by this stage the third option was no longer a practical possibility; besides, plague was already sweeping through northern England, adding a fresh layer of devastation to that wreaked by Norfolk and his men.[111] Since obeying the summons often seemed the only realistic choice, yet it was tantamount to signing their own death sentences, some of the gentry tried to avoid the inevitable by claiming that they were too ill to make the journey south, but Henry was implacable. By the end of March, with executions being carried out at Carlisle, York and Lincolnshire – there were even a dozen grisly hangings in London – it must have seemed obvious what was going to happen to all ex-Pilgrims. Yet Aske, Constable, Darcy and many others all trooped down meekly to London in late March and early April. Did they think the game was up and that further resistance was useless? Or did they imagine that, as they had done nothing rebellious since the truce was agreed since early December and had received a royal pardon, they were safe?[112]

Towards the end of March 1537 Darcy set out for London; on 7 April he was committed to the Tower. Henry VIII now let it be known that he and the other Pilgrims would be tried for treason as they had secretly abetted the Bigod–Hallam rising. Virtually everyone in the kingdom, including the king, knew that this was a grotesque falsehood, but Henry had always been determined, since day one, that all Pilgrim leaders would end up on the scaffold. He now falsely and treacherously used the Bigod–Hallam fiasco as a pretext for abrogating his own pardon. Even some of his own most craven courtiers thought such duplicity set a dangerous precedent, for if the commons ever rose again they would certainly never trust the words of the king or his nobles. The utterly unscrupulous bad faith of the king found its predictable coda in the failure to summon the promised parliament.[113] Darcy came to trial before a jury of his peers on 15 May 1537 in Westminster Hall and was found guilty; there could be no other verdict unless the peers themselves wished to taste the headsman's axe. Henry delayed Darcy's execution for a while as he dithered about whether to execute him in London or Yorkshire, but finally ordered him to be beheaded on Tower Hill on 30 June.[114] On 7 April Aske was arrested – there was no further spurious nonsense about 'my good Aske' – and tried by a specially picked jury of nine knights and three gentlemen, charged with meting out 'justice' to all the Pilgrim leaders. Henry treated Sir John Bulmer and his wife with egregious cruelty. Bulmer knew the fate that awaited him and tried to put off obeying the summons, but soon enough he was forced down to London; executed on 25 May, he at least was spared the hideous spectacle of seeing his wife burned at the stake. Bigod and Hussey met their fate on 16 May, as did Adam Sedbergh, Abbot of Jervaulx.[115] Constable, the one Pilgrim leader who had seen through Henry VIII from the very beginning, was executed on 6 July at Hull, after Henry decided that Constable and Aske would be best disposed off in the north for exemplary purposes; Aske was turned off in York. Whereas Aske virtually gave up and even confessed to treason, Constable was made of sterner stuff. The quatrain he composed on the date of his execution displays his sustained contempt for the king:

> Let the long contention cease
> Geese are swans and swans are geese
> Let them have it as they will,
> Thou art tired, best be still.[116]

Henry took particular pleasure in extirpating the entire clan of the Duke of Northumberland and breaking the power of the house of Percy for ever; never again could they threaten the throne. Sir Thomas and Sir Ingram Percy were lodged in the Tower and quickly executed. Their brother, the Earl of Northumberland, who had taken no part in the Pilgrimage and had even opposed it, would certainly have been beheaded had his fatal illness not swept him away first. Such was Henry's maniacal thirst for blood that he even found an excuse to murder the guiltless Thomas Miller, the Lancaster Herald. For the 'crime' of having been present at the early Pilgrim deliberations, Miller was tried in the summer of 1538 and hanged in chains in York.[117] Henry VIII's apologists like to point out that he executed 'only' 216 people as a result of the Pilgrimage, as contrasted with the 100,000 who were slaughtered in Germany after the Peasants' Revolt of 1525. They omit to mention that the tens of thousands who died in Germany were the victims of bloodthirsty armies that were unleashed on them; they were not put to death by a judicial process sanctioned by a parliament.[118]

Elated by his almost miraculous success against the Pilgrims, Henry went on to eliminate the entire Pole family in revenge for the cardinal's 'treason'.[119] He then decided to settle once and for all with the White Rose faction. The Marquis of Exeter, leader of the Yorkists, had not lifted a finger to help the rebels during the Pilgrimage. If he had raised the West Country for the rebels, as he could easily have done, the tide of rebellion in England would have become a tsunami that would have swept away Henry VIII and the Tudors for ever. Yet Exeter's loyalty availed him nothing. In 1538 he and his associates were arrested on a trumped-up charge of conspiracy. The sequel was predictable. Exter was tried and found guilty of supporting the Poles on 3 December 1538, and was beheaded six days later; the rest of his Yorkist party were also executed.[120] Henry, grotesquely fat and suffering from an ulcerous and suppurating leg, survived another ten years – a decade in which his homicidal fury reached new heights. The architect of his victory over the Pilgrims, the Duke of Norfolk, nearly became one of his victims when his son, the courtier-poet Earl of Surrey, offended the king in a trivial matter over a coat of arms. Both Surrey and Norfolk were found guilty of treason, and Surrey was executed, Henry VIII's last major victim. Norfolk was gazetted to die shortly afterwards, but the day before his execution the king expired, and the interim shepherds of his successor Edward VI decided not to inaugurate his reign with a decapitation. Norfolk was kept in the Tower but was reinstated under Mary Tudor in 1553 and spent the last year of his life in something like his former glory.[121]

The main consequence of the failure of the Pilgrimage was that the dissolution of the monasteries continued unimpeded, making the Crown richer by around £150,000 a year from the revenue of abbey lands and, incidentally, giving the same kind of inflationary push to the English economy the precious metals of the Americas had given to Spain in the same period.[122] It is generally considered that the Pilgrimage of Grace was a total and lamentable failure, but a more nuanced view is possible. In the first place, the rebellion set Henry thinking about Thomas Cromwell, and was one factor in the multi-causal downfall of the Catholics' mortal enemy. At the economic and financial level the rebellion occasioned second thoughts in many areas. The Statute of Uses was negated by a Statute of Wills. Customary rights of tenure were largely secured as landlords abandoned the manorial system and switched to demesne leaseholds. By the end of the sixteenth century gressums were no longer arbitrary but fixed. In general the protest against Henry's fiscal reforms was successful, possibly thereby stopping a major overhaul in Tudor government.[123] Even at the religious level something was achieved. The pace of the Reformation was slowed down, so that it is generally considered that the real parting of the ways between Catholicism and Protestantism in England came in the reign of Elizabeth I. It is perhaps significant that four of the seven sacraments that Henry had omitted from his Ten Articles were restored in the Bishop's Book in 1537.[124] More controversially, some historians suggest the defeat of the Pilgrimage was overall a 'good thing' as England could scarcely have survived a protracted civil conflict so soon after the Hundred Years War and the Wars of the Roses.

Perhaps most significantly, the unsolved commoner grievances of the Pilgrimage of Grace triggered another rebellion shortly after Henry's death. The year 1549 saw two simultaneous but disparate risings in England, sucking in no fewer than twenty-six counties and showing the massive potential discontent with the Tudors that intelligent leadership of the Pilgrimage could have tapped. The curiosity of 1549 was that, whereas the Pilgrimage had managed for a time to unite the religious and socio-economic strands in the rebellion, this time they bifurcated, with the West Country being the focus for religious discontents and Norfolk the fulcrum for the social and economic issues.[125] The most striking outer symbol of the Pilgrimage of Grace was the badge displayed by the Pilgrims on their banners, which depicted the famous Five Wounds of Christ. This symbolism was revived in the West Country and in Hampshire, where the trigger for rebellion was the imposition of a new English Prayer Book which jettisoned many of the much loved traditional elements of liturgy. The revolt, at its apogee in Devon, was another nostalgic Catholic one, emphasising Latin, orthodoxy and traditional modes. Yet it was ill led. It began promisingly with the siege of Exeter by a sizeable rebel army, but Somerset, the Lord Protector, was able to defeat the insurgents easily, bringing them to battle and slaughtering 4,000 of them.[126] The revolt in Norfolk, uncoordinated with that in the west, was a more serious affair but very different in tone and temper. Here the great issue was enclosure, which some historians see as the locus classicus of inchoate capitalism. Enclosure has sometimes been portrayed as an economic imperative of the wool and cloth industries, and to an extent that is true, but its real impetus was the lust for profit. By 1500 about 45 per cent of arable land in England was enclosed, for landlords could rent enclosed land for three times the price of unenclosed land: in short, enclosure increased the wealth of landowners at the expense of wage labourers and tenant farmers.[127] A spontaneous uprising of countrymen who began pulling down enclosure hedges in Norfolk – the first such incident was reported on 20 June 1549 – turned into something more serious when a local landowner, Robert Kett, joined the rebels, organised them, marched on Norwich with a force of 16,000 and set up a camp on Mousehold Heath – the same spot used by the Norfolk rebels in 1381. At this camp Kett held a mini-parliament under an oak tree, which became known as the 'oak of Reformation'. The basic idea was taken up with enthusiasm and altogether another eighteen camps sprang up, thus gaining 1549 the reputation of being 'the camping time' or the 'commotion time'. The camp movement soon spread to Kent, marking that county's third significant entry into the annals of revolt. Although attempts have sometimes been made to portray Kett and his movement as forerunners of the Civil War radicals in the 1640s, this is unconvincing. Kett's ambitions were purely local, not national, and his ambitions were modest. He called on the Crown to act as honest broker in the disputes over enclosure and for rents to be fixed at 1485 levels.[128]

The social composition of the rebels reveals the important role of small merchants, tradesmen, minor officials and bailiffs. It was thus in no sense a proletarian or peasant rising and, given its local nature and modest names, certainly does not merit the title of revolution. Yet to the rulers of Tudor England even the mildest socio-economic demands were construed by the elite as a challenge to its credibility. Kett's threat to Norwich was the excuse Somerset needed to send an army against him. First into the fray was the Marquis of Northampton with a force of Italian mercenaries, but these were heavily defeated by the rebels on 1 August. The prelude to the battle saw taunting by the rebels in the form of 'mooning', which was to become a feature of the rising.[129] Kett enjoyed a three-week run as chief magistrate of his oaken parliament, but on 23 August the Earl of Warwick arrived in the environs with a fresh army of 12,000 men. Norwich itself became a battleground. For three days there was desperate hand-to-hand fighting in the streets and alleyways of the city. By the evening of 25 August Warwick's men were close to defeat and begged him to surrender. He called for one final do-or-die effort, and his energy was rewarded by the fortuitous arrival of reinforcements. The new troops tipped the balance, the rebels were routed and a huge slaughter resulted as Warwick's men sought to assuage their cowardice by mayhem and atrocities. Forty-nine rebels were hanged after the battle as exemplary punishment.[130] So subsided the final ripples from the Pilgrimage of Grace. The failure of the Pilgrims to arrest the Reformation may have had profound cultural effects. The high tide of Protestantism that ensued resulted in a fanatical hatred of statues, icons, sacred images and all the farrago of traditional Catholicism. Devotional art in particular was perceived as Romish idolatry. Altar screens were torn down and replaced by bare boards listing the Ten Commandments. The possibility of an English Renaissance in painting to match that on the continent was killed stone-dead.[131] It has been convincingly argued that in English culture the visual was replaced by the verbal. There were no Titians, Raphaels or Michelangelos in England, and even music went into abeyance, with no significant composer between

Thomas Tallis and Elgar (Handel was German). In compensation in literature Protestant England produced Marlowe, Donne, Ben Jonson, Milton and Shakespeare (though there is a school of thought that Shakespeare was a secret Catholic). The truly revolutionary nature of the Pilgrimage reveals itself not just in the religious and social road not taken as a result of its failure but in the cultural consequences of Henry VIII's triumph.

6
Cromwell and the Levellers

As so often happens in human affairs, the egregious errors and despotism of one generation are paid for by subsequent ones. Just as the weak and ineffectual Louis XVI of France would eventually carry the can for the excesses of Louis XIV and Louis XV, so the 'sins' of the Tudors were requited in blood by the Stuarts. Charles I, the second Stuart king (1625–49), was weak, vacillating, autocratic, devious, duplicitous and even treacherous, but was unlucky to spend his last minutes on earth under a headsman's axe. If human affairs were ever governed by justice – and we know that they are not – that was the fate that should have attended the loathsome Henry VIII, who died in his bed. All the traits of despotism, hypertrophied willpower, cunning and sheer malice were inherited by his daughter Elizabeth – perhaps not surprisingly, as we would expect the issue of a pairing between Henry VIII and Anne Boleyn to produce a monster. Yet the Tudors have enjoyed an overwhelmingly favourable press: Henry VIII is known as 'bluff King Hal', while Elizabeth is 'Gloriana' or the 'Virgin Queen'. It was the misfortune of the Stuart dynasty to inherit the throne of England at the very moment Europe was undergoing a 'general crisis'.[1] Whereas the sixteenth century in Europe had been an era of optimism, fuelled by the age of discovery and the Renaissance, by the seventeenth the mood was dark and pessimistic. It was true that the Reformation had unleashed violent religious conflicts, but these were as nothing compared with the holocaust of the Thirty Years War (1618–48), a conflict which saw the population of Germany decline from 21 million to just 13 million. While the radical empiricists deny that Europe suffered a general crisis in the seventeenth century – there is a breed of scholar that invariably denies *all* general manifestations and believes only in unique, minute particulars – the weight of evidence for such a phenomenon is overwhelming. Its principal obvious signs were the revolt against all-powerful and hegemonic Spain by Portugal, Naples and Catalonia in three separate revolts, the Fronde rebellion in France, and the Thirty Years War itself.[2] Some historians would go even further and insinuate a general crisis of worldwide dimensions, whose other overt expressions would be the collapse of the Ming dynasty and rise of the Manchus (Qing) in China (1644–62), the Shimabara uprising in Japan in 1638 and the implosion of the Ottoman Empire. In Europe some of the common factors are patent and palpable. Massive inflation was caused by the influx of precious metals sucked in from Bolivia, Mexico and China. A precipitate demographic decline accompanied the coming of climate change (the 'Little Ice Age'). There was tension and conflict between the highly bureaucratised royal courts and the regional, land-based aristocracy and gentry – the first appearance of the 'Court versus Country' collision that would last well into the eighteenth century.[3] And there were the highly significant intellectual and religious changes introduced by the Reformation and the Renaissance.

In England two factors were especially salient. By the reign of Charles I three-quarters of the population still lived in the countryside and the economy was still overwhelmingly agricultural, with tin being the only important mineral mined. Out of a population of perhaps 5 million – there had been a great spurt since the beginning of Elizabeth's reign – London already boasted half a million inhabitants, at least ten times larger than Bristol and Norwich, the most populous cities thereafter. East Anglia indeed was probably the most advanced area, with a class of small farmers enjoying economic prosperity and some local political independence. The social structure had not changed greatly in its essentials for more than a century: there was still the same fairly rigid hierarchy of great nobles, landed gentry, artisans and merchants, small peasants and agricultural labourers, plus a mass of paupers. Perhaps the truly significant class was the gentry, and it is no accident that there has been a frenzied polemic among academic historians as to whether this class was rising or declining on the eve of the English Civil War.[4] Ironically, the gentry, the cutting edge of the Pilgrimage of Grace, turned out to be the major beneficiaries of the dissolution of the monasteries. Elizabethan England seemed to have frozen the class structure on an 'as is' basis, particularly with the Statute of

Labourers, which aimed to break up all associations of working men and to control tightly the supply of peasant labour. This statute prescribed a seven-year apprenticeship for any given trade, and set the wages in each trade annually at Easter through the justices of the peace.[5] The wool industry was still important in the 1590s, but there were signs of latent economic crisis in the intense conflict between weavers and merchants. Another sign that beneath the surface all was not well was the violent oscillation in priorities, whereby the English economy seemed unable to decide whether it should concentrate on the cultivation of corn or cattle.[6] Aside from the socio-economic rumblings, by the reign of James I (1603–25) the Protestant religion was beginning to fracture. The reign of Elizabeth is rightly seen as an epoch when Protestantism in England finally demolished Catholicism, but another of history's iron laws was about to be triggered thereby. The French writer and philosopher Jean-Paul Sartre sagely prophesied in 1956, when Nikita Khrushchev famously denounced Stalinism at the 20th Communist Party Conference: 'Les déstaliniseurs se déstaliniseront.'[7] In other words, reformers always have to beware because they in turn will become the target for even more radical reforms, and so it proved with English Protestantism. The new Protestant winds blowing from central Europe would not leave the English dispensation unscathed. By the end of James I's reign, the effect of the Thirty Years War was to fracture Elizabeth's 'Protestant settlement'. The new rival to the Anglican Church was Puritanism, bringing in its wake many even more radical belief systems. Puritanism called for an even greater distance between Church and State, the abolition of a State religion, the destruction of all remaining Catholic residues and the refinement of doctrines. Heavily influenced by the Lollards, who seemed to have been routed in the fifteenth century – to such an extent that Lollardism has been dubbed 'the childhood of Puritanism' – the new religion's great strength was that it was a trans-class phenomenon. Ominously, its major stronghold was the prosperous East Anglia, virtually a byword for the power of the gentry.[8] In the train of the Puritans came other dispensations born in German Europe: the Anabaptists, who appealed mainly to the lower classes, and Calvinism, mainly an urban and middle-class phenomenon. Side by side with the fracturing of Protestantism went a not-unconnected exponential increase in the power of Parliament. Henry VIII, who used the House of Commons as his pet poodle, would have been appalled at the 'treasonous' growth in the powers of MPs by 1625.

Charles I was one of those people who displaced or rationalised his own inadequacy by systematic duplicity. Swept along by historical currents with which he was incompetent to deal, Charles was a pathetic figure who reaped what the Tudors had sown and has some residual claims on sympathy, if not as 'Charles the Martyr' or the 'holocaust of direct taxation', as Disraeli dubbed him,[9] then at least as someone caught up in the whirlwind of history. James I had left him a poisoned chalice in the shape of the violently anti-Puritan churchman William Laud. James had turned to the religious conservative Laud in alarm at the inroads of Calvinism. Though non-Catholic, Laud was a 'high' Anglican who favoured stained glass, altar rails and sumptuous clerical dress in religious ritual, and order, obedience and ceremony in the political sphere. Bishop of London in 1628 and Archbishop of Canterbury in 1633, Laud regarded Puritanism and all the dissenting Protestant breakaway movements as schismatic in the theological sense and punished them severely. To the Puritans Laud seemed merely popery in another guise or the Counter-Reformation by another route – fears heightened by the fervent Catholicism of Charles I's wife Henrietta – and the fact that Laud persecuted them with all the ferocity of a latter-day Thomas More lent credence to the belief.[10] Laud and Wentworth, Earl of Strafford, were Charles I's right-hand men, and the religious conflict between Puritanism and orthodoxy went in tandem with the struggle for mastery between Charles I and Parliament. The first test of strength between monarch and House of Commons came over the royal favourite, the Duke of Buckingham who, in some ways conveniently, was assassinated in Portsmouth in 1628. When Parliament moved to impeach Buckingham, Charles 'solved' the crisis by dissolving it. Thereafter, from 1629, he ruled as a far from enlightened despot in the eleven-year period of his 'personal rule'. The notorious Court of Star Chamber was Charles's favourite method of control.[11] The problem any king faced in trying to do without Parliament was that only the Commons could vote for subsidies, so where was the money for government to come from? Charles hit on the expedient of Ship Money. Traditionally, in wartime a king had been able to call on all littoral shires to raise money for the navy, each county contributing the cost of one ship. Charles introduced a new version of Ship Money and broke the conventions of government in two ways. First, he decreed that *all* counties should pay it, and, secondly, he made it a permanent tax, obtaining even in peacetime. It was first levied in 1634 and made permanent in all counties in 1636.[12]

The battle lines between Parliament and monarch hardened as the disbanded Commons found other ways to oppose both Ship Money and the Laudian project. The danger for Charles was that the prosperous middle classes had now taken over the role previously assumed by the barons or pretenders to the throne. Both sides thought that God was on their side and the other side was the devil – a prequel to armed conflict that always presages future huge casualties, atrocities and war crimes. Two famous cases in the 1630s showed the opposition in action. In 1638 John Lilburne, later to be famous as a leading Leveller, was punished by the Court of Star Chamber for his verbal onslaughts on Laud by being flogged all the way from Fleet Prison to Westminster and then pilloried and jailed for two years; it was the foundation of his fame.[13] Meanwhile in 1637 the wealthy Buckinghamshire landowner John Hampden refused to pay Ship Money and challenged Charles's legal right to levy it. His was a principled stand of 'Won't pay' rather than 'Can't pay'. In 1638 the judiciary ruled in Charles's favour, but very narrowly, with the judges voting 7–5 for the legality of Ship Money. A more cautious ruler might have read the implicit warning signs in this narrowly favourable judgement. Hampden publicised his stance, mainly on the grounds that Ship Money was part of a wider popish plot, but he touched a nerve, for Ship Money was profoundly unpopular and distasteful to the tax-paying classes on a number of grounds. Obviously financial self-interest was involved but, more seriously, the exiled Parliamentarians sincerely believed in the slogan 'no taxation without representation' and feared that the illegal tax meant the king would escape ever having to summon Parliament again. It was but a short step from this to the belief that the tyrant Charles could be halted only by force.[14] Meanwhile the personal rule of the king was assiduously challenged at a number of levels: by Sir Edward Coke in the name of the 'rule of law' and by the displaced Parliamentarians in the name of the sovereignty of Parliament: this was the essential 'soul' of the body politic and its aim should be the overthrow of the Stuarts' belief in the divine right of kings in favour of the notion of kingship as a trust, which could be revoked by Parliament for bad behaviour.[15]

Yet what really triggered Charles I's ultimate downfall was the unfortunate fact (for him) that he was the King of Scotland and Ireland as well as England (the Stuarts were a Scottish dynasty). Laud's reforms resulted in a New English Prayer Book, which to Scots, now deeply attached to Calvinism, was a 'Popish' tome. The swearing of a formal 'Covenant' to oppose the encroachment of Catholicism and the high Anglicanism of Laud led very quickly to armed insurrection north of the border. Charles's forces performed shamefully badly in the ensuing 'Bishops' Wars', waged in 1639–40. The Scots gained the upper hand, defeated the royal army at the Battle of Newburn in 1640 and even occupied the city of Newcastle. A humiliating peace was patched up towards the end of the year.[16] Determined to have a military solution to the problem of the rebellious Scots, Charles abandoned his personal rule and summoned the 'Short Parliament' of 1640 so that he could raise the money to equip a credible army. The new assembly soon showed it would not be the king's creature: instead of meekly voting the sums Charles required, it objected strenuously to the Court of Star Chamber, arbitrary taxation (especially Ship Money) and the economic monopolies granted by the monarch. Charles's nemesis turned out to be the firebrand John Pym, a fanatical anti-Catholic and permanent thorn in the royal side, whose speech on 17 April 1640 is regarded as one of the timeless House of Commons classics.[17] After three weeks of intransigence from the Short Parliament, with nothing achieved and no money voted, Charles angrily dissolved it. Having second thoughts with the military debacle on the borders, he hastily summoned another conclave, this time the famous 'Long Parliament'. If he thought he had suffered slings and arrows from the Short Parliament, they were as nothing to the invective with which Pym and his colleagues now assailed him. Almost the only thing to be said in Charles's favour was that he had kept Britain out of the Thirty Years War – the only time from 1066 to the present day that the nation has avoided involvement in a major continental conflict. The blistering attacks on Charles, Laud, Strafford and all the royal policies in 1640–2 have justifiably been called 'the revolution before the revolution'.[18] The Laudian system was a particular target for Pym and his associates. Once again the time-honoured distinction between a monarch to whom loyalty was owed and evil counsellors who had led him astray was resurrected. Parliament ordered the arrest of the four most prominent: Laud, Wentworth, formerly Charles's deputy in Ireland and ennobled as the Earl of Strafford in 1640, Sir Francis Windebank and Lord Keeper of the Seals John Finch.[19]

Windebank was a target for his anti-Puritan zealotry and his encouragement of Charles in his desire to impose a military solution on Scotland, while John Finch was in the line of fire for having presided over the trial of John Hampden. These two made good their escape to the continent, Windebank to France and Finch to Holland, but Strafford and Laud were caught securely in the net and so well guarded that Charles's attempts to spring them clandestinely from jail came to nothing. Strafford, still bearing his grandiose title of lord deputy in Ireland, was initially impeached for treason but the charges would not stick.[20] Parliament then acted just as despotically as Charles by resurrecting the medieval Bill of Attainder, which basically allowed Parliament to put to death anyone it chose without giving further reason, subject only to a simple majority in the Commons. A campaign of intimidation secured the required majority, by 204 to 59. Despite promising Strafford faithfully that he would not allow him to be put to death, Charles weakly gave his assent to the Bill of Attainder, effectively abandoning him and Laud to their fate. Three weeks later Strafford was executed on Tower Hill (12 May 1641), after being given the last sacraments by his friend the tearful and distraught Laud.[21] The archbishop himself languished in prison until his execution in 1645. Charles seems to have thought that his assent to the attainder would conciliate Parliament, but MPs knew well enough that this time around he was not in a position to dissolve the House to avoid the attainder proceedings, as he had done in the case of Buckingham in 1628. Pym and his friends were in no mood to extend olive branches to a man they considered a popish tyrant, so pressed on with a wholesale programme of reform: gelding the Star Chamber, abolishing Ship Money and customs duties, enacting a law that stipulated that only Parliament could dissolve itself. The Triennial Bill required Parliament to be summoned every three years, whether or not the monarch called it.[22] Whereas the constitutional changes might have been considered mild, in the sense that they simply took the country back to the status quo as in the reign of James, the religious measures the Long

Parliament enacted were radical and revolutionary. Radicals like the poet John Milton hailed the coming extirpation of episcopacy.[23] In vain did Charles I lament that the country was heading down the road of Tyler and Cade.[24] His counter-strikes were hamfisted and amateurish, such as his dabbling in a plot by Scottish sympathisers to seize Covenanter leaders. He still imagined that if he could forge a lasting peace in Scotland, he might be free of the financial shackles of the Long Parliament and thus able to dissolve it.

The outbreak of rebellion in Ireland in 1641 took away the last vestiges of royal manoeuvring space. The shocking outburst of violence there had many causes, all exacerbated by Strafford's despotic rule, but the ensuing massacres and atrocities lost nothing in the telling and were used as black propaganda by Protestant Parliamentarians insisting that Britain was already involved in a ferocious religious war. Some of the more extreme elements even alleged that Charles was complicit or in sympathy with the Catholic rebels. It was Ireland more than anything else that allowed the Puritans to claim that the general war that broke out in 1642 was a war of religion; some historians have agreed with them, dubbing the events of 1642–5 not a British revolution but the last European war of religion, and that what is termed the English Revolution should really be called 'the second Reformation'.[25] Pym used the occasion of the Irish rebellion to move in for the kill. First he got the Long Parliament to sign up to a bill that ensured the king could only use councillors approved by Parliament. Perhaps the pace of change at a moment of crisis was too much for some Parliamentarians, for this engendered surprising opposition and was passed only by 151 votes to 110. Nothing daunted, Pym next persuaded the Long Parliament to draw up a 'Grand Remonstrance' for presentation to the king.[26] This was a lengthy and devastating indictment of the king's entire reign and a wholesale assault on the royal prerogative and squeaked through the Commons very narrowly, by 159 votes to 148. Predictably Charles repudiated the charges, refused to accept the document and declared defiantly that he was now the sole bulwark against the floodgates of anarchy Pym was opening.[27] Pym followed up with the Militia Bill, which effectively transferred control of England's armed forces from the king to Parliament, but was thought a step too far by a significant minority in the Commons and probably by a majority in the Lords.[28] Finally Charles heard the false rumour that Pym intended to impeach his queen, Henrietta, for her Catholicism. The provocation by Parliament led Charles to what some consider his most egregious act of folly. On 4 January 1642 he entered Parliament with some 200 armed men, intending to arrest six Parliamentarians, including Pym, but found, to use his own famous phrase that 'the birds had flown'. Forewarned, Pym and the other potential detainees had slipped out of the chamber by a side door.[29] The resulting uproar in overwhelmingly pro-Protestant and Parliament London was so great that the king fled the hostile capital, in mortal fear of the mob. There followed a period of low-level hostilities and guerrilla warfare between armed bands of the king and Parliament while Charles tried, with some success, to appeal over the heads of his Parliament to his people. Finally he raised the royal standard at Nottingham in August 1642 and declared Parliament and its forces to be in treasonable revolt against his own divinely constituted authority. The English Civil War had begun.

The bloody conflict that began was prolonged and merciless because for a long time neither side had a decisive advantage. Charles probably won the first major battle, Edgehill (23 October 1642), on points but lacked both the resources and the military skill to follow up with a knockout blow. The parliamentary armies, initially under the command of the Earls of Manchester and Essex, had to tread carefully and to try as far as possible to avoid potentially decisive battles, for, if they beat Charles on the battlefield, he would still be king, but if they lost he would undoubtedly execute the vanquished as traitors.[30] The war settled into a stalemate of ineffectual sieges, small-scale skirmishes and guerrilla activity, with the royalists broadly controlling the west of England and Parliament the east. It was not until 1644 that Parliament felt confident enough to risk a major battle, but the result, at Marston Moor in July, was nearly decisive. Charles and his Cavaliers suffered a severe reverse in an engagement that has the dubious distinction of being the bloodiest battle ever fought on English soil.[31] Marston Moor should have been the effective end of the Civil War, but Essex and Manchester made serious blunders in the winter of 1644–5, allowing Charles to survive and regroup. By this time the rising star in the parliamentary ranks was Oliver Cromwell, who saw that victory would come only when Essex and Manchester had been demoted. Always a consummately skilful politician, Cromwell persuaded the

Commons to pass the Self-Denying Ordinance, which stipulated that members of parliament should not serve in the army. This was his clever way of getting rid of Essex and Manchester, whom Cromwell replaced with his faithful acolyte Thomas Fairfax. It was symptomatic of Cromwell's political guile that he engineered a situation whereby he himself was not subject to the Self-Denying Ordinance so that, still a serving MP, he was also in effect the generalissimo of the army.[32] The Ordinance also called for a professional fighting force, to be termed the New Model Army. It was supposed to be – and to some extent was – a 'People's Army' a forerunner of similar bodies in the French and later revolutions. Well trained and equipped, the new force proved its mettle at the Battle of Naseby in June 1645 when Parliament finally won the decisive victory that had so long eluded it.[33] Cromwell distinguished himself in the fighting, and Charles fled north to Scotland, but surrendered to the Scots at Newark in 1646. The winning over of Scotland was another of Cromwell's triumphs, achieved on the understanding that Presbyterianism would be introduced as the national religion in England. Charles was then handed over to Cromwell and Parliament by the Scots on payment of a 'ransom' of £200,000 and placed under house arrest at Holdenby, Northamptonshire.

It is difficult to overstate the objective devastation and sense of chaos engendered by the Civil War, and the later hostilities ending with the Battle of Worcester in 1651. The whole of the British Isles had suffered grievously in what some analysts rank as one of the most brutal wars of all time. There is fairly general agreement that some 190,000 died in the fighting in England (90,000 battle casualties and another 100,000 who died of wounds and disease), and 120,000 were taken prisoner. At least 60,000 (a very conservative estimate) died in Scotland, while in Ireland the colossal fatalities are generally considered unquantifiable.[34] The high estimate of 618,000 dead (112,000 Protestants and 504,000 Catholics) may not be an exaggeration. This would provide a total fatality of nearly 900,000; even the most conservative 'down-sizing' appraisal provides a figure of no fewer than half a million.[35] To put it another way, England suffered a 3.7 per cent loss of population, Scotland 6 per cent and Ireland a staggering 41 per cent. Placing these figures in context, we should remember that the entire four-year holocaust of the American Civil War of 1861–5 produced 620,000 deaths, while even the Great Hunger in Ireland in 1845–52 resulted in 'only' a 16 per cent loss of human life (mass emigration was another matter). The most horrendous bloodletting in modern times, by the Soviet Union in the 'Great Patriotic War' of 1941–5, caused a death toll of 25 per cent of the population.[36] Small wonder that many people living in 1645 felt they had been sucked into a black hole and that they were living in 'a world turned upside down'. Even at the military level the situation was chaotic, for many vigilante bands and groups of thugs and gangsters appeared on the fringes of the fighting, further complicating campaigns and issues. The most significant 'third party' were the Clubmen, local self-help groups or vigilantes, as their name suggests usually armed with only primitive weaponry. Wearing white ribands and declaring a plague on both houses, the Clubmen hoped to emerge as a viable *tertius gaudens*. Because their natural inclination as conservative groups was to support the royalists at a pinch, Cromwell identified the Clubmen as an enemy who should not be ignored. Their heartland was Dorset and Hampshire, and in an hour's stiff fighting on Hambledon Hill, Dorset, in August 1645 Cromwell's men encountered ferocious resistance before dispersing the Clubmen; out of some 2,000 who engaged with the Parliamentarians that day, 60 lay dead on the field, 200 were wounded and another 200 taken prisoner; the rest fled into the Dorset wilderness, never to regroup.[37]

The most obvious sign of the chaos world of the 1640s was the shivering of Protestantism into myriad sects and cults. While mainstream Protestantism largely took the form of Prebyterianism and Puritanism, themselves offshoots of the original episcopal Protestantism, the fractionalism of even those radical sects continued apace. It was these seventeenth-century manifestations of religion that became particularly associated with the rise of capitalism, as shown in the classic works by Weber and Tawney.[38] The historiography of 1640s England mirrors this splintering. Vulgar Marxism has sometimes been too ready to conclude that religion must always be the opium of the people, or the fantasy of Man afflicted by his own inadequacy, and that therefore the Protestantism of the Parliamentarians must have been 'nothing but' the interests of a rising (and temporarily ruling) class, a mere epiphenomenon. Vulgar anti-Marxists have been too ready to indict Marxist historians of believing in an overschematic and reductive 'transition' from feudalism to capitalism, somehow choosing the English Civil War as its epiphany.[39] The truth is that in the 1640s religion and politics interpenetrated to an extent that is hard for the modern mind to encompass. Whereas a modern thinker might frame arguments for the ideal society in terms of economic and social statistics, the men of the 1640s invariably referred the issue to the Bible. A nuanced class interpretation of the 'English Revolution' is perfectly valid and possible as long as it does not become hypostasised as mere theory, and as long as it includes the religious factor. The more sophisticated Marxists were always aware that religion and socio-economic thought could not be reduced to 'superstructure' and 'base'. Engels himself preferred to use 'correlations', pointing out that there was a connection between capitalism and Calvinism, in that predestination (the religious doctrine) was analogous to the theory of the market. Just as good works would avail a man nothing in the quest for Heaven, as only predetermined grace was efficacious, so mere entrepreneurial talent did not suffice in capitalism, as the market had its own iron rules.[40]

By the end of the Civil War the Presbyterians, in the majority in Parliament, were becoming seriously alarmed by the rise and proliferation of dissenting and left-wing sects within Protestantism; it even seemed to them that Charles I might have been right after all when he prophesied that the end of episcopacy was also the end of order and the beginning of chaos. The principal strand in what has been called 'the Radical Reformation' was furnished by the Anabaptists, who began in Germany and influenced the Peasant Rising there.[41] Whereas Martin Luther had believed in the importance of grace, he drew the line both at predestination and the abolition of churches and hierarchy, as also the concomitant social doctrines; it was no accident that he was an arch-denouncer of the German Peasants' Revolt. The Anabaptists by contrast believed in adult baptism and the literal interpretation of the Sermon on the Mount, rejected oaths, capital punishment and all the trappings of magistracy. Bitterly opposed to feudal oppression as they were, it was not surprising to find Anabaptists opposed to all constituted authority and headed in the direction of political radicalism. By 1640, more than a century into its existence, Anabaptism was a creed whose tenets were absolute social equality and revolution to achieve the ideal Christian commonwealth. Anabaptism, itself an offshoot of Protestantism, loathed all established churches, priests and other religious elites or intermediaries, but soon spawned a number of breakaway movements in turn, principally the Mennonites, the Hutterites and the Amish. Perhaps its most important offspring were the Quakers or Friends, rightly identified by Voltaire as the 'children' of the Anabaptists.[42] Quakerism went beyond the Anabaptists by rejecting not just baptism but *all* sacraments; religion was to be entirely a matter of communion between the individual and God, the Friends would congregate merely to share each other's personal revelations reached by meditation; pacifism was mandatory and there was to be complete equality for women.[43] Many of the sects in the Radical Reformation emphasised the original teachings of Jesus, as opposed to the later Christology of St Paul; the difference between the doctrines of Jesus of Nazareth and Paul of Tarsus has rightly been compared to the gap between orthodox Marxism and Marxism–Leninism. Yet many others emphasised mostly the core idea of antinomianism – the idea that there was no need to obey human laws, as faith alone was sufficient for salvation. The emphasis on faith rather than good works had been there in the beginning of Protestantism with Luther, but he vehemently denounced antinomianism. Finding it difficult to make out the antinomian case convincingly from the Gospels, sects with this notion as their core belief tended to gravitate to St Paul, from whose writings a specious case for the ideology could be made out.[44]

By the 1640s, with Puritans, Quakers, Baptists and Anabaptists well to the fore, the splintering of Protestantism seemed to have gone as far as it could. Yet all these creeds were recognisably Christian; already they were being overtaken by the second wave of cults and sects, which increasingly detached themselves from a Christian base. The Muggletonians were perhaps just still inside an ecumenical broad tent. Unitarian (deniers of the Trinity), hostile to reason and with a fondness for publicly cursing all who criticised them, the Muggletonians held the self-contradictory belief that Jesus Christ was indeed the Son of God but that God never intervened in the affairs of the world. God himself was precisely defined as a man between five and six feet who lived in a physical heaven about six miles above the earth.[45] Another eccentric notion was that when Jesus was crucified, there was a temporary power vacuum in heaven, and God the Father had to deputise Elijah and Moses until the Resurrection. Muggletonians also rejected the mind–body dualism, and argued that with no 'spirit' it followed that there could not be ghosts, witches or other supernatural phenomena. In rejecting the rigid separation of mind and matter, they anticipated by a couple of centuries William James's later notion of 'neutral monism'. As a Quaker-like community, the Muggletonians survived until late in the eighteenth century.[46] Another sect with superficial similarities to the Quakers was the Seekers, a religion founded by the three Legate brothers in the 1620s. Starting from an anticlerical and anti-Trinity stance, the Seekers soon left Christianity further and further astern as they embraced millenarianism, hermeticism, mortalism (the soul is not immortal), gnosticism and occultism in a seam-bursting eclecticism that focused mainly on Hermes Trismegistus as the true god; the Seekers' one saving grace was that they advocated religious tolerance.[47] Yet another sect to abandon Christianity were the Ranters, who explicitly embraced antinomianism and pantheism. Starting from the Calvinistic premiss of predestination or predeterminism, they argued that this must logically provide a licence to do as one pleased. Scripture, tradition, authority, a personal god, conventional morality were all jettisoned. A Ranter, they claimed, was free from all conventional restraints, sin was purely the product of the imagination, and private property was wrong.[48]

Yet another wacky sect was the the Adamite persuasion. The Adamites believed in nudity, the rejection of private property, communal living, no marriage but the sharing of women in common.[49] Also at a non-Christian, secular level were the pressure groups such as the Divorcers, influenced by John Milton who, having been refused a divorce after a deeply unsatisfactory marriage, campaigned for its legality.[50] Most of these cults vaguely and ultimately derived from the antinomian or Anabaptist tradition of the Radical Reformation. Yet there were other highly eccentric (to put it no stronger) groups who took their inspiration from mainstream religion and belief. Devotion to eschatology, chiliasm and millenarianism was rife in the 1640s. The Fifth Monarchy Men, for instance, believed that the execution of the king would trigger the end of times and the Second Coming.[51] More sinisterly, and in keeping with the tenets of the Puritans and the Presbyterians, there was a 'witch craze' or revival of the belief in black magic. This was particularly associated with the areas that had been Roundhead strongholds in the Civil War: Essex, Norfolk and Suffolk. Cynical individuals promoted the idea that women were witches and men warlocks or maguses in order to collect bounties (equally cynically offered by the parliamentary authorities) or to settle private scores or vendettas. The most sinister individual connected with the 'witch craze' was the self-styled Witchfinder-General, Matthew Hopkins (c. 1620–47), who claimed judicial powers never actually granted by Parliament but nonetheless connived at. Combing through Essex and East Anglia in the two years from March 1645 Hopkins and his associates hanged more than 200 people for 'witchcraft'.[52] All of these effusions of craziness and lunacy were aspects of the 'world turned upside down'. Cromwell and his Parliamentarians had, so to speak, gone through the mental sound barrier and were now in uncharted territory. They had done what no previous revolutionaries had ventured to do: opposed a king in battle and overthrown him. With all the old certainties gone, it was possible to believe in grand projects and to dream impossible dreams. In the famous words attributed to G. K. Chesterton, when men have ceased to believe in God, they do not believe in nothing, they believe in anything.[53] With no boundaries or limits anywhere in sight, a truly revolutionary vacuum had opened up.

By 1645, too, there was palpable tension even among the victors, between army and Parliament. The New Model Army prided itself on being a force whose officers were meritocrats, recruited from the same social level as its troopers, from peasants, labourers, journeymen, yeomen and artisans, with the last two especially prominent in the cavalry, where one had to pay for one's horses. Politically the New Model Army was represented by the Independents. Parliament, by contrast, was the stronghold of the big landowners and the bourgeoisie. Thus far at least the army–Parliament split could be regarded as a form of class conflict. In religious terms the division was between Congregationalists (Puritans) in the army and Presbyterians in Parliament, with the Presbyterians determined to deliver on Pym's promise to the Scots (before his death in 1643) that he would unite Scotland and England in a Kirk-based Presbyterian worship.[54] Milton was particularly incensed by this ambition and declared that the attempt to replace the Church of England with a new breed of religious authoritarianism would in effect take England back to the days before the Reformation: 'New Presbyter is but old priest writ large,' was his quip.[55] The Presbyterian Parliament made no secret of its desire to disband the New Model Army after Naseby, without, however, giving its troops blanket amnesty for any war crimes committed or guaranteeing back pay. Parliament was reluctant to make up the army's huge pay arrears and, backed by important figures like the Earl of Manchester (who had not wanted to fight on after Marston Moor), was suspected of wanting a 'cheap peace' – basically accepting Charles I back on a revised basis and letting bygones be bygones. The tension between Parliament (relying on the heavily Presbyterian capital city of London) and the Independents (Congregationalists) had been evident since late 1643 when a bitter pamphlet war was waged between the two sides, with Presbyterians making the allegation, which would become a standard canard, that the religious freedom wanted by Independents would lead to anarchy and the euthanasia of private property.[56] The Presbyterian programme was the execution of Archbishop Laud (achieved in 1645), the marginalisation of the Independents and strict press censorship – the issue against which Milton inveighed in *Areopagitica*.[57] Cromwell himself made press censorship a difficult ambition by telling Parliament in clear terms after Naseby: 'He that ventures his life for the liberty of his country, I wish he trust God for the liberty of his conscience and you for the liberty he fights for.'[58] When the New Model Army arose to thwart their plans, the Presbyterians hatched a new project: causing disaffection and mutiny by haggling over arrears of pay, dismissing the malcontents and then sending the lumpen remainder to the wars in Ireland. There was particular hatred of the egalitarianism and meritocracy in the reformed army, which the Presbyterians tried to express with withering contempt.[59]

As a counter to this hard-line Presbyterianism, a 'leftist' faction of the Independents manifested itself, which a little later would acquire the label 'the Levellers'. This was a term with a curious ancestry. 'Leveller' was first used in seventeenth-century England as a term of abuse for rural workers: in the Midland Revolt of 1607 the name had been used to refer to those who 'levelled' hedges in the fight against enclosure.[60] Almost everything about the Levellers is disputed by historians. Some doubt that they were ever very important or influential, others question whether they were in any real sense radicals, and others again see their real significance as being in theology rather than politics (that is, if one can in fact make such a neat division about affairs in the 1640s).[61] Yet some generalisations are possible. The Levellers formed something like a third stratum, being drawn largely from the lower-middle classes: skilled craftsmen, cobblers, printers, small farmers, small traders, shopkeepers, weavers from Spitalfields, lead miners from Derbyshire.[62] The Levellers stressed the sovereignty of the House of Commons and the possible abolition of the House of Lords. They wanted elections for a new parliament on an extended franchise, drastic reform of the legal system with particular emphasis on strong protection for the individual against the State, legal protection for all dissenting Puritan sects, and a number of key economic reforms: reform of taxation towards a progressive system; the abolition of excise tax and compulsory tithes; and the extirpation of all monopolies, including corporate ones like those of the Merchant Venturers and Stationers Companies. In Leveller ideology there was a particular hatred of lawyers, viewed as 'caterpillars of society'. Influenced by the Anabaptists, though often deists, the Levellers advocated communal living and equality of the sexes (though not full economic equality) and particularly detested wars and capital punishment.[63] The main influences on them were, in very broad and general terms, the Calvinism of the Reformation, the rationalism of the Renaissance and an indigenous English tradition connoted partly by attachment to Magna Carta and partly by the myth of the Norman yoke. The most abiding strand in the movement was the emphasis on the supremacy of local autonomy and conscience over any putative loyalties to economic overlordship, monarchy or the State.[64] Naturally the appearance of such a grouping on the Independent side was manna to the Presbyterians, who falsely claimed that their opponents were all communists. As one of them put it, their enemies went 'by the name of Levellers, a most apt title for such a despicable and desperate knot to be known by, that endeavour to cast down and level the enclosures of the nobility, gentry and propriety, to make us even, so that every Jack shall vie with a gentleman and every gentleman be made a Jack'.[65]

The three most important figures in the emerging Leveller movement were John Lilburne, William Walwyn and Richard Overton. Lilburne, who had made his name after his ordeal at the hands of the Star Chamber, is the best known and the most feted, perhaps because he was in liberal terms a moderate, the kind of turbulent individual who is a rebel, rabble-rouser and generally 'agin' things without in any sense being a revolutionary. A colonel in the Roundhead army, he was at one stage captured by the royalists and threatened with execution for high treason until Parliament threatened retaliation in kind against Cavalier prisoners.[66] From 1640 until 1646 he was close to Cromwell and supported him in his struggle against Edward Montagu, 2nd Earl of Manchester – a struggle which ended with Cromwell triumphant. The future Lord Protector's critics claimed that he was an ingrate for having betrayed the man who was his commanding officer – for Manchester, having begun the Civil War as a protégé of Essex, in August 1643 received an independent command as leader of all parliamentary forces in the eastern counties of England, with Cromwell as his second-in-command. Lilburne was a vociferous supporter of Cromwell in his campaign against Manchester via the Self-Denying Ordinance, which ended with Manchester's resignation.[67] Lilburne acquitted himself well at the Battle of Marston Moor but resigned his commission as lieutenant-colonel before Naseby, in April 1645, on grounds of conscience: he was angry about Parliament's attempt to make its supporters sign the Solemn League and Covenant, committing them to Presbyterianism. Still in his early thirties, in July he received the first of the prison sentences that would lead later students of revolution to compare him to the nineteenth-century thinker Auguste Blanqui, who spent most of his life in prison.[68] In Presbyterian eyes he had committed two grave offences: he denounced MPs who lived in comfort while soldiers continued to die, and he slandered the Speaker of the House of Commons by alleging that he was in correspondence with the royalists.[69] In October he was released after a petition by over 2,000 leading citizens in London, only to be jailed once more in July 1646 when he denounced Manchester as a traitor and royalist sympathiser. The latter part of the charge was true: Manchester was a peace-loving individual who had taken up arms only reluctantly for Parliament, took no part in the trial of Charles I in 1648–9, retired into private life in the 1650s and was rewarded with high honours by Charles II after the Restoration.[70]

1646 also saw Lilburne's breach with Cromwell. There were both rational and irrational elements in this rupture. Cromwell was always a natural conservative while Lilburne was a born rebel; Cromwell was a natural politician, used to compromise, cabals and committees, whereas Lilburne was a sea-green incorruptible, impatient with the short change of politics; one critic indeed has justifiably complained that he was lacking in common sense.[71] Moreover, there are some grounds for thinking that Lilburne suffered a 'father complex' and that this may have played a part in his hostility to the 'father figure' Cromwell, fifteen years his senior.[72] Whatever the reason, the sudden and pronounced hostility to Cromwell that appeared at the end of 1646 and intensified with every year that passed was dangerous: as has been well said of Cromwell: 'When Cromwell feared a man, he struck him down, were he monarch or Leveller,' and it seems Cromwell genuinely did fear the power of Lilburne's oratory and skill as a propagandist.[73] At the beginning of Lilburne's pamphlet campaign his targets were also Cromwell's targets. *England's Birthright Justified* of October 1645 called for Parliament's powers to be limited by law and attacked monopolies, not just in economic life but in the Church and the law. Even here one could discern the glimmer of a criticism of Cromwell in the remark that the Self-Denying Ordinance should be strictly enforced – everyone was aware that the great leader had evaded its provisions.[74] In March 1647 Lilburne produced his masterpiece of pamphleteering *The Large Petition*, which called for religious freedom, the abolition of tithes, the dissolution of the Merchant Adventurers' monopoly, demanded that all laws be in English, that self-incrimination in courts be abolished, and that criminals should receive humane treatment.[75] This document contains many of Lilburne's most common predilections and preoccupations. He despised the Long Parliament for its Presbyterian dominance and especially its habit of voting public moneys for the enrichment of its members.[76] He hated the monopoly of the Merchant Adventurers and those of other large corporations such as the East India Company. In economics he was for free trade but wanted some import quotas. And he was adamant that the use of Latin and Norman French in law courts was simply another attempt at obfuscation by venal lawyers; his suspicion of the legal profession was justified, for lawyers managed to defeat every attempt in the years 1645–59 at an organic reform of the common law; there would be no great codes like those of Napoleon or Lenin. The clauses relating to humane treatment of prisoners probably indicated that uppermost in Lilburne's mind was his abiding hatred of imprisonment for debt – a bugbear common to the Levellers, but once again indicating the class element in their programme, as draconian penalties for debt were in the interests of big capitalism but against those of craftsmen and small traders.[77]

Lilburne has always had his fervent admirers among later libertarians and socialists, perhaps most notably William Godwin.[78] Others, perhaps put off by Lilburne's relentless pose as man of action, have preferred the quieter William Walwyn or the genuinely radical Richard Overton. The great scholar Christopher Hill once confidently declared that among the Levellers only Walwyn and Overton truly deserved the title of revolutionaries, with Lilburne as an obvious reformist.[79] Walwyn, perhaps in his mid-forties by the time of the decisive Battle of Naseby, was a meritocrat and ex-master weaver who genuinely admired Lilburne, but was not overawed by him and quite prepared to convict him of political naivety. In the October 1645 pamphlet *England's Lamentable Slavery*, for instance, Walwyn eulogised Lilburne but pointed out that he seriously overrated Magna Carta, which he called 'a mess of pottage'.[80] Nevertheless, Walwyn rallied Leveller sympathisers in London to protest against Lilburne's first arrest and produced a small masterpiece (possibly in co-authorship with Overton) in the pamphlet *Remonstrance of Many Thousand Citizens*, which is often claimed as the founding document of the Leveller movement. Emphasising again and again that the people command Parliament and not vice versa, Walwyn demanded complete press and religious freedom; he used the case of Lilburne's imprisonment to reiterate the Leveller opposition to being jailed for debts.[81] In October 1646 he followed this up with another pamphlet extolling freedom of speech and religion – *A Demur to the Bill for Preventing the Growth and Spreading of Heresy* – another clampdown the Presbyterians were able to push through a tame Parliament.[82] The power of Walwyn's pen irritated the opposition, and they made him the target for the most sustained character assassination in a scurrilous pamphlet entitled *Walwyn's Wiles*, accusing him of being 'a Jesuit, a bigamist and a man who drove women to suicide, a hatred of all lawyers and all governments'. Walwyn swatted this away easily in his *Just Defense*,[83] but perhaps he was already becoming alarmed at his exposed position and the possible repercussions. Although he co-wrote the later key Leveller document *An Agreement of the People*, he perhaps significantly took no part in the famous Putney Debates of November 1647, and was severely shaken when arrested in 1648 with the rest of the Leveller leaders. On his release he moved in the opposite direction from Lilburne, declared his loyalty to Cromwell, retired from public life, retrained as a physician and kept his head down during the Commonwealth. He had two parting shots as a pamphleteer: *Juries Justified*, a defence of trial by jury (1651), and the following year *For a Free Trade*, an unsuccessful attempt to persuade Cromwell's Council of State to abolish the Levant Company's monopoly of trade with the Middle East, some of the arguments in which anticipate Adam Smith.[84]

In some ways the most impressive of the Leveller leaders was Richard Overton, in 1645 yet another man in his mid-forties (i.e. roughly the same age as Cromwell). Little is known of his early life, though some say that he was an ex-actor and playwright.[85] A devotee of popular sovereignty, social equality and the abolition of monarchy, he had little time for the troika of king, House of Lords and nobility, and some have identified him as the most revolutionary of all the Levellers.[86] Though ostensibly a man of God (probably a deist), the main thrust of Overton's thought was materialist. In the dark years before the outbreak of war in 1642, Overton was the leading figure in the underground Cloppenburg Press, which violently attacked Laud's religious programme and called for the dismantling of State religion and the Church of England.[87] A further venture into publishing in 1646 saw him arrested on the nugatory grounds of printing without a licence; he was imprisoned in August and not released until September 1647. Jail did not soften him. He was the author of the hard-hitting pamphlet, *An Appeal from the Degenerate Representative Body to the Free People of England*, published in July 1647, which violently attacked a 'tyrannical' Parliament.[88] Doubtless concluding that there was little point in holding him in prison unless they could silence his thought, Parliament released him in September 1647. Without question Overton was the most interesting of the three Leveller leaders. He lacked Lilburne's talent for high drama and self-advertisement or Walwyn's cool analytical style, but managed to combine the dauntlessness of the one with the cerebration of the other. Influenced by Thomas More's *Utopia*, he argued for a 'welfare state' on a county, not national, basis.[89] More original than his comrades, Overton made an outstanding case for religious tolerance while lambasting the Presbyterians. Religious tolerance was what made for stable and prosperous societies, he averred, instancing the Dutch Republic. More to the point, he argued convincingly that religious tolerance could lead to a genuine Catholic–Protestant rapprochement, which would make horrors like the Thirty Years War outmoded.[90] In the *Appeal from the Degenerate Representative Body* Overton began to investigate the social and economic roots of society, but his edging towards social equality was meat too strong even for most Levellers, who managed to sidetrack him onto the 'softer' issues of suffrage and Church–State relations.[91]

By early 1647 political England was effectively divided into four factions. The severe divide between Parliament/Presbyterians and New Model Army/Independents remained, with Charles I hovering in the wings, intriguing and hoping to turn this split to his advantage. But a new feature on the landscape was the factionalism within the army itself, between conservative elements led by Cromwell and Fairfax and the radical wing represented by the Levellers. By 1647 the Levellers were already a force to reckon with: all the most original ideas were theirs and they had built up an impressive organisation in London, complete with a central committee of twelve and elected treasurer, weekly subscriptions from members and regular public meetings.[92] The Levellers even had tendrils in Parliament, since Overton, Walwyn and Lilburne had close links with radical MPs such as Thomas Rainsborough and Henry Marten.[93] It was true that both Lilburne and Overton were in the Tower early in the year, but the repression connoted by this seemed heavy handed and likely to backfire. A significant moment came in March when Lilburne told Cromwell explicitly that he no longer reposed any confidence in him and looked for no good from him; as the year progressed, Lilburne's distaste for 'Noll' hardened to extreme dislike and then outright hatred. Lilburne was feeling particularly outraged that, when he asserted the simple principle of parliamentary sovereignty in his March pamphlet *The Earnest Petition of Many Freeborn People of this Nation*, the very Parliament to whom he was ascribing the sovereignty voted (by 94 votes to 86) that the pamphlet should be burnt by the common executioner. Cromwell tried negotiating with 'Freeborn John' throughout the year, hoping for a compromise, and visited him in the Tower on many occasions, but Lilburne remained uncompromising and obdurate.[94] Lilburne's sticking point was that the Presbyterians in Parliament were secretly negotiating with Charles I to patch up a pact which would simply slap the king on the wrist and accept that the entire Civil War was just a case of royalist 'boys will be boys'; Cromwell meanwhile seemed to connive at this and appear as a complaisant partner. The bad faith of the army was anyway soon apparent when it tried to disband the New Model Army without settling its back pay and without issuing a blanket amnesty for actions committed during the war; even worse, the spectre arose of a long war in Ireland for which men would be drafted.[95] This was the genesis of the election, in April 1647, of representatives of the army rank and file known as 'Agitators' – a confusing term because of the freight of later, anachronistic associations. However, it is *not* anachronistic to remark that the appearance of the Agitators marked a definite leftward shift in the army, since nothing like them would be seen again until the workers' and soldiers' councils in Russia after October 1917.[96] When the Agitators threatened mutiny, Cromwell and Fairfax called a meeting of the entire army on Newmarket Heath. The rank and file vociferously defied Parliament and vowed they would not disband until their just demands were met. A General Council of the Army was formed, with Cromwell and senior officers (the so-called 'Grandees') serving alongside the Agitators. This hastily improvised council held a second meeting on Triploe Heath, Cambridgeshire, and agreed to formal elections in September. Meanwhile, as a sop to the Levellers, Cromwell persuaded the Council to agree to some of Lilburne's ideas.[97]

While this intense struggle was going on inside the army, the other two main actors had not been idle. Charles I's intrigues with Parliament for a restored monarchy and a State religion of Scottish Presbyterianism so alarmed Cromwell that he considered a number of countermeasures. Whether he directly instigated the seizure of the king in June 1647 cannot be proved by the standards of evidence required in a court of law, but two matters are salient: on 31 May he met Cornet George Joyce of the parliamentary cavalry, and a few days later Joyce and a troop of cavalry snatched Charles I away from Holmby House and brought him to Newmarket, where the army was convened.[98] This coup was expressly aimed at preventing the king from striking a separate deal with Parliament. The Presbyterians struck back with fury. In July they managed to whip up the London mob, which invaded Parliament and forced members to pass motions taking control of the

London militia and inviting the king for talks. The Presbyterians were now confident that their trained bands (20,000 strong) could see off any military threat from the army, but they underrated Cromwell. Whatever his dithering and indecision on political matters, militarily he always acted with crisp decisiveness, as he would prove over and over again. On 7 August Fairfax and the army entered the capital without bloodshed or opposition. Parliament immediately rescinded the motions that had so offended Cromwell.[99] With the struggle between Parliament and the army clearly resolved in favour of the latter, the Grandees now had to deal with the Levellers, who went from strength to strength. In September Overton was released from imprisonment and added his voice to the clamour for reform. A particular cause of Leveller discontent was the Grandee manifesto, possibly written by Henry Ireton, *The Heads of the Proposals*.[100] This document, often considered more liberal than the 'settlement' in the Glorious Revolution of 1688, was remarkably lenient to Charles I. It agreed to restore him as monarch and granted an amnesty to royalist officers, on the sole condition that they were banned from public life for five years. The king would be required to summon a parliament every two years, and there would be no royal control of the armed forces for a decade.[101] *The Heads*, in effect Cromwell's personal charter, clearly revealed him as a highly conservative figure. He had no principled objection to monarchy or the House of Lords, both of which stuck in Leveller throats, but its assessment of the devious Charles I was amazingly naive; the Levellers could always see through the king's duplicity whereas Cromwell struggled to absorb his perfidy.[102] Charles, who like the Bourbons in France after 1815 had learned nothing and forgotten nothing, predictably tried to use *The Heads* as an entering wedge and to play Parliament and the army off against each other.[103] More ominous for the Levellers was the revelation that Cromwell was a man of the past, who believed in the sanctity of property and the efficacy of the old system, provided it was given a few tweaks.

The Levellers' response to *The Heads* was outrage. Indignant statements, not just whispered, but openly delivered, expressed the widely held view in radical circles that things were worse now, in 1647, than they had been in 1642 when Charles I's tyranny provoked armed opposition: better Ship Money than the Excise was one watchword.[104] The Levellers reponded to Cromwell and Ireton with *The Case of the*

Army Truly Stated, which repudiated all deals with the king, accused Cromwell and Henry Ireton of negotiating with Charles I behind everybody's back, demanded the abolition of the Long Parliament, its replacement by a representative body and called for universal suffrage to the new parliament for all males over twenty-one (with ex-royalists excluded). Other demands included biennial elections and the abolition of all monopolies – many of the demands being almost word-for-word repetitions of the *Large Petition*.[105] It is thought that the *Case of the Army* was the work of a new and rising star in the Leveller movement, Edward Sexby, another meritocrat in his early thirties who had risen from the ranks to become a colonel in the army. Something of a hothead, Sexby has been aptly described as 'brilliant but unstable'.[106] Already by 1646 he was working as Lilburne's agent while Freeborn John languished in jail. The Levellers followed up the Sexby manifesto with *An Agreement of the People* (October 1647), the work of Walwyn and John Wildman, which stressed political, religious and legal aspects of the settlement they hoped for in the future. Common law, Habeas Corpus and Magna Carta were all to be enshrined in a written constitution. Developing the motif of biennial parliaments, they stressed that the electoral districts should not be unfairly weighted and should all contain roughly the same number of inhabitants; in short, rotten boroughs were to be extirpated. There should be no conscription but strict equality before the law and total religious freedom, with a provision written into the constitution that Parliament could never violate it. The negotiations with the king were again denounced as the soldiers being 'made to depend for settlement of our peace and freedom upon him who intended our bondage and brought cruel war upon us'.[107] In contrast to the fire-eating *Case of the Army*, the *Agreement* was a very conciliatory document. It barely mentioned the House of Lords and other controversial matters and was really a sketch for a draft constitution; some say that it anticipated the Glorious Revolution settlement of 1689 and the constitutional convention at Philadelphia in 1787, which framed the US Constitution. The two documents together show both the evolution and the tension in Leveller doctrines. In philosophical terms the Levellers could never quite agree whether their claims for freedom rested on an appeal to history or to natural rights. Political liberty was the cornerstone of Leveller thought, to the point where some commentators have referred to them as the 'Arminians of the Left' – exponents of an essentially practical Christianity expressing social concern and social action – perhaps a forerunner of what we might nowadays term 'liberation theology'.[108]

Cromwell decided that the differences between the Grandees and the Levellers should be thrashed out in public meetings. The venue chosen for the historic clash of Roundhead ideologies was St Mary's church, Putney, where for two weeks from the end of October 1647 a titanic dialectical struggle was fought. Much of the defence of the Grandees was conducted by Cromwell himself and his son-in-law Henry Ireton, one of Noll's particular favourites, and a man to whose intellectual prowess he usually deferred. Clever yet arrogant, Ireton had distinguished himself in the Civil War and married Cromwell's daughter Bridget in June 1646. He particularly rankled with the Levellers, who (Lilburne excepted) still had a soft spot for Cromwell but could not abide the imperious 'Prince Ireton'.[109] It is a curiosity of the Putney Debates that none of the 'big three' Levellers was present: Lilburne was still in jail, Overton had just been released and Walwyn kept away out of natural timidity. Yet the Levellers still fielded a formidable team. Among the Agitators they featured Edward Sexby and William Allen as their principal speakers, while their civilian representatives were John Wildman and Maximilian Petty. Wildman, at Putney aged only twenty-six, was a born politician and intriguer, who would plot successively against Cromwell, Charles II and James II and end a long life as William III's postmaster-general in the 1690s.[110] It is possible that he was at root no more than an inveterate plotter, and Disraeli, in *Sybil*, certainly seems to have overrated him by calling him 'the soul of English politics' during the 1640s.[111] Intellectually gifted and with a taste for anagrams – he liked to refer to himself as John Lawmind – Wildman had a fluent tongue and pen and had collaborated with Walwyn in polemical pamphleteering, but in certain radical circles there was a suspicion that he was not quite sound. Overton particularly disliked him as a political trimmer, prepared to cut his conscience to the prevailing fashion and to 'sell out' his radical comrades if he was offered pensions and places.[112] The joker in the Leveller pack turned out to be Colonel Thomas Rainsborough, perhaps the ablest officer in the New Model Army and the only Leveller among the field officers. A member of parliament since 1646, famous for his courage and recently appointed head of the parliamentary navy – a move, some thought, designed to steer him away from political 'meddling' – Rainsborough lacked the polished classical learning of some of his contemporaries, but made up for that with plain, economical and lucid English, pointedly refusing to quote classical literature.[113] Some maintain that he was not Ireton's equal in the dialectical passage of arms, but such a view is not borne out by the verbatim transcripts of the Putney meetings made by Secretary Clarke.[114]

The great debate began on 28 October 1647. Cromwell announced that the meeting would not be tied down with procedural details but that the floor would be offered to anyone willing to speak. Edward Sexby was first on his feet, denouncing *The Heads* as a humiliating peace treaty with Charles I and adding that the leadership seemed to be serving everyone's interest except the army's; facing Cromwell and Ireton squarely, he told them that their 'credits and reputations had been much blasted'. As for Charles I, negotiating with him was a waste of time: 'except we go about to cut all our throats, we shall not please him'. Parliament, too, was a nest of knaves, 'a company of rotten members'.[115] Cromwell replied that he was prepared to give further consideration to both *The Case of the Army* and the *Agreement*. However, when the latter manifesto was read out, Cromwell described it as 'specious' and said he would need time to consider its detailed arguments. He entered the interim judgement that to adopt the *Agreement* would make England another Switzerland, with cantons competing against each other. When he went on to mention a number of unspecified 'difficulties', Rainsborough, who was always quick-tempered, remarked with heavy irony: 'Oh unhappy men are we that ever began this war! If ever we had looked upon the difficulties, I do not know that ever we should have looked the enemy in the face.'[116] Cromwell then opened a second front in his defence, claiming that both *The Case of the Army* and the *Agreement* were in conflict with commitments the army had already entered into at Newmarket, to support the existing king and Parliament. This was the point where Wildman entered the fray. Correctly intuiting that Cromwell was stalling, he made the irrefutable point that no agreement is meant to be eternal, that all accords can be modified or supplanted by later, juster ones. Wildman and Ireton then got bogged down in a somewhat abstract discussion about whether one is morally committed to observe unjust agreements, with Wildman answering categorically in the negative while Ireton took the classical legalistic 'a contract is a contract' line.[117] A douche of common sense was added by one identified only in the transcripts as 'a Bedfordshire man' but thought to be trooper Matthew Weale, one of the signatories of *The Case of the Army*. He made the point that one definition of 'unjust' would be if the army had already promised Charles I, 'that man of blood', what rightly belonged to the people.[118]

Just when the debate seemed to have ground to a halt in a spectacular display of logic-chopping and prevarication from Cromwell and Ireton, to the Grandees' evident relief an Anabaptist colonel named William Goffe intervened to say that in all the sound and fury the central issue of God was being lost sight of; it would therefore be better if all present prayed for guidance. A long prayer meeting followed, which was prorogued until the following morning and then continued. This was especially irritating to Wildman, who thought that reason rather than biblical quotations was the key to political reform and objected to the Grandees' attempt to bring religion into everything.[119] The first day's discussions had revealed the strengths and weaknesses of all the dialectical combatants. On the Leveller side Sexby was revealed as intemperate, Wildman silky and serpentine and Rainsborough crossgrained and irascible.[120] To add to the sequence of fleas biting each other ad infinitum, incredibly a split manifested itself even *within* the Leveller ranks. While Wildman and Sexby were foaming-mouthed anti-royalists, baying for the blood of Charles I, Rainsborough felt that this concentration on the monarch was playing Cromwell's game for him, allowing him to obfuscate the truly important issues of religious freedom, universal suffrage and social equality. In a break in proceedings on 31 October Rainsborough visited Lilburne in the Tower and complained about the conduct of Wildman and Sexby, who, he thought, were distorting things with their rabid republicanism.[121] Rainsborough was agnostic on the subject of the king and Lilburne agreed with him: in jail he had made friends with royalist prisoners and was at the point where he would almost have preferred the 'old tyranny' of Charles I to the new variety of Cromwell. The striking thing about the debates is how they were dominated on the radical side by a few outstanding individuals. Occasionally Clarke and his stenographers mention the odd interjection, as by the 'Bedfordshire man' or the individual identified as 'Buff Coat', who turns out to have been Robert Everard, soldier and religious controversialist.[122]

Meanwhile for the Grandees Ireton had not lived up to his reputation as an intellectual jouster and had been worsted in debate by Rainsborough. He had also made a poor impression on army rankers with his cold, desiccated, dispassionate demeanour. Cromwell still retained the affections of the rank and file. He tended to reply to personal criticisms with dignity and calm, but the jibes clearly rankled, for as the days wore on he would more and more assail the Agitators with heavy sarcasm.[123] It is interesting to observe the differential attitudes of Cromwell and Ireton towards their opponents. They seem to have genuinely detested Sexby and Wildman but been tolerant and accommodating with Rainsborough. Cromwell could ride out Rainsborough's abstract arguments, but he found Sexby's venom hard to take. The taunt that particularly nettled him was when Sexby later said that Roundhead soldiers had fought a great war for an illusion, as it now transpired that the ordinary soldiers had no rights in the kingdom and were no better than mercenaries.[124] Despotic, theocratic, with no patience for notions like egalitarianism, popular or even parliamentary sovereignty, Cromwell was ill at ease throughout the Putney Debates. He refrained from telling the assembled troopers that he did not believe in a free press and would accept only 'guided' democracy (he was always a great one for telling people only what they wanted to hear). Impatient with political theory, he took the attitude summed up a century later byAlexander Pope: 'For forms of government let fools contest, whate'er is best administered is best.'[125] He had no problems with limited monarchy or the House of Lords, secure as he was in his belief that if there was dysfunction in the political system God would intervene. Uncomfortable with the set-up of the Putney Debates, Cromwell may have felt seriously out of his depth, perhaps exhibiting what one commentator has termed an 'inferiority complex'.[126] Yet for the most part he reined in his despotic impulses. Only occasionally did the theocracy seep out, as when he blurted out that he rejected all 'temporal things' as 'but dross and dung in comparison of Christ'.[127] What we most of all discern in Cromwell is that hesitancy and seeming irresolution he seemed always to display off the battlefield; whenever the prospect of real change threatened, Cromwell would usually react initially in a pusillanimous way and later, under pressure, turn seriously reactionary.

On the afternoon of 29 October the Putney Debates resumed in earnest, and this was the moment when the discussions reached their high-water mark. The occasion was an impassioned verbal contest over universal suffrage. Rainsborough produced a declaration that has become the most famous single quotation from the entire debates, and echoes down the ages (only feminists who dislike his use of the masculine pronoun have reservations: 'I think that the poorest he that is in England hath a life to live, as the greatest he; the poorest man in England is not at all bound in a strict sense to that government that he hath not had a voice to put himself under.'[128] Ireton's response to this plea for universal manhood suffrage is almost equally well known, as propounding the favourite theory of ruling classes until the modern era: that only the possession of property gives one the vested interest to vote for what is truly beneficial for the nation. In the eighteenth century this notion would be developed by the Tory landed interest contending against the post-1688 Whig financial interest into a refinement that land alone guaranteed full patriotic commitment, since those with their wealth in bonds, stocks and shares could decamp abroad with their money.[129] And thus Ireton:

> I think that no person hath a right to an interest or share in disposing of the affairs of the kingdom, and in determining or choosing those that shall determine what laws we shall be ruled by here – no person hath a right to this, that hath not a permanent fixed interest in this kingdom . . . Give me leave to tell you, that if you make this rule I think you must fly for refuge to an absolute natural right and you must deny all civil right; and I am sure it will come to that in the consequence . . . I would fain have any man show me their bounds, where you will end, and why you should not take away all property.[130]

Ireton, one of the first in a long line of conservative thinkers (and even some liberal ones like John Stuart Mill) who thought that the enfranchisement of the economically dispossessed would bring chaos, argued, according to his lights quite correctly, that once the political and constitutional arguments for private property were discarded, sheer logic would compel the majority of voters (who were propertyless) to question the socio-economic necessity for the institution. The only remaining argument for gross economic inequality would then be sheer selfishness and greed. It is interesting that Ireton was fearful in this way, for none of the Levellers actually advocated complete equality or perfect freedom – which was why the Diggers, who appeared later, would style themselves 'True Levellers'.[131]

There followed some semantic jousting on the various meanings of 'property'. The flavour of the debate on the afternon of 29 October is best conveyed by verbatim quotes from the transcripts made by Clarke and his stenographers:

> RAINSBOROUGH: 'As to the thing itself, property in the franchise, I would fain know how it comes to be the property of some men and not of others. As for estates and those kind of things, and other things that belong to men, it will be granted that they are property; but I deny that is a property to a lord, to a gentleman any more than to another in the kingdom of England. If it be a property, it is a property by law; neither do I think there is very little property in this thing by the law of the land, because I think that the law of the land in that thing is the most tyrannous law under heaven, and I would fain know what we have fought for, and this is the old law of England, and that which enslaves the people of England, that they should be bound by laws in which they have no voice at all. The thing that I am unsatisfied in is how it comes about that there is such a property in some freeborn Englishmen, and not in others.'[132]

> WILDMAN: 'Our case is to be considered thus, that we have been under slavery. That is acknowledged by all. Our very laws were made by our conquerors, and whereas it's spoken much of chronicles, I conceive there is no credit to be given to any of them; and the reason is that those that were our lords, and made us their vassals, would suffer nothing else to be chronicled.[133] We are now engaged for our freedom. That is the end of Parliament, to legislate according to the just ends of government, not simply to maintain what is already established. Every person in England hath as clear a right to elect his Representative as the greatest person in England. I conceive that is the undeniable maxim of government, that all government is the free consent of the people. And therefore I should humbly move that if the question

be stated which would soonest bring things to an issue – it might perhaps be this: Whether any person can justly be bound by law, who does not give his consent that such persons shall make laws for him?'[134]

SEXBY: 'We have engaged in this kingdom and ventured our lives, and it was all for this: to recover our birthright and privileges as Englishmen – and by arguments argued there is none. There are many thousands of us soldiers that ventured our lives: we have had little property in this kingdom as to our estates, yet we had a birthright. But it seems now, except a man hath a fixed estate in this kingdom, he hath no right in this kingdom. I wonder we were so much deceived. If we had not a right to the kingdom, we were mere mercenary soldiers. There are many in my position that have as good a condition, it may be little estate they have at present, and yet they have as much right as those two [Cromwell and Ireton] who are their lawgivers, as any in this place. I shall tell you in a word my resolution. I am resolved to give my birthright to none. Whatever may come in the way and be thought, I will give it to none. I think the poorer and meaner of this kingdom (I speak as in that relation in which we are) have been the means of preservation of this kingdom.'

RAINSBOROUGH (to Ireton): 'Sir, I see that it is impossible to have liberty but all property must be taken away. If it is to be laid down as a rule, and you will say it, it must be so. But I would fain know what the soldier hath fought for all this while? He hath fought to enslave himself, to give power to men of riches, men of estates, to make him a perpetual slave. We do find in all presses that go forth none must be pressed that are freehold men.[135] Unless these gentlemen fall out among themselves they shall press the poor scrubs to come and kill each other for them.'

IRETON: 'First, the thing itself [universal suffrage] were dangerous if it were settled to destroy property. But I say that the thing that leads to this is destruction to property; for by the same reason that you will alter this Constitution, merely that there's a greater constitution by nature – by the same reason, by the law of nature, there is a greater liberty to the use of other men's goods which that property bars you.'

So the fiery debate continued. Rainsborough's younger brother Major William asked to speak and asserted that without universal suffrage, the army would simply be replacing Charles I's tyranny with one by plutocracy; rich men could enslave all others in the nation and 'the one part shall make hewers of wood and drawers of water of the other five'. Inevitably, Major Rainsborough finished his speech with the now familiar mantra: 'I would fain know what the soldier hath fought for all this while?' Ireton constantly tried to patronise his opponents but was worsted in debate not just by Rainsborough but by Wildman and Sexby also.[136] Ireton's sticking point was that it was irresponsible to give the franchise to anyone who did not own a freehold worth forty shillings. To the arguments about an Englishman's natural rights, Ireton declared that the right to breathe air and to travel the highways was indeed a natural right, but this was by no means the same thing as political participation; here the rights were secured by land, since only property gave one a legitimate stake in government. Rainsborough's refutation of this was threefold: that the key was reason, and God gave all men reason, not just those with property worth forty shillings; that if people were the foundation of all laws, it followed that people must have a say in framing laws; and that it was monstrous to suggest, as Ireton did, that those who had actually *lost* property by fighting in the Civil War should now be deprived of a say in the new government.[137] Ireton could find nothing to say to this except a reiteration of his credo that the suffrage must be grounded in property, for otherwise the result would be chaos and anarchy; universal suffrage opened the floodgates to a hellish world. Rainsborough replied that this was casuistry. He resented being called an anarchist, and anyway the basic moral law (thou shalt not steal) protected landowners from expropriation.[138] At this point Cromwell had to intervene to cool raised tempers. Emolliently he reassured Rainsborough that of course no one could call him an anarchist; nevertheless, he entirely agreed with Ireton's fundamental thesis, that votes for all men would lead to anarchy.[139] The Levellers then zeroed in on the forty shilling requirement. In a pre-echo of eighteenth-century arguments, they pointed out that a property qualification in land disenfranchised both those whose wealth was 'portable' or in cash, or those who had leasehold rather than freehold arrangements. Cromwell backtracked at this point and conceded that leaseholders would have to have the vote; he also agreed that *The Heads* was defective in not calling for electoral reform. Seeing that Rainsborough was winning the argument and clearly had the audience on his side, Ireton tried to make up ground by some rather lame interjections. First he raised the 'straw man' argument of a foreigner who would enjoy the vote while visiting England if the vote was divorced from a stake in the kingdom. Then he claimed that it was easy for the ordinary propertyless man to ascend the social ladder by engaging in commerce or trade, seemingly forgetting that only a minority of the parliamentary soldiers were tradesmen. Most of them were yeomen or craftsmen – the very groups whose historical fate was to be overwhelmed by Ireton's men of property and thus largely sink into the proletariat.[140] In reply to the reiterated Leveller theme of 'What did we fight the war for?' he tried to argue that the war was not fought for general, abstract principles but for the simple cause of combatting Charles I's arbitrary government. The effect of this was immediately blunted by a blundering intervention by Cromwell's chaplain, Hugh Peters. Here was yet another fascinating character in that gallery the 1640s produced. A 49-year-old preacher, who had met the Swedish hero Gustavus Adolphus in the Thirty Years War and done pioneering work for the Church in Boston and Salem, Massachusetts, in 1635–41, Peters was valued by Cromwell as a talented negotiator and peacemaker who, in successive interviews with Charles I at Newmarket and Windsor, seemed to have talked the king round to a more accommodating frame of mind.[141] Yet at Putney he can scarcely have impressed his patron, for now Peters proposed that all who fought against Charles I should automatically have the vote. Finally the day's proceedings came to an end when a committee was formed to discuss the franchise. A motion was proposed and passed that in any case no servants, beggars or apprentices be given the vote, as they were dependent on others and could be browbeaten.[142] A straw vote was taken before the meeting adjourned on the general framework and terms of reference of the committee and only three voices were raised against the majority opinion.[143] Cromwell's parting words on the evening of 29 October were that after a couple of days for prayer and reflection the delegates should reassemble on 1 November.

Cromwell doubtless thought he had been very clever in diverting his officers and men from questions of political theory to a contemplation of the Almighty. In fact he had made the most elementary mistake in the politician's book: asking a question to which you do not already know the answer. When the debates resumed on 1 November, he asked his men what answer God had given to their prayers, perhaps expecting a litany of homiletic bromides. The Levellers pounced: they had been told on no account to negotiate with Charles I, described by a Captain Bishop as 'that man of blood'.[144] Speaker after speaker complained that the Grandees' determination to preserve the king at all costs would end by destroying the country. Cromwell was taken aback, and his humour did not improve when a bad-tempered debate ensued on whether God had a role in civil affairs anyway. Once again Cromwell's instinct was to stall and to dissolve the fractious plenary sessions into committees, where the 'trouble-makers' could be more easily marginalised. On 5 November Fairfax, just recovered from a bad illness, presided over a meeting of the General Council.[145] Here was more ill-humour. When Rainsborough got a motion passed that a letter should be sent to Parliament, ordering it to repudiate all negotiations with the king and forbidding any future overtures, Ireton stormed out in a fury.[146] On 8 November the debates effectively came to an end. Cromwell proposed a harmless-looking motion that the Army Council be temporarily suspended. The motion was carried, but then Cromwell ordered the Agitators back to their regiments, on the grounds that the legitimating authority for the debates (the council) was no longer in existence. Meanwhile he formed a new committee formed of officers only, thus giving the Grandees an automatic majority, which was instructed to draw up a manifesto in the name of General Fairfax which would replace the *Agreement*.[147] The original accord, hammered out with such difficulty on 29 October, required the General Council to convene another meeting of the entire army to ratify the decisions taken at Putney. After further stalling, Cromwell hit back on 9 November with a small masterpiece of chicanery. In the first place he sent a second letter to Parliament, in defiance of the Putney mandates, repudiating Rainsborough's earlier letter and stating that negotiations with the king could continue. Even more seriously, he changed the arrangements for the general summoning of the army. The rendezvous was now to be in three separate places, staggered between 15 and 18 November.[148] This would allow the Grandees to cherrypick the locations with the most pro-Cromwell regiments and also to pack them with a roving claque of their supporters. Cromwell's high-handed despotism was egregious. The Levellers rightly read all this as a quite obvious ploy to stop them getting the *Agreement* adopted by general acclamation of the army. And so the Leveller hopes, which had soared so high during the opening days of the debates, came crashing to earth. 'One man, one vote' had been rejected in favour of property qualifications for the suffrage, giving *plural* votes to the rich. Biennial parliaments, freedom from conscription and indemnity from prosecution for war crimes had all been shelved. Freedom of worship was allowed only in the sense that Cromwell forbade direct compulsion in religious matters, but there was no freedom of belief, since Cromwell banned certain creeds deemed injurious to the public good. He did not allow the House of Commons full sovereignty or the power to overrule the monarch or the House of Lords and, ominously, retained the press gangs for conscription.[149]

The last committee meeting at Putney took place on 11 November, but any chance that Leveller disappointment with Cromwell might manifest itself in significant armed opposition vanished with the much more dramatic news on that day. Having been housed at Oatlands Palace in a village near Weybridge, Surrey, Charles I was moved to the greater security of Hampton Court. It was from there on 11 November that he made a dramatic escape with the intention of rallying his Scottish supporters. Some claim that Cromwell connived at the escape, since he wished to use the king as a pawn in his struggle with the Levellers. The more conventional view is that Charles was already intriguing with the Scots, that the army had become suspicious, and that he therefore had to escape to continue his dealings with Scotland. He could easily have got away to France but, in an evil hour, somehow got it into his head that Colonel Robert Hammond, governor of the Isle of Wight, would be sympathetic to his cause. The king arrived on the island, justifying his breakout on the many threats and references to 'man of blood' at the Putney Debates, which had been reported to him. Hammond, though, another of the young men who rose to high position through wartime exploits (he was just twenty-six), turned out to be a Cromwellian loyalist and imprisoned the monarch in Carisbrooke Castle.[150] Nonetheless, Charles successfully intrigued with the Scots Covenanters: they would raise an army, defeat

Cromwell and restore Charles, and in return he would make Presbyterianism the State religion.

The outbreak of what became known as the Second Civil War effectively killed off Leveller aspirations, since the army had to unite behind Cromwell in face of the common danger. Yet even before the renewed civil war gave him the perfect excuse to ignore the Levellers, Cromwell had dealt them a devastating blow. On 15 November the first of the three planned rendezvous took place at Corkbush Field near Ware, Hertfordshire. All officers and men were required to take an oath of loyalty to Fairfax and the Army Council and to accept *The Heads* as the army's ideological gospel; in return Cromwell promised there would be full payment of arrears of wages. The Machiavellianism of Cromwell can be seen in a twofold way. First, he argued that if soldiers refused to sign, Parliament would use this as an excuse to welch on back pay or pay only those who had signed; this was a blatant appeal to the most naked aspect of human nature. Second, he ensured that the oath would bind the troops to loyalty to the Army Council, not Parliament.[151] Rainsborough made a valiant attempt to counter these shenanigans, but when he tried to present Fairfax with a copy of the *Agreement*, he was brushed aside. All officers encouraging their men not to sign were arrested by Cromwell's elite bands. Even so, he had to use physical force to browbeat and overawe the dissidents in the ranks. Seven regiments were present at the rendezvous, but two of them proved particularly troublesome and displayed copies of the *Agreement* in their hatbands. Colonel Harrison's regiment of cavalry was at first openly defiant, but Fairfax cajoled them and talked them round, stressing that he would resign as army commander if he did not get his way. Robert Lilburne's regiment of infantry was made of sterner stuff (Robert was Freeborn John's brother). Making no headway with exhortation and abstract advocacy, Cromwell and his men eventually rode in among them with drawn swords and arrested nine ringleaders; the colourful story that Cromwell personally pulled the *Agreement* out of their hatbands is, alas, apocryphal.[152] Three of the arrested ringleaders were court-martialled and sentenced to death. Cromwell decided to execute just one of them *in terrorem*; the luckless man turned out to be Private Richard Arnold. After the execution Cromwell, sensing a grim and sullen mood in the army, commuted all other sentences on the mutineers.[153] Fairfax too played a conciliatory role. He told the men that the harsh but necessary treatment meted out to Arnold did not mean that he was going back on his promise to guarantee a regular and representative Parliament. The mixture of carrot and stick was effective: at the other two rendezvous, at Ruislip Heath and Kingston, the cowed troopers signed up to *The Heads* without demur.[154]

7

England's Revolution Manqué?

Meanwhile Charles's machinations had so far prevailed that a serious royalist uprising broke out, triggering what would be known as the Second Civil War. Although the sheer numbers of rebels declaring for Charles should on paper have given him his best chance since 1642, the Cavaliers this time were hopelessly divided and uncoordinated. The outbreaks in support of the king in England and Wales broke out long before the Scots were ready to cross the border, giving Cromwell and his lieutenants the opportunity to defeat them piece-meal. Beginning at the end of February 1648, South Wales, Cornwall, Kent and Essex provided the focus of the royalist attempt, with minor skirmishes in Surrey, Northamptonshire and Lincolnshire. Evident in the hostilities and campaigns in 1648 was a hardening of attitudes on the parliamentary side and hence a greater incidence of atrocities and war crimes even as compared with 1642–5, which had hardly been a civilised tea-party affair; this time around many captured royalist commanders were simply executed without trial.[1] The great Scottish invasion, when it finally came very late in the day, was an acute disappointment: whereas Cromwell and his brilliant new 29-year-old general, John Lambert, seemed to have an intuitive mutual understanding and instinctive rapport, the Scottish commanders quarrelled with each other and with the putative royalist commander-in-chief in the south-west of England. Cromwell once again proved himself an energetic and inspired general and on 17–19 August routed the Scots at Preston. Though he had only about 8,600 troops against 20,000 of the enemy, Cromwell caught them when they were strung out and thus achieved local superiority of force. For just 100 admitted casualties, he killed 2,000 Scots and took another 9,000 prisoner.[2] This was almost the final nail in the coffin for the Levellers' fantasy of exciting the army against the Grandees. 1648 saw the Levellers in generally subdued mood, aware that they could be dubbed unpatriotic and treacherous for rocking the boat while Cromwell was engaged against the royalists. They concentrated on building up their organisation in London, and in July brought out the first edition of their newspaper, *The Moderate*.[3] In January a very conciliatory petition to the Army Council accepted the Grandees' compromise on the suffrage that beggars and servants should not have the vote. The Levellers were shaken, not just by Cromwell's defeat of them in the army but by their failure to make headway on the issue of equality, with both the Baptist and Independent churches disappointingly distancing themselves from the movement on this issue.[4] The exception to the generally sober tone of the chastened Levellers was, not surprisingly, Freeborn John. Lilburne had been released from jail in November 1647, in effect granted bail without asking for it, as one student of the movement has put it.[5] Made not a whit more compromising by his spell in prison, Lilburne at once began to campaign for an armed rising against Cromwell and the Grandees, arguing that an army coup was imminent, and that radicals in the ranks should beat Cromwell to the punch. It was generally remarked that early in 1648 Leveller fears about Cromwell's repressive intentions became more paranoid than ever and consequently the idea of armed insurrection seemed positively to haunt their movement.[6] Finally Lilburne went too far and in a House of Commons debate expressly accused Cromwell of high treason. He was then himself immediately arrested for treason and once again incarcerated. Following his amazing zigzag, in–out pattern of freedom and imprisonment, Lilburne was again released in August 1648 after a massive petition to the House of Commons, including tens of thousands of signatures from London, evincing the growing power of the Levellers in the capital.[7]

The defeat of the royalists in the Second Civil War and the revelation of Charles I's duplicity, double-cross and treachery finally disgusted Ireton and Cromwell, who concluded that a deal with the king was no longer possible. Amazingly, even though Parliament had voted in January 1648 to cease all negotiations with the monarch, by September, with Charles no longer a military danger, that resolution was fading, and the Presbyterians in Parliament, still hankering for the imposition of their creed as a State religion, were disposed to begin talks yet again with the wayward Stuart king. This stupefied the Levellers and roused them to a new initiative. A petition from them in September called for three main things: an end to all talks with Charles or even the disconcerting talks about talks; enclosure to be abolished or admitted in individual cases only if it could be demonstrated to redound to the benefit of the poor; and a declaration that Parliament would never abolish private property or seek to level and equalise by force. This last was a rebuttal of the Levellers' critics, and Cromwell himself, who were apt to refer to them as communists or 'Switzering anarchists'.[8] Wildman and the Independents also pressed hard for an amendment to a draft *Remonstrance* drawn up by Ireton which both called for the execution of Charles and insisted that any new monarch should only be allowed to come to the throne once he had signed up to the *Agreement*; nearly a year on from the Putney Debates the Levellers had still not entirely given up on their favourite project. The interesting thing about the amendment was that it was not a republican document but, by attaching conditions to the coronation of a king to succeed Charles I, hoped to secure radical change. Ireton and Cromwell agreed between themselves that Noll would have to conduct mopping-up operations in Scotland after the victory at Preston and that, in view of this and their resolve to execute Charles I, to say nothing about dealing with a still recalcitrant Parliament, it would be best to settle accounts with the Levellers at a later date; Wildman's amendment was then allowed through. Ireton told Cromwell he was hopeful that the man in the street would forget all about the *Agreement* in the excitement over Charles I's execution.[9] Only Lilburne was shrewd enough to see how his enemies' minds were working and began to campaign against bringing the king to trial on a charge of war crimes. Whether Lilburne secretly intrigued with Charles I in 1648 is still debated; it is not impossible, given that he now regarded Cromwell as a more egregious tyrant than Charles ever was. It is probable that at bottom he was indifferent to the king's fate. But the sticking point for him was popular sovereignty. Lilburne's analysis and advocacy were threefold. He considered it essential that the *Agreement* should be ratified by Parliament before the king was brought to trial. He thought that to execute Charles was a tactical mistake; what the anti-Cromwell faction should do was to keep the monarch in play as a pawn and counterweight to Cromwell. Most of all, he insisted on the point of principle that Cromwell and the Grandees had no right to try Charles, as there was as yet no settled legal authority or constitution in England. To execute the king before parliamentary elections had been held under universal suffrage (excluding servants and beggars) and the future shape of politics determined by a genuinely popular vote would not just be jumping the gun; it would be judicial murder plain and simple.[10]

While Lilburne campaigned thus, two dramatic events entirely changed the picture. First, the gallant Colonel Rainsborough was killed in almost the last fighting of the Second Civil War. Fairfax had sent Rainsborough north, far from London, so that his eloquence and advocacy would not be available to the Levellers. Appointed parliamentary commander-in-chief in Yorkshire, Rainsborough arrived at Pontefract (where the royalist-held castle was under siege) and found to his amazement that the Puritan commander on the spot, Sir Henry Cholmly, violently objected to the appointment, refused to accept his authority and declined to follow his orders. Since Cholmly's troops remained loyal to him, and Rainsborough had brought only a personal bodyguard, the only way to resolve the conflict was to write to Fairfax in London. While this wrangling continued, Rainsborough took up his quarters in Doncaster. On the night of 30 October four officers sallied from Pontefract in an attempt to kidnap Rainsborough; there was a scrimmage in the colonel's lodgings and Rainsborough was run through with a sword and sustained a mortal wound.[11] The death of the great radical hero was the occasion for loud lamentations by his followers, who, at his funeral in London (attended by more than 3,000 troops), wore sea-green ribbons in their hats. The death was, from the Grandees' point of view, more than a little convenient. Suspicions were immediately voiced and Cholmly implicated. It was queried how he, supposedly besieging Pontefract Castle, had allowed four royalist assassins to slip through his lines and then enter Doncaster without let or hindrance; the tale of abduction was widely scouted, and radicals whispered that it had been a murder raid in which Cholmly had colluded. The wider suspicions were that Cromwell himself and Fairfax were implicated.[12] Even as the Levellers reeled under the impact of Rainsborough's loss, Cromwell effectively took out all his enemies with one blow. Ireton's *Grand Remonstrance*, incorporating the Walwyn amendment, was rejected in the House of Commons on 20 November by 125 votes to 58. Even worse from the army's point of view, the parliamentary commissioners who were treating with Charles I brought back a highly unsatisfactory answer from the king to the points put to him, yet Parliament accepted their report on 5 December by 129 to 83.[13] The army's response was immediate. On 6 December army detachments under Colonel Pride barred the entrance to the Commons and arrested all Presbyterian members in what has sometimes been described as England's only military coup. The Presbyterian MPs were arrested, held for a few days and later released, but the result was that Parliament was now truncated, with just 200 members left, all loyal to Cromwell and the army. This was the beginning of the so-called Rump Parliament, which would endure until 1653.[14] Once again Cromwell, though clearly the brains behind the operation, ensured that there was no paper trail that would lead directly to his door. Located in Pontefract on 6 December, but undoubtedly privy to all that was going on, Cromwell immediately raced down to London to take charge.

Having solved the problem of parliamentary opposition, Cromwell now pressed hard for the trial and execution of the king. Perhaps oddly, he simultaneously sought to deal with the Levellers in another series of debates, the so-called Whitehall Debates of 14 December–13 January, narrower in focus than the famous ones at Putney a year before and concentrating mainly on the issue of religious toleration. The Levellers presented the *Second Agreement of the People*, which contained detailed proposals for a new parliament with universal male suffrage (conceding the Grandees' point about the non-eligibility of servants and beggars), requiring the new body to abolish base tenures and making the accommodating gesture that eight issues could be reserved from the decision-making of MPs. In a supplementary pamphlet *No Papist nor Presbyterian*, they argued controversially that Catholics should have religious freedom.[15] Cromwell's policy was to string the Levellers along until he had finally closed accounts with the king. Cromwell's animus against Charles was now white-hot. He considered his actions in the Second Civil War, and especially the secret treaty with the Scots, to be 'prodigious treason' and he moved swiftly to take the king out of the political equation. One of the first acts of the Rump Parliament was to pass an act creating a new High Court of Justice. Even though the Lords refused their assent, Cromwell invoked popular sovereignty and declared that the will of the Commons was law. The High Court in turn established 135 commissioners, of whom 68 would sit in judgement on Charles I. The Stuart monarch meanwhile was moved from the Isle of Wight to Hurst Castle near Portsmouth, thence to Windsor Castle and finally brought to trial in Whitehall on 20 January 1649. The High Court had its first sitting under Chief Justice John Bradshaw, while Solicitor-General John Cooke conducted the prosecution. Charles was accused of treason, specifically of using his power for personal interests rather than for the good of England and thus causing the deaths of at least 5 per cent of the population. The indictment charged the king with being 'guilty of all the treasons, murders, rapines, burnings, spoils, desolations, damages and mischiefs to this nation, acted and committed in the said war, or occasioned thereby'.[16] The trial began on 20 January, but Charles refused to plead, on the ground that the High Court was not a legally constituted body and that the king could do no wrong. The commissioners heard evidence of all the depredations carried out during the war and constantly asked Charles to speak. All he would say was that he demanded to know on what authority he was brought there. Illogically, after refusing to speak, the king then demanded the right of reply when he was found guilty on 27 January, but this was not conceded. Fifty-nine commissioners, including Cromwell, signed the death warrant, but not Fairfax; his refusal to do so undoubtedly saved his life at the Restoration in 1660 when Charles II systematically and vengefully consigned all surviving regicides to traitors' deaths.[17]

Charles's execution on 30 January seemed to open up an entirely new chapter in history. Kings had been deposed before (Henry VI) and even assassinated (Richard II), but this was the first time one had been killed after judicial process. The Fifth Monarchists thought Charles's death presaged a new millennium, and in radical circles the idea of a fresh dawn manifested itself most dramatically in the appearance of the Diggers. The Digger movement was almost entirely the brainchild of one man: Gerrard Winstanley, a forty-year-old ex-cloth merchant, a gentleman born in Wigan who had been bankrupted in 1643, the victim of fraud. Winstanley moved to Cobham, Surrey in 1643 and became a farmer, and it was there that he became a radical thinker.[18] Historians have not usually been kind to Winstanley, and judgements vary between those who perceive him as a hopeless dreamer and those who see him as having been (in the years 1649–50) in the grip of temporary psychosis. Here is one patronising judgement: 'Gerrard Winstanley, a small businessman who began his career wholesailing cloth, ended it wholesailing grain, and in between sandwiched a mid-life crisis of epic proportions.'[19] In 1648 he started his short-lived term as a writer, pamphleteer and agitator with some mystical musings on religion and Christianity clearly influenced by the Anabaptists, the Quakers and the importance of the 'inner light'. Some have seen Winstanley as a kind of locus classicus of the chaos world opened up by Puritan victory in the Civil War and the execution of Charles I. All the following heterodox or heretic views can be discerned in his work: radical Arminianism, anti-Trinitarianism, repudiation of the doctrine of original sin, scepticism about Heaven and Hell, moralism, soul-sleeping, antinomianism, the creation of the world by God, allied to millenarianism and a belief in the imminent arrival of the kingdom on earth, not to mention virulent anticlericalism.[20] His views on God and religion can be simply stated. Like so many mystics, he believed in the 'God within' and denied the existence of a transcendental and interventionist deity. For Winstanley, Christ was not a real person and the biblical stories he cited so often were allegories not statements of fact or history. The Second Coming for him was not the glorious return of a Trinitarian God in a cloud of angels but what he called 'the rising up of Christ' or the spirit of Reason becoming triumphant.[21] The hopes of immortality which official religions peddled – and especially the story of the Resurrection – were delusional; to this extent Winstanley would have agreed with Marx's famous later judgement that religion was the opium of the people.[22] However, unlike Wildman, he liked to quote massively from the Bible, always interpreting the stories, whether the Genesis tale of the Garden of Eden, Exodus, Jacob and Esau, Daniel or Revelations, in a figurative or allegorical way. He also liked to cherrypick passages from the Bible to prove a point – the scepticism about rulers in the Book of Samuel, for example, or the famous saying of St Paul that under the new covenant there were neither masters nor slaves, Jew or Gentile, male or female.[23] Some critics have found it hard to reconcile this visionary and mystical Winstanley of 1648 with the radical egalitarian of 1649. Yet the alleged conundrum does not seem insoluble. There are a number of possibilities. Perhaps he was at root a mystic and his socio-economic analysis should be interpreted symbolically. On the other hand, maybe the political writing is primary and the numinous items secondary or allegorical. Or it could be that, like so many thinkers and artists – Cobbett, Henry James, C. G. Jung, A. N. Whitehead, Ludwig Wittgenstein etc, etc – he had distinctive early and late periods in his work. The most likely explanation is that the mysticism and the social and economic radicalism were unintegrated aspects of his thought, or linked by the simple proposition that a true understanding of Christianity would lead one to socialism. Significantly Winstanley was fond of the famous passage in the Acts of the Apostles where the early members of the Church are seen sharing everything in common.[24]

If Winstanley's religious thinking is sometimes a muddle, his socio-economic thought is reasonably clear-cut. He started from the unexceptionable proposition that vague talk of equality is meaningless without social equality. He grasped that 'equality of opportunity' must be a meaningless slogan if the parties concerned start from vastly different economic, social and financial bases. As for 'equality before the law', as Anatole France famously remarked this means that rich and poor are forbidden to sleep under the bridges of the Seine.[25] Winstanley thought that the first step towards social equality was the foundation of self-help and self-sustaining agricultural communities, communistic in nature, and that this would be the germ from which the eventual sharing of all property in common would grow.[26] His 'take notice' declaration became as famous in its own way as Rainsborough's 'the poorest he' (see above, p. 178): 'Take notice that England is not a free people, till the poor that have no land have a free allowance to dig and labour the commons, and so live as comfortably as landlords that live in their Inclosures.'[27] Winstanley's *oeuvre* evinces in socio-economic affairs the same hatred for landlords and their 'jackals', the lawyers, that is expressed for priestcraft in the religious writings. He particularly detested the landlords' practice of selling timber from common land at a profit to provide dowries and portions for their children. Taking up John Ball's old mantra about the absence of a leisured non-productive class in the Garden of Eden, he stressed both the justice, desirability and redemptive power of the 'gentleman' undergoing manual labour and picking up a spade.[28] Of course this aspect of communist thought became especially notorious in the 1960s and 1970s when both Mao in China and Pol Pot in

Cambodia tried to break down the division of labour by forcing intellectuals, bureaucrats and other 'parasites' to labour in the rice fields; naturally, when pushed too far, what sounds like a reasonable prescription becomes an example of what the poet Wallace Stevens called 'logical lunacy'.[29] Winstanley's view of the world was Manichean, a permanent struggle between the forces of light and darkness. He saw 'Christ' as the great leveller, emphasised the Sermon on the Mount – the meek shall inherit the earth, etc – and regarded private property as a form of blasphemy against Christ. Anticipating Rousseau and Wordsworth, he excoriated the notion of original sin as the explanation for evil in society and underlined the primal innocence of the child: 'Look upon a child that is new born, or till he grows up some years: he is innocent, harmless, humble, patient, gentle, easy to be entreated, not envious. And this is Adam, or mankind in his innocence; and this continues till outward objects entice him to pleasure, or seek content without him. And when he consents, or suffers the imaginary Covetousness within to close with the objects, then he falls, and is taken captive, and falls lower and lower.'[30] In short, Winstanley discounted the notion of an incorrigible human nature and thought that environment and society were the corrupters – from which it followed of course that schemes of social amelioration were feasible and that the 'New Man' could be created, in Winstanley's view by manual labour in the first instance.

It is important to be clear that Winstanley's ideas, in some ways highly original, did not appear in a vacuum, nor were they the product of, as it were, an intellectual devising a bright idea in his study of an afternoon. The years 1620–50 are generally considered the worst that the poor and dispossessed of England ever suffered. Indeed the entire century roughly from the Pilgrimage of Grace to the outbreak of the English Civil War (1540–1640) was miserable except for the privileged classes, with wages halved, unemployment high, taxation heavy, harvests bad and the impact of war especially horrendous, not just in terms of the free billeting and quartering of troops and military looting, but also the famine and disease that always followed sustained warfare. One scholar indeed has characterised the years 1647–50, when Winstanley's radical ideas were coming to light, as 'the seventeenth, eighth and sixth most serious depressions of the entire early modern period'.[31] The irony for Winstanley and those who thought like him was that the century of immiseration coincided with a vast influx of wealth to central government from the confiscated 'abbey lands' and other property forfeited for treason, real or simply alleged; Digger propaganda often contrasted this paradoxically with food shortages and high prices.[32] The other main 'deep structure' element of the Digger movement was that it was the culmination of a century of unauthorised encroachment on forests and wastes by squatters and local commoners, impelled both by the above immiserating factors and by land shortage and population pressure.[33] It is often said that Winstanley's thought was idiosyncratic, creative and up to the moment with a savage irony that anticipated Swift and Orwell.[34] Nowhere is his capacity for melding ideas from different sources to form a kind of 'syncretism' more evident than in his 'light on the road to Damascus' essay written in January 1649, at the very moment Charles I was on trial. While all the above elements were clearly influences, Winstanley managed to weave in the fate of the king as a salient feature.[35] The execution of the monarch would be a turning point and not just in a millenarian sense, as the Fifth Monarchists understood it. For Winstanley, the Digger programme of communism was a logical consequence of Charles's death. The abolition of monarchy and the introduction of a 'free Commonwealth' would, in his view, invalidate all laws introduced since the Norman Conquest and restore to the common people their ancient legal rights to the commons and wastes of England. Moreover, Parliament was obligated to the common people, as without their help the royalists could not have been defeated. The Diggers were the backbone of the new covenant. Parliament would be in breach of this covenant if, having secured the support of the dispossessed to defeat Charles and his Cavaliers, it then shut them out from the fruits of victory and kept these solely for the gentry and aristocracy. It is at this point that we see most clearly the convergence of Digger ideology and the thought of radical Levellers like Sexby. The other interesting aspect of Winstanley's ideas was the continuing interpenetration of religious and socio-economic motifs, for talk of a 'Covenant' irresistibly recalled the very different meaning put on the word by the Scots and the Presbyterians.[36]

Despite its power and originality, Winstanley's thought is vulnerable to some criticisms that have always been thought definitive by those who disparage him. Feminists claim that his work is 'chauvinistic' in that, despite his radicalism, he still advocates patriarchy and female chastity; this is true enough, though parts of his work can be read as feministic.[37] Such is his hatred of private property that he proposes the death penalty or slavery for those who would refuse to participate in his utopia, who profiteer or show interest in money, dividends and any form of private profit. Once again the charge can be sustained, but it should be remembered that Winstanley's ideal penal code had far fewer offences for which the penalty was capital than the law of England in the seventeenth century and – even more so – the Bloody Code of the eighteenth century. More seriously, Winstanley often claimed that his theory of communism was a direct revelation from God, or that God was 'our common Father' and the earth our common mother, but if the Supreme Being did not exist except as 'the God within', it is difficult to see what meaning the statement could have. For that matter, what did his statement mean that it was offensive to God for destitution to exist in a land as rich as England? If the God was within, this could mean only that it was offensive to Winstanley. In fairness to Winstanley it should be conceded that all who posit a quasi-Buddhist introjected deity labour under acute difficulties with language when they speak of 'God'; the classic case is that of the psychologist C. G. Jung.[38] At a deeper level there is tension and ambiguity in Winstanley's thought as between his belief in a wholesale root-and-branch transformation of the *entire* society and the creation of a system of landless and propertyless communities in the here and now, existing alongside but independent of the official legal and property system. Doubtless Winstanley saw the second option as an interim solution – it would be his equivalent of the 'dictatorship of the proletariat' – but there are difficulties about how the passage from one to the other is effected which Winstanley never clears up; the most there is is the admission in his later writings that the transition would be a much longer haul than he originally thought.[39] Whatever defence can be entered on Winstanley's behalf in these matters, there can be no disputing that his discussion of the origin of 'covetousness' and private property is a tissue of confusion. He said that the obstacle to achievement of the Digger programme was man's sinfulness, but as the origin of sin itself was supposed to be private property, the argument was circular: it amounted to saying that one could not abolish private property because it existed. Besides, if man originally lived in a

Rousseauesque 'state of nature' and human nature was innocent and childlike, how could private property, allegedly the cause of sin, have arisen in the first place? Additionally, Winstanley oscillated in his explanation of the origin of inequality. Sometimes he located it in the mists of time, as Rousseau later would, and ascribed it vaguely to 'covetousness' (a key Winstanley concept but one that was never properly unpacked). For him the Digger movement was essentially a spiritual struggle, exhibiting the Manichean conflict between the power of love and the power of covetousness.[40] At others, he insisted that Anglo-Saxon England had been a Golden Age and that it was only after 1066, with the coming of the 'Norman yoke', that social inequality really took a hold. The 'Norman yoke' became something of a rallying cry for the Diggers; for them it was the essence of Cromwell's sinfulness that he arrested the otherwise inevitable fresh start and return to the Golden Age that England would enjoy.[41] On the other hand, he always pointed up the moral that the removal of the Norman yoke was merely a *necessary* condition for utopia; the sufficient condition remained the achievement of the state of perfection of the early Christians in the Acts of the Apostles.

Yet Winstanley was no mere armchair theorist, anticipating Proudhon in his declaration that property was theft or adumbrating ideas that would be more comprehensively developed a century later by Rousseau. In line with his conviction that the division of labour between workers by hand and workers by brain was a symptom of human sinfulness, in April 1649 he began his great social experiment in Surrey. With a dozen comrades he began sowing carrots, parsnips and on St George's Hill, Crown land and therefore, in the post-execution context of early 1649, of uncertain status. Those who worked on St George's Hill included a shoemaker, a cloth-maker, a householder, a blacksmith, a maltster, a baker and a baker's apprentice. Because of the apparent connection with the brewing trade, hostile propagandists spread the canard that the Diggers were a band of drunkards.[42] The social composition of the Diggers closely resembled that of the early Quakers, in that the middling sectors were attracted as well as the poor. At first they were not molested in their agriculture, as it was thought they had the protection of the army. When it became clear that they did not, they became the target for violent attacks, accused of being godless and of sharing women in common. Forced off the hill by a violent mob, the Diggers were first imprisoned in a church and then haled before magistrates; meanwhile their houses were destroyed. When the justices could no longer find any excuse to hold them, the Diggers tried to return to the hill with horses to carry away wood, but they were savagely beaten up by an angry mob who also killed their horses and maliciously destroyed their crops.[43]

Winstanley made a number of appeals to different quarters, protesting about this savagery and particularly upset about the presence of 'ignorant bawling women' in the aggressive mobs. His pamphlets went out to the House of Commons, the City of London, the Army Council and to Fairfax himself. He used the selfsame arguments throughout: the Diggers were respectable men trying to grow crops on unpromising soil, in other words they were socially useful, peaceful citizens who made no attempt to invade or expropriate private land.[44] It is noteworthy that in his attempt to get Fairfax on his side – which would certainly have scared off the local roughnecks – Winstanley linked the idea of private property with the 'Norman yoke', which he claimed had now ended with the death of Charles I. So far from advocating revolution, he claimed to be in daily expectation that Cromwell himself would usher in the new age, and that he had merely anticipated it; it is an open question whether Winstanley really believed this. Fairfax agreed to receive Winstanley and his de facto Number Two, William Everard; the two waited on Fairfax on 20 April but offended him by refusing to remove their hats in his presence, to signify their commitment to absolute equality.[45] The general's bemused and noncommittal stance encouraged the naive Diggers to conclude that he was on their side. In July 1649 Winstanley learned the truth when Fairfax sent troops to clear the Diggers off St George's Hill. Winstanley decided to try again in another location. Whereas from April to July, for all the persecution, he had been among friends and kinfolk, in August he made the tactical error of switching his operations from St George's Hill to Cobham, hoping to avoid club-wielding mobs. The move simply exposed the reality of post-execution army rule. Persecution continued: when the Diggers tried to prosecute their assailants, their bills were thrown out by the Grand Jury. Winstanley realised that Fairfax was a false friend and that he had moved from a mere bush fire to an inferno.[46] This time the main persecuting impetus came from the army itself, on the grounds that the Diggers were a crypto-royalist faction secretly working to restore Prince Charles (the later Charles II). A veritable reign of terror began. Cobham tenants were ordered by the Army Council to evict all Diggers and their sympathisers and to deny them food and lodging. By the spring of 1650 the Diggers were decisively beaten. Although the movement limped on outside Surrey – for Everard especially had managed to proselytise in Wellingborough, Northamptonshire and Iver, Buckinghamshire and to a lesser extent in Barnet, Enfield, Dunstable and Bosworth in Nottinghamshire – the game was up and Winstanley knew it.[47]

An obvious question is: How did the Diggers relate to the Levellers? Whereas the Diggers were a tightly knit, homogeneous movement, the Levellers ran the gamut from republican reformism to communism – roughly the difference between Lilburne and Walwyn, the most left-wing of the Levellers – and at the leftward end there was virtually no difference between a radical Leveller and a Digger. The Diggers liked to pre-empt this debate by calling themselves the 'True Levellers'.[48] The essential difference between a mainstream Leveller and a Digger was that the former believed in political equality only, not social and economic equality, though most Levellers would have had little difficulty with Winstanley's characterisation of clergy, lawyers and king as three heads of the same monster.[49] It would be incorrect to take an intellectual short cut and say that the Levellers were an urban phenomenon and the Diggers a rural one, for most Levellers had some interest in the countryside and were in favour of opening enclosed commons and fens and abolishing tithes and base tenures, as their manifestos indicate. It is, however, true that rural Levellers tended to be more sympathetic to the Diggers than their urban brethren. The basic Leveller thrust was towards helping agricultural labourers without communalism, while still preserving private property and social hierarchy.[50] The Levellers were naturally angry and contemptuous about Fairfax's use of troops on St George's Hill, which they considered heavy-handed despotism or the sending of 'divers troops of Janissaries . . . prancing into Surrey'.[51] However, among Leveller leadership there was irritation that the 'extremism' of the Diggers was allowing the Grandees to portray the entire Leveller movement as a band of foaming-mouthed communists and revolutionaries. It is undoubtedly true that in 1649 the army's attitude to both Levellers and Diggers evinced the same kind of purblind paranoia exhibited by Senator Joseph McCarthy and his acolytes towards a handful of American communists who supposedly constituted a 'red menace'. The most popular Grandee slur was that the Diggers were simply the acceptable face of Ranterism and that they shared women in common. Winstanley was particularly incensed by this, as he despised the Ranters for their cavalier attitude to female chastity and for promoting idleness; he therefore directed particular vituperation and scorn against them.[52] It was almost predictable that the Leveller who most distanced himself from the Diggers was John Lilburne, for Lilburne's personality dictated that he must always be in the van of any opposition to Cromwell. In his contrarian desire always to be 'agin' orthodoxy, he even perceived the Diggers as the enemy on this score and poured scorn on Winstanley and his social experiment:

> In my opinion and judgement this conceit of levelling property and magistracy is so ridiculous and foolish an opinion as no man of brains, reason or ingenuity can be imagined such as to maintain such a principle, because it would, if practised, destroy not only the individual in the world, but raze against the very foundation of generation and of subsistence . . . As for independence and valour, by which the societies of mankind are maintained and preserved, who will take pains for that which when he hath gotten it is not his own but must equally be shared by every lazy, simple, dronish sot.[53]

While Fairfax dealt decisively with the Diggers, Cromwell completed the political extinction of the Levellers. 1649 was undoubtedly his annus mirabilis, for in that one year he executed a king, laid Ireland waste in a campaign that would live in infamy and make his name resonate with purulent hatred to this very day, and finally put paid to all hopes of political improvement and liberty.[54] Levellers' expectation rose momentarily in February, when the House of Commons abolished both the monarchy and the House of Lords and appointed a Council of State of forty-one members (all Grandees) as executive authority, but populist aspirations were immediately dashed when the Grandees countered increasing Leveller activity in the army by banning all petitions to Parliament from serving troops. Lilburne, by now disillusioned with politics and genuinely wishing to spend more time with his wife and family, told Hugh Peters bitterly that he would rather live seven years under Charles I than a single one under the new regime and was even thinking of switching his support to 'Prince Charles' (the future Charles II).[55] The miserable plight and discontent of the soldiers he had fought with encouraged him to make one last effort on their behalf. In *England's New Chains Discovered*, of March 1649, usually considered his polemical masterpiece, he went for the Grandees' jugular. His theme was the one he had already expressed to Peters: that the king had gone but the nation had merely exchanged one species of tyranny for another. The new Council of State was clearly a souped-up version of the old Star Chamber, the Rump Parliament was not going to submit itself to elections, and Cromwell and his gang were using censorship and the law of libel to gag all opposition. Denouncing Cromwell and Ireton as 'the grand continuers', who were cynically manipulating a docile Commons for their own ends, he appealed to the army to rise up against Cromwell's imminent dictatorship. The rhetoric was compelling: 'We were before ruled by King, Lords and Commons, now by a Council, Court-Martial and House of Commons: and we pray you, what is the difference?'[56] Another pamphlet, *The Hunting of the Foxes*, possibly written by Overton (or maybe Lilburne or perhaps both) was a withering indictment of the hypocrisy of Cromwell and Ireton and no longer pretended there was room for dialogue between Grandees and Levellers; political life in England was now a naked struggle for power.[57] Cromwell was seriously alarmed by this powerful rhetoric. He knew that the rank and file of the army were severely disillusioned on a number of counts, principally the failure of the new regime to introduce even the mild reforms promised in Ireton's *Remonstrance*, and the rumour that they would be required to serve in Ireland, which they had not signed up for. He called for stern measures and told the Council of State: 'I tell you, sirs, there is no other way to deal with these men (the Levellers) but to break them in pieces.'[58] In March the radicals saw the first signs of iron in the new order. Eight Leveller troopers went to see Fairfax to ask for restoration of the right to petition the Commons; he dismissed them brusquely and cashiered five of them on the spot. Shortly afterwards (when *England's New Chains* appeared), Lilburne, Walwyn, Overton and the Leveller treasurer, Thomas Prince, were arrested for treason by order of the Council of State.[59] This event precipitated the first clear appearance of women as a force to be reckoned with in the Leveller movement. Several hundred marched to Westminster to petition Parliament for the release of their leaders. Members of parliament predictably taunted them as being 'mere females' meddling in affairs they did not understand. Nothing daunted, Katherine Chidley, a woman in her thirties who was the Boadicea of the movement, collected 10,000 signatures from the radical sisterhood and petitioned Parliament again; Chidley wrote a pamphlet for the occasion.[60]

Walwyn, Overton, Lilburne and Prince spent most of 1649 in the Tower. They (perhaps especially Walwyn and Overton) were in chastened mood once they saw the vehemence with which Cromwell intended to suppress them. Scribbling away furiously in their cells, they produced a series of pamphlets that were notable for their moderation and conciliatory tone. Walwyn's *A Manifestation* seemed more a dig at the Diggers than an attack on the Grandees. It rebutted absurd charges that the Levellers were pro-popery, crypto-royalists, atheists, anarchists and anti-scripturists and emphasised that equality of wealth and common ownership could only ever be justified if the people freely chose it; it could never be achieved by duress or forced on an unwilling population.[61] Walwyn was much preoccupied by a Grandee pamphlet entitled *Walwyn's Wiles*, which had accused him not just of political Machiavellianism and extremism – allegedly he wanted to destroy all government and execute all lawyers – but also of being a crypto-Jesuit, a bigamist and a man known to have driven several women to suicide. In *Walwyn's Just Defence*, written in June, he had no difficulty showing all this up for the scurrilous nonsense it was.[62] Meanwhile Overton and Lilburne were collaborating on the *Third Agreement of the Free People of England*, which was essentially a peace offering to Cromwell and the Grandees, eschewing most controversial issues and concentrating on the franchise and electoral reform. It asked for suffrage for all males over the age of twenty-one with no exceptions; an annual parliament with 400 paid members; rotation of political offices as in ancient Athens; abolition of tithes and religious toleration for all denominations except Roman Catholics; no more parliamentary interference with the law courts and no more legal exemptions and privileges; trial by jury with jurors openly chosen; the army to be commanded by officers appointed by Parliament; the ending of all trade monopolies, and indirect taxation replaced by direct; freedom of the press; a maximum rate of interest of 6 per cent and legislation to change base tenures into freehold. As a clear sop to the Grandees, there was to be a total ban on communism in any form. Most of the radicalism in the document came in the proposals for legal reform: no court proceedings to last longer than six months, defendants' right to silence, capital punishment to be retained only for murder and treason, and debt to be unpunishable by imprisonment.[63] Not only did this manifesto give no comfort to the Diggers or the Levellers' left wing, it sought to calm the panic induced in London merchants, traders, businessmen and financiers by all the talk of socio-economic equality. As has been well said: 'The fear of communism that haunted the wealthier Puritans was doubtless an expression of the unconscious guilt they felt when they contrasted their own prosperity with the hunger of the poor around them. What if there were, after all, a God who would avenge the widows and the fatherless?'[64] The Grandees showed their contempt for this overture by passing a Treason Act making it an express act of treason to say that the existing government was unlawful.

While the Leveller leaders languished in jail, their followers experienced the sharp end of the Grandees' backlash. By now Cromwell, Ireton and Fairfax were in agreement that sterner measures were needed to arrest the levelling 'cancer' in the army. In April there occurred the 'Bishopsgate mutiny'. Three hundred troopers of Colonel Edward Halley's regiment stationed in Bishopsgate demanded the immediate implementation of the full Leveller programme as the price of their agreeing to serve in Ireland. After Fairfax appealed to them, the mutineers laid down their arms. All 300 were cashiered with loss of pay including arrears, 15 of the 'ringleaders' were arrested and court-martialled, and 6 were sentenced to death; 5 of these were pardoned but 23-year-old Robert Lockyer was hanged. The death and funeral of Lockyer on 27 April was the occasion for a massive Leveller demonstration, and a fortnight later there was a tense confrontation in Hyde Park when Cromwell faced down hundreds of defiant Leveller soldiers with sea-green ribbons and bunches of rosemary in their hats.[65] From the Tower Lilburne and Overton wrote to Fairfax that the sentence of execution on Lockyer was not just murder but treason as well. Tempers were running very high. If the Grandees thought that a show of toughness would intimidate the army, they were soon disabused. On 1 May troopers of Scroop's horse at Salisbury categorically refused to serve in Ireland, adducing as grievances also the imprisonment of the Leveller leaders and the execution of Lockyer. Faced with mutiny, the officers at Salisbury simply decamped, and for twelve days there was anarchy and chaos. An even more serious manifestation followed at Oxford. Captain William Thompson and a large band of cavalry effectively declared themselves rebels by going far beyond the negative mutiny of their Salisbury *confrères*: they actually called for armed insurrection to overthrow Cromwell.[66]

Fairfax and Cromwell did not underrate all these warning signs and realised they would have to act fast to stop the contagion from spreading; if Thompson could unite all mutineers between Salisbury and Oxford he would have a formidable fighting force of 3,000 men at his disposal. Cromwell sent ahead, by flying columns and post horses, a handful of officers, in essence political commissars, whose task it was to talk the mutineers into laying down their arms or least stalling them and slowing them up by pointless talk. One of these agents was a Major White, who seems to have been particularly successful.[67] A campaign of disinformation managed to detach a number of the mutineers on 11 May, but Thompson himself escaped from the attempt to encircle him, taking nearly 1,000 armed rebels with him. Tired, wet and hungry, Thompson's men billeted themselves overnight in the grey-stone cottages of Burford and environs. Decisive action in times of military crisis was always Cromwell's strong suit. Relying on speed and forced marches to confound enemy expectations, Cromwell and Fairfax put together an elite squad of 2,000 men to ride fifty miles a day and strike back fast. At midnight on 14–15 May he came upon the sleeping rebels at Burford and smote them with biblical fury, scattering the confused and panic-stricken foe in short order.[68] A few shots were fired, but resistance seemed useless. Five hundred fled into the night (Thompson among them), but 340 were taken prisoner. Fairfax's court martial selected four victims for the death sentence. Cornet Dene won a reprieve after the most abject display of grovelling recantation and a promise to preach his 'reformation' throughout the army, but the other three were executed: Cornet James Thompson (the rebel leader's brother) and Corporals Church and Perkins. Thompson himself was killed a little later in a shootout at Northampton.[69] In contrast to the cowardice of 'Judas' Dene, most of those captured were defiant. Among them was William Eyre, a veteran of Edgehill and Cromwell's 1643 campaign in Lincolnshire, who told Fairfax at the court martial: 'If but ten men appeared for the cause, I would make eleven.' Eyre and certain others got off lightly, possibly because they were lower-middle-class officers of the kind Cromwell favoured, the famous 'plain, russet-coated captains'.[70] The proletarian rebels were more roughly handled, including a number who were locked up for a week in Burford church on bread and water.

Although there was another small mutiny in Oxford in September, resulting in another two executions, the Levellers had shot their bolt. Cromwell departed for his slaughterous campaign in Ireland, confident that he had defeated his most persistent critics. A significant pointer was that *The Moderate* ceased publication in September. The defeated and disillusioned Levellers and Diggers largely drifted away into Quakerism and other forms of quietism; a few opted for millenarianism.[71] Cromwell judged the time was right to put Lilburne on trial for his life but, as with all his most despotic decisions, he liked to delegate the details to underlings while he was absent. The charge was treason. Since under the Treason Act it was treason to question the legitimacy of the Council of State, it followed that Lilburne must clearly be guilty, for he had described the 'Army junto' as one run by 'tyrants and weasels and polecats'. In a two-day trial in October, conducting what they thought would be an open-and-shut case, the judges directed the jury to convict but instead, after an hour's deliberation, they acquitted him of all charges. In Ireland Cromwell heard to his fury that Lilburne had been carried back, shoulder-high, to the Tower by a jubilant crowd. It was two weeks before the Council of State thought it safe to release him, but they finally did so in November, freeing Overton, Walwyn and Prince also. So popular was Lilburne that Cromwell and the Council did not dare to proceed against him again until 1651. This time they found a way to avoid the 'inconvenience' of jury trial and held him in contempt for having libelled a member of parliament; this allowed them to exile him. Lilburne departed for a two-year sojourn in Holland.[72]

The delay in having, so to speak, a second shot at Lilburne was partly occasioned by the eventful nature of the years 1650–1. After spending nine months in Ireland, Cromwell was forced to return to

Great Britain in May 1650 to oppose a new royalist rising engendered by Charles II's landing in Scotland and his acclamation by the Covenanters there. Cromwell always had as soft a spot for the Scots as he had a pathological loathing for the Irish, and at first he tried to talk them round. His appeal to the General Assembly of the Church of Scotland, rebuking them for the royal alliance, has become famous: 'I beseech you, in the bowels of Christ, think it possible you may be mistaken.'[73] Rebuffed, he prepared for war. He won a great victory at Dunbar in September 1650, but it was another year, until September 1651, before he extinguished the threat from Charles with a smashing victory at Worcester, which many military historians think was his finest martial hour.[74] This triumph was overshadowed a little later by the death of Ireton, whom Cromwell always loved like a son. Ireton, left in command of the New Model Army in Ireland when Cromwell was forced to return, died of fever just after successfully completing the siege of Limerick; Cromwell was devastated. Returning to London, he struggled through more than a year's unsatisfactory dealings with the Rump Parliament before dissolving it in April 1653; the immediate trigger was the Rump's threat to disband Cromwell's 50,000-strong army as 'too expensive'. Cromwell's harangue on that occasion produced another of his famous sayings: 'You have sat too long for any good you have been doing lately . . . Depart, I say; and let us have done with you. In the name of God, go!'[75] It was a choice irony that Cromwell, who had regarded Charles I's irruption into the Commons in January 1642 as the ultimate blasphemy, should easily have outdone the king in despotism by dissolving *two* parliaments, the Long in 1648 and the Rump in 1653. The phantom-like Barebones Parliament, a hand-picked assembly, lasted a mere six months in 1653, after which Cromwell had himself declared Lord Protector for life.[76]

Cromwell's total and unalloyed triumph was the end of the road for most of the Levellers and Diggers. Walwyn, Overton and Winstanley most obviously came to heel. Walwyn's later pamphlets were reformist and tame. In December 1651 he wrote a defence of trial by jury, but as this was the sole Leveller achievement left standing, his advocacy seemed supererogatory. In May 1652 he made an unsuccessful attempt in *For a Free Trade* to persuade the Council of State to abolish the Levant Company's monopoly of trade with the Middle East, using some arguments which anticipated Adam Smith.[77]

Although he was rearrested as a precaution when Lilburne returned from exile in 1653, he soon proved his loyalty to the new regime and retired into private life, where he 'retreaded' and worked as a physician until his death at eighty in 1681. Richard Overton at first proved defiant, moved to Holland and began plotting with John Wildman and Edward Sexby to overthrow the Protectorate. He soon saw that the various conspiracies were wildly impractical, cut his losses and returned to private life in obscurity in England; he died in 1664 in his early sixties.[78] Winstanley maintained his socialistic stance until 1652, then gave up and joined the Quakers. He inherited an estate, became a man of property, a churchwarden and later chief constable of Elmbridge. Like Walwyn and Overton, he survived well into the reign of Charles II and died aged sixty-seven in 1676.[79] Another long-lived Leveller was John Wildman, the inveterate plotter and intriguer, who conspired against Cromwell and the restored Stuart monarchs and ended up knighted by King William III after the Glorious Revolution. His parting shot, while safely out of Cromwell's reach on the continent, was a splenetic attack focusing on the Lord Protector's distasteful personality.[80] The two most courageous Levellers were destined, perhaps as a consequence, to die young like Rainsborough. Edward Sexby, unlike Overton and Wildman his two early collaborators in plotting, did not get out when the going became dangerous but seemed almost to redouble his efforts. He recruited as his chief accomplice an intemperate young man named Miles Sindercombe, and the two became enmeshed in a complex plot to assassinate Cromwell. Charles II had put a bounty on the head of the Lord Protector, offering an annuity of £500, the rank of colonel and other honours to 'whosoever will, by the sword, pistol or poison, kill the base mechanic fellow, by name Oliver Cromwell'. While secretly loathing the royalists, Sexby conspired with them on the continent and hatched what he thought a credible plot to liquidate Cromwell. Returning to England with Sindercombe early in 1657 to implement the conspiracy, the plotters were betrayed to Cromwell's chief of police. Sentenced to a traitor's death, Sindercombe committed suicide in the Tower in February to avoid being hanged, drawn and quartered. Sexby remained at large until July, but was then kept in the Tower and interrogated personally by Cromwell. He allegedly caught a fever and then went insane, but the probability is that he was so badly tortured that his health simply gave way. He died in the Tower in January 1658, still in his early forties.[81] Lilburne also died young. After a restless exile in Bruges and the Netherlands, he suddenly reappeared in England on 14 June 1653, claiming that since the Rump Parliament no longer existed, in logic he could hardly still be punished for having impugned its integrity; after all, Cromwell himself had done that. The Lord Protector was having none of it; 'Freeborn John' was arrested and lodged in Newgate jail. For the second time he had Lilburne put on trial for his life. The trial began on 13 July in an atmosphere of great tension, with soldiers barring the entrance to the Old Bailey against a huge hostile crowd. A popular ditty ran round London:

> And what, shall then honest John Lilburne die?
> Three score thousand will know the reason why.[82]

This time the proceedings were protracted, but the result was the same as before. Lilburne cleverly appealed to the jury on the general morality of his banishment, not the technicality of whether he had breached its terms. On 20 August Lilburne was acquitted, with the jury recording this verdict: 'John Lilburne is not guilty of any crime worthy of death.'[83] In fury Cromwell insisted that the jurors be interrogated by his secret police and the Council of State to discover why they had delivered such an unsound judgement. Thus were all the accusations adequately fulfilled, that England under Cromwell had not advanced beyond the Court of Star Chamber. The move was, however, in vain. The jurors all met at the Windmill Tavern before their interrogation and concerted the answer which all then gave: 'I gave the verdict with a clear conscience and I refuse to answer any questions about it.' Cromwell refused to allow Lilburne to go free. He was taken from Newgate to the Tower and then to Mount Orgeuil Castle in Jersey, where the governor found him 'more troublesome than ten cavaliers'. He was brought back to England in 1655 and placed under house arrest in Dover Castle. He then converted to Quakerism, allowing his friends finally to persuade Cromwell to give him his liberty. After a very short spell of freedom he died aged forty-three at Eltham in Kent.[84]

The years 1646–9 undoubtedly constituted a revolutionary moment, a time when, in principle, momentous changes were possible. The

Puritans broke through the 'credibility barrier' which had so afflicted Tyler, Cade and the Pilgrims of Grace and, by executing the king, demonstrated that they were not afraid to sail into uncharted waters. Whether significant social change really was feasible remains debatable, and part of the reason lies in the political, personal and ideological weaknesses of the Levellers themselves. After all their grandiose proposals, only trial by jury survived as a solid achievement; even the abolition of monarchy and the House of Lords, which seem to have been achieved by 1649, were later rescinded. Universal male suffrage did not arrive until 1918, and biennial parliaments have never been achieved in England. The mistakes of the Levellers were legion. They sacrificed the art of the possible for utopian and chimerical goals. One of the feasible reforms which they did *not* ask for was the secret ballot and this omission is very odd, since it was a prescription contained in all the best-known works of political theory, such as More's *Utopia* or Harrington's *Oceana*. They made their only serious move – trying to provoke mutiny and revolt in the army – much too late, in 1649, by which time large numbers of their comrades had already been sent to Ireland and a good deal of discontent in the ranks had been allayed by Cromwell's use of Crown lands (in part) to settle the arrears of military pay (the other part was sold off at rock-bottom prices to land-grabbing senior officers and civilian property speculators). They were guilty of the besetting sin of the Left through the ages – internal factionalism and squabbling instead of concentrating on the common enemy. Here Lilburne, idiosyncratic, individualist and a non-team-playing prima donna must bear a considerable burden of blame; not only did he quarrel with his fellow Levellers but in his boastfulness and arrogance, which Thomas Carlyle so disliked, he often alerted Cromwell to Leveller intentions and strategy.[85] At a deeper level, one can say that the Levellers had no awareness of the deeper currents of history or even the social and economic imperatives of their own world. Their economic theory was primitive and related to an ideal world of owner-occupiers, independent tradesmen and self-employed craftsmen, freed from the shackles of economic monopoly. Typically the 'middling sort' themselves – skilled craftsmen, cobblers, weavers, printers, lead miners, small traders, shopkeepers, etc. – still clung to a property qualification for the suffrage and had nothing to offer the agricultural workers, who, after all, made up three-quarters of the

English economy.[86] Most of all, they had no idea of the possibilities latent in capitalism and were lacking in revolutionary consciousness. Marxists would say they were premature revolutionary utopians, since capitalism could be overthrown only with the emergence of an industrial proletariat, and were thus vulnerable to Marx's general critique of utopian socialism as mere wishful thinking.[87] It should have been clear that the great land-owning classes would not give up their privileges without a ferocious struggle, inevitably involving armed conflict. Not only was the Left in the 1640s not ideally placed for this – the Diggers were actually pacifists – but they had not thought through the implications of their demands in terms of revolutionary violence. This was supremely ironic in light of the fact that they had just fought a bloody civil war to achieve lesser changes. However, it is possible to imagine, counterfactually, the England that might have emerged if the Levellers had had leaders of the calibre of Cromwell and their opponents lacked them. The likelihood is that the nation would not have acquired an empire but would have developed along the lines of Switzerland or Scandinavia.[88] Certainly on the question of Ireland the Levellers had the best ideas. John Bull's other island would not have been subjected to a further three centuries of repression, exploitation, bloodshed and famine. What the Levellers wanted from Ireland – partnership with a benevolent neutral, pledged never to sign up with England's enemies, much as in the 1921 treaty granting independence – could theoretically have occurred in 1649.[89]

Most of all, they underrated Cromwell and were no match for him in political terms. He was always a much more traditional figure than Lilburne, Overton and Winstanley imagined. The pre-1642 social system would have suited him well; it was only the autocracy of Charles I that was the problem. A deep-dyed, innate conservative wedded to private property, regarding social caste as just as much part of the natural order of things as the law of gravity, Cromwell never wanted manhood suffrage or religious toleration, and in foreign affairs was a throwback to Elizabeth I, basically an English anti-Spain imperialist. Clear-sighted, Cromwell saw that he had to defeat the royalists and the Presbyterians in Parliament before turning on the Levellers, which accounts for the apparent tolerance in evidence at the Putney Debates. It has been argued that for a short time after the Battle of Worcester in 1651 he seemed sympathetic to radical aims[90] but, if this really was the case, his hesitation did not last long. His attitude to the Left is well summed up in another of his sayings: 'It is some satisfaction if a Commonwealth must perish, that it perish by men and not by the hands of persons differing little from beasts. That if it must needs suffer, it should rather suffer from rich men than from poor men who, as Solomon says, "when they oppress leave nothing behind them, but are a sweeping rain".'[91] His essential problem, after the dismissal of the Rump Parliament in 1653, was that he ended in a political cul-de-sac. His Barebones Parliament, designed as a 'house of godly men', failed through lack of popular support and his general Instrument of Government declined into local military satrapies ruled by his major-generals. When asked to nominate a successor, he named his son Richard, who turned out an egregious failure. By the time of his death in 1658, Cromwell had solved not one of the nation's essential problems and left it in a state of confusion paralleled in the modern era most closely by Marshal Tito's legacy to the former Yugoslavia. Facing uncertainty and chaos, Cromwell's lieutenants opted for the restoration of the Stuarts rather than the political equivalent of open-ocean navigation, which opened up the possibility of a resurgence of the radicals.

From their own selfish point of view, the Grandees did well. The years after 1660 saw a notable return to power of the aristocracy, albeit modified by the post-1688 financial revolution. The ordinary man and the common people, so prominent in the 1640s, did not really revive for another 200 years. Cromwell understood the tides of history as the Levellers did not. To say that he was a mere 'epiphenomenon', as vulgar Marxists used to, and that he was simply the man required by a certain social situation of course begs the question; the only proof of the socio-economic requirement is the actual appearance of the man himself, so that the argument is circular. Sober historians are wary of 'lessons' taught by Clio, but the 1640s do seem to have reinforced two of history's constants. One is that revolutionary turmoil, of our Categories Two and Three (see Appendix) inevitably ends with the man on horseback. Those, like Thomas Carlyle, fascinated by the parallels between the English and French Revolutions have constructed a fanciful scenario whereby the Presbyterians are the analogue of the Girondins, the Jacobins the equivalent of the Independents and the Levellers are paralleled 150 years later by Hébert and Babeuf. One adaptation of this thesis ends in absurdity, with Cromwell as the Directory and the Glorious Revolution of 1688 featuring as Napoleon.[92] More convincing is the obvious parallel between Cromwell and Napoleon himself and with other 'strong men' or dictators who emerged from the chaos of real revolution: Lenin and Stalin in the Soviet Union, Mao in China, even Álvaro Obregón and the PRI in Mexico in the 1920s. The other constant is that warfare and military defeat are the mothers of revolution. Apart from the parallel between the 1640s in England and the 1790s in France, there is the emergence of the Paris Commune after the debacle of the Franco-Prussian War in 1871, the 1905 rising in Russia following defeat by Japan, 1917 in Russia and the rise of the Communist Party in China after the failure of the Kuomintang in the war against Japan in 1937–45.

8

The Jacobite Rising of 1745

The Jacobites were the adherents of the Stuart dynasty exiled from England in the 'Glorious Revolution' of 1688 and so called from the Latin for James (*Jacobus*), since James II was the luckless monarch ousted that year. For seventy years (1689–1759), they sought the return of the Stuarts by means of armed insurrection, coup d'état or foreign invasion. Jacobitism was also an international movement, with tentacles in trade, finance, industry and, especially, the military, and many regiments of Irish and Scottish exiles were formed in France and Spain. The Jacobites' military talents saw them employed by a wide range of foreign governments from Versailles to Moscow.[1] Curiously, until the 1970s, historians refused to take Jacobitism seriously, regarding it as, at best, capable of fomenting 'a little local difficulty', to use Harold Macmillan's famous phrase when he purged his cabinet in 1962. The usual view was to dismiss the Jacobite movement as a benighted anachronism, hopelessly wedded to the past and crippled by nostalgic hankerings for absolute monarchy and the divine right of kings. In fact Jacobitism was at once simple and highly complex.[2] Simple because it had a clear, focused aim, unlike Wat Tyler, Jack Cade and the Pilgrimage of Grace. There was no ambivalence about the colossus standing in their path, such as the Levellers and Diggers entertained for Cromwell. The usurping foreign monarchs (first the Dutch William and Mary, then Queen Anne, finally the first two Hanoverian kings, George I and George II) were the enemy and had to be displaced by whatever means, including assassination. Complex, because Jacobitism evolved over time and took protean forms. Part of the muddle anti-Jacobite historians have got themselves into is to predicate attributes of the entire movement which can only be predicated in closely defined eras. In short, those scholars who take a cavalier view of Jacobitism commit the most basic fault in writing history: unawareness of chronology. What can be said about the movement in the years 1689–1715 cannot be said about the years 1715–45, and still less about 1746–59.[3] There are complications in space, too, as well as time. From 1689 to 1713 James II and his son James Francis were domiciled at the Château Vieux at St Germain, outside Paris, running an 'alternative' court and constantly beset by money problems. When Louis XV was compelled by the terms of the Treaty of Utrecht to expel the Jacobites, James and his courtiers flitted phantom-like to two different makeshift abodes, first Bar in Lorraine, then Avignon, and finally to the ducal palace in Urbino in 1717. Finding James Francis discontented here also, Pope Clement XI persuaded him to move to the security of the Papal States, using James's marriage as the pretext. From 1719 until his death in 1766 James was ensconced in the unprepossessing Palazzo Muti, a step down from the grandeur of St Germain and Urbino but secure and permanent. From here James (by now 'the Old Pretender' to the Hanoverians) directed (or tried to) the heterogeneous Jacobite movement, attempting to draw together strands in England, Scotland, Ireland, France, Spain, Russia and a host of minor states and principalities.[4]

It is customary to say that there were four Jacobite rebellions in Britain, those of 1708, 1715, 1719 and 1745, though 1708 does not really count as an authentic rising. In that year the Jacobites' staunch ally, Louis XIV of France, sent the twenty-year-old James Francis Edward, son of James II, with 6,000 French troops to attempt a landing in Scotland. The half-heartedness of the French commanders ensured that the young man never even set foot on Scottish soil; the most he did was sight Edinburgh from the Firth of Forth before the Royal Navy chased the French flotilla away.[5] In 1715 the Jacobites, this time on their own, since the French had signed the Treaty of Utrecht in 1713 bringing to an end the War of Spanish Succession, organised a rising which on paper was formidable, envisaging as it did simultaneous armed outbreaks in south-west England, northern England and Scotland. This time the main factor bedevilling the Jacobites was lack of a credible commander. The rising in the south-west collapsed ignominiously in September, but at first the Jacobite Earl of Mar seemed to carry all before him, and quickly had most of Scotland at his feet. In northern England the rebels were led by Thomas Forster,

MP, and the young James Radcliffe, 3rd Earl of Derwentwater. Both Mar and Forster proved hopeless as generals. On 12 November Forster and the English Jacobites confronted the Hanoverian enemy at Preston and at first gave a reasonable account of themselves. The arrival of a second loyalist army sealed their fate, and Forster surrendered on 14 November, without securing any terms or concessions for his men. 13 November was also the date of the battle that sealed Scotland's fate. Mar brought the enemy to battle at Sheriffmuir, north of Stirling. Despite having a three-to-one numerical superiority, he botched the direction of the battle, which ended indecisively.[6] At this setback Jacobite morale plummeted and there was mass desertion from the ranks. The cause of the Stuarts was all but extinguished in Scotland when James Francis (the 'Old Pretender' to the Hanoverians) landed in Scotland, intending to have himself crowned at the traditional site of Scottish coronations, Scone. Expecting to find Mar victorious and the Jacobites piling success on success south of the border, he was flabbergasted by the debacle he found. Never a tough or gritty individual, James cracked under the stress. Totally lacking in charisma, he depressed his Scottish followers rather than enthusing them. Even as he made futile attempts to rally them, news came in that his treasure ship, containing all the money to finance operations in Scotland, had run aground on the Dundee sandbanks. The Scottish nobles who supported James decided to melt away into the islands, effectively abandoning their leader, who embarked for France on 4 February 1716, a broken and disconsolate man.[7]

The 1719 rising was nothing like so ambitious or elaborate as the '15 but ended equally disastrously. This time the Jacobites had the nominal advantage of foreign backing. War had broken out between Spain and England in 1718 over the Spanish seizure of Sicily and Sardinia. Spain's first minister Cardinal Alberoni endorsed a two-pronged Jacobite rebellion, with risings in England and Scotland. The Spanish fleet bearing the troops supposed to land in England was shattered by a force-twelve storm in the Bay of Biscay. The Spanish force for Scotland got through and rendezvoused with pro-Jacobite lords in Stornoway on the Isle of Lewis. But then the besetting sin of Jacobitism – factionalism – took a hand. The commanders could not agree a common strategy for Scotland. The Jacobite Earl Marischal, who had the ear of the Spanish, prevailed and landfall was made on the mainland at Eilean Donan opposite the Isle of Skye. Blockaded there, Marischal withdrew inland but was cornered by Hanoverian troops at Glenshiel. With overwhelming superiority in artillery, the Hanoverians won an easy victory and compelled the Spanish to surrender; Marischal and the other Jacobite commanders made good their escape.[8]

For twenty-five years thereafter the Jacobite cause was in the doldrums. James Stuart kept hoping for the elusive 'favourable conjuncture' that would tempt a foreign power to aid the Jacobites in another rising, but no offers were forthcoming. Part of the problem was the long European peace between the Treaty of Utrecht in 1713 and the War of Jenkins' Ear in 1739. There *were* minor wars, such as that of the Polish Succession in the 1730s, but a general conflict was avoided by the 'peace at any price' policies pursued simultaneously by Robert Walpole in England and Cardinal Fleury in France. Just when Jacobitism seemed doomed to euthanasia, a new star appeared. In 1719 James contracted a marriage with Clementina Sobieska, a fabulously wealthy Polish princess, granddaughter of the Jan Sobieski who had turned back the Turks at the gates of Vienna in 1683.[9] Late the following year Clementina gave birth to a son, Charles Edward Casimir. Charles Edward Stuart was destined to be one of the great heroes of the age. To the Scots he was 'Bonnie Prince Charlie', to his admirers the Young Chevalier or the Young Adventurer, to hagiographers Ascanius – though since Ascanius's father in the myth was Aeneas, who fled from Troy to found Rome, this was hyperbole pure and simple: the ineffectual James Edward was no Aeneas. From a very early age the young prince set himself to become a great warrior: he mastered firearms and swordplay, hunted assiduously, managed to serve in a campaign at Gaeta, Italy, at the age of thirteen and prepared himself like a knight of old for the ordeal to come.[10] The one defect in his character – and it was to be as significant a one as the *hamartia* or fatal flaw in all great tragic heroes – was an unintegrated ego. In times of good fortune, when his star was in the ascendant, the prince was brilliant, charming, charismatic, inventive, creative, even original. When things went badly, he fell apart rapidly, descending into illness, depression, rage and, in later years, alcoholism. He had no middle range, either of emotions or rationality, he was an 'all or nothing' personality, with all the problems such a psychology engenders.[11] His mother was a neurotic and religious maniac, who mortified the flesh in hopes of salvation and posthumous canonisation. His father was cold, pious, timid and unemotional. The marriage was a disaster which it needed papal intervention to patch up. Charles Edward therefore lived his early years in an emotional cauldron and lost his mother when he was fourteen, when Clementina in an excess of pietistic zeal virtually starved herself to death and succumbed to scurvy. The loss exacerbated the instability and volatility in the prince, and helped to nurture a growing antagonism towards his father, at first unconscious, later manifest and overt. Charles Edward and James Francis seemed incapable to getting on at any level, personal, emotional, political. As he neared his twentieth year, Charles became almost visibly impatient with his father's dedication to the 'art of the possible', his political naivety, his lack of worldliness and cynicism. One clear result of his distancing from both parents was the rejection of their religion. While James and Clementina were fervent Catholics, Charles Edward gradually rejected religion. Once the break with his father was complete, he threw off the mask and revealed himself as a freethinker and deist; some would say he went beyond this into outright atheism.[12]

Thirsting for action, Charles welcomed the coming of a general European conflict in 1740, when the War of Austrian Succession broke out. For three years he waited patiently for England to be sucked into warfare with France, which would give him the chance he was waiting for. The opportunity came in the winter of 1743–4. In January 1743 Cardinal Fleury died, and the 32-year-old Louis XV, at last emerging from his shadow, made it clear that from now on he was the prime decision-maker in France. Piqued by English provocations both in Europe and around the world, Louis laid a master plan for a surprise invasion of England without a declaration of war. He began by sending his master of horse James Butler on a reconnaissance tour of England to gauge the strength of the Stuart party there. Butler reported favourably.[13] Louis now had to implement the most difficult part of his plan. He had somehow to incite the Jacobites in Britain to rise simultaneously with the landing of French troops, but faced the dilemma that if he involved James and his son, known to be agog for military glory, this would alert the government in England to his hostile intentions. He therefore asked James in Rome for copies of manifestos and declarations of intent, plus a commission of regency for Charles Edward, against the day he finally decided to give the green light to the cross-Channel invasion; he hinted that this was still about a year in the future. He then intended to land his troops, publish the various Jacobite manifestos and then summon Charles Edward to come to England as Regent. Unfortunately for him, there was more than a whiff of 'too clever by half' about this plan and, as often happens in such cases, he became tangled up in the coils of his own deceit. He used a Scottish Jacobite, William MacGregor of Balhaldy, as his go-between for the messages conveyed from Versailles to Rome, informing James that he could not send him a formal letter because of security considerations. James partially took the bait, but Balhaldy had smelt a rat and told Charles Edward of his suspicions.[14] The prince had been champing at the bit for months, vainly pleading with his father to let him escape from the Palazzo Muti to the wider world to organise another Jacobite rebellion. He now re-exhorted his father, cajoling Balhaldy to plead on his behalf that that was what Louis XV really wanted. Reluctantly James signed the commission of regency and allowed his son to depart. On 8 January, using a series of elaborate subterfuges to throw Hanoverian spies off the scent (the Palazzo Muti was under permanent surveillance by agents of the British government),[15] Charles Edward slipped out of Rome. He would never see his father again and would return to the Eternal City only when James died in 1766.

After a month of incredible adventures in deep midwinter in Italy, on the Mediterranean coast and in France, the prince reached Paris on 8 February. His arrival came like a thunderbolt and seriously disconcerted the French ministers, whose elaborate planning for the invasion of England was already running into difficulties. 15,000 troops had been assigned to the task, under the command of France's greatest soldier, Maurice, Comte de Saxe. The invasion force was assembling in the northern ports of Gravelines and Dunkirk, ready to cross the Channel in flat-bottomed boats as soon as it was certain that the Royal Navy could not intervene, and the English Jacobites had sent pilots to guide the French armada through the tricky Thames estuary. To ensure success French Admiral Roquefeuil was given the task of sortieing from Brest and luring the British fleet under Admiral Sir John Norris down the Channel towards the western approaches; the invasion force would then proceed to a landfall at Maldon in Essex.[16]

Everything then seemed to go wrong at once. First the English Jacobites switched their desired landfall from Maldon to Blackwall a few miles from London, which meant that extra pilots had to be found. Then the first pilot sent to France to coordinate operations unaccountably got lost and landed further down the coast from Dunkirk; unable to speak any French he floundered around hopelessly for a few days before returning to England. Then Saxe decided that even if the Brest fleet was successful he still needed an escort of warships across the Channel, leading Roquefeuil to divide his forces and send one squadron back to Saxe. Next Admiral Roquefeuil notified Saxe that he had successfully decoyed the Royal Navy and the coast was clear, but immediately countermanded the signal to say that he had not been able to dupe Norris, who was now retreating towards Gravelines. Almost incredibly, while this welter of confusion was taking place, the prince suddenly arrived in Paris. The victim of his own Machiavellianism, Louis XV was forced to treat the uninvited interloper as an honoured guest. But the British government was not deceived. So far Saxe had had the element of surprise on his side, and the authorities in London had not had an inkling that an invasion was afoot.[17] The arrival of the Stuart prince let the cat out of the bag, for his advent could mean only one thing. Both Saxe and the ministers fumed that the Stuart prince's blundering onto the scene at that precise moment effectively destroyed their plans, and ever afterwards claimed that the Jacobites themselves by their ineptitude had destroyed the best-ever chance of a Stuart restoration.

None of this weighed with Charles Edward. He barely took the time to recover his strength before he was on the road to Gravelines. Once on the coast he became involved in furious altercations both with Saxe and the Earl Marischal, who had never liked the prince. Marischal additionally was a prima donna and a defeatist. When Charles Edward furiously denounced Saxe to what he thought was a cabal of sympathisers, Marischal spoke up for Saxe. Meanwhile events in the Channel seemed to be reaching a crisis as Roquefeuil and Norris prepared to give battle. Suddenly, on the afternoon of 7 March, both fleets were hit by a force-twelve storm; the wind speeds were of hurricane strength. Eighteen of Norris's warships were badly damaged, but Roquefeuil managed to slip anchor and run before the wind to Brest, sustaining only minor damage. The real devastation occurred in Gravelines and Dunkirk. Eleven transports and many smaller craft were wrecked and, worse, six months' supplies and materiel destroyed, along with anchors and tackle. Saxe wrote to Versailles to request permission to abandon the invasion, which obviously could not now take place. Even as he awaited the answer, a second ferocious storm on 11 March delivered the coup de grâce to his shipping. Saxe coldly informed the Stuart prince that the expedition had been cancelled.[18]

It was now that the prince revealed one of his most serious weaknesses: he was no diplomat or politician, and never learned to take no for an answer once he had set his mind on something. The abandonment of the invasion scheme was the only sensible course in the circumstances, but Charles chose to see it as an example of French perfidy and treachery; never afterwards would he trust Louis XV and his ministers. The French were far from blameless: they had been tardy, inept and incompetent, with even the great Saxe scarcely appearing to advantage. Yet, as Saxe reasonably pointed out, he was no Aeolus who could command the winds. The prince would have none of it. Learning that Norris's fleet had reformed and was again barring the way across the Channel, he asked Saxe and the ministers in Versailles how even a so-called 'Protestant wind' could disperse the French armada yet leave the Royal Navy intact.[19] His angry missives caused serious embarrassment at Versailles. Louis XV 'solved' the problem by ordering the prince away from the coast to live incognito in France, pending a possible second chance at the invasion of England. Charles wrote to his father, fuming at the shabby treatment meted out to him; this time James, who habitually took the side of caution and expediency, agreed that the French behaviour was shoddy. In his internal exile and forced to remain incognito, the prince fumed at French double-dealing and rationalised his rage by visiting Paris on many occasions, though strictly forbidden by Louis from doing so. For more than a year (March 1744–July 1745), he fumed impotently in France, dependent on French money for his very subsistence but loathing everything about the French king and his ministers.[20] Gradually Charles Edward convinced himself that he should look for nothing from France and should go it alone. It was now that he revealed himself a most modern figure, a born revolutionary in his thinking. There were three aspects to this. The first was his understanding that the Whig/Hanoverian/Protestant ascendancy rested on far too narrow a base; there was a handful of major beneficiaries, but the majority of people in all classes were excluded and alienated. Second there was his voluntarism, the belief that willpower could move mountains and that elan, enterprise and initiative could overcome what looked like insurmountable obstacles. In modern revolutionary terminology we might say that Charles Edward was a believer in 'subjective conditions' while his father believed in 'objective conditions' (that elusive 'favourable conjuncture').[21] As the prince rightly saw, one could wait a lifetime for objective conditions and even when they occurred, as in 1743–4, a series of casual chances could still ruin everything; better by far to trust in one's own star and devise a rolling strategy, a snowball of accelerating momentum. The second original facet of the prince's thinking anticipated some of Lenin's thinking. Lenin believed that revolution had to take place in the most advanced European countries, but later modified his theories to accommodate the situation in Russia in 1917 and then posited that it did not matter if the revolution broke out *first* in a backward country as long as the advanced nations then joined in the revolutionary moment.[22] Similarly, Charles Edward accepted that a French invasion followed by a Jacobite rising in Britain was the best-case scenario. It followed that his destination must be Scotland, for in the Highlands the tradition of bearing arms was an everyday business, and many of the clan chiefs were Jacobite, so that he would have a ready-made army. However, he saw no reason why a rising in Britain *first* should not then trigger the hoped-for French intervention. It is a travesty of his thinking – and really would make him the blockhead some allege him to have been – if he thought a rising in the Highlands *unaided* would secure him his dreams.

Using the services of a shady Scots banker Aeneas MacDonald, and through him the Paris-based firm of Waters and Son, depending ultimately on the family (Sobieski) jewels in the deposit bank of the Monte de Pietà in Rome, the prince assembled a cache of arms in a warehouse in Nantes amounting to twenty small field pieces, 11,000 guns, 2,000 broadswords and a good quantity of powder, plus a war chest of 4,000 louis d'or in cash. But how to clear it from French ports without alerting the authorities? Charles Edward solved this by recruiting a clique of rich Jacobite exiled ship-owners based in Nantes and St Malo, unscrupulous men who had made fortunes from slave-trading and piracy.[23] With their aid, he double-bluffed the Minister of Marine, Comte de Maurepas, into thinking he had rented a ship to convey messages to and from Scotland. Having secured the necessary paperwork to enable him to sail from the port of St Nazaire, he had his secret cache loaded on board and embarked himself with about a dozen retainers, including the famous 'Seven Men of Moidart' – actually an assemblage of ne'er-do-well adventurers, crooked counsellors and irresponsible drunks (one of them Aeneas MacDonald).[24] At the last moment the doyen of the Jacobite ship-owners, Antoine Walsh, who had pledged himself to convey the prince to Scotland, announced a great coup. He had secured Maurepas's permission to take 700 of Lord Clare's regiment of Irish exiles on a privateering expedition – Versailles often authorised such use of manpower to its freebooters who operated under letters of marque; as in all eras the dividing line between privateering and piracy was thin. Walsh agreed that Charles Edward could take the 700 to Scotland as the nucleus of an army and an earnest of the French government's good faith.[25] He had gulled the French government and now proposed gulling the Scottish leaders as well. Walsh and Charles Edward laid their final plans. The adventurers would rendezvous at Nantes under assumed names, proceed to St Nazaire and board the frigate *Doutelle*. They would then sail to the island of Belle-Isle near Quiberon in Brittany, where a more powerful warship, the *Elisabeth*, would be waiting to embark Clare's regiment. Together the two ships would then stand away for Scotland on a north-westerly track. All went smoothly, and after the rendezvous at Belle-Isle on 12 July and final preparations, the two vessels put to sea on 16 July. So far luck had been with the adventurers, but on 20 July came a near-fatal blow to the enterprise. A British warship, HMS *Lion*, intercepted them, and a dreadful, pounding battle raged for four hours until sunset. Technically, the *Elisabeth* was the victor, as she forced the stricken *Lion* to return to Plymouth, but she herself was disabled and unable to continue. Even worse, she was listing so badly that she was unable to heave to to allow Walsh to transfer the men of Clare's regiment to the *Doutelle*, which had lain out of range of the English guns during the battle and was thus unscathed. Forced to return to Brest, she bore away with her not only Charles Edward's embryonic army but 1,500 muskets and ammunition and 1,800 broadswords.[26] A lesser spirit than Charles Edward would have abandoned the enterprise there and then.

The prince persevered, and pressed on to Scotland. He had originally intended to land on Mull to be acclaimed by the pro-Jacobite Maclean clan, but the clan chief Sir Hector had been suddenly arrested by the government on suspicion earlier in 1745. It was therefore decided to make landfall in the country of the Clanranald MacDonalds, a Catholic clan in the remote western Highlands. After surviving two bad storms, the prince and party landed on the island of Eriskay on 3 August, one of the most impoverished of all Hebridean islands. Here Charles was visited by MacDonald of Boisdale, brother of the Clanranald clan chief, who advised him that the great Skye chiefs would not rise for him and that he had better therefore return home. 'I am come home,' the prince replied.[27] Boisdale shrugged and stressed that none of the Clanranalds would ever serve under the Stuart banner, then curtly departed. There was a clamour among the prince's supporters for him to cut his losses and return to France, which he was able to beat off mainly with Walsh's help. Instead, he crossed to the mainland, making a famous landfall at Loch-nan-Uamh in Arisaig. Here young Clanranald, son of the clan leader, visited him and was as discouraging as Boisdale had been. Charles blunted his defeatism by sending him on a mission to the great Skye chiefs to urge them to reconsider. But when they reiterated their refusal to 'come out', even Walsh lost heart; the prince was now alone in his desire to continue. It was now that Charles displayed that cunning which always, confusingly, coexisted with his general political naivety. He, so to speak, went under young Clanranald's head to his younger kinsman Ranald MacDonald. This rash youth declared he would follow the Stuart prince to the ends of the earth even if no other Scotsman drew his sword. The prisoner of traditional clan notions of honour, young Clanranald had no choice but to declare himself also a volunteer. His adherence in turn persuaded the lesser MacDonald chiefs Keppoch and Glencoe to sign on.[28] The rolling strategy was beginning to work, but to attain credibility Charles needed the backing of a major clan chief. This he obtained with Donald Cameron of Lochiel. Legend says that Lochiel, a sobersided, 'improving' capitalist was seduced by the siren-like magnetism of the prince, but the truth was that Charles Edward persuaded him that France was just waiting to intervene, that Louis XV just needed the flicker of a rebellion in Scotland to win over his recalcitrant ministers. After much soul-searching, Lochiel allowed himself to be persuaded, but he took the precaution of taking security for his estate. The prince gave him an IOU, pledged against the Sobieski jewels (which, unknown to him, his father had already mortgaged). Charles had reached first base, and it was agreed that the Stuart standard would be raised at Glenfinnan on 19 August. Walsh was sent back to France to report the prince's success.[29]

After the gathering of the clans at Glenfinnan on the banks of Loch Shiel, Charles and his tiny army of 3,000 men set out to conquer Scotland. He had to jettison his original strategy of capturing all forts and castles because the artillery to accomplish this had gone back to France on the *Elisabeth*. The untalented John William O'Sullivan, one of the 'Seven Men of Moidart', was appointed major-general. Encouraged by messages from the head of the Fraser clan, Lord Lovat (who was playing a double game), Charles decided on the earliest possible battle with the forces of the commander-in-chief in Scotland, Sir John Cope, who had been ordered north from Edinburgh to seek out and destroy the inchoate rebellion. Like ships passing each other in the night, the two small armies (Cope had no more than 3,000 troops) both traversed Corriearack but did not meet. Surprised not to find the enemy in possession of the defile, Cope pressed on north to try to pacify any wavering clans who might be thinking of joining the Jacobites. The Highland army arrived, advanced cautiously, expecting to find Cope waiting for them, reached the other side of the pass and realised, to their great joy, that they were thereby masters of central Scotland.[30] From then until the end of the month there was nothing but good news for the Jacobites. One of Charles's 'Seven Men' the *de jure* Duke of Atholl and titular Marquis of Tullibardine, put his pro-Hanoverian brother (the de facto duke) to shame, and raised the numerous Atholl sept for the Stuarts. Lord Nairne, an important Atholl scion, joined the prince, as did John Roy Stewart, warrior, poet and adventurer, whom Charles commissioned to raise a regiment from among the discontented in the slums of Edinburgh. Another recruit, ambivalent and reluctant at first but later true gold, was Cluny MacPherson, head of the eponymous clan, but he agreed to serve only when the prince granted him the same terms as Lochiel, i.e. full security for his estates.[31] On the evening of 4 September, Charles

Edward entered Perth and proclaimed his father King James (and himself prince regent). At Perth he was joined by David, Lord Elcho, one of the first of the Lowland lairds to come out, but Elcho donated a shirt of Nessus that would bedevil all future relations with the prince when he made him a loan of 1,500 guineas to tide him over his immediate financial problems. The prince always took the line that this was a variant of a stock-exchange investment, that Elcho stood to gain hugely in the event of a Stuart restoration, but could not expect to be repaid if this failed to occur; Elcho, by contrast, regarded the loan as a commercial transaction, pure and simple.[32] While the Jacobite army rested at Perth, more high-profile aristocratic recruits came in with their levies: the Duke of Perth, Robertson of Struan, Lord Strathallan, Oliphant of Gask, Lord Ogilvy (who was immediately made a regimental commander). Finally there arrived the prince's evil genius: Lord George Murray. An inspired military tactician but a plodding by-the-book strategist, Murray also possessed the most fatal of flaws: he could never get on with the prince. The clash of personalities was of an ancient type: a dour, cold, aloof, blunt-spoken oligarch who prized the truth (as he saw it) above all things and found it impossible to defer like a true courtier was ranged against an extrovert, charismatic, charmer. Murray, like Marischal, had the disadvantage that he was in the same age range as James Francis and the Earl Marischal and, in the prince's mind, became conflated as a despised authority figure of the kind who could always point out the flaws in any plan and forever see the negative side, while seemingly temperamentally averse to sanguine prospects, geniality and eupeptic optimism. Where the prince was the avatar of 'subjective conditions', Murray had an almost pedantic and pedagogic commitment to objective conditions. It was a match made in hell.[33]

Charles Edward always had enough common sense to 'balance the ticket' – after all the Seven Men of Moidart had comprised four Scots and three Irishmen – and now in selecting his lieutenant-generals he allowed experience and prestige to override his personal feelings. Accordingly he appointed Lord George Murray and the Duke of Perth as his lieutenant-generals, with O'Sullivan under them as major-general, Strathallan brigadier-general, Sir John MacDonald the cavalry commander, and other leading Jacobites made colonels as regimental commanders. Unfortunately Perth did not get on particularly well with Lord George either, and this exacerbated the already endemic factionalism in the Jacobite army. In France in 1744–5 the prince had had to contend with the strife between the Paris-based Jacobites loyal to James (the 'king's party') and those loyal to himself (the 'prince's party'), and this tended to bifurcate in turn into Scotsmen and the Irish.[34] Since the Scots he took with him as part of the 'Seven Men' were all loyalists, that seemed to have ended one aspect of Jacobite factionalism, but by the time he reached Perth another had sprung up to take its place. There were those like Perth and O'Sullivan who always backed the prince in decision-making, but the clan leaders like Lochiel tended to heed the advice of Lord George. When the pro-Stuart feudal lords from north-eastern Scotland and the Lowlands came in – men like Lords Pitsligo, Glenbucket and Lewis – they too tended to side with the prince rather than Lord George, giving him in most circumstances a bare majority if controversial issues were put to the vote. In a good working partnership the inspirational leadership of the prince would have complemented the down-to-earth common sense of Lord George, but their innate clash of personalities meant that the two sides tended rather to pull apart.[35] This was a weakness in the Jacobite army that was never overcome. Overlaying the prince–Murray mésalliance was a largely unspoken divergence of view between Charles and his Scottish followers. Whereas for the prince the aim of the rising was to recoup the three kingdoms of England, Scotland and Ireland for the House of Stuart, for most Scottish Jacobites the aim was repeal of the Act of Union and an independent Scotland.[36] This divergence of aims was always shelved for another day, never discussed and allowed to fester, but it was to re-emerge at times of crisis with devastating effect. As part of his 'all or nothing' mentality the prince always insisted that he would have all three kingdoms or none (*rien de partage: tout ou rien* – 'no dividing up or partial shares' was his watchword).

So far the Highland army had proved superior to the Hanoverian enemy in speed and mobility, but now George II's government hit back with a valuable weapon of its own with which the Jacobites could not compete: seapower. Although the effect and importance of seapower in the '45 has been absurdly overdone, usually by devotees of historical inevitability, it *did* play a significant part in the early and late stages of the rising, while being irrelevant to the crucial middle chapters.[37] In September the immediate consequence was that Cope, learning that the Jacobites were threatening Edinburgh, marched his army from Inverness to Aberdeen, embarked them and landed them on the Firth of Forth at Dunbar, east of Edinburgh. Meanwhile the Highland army was within striking distance of the Scottish capital, having marched to Falkirk, within cannon shot of Stirling Castle, and then to the environs of Edinburgh, whence they sent out a demand for surrender to the burghers of that city. Within Edinburgh there were divided counsels, with some advocating a fight to the death but a majority, fearful that the city would be put to the sword and sacked as thoroughly as Rome by Alaric or Geiseric, or given over to mass atrocity like Magdeburg in the Thirty Years War, in favour of submission. The surrender terms were all but agreed when the burghers suddenly heard that Cope had landed at Dunbar. This encouraged them to stall, but Charles Edward, abandoning his usual humanitarian 'softly, softly' stance, warned them that he would burn the city to the ground unless he received an immediate surrender. The browbeaten citizens gave in but saved themselves from later accusations of treason by 'accidentally' leaving some of the city gates open, allowing the clansmen to pour in.[38] The upshot of this confused period of alarums and excursions was one of the golden moments in Charles Edward's life when he entered Edinburgh in triumph on 17 September. While the diehard Whigs held aloof, most of Edinburgh was swept up in a maelstrom of euphoria, nostalgia and triumphalism, with the prince at his magnetic best, and Edinburgh's women particularly impressed by his charms. He entered Holyrood House as a conquering hero, and indeed had every reason to feel pleased with himself for, just twenty-eight days after raising the standard at Glenfinnan, he was almost master of Scotland.[39]

There was just one obstacle left: Cope. On paper he easily held the advantage over the Jacobites for, advancing to the relief of Edinburgh, he had the luxury of selecting the field of battle on which he would confront the enemy. This was at Gladsmuir or Prestonpans to the east of the capital, in a strong natural position, with the sea as a natural defence to the north protecting his right flank. He also disposed of powerful artillery, which could have devastated the Highland army if it had made a frontal assualt from the west or south. There was one weak point, which Lord George Murray, who had a superb eye for ground, spotted at once. On the eastern side of Cope's forces was a seemingly impenetrable morass, but one of the men John Roy Stewart had enlisted in Edinburgh knew of a narrow path through it. Travelling at times in Indian file, the clansmen picked their way through the marsh on the night of 20–1 September and fell on Cope's flank at first light. The big guns were captured first, after the inexperienced gunners panicked and fled. Then wave after wave of claymore-wielding clansmen smashed into the Hanoverian army. They acted so quickly that the enemy cavalry were routed almost before they realised what had hit them. Panic spread to the infantry, and the short-lived battle quickly became a rout. The Jacobite officers lost control of their men at this point, with the result that the Highlanders cut loose and butchered as many of the fleeing redcoats as they could catch up with. Cope's army lost more than 300 dead and over 400 wounded, while the Jacobite casualties totalled barely a dozen.[40] Cope fled to Dunbar where, according to Robert Burns, though inaccurately, he was the first general to come with news of his own defeat. The consequences of Prestonpans were dramatic. Except for isolated fortresses like the castles at Stirling and Edinburgh, all of Scotland was in Jacobite hands. The regime in London finally realised the gravity of the situation that faced it, and the London stock market reacted badly, triggering a financial crisis. In a panic George II and his principal minister, the Duke of Newcastle, recalled regular troops from the battlefields of northern Europe (where the king's son the Duke of Cumberland had recently been devastatingly defeated by Marshal Saxe at the Battle of Fontenoy), and called on the Swiss and Dutch to honour their treaty obligations, committing them to provide mercenaries to fight in England in a dire emergency.[41] Charles Edward returned to Edinburgh in triumph and made another stunning entry into the city, this time as a proven conqueror. For a full month he held a glittering court at Holyrood House, with levées, receptions, banquets and balls. On 10 October he issued his manifestos on future policies in England and Scotland, disappointing his more perceptive supporters by the vagueness of his proposals. But, this issue aside, the prince's sojourn at Edinburgh in October 1745 was the high point of his life. These were his great days, the ones he would look back on forever through a nostalgic mist.[42]

The most dramatic consequence of Prestonpans was that the French decided, albeit hesitantly, to commit themselves to the Stuart cause, thus proving the soundness of the prince's voluntarist approach. Astounded at first by his 'go it alone' strategy, Louis XV was sufficiently intrigued to send an envoy to Scotland, the Marquis d'Eguilles, to sound out the true state of affairs. The question of whether to support the Stuart prince occupied many sessions of the Council of State, Louis's inner cabinet, composed at that time of just six ministers of state, of whom only two were outright Jacobite supporters. To make matters worse for the Jacobite cause, their two supporters, the Marquis d'Argenson and Cardinal Tencin loathed each other and supported different factions: Tencin was a supporter of James Francis, while d'Argenson admired the prince. Of the other four, both finance minister Philibert Orry and the man who succeded in late 1745, M. Machault d'Arnouville, were most concerned about the costs of an expedition to Great Britain, while the Comte d'Argenson (the marquis's brother) wanted to concentrate on European warfare. The Duc de Noailles was an advocate of the Americas as the primary focus for French energies, while navy minister the Comte de Maurepas opined that a restored Charles Edward would be more of a threat to France than George II had ever been.[43] Faced with such divided counsels among his ministers, the pathologically indecisive Louis XV opted for a peculiarly modern solution – 'more research' – which was the genesis of the d'Eguilles mission. What the French king should have done was get down to serious planning for an invasion the moment he heard that the clans had risen for the prince, but he believed that he who hesitates is king.[44] His decision to stall was probably the single most important cause of Charles Edward's eventual defeat. Had he acted at once, the entire history of 1745–6 would have been different. The d'Eguilles mission yielded some useful data on the Jacobite grandees, but all the hard intelligence he had to transmit had already been conveyed by the envoys the prince sent from Scotland to Versailles, first the Machiavellian parson George Kelly, one of the Seven Men of Moidart and then an emissary of an altogether superior calibre, the distinguished economist Sir James Steuart of Goodtrees.[45] D'Eguilles's arrival in Scotland on 14 October 1745 was a tremendous fillip for the Jacobites, as it seemed to confirm the truth of all the prince had told them. Even more encouraging was the sequel to Prestonpans when Louis XV concluded a formal pact with 'King James' – the Treaty of

Fontainebleau – giving him co-belligerent status. The Jacobites had thus achieved a level of recognition in wartime which had eluded them for fifty-six years. Moreover, the treaty prevented Dutch troops from serving against the Jacobites, since they were constrained by the articles of a previous capitulation to France. From late October to late December the French worked hard to mount a credible cross-Channel expedition. 15,000 troops, including most of the Scottish and Irish exiles in the service of France, were earmarked for the enterprise, the command was given to the high-born aristocrat the Duc de Richelieu, who thirsted for a marshal's baton, and all necessary shipping assembled in a chain of Channel ports stretching from Ostend to Dieppe.[46]

One of the profound problems that beset the Jacobites (and the French) in 1745–6 was that it took twelve days for events and decisions taken in either Scotland or France to be conveyed to the other side. They were both thus in the position of astronomers gazing at distant stars that had already ceased to exist. The debacle this would engender was realised only gradually, and meanwhile d'Eguilles's presence buoyed up the prince's newly formed council. To this were appointed his Irish favourites O'Sullivan and Sheridan; Perth and Lord George Murray automatically qualified as lieutenant-generals; also coopted were the lords of the feudal north-east and the Lowlands: Pitsligo, Balmerino, Glenbucket, Elcho, Ogilvy, Lewis Gordon, Murray of Broughton – most of whom tended to support the prince in the council's decision-making.[47] Most bizarre of the Lowland lords with a council place was the Earl of Kilmarnock: his motive for joining the Jacobites was bankruptcy, and he famously declared that he would have joined Saracens, Turks or Moslems who set up a standard in the Highlands if he could thereby be relieved of his debts. The other faction on the council largely comprised the clan leaders or (in the case of chiefs who elected not to 'come out' in person but to send a senior representative to lead their men) their deputies: Lochiel, Cluny MacPherson, Keppoch, Lord Nairne, young Clanranald, Stewart of Ardshiel (commanding the Stewart clan), MacDonald of Keppoch, Mackinnon of Skye and Lochgarry (heading the Glengarry regiment).[48] The council met every day to discuss not just policy and grand strategy but day-to-day administration and the conduct of the continuing siege of Edinburgh Castle. Having ridden out the curse of factionalism between 'king's party' and 'prince's party' in France in 1744–5, and then prevented the worst aspects of an Irish-Scottish rift among his followers, the prince found that a new division had arisen: between those invariably loyal to him (Sheridan, O'Sullivan, Tullibardine, Murray of Broughton, Kilmarnock, Pitsligo, Perth, Lord Nairne) and those who took their cue from Lord George (Lochiel and the other clan leaders); invariably there were a few floating voters who oscillated between the two sides. The heterogeneity of motivation among council members was striking. Sincere ideologues joined forces with political adventurers; those excluded from office through proscription of the Tory Party made common cause with politicians taking out an insurance policy; clan chieftains sat in conclave with bankrupts; banished Irish Catholics plotted with covert Scottish republicans. Scottish nationalists hoped to throw off the English yoke; the English working man looked forward to the root and branch dismantling of the regime of money.[49] Like most historical events, the Jacobite rising of 1745 cannot be fitted into any general category without omitting most of the nuances, undertones, subtexts and unique factors of contingency which went into its make-up.

There were perhaps half a dozen days of decision, when momentous issues were decided, during the rising. One of these came on 31 October 1745 when the council passed a motion to invade England. This was one of the most hard-fought triumphs for the prince, and the decision was taken by just one vote. He would not have succeeded at all if John Roy Stewart, colonel of the newly formed Edinburgh regiment, had been on the council. On the other hand, many of his natural supporters were absent that day raising recruits: Pitsligo, Glenbucket, Ogilvy, Lewis Gordon. The prince was supported by his 'old faithfuls': Sheridan, O'Sullivan, Tullibardine, Kilmarnock, Murray of Broughton, Perth and Lord Nairne: Lord George mustered Lochiel, Clanranald, Keppoch, Ardshiel, Glencoe and Lochgarry.[50] The clan leaders objected vociferously to crossing the border into England and advocated sitting tight and consolidating a united Scotland, confident that the French would send an army. One of Murray's best arguments was that if the Jacobites invaded England, the Hanoverians would simply take the opportunity to reconquer Scotland.[51] The prince assured the doubters that he was confident of raising enough men both to invade England and to maintain their position in Scotland, pointing out that the projected French invasion was being launched at *England*, not Scotland, which would prevent George II and his ministers from sending an army north, lest they suffer the notorious fate of Harold Godwinsson in 1066, caught between Harald Hardrada in the north and William of Normandy in the south. The French factor, indeed, was one of the four motifs the prince plugged away at in a bravura display of dialectical skill – a feat impossible to achieve if he really was a Polish blockhead, as his critics allege.[52] It was essential to keep up the momentum and make the French believe they were backing winners, not abject losers. Lord George's alternative strategy was to retreat to the Highlands for a massive recruiting drive, which he alleged could net 24,000 fighting men in all, but to foreign eyes this would look like a craven retreat. Momentum was also the pith of the prince's second main argument, which was that to remain in Scotland risked losing the army through inanition and low morale. Clan armies were notorious for their part-time nature, with warriors slipping away home for the harvest or to visit families, and many a promising anti-English venture in Scotland had perished on just such a rock. Weeks of boredom and guard duty in Edinburgh, with no prospects of hard fighting, good living or loot, would sap and drain away Highland esprit de corps. Continuing his theme of momentum, the prince stressed the need for a second victory, over the armies of Marshal Wade, currently converging on Newcastle. Vanquishing Wade would set England alive, and all the latent Jacobite support there, both in the Tory gentry and among the common people, would then manifest itself.[53] As his fourth and final point, the prince sharply posed the question of how the Highland army was to be financed, fed and equipped if it remained on the defensive in Scotland. The promised treasure ships from France had yet to arrive and would have to run the gauntlet of the Royal Navy to do so. The Hanoverians had cunningly secreted most of the silver in Scotland inside their impregnable fortresses, and soon the Jacobites would either run out of money or be forced to collect the hated Malt Tax, the very impost that had made the Hanoverian regime so unpopular. South of the border, however, were rich pickings. The Jacobites, claiming *de jure* right, had already begun collecting the public moneys, principally the cess and the excise, but the revenue base in Scotland was small, and in England huge.[54]

Yet if the prince won the argument for an invasion of England, he lost the secondary one concerning the itinerary. Charles's instinct was to head straight for Newcastle and a decisive trial of strength with Wade. All the Scots leaders, however, who never relished the prospect of penetrating into England, wanted to postpone the final day of reckoning and therefore grasped eagerly at Lord George's suggestion that the route south should be a western one. If there was latent Jacobite support in England – and Lord George always doubted there really was – it was supposed to be found in Lancashire, Staffordshire and Wales. A march through the north-west, admittedly at first through hostile territory, would soon take them into these promised lands and give the squires of north-west England and Wales the chance to do something more than drink the health of the 'Pretender'.[55] The prince fumed that Lord George's ideas undermined the logic of his own carefuly reasoned scenario for an invasion of England and was really his lieutenant-general's way of securing by the back door what he had failed to accomplish at the front. But this time Lord George won a clear majority for his ideas. It was to be invasion, then, but by the north-westerly route, down through Cumbria into Lancashire and on to Staffordshire, a sweep through the alleged Jacobite heartland. Some of the prince's ideas were still valid, as the prospect of battle with the detested English ended all signs of dropping away in morale among the clansmen, his continued progress south encouraged Versailles, and large amounts of public money were uplifted by an efficient system of tax collection – something that so infuriated the Hanoverian government that they declared all tax collection for the 'Pretender' an express act of treason.[56] Nevertheless, both Charles Edward's original scheme and Lord George Murray's emendation contained some serious flaws. In the first place, the intelligence, communication and espionage system of the Highland army was lamentable. Next, there was no effective communication between the Jacobites and either of their putative allies, the French and the English Jacobites. The prince did not know from day to day what stage French preparations had reached or what their immediate intentions were.[57] In the case of the English Jacobites, he sent a few letters south to the pro-Stuart grandees like Sir Watkin Williams Wynn and the 4th Earl of Barrymore, but these were intercepted. Beyond this, Charles seems to have expected that once he crossed the border he would be greeted with rapture and there would be spontaneous armed insurrections on his behalf. He was right that the Whig/Protestant/Hanoverian nexus rested on too narrow a base, but wrong to think that necessarily implied a commitment to Jacobitism.[58] The blunt truth was that 90 per cent of the population of Great Britain did not care who won the dynastic struggle, but would join in on the winning side once it was clear which that was.

It was agreed that the Jacobite army, only 5,000 strong – a perilously small number for such an ambitious operation – would march through the Lowlands by two different routes (one easterly, the other westerly) and rendezvous outside Carlisle. Meanwhile the prince laid his plans to ensure that the enemy did not recover Scotland while he was away and thus cut him off from his base. He appointed the Earl of Strathallan to head the second army being recruited in Scotland, with Oliphant of Gask as his deputy, Lord Lewis Gordon to be his strong right arm in the north-east and young Glengarry to raise the hesitant or still recalcitrant clans in the Highlands proper; the Glengarry regiment in England would meanwhile be commanded by his kinsman Donald MacDonald of Lochgarry. The prince set off for the border on 1 November, taking Elcho's cavalry and the clan regiments with him on an easterly route as if he intended to attack Newcastle, then swung west to rendezvous at Dalkeith with Lord George Murray, the Athollmen, the newly formed Edinburgh regiment and the Lowland contingents, who had marched via Peebles and Moffat with the baggage and artillery.[59] The prince spent his first night on English soil on 8 November, then proceeded to a vigorous siege of Carlisle. Marshal Wade, who had marched north with an army in early October, tried to cross the Pennines to relieve Carlisle but was driven back by heavy snowdrifts. In despair at news of the Wade debacle, the citizens of Carlisle surrendered both town and castle on the 18th after perfunctory resistance.[60] Murray's column had disappointed the prince by somehow losing all their tents on the march through the Lowlands, so that henceforth the warriors of the Jacobite army had to be billeted in towns and, because of the pressure on accommodation, the march south through Cumberland and Westmorland was again a two-column affair, with the prince's contingent always a day behind Lord George's until they reached Preston.[61] The heroism of the clansmen and other Scots in braving snow, rain, freezing temperatures and steep gradients in the fells south of Penrith can never be overemphasised: in such conditions their rate of march was amazing, sometimes up to twenty-seven miles a day. The prince, euphoric and exuberant, marched at the head of his troops, enduring all the hardships of fording rivers and uphill treks, refusing to go on horseback. A few English recruits dribbled in, notably an educated young man named John Daniel, who famously described Charles Edward on the road to Preston:

> The first time I saw this loyal army was betwixt Lancaster and Garstang: the brave Prince marching on foot at their head like Cyrus or a Trojan hero, drawing admiration and love from all those who beheld him, raising their long dejected hearts and solacing their minds with the happy prospect of another Golden Age. Struck with this charming sight and seeming invitation *leave your nets and follow me*, I felt a paternal ardour pervade my veins.[62]

The two columns reunited at Preston, and another tense council meeting followed, when Lord George suggested that the prince should cut his losses and return to Scotland: they had marched into Lancashire to give the English Jacobites ample time to join them, but there was still no sign of them. On this occasion the prince produced the Marquis d'Eguilles as his trump card, with the French envoy stressing the bad impression that would be created in Versailles. Grudgingly, Lord George agreed to march to Manchester and into Staffordshire, but the atmosphere as the council broke up was ominous, with all present feeling that the real issues had merely been shelved.[63] The two-day sojourn in Manchester on 29–30 November seemed to prove the prince right, for the advent of more than 300 volunteers enabled the Jacobites to form a Manchester regiment, and the prince's party further pointed out that here was a large town of 30,000 people that could conceivably have resisted them but showed no inclination to do so. Nevertheless, there was yet another acrimonious council meeting, this time with Lord Nairne's vote only just swinging things in the prince's favour.[64] Charles Edward was still euphoric and confident and seemed to take Lord George's warning that he would march the length of Derbyshire but no further as a mere rhetorical flourish. Murray was at his best as a tactician in the following days, and all of his skill was needed for, having easily outpaced Wade, whose army was following south in a ponderous track on the other side of the Pennines, the Jacobites were now entering the orbit of a second Hanoverian army commanded by the Duke of Cumberland. To make Cumberland think that Wales was still the Jacobites' destination, Lord George brilliantly decoyed him. Learning that Cumberland was nearby, at Stafford, he feinted towards Congleton as if his target was Wales, then swung back in an arc to Ashbourne, which the prince had already reached.[65] With the two columns once more united, the Highland army entered the town of Derby in triumph on the evening of 4 September, just 127 miles from London. Morale among the clansmen was sky-high as they cleaned their guns and honed their claymores. Everyone expected a battle with Cumberland within forty-eight hours and all were confident they would win it. The prince meanwhile had moved from aplomb to complacency and even arrogance. Convinced he was on a winning streak, he made no attempt to lobby or win over the Scots leaders ahead of the council Murray convened for 5 December. He remained convinced that the meeting had been called purely to decide on the itinerary and dispositions as the army approached London.[66]

To his stupefaction he learned that Murray and the clan leaders had had enough and were determined on retreat. Calmly Murray explained that he had given the English Jacobites every chance and there was still no sign of them; it was therefore better that the army return to Scotland before it was engulfed by superior numbers. All the signs were that there were three Hanoverian armies in the field: Cumberland close at hand, at Stafford; Wade somewhere in their rear; and a third force barring the way to London at Northampton. Since Jacobite intelligence was so lamentable, neither Murray nor the prince knew what the enemy's true situation was, but Charles made the mistake of rebutting this tactical appraisal with another general exhortation for 'just one last push'. The problem was that the council members had heard all this before, at Carlisle, at Preston, in Manchester. Now they demanded to see documentary evidence from the prince of his putative support – letters from the English Jacobites or from Louis XV. To general astonishment the prince was forced to admit he had neither.[67] At this even erstwhile supporters like the Duke of Perth became disillusioned and sided with Murray. Sensing the game slipping out of his control, Charles asked for an adjournment until the early evening, hoping to rally support by one-to-one lobbying. He made little progress with this during the afternoon, but by the time of the second council meeting, around 6 p.m., Murray was able to produce his trump card in the form of 'solid' physical evidence. He introduced into the council a man named Dudley Bradstreet, a paid agent of the Duke of Cumberland and an operative of high calibre, a master of disinformation. Calmly and lucidly Bradstreet told how he had just come from London and that there was an army of 9,000 men under Generals Hawley and Oglethorpe barring the way to the capital at Northampton. At this the prince became distraught. 'That fellow will do me more harm than all the Elector's army!' he bellowed.[68] Bradstreet was then ushered out and a vote taken. Although young Clanranald was the lone voice supporting him, the prince later claimed that 'he could not prevail upon one single person to support him'. Faced by an almost unanimous vote to return to Scotland, he fumed, raged and blustered: 'You ruin, abandon and betray me if you do not march on,' were his reported words.[69] Finding even his 'old faithfuls' like Tullibardine among the ranks of his opponents, Charles salved his hurt pride with the following outburst: 'In future I shall summon no more councils, since I am accountable to nobody for my actions but to God and my father, and therefore shall no longer ask or accept advice.'[70]

The decision at Derby has long been disputed, but in revolutionary terms it is unquestionable that Charles Edward was right and Lord George wrong. The '45 had been a gamble from day one, and the gamble had paid off spectacularly. All the evidence suggests that Murray and the clan leaders lost their nerve and folded their cards at the crucial moment. From a military point of view, Lord George's arguments were bogus. Wade was still lumbering in a long way to the north and on the other side of the Pennines, so was out of the picture; Cumberland could at most have got 4,000 weary troops between the Jacobites and London, and who could doubt the outcome of a fight between such men and 5,500 zealous Scots? As for the wholly fictitious third army at Northampton, Bradstreet's own words are eloquent: 'Observe that there was not nine men at Northampton to oppose them, much less 9,000.'[71] Murray and the Scots leaders were defeatist at the vital moment, with Murray asserting that if the Jacobites advanced, the enemy would grow stronger as they grew weaker; all the evidence is against this, and Murray had only his own gloomy thoughts to buttress the argument: it remained a mere assertion. In fact, the authorities in London were by this stage in a state of panic 'scarce to be credited', in Henry Fielding's words. They knew very well that the proletarians and poor of London had no love for them and would stand idly by until they saw who the winners were. Moreover, even historians who attempt to prove the impossible by claiming that Cumberland still had the military whip hand, concentrate narrowly on the purely military situation and ignore the wider political dimensions of the crisis in December 1745. The index of Bank of England stock fell from 141 in October 1745 to 127 in December, then fell further and did not rise above 125 until mid-January 1746.[72] French observers thought an advance from Derby on 6 December would have had one of two consequences. Either there would be a general collapse of business confidence, with panic-stricken investors trying to withdraw funds, or national debt fundholders, seeing their investments in danger of annihilation, would have colluded with London Jacobites and arranged a coup d'état ahead of the arrival of the Jacobite army. As it was, the retreat from Derby let the cat out of the bag in spectacular fashion. It freed the Hanoverians from the abiding nightmare that they might havc to fight a war on two fronts; it alerted them that there was no prior collusion between Charles Edward and Versailles, and that the expedition being prepared at Boulogne by Richelieu was an independent venture; and it proved once and for all that the alleged fifth column of English Jacobites was a paper tiger.[73]

The trek back to Scotland in December was a dismal and dispiriting affair. Once the clansmen realised they were not going on to London but retracing their steps on 6 December, there was an eerie, ululating whoop of despair as they began the march. No longer did the prince march at their head like a hero, but rode in the rear, sullen, depressed and broken. 'It is all over, we shall never some back again,' Sheridan remarked.[74] The prince never recovered from the psychic shock of Derby. Whereas on the march south he had regularly gone to bed at 11 p.m. and been up again, at 3 a.m., almost panting for the day's trek, on the retreat he slept late, drank a lot and often delayed the day's march. Now too the Highland army faced an entirely different situation. They had Cumberland at their heels, Wade ahead of them, and a hostile civilian population to face. The English who had cheered them or at least acquiesced in their presence in the towns, now exhibited a defiant and peevish face. Discipline, so impressive on the way south, also broke down, never entirely, it is true, but still to an alarming extent.[75] There were elements of both bluff and reality in the way officers distributed powder and cartridges to the men in expectation of a battle with Wade. Partly it was a morale-building exercise, but partly it was genuine fear. The truly amazing thing about Marshal Wade's supine performance was that he failed to intercept the Jacobites both on their way south *and* their way north. If he had been even halfway competent, he should have crossed the Pennines after the Jacobites moved south from Carlisle and cut off their retreat to Scotland.[76] As it was, the retreat to Scotland was a sombre affair. The Jacobites had to put up with sniper fire and summary execution of any stragglers. This was the pattern in the towns of Ashbourne, Leek, Macclesfield and Stockport. At Manchester the prince's patience snapped, and at the first sign of disloyalty, he exacted a hefty fine of £2,500 from the burghers.[77] There was further tension between him and Lord George, for Charles resented any semblance of 'running away' from the pursuing Cumberland, and was only narrowly talked out of spending a second night in Manchester out of sheer bravado. At Preston, though, he dug in his heels and insisted on a two-day stopover. The consequence was that both Cumberland and Wade's vanguard came perilously close. Charles Edward still insisted he was returning to 'prepared positions' and was itching for a fight with the Hanoverian troops for reasons of credibility. Leaving Lancaster for Kendal on the morning of 15 December, Lord George could not resist a taunt: 'As Your Royal Highness is always for battles, be the circumstances what they may, I now offer you one in three hours from this with the army of Wade which is only three miles from us.'[78]

The prince took his revenge by entrusting the artillery and baggage in the rearguard to Lord George, with strict orders that not a cannonball was to be left behind. Not surprisingly, for every day of the march Cumberland closed the gap on the retreating Jacobites. Finally, on the afternoon of the 18th, he caught up with Lord George and the unwieldy baggage wagons as they toiled up the dreadful road to Penrith. All afternoon a running fight raged in and around the approaches to Clifton village. As dusk fell and the Highlanders seemed in danger of being surrounded, Lord George learned that his assailants were not Cumberland's main force but the 2,000 men of his vanguard. Here was a great opportunity to commit the entire Jacobite army, wipe out Cumberland's front-runners and tarnish his image with another Hanoverian defeat.[79] Yet the prince refused to heed Lord George's pleas, pressed on to Carlisle, and sent back only sufficient numbers to prevent Murray and the rearguard from being engulfed. The Scots leaders were infuriated at the lost opportunity. As Lord Elcho remarked tartly: 'As there was formerly a contradiction to make the army halt when it was necessary to march, so now there was one to march and shun fighting when there would never be a better opportunity for it.'[80] Lord George made the best of the reinforcements, fortunately the crack troops under Cluny MacPherson and Stewart of Ardshiel. As dusk fell Cumberland's men took up defensive positions in the enclosures around Clifton village, but they were soon winkled out by yet another claymore-wielding charge from the intrepid Highlanders. For half an hour there was some nasty fighting, sometimes euphemistically described as a 'skirmish'. The casualty figures convey the reality. About 100 of Cumberland's men joined the casualty lists, but only about a dozen were listed as dead; the Jacobites recorded the same number of dead with only one wounded – an indication of the courage displayed in their frontal assault – but they decisively stopped Cumblerland's pursuit.[81] He paused for a day to lick his wounds while both detachments of the Jacobite army pressed on to Carlisle. Here the prince made another bad decision. He elected to leave a garrison behind in the city to defy Cumberland. The 250 members of the Manchester regiment plus about 100 Jacobites in the service of France were left behind in what was to any sober observer a suicide mission. When Cumberland arrived, he used his heavy cannon to blast his way through to the castle and compel an early surrender; the luckless men of the Manchester regiment, unprotected by any cartels of war, were led away to trial and barbarous execution for treason.[82]

The prince crossed back into Scotland on his twenty-fifth birthday, having completed one of the great exploits in the history of warfare, albeit unsuccessful. On a 500-mile round trip he had lost just two dozen men and given the slip to two separate armies. He found a mixed picture awaiting him. As soon as he had crossed the border south, the Hanoverians, as Lord George had predicted, reoccupied Edinburgh. Although Cumberland returned to London after Carlisle, a second Hanoverian army had been formed under General Henry

'Hangman' Hawley, a brutal martinet who had been appointed to succeed Wade; that was the elderly marshal's sole punishment for his lacklustre performance in 1745.[83] To balance this, the Jacobites had achieved some signal successes: Lord Lewis Gordon had routed loyalist forces assembled by the turncoat Skye chief Norman Macleod; Lord Lovat had finally brought out his Frasers for the prince; a second Jacobite army had been formed after some barnstorming recruitment drives; and, most gratifying of all, Lord John Drummond had arrived from France with 1,100 men of the Irish Brigade.[84] This seemed to indicate that the French were finally coming, but in fact Richelieu and his political masters were already losing their appetite for anything other than 'pump-priming' the rebellion in Scotland; the logistical problems of switching an army originally earmarked for an invasion of England to one destined for north of the border were simply too much for them. By the beginning of February 1746 Louis XV had laid aside all thoughts of a major pro-Stuart enterprise.[85] Yet, ignorant of these developments, Charles Edward temporarily recovered some of his composure. His army occupied Glasgow, where more money tributes were exacted. After a week in the city, where hostility to the Jacobites was far more evident than in the Scottish capital, the clan chiefs proposed a reoccupation of Edinburgh, to force Hawley to come to them. The prince demurred and opted instead for a siege of Stirling Castle – another attempt at siegecraft doomed to failure; the taking of citadels was simply not the Jacobites' strong suit.[86] Decision-making entered a limbo period when the prince fell ill with influenza and lay on his sick bed from 5 to 16 January 1746. This was the first of three major illnesses that were to prostrate him in the next months: flu in January, pneumonia in February and scarlet fever in March, unquestionably all maladies that were stress related.[87] Lord George exhibited his usual blundering lack of empathy by choosing the prince's invalid period to add another notch to the escalating series of conflicts with him. Since Charles had declared at Derby that he would no longer summon councils, Lord George told him it was now imperative to appoint an inner cabinet of five or six regimental commanders. An invalid still, the prince hit back with one of his most lucid and incisive letters ever, pointing up all Lord George's faults and containing the typical (and very modern) Charles Edward flourish: 'When I came into Scotland I knew well enough what I was to expect from my enemies, but I little foresaw what I would meet with from my friends.'[88]

The siege of Stirling quickly petered out in fiasco, as the French so-called expert in siege warfare who had come over with Drummond proved spectacularly incompetent. Meanwhile Hawley's advance guard and the Jacobite van had a number of inconclusive skirmishes, clearly the prelude to a major battle. With 8,000 men now under his command, Lord George Murray faced the prospect with confidence. On two successive days he drew up his army near Bannockburn, hoping to tempt Hawley to attack him and thus repeat Robert the Bruce's glorious victory over the English in 1314. When Hawley refused to take the bait, Murray decided to seize the high ground to the south-west of Falkirk, a mile from Hawley's camp, effectively forcing him into combat. When Hawley realised around noon on 17 January that the entire Jacobite army (except for some 1,200 still futilely pursuing the siege of Stirling) was moving into position on Falkirk moor, he ordered his own troops to the summit to contest the high ground. The two sides were almost equally matched in numbers and firepower.[89] After probing for two hours and failing to winkle the well-disciplined clansmen from their positions, at around 4 p.m. Hawley ordered a frontal attack; Clifton had taught him that the Highlanders were more adapted to night engagements, so he wanted to settle the issue before dark. Yet only a madman would have done as Hawley did, and order 700 dragoons to charge a wall of 4,000 clansmen. The cavalry took a devastating volley at a ten-yard range, and 80 of them fell dead on the spot. Their comrades broke and fled: two of the regiments rode down their own infantry while the third was cut to pieces by Highland berserkers. The blood of the Jacobite warriors was now up, but unfortunately this meant a breakdown of discipline. Two of Murray's best regiments broke away to pursue the dragoons and the weak Glasgow militia, momentarily exposing the Jacobite flank to Hawley's infantry, but Lord George's reserves charged, claymore in hand, and routed four of the six regiments on the Hanoverian left in a matter of minutes.[90] Total catastrophe loomed for Hawley but, fortunately for him, his best commander General Huske made an orderly retreat with the three regiments he commanded. In the gathering gloom it soon became impossible for the Jacobites to see what was going on, and they had to infer the course of the battle from noises and sounds.

Ultra-caution led the confused Jacobite chain of command to be uncertain of the outcome on the Hanoverian right, Murray did not press his advantage, and so Hawley escaped the annihilation which would surely have been his fate if darkness had not supervened. Although the Jacobites were left in possession of the field, and proceeded to occupy Falkirk that night, their victory was not the total triumph it would have been if battle had been joined a couple of hours earlier. The fighting had been fierce, with some 50 Jacobites killed and 70 wounded, but Hawley sustained much greater losses, with a casualty roster of over 1,000, including more than 400 men and 20 officers killed.[91]

Seldom has a victory been greeted with less elation. Recriminations flew thick and fast as each of the Jacobite commanders tried to blame the others for the bitter outcome that total victory had slipped from their grasp; Hawley had made good his escape and could be reinforced by sea. With the prince still ill at Bannockburn, where he was being nursed by his mistress Clementina Walkinshaw, the Highland grandees seized the chance to implement the idea they had nurtured ever since Prestonpans: a retreat to the Highlands in an attempt to raise the entire fighting strength of the Jacobite clans. Murray claimed that retreat was essential, since 2,000 disgruntled clansmen had deserted in the bitterly disappointing aftermath of Falkirk. No historian has ever been able adequately to explain how the Jacobite leadership imploded in the ten crucial days of 17–28 January, but Lord George Murray for one seems to have suffered some kind of a breakdown. Whatever the causes, on the evening of 29 January he sent the prince a remonstrance, signed by Lovat, Lochiel, Clanranald, Keppoch, Ardshiel and Lochgarry, demanding an immediate withdrawal to the Highlands. When he read the document, the prince was incandescent with fury. 'Have I lived to see this?' he exclaimed.[92] In vain he expostulated that history had never before known a case of an army retreating after winning a victory. Lucidly, he rebutted Murray's specious arguments and demonstrated with faultless logic that the new 'strategy' would lead to disaster. But he bowed to the wishes of the majority, albeit with bad grace: 'After all this I know I have an army that I cannot command any further than the chief officers please, and therefore if you are all resolved upon it I must yield; but I take God to witness that it is with the greatest reluctance, and that I wash my hands of the fatal consequences which I foresee but cannot help.'[93] Reluctantly Charles Edward agreed to take the clan regiments into the Highlands, while Murray, the cavalry and the Lowland regiments wound round the east coast via Aberdeen and Montrose to Inverness. The prince was soon deep in his second bout of illness, while his men ploughed through snowdrifts and winter conditions so ferocious that Cumberland, newly arrived in Edinburgh, did not even attempt to follow. Murray's march round the coast encountered even more terrible conditions, especially on the road out of Aberdeen.[94] Three weeks later Cumberland advanced cautiously up to Aberdeen, taking care to build up his commissariat and provision his forces adequately. His long stopover there handed the initiative to the Jacobites. Murray and the clan leaders implanted their Highland strategy, overly confident since at this stage Cumberland made few attempts to impede them. Murray's strategy was fourfold: somehow to pen the Hanoverians in Aberdeen so that French ships bringing troops and money could continue to land on the east coast; besiege Forts William and Augustus; beat off any enemy reinforcements entering the Highlands; and disperse the hostile forces under Lord Loudoun in the territory to the north of Inverness. March 1746 at first saw the Jacobites everywhere successful, but it was the falsest of false dawns. Fort Augustus fell after two days, but Fort William proved a tougher nut. The Jacobite Earl of Cromarty ended the Hanoverian presence north of Inverness with a forceful campaign. Murray, taking personal command in the central Highlands, scored success after success but was once again defeated by a fortress – this time the Duke of Atholl's stronghold at Blair Castle which Murray lacked the numbers to reduce.[95]

As if by a kind of malign pre-established harmony, no sooner was the prince well again after three months as an invalid than Jacobite fortunes dipped alarmingly. Although the failure to take Blair Castle was essentially because of superior Hanoverian numbers, the debacle at Fort William was the result of incompetence pure and simple (and once again the French 'expert' in siegecraft was to blame). Seeing the inept way the siege was being conducted, the Fort William garrison made a sudden sortie, destroyed most of the Jacobite heavy artillery and captured the rest.[96] Meanwhile failures in administration and commissariat plus shortage of money were leaving Charles Edward's troops hungry, and so the desertion rate multiplied. The crisis over money became catastrophe with the loss of the *Prince Charles*. This was a French ship specifically designed for the relief of France's ally in the Highlands: it was conveying not just Berwick's regiment of Scots and Irish exiles in the service of France, but 14 chests of pistols and sabres, 13 barrels of gunpowder and, crucially, £13,600 in English gold and 1,500 guineas laden in 5 chests. On 25 March the *Prince Charles* reached Pentland Firth but was spotted by four Royal Navy cruisers. After a five-hour chase the French treasure ship ran aground; not only were all Berwick's men taken prisoner but the money was lost.[97] This was a disaster of almost inconceivable magnitude. There was now no hope for the Jacobites unless there was a sudden rising in London or a massive French landing, but at this very moment a courier arrived from Versailles to inform the prince that Louis XV had abandoned all thoughts of a major French expedition to Scotland. Instead of a coup d'état in London, Charles Edward now received the coup de grâce from Cumberland. Travelling at unwonted speed, the Hanoverian duke left Aberdeen on 8 April, heading for Inverness and in command of a well-fed and well-equipped army of 9,000 men. He took the Jacobites by surprise, for their regiments were still scattered all over the Highlands in pursuit of Lord George's heterogeneous strategy.[98] In something close to panic the prince ordered them back to Inverness with all speed. Yet the velocity of Cumberland's advance took him to Nairn, just ten miles from Inverness, on 14 April, at which date the contingents of Cluny MacPherson, Lord Cromarty, Mackinnon, Barisdale and Lord Lovat were still absent, as well as large numbers of Camerons, Clanranald MacDonalds, MacGregors and Mackenzies, leaving the prince about 3,000 short of his nominal muster roll.[99] To try to square the circle or at least significantly reduce the odds against him, the prince elected for a night march on Cumberland's camp at Nairn on the evening of 15–16 April. The idea was for three columns to travel through the heather by separate routes, rendezvous at 1 a.m. outside Nairn and then fall on the Hanoverian encampment at first light, in a rerun of Prestonpans. Yet everything that could go wrong with this stratagem did so. The columns were late in setting out, frequently got lost because the so-called guides provided by the Mackintoshes turned out not to know the terrain in any detail and had grossly underestimated the time it would take to complete a ten-mile march on narrow tracks, and the moor over which they marched was plashy and foggy; fiasco was almost complete when the three columns ended up blundering into each other. At 1 a.m., the time set for rendezvous, the Jacobite vanguard was still four miles from its target, having completed little more than a mile an hour since departure. Amid a welter of recriminations and blame-shifting among the leaders, with Charles Edward once again claiming that he had been betrayed, the decisions was taken to return to base.[100] The weary clansmen arrived back at headquarters at Culloden House on Drummossie Moor around 6 a.m. Exhausted and famished Highlanders threw themselves to the ground to grab a few hours' sleep before the battle which everyone now knew was imminent.

Much has been written about the half-hour battle that commenced shortly after midday, but the essence of it was that the Jacobites were beaten before they began. In one of his self-destructive moments, increasingly frequent after Derby, the prince had already (14 April) rejected Lord George Murray's advice to fight on a far more advantageous battleground on open ground near Dalcross Castle and had insisted on Drummossie Moor, terrain far less suitable for the Highland army's main weapon, the frontal charge. His men were tired and starving, and because of the regiments still straggling in or miles away on the road, he had just 5,000 men to pit against Cumberland's 9,000. O'Sullivan, the prince's military adviser, had failed to take into account the funnelling effect of the stone walls in Culloden Park, which hemmed the Jacobite front line into a narrow space no more than 300 yards wide. The Jacobites were drawn up in a higgledy-piggledy way, with men joining the left wing at the very last moment and the MacDonald clansmen sullen because they had not been given the 'place of honour' on the right wing.[101] Instead of giving the order to charge once the enemy were within range, the prince, acting as battle commander for the first and only occasion, wasted time by attempting complex but futile flanking manoeuvres, meanwhile exposing his troops to accurate artillery fire.[102] When the order to charge was finally given, the clansmen achieved all that raw courage could achieve but it was not enough. Clan Chattan (the confederacy of minor clans) positioned in the centre hurled themselves on the enemy and nearly succeeded in breaking the front line until being repulsed by sheer weight of numbers. The Athollmen on the right supported them but were badly mauled by close-range fire from Cumberland's best regiments.[103] Many of the other clan regiments did not distinguish themselves. The Camerons behaved badly and fled after taking flanking fire from Cumberland's Scots allies, the Campbells, not even bothering to attend to their chief, Lochiel, who had been wounded in both legs; fortunately for him, he was helped off the field by a handful of loyal retainers. The MacDonalds on the left never got into the fight. Keppoch was so enraged by their behaviour that he charged back alone towards the enemy to shame them and was at once dropped in his tracks by a Hanoverian marksman, thus becoming the only battlefield death among the Jacobite council members.[104] Cumberland's men next advanced on the Jacobite second line, mainly comprising the Scots and Irish regulars in the service of France. The Irish under Brigadier Walter Stapleton on the Jacobite left gave a good account of themselves, retreating in good order while providing covering fire for the fleeing MacDonalds, while on the right Elcho's cavalry were the heroes of the hour, halting by staunch courage an encircling movement by Cumberland's dragoons that would have scooped Charles Edward himself into the net. The defeated Jacobites streamed off the field, but only those mounted or fleet of foot escaped the fury of Cumberland's pursuers, who butchered without mercy all those they overhauled; even some of the exhausted veterans of the night march who had never woken from their slumbers to take part in the battle were cut down as they slept. About 1,000 Jacobites perished on the field of battle, but another 1,000 or so were slaughtered in the 'no quarter' aftermath. Cumberland, who habitually under-reported his losses, posted a casualty list of around 400 omitting any seriously wounded who later died of their injuries. Nevertheless, there could be no disguising the fact that the Jacobites had sustained a major defeat.[105]

It had been agreed that in the event of a defeat the Jacobites would muster at Ruthven in Badenoch between 17 and 20 April. About 4,000 Jacobites foregathered there, including the fresh and intact regiments of Lord Ogilvy and Cluny MacPherson. Considering the gravity of the defeat at Culloden they were in remarkably good heart and, if they could only secure reliable food supplies, were willing to carry on fighting or at the worst disperse into the Highlands and fight in guerrilla warfare. Yet all their hopes were dashed by a *sauve qui peut* message from the prince: 'Let every man seek his safety in the best way he can.'[106] Although Charles assured them he intended to go back to France and return with a powerful army, the impression was left that he was running away. Depressed, dispirited and fuelled by paranoid feelings of betrayal, badly advised by evil counsellors like Sheridan, who exaggerated the disaster at Culloden, the prince had got it into his head that he could trust no one and had to get away to France as fast as possible. His disconsolate army drifted away, now an easy prey to Cumberland's dubious mercy. The prince to some extent retrieved his reputation by his six-month escapade in the heather, forever one step ahead of the questing redcoats and, in refutation of his paranoia, never betrayed by the Scots even with a bounty of £30,000 (about £2 million in today's money) on his head.[107] He arrived in France in October, was greeted as a hero, but soon fell foul of Louis XV and was expelled from French territory in 1748. After eleven years of ineffectual plotting, he saw Jacobite hopes finally extinguished by Admiral Hawke's crushing naval victory at Quiberon in 1759. He spent most of the rest of his unhappy life as an alcoholic.[108] Cumberland and the government in London exacted a harsh and ferocious reprisal for the rebellion. Around 120 rebels were executed, including most of the high-ranking Jacobite lords who were captured, and 936 men were transported to penal colonies in the Americas. A raft of legislation in 1746–7 banned Highland dress (such as the plaid) and destroyed the clan system. The Abolition of Heritable Jurisdictions Act of 1747 ended the judicial and military power of clan and feudal leaders in Scotland. The ordinary crofters' herds of sheep and cattle were systematically pillaged, and the estates of all landowners who had come out for Charles Edward were confiscated.[109] Government troops were stationed in the Highlands, and Scotland was for at least a decade an occupied country. The vindictiveness of the authorities evinced the fear they had been living under and their tacit acknowledgement that they had just faced what was to be the greatest revolutionary threat to the State in the eighteenth century. The Stuart prince never deviated from his belief that at Derby he had had a heaven-sent opportunity to topple the Hanoverian government but that the Scottish leaders, with their tunnel-vision state of mind, had prevented this – though, as has been pointed out, in a crisis states of mind are all important and cannot be gainsaid.[110] The consensus of historians is that Charles Edward was right. Had he been successful, he would have been regarded as one of the great revolutionaries in history instead of a heroic failure. The most learned commentator on the military aspect of the '45 concludes thus: 'Yes, Prince Charles should have advanced from Derby, for that course offered a realistic, if incalculable chance of success, as against the near certainty of the destruction of the armed Jacobite cause.'[111]

9
Evolutionary Jacobitism

The '45 was a stunning demonstration of revolutionary voluntarism which failed only because of the human weakness of Charles Edward's accomplices. But was it in the end anything more than a transfer of power within a given socio-economic system, a change of ruling dynasty, simply a violent version of the meaningless oscillation that takes place between two parties in a modern social democratic nation-state, at best a coup d'état against the ossified one-party system of the Whigs? The transfer-of-power view has been popular but it is heavily dependent on a perception of Jacobitism as purely a movement of nostalgic reaction, sustained by outmoded ideologies such as the divine right of kings. In fact, even at the level of ideology the Jacobite movement had undergone numerous transmogrifications, and once again it must be stressed how important is an awareness of chronology. Whereas divine right was important in the period 1689–1715, after the 1715 rising it was increasingly replaced by the 'Country' ideology, with its emphasis on government corruption and, in Scotland, by the mystical providentialism typical of the Episcopalian north-east. In the period 1745–59 the ideology of Jacobitism mainly focused on social grievances, anticipating John Wilkes and the radicals.[1] Charles Edward, under the tutelage of men like Sir James Steuart of Goodtrees and the industrialist John Holker, held himself forth as the champion of the dispossessed and the wretched of the earth. Part of his high talent as a revolutionary was his understanding that a man who could raise the entire body of forty-odd Scottish clans under his banner would have an almost irresistible army of 30,000 men at his command. It was only clan Campbell, the richest, most populous and most powerful clan in the Highlands that stood in his way. It is significant that the Campbells were present in numbers at Culloden on Cumberland's side and that their stranglehold on the Highlands was the very factor that persuaded most of the other clans either to declare for the Stuart prince or remain neutral.[2] In short, anti-Campbell sentiment rather than pure ideological commitment to the Stuarts was the main spur in the Highlands, which was why chiefs with a lot to lose, such as Cameron of Lochiel and Cluny MacPherson took security for their estates from the prince and also why the struggle in the Highlands in 1745–6 so often took on the appearance of small clans ranged against the Campbells.[3] It would become clear later that this was no accident, that Jacobitism as the shield and buckler of the weak and dispossed was an important part of its profile.

The appeal of the Jacobites for what was usually referred to in the eighteenth century as 'the lower sort of people' is a complex issue to resolve, for three main reasons. The first is that the common people in the eighteenth century – whether we refer to them contemptuously in the manner of the Hanoverians as 'the mob' , or more respectfully, following the example of George Rudé, as 'the crowd' – used Jacobite slogans to sanctify and legitimate riots about immediate and obviously economic issues: prices, turnpike roads, enclosures, the seizure of profiteerers' goods, the introduction of a new industrial process, the curtailment of a traditional form of transport or any other customary right. The second is that the proscribed nature of the English Jacobite party on the one hand, and the passage of the Riot Act on the other, make the subject peculiarly difficult to explore, so that much work on popular Jacobitism is of a pioneering variety.[4] The third is that economic and social issues which had a negligible or merely tangential relationship to Jacobitism were invariably associated with it by government propaganda – during the 'Robinocracy' (the twenty-year dominance of Sir Robert Walpole in English politics in the 1720s and 1730s) this was a reflex Walpolian ploy to try to discredit the opposition. The Jacobites were 'fed back' by black propaganda into any and every social disturbance, as can be seen in the agitation over the Excise Act in 1733.[5] Despite the excesses of Walpole and his acolytes, anticipating in many ways the outrageous hyperbole of Senator Joseph McCarthy over communism in the USA of the 1950s, the Whig/Hanoverian ruling nexus was right to fear the appeal of Jacobitism for the common man and to identify a strong strain of Jacobitism in the Tory Party, which endured long years of exile in the political wilderness. The alleged Jacobitism of the Tory Party in 1715–45 is highly disputed academic territory,[6] but the convergence of the principles and ideas of the banished Stuarts with political radicalism receives interesting confirmation from an examination of the personalities and electoral support of the Tories in this era, which make it clear that eighteenth-century Tories were already showing signs of the heterodox orientation Disraeli would urge on them in the nineteenth.[7] In cases where we have a complete picture, as in Derby in the 1734 election, we see that Tory voters are frameworkers, knitters, butchers, tailors, brick-makers, wool-combers, blacksmiths and tanners, in contrast to those voting for the Whigs: lords, squires, aldermen and lawyers.[8] This was in line with the general tenor of the Tory Party. Gilfrid Lawson, a Tory MP (for Cumberland) opposed Walpole's 1732 Salt Tax on the ground that it would fall hardest on the poor. Thomas Brampton, who was to have led the Essex Jacobites in 1744 in an uprising to coincide with the French landing at Maldon, was clearly something of a radical.[9]

Assertions that there was an attachment to the House of Stuart among the labouring classes were frequently made by Jacobite partisans, and in many cases they were strongly warranted. As often with Jacobitism, one of the principal sources is the Jacobite historian, Thomas Carte (1686–1754), though for obvious reasons his testimony has to be regarded with circumspection. In a lengthy report to James Francis ('King James') in 1739 Carte gave a list of working men who he declared would be ready, given leadership, to take up arms for the Stuarts. In the south-west he instanced clothing workers and colliers in Somerset and tin miners and fishermen in Cornwall ('20,000 people employed in the pilchard fishery and 40,000 in tin and copper mines') whose misery and exploitation could be turned to good advantage in a Jacobite rising.[10] In the Midlands he pointed to the area around Birmingham and Wolverhampton: 'in a tract of country but 24 miles in circumference, taking in Walsall and Dudley, there are above 80,000 fighting men, colliers and iron workers'. Another area worth the attention of Jacobite plotters, according to Carte, was the West Riding of Yorkshire, where the clothiers and colliers of Leeds, Wakefield, Huddersfield and Halifax were ideal Jacobite materal. Carte's ideas were reproduced by Louis XV's agent James Butler in 1743 following his reconnaissance trip to England and were taken very seriously in

Versailles.[11] One contingency plan for a French invasion stated that if no more than 5,000 troops could be spared for a descent on England, then landfall should be made in Dorset, where the French could expect to be joined by the discontented clothing workers. Likely Jacobite supporters were also assessed in terms of the kind of support they could enlist or levy among their workers. Henry Portman (an English MP) was said to be an important Jacobite because of the size of his estates and the number of his tenants employed in woollen manufacture.[12] Nathaniel Curzon of Kedleston, Derbyshire, was thought a significant figure because he had 10,000 miners in his employ.[13] Similarly George Chaffin was thought an important Jacobite since his workers might assist a rising in Dorset.[14]

Another of Carte's ideas was that only a standing army stood between the Whigs and an angry populace, but that this was itself dangerous for the Hanoverians, since the rank and file of the army were drawn from the working people. In a letter to James Stuart on 9 February 1738, Carte attempted a 'grand slam' of arguments purporting to show that the English army was a negligible force to pit against a foreign invasion or a domestic rising. Without the army the Whigs 'would else be knocked on the head by the people . . . the present number of forces is absolutely necessary for the support of King George and his government and if that army was once broke, he would be rooted out of the nation by the mob in three months' time.[15] Carte's argument was that the army was composed of 'Englishmen who conversed with the common people, imbibed the same sentiments and were full as dissented as they'. Moreover, he added, a standing army was in flat contradiction to those liberties for which the 1688 Revolution had been ostensibly brought about; to get rid of a standing army, therefore, people would not mind whether they were ruled by a Catholic or Protestant king.[16] It has been objected that Carte and other Jacobites were simply telling 'King James' what he wanted to hear and critics have been ready to pounce on his smallest slip. It has to be acknowledged that he was sometimes confused in his thinking, since we are told both that the working classes would rally to the Stuart standard at the request or their lords and employers *and* that the misery and exploitation they suffered (presumably caused by the activities of these same masters) would lead them to flock to the French if they invaded. Yet for all Carte's exaggerations, the core of his analysis was sound: there *was* much working-class unrest which the Jacobites could have exploited to greater advantage. The proof came in 1745. It is sometimes overlooked that there was a strong proletarian element in the composition of Charles Edward's army.[17] Artisans, shopkeepers, farmers and labourers made up a large part of the non-clan element of the army, many of them holding commissions of company rank.[18] Almost the whole of John Roy Stewart's regiment was recruited from the slums of Edinburgh. The Manchester regiments, commanded by Francis Towneley, contained a strong component of weavers, drapers and apothecaries – exactly the kind of men who made up Wilkes's supporters in the 1760s, and whose anti-Scottish and anti-Catholic sentiments are sometimes cited as conclusive evidence that the English mob could never have held Jacobite sympathies.[19] And it is certain that the pitmen, keelmen and sailors of Tyneside, if mobilised, could have made up another regiment just as strong as the Manchester one – illustrating once again, to cite Sir Alexander of Sleat, that Charles Edward really was the best strategist in his army, and that the invasion of England should have aimed straight at Newcastle and Marshal Wade.[20]

Yet another manifestation of 'radical Jacobitism' was the many covert and crypto-republicans who used the Jacobite movement as cover because an overt declaration of such principles was too advanced for eighteenth-century Britain. The prime example of such a disguised republican was George Keith, 10th hereditary Earl Marischal of Scotland, Charles Edward's nemesis and bête noire and later confidant to such diverse figures as David Hume, Frederick the Great and Jean-Jacques Rousseau.[21] One of the factors in this strange affair of lions in tigers' clothing was that as the Whigs in the first half of the eighteenth century became clearly established as the party of finance, big business and the moneyed interest, the Tories swung left into the ground of earlier Whig republicanism. This swing has sometimes been dismissed as a purely negative phenomenon – an alliance of the two defeated classes, urban poor and backwoods gentry – but it bears closer examination. Surely no stranger political turnaround has been witnessed than that whereby the House of Stuart in the eighteenth century became in effect the standard bearer for the very ideas it had fought against in the Civil War of the 1640s. Jacobites in 1700–50 found support among the Derbyshire miners, framework knitters, wool-combers, butchers, tailors, brick-makers, blacksmiths and tanners, whose ancestors had been Levellers in 1649,[22] and among the weavers of the south-west, who had supported Monmouth in 1685. John Burton of Corpus Christi College, Oxford, a bitter enemy of Dr William King (who made a famous and vehemently pro-Jacobite speech at the dedication of the Radcliffe Camera in 1749), pointed out the similarities of that speech to 1640s republicanism; 'What were republican principles in the last century are Jacobite principles in this.' The *London Evening Post* endorsed Burton's remarks and pointed out that had Dr King's speech been published 120 years earlier, it would have been considered a republican libel.[23] Something strange had happened to the Leveller and other radical movements of the 1640s. Anabaptists, Commonwealthmen and republicans supported Monmouth's rebellion against James II in 1685 but showed little support for William of Orange in 1688.[24] After the rise of Jacobitism and the coming of the Whig ascendancy, this radical political fringe seemed to lose its identity. Of the two radical tendencies, those of the Jacobites and the eighteenth-century Commonwealthmen – who were left on the periphery of politics by the centripetal Whig/Tory struggle – only the Jacobites thrived. The Commonwealthman ideas of liberty of conscience, extension of the franchise, redistribution of parliamentary seats, rotation in office, separation of powers, and a federal United Kingdom, did not seem attractive in the eighteenth century and seemed to many Jacobites a luxury or an irrelevance, a case of fiddling while Rome burned.[25] Also, non-Jacobite radicals were marginalised in 1700–50 because, in closing ranks against the Jacobites, the Whig aristocracy closed the door on other forms of 'deviance'. The very existence of the Stuarts played into the hands of the Hanoverian Whigs, for they were able to stifle the Tories and muzzle republicans and Commonwealthmen by crying up the fears of foreign invasion, civil war and anarchy that the Jacobites were held to portend. The one place that remained for radical ideas was within the only effective opposition left – the Jacobites – who were also the only group prepared to resist the existing regime by force. So it is that a paradoxical link can be found between the radical Jacobites of the 1740s and the Levellers of the 1640s. It was no accident that in Scotland during the '45 there appeared a pamphlet called *Liberty and Right*, which in its advocacy of payment of MPs, readjustment of constituencies, more frequent elections and the abolition of primogeniture was a harbinger of Chartism.[26]

Jacobitism was also radical in its embrace of what in modern times would be called 'social crime'.[27] There are two aspects to this. One is the tenet that many 'criminals' were forced to defy the law simply because of the egregious injustice of eighteenth-century England's 'Bloody Code' and the rampant corruption of central government. The other is that the Whig/Hanoverian ruling nexus designated as crime activities which had the sanction of social custom, ancient habit and local folkways. Whereas certain actions – murder, rape, infanticide, etc – are regarded as crimes by all societies, others are culturally defined or are simply the results of statutes issued by dictators or other repressive governments. The ideological stance of the Jacobites was that the epidemic of highway robbery in eighteenth-century England was directly caused by the gross inequality and misery deliberately produced by a narrowly based elite that had allied itself to usurping dynasties – initially the House of Orange, then (after the interim period of Queen Anne), the House of Hanover. For this reason there was a clear correlation between highwaymen and Jacobitism.[28] The contrast between the fuss made over a highway robbery involving £10 and the insouciance with which society regarded the bribery and peculation of Sir Robert Walpole, involving hundreds of thousands of pounds, was a staple comment of the day and appears explicitly in John Gay's *The Beggar's Opera*.[29] The Jacobites encouraged this line of reasoning. Since the post-1688 regime was illegitimate, it followed that in a sense all its property relations were bogus, and that the highwayman was merely claiming back what had been stolen. Anticipating Proudhon, the Jacobites insinuated the idea that all Hanoverian property was theft. The proposition that crime was a function of destitution, and destitution was itself a direct consequence of Whig economic policies, was a hardy annual in the reportage of the Jacobite journalist Nathaniel Mist.[30] A report to James Stuart at the end of 1728 (the year Gay's opera appeared) made the point explicit:

> Highway robberies prevail in England more than in any other nation of Europe. Are not the persons who commit them frequently such as are unwilling to make their distress public, and, finding themselves sunk in spite of industry, grow desperate and run the risk of an

> ignominious death to satisfy these voracious harpies the Whigs that occasion all their misery.[31]

There was a Jacobite flavour to several of the early eighteenth-century highwaymen. John Lunt moved from being a secret agent for James Francis in 1694 to becoming a 'gentleman of the road', and was one of several men at the time who made the transition from robber to Jacobite or vice versa.[32] Thomas Butler (executed 1720) fought for the 'Pretender' and was employed as a spy in the 1715 rising by the Duke of Ormonde. When luxurious living exhausted his money on the continent, Butler came to England and took up highway robbery. He and his trusted servant lived a double life for years. They would alternate periods 'on the road' with residence in London, where they lived in some style and were received in polite society.[33] Thomas Neale, a highwayman who was hanged in 1749, invoked the Jacobite martyr Lord Balmerino, beheaded two years earlier, as a fellow-sufferer; both were the victims of an illegitimate government.[34] According to this line of argument, the highwayman was a political criminal; as Chevalier Ramsay, the Jacobite ideologue, argued, if you deny the hereditary principle in kingship, you cannot retain it in property. The highwayman, when taxed with his actions, can reply: 'Rich men have violated this contract; they have seized upon everything, nothing remains for me. I will enter upon my natural right. I will take it and seize upon that which naturally belongs to me. The hereditary right of lands is a mere chimera.'[35] To the Hanoverians, for the Jacobites to condone highway robbery was outrageous, and even more so was their fondness for pirates, for these were individuals, by definition, outlawed by the *ius gentium* or what we would nowadays call international law. The Jacobites replied that implicit in the *ius gentium* was the doctrine of divine, hereditary and indefeasible right, and that the ousting of the Stuart dynasty in 1688 was itself an act of piracy. And so it is not so remarkable to find, in the decade after the Treaty of Utrecht, that last flowering of piracy in the Atlantic, Indian and even Pacific Oceans, a close alliance between the Jacobites and some of the most notorious pirates of the age. French corsairs operating out of Channel ports in wartime under letters of marque did not always take the trouble to put their activities within a legal framework when they freelanced in peacetime in remote oceans.[36] Not only did the

Jacobites of the post-1715 period retain close contacts with the famous pirates of Madagascar and the Seychelles, but the pirates of the Bahamas offered to support 'King James' openly against the house of Hanover.[37] Fully to explicate all the interlocking strands of Jacobitism and piracy would, however, take us very far from the world of the Jacobite rising of 1745. One example must suffice. Using as their military arm the pirates of Madagascar, James's agents in the 1720s dreamed of a Jacobite commercial empire to rival the official one, based also on friendly relations with the Dutch at the Cape of Good Hope, the Portuguese at Rio de Janeiro and the Spanish both at Buenos Aires and in the Pacific. Once such a commerical bloc was established, the plan was to begin trading with China.[38]

Perhaps the closest of all convergences between Jacobitism and crime was that with smuggling. Many observers, most of them very far from being Jacobites, inveighed against eighteenth-century fiscal policy in England on the grounds that the extremely high level of contraband – one estimate is 20,000 persons employed full-time in the trade in a century when the population rose from 6 to 8 millions – was a direct consequence of punitive levels of taxation and could be halted if governments would content themselves with modest tax yields. One such critic was Adam Smith, whose 'take' on contraband was devastating. He defined a smuggler as

> a person who, though no doubt highly blameable for violating the laws of his country, is frequently capable of violating those of natural justice, and would have been, in every respect, an excellent citizen had not the laws of his country made that a crime which nature never meant it to be . . . To pretend to have any scruple about buying smuggled goods would in most countries be regarded as one of those pedantic pieces of hypocrisy which, instead of gaining credit with anybody, serve only to expose the person who affects to practise them to being a greater knave than most of his neighbours.[39]

The Jacobites took up the theme of high taxation with gusto, alleging that the main reason they were high was the need to pay bondholders of the national debt. Jacobite contacts with smugglers were partly for reasons of opportunism and financial self-interest by the latter, but there is also much evidence of sincere ideological commitment to

'King James'. The exiled Jacobites maintained regular contacts with smugglers – hardly surprising since many Jacobite ship-owners were specialists in privateering, outright piracy and even the slave trade.[40] Smugglers were also instrumental in the many Jacobite schemes (and some actual enterprises) for landing arms in the Highlands. In 1727 the Jacobite David O'Brien wrote James a long memoir, explaining how arms bought in Holland could be taken to the Western Isles with the help of their smuggler friends. The memoir reveals a deep knowledge of the entire contraband trade from Barbados to Hamburg.[41] Smugglers were also invaluable in providing information on the strength and disposition of British forces when the French were attempting to launch invasions on behalf of the House of Stuart. The Irish Jacobite Comte de Lally, who commanded a regiment of the Irish brigade in both the 1744 and 1745 invasion attempts, was the directing force behind the smugglers and would go on to become the hidden hand behind the most notorious band of Sussex desperadoes, the Hawkhurst gang.[42] He it was who arranged for the French expedition of 1743–4 to be piloted by two masters of contraband vessels, Thomas Harvey and Robert Fuller. In 1744 the smugglers took several officers of Lally's regiment over to England to spy on the troops guarding London.[43] Lord Caryll, later Prince Charles Edward's private secretary, was another Jacobite grandee who was a vital link in a broad smuggler–Jacobite nexus.[44] This Jacobite–smuggler symbiosis continued into the Seven Years War. When yet another French invasion was broached in 1755, Duncan Robertson, 11th Laird of Struan suggested to James Francis that the obvious thing to do was use the many friendly smugglers as pilots for the invading fleet.[45]

The Jacobites were also behind the most daring exploit by the Hawkhurst gang. When a revenue cutter intercepted their vessel bringing 30 hundredweight of tea, value £500, and took it to the customs house at Poole, the Hawkhurst men decided to break into the customs house and regain the loot. A raid by 60 armed men on 7 October 1747 easily achieved its objective: in triumph the raiders divided up the spoils and gave each participant 27 pounds of tea. Unfortunately, careless talk in an inn allowed a shoemaker to identify the gang. He made contact with a minor excise official, and the 2 men set out for Chichester to make a formal deposition before a Customs and Excise board. Alerted about this by a sympathetic publican, the smugglers ambushed the 2 men on the road, beat them up, murdered and then mutilated them.[46] This was direct defiance of the government, and one of the most notorious Whig hard liners, the Duke of Richmond, determined that the culprits should be brought to book and turned the hunt for them into a personal crusade. He offered a huge reward for information, human nature duly asserted itself, and the Hawkhurst men were identified, arrested and brought to trial. The ringleaders were hanged at Tyburn and, by the time of his death, Richmond's almost monomaniac crusade, plus his largesse, had secured 45 deaths among the Hawkhurst gang: 35 executions and 10 more smugglers who died in jail while waiting for the hangman's rope. Richmond's pogrom against the Hawkhurst gang has puzzled many historians, who can see no clear motive for the money and energy he was prepared to expend on his campaign except an (unexplained) hatred of smugglers.[47] Yet the hidden motive was almost certainly his fanatical anti-Jacobitism. Richmond had been a creature of the Duke of Cumberland's during the '45 and was a close friend of the Pelham brothers (Henry Pelham and the Duke of Newcastle), who between them virtually ran the Whig government during the 1745 rising. Pelham's papers explicitly reveal that fear of the Jacobites was one of the prime motives in the unprecedented campaign against the Sussex smugglers.[48] When the purge of the Hawkhurst gang finally ended, Horace Walpole (Sir Robert's son) thought that their extirpation came about because Newcastle managed to 'turn' rival gangs in Sussex against the exiled Stuarts.[49] Scholarly research has revealed that the mastermind behind the entire daring escapade of the raid on the Poole customs house that triggered the great crisis for the Hawkhurst gang was none other than the dauntless Comte de Lally.[50]

Whereas the connection between smugglers and Jacobites is clear, that between poachers and the House of Stuart is not only turbid but has generated a variety of interpretations, mainly centring on the issue of the poachers of Berkshire and Hampshire (and especially the royal forest at Windsor) – the so-called Waltham Blacks, from their habit of blacking their faces while illegally taking deer and rabbits. There are three main views of the Blacks. One is that they were simply ordinary criminals and cut-throats whose importance has been blown out of all proportion. Another is that they were the 'social criminals' par excellence, defending customary rights to take game against a repressive and draconian legal system. The third is that the poachers were mainly crypto-Jacobites, and that this explains Walpole's obsession with them in the 1720s.[51] The existence of the Waltham Blacks gave Walpole the excuse to enact one of the most notoriously catch-all penal statutes in English legal history – the Waltham Black Act of 1722. Together with the Riot Act, this legislation gave Walpole and the Whigs virtually unlimited powers to proceed against suspected poachers, abolishing all pre-existing legal safeguards; the two statutes were the centrepieces of eighteenth-century England's notorious 'Bloody Code'. 1722 was also the year of one of the most complex Jacobite conspiracies, the Layer–Atterbury plot, and in Walpole's mind the Black Act was probably mainly conceived as his ultimate deterrent against Jacobitism. Other Whig ministers thought the Jacobite threat overrated and perceived the greatest menace to be that from the 'lower orders'. Much unnecessary academic debate has arisen concerning which of these two motives was primary, yet there is no law of excluded middle that prevents us from saying that both were important. The other impassioned debate concerns the identities of the Waltham Blacks: were they Jacobites, non-political or even anti-Jacobite? Certainly some Blacks bitterly objected to being called Jacobite,[52] but that is not necessarily the end of the matter. As one historian of the subject has rightly commented, 'The issue of Jacobitism is complicated and made immensely more so by the double talk of the times and by a press blanketed with censorship.'[53] In Windsor the correlation between Blacks and Jacobites was particularly strong; and although the property of Jacobite sympathisers was sometimes attacked, it must be allowed that this could well have been camouflage. Walpole's branding of all political opponents, of whatever hue and from whatever stratum, as Jacobite was a classic of crying wolf but, as in the original fable, there was a wolf: some of the Blacks were Jacobite sympathisers. There was in particular a 'crossover' between poaching, smuggling and acting as a pro-Stuart agent.[54] The convergence of the Waltham Blacks and Jacobitism was most clearly seen in March 1746, when Prince Charles Edward's adventure was on its last legs in Scotland. Suddenly there was a re-emergence of the Black phenomenon, which Walpole thought he had destroyed forever in the 1720s.[55]

Yet of all species of criminality, whether we regard the offences as crimes against humanity sub specie aeternitatis or the bogus delinquency of men who were really primitive rebels or 'social criminals', the manifestation most clearly linked with Jacobitism was rioting. It is a commonplace that eighteenth-century England was a turbulent society where rioting was rampant, and it has been argued that the rioters of that era, seldom mindless hooligans but usually 'other directed', were really the unleavened raw material that in a later era would have been processed through trade unionism or socialist politics.[56] The link between rioting and popular Jacobitism is so intimate that in the period 1689–1715, the two phenomena virtually operated as synonyms.[57] Even in 1716–44, when the Jacobite movement was supposedly moribund, and in 1747–54, when Charles Edward's defeat was supposed to have killed it off for good, the level of convergence between rioting and Jacobitism was astonishing. It is important to be clear: not all post-1715 rioting was actuated by pro-Stuart sentiment or used Jacobitism as a legitimating cloak. Sometimes rioters and strikers refused to have their activities politicised, as in 1719 when a Stuart sympathiser tried to turn a weavers' strike into an insurrection in support of the '19 rising in Scotland.[58] It is perhaps not so surprising that 'between 1715 and 1722, popular Jacobitism disturbed the peace of almost every important town'.[59] The aftermath of the '45 in England showed clearly that, as all contemporaries felt, Jacobitism had not been dealt a death blow at Culloden (which is what most modern historians, with the benefit of hindsight, now allege). Pro-Jacobite riots and strikes were at a new high in 1747–54 and continued even into the first three years of the Seven Years War. In 1747–54 there were pro-Jacobite riots and demonstrations in all the following cities: Manchester, Lichfield, Oxford, Bristol, Newcastle, Walsall, Shrewsbury, Norwich, Leicester and Exeter.[60] Staffordshire was always a Jacobite stronghold, and Lichfield saw major demonstrations in support of the exiled dynasty at both the by-election of 1747 and that of 1753. At Lichfield races in 1747 the overt contempt for the Hanoverian dynasty would certainly have merited prosecution under Hanoverian treason laws, which might have netted some very big fish, since both Sir Watkin Williams Wynn, supposedly the doyen of English and Welsh Jacobites, and the 'Bonnie Prince's' confidant Sir James Harrington were present. Some claim that only the timorousness of the Tory baronets prevented a spontaneous Jacobite uprising there and then.[61] On this occasion the Whig authorities decided to let sleeping dogs lie. They were not so accommodating in 1750 on the occasion of a serious riot in Walsall, when six troops of cavalry were needed to quell the disturbances.[62] Yet the most amazing proof of the durability and survival of popular Jacobitism is provided by the outbreaks that occurred in England as late as 1756 and 1757, when the Hanoverian state was once more engaged in a life-and-death struggle with Ancien Régime France. Election riots in Tamworth (Staffordshire) in 1756, and in Harrogate and Halifax the following year had a clear Jacobite tincture. In 1756 food rioters in Warwickshire invoked 'the Pretender' and refused to disperse until 'King James' came to stop them.[63] The ill-considered idea of rushing through a Militia Act in 1757 as additional security against foreign invasion inflamed a volatile population, particularly disgruntled after the poor showing of the nation in the first two years of the war, with severe setbacks at Minorca and Fort William Henry in North America. The Militia Act was perceived by ordinary people as a typically dishonest Whig wheeze to try to get the unwilling to fight overseas. Opposition was ferocious, and many localities expressly invoked the Jacobites as the legitimate sovereigns and guarantors of the legitimacy of their own disaffection.[64] Not until the annus mirabilis of 1759, when Britain won a string of military victories worldwide, did the tide of Jacobite sentiment ebb.

It should not be thought that popular Jacobitism manifested itself only in areas which the Hanoverians could subsume under the rubric of criminality. Certain regions evinced a persistent Jacobitism which only the defeat of the French fleet at Quiberon Bay in 1759 could extinguish entirely. One such area was Tyneside, where a new class of Jacobites had arisen in the shape of keelmen and colliers. Troops were used against the keelmen's strike in Newcastle in 1710 and again in 1719, while there was a particularly bloody clash between the Hexham colliers and the army in 1761. These two groups were the most active of proletarian dissidents. The authorities could never quite make up their minds whether the colliers were actuated more by levelling or Jacobite principles.[65] As for the keelmen, their grievances were legion: seasonal employment, erratic relief 'charity', being in bond to fitters but having coal owners as their masters, annual indentures, and much more.[66] Small wonder that one of their favourite pastimes was proclaiming 'King James', which they continued to do as late as 1750. In that year, however, they slightly muddied the waters by proclaiming *Charles Edward* king (James did not die until 1766) and then confusingly adding: 'King of England, *France* [italics mine] and Ireland'.[67] A combination of keelmen's action and a Jacobite rising could have paralysed Newcastle and cut the coal lifeline, as was feared in 1716–18 and could easily have happened in 1745 if the members of the prince's council had heeded his advice and taken the eastern route for a showdown with Wade. In 1715 the keelmen's rising had come within an ace of securing the city for the Jacobites and would have done so but for the ambivalence of the faint-hearted Jacobite Sir William Blackett.[68] In 1745–6 the keelmen were again to the fore, and in April 1746 the city authorities had to act fast to nip in the bud a plot to spike the cannon in Newcastle and raise 1,500 recruits for the house of Stuart – and this was at the very moment of Culloden.[69] What made the situation on Tyneside in 1745–6 so dangerous for the Hanoverians was that there is strong evidence of significant aristocratic and gentry support for the keelmen. Displaying the customary class prejudice, government sources ignored the fact that the heart and mind of the conspiracy was provided by the keelmen and preferred to concentrate on the '15 or 16 gentlemen' actively involved in the plot.[70]

Manchester was another urban centre with strong Jacobite sympathies, strong enough to provide 200 or so volunteers for Charles Edward's Manchester regiment in 1745. As against those who claim that Jacobitism was a movement of benighted reaction, the evidence rather is that it appealed to the new kind of social grouping that arose with the northern textile industry; the officers of the Manchester regiment were weavers, drapers, dyers and mercers. Other members came from a new kind of middle class, dependent on the wealth and consumer tastes generated by the textile industry, apprentices to professions such as pharmacy, medicine and the law.[71] It was a staple part of Whig propaganda to make 'Jacobite' and 'Catholic' synonymous, despite the fact that most Jacobite supporters, and even soldiers in Charles Edward's army, were not Catholic, but Scots Episcopalian, Presbyterian, and non-juring members of the Church of England.[72] It was not the shires, presided over by claret-swilling squires like those portrayed in Fielding's *Tom Jones* (especially Squire Western) but the cities that provided Jacobitism's cutting edge, proving over and over again that the conflation of 'Jacobite' with 'reactionary' simply will not hold water. Around 1715 the Jacobite propensity of the City of London was undoubted.[73] The question that has been debated is how much of this sentiment survived in 1745? The conventional view is that London Jacobitism was still a considerable force in 1745, and the perception has not been seriously shaken.[74] Certainly the Duke of Newcastle's secret agent Dudley Bradstreet, who caused such havoc at the council at Derby on 5 December 1745 and was unusually well informed, was convinced that the mob would have joined the Stuart army once it reached London.[75] And perhaps the most eloquent testimony to the likely scenario had Charles Edward reached London was provided by William Pitt the Elder, a fervent anti-Jacobite: 'If the rebels had made themselves masters of London, I question if the spirit of the population would not have taken a different turn.'[76]

The Hanoverians deeply feared the urban crowd and the secret political sympathies of the toiling masses and knew there was no love there for them. The government realised that if the status quo was in danger from the Stuarts, ordinary people could not be relied on to defend it – indeed that they would probably join the Jacobites once their cause seemed in the ascendant. For this reason the defence of England in 1745 against the Highland army was extraordinarily difficult.[77] The militia was considered an unreliable body to call out, as it might take the wrong side; the political danger of this and thus the inoperability of the militia as a defence bastion is yet another reason why the '45 rebellion could have been successful.[78] In Scotland the militia idea was always opposed because disarming laws were thought essential against Jacobites. Such was the apprehension about popular Jacobitism that it was considered sinister that the militia idea had been popular in those areas where Charles Edward received support.[79] The Hanoverians therefore faced a dilemma: either the militia could not be called out because of local reluctance or obstructionism during the rising or, if it was called out, it was to be feared as a potential Jacobite fifth column.[80] Faced with all this, the only tactic for the Whigs to adopt was classic 'divide and rule': somehow to foment the masses against the Jacobites. As one pro-government correspondent in Staffordshire in 1745 put it: 'I apprehend no tumult unless the common people should attack the papists, which they show some inclination to do, and should that ungovernable monster make the first move, it would be prudent to direct his head towards the cause of these our troubles.'[81] Yet in most government quarters the fear was not so much that the common people would bring about a Jacobite restoration by their own spontaneous efforts as that local disorders would create chaos, allowing the gentry to rise and/or a foreign power to invade. In some ways what the Hanoverians feared most was not so much hostility from pro-Jacobite crowds as the apathy and indifference of the mass of the people as to who won the dynastic contest; this was particularly in evidence during the '45 as, despite all the loyal proclamations, the local volunteer forces simply melted away as the Jacobite army marched further south.[82] Indirect evidence for the apprehension entertained about the possible reactions of the ordinary man (and woman) to the Jacobite risings comes in the plethora of pamphlets directed to this class in 1745.[83] The anonymous *Drapier's Letter* of 1745 (which attempted to ape the more famous *Drapier's Letters* of Jonathan Swift) contained some first-class propaganda directed at an audience of 'Labourers, Farmers, Artificers and Tradesmen', of which a few excerpts will suffice to convey the flavour. The author argues that the issue between Jacobite and Hanoverian should be a matter of concern for the gentry and aristocracy alone, and that for the working man to take part or show interest would be to manifest 'false consciousness':

> What are the poorer sort the better all this while? Will the labourer get one farthing a day more? Will the farmer's rent be allowed? Will the artificer be more employed or better paid? Will the tradesman get more customers or have fewer scores in his book? . . . If the poor labourer, when all is over, is to be a labourer still and earn his groat a day, as hardly as he did before, I cannot find why he should fancy it worth his while to venture a leg or an arm and the gallows too into the bargain, to be just where he set out . . . It well deserves your thought whether it is worth your while to beggar yourselves and your family that the man's name upon the throne be James instead of George.[84]

Such propaganda would have been otiose if there were genuinely nothing to fear from popular Jacobitism.

The view, so widely held that until recently it has almost been a dogma among historians, that Culloden finished off the Jacobite movement for good, cannot be sustained and has recently been subjected to devastating analysis. To sum up: Ireland and Scotland remained in turmoil until Hawke's victory at Quiberon in 1759, with Scotland in some ways even more pro-Jacobite than in 1745; the French planned to invade England with 100,000 men as against the 15,000 in 1745–6; the working classes had still not decisively shifted their allegiance to Methodism or the new radicalism of John Wilkes; and, as has been demonstrated above, large sections of urban England remained disaffected.[85] It has been convincingly demonstrated that one in four of the aristocracy and gentry under George I and George II harboured Jacobite sympathies.[86] Moreover the attachment to the House of Stuart by the gentry was not simply empty posturing, even though the record of the English Jacobite grandees, such as Lord Barrymore, Sir John Hynde Cotton and Sir Watkin Williams Wynn was not impressive.[87] The most formidable of these was supposedly Williams Wynn, but history has been kind to the Welsh baronet, with no less than three separate explanations put forward to explain his non-appearance in the field with his feudal levies on Charles Edward's behalf. One is simply that by pure bad luck he was in London when the prince invaded, was being tagged by government agents and could not get away.[88] Another is that he sent a letter to Charles Edward at Derby, promising to join him with his men, but that the messenger got to Derby on 8 December, two days after the Highlanders had begun their retreat. Very convenient, the sceptic may mutter but, surprisingly Williams Wynn has found historians to believe him.[89] Yet a third explanation is that Williams Wynn has been much maligned but was actually a victim of the yawning gap between the Whigs (representing financial interests) and the Tories (the landed interest). According to this view, which was circulated by Aeneas MacDonald, one of the Seven Men of Moidart, it so happened that when the prince crossed into England, Sir Watkins had just £200 in ready cash; his wealth was vast but his liquidity was low. MacDonald, always a treacherous acolyte of the prince, alleged that if Charles Edward had given the Welsh grandee adequate notice, he could have raised, not £200 but the £120,000 he had spent on the previous two general elections.[90] However, it is important not to extrapolate from the disappointing behaviour of the three most important English Jacobite nabobs to the behaviour of the Tory gentry as a whole. Once again, more recent research establishes the bulk of them as sound, true and loyal to the Jacobite cause.[91]

Wherever one looks in 1745 one sees evidence of deep discontent with a dangerously narrowly based Whig/Hanoverian elite. It was part of Charles Edward's revolutionary acumen to intuit how deep the malaise went, and it was not his fault that more was not made of this. To an extent he was right in his frequent fulminations against his father and the older generation of Jacobites, who tended to have a naive faith in the workings of providence whereby, in the case of the 1733 Excise Act, say, popular tumult was somehow supposed spontaneously to lead to a Stuart restoration without any effort on their part.[92] The potential for an organic working-class Jacobitism did exist: the agitation against the Excise Act, the Porteous riots of 1737, the turnpike riots in Bristol and Hereford, to say nothing of the specific grievances of keelmen, colliers, weavers and miners already mentioned, could all have been mobilised and turned to advantage by skilful Jacobite agents. Sadly, men of the right calibre were usually lacking and, even when they were available, they did not receive enough encouragement from 'King James' and the other grandees.

Partly it was snobbery directed against too close an association with the lower orders and a fastidious distaste for the more unscrupulous methods sometimes proposed. For example, James specifically vetoed plans to counterfeit currency, to clip coins or indulge in other forms of 'coining' – which would, ironically, have produced a double charge of high treason under the Bloody Code, since the two offences expressly identified there as treason were denial of the validity of the Protestant Succession and tampering with coinage.[93] Mainly, though, it was the absurd belief that revolutions can spontaneously generate themselves; James and his henchmen forgot the oldest wisdom of all – God helps those who help themselves.[94] It does not pay to be anachronistic about revolution and the Jacobites. The organisation of a large number of men in the service of a proscribed organisation – when Tory ranks were honeycombed with spies and the Hanoverians had all manner of extra-legal weapons at their disposal, such as general warrants and automatic suspension of Habeas Corpus – with the concomitant requirement of secrecy, was a tall order even for quasi-feudal lords like Sir Watkin Williams Wynn.[95] This is quite apart from the fact that the kind of revolutionary consciousness which could direct a mass movement did not appear in Europe until the French Revolution. It would therefore be unreasonable and anachronistic to fault the Jacobites for not doing what it would not have occurred to anyone in the mid-eighteenth century to do.[96] Yet these arguments cannot be pushed too far. Charles Edward proved that an alliance between the Stuarts and the dispossessed was not chimerical when, in 1759, hoping for a successful French invasion of Britain, he produced a manifesto of 107 clauses. This was a thoughtful tour d'horizon of the policies to be followed by a restored Stuart dynasty and had been written in close consultation with John Holker, ex-Jacobite officer in the Manchester regiment, founder of the French textile industry and currently the French inspector-general in charge of foreign manufactures.[97] Much of the manifesto deals with subjects traditionally dear to Jacobite ideology – the corruption of the Hanoverians, the national debt, the issue of standing armies, even the prince's own conversion to Protestantism in 1750. The truly original part of the document deals with socio-economic problems. Simplifying, we may say that Charles Edward threatened to dethrone the financial capitalism rampant in England since 1689 with a moderated industrial capitalism, centred on textiles, fisheries, the linen industries and export-led growth. Finally the prince ended with a flourish. He made the revolutionary promise to put the poor and needy under the protection of the State – a form of welfarism that would not be seen in England for another 200 years.

> Is not the poor in a starving condition? But what makes poor but a neglected education of youth, or heavy taxes? Are these poor cared for, notwithstanding the large fund raised upon the nation for that purpose? . . . We shall take under the protection of the state the children of poor parents, whereby the latter may be encouraged to propagate, and the former be properly cared for and become as by nature they are intended, the fountain of wealth in an industrious nature.[98]

That the '45 posed a revolutionary threat to eighteenth-century Britain should already be clear, making the rising that year an obvious candidate for a close encounter of rank one. James Francis and Charles Edward (his regent in the case of a restoration and, probably, soon-to-be king after James's likely abdication) would have had debts to pay off and promises to keep, both to the gentry and to the toiling classes. Not only would the masses necessarily have been coopted in a way not seen hitherto, but there would be a clean sweep of the elite, with both the members of the prince's council and the English Jacobites like Williams Wynn, Cotton and Barrymore jockeying for positions. There could thus be no question of a mere transfer of power or the continuity of the old elites. There could be no Marlboroughs (military victor under the Stuarts at Sedgemoor and later under Queen Anne at Blenheim), of Benjamin Franklin (trusted British agent, then cutting-edge ideologue of the US constitution) making a smooth transition into the new regime. The more problematical issue is whether the entire direction of British economic and foreign policy would have changed under the restored Stuarts and, thus, whether the entire course of British history would have been different. To an extent we are faced with the head-on collision of historical inevitability and counterfactual history. Would the Stuarts have been compelled by Parliament to carry on much as before or would they have had the power to take the nation in a new direction, possibly ending up like Switzerland or the Scandinavian countries? Unavoidably, then, we have to ask whether the rise of the British Empire was inevitable, with an unstoppable momentum beyond human agency.[99] Any such argument has to be carried out with great care and nuance, steering a middle course between the reefs of 'what if' history and the wilder shores of historical inevitability. For example, it was a favourite motif of John Buchan that the restoration of his beloved Bonnie Prince Charlie would have meant that the loss of the American colonies would not have happened. Better by far is the famous argument by Tom Paine in his 1776 pamphlet *Commonsense* that for all kinds of reasons the separation of the American colonies from the mother country and their establishment as an independent nation-state was inevitable in an overdetermined way.[100] The question of whether Britain and France were doomed to fight each other in the 'Second Hundred Years War' (1689–1815) is a fascinating one, all the more intriguing since it was the very issue posed by the French Ministers of Louis XV's council in 1745–6 when they debated the nature and extent of their support for Charles Edward's allegedly rash adventure.[101]

Jacobitism was always linked in Whig and Hanoverian minds with support for their commercial rivals: the establishment of the short-lived Ostend Company (1717–31) by the Austrian emperor, for example, was regarded as a device by the Jacobites to undermine the Protestant Succession.[102] It was widely felt that the Stuarts could be restored only with French help, and that if a restoration was accomplished, the French would inevitably exact as their price commercial privileges which would lead to their victory over England in the worldwide struggle for economic supremacy. After all, it was reasoned, the early Stuarts had ended the 'inevitable' conflict with Spain, until this was revived by Cromwell in the 1650s, and the later Stuarts had both preserved pro-French policies (France having displaced Spain as England's putative Public Enemy Number One after the great victory over the Spanish *tercios* at Rocroi in 1643) for political, fiscal and religious reasons, regardless of the commercial interests at stake.[103] With the exception of the East India Company, which favoured trade with France as it needed French bullion, all sections of the Whig mercantile interest were opposed to France and identified her as the natural enemy. Anti-French policies were needed precisely because France was the chief competitor for world trade, and the idea of a commercial treaty with France after 1713 had been repudiated by Parliament through an alliance of Whigs and Hanoverian Tories.[104] The principal prize in the global struggle was perceived on both sides to be the Spanish American colonies.[105] As early as the War of Spanish Succession, Louis XV had made it clear that he intended to exclude English merchants from the entire Spanish Empire and to open it to French traders. But with the Treaty of Utrecht and its *asiento* provisions, the English seemed to have gained the upper hand in the struggle for the possession of the decaying Spanish Empire in the Americas. If the Jacobites were successful in restoring their king with French aid, France would certainly demand as a quid pro quo that the provisions of the Treaty of Utrecht be undone.[106] The Hanoverian pamphlet, *A Calm Address*, argued that if the Pretender succeeded in regaining the throne of England. he would be bound on principles of gratitude to cede to the King of Spain the important ports and fortresses of Gibraltar and Fort Mahon (Minorca). France would have to be given back the recently taken Cape Breton and in addition would demand the reduction, if not outright repeal, of the various heavy customs duties on French goods, especially wine; this would damage both the Portuguese trade and British commerce.[107] The close identification of the exiled Stuarts with France lost their dynasty considerable support. At the trials of the defeated Jacobites in 1746, much bitterness was directed at their alleged treason in betraying English interests to the French.[108] Sadly for the Stuarts, many French ministers and advisers doubted a Stuart king would be able to force through such concessions against a recalcitrant Parliament, and that the English projection of future benefits to France was chimerical. This was why many of them – the Duc de Noailles, the Comte de Maurepas and the foreign policy adviser Pierre André O'Heguerty advocated that Louis XV should strive to make Charles Edward king of Scotland or Ireland, but not of England, thus allying them with the clan leaders and against the wishes of the prince.[109]

Uncertainty over land and real estate is all but definitional of a revolutionary situation – it was, after all, worry and concern over this issue that swung the peasantry and the owners of so-called 'national property' (i.e. that confiscated from émigrés) away from revolution and into the dictatorial embrace of Napoleon. Here again we see the revolutionary implications of the '45, for the question of land titles was one of the hidden but profound issues in oligarchic opposition to Jacobitism in England.[110] Many of the eighteenth-century Whig families, the Hollises, Pelhams, Russells (and dozens of other aristocratic families), enjoyed property which had once belonged to the Catholic Church at the time of the Reformation – the so-called 'Abbey Lands'. Naturally, they were fearful about what might happen to these lands if the Stuarts were restored. There even existed a special law, praemunire, second only to high treason itself in gravity, aimed at the pope and all his works. One of the factors constituting a praemunire was 'to molest the possessors of Abbey Lands'.[111] In the seventeenth century the political theorists Sir William Temple and James Harrington had drawn attention to this as a potentially contentious legacy in English politics, an unwelcome legacy from the Reformation.[112] In 1687 James II went so far as to order his favourite physician Nathaniel Johnston to write a tract reassuring owners of 'Abbey Lands' about his intentions, even if the King of England (he presumably meant himself) were to return permanently to the Catholic Church.[113] It is usually considered that these Whig fears were largely chimerical. It was already 200 years since the dissolution of the monasteries, and the 'Abbey Lands' had been sold and resold, divided and subdivided many times since. Even if the Jacobites had wanted to restore them, the task would have been impossible. But what counts most in a revolutionary situation is *perception*, not reality; what mattered was not that such fears were irrational but that they existed and could be exploited to make political capital. Nobody was unaware of the immense significance of the land issue to the outcome of the dynastic struggle between Stuart and Hanoverian. It was said that some Jacobite magnates drew back from outright rebellion in 1715 because of worries on this score.[114] Louis XV's agent James Butler pointed out in 1743 in his report to the French court that Cumberland was a county totally committed to the Hanoverians because former Crown lands had been alienated to the local aristocracy. Great play was made of the issue of 'Abbey Lands' during the 1745 rising.[115] That masterly propagandist Henry Fielding devoted a good deal of attention to it in his *Serious Address*.[116] Horace Walpole remarked to Sir Horace Mann in September 1745 that, with the Young Pretender already in Scotland, priests would by then have set out from Rome in expectation of repossessing the 'Abbey Lands'.[117] Such was the emphasis placed on this issue in government propaganda that Charles Edward himself wrote from Perth in September 1745 in great indignation that the Whigs should have attempted to smear him by imputing to him the intention of restoring Church land.[118]

The Jacobites themselves were well aware of their vulnerability to hostile propaganda on this issue. They realised that, even if they could overcome the byzantine complexities involved in restoration of these lands, they would simply cause hardship and suffering to hundreds of powerful families and thus drive them to eventual revolt. Yet the fear that these fertile properties, about one-third of all the real estate in England, might one day be restored to their original owners, had always been the economic base on which the ideological superstructure of 'anti-popery' had been built.[119] To get round this, James Francis's advisers put it to him in 1724 that he should obtain a decree from the pope, in which the Catholic Church renounced all claim to these lands.[120] The advice was never acted on for a number of reasons. James felt that such a disclaimer would harden rather than weaken the opposition to Jacobitism in England, as it would be construed as a pre-emptive bid to win hearts and minds, prior to a Jacobite invasion. Others raised the possibility of later popes annulling such a decree.

THE PEASANTS' REVOLT, 1381

(*Right*) John Ball (mounted) meets Wat Tyler (standing front left) and his supporters at the gates of London; illumination from Jean Froissart, *Chroniques de France, d'Angleterre*, *c.*1460–80.

(*Left*) Wat Tyler is wounded by William Walworth, Lord Mayor of London, and taken to St Bartholomew's Hospital; nineteenth-century lithograph.

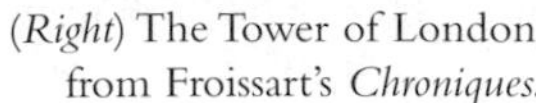

(*Right*) The Tower of London, from Froissart's *Chroniques.*

THE JACK CADE REBELLION, 1450

(*Above*) Jack Cade attacking London at night; illustration from *History of England* by Henry Tyrell.

(*Below*) Lord Saye and Lord Sele are brought before Jack Cade in 1450; illustration from *Hutchinson's Story of the British Nation*, *c.*1923.

THE PILGRIMAGE OF GRACE, 1536

(*Above*) Aske affixing his proclamation to the door of York Cathedral; illustration from *The Church of England: A History for the People* by H.D.M. Spence-Jones, published. *c.*1910.

(*Left*) Letter from Lord Darcy to Robert Aske.

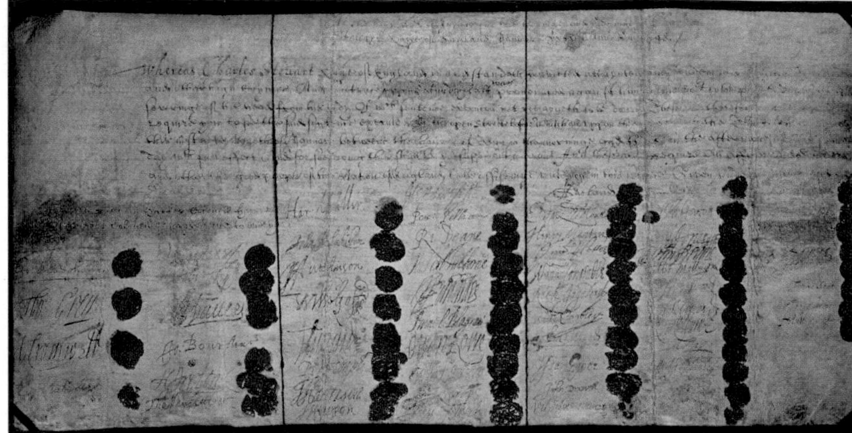

(*Above*) The death warrant of Charles I, signed and sealed by the fifty-nine commissioners on 29 January 1648 (old style calendar, 1649 new style calendar).

(*Above*) The Battle of Naseby, 14 June 1645.

THE JACOBITE UPRISING, 1745–6

(*Left*) Prince Charles Edward Stewart, pastel portrait by Maurice Quentin de la Tour.

(*Below*) The Battle of Culloden, oil painting by David Morier, *c.*1746.

(*Left*) Lord Lovat, Simon Fraser, being executed on Tower Hill for his part in the second Jacobite uprising; copper engraved print, *c.*1754.

(*Above*) An early daguerrotype taken in 1848 by William Kilburn, showing the Great Chartist Meeting on Kennington Common.

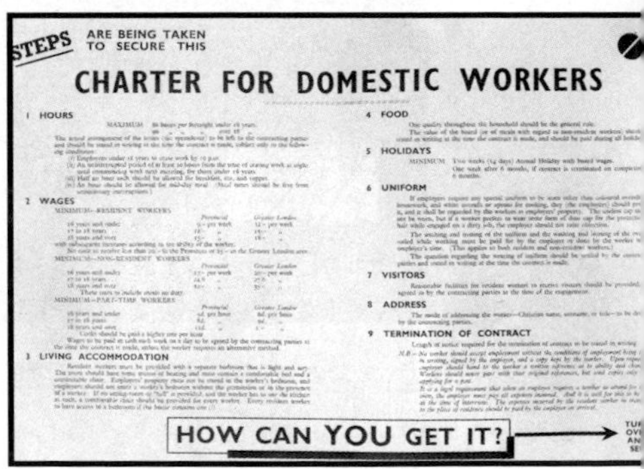

STEPS ARE BEING TAKEN TO SECURE THIS

CHARTER FOR DOMESTIC WORKERS

1 HOURS

2 WAGES

3 LIVING ACCOMMODATION

4 FOOD

5 HOLIDAYS

6 UNIFORM

7 VISITORS

8 ADDRESS

9 TERMINATION OF CONTRACT

HOW CAN YOU GET IT?

(*Above*) The charter for domestic workers.

(*Left*) An attack on the Westgate Hotel, 4 November 1839, during the Newport rising; nineteenth-century engraving.

(*Above*) The wreckage of a bus after having een set on fire by strikers in South London.

(*Right*) Women on horseback lead an Anti-Strike demonstration of 25,000 women marching from Victoria Embankment to the Royal Albert Hall.

(*Left*) Volunteer transport and their police protection following the government's successful call for recruits.

(*Left*) Commuters at Paddington Station on the third day of the Strike, 6 May 1926.

(*Right*) Congestion along the Embankment as commuters attempt to get to work during the Strike; photograph from *The Illustrated London News*, 8 May 1926.

(*Left*) Trouble breaking ou in Hammersmith Broadw during the passing of a milk lorry; photograph from *The Illustrated Londo News*, 15 May 1926.

William Shippen, the English Jacobite, objected that if James obtained such a decree, he would make himself appear more, not less, of a papal poodle; he would seem to be a man who did no more and no less than the pope ordered him to do.[121] The issue was left in limbo, to provide wonderful propaganda for the Whigs. However, the matter was a running sore and even more acute in Ireland, always (and rightly) considered crypto-Jacobite, where further lands had been alienated as a result of the conquests by Cromwell and William: the effect of these had been to leave only one-seventh of Irish land in Catholic hands; hence for the Protestants a return even to 1640 was dreaded.[122] Much of this expropriation, however, had taken place in the Cromwell era and, significantly, had not been reversed by Charles II, whose abiding concern, as he put it, was not to go on his travels again. Yet the land question was even more complex in Ireland since, as Bishop Berkeley (he of the *esse est percipi* principle in philosophy) pointed out in 1745, many Catholic landowners by that time held their property under the Act of Settlement of 1701; it was most unlikely, he alleged, that their titles would be recognised by an incoming Jacobite regime.[123]

Of all the revolutionary motives imputed to the Jacobites, the most worrying was the fear in Whig minds that an incoming Stuart regime would repudiate the national debt. The Whigs had ingeniously linked the fortunes of the Act of Settlement, which essentially outlawed Catholicism, with the national debt. To defeat Louis XIV in the war of 1689–97 William of Orange had needed huge sums of money, and to get these by new mechanisms he was prepared to trade off most royal prerogatives to Parliament.[124] This was the genesis of the distinctive financial capitalism introduced after 1688, symbolised by institutions such as the national debt, the Bank of England (founded in 1694) and the South Sea Company, which gave Parliament full powers to approve all borrowing by the Crown.[125] It was an abiding motif in Whig propaganda that the restored Stuarts would cancel the national debt and ruin bondholders. Pro-Hanoverians argued that to oust their regime was not just a matter of revoking the Act of Settlement, which could be done by a hastily convened Parliament after Stuart restoration but to ruin thousands, precisely since the Protestant succession and the post-1688 system rose or fell together. Under the Hanoverians, it was argued, Parliament was sovereign, but under the Stuarts this had never been the case and never would be. A monarch who could act on his own initiative, untrammelled by Parliament, had difficulty borrowing on the open market since he could not credibly commit to repayment in all circumstances and was likely to default if the going got tough, just as Charles II had done in 1672.[126] Quite apart from the problems debt repudiation would cause to traditional allies like the Dutch (who were major debt-holders), cancellation of the national debt would mean destroying wealth: the author of the 1745 *Calm Address* argued that the debt was an interest-bearing form of wealth which the *public* owned.[127] Charles Edward was well aware that this was a crucial issue but was determined not to give hostages to fortune. In a rare demonstration of political nous he decided to stall. In a proclamation dated 10 October 1745, issued during the prince's halcyon sojourn in Edinburgh, he said the following about the national debt: 'That it has been contracted under an unlawful government, nobody can disown, no more than that it is now a most heavy load upon the Nation; yet in regard that it is for the greatest part due to those very subjects whom he promises to protect, cherish and defend, he is resolved to take the advice of his Parliament concerning it.'[128]

The wide spread of the debt was in some ways the nub of the matter. By increasing the number of bondholders battening off the national debt, the post-1688 elite had coopted them into the new political and dynastic system. The countervailing lever the Jacobites had to play on was the interest of the gentry, who had to pay the land tax to service the debt. The Jacobite risings were the most severe manifestation of an underlying court/country fracture, pitting the moneyed interest against the landed interest; in post-1715 terms this meant Whig versus Tory. Jacobite propaganda therefore concentrated on the increasing load of taxation that had to be paid to service the debt. The crushing burden of taxation, it was alleged, affected agricultural production, made English trade goods dearer, and thus enabled England's rivals to undercut her in world markets.[129] For this reason many of James Stuart's advisers counselled him to repudiate the debt altogether; mere cancellation with compensation to debt-holders was too onerous.[130] From this it was a short step to the widely held perception that the restored Jacobites would cancel *all* debts and financial obligations incurred since 1689, and especially those that had accrued after 1714. The perilous relationship between debtors and creditors in itself underlines the much graver social dislocation portended by a successful Jacobite rising than by, say, the transfer of power in the 'American revolution'.[131] The Philadelphia Convention of 1787, which established the United States, set its face resolutely against any concessions to debtors. There was thus a huge class of actual or potential Jacobites among men who had nothing to gain from the post-1688 regime. It was a common gibe in Ireland in 1745 that Catholic debtors were withholding payment from their creditors until they could see the outcome of the rebellion.[132] Bankrupts, too, were particularly likely, for obvious reasons, to be Jacobite. The correlation can be well observed in the career of Charles Caesar, MP for Hertfordshire – almost a textbook example of the connection between bankruptcy and Jacobitism.[133] The Duke of Wharton – the so-called 'Hell-Fire Duke', who dabbled in freemasonry and the occult and performed occasional services for James Stuart in the 1720s – is another good example.[134] In 1745 many financially ruined men were led into rebellion in the hope of recouping their place in the world. Leading examples of Jacobite bankrupts in that year were the prince's secretary, John Murray of Broughton, and the Earl of Kilmarnock, who paid for revolt with his head.[135] Government records contain much more evidence. Among members of the Scottish gentry alone we find in one indictment for rebellion in 1746 the following list of bankrupts: Sir John Wedderburn of Blackness, David Fotheringham of Powrie (who acted as the Jacobite governor of Dundee), James Lindsay of Glenquist, James Hepburn of Keith, Patrick Walland of Abertrothock and David Carmichael of Balmeddie.[136] There was also a string of bankruptcies caused by agricultural depression in the 1730s that added a quiverful of 'economic Jacobites' to the ranks of the malcontent. One interesting contrast between the 1715 and 1745 risings concerns the motivations of the Catholics of northern England. In 1715 there was hardly a single Catholic gentleman in Northumberland who was not on the brink of ruin with a heavily mortgaged estate, and it was this which had brought them out for the 'Pretender'. By 1745 this grouping had completely disappeared.[137]

Yet it was always the national debt, and the uncertainty about Jacobite intentions in this regard which most concerned supporters of the post-1688 regime and especially the Hanoverian succession. Almost nobody expected continuity with the old system: the options seemed to be cancellation, with compensation for bondholders, or outright repudiation. Most of James Stuart's counsellors advised that the soft option was simply too expensive and was self-defeating. It was estimated in the early 1730s that if James Stuart was restored and wished to liquidate the debt, he would have to raise £3 million a year in compensation. At the same time he would have to pay £1,500,000 yearly for the army and foreign mercenaries and raise another £500,000 for the civil list and to maintain foreign diplomatic representation. A Stuart monarch would then be faced with the option of cutting down the latter two items of expenses to defray the payment on the debt and thus losing popularity fast. The hard liners among his counsellors warned him that squeamishness over repudiation would cost him dear. If he repaid bondholders, they would simply use the money to conspire against him. Besides, Jacobites had been deprived of the fruits of their estates since 1688; it was time for the Whigs to suffer for their beliefs.[138] Meanwhile, a very shrewd move would be to win over the landed classes definitively to the Stuarts by making an outright gift of those entailed estates that came into the hands of certain great families in the reign of Edward VI and Elizabeth I; many noble families without a male heir lost estates worth £20,000 a year when such entailed estates reverted to the Crown. Such a gesture, moreover, would turn the tables on propagandists of 'Abbey Lands' and conciliate important sectors of the aristocracy.[139] The key was to win over almost the entire landed interest, so that repudiation of the debt would cause hardship only to the Dutch or London financiers who had no military capability in England.

It is difficult to overestimate the fears caused by the Jacobite threat to the hegemony of financial capitalism. Supporters of the post-1688 dispensation otherwise as different as Daniel Defoe and David Hume were at one in seeing this as the gravest threat of all from the Stuarts.[140] The national debt issue most clearly defines the Jacobite threat as revolutionary or, if the nomenclature is preferred, counter-revolutionary, but at any rate a phenomenon much more serious either than the original 'Glorious Revolution' or the 'American Revolution'. Modern econometric studies underline the gravity of the threat, with violent market oscillations in evidence whenever there was a Jacobite rising or even when there were rumours of one.[141] How could one seriously imagine that the Bank of England would survive in its pre-1745 form when it had lent money to the very people who had driven the Stuarts into exile and prevented their return for fifty-seven years? It is impossible toto dissent from the verdict of modern economists who have studied Jacobitism, viz. that the Jacobite threat was of a genuinely revolutionary variety.[142] It is possible to speculate counterfactually how England might have evolved if Charles Edward had been successful in 1745. Despite the scepticism of Maurepas et al., the commitments to France could not be easily shrugged off, so that it is unlikely that the great conflict of the Seven Years War, settling the issue of global hegemony between Britain and France, would have been fought. England would probably have settled into a quasi-Scandinavian mode of development, with no far-reaching British Empire. *Pace* John Buchan, King Charles III (for James had already announced his intention of abdicating in favour of his son) would not have been able to prevent the separation and independence of the American colonies, as this was historically overdetermined. In economic terms, Charles Edward probably would have delivered some of his promises to the poor and dispossessed, especially given the strong Jacobite opposition to the anti-common people thrust of phenomena such as enclosure.[143] Late eighteenth-century England under the Jacobites might not have been a brave new world but it would have been a very different one from the universe of Adam Smith, Captain Cook and Pitt the Younger.

10

The Advent of the Chartists

One of the surprise outcomes of the English Civil War was the retreat, evinced both by the 1660 Restoration and the Glorious Revolution of 1688, from any notion of power to the bourgeoisie, let alone the toiling classes. For almost 200 years the landed aristocracy had a fairly clear run at power and hegemony. After the defeat of the Jacobite rising at Culloden in 1746, there were no real challenges to their position for another another 100 years, though the repeal of the Corn Laws in 1846 signalled a fairly clear-cut victory over the landed interest by the new class of capitalists produced by the Industrial Revolution. More significantly, there were no revolutionary challenges to the ruling class. During these 100 years, it is true, the elite had to deal with serious outbreaks of rioting and even the rise of the crowd as a new factor in politics. The Wilkite riots of the 1760s were really the pursuit of mainstream politics by other means.[1] The Gordon riots of 1780 were far more serious, and some have even seen them as a *révolution manquée*, working from the fact that the rioters, ostensibly enraged against Catholics, took care mainly to target the property of *wealthy* Catholics; Romish craftsmen and labourers, from the same social stratum as the rioters, were left alone.[2] In fact, all the Gordon riots did was to expose the unreality of 'spontaneous combustion' (a theory later avidly exposed by Rosa Luxemburg) as a means to revolution. Extrapolating from the Gordon riots, many observers then and since have wondered why England did not follow France into revolution in 1789 or even beat the French to it. On superficial indices England in the 1780s seemed more vulnerable to revolution than France. The Bourbon monarchy appeared stable while the British constitution was riddled with corruption; France's ruling dynasty was at least homegrown, where the Hanoverians were boorish Germans; England emerged from the American War of Independence a beaten nation militarily, while France was on the side of the victors; and the entire lengthy tradition of rioting and popular disturbances in England made its population seem more refractory and rebellious than the cowed French. There can be many answers to the question of why France swung hard left into revolution while the English sailed the seas of continuity. Some of them are obvious. The peasantry was not an issue in England, the British had not emerged from the American war bankrupt as the French had, and their economy was in better shape.[3] Not insignificantly, the Gordon riots were a false dawn if viewed as inchoate revolution. From 1792 to 1815 almost continual war in France coupled with severe repression at home – principally Pitt the Younger's 'white terror' and his Two Acts (against Treasonable Practices and Seditious Meetings) – put most thoughts of even mild social protest on the backburner.[4]

After Waterloo, British politics was dominated for a long time (until 1832) by the issues of Catholic emancipation and electoral reform. The former was achieved by 1828, but the latter was altogether more intractable. There had been pressure for the extension of the franchise ever since the founding of the London Corresponding Society in 1792. In the immediate aftermath of the Napoleonic Wars, a campaign for universal male suffrage, annual parliaments and the secret ballot was led by the charismatic Henry 'Orator' Hunt. Government cracked down hard, first in the notorious Peterloo massacre of 1819, when a peaceful radical movement in Manchester was broken up by the military, leaving some 700 demonstrators seriously wounded; 15 were killed outright and many others crawled away to die from their wounds afterwards.[5] In some ways this was the most heinous reponse to popular protest ever seen in English history, for the troops were not facing armed and destructive rioters but unarmed demonstrators; moreover the level of vicious, misogynistic violence meted out to women protesters shocked even those with no sympathy for radical causes.[6] Peterloo was followed by Hunt's imprisonment for nearly three years and the passage of the Six Acts, suppressing radical meetings and publications, limiting the numbers of people who could assemble for political discussions, curtailing civil liberties and making it a crime even to discuss certain books and journals. As one historian has remarked: 'It is not fanciful to compare the restricted freedoms of the British worker in the post-Peterloo period in the early nineteenth century with those of black South Africans in the post-Sharpeville period of the late twentieth century.'[7] It is a myth that Peterloo led to any softening in elite attitudes or that it influenced MPs to pass the Reform Act of 1832. What operated most forcibly was the law of unintended consequences. The Tories under the Duke of Wellington repealed the anti-Catholic penal laws out of a sense that the situation in Ireland was reaching boiling point. However, many Tories argued that the danger from northern cities was just as great and, in any case, the people there were largely nonconformists who would offset the newly emancipated Catholics. It became even more difficult for the diehards to hold the pass against parliamentary reform when Wellington alienated his own party with a fatuous no-change speech. After losing a vote of no confidence in the House of Commons, Wellington resigned and the parliamentary initiative passed to the reform-minded Whig Lord Charles Grey. He it was who managed, at the third attempt, to enact the so-called Great Reform Act.[8]

However, the Whigs made it clear that the Reform Act was as far as they were prepared to go in granting concessions to the lower orders. Accordingly, in the 1830s social unrest and agitation grew exponentially. There were many reasons for the tense and febrile politics of the decade, but four may be identified as salient. In the first place, in all but elite circles the much-trumpeted Reform Act was a severe disappointment. It was true that 143 rotten boroughs had been abolished and 135 new seats created in the northern industrial areas, thus aligning the electorate to some extent with demographic reality, but even at this level not all the 'pocket boroughs' had been phased out. In its other aspects the Reform Act was a grave let-down. Much was made of the increase in the electorate from around 400,000 to 653,000 (out of a population of some 13 million in Great Britain) – about one in six of the male population – but these men comprised a smaller proportion of the population than those eligible to vote in 1640.[9] In Ireland the situation was even worse, with just 90,000 eligible to vote out of a population of 7.8 million. Moreover, as well as extirpating most rotten boroughs the act swept away the ratepayer 'scot and lot' franchise that had existed in 37 boroughs, including radical strongholds like Westminster. Whether through ineptitude or Machiavellianism the 1832 act disenfranchised large numbers of working-class men by opting for a £10 property qualification instead of a ratepayer franchise. On the other hand, it enfranchised the £50 tenants at will, whose lack of security of tenure made them essentially the creatures of their landlords at election time. Though more people could now vote, it was simply more of the wealthy, making the electoral system in net terms less democratic than before.[10] To the fury of early nineteenth-century feminists, women were now expressly forbidden the vote in general elections; hitherto a few wealthy female landowners had squeezed in. The essential factor of the secret ballot to prevent intimidation, for which Orator Hunt had striven, was not conceded. It is not surprising that, in the opinion of most later historians, the 1832 act changed very little at all. It was a classic illustration of the Lampedusa dictum in *The Leopard*: 'Everything must change so that everything remains the same.'[11]

A second reason for working-class ferment was the introduction of the New Poor Law in 1834. Since 1795 indigence had been tackled through the 'Speenhamland system', which doled out relief to paupers according to the size of families and the prevailing cost of bread, but by the early 1830s this approach was deemed ruinously expensive, since it cost the Exchequer £7 million in 1832 alone. The 1834 act ended out-relief to the poor and instituted workhouses, which were to become a shibboleth of horror to the working class. The workhouse system was directed by a central department and three commissioners. Paupers were separated by age and sex and made to work in dreadful conditions for a stipend below the level of the lowest-paid worker in regular employment. Rather than enter the dreaded workhouses the unskilled would accept almost any job and at almost any level of pay; some families even starved to death rather than accept the humiliation and stigma of the workhouse. One of the aims of the radical movement after 1834 was to end this iniquitous system.[12] Yet another proletarian grievance was the ferociously hostile attitude of all governments to the nascent trade union movement. In the 1790s William Pitt the Younger, that unregenerate foe of all things radical and progressive, had effectively made trade unions illegal with his Combination Act. Pitt's law was repealed in 1824 after assiduous lobbying by a fascinating troika of individuals: Francis Place, Joseph Hume and Sir Francis Burdett. Hume (1777–1855) was the most interesting of the three since his radicalism evolved, and he eventually became a 'moral force' Chartist. Burdett (1770–1844), who had earlier suffered imprisonment for his beliefs, gradually became more and more conservative as he grew older and eventually abjured all his earlier beliefs. Francis Place (1771–1854), often thought of as the key link between the eighteenth-century politics of crowd agitation and the mass movements of the 1840s, was an anomalous figure. Supposedly a leader of the Labour movement, he was a Benthamite who thought that unions were a fetter on free trade and the workings of the market; he confessed that his motives for working so hard for the repeal of Pitt's Combination Act was that he thought a carefully revised act – the one he achieved in 1825 – would kill off trade unions for good.[13] Instead they grew rapidly in the years thereafter. The 1825 Combination Act accepted the legality of unions but imposed limitations on the right to strike and confined unionism within severe guidelines: men could meet to bargain over wages and conditions but anything beyond this – intra-union solidarity, sympathetic strikes, unions with political aims – was to be considered a criminal conspiracy. Trade unions were informed that they could not 'molest, obstruct or intimidate' anyone, with the precise meaning given to these verbs to be decided by judges, not a group known for their working-class sympathies.[14]

The most sensational manifestation of government attitude to trade unions came in 1834 when six Dorset farm labourers were arrested and charged with administering unlawful oaths during a meeting of an agricultural labourers' friendly society. Their actions were not in any way sinister – no different from the oaths taken at masonic or Orange lodges, as the Irish Nationalist leader Daniel O'Connell, 'the Liberator', pointed out – but the government chose to take the line that the Tolpuddle men were planning a violent uprising. The real purpose was to arrest the burgeoning trade union movement, which had alarmed Place and those who thought like him by its rapid take-off after the passage of the 1825 Combination Act. The 'Tolpuddle Martyrs' were each sentenced to seven years' transportation to Australia. A national outcry convinced Lord Melbourne and his cabinet the sentences were excessive and they were pardoned, but not before the seven men had endured two years of the harshest conceivable treatment in Australia's penal colonies. Although the men returned to England and a heroes' welcome, the Labour movement had been made aware, as had the reformists at Peterloo, that in the English ruling class they faced a ruthless and bloodthirsty enemy.[15]

Nonetheless middle-class reformers plugged away at the Ten Hour Movement to limit the working day. Perhaps the three most powerful streams feeding into the river that finally became Chartism were opposition to the new Poor Law, the movement for factory reform and the campaign for the ten-hour day. There were other important issues, too, such as the campaign for repeal of the newspaper stamp duty and, for middle-class radicals, the worsening situation in Ireland, exacerbated by the government's Irish Coercion Bill of 1833.[16] All this took place against a background of worsening factory conditions as industrialisation reached its apogee, increasing unemployment in the weaving industry, rising prices – the price of wheat rose from 39 shillings a quarter in 1836 to 68 shillings in 1840 – resentment at factory discipline and especially the employment of women in textile mills, as this was thought to break up family life, and general hatred of the Whig government. Although radical concern over the ancient issues of 'old corruption' and the powers of the Crown lessened in the 1830s, in part because of the 1832 act and the accession of Queen Victoria in 1837, the working classes and their supporters loathed the Whigs for their actions over the Poor Law, the Tolpuddle martyrs and the repression of the Captain Swing riots in southern England. Most of all they detested them for not passing on the perceived benefits of increasing prosperity to the proletariat.[17]

All of these issues at play simultaneously created the 'perfect storm' of radical opposition that came to be known as Chartism. It was the abiding ambition of Chartism, never fully realised, to build a national, coherent mass movement that would fuse all these discontents. The spectrum of opposition to the 'bloody Whigs' ran all the way from the Tory leader Sir Robert Peel, who particularly disliked the 1834 Poor Act, through Robert Owen and other like-minded cotton-mill owners to the benighted paupers themselves. The Ten-Hour Movement was headed by Tory gentry in Yorkshire, where an alliance between Tories and working-class radicals was particularly evident. There was considerable overlap between trade union membership, the campaign for shorter working hours and action against the poor law. The first man to try to integrate all this into a single movement was William Lovett, whose London Working Men's Association (LWMA) was formed in June 1836.[18] The essential problem with the LWMA was that its aim was a trans-class coalition. Seeking to reach out to the middle classes, it was expensive to join and restricted to 'persons of good moral character'. This reflected William Lovett's essentially conservative temperament.[19] Partly as a reaction to this, a rival organisation, led by Bronterre O'Brien arose in 1837, known as the London Democratic Association (LDA) and dedicated to the principles of Tom Paine. Meanwhile an Irish politican named Feargus O'Connor, who in 1835 lost his seat as an MP through allegedly not having the proper property qualifications, founded yet another radical organisation in London, the Marylebone Radical Association; London thus had three rival radical organisations. By 1837, with a worldwide economic depression beginning to bite, the provinces began to get in on the act. The Birmingham Political Union, like the LWMA a reform movement reaching out to the middle classes, was the first to adopt all six points of what would later be the People's Charter, the manifesto of Chartism. These were the very far from revolutionary Six Points: universal male suffrage, payment of members of parliament, equal constituencies, no property qualifications for members, the secret ballot and annual parliaments.[20] The upshot of all this activity was the first explicitly Chartist national meeting at Kensal Moor near Manchester on 24 September 1838 attended by a crowd estimated at anywhere from 100,000 to 250,000 and called to organise a national petition to Parliament. It was agreed that fifty delegates from the meeting would meet in London early the following year at a national convention to plan strategy. A further triumphal and highly optimistic meeting was held at Hartshead Moor in Yorkshire on 15 October.

And so the Chartist movement was born. Two key questions immediately present themselves. What was the social composition of Chartism, and who were its leaders? In general Chartism appealed most strongly to radical intellectuals and the skilled workers of the northern and Scottish industrial cities and, to a lesser extent to the artisans and craftsmen of London. One analysis of recruitment into the movement in 1838–9 finds four main groupings: the hard core of radical reformers, some of whom would go on to embrace socialism; young men keen to see action who were new recruits to working-class politics; a large body of 'infantry' – loyal supporters who could be relied on to attend meetings, march in processions and sign petitions – or what one might call the 'fellowship' of Chartism; and a rank and file fluctuating between enthusiasm and apathy, depending on the fortunes of the movement at any given time.[21] The horrors of the industrial north and the 'Satanic mills' in the early nineteenth century, as in Dickens's Coketown, with its giant factories and clouds of choking smoke, are too well known to require elaboration and were famously described in Engels's classic, *The Condition of the Working Class in England*.[22] Another study of London Chartism identifies all the following groups as supporters: boot and shoemakers, tailors, members of the building trade (carpenters, joiners, stonemasons, bricklayers, plasterers, plumbers, painters, glaziers), silk weavers, hatters, jewellery and watchmakers, bakers, labourers, and members of the furniture, leather, printing and book trades, as well as those working in metals (coppersmiths, braziers, tinplate workers, boiler-makers, engineers).[23] Moreover, at least in its early days, Chartism had a strong appeal to women, who played an important role in the movement, albeit largely as 'spear carriers' to the disgust of later feminists.[24] By drawing support from such wide and diverse sources, Chartism was able to establish itself as the first modern political party, drawing strength from Scotland, Ireland and Wales as well as England. The appeal of rival movements and ideologies, such as Luddism or Captain Swing, was minimal, as their potential supporters were swallowed up by the overarching ideology of Chartism.[25] Modern techniques such as mass demonstrations, the raising of election funds and the disruption of rival meetings, were all perfected by the Chartists. The movement also appeared at a historical hinge, for the 1840s was a decade of industrial, technological and demographic change. Railways, the telegraph, the penny post and urbanisation all played their part in 'shrinking' the nation, and the plethora of newspapers meant that the English public was the most politically informed in Europe.[26]

The early leaders of the Chartist movement spanned the spectrum between a modest, almost deferential attitude to the ruling elite and a commitment to gradual reform on one hand and a foaming-mouthed rhetoric of revolution on the other. The two representative figures in the period 1838–40 were William Lovett and the Rev. J. R. Stephens. Lovett (1800–77), a ropemaker, Methodist and union organiser, claimed to have inherited the mantle of Orator Hunt – an absurd claim as he had neither Hunt's eloquence as an orator nor his skill as a politician. He did, however, have respectable credentials as a veteran of the campaign to pardon the Tolpuddle martyrs and he was a prolific journalist.[27] A working-class intellectual, he had a naive belief in the automatically prevailing power of truth. For O'Connor he always had a visceral loathing. The leading advocate of 'moral force' as against O'Connor's espousal of 'physical force' he fell out with the Promethean Irishman as early as 1837 when O'Connor criticised his 'softly, softly' handling of government repression of a Glasgow spinners' strike. Lacking all O'Connor's ability as a politician, his charisma and his power as an orator, Lovett was soon reduced to making peevish attacks on his rival. During his bitter quarrel with O'Connor in 1838 he accused the Irishman of always wanting to take credit for the achievements of Chartism and for ruthlessly cutting all other leading actors out of the historical record: 'You carry your fame about with you on all occasions to sink other topics in the shade – you are the great "I AM" of politics.'[28] The general opinion among historians is that Lovett was a distinctly minor figure, that both he and the LWMA have been overrated, and that he was unfitted to be either a tactician or a theorist of a revolutionary movement.[29] Lovett's obtuseness would later bring him, unwittingly, to deliver London Chartism into the O'Connorite camp, whereas originally O'Connor had concentrated on the provinces. But Lovett did not lack courage and later served a prison sentence in appalling conditions for his Chartist beliefs. To his credit, he detested O'Connell the 'Liberator' even more than O'Connor. In 1843 he made a bitter attack on the Liberator and, comparing O'Connor with O'Connell as both 'most preeminent in the art of gulling', called down a plague on both their houses.[30]

No greater contrast could be imagined than that between the mild Lovett and the tempestuous, fire-eating Methodist preacher Joseph Rayner Stephens, though Stephens was later to prove himself no more than a 'talking horse', to use racing parlance. An early Chartist, though he never called himself one, Stephens had distinguished himself in the campaign for the ten-hour day.[31] An impassioned advocate of violence, Stephens had three main themes in his orations. One was that Christianity and radicalism/socialism were co-extensive. To this end he often claimed comradeship with John Ball and Jack Cade and, at the meeting at Hartshead Moor in October 1838, famously declared: 'The Lord Jesus Christ was the prince of Jack Cades!'[32] A second motif was that the Charter had an organic connection with the original Great Charter or Magna Carta. In his Hartshead Moor speech Stephens expressed this as follows: 'We stand upon our rights – we seek no change – we say give us the good old laws of England unchanged . . . What are those laws? Aye, Magna Carta! The good old laws of English freedom – freedom of worship – freedom of homesteads – free and happy firesides, and no workhouses.'[33] A third theme was the egregious wickedness whereby working-class men had to send their wives to work in factories merely to survive. In his own, admittedly paternalistic, way Stephens always cared about women. One of his mottos was: 'For children and wife we'll war to the knife.'[34] Even O'Connor, no slouch at demagoguery himself, felt that Stephens's over-the-top effusions damaged the cause by frightening the middle classes away. Posterity has not been kind in its judgement on Stephens. Dorothy Thompson summed him up thus: 'He was much more the kind of charismatic, irresponsible demagogue that the historians have presented O'Connor as being, than was O'Connor himself . . . his staring eyes and emotive language aroused crowds to hysteria . . . the Savonarola of the early Chartist movement.'[35] A kinder assesment is this: 'It was the impassioned platform oratory of men like O'Connor and Stephens that drew working-class supporters to the Chartist movement, rather than the dry fare dished up by Lovett and the LWMA.'[36]

Yet by any reckoning the titanic figure of the early years of Chartism was Feargus O'Connor (1794–1855) and, unlike Lovett and Stephens, who quickly faded from the scene, O'Connor dominated English radical politics for the next twelve years. O'Connor, an Irish Protestant aristocrat, was in the classic tradition of 'gentleman radicals' exemplified by Sir Francis Burdett and Orator Hunt in the Regency years, and by Sir Charles Dilke, Henry Hyndman and Sir Wilfred Lawson at the end of the nineteenth century. He was in many ways a quintessential Irishman, a fine horseman and expert whist player with an over-endowment of 'blarney'. Allegedly a descendant of one of the high kings of Ireland, he inherited an estate from his uncle, was educated at Trinity College, Dublin, and called to the bar in 1820. He began his political career as a liberal organiser and was elected MP for Cork in 1831, but was unseated four years later on the grounds that he lacked the requisite property qualifications.[37] At first he was a follower of Daniel O'Connell the 'Liberator' but fell out with the leader in the mid-1830s after growing disillusionment on a number of issues. O'Connell was something of a tunnel-vision politician, who had but two main aims: Catholic emancipation and the repeal of the 1801 Act of Union, which made Ireland part of the United Kingdom. His success on emancipation in 1829 led him thereafter to a monomaniac concentration on repeal, which, as O'Connor saw, was only a beginning to the solution of Ireland's problems, not the end piece. Moreover, O'Connell was a Benthamite, in favour of laissez-faire economics and in politics believed in unwavering support for the Whigs. In everyday politics O'Connor found him much more interested in the health of the Irish party in Westminster than in Ireland itself.[38] At any rate the split between the two men was not long in coming. Some see O'Connor as a divided self, with one half devoted to an independent Ireland and always hankering to lead the Irish to this promised land, and the other half committed to Chartism and the English working class. O'Connell's vast power in Ireland cut O'Connor off from his Irish taproots and, so to speak, marooned him in English politics. Some see this as an inevitable consequence of O'Connor's rebellious nature but others, more shrewdly, suggest that, once O'Connell discerned the political talent in the younger man, he wanted him ousted. He disliked O'Connor's growing popularity as he could not bear 'a brother near the throne'.[39] After the split the antagonism between the two men became palpable. O'Connell could not bear O'Connor's ferocious attacks on the English Whigs and dubbed him a Tory radical, though O'Connor was surely correct to discern in O'Connell much more kinship with the English propertied class than the Irish peasantry. In a series of pamphlets in 1837 O'Connor accused O'Connell of autocracy, corruption and servility to the English elite and would continue to assail him for his inept handling of Irish affairs; always in the back of his mind was the thought that one day he might supplant O'Connell as leader of the Irish.[40] There is no question but that O'Connor won the propaganda war in the minds of all but the English elite. O'Connell replied with many savage and withering denunciations of Chartism, which he loathed viscerally and saw as a danger to civilisation itself.[41]

O'Connor has always divided commentators, and a balanced and nuanced view of him is not easy. Some have seen him as an utterly negligible figure, vain, arrogant, self-regarding, intellectually incoherent, a gadfly or butterfly, a demagogue who lusted after popularity and basked in the pleasure of being a popular idol but had essentially nothing to say and nothing to contribute: 'the ruin of the Chartist movement' in one view.[42] We must concede the critics many of their points. He was all things to all men, hail-fellow-well-met when meeting the workers, a figure of gravitas when dealing with the Establishment. He could not collaborate with equals and fell out with all other leaders of the Chartist movement, wanting always to be centre-stage. His espousal of 'physical force' was insincere. Basically he agreed with the 'moral force' faction, but he knew that if he came out openly on their side he would alienate the masses, who wanted stronger meat. He was one of those maddening 'revolutionaries' who claim that violence is necessary to achieve desired ends but only in certain circumstances which he would never specify; needless to say there never was a time when the 'favourable conjuncture' for violence presented itself. He lacked courage and was an irresponsible mob orator, whipping his audience up to expectations he knew in his heart he could never satisfy. In his vanity he claimed to be a theoretician yet he contributed nothing to Chartist thought.[43] Quick-witted and cunning, he was nonetheless deficient in real intellect. As one hostile critic has remarked: 'His mental culture was surprisingly limited, his legal education was neither comprehensive nor profound enough to separate him from the masses.'[44] Some even condemn him because he was a habitual womaniser. The phrase 'he never married', which usually carries the connotation of homosexuality, in O'Connor's case simply meant that he had a multitude of mistresses, girlfriends and one-night stands, though, as always with O'Connor, when the source for the philandering is his own 'memories', one should beware. All that is on one side. Yet the suspicion arises that O'Connor has been underrated and unfairly traduced simply because he ended as a failure. Alongside these (admittedly grave) defects were many virtues. O'Connor was a deeply attractive human being in many ways. A natural actor, with a bell-like voice that put him in the class of Pitt the Elder, Danton or Orator Hunt, he was supremely witty, a first-class mimic and a brilliant raconteur with an inexhaustible fund of anecdotes.[45] He had a shrewd understanding of power and human nature and realised, unlike Lovett, that Parliament would never concede the Charter simply on the basis of quiet, peaceful lobbying. He had the common touch and could enthral working-class audiences by knowing exactly the right note to hit, exactly the right mixture of indignation and exhortation to work into his orations. He knew precisely how to articulate their hopes and fears. Amazingly, he very quickly overcame the innate prejudice of the English proletariat against the Irish, won them round and enthused them to the point where he became their idol. Nor was he a mere 'champagne socialist' of his times. His sympathy for the wretched of the earth was deeply sincere and he poured his own money into the cause. He could have become comfortable and wealthy by practising the law and would have had fewer interruptions to his hedonistic pursuits as a lawyer, but chose to commit himself to the working class.[46] He never enjoyed robust health and was frequently ill during his Chartist heyday but drove himself on through willpower. His work rate was phenomenal. Between June 1838 and August 1839, he spent 123 days on the road, during which he made 147 major speeches as well as attending innumerable conferences, committee meetings and court hearings.[47] His faults were legion but there can be no doubting his fundamental sincerity.

Other significant leaders of early Chartism were Thomas Atwood (1783–1856), the leading light of Birmingham Chartism and Peter Murray McDouall (1815–54), a Scottish surgeon in favour of physical force and the general strike.[48] More formidable and prominent were the intellectuals of the movement, James Bronterre O'Brien and George Julian Harney. Bronterre O'Brien (1805–64), another Irishman, had aspects of his personality that were uncannily like O'Connor's: like him he was educated at Trinity College, Dublin, trained as a lawyer and suffered the same pattern of frequent ill health, ending with mental illness. Intellectually, he had a finer mind than O'Connor's. As an undergraduate he had won the college's gold medal for science and was deeply and widely read. He was radicalised by his intense study of the French Revolution, from which he derived a fervent admiration for the men of the Left, especially Robespierre and Gracchus Babeuf, and also by his leading role in the fight against stamp duty on newspapers.[49] Faced with the elite's blatant attempt at censorship by price, thus placing newspapers beyond the reach of the ordinary man, O'Brien hit back by publishing *Bronterre's National Reformer*, which consisted of 'essays' rather than news items and so escaped stamp duty. The scale of the authorities' paranoia about words written by dissidents can be gauged by the police raid on O'Brien's house in 1838, when they seized a manuscript he was writing on the

French Revolution! Known as the 'schoolmaster of Chartism' he deeply influenced Harney at the start of his career and continued to write voluminously.[50] Despite his fine brain, O'Brien was a poor strategist and politician and, even at the abstract level, his thinking could be confused and incoherent – which some attributed to alcoholism. The seam-bursting eclecticism of his thought led him to some bizarre notions, such as that technology alone and unaided would bring about classlessness without the loss of any wealth or property or the loss of a single life. After 1840 O'Brien abandoned his early leftism, swung hard right and ended as a mild reformist, dedicated to cooperation with the middle class. Many contemporary observers thought him the most intellectually gifted of the Chartists, and this included Engels, who strongly disliked him at the personal level.[51] His last decade was blighted by severe illness and tuberculosis; scholars dispute about whether mental illness or alcoholism was his bane. O'Brien's main problem as a would-be political leader was that he was a perfectionist who hated compromise; he was also unstable, unable to hold down any job long, a Jonah figure and paranoid with it.[52]

In contrast to O'Brien, who made the conventional passage from youthful firebrand to elderly conservative (the political equivalent of *jeune cocotte, vieille dévote*), his early pupil George Julian Harney (1817–97) moved ever leftwards, ending as a Marxist. Trained as a seaman, Harney was radicalised when he was arrested as a paper boy for selling an unstamped newspaper. Already by 1839 the most left-wing of the Chartists, he later became a close friend of Marx and Engels.[53] He too was a great admirer of Robespierre but, unlike O'Brien, never recanted. A fine writer, he was never much of an orator – a facet of his personality seized on by his many critics in the Chartist movement – but on any rational analysis he emerges as more clearsighted than Lovett, O'Brien or O'Connor. The flavour of Harney's thinking is well conveyed by one of his utterances in January 1839:

> We demand universal suffrage, because we believe thc universal suffrage will bring universal happiness. Time was when every Englishman had a musket in his cottage, and along with it hung a flitch of bacon; now there was no flitch of bacon for there was no musket; let the musket be restored and the flitch of bacon would soon follow. You will get nothing from your tyrants but what you can take, and you can take

> nothing unless you are properly prepared to do so. In the words of a good man, then, I say, arm for peace, arm for liberty, arm for justice, arm for the rights of all, and the tyrants will no longer laugh at your petitions. Remember that.[54]

To his delight Harney found ironworkers in Winlaton, near Newcastle upon Tyne, making weapons. At a meeting of the London Democratic Association, Harney proposed and passed a motion 'to meet all acts of oppression with immediate resistance . . . we hold it to be the duty of the Convention [the forthcoming General Convention of Chartists] to impress upon the people the necessity of an immediate preparation for ulterior measures'. This meant that at the Convention O'Connor had to head off flank attacks from both the intellectuals, O'Brien and Harney. Whereas O'Brien always rather resented the fact that O'Connor kept him on a tight leash, Harney was more sympathetic to his leader and regarded him as indispensable. He appreciated that O'Connor was far more accommodating to his followers than Orator Hunt or William Cobbett had been and that he had sacrificed a lucrative career as a lawyer for the cause.[55]

Harney came into his own at the General Convention of the Working Classes held in London on 4 February 1839, especially as O'Connor was absent. The great Irish leader had a distaste for such assemblies and preferred to campaign mainly through the hugely influential newspaper he founded in Leeds, the *Northern Star*. Fifty-three delegates foregathered for what was intended to be a grand strategy meeting, including 6 newspaper editors, 2 doctors, 2 religious ministers, 3 magistrates and a plethora of shopkeepers.[56] Straight away there was tension between the 'moral force' and 'physical force' factions, with Harney openly expressing impatience and discontent with Lovett's chairmanship. There was already bad blood between the LWMA and the O'Connorite faction, not just because of the general poor state of relations between Lovett and O'Connor but because the 'physical force' people accused Lovett and the LWMA of collusion in a parliamentary witch-hunt of trade union activities following the turbulent strike of Glasgow cotton-spinners in 1837. Factionalism – that besetting sin of the Left throughout history – was the most striking thing about a Convention that should have been preparing a common, united strategy. The general ambivalence has been well summed up by one student of the conference: 'Some were prepared to threaten force, others were anxious to regard it as a last defence. Some dabbled in the rhetoric of revolution; others, a tiny minority, thought seriously but not very effectively how a revolution might be accomplished.'[57] The main aim of the Convention was to prepare a national petition demanding the Six Points, to be presented to Parliament. Although there were minor and inconclusive debates about the correct attitude to take to the growing middle-class movement to repeal the Corn Laws, most of the discussion concerned the correct moral stance of the so-called 'loyal rebel'. What was to be done if Parliament rejected the petition? And what was the role of violence? Harney reported that talk of violent action was in the air. The delegation from Tyneside stated defiantly: 'If they Peterloo us, we'll Moscow them.'[58] Hardly surprisingly, with so many different factions jostling for supremacy, no firm decision was taken except for the anodyne resolution to meet all acts of government oppression with 'immediate resistance' (type unspecified).[59] From afar O'Connor endorsed the formula 'peacefully if we may, forcibly if we must'. Yet his most favoured formula – an alliance of the labouring classes in England and Ireland – met with indifference and sometimes outright hostility.[60] Lovett seemed convinced by the 'success' of the Reform Act of 1832 that the Chartists could achieve their aims by incessant nagging and chivvying, almost as though he thought the government could be bored into granting the Six Points. The Convention can only be considered a failure and a wasted opportunity. The delegates did not seek to coopt the all-important London proletariat, nor did they make any realistic contingency plans in case the national petition was rejected.[61] Always absent from Chartist deliberations was the chessplayer's mentality, planning four or five moves ahead. They preferred to react to government initiatives, which meant they were permanently on the back foot. 'Immediate resistance' was given no realistic content.

While the Convention relocated itself to Birmingham in May 1839, social tensions were at white heat. Alarming reports were coming in of the arming of the working class and Chartists' supervising military drills in secret bases. A bogus rumour stalked Whitehall that there would be a general insurrection on 6 May.[62] By this time the Whigs had entered their second ministry and the prime minister was Lord Melbourne, by nature a jittery hard liner. His government secretly encouraged magistrates in the north to break up Chartist meetings and make arrests; McDouall was one of the first swept up in this net. Meanwhile the mass meetings in the north went on: Newcastle Town Moor on 20 May, Kersal Moor on 20 May. Hartshead Moor on 21 May. The firebrand Joseph Stephens told his impassioned listeners that God's law called for the use of force against evil men.[63] In June the Chartists presented the national petition to Parliament. There were 1,280,000 signatures – representing more than 50 per cent of those who had voted in the 1837 general election – and the document containing them was three miles long. Despite this signal demonstration of the popular will, Parliament contemptuously rejected the Charter by a vote of 235–46. This hit the delegates to the Convention, still in session at Birmingham, like a thunderbolt.[64] The Convention had opted for petitioning for four main reasons: since they were disenfranchised, there was no other way for the working class to communicate with Parliament; the petition bound together the disparate groups operating under the umbrella of Chartism; women could take part in the activity as they could not in violent clashes; and it was thought that no deference was involved in petitioning.[65] O'Brien, however, was vehemently opposed from the beginning. He argued that to petition *was* to show deference.[66] He argued that the Convention had to collect 2–3 million signatures before it presented a petition or called a general strike; an overwhelming mandate was necessary. O'Connor, who attended the Convention in Birmingham, maintained that signatures were consequences not causes of Chartist activity; that presenting the national petition and preparations for a general strike should proceed *pari passu*. Overemphasis on *numbers* of signatures, he argued, missed the point, for a million signatures could not dislodge a single troop of dragoons.[67] When the national petition was rejected, O'Connor and the Convention discussed countermeasures that stopped short of an armed uprising. These included the withdrawal of savings from banks and the conversion of paper money into gold and silver. Most popular of all counterstrikes was the option of a 'sacred month' during which the proletariat would do no work at all – a euphemism for a general strike.[68]

Why was the government so uncompromising in its rejection of the Charter, which, on the face of it, contained no revolutionary demands and could be construed as mild electoral reformism? The main evidence comes from Lord Melbourne and his home secretary,

Lord John Russell. William Lamb, 2nd Viscount Melbourne, was an oddity who earlier in life had suffered the indignity of being cuckolded by Lord Byron. Perhaps in compensation he turned to sado-masochism: spanking sessions with aristocratic ladies and, more sinisterly, brutal whippings of orphan girls he had taken into his household, allegedly out of charity.[69] Melbourne was not, like the Duke of Wellington, an unregenerate reactionary, though he listened to Queen Victoria, whose favourite he was and whose hatred of Chartism was well known. Deeply influenced by Russell, he suppressed his natural hard-line instincts and determined on constitutionalism, prepared to use the military against the Chartists but only when he deemed it absolutely necessary.[70] Lord John Russell, grandfather of the famous philosopher Bertrand Russell, had few popular admirers, being despised for his diminutive size (5' 5"), but his view of the Chartists was nuanced. Contemptuous of the Charter and its ideology, he was one of those who affected to patronise its benighted believers. He remarked disdainfully that the Chartists were really concerned about economic advancement while pretending to be interested in suffrage. But, he pointed out, surely the Chartists were not so stupid as to confuse the two; the example of the USA proved that economic prosperity had nothing to do with suffrage.[71] He genuinely believed that universal suffrage would mean the death of property, that the Chartists had swallowed whole the myth of the French Revolution, and that the vengeful majority would sweep away all vestiges of privilege. For Russell, Chartism meant the end of the House of Lords, the monarchy and the equalisation of property. On the other hand, he was not so intemperate as O'Connell, who denounced 'physical force' Chartists as treasonous. Russell distinguished between abstract advocacy of the Charter, as plugged assiduously in O'Connor's *Northern Star*, and genuinely revolutionary activity. There were some nervous moments for the Whigs in the winter of 1838–9 when Russell temporarily left his post to attend to his wife Adelaide's illness and death, and the more volatile Melbourne took over his portfolio. Russell returned to the Home Office in early 1839, only to find himself accused by *The Times* of excessive leniency towards the Chartists.[72] He was sufficiently alarmed by the reports of drilling and arming among the Chartists to persuade Melbourne to recall three regiments from Ireland.

After the rejection of the national petition, Chartist anger reached a diapason, and the aggressive stance from the government once they got wind of the 'sacred month' made it seem likely that a major conflagration would sooner or later erupt. Typical of the heavy-handed approach from the authorities was an incident in Birmingham on 8 July. A peaceful meeting of Chartists in the Bull Ring was violently attacked by the police and many were injured.[73] As a response to the intolerable provocation of a radical meeting the government arrested William Lovett, who was found guilty on public order charges and spent a dreadful twelve months in jail. Tempers were running high, and O'Connor had to use all the persuasive power of his *Northern Star* to dampen tensions.[74] For a while England hovered perilously close to revolution. Lord Broughton told the cabinet, 'As the object of the Chartists was to knock us on the head and rob us of our property, we might as well arrive at that catastrophe after a struggle as without it; we could only fail and we might succeed.' To which Melbourne replied ominously, 'Exactly so.'[75] A general strike would probably have led to more violence and a nationwide rising, with unpredictable consequences. This was the juncture at which O'Connor persuaded the Convention to call off the 'sacred month'. As he correctly pointed out, the Convention had made no proper arrangements for coordinating such an upsurge. The outright rejection of the national petition had shaken him, and made him realise that he had not thought through the consequences and implications of his call for 'physical force'. He felt that he needed more time and that the Chartists, instead of winning a quick victory, would have to settle in for a long haul.[76] Perhaps he did not dare to admit to himself the awful truth: that he had used the exhortation to violence as a bluff, which the government had now called. Some of the Convention members admitted other fears: either that government repression would be terrible and bloodthirsty or, even worse, that workers would fail to heed the call and the sacred month would fail spontaneously. To the fury of Harney, the Convention voted against a general strike in July.[77] The 'sacred month', due to begin on 12 August 1839, was cancelled and a pointless three days of protest meetings substituted. Disgusted by the betrayal by their leaders, the workers scarcely heeded the Convention's call for the three-day protest, and from this date the would-be ruling committee began to disintegrate as an effective body. Its dissolution in September signalled the end of the LWMA's leadership of the movement.[78]

We shall have occasion later to discuss the extent to which revolutions can fail through sheer bad luck or, conversely, how elites can survive through good fortune. Among the happy circumstances for Melbourne's Whig government was the appointment of Major-General Sir Charles Napier as army commander in northern England (his official title was General Officer Commanding the British Northern District). Some of Napier's sayings might have seemed ominous in the mouth of a man appointed to police Chartists: 'The best way to quiet a country is a good thrashing, followed by great kindness afterwards. Even the wildest chaps are thus tamed.' 'The human mind is never better disposed to gratitude and attachment than when softened by fear.'[79] Yet, far from being a blimp, Napier was one of the most impressive and intelligent individuals the British armed forces have ever produced. He was as talented at administration as at conducting military campaigns, as he had proved in a memorable posting as British governor (resident) of the island of Cephalonia during the wars of Greek independence. Veteran of the Peninsular Wars and a man of leonine courage who had already survived three close encounters with death, Napier was also an intellectual with a wide range of interests. In politics he was a radical who had clashed bitterly with the reactionary O'Connell over the Poor Law and his visceral sympathies were with the Chartists. During his varied and fascinating life he won the admiration of at least two men of genius, Lord Byron and Sir Richard Burton.[80] He was also witty, as he showed later when sending his one-word dispatch announcing the conquest of Sindh in India (*Peccavi* – Latin for 'I have sinned'). Immediately on taking over military command in northern England, Napier showed his calibre. He made extensive preparations in Manchester, Nottingham and Derbyshire, while warning the Chartists in a friendly way that an armed rising was suicidal. At a personal level he liked O'Connor, admiring him for his wit as well as the way the Irishman seemed always to wear an expression on his face as though he expected all to be done with good behaviour and fair play. Napier attended Chartist meetings and was impressed by the power of O'Connor's authority and the seemingly magical way in which the crowds would melt away after he had finished speaking.[81] In his private correspondence Napier told his friends that he could find nothing to object to in the Chartists' political programme, that they were right when they said that the people of England were ill-treated and ill-governed.

Whatever his private sympathies, Napier was a soldier and determined to do his duty. Informally he told the Chartist leaders that he deplored the prospect of large-scale casualties but considered them inevitable if the workers took up the sword. In his private correspondence he railed at the narrow-minded and bigoted magistrates (mainly recruited from the gentry) he had to work with and, in defiance of the general directives from the Melbourne government, warned them not to try to break up mass meetings like the one on Kersal Moor. He also despised the cowardice of his civilian collaborators, while grudgingly admitting there were reasons for it: 'Funk is the order of the day . . . there is some excuse for the people seem ferocious enough.'[82] Nevertheless Napier was confident that in any armed conflict with rebels he would prevail, confident of the discipline and massive firepower of his troops, knowing too that he held most of the cards, since the government ran an efficient system of spies, secret agents and postal interception. What he most feared was either that a hot-headed, fire-eating magistrate would start a conflagration by trying to break up one of the mass meetings, or that armed Chartists might score an isolated success against a small army detachment: 'If only a corporal's guard was cut off it would be "total defeat of the troops" ere it reached London, Edinburgh and Dublin; and before the contradiction arrived the disaffection, in the moral exaltation of supposed victory, would be in arms. This is more especially to be apprehended in Ireland, where rivers of blood might flow.'[83] Napier's combination of firmness, moderation and diplomacy paid off. He it was more than anyone who convinced the Chartist leaders that the government could not be cowed by mere threats and calls for revolution and convinced O'Connor that the ruling classes could not be panicked or stampeded into taking rash retaliatory measures, as they had done on the continent. This was all the more telling since Napier's private criticisms of the government increased almost daily.[84] The deeply impressive Napier made sure all the time that the ball was in the Chartists' court while making them aware of the deadly consequences. It was the technique he was to use many years later at the end of his triumphant period in India. When faced with the custom of *suttee* (widow burning) after his conquest of Sindh, he called together the province's tribal elders and played the Dutch uncle as follows: 'You say that it is your custom to burn widows. Very well. We also have a custom. When men burn women alive, we tie a rope around their necks and we hang them. Build your funeral pyres; beside it, my carpenters will build a gallows. You may follow your custom. And then we shall follow ours.'[85] It is hard not to see this, mutatis mutandis, as Napier's posture towards the Chartists in 1839.

Nevertheless, the avoidance of major armed conflict in 1839 was a 'near run thing', to quote Napier's one-time mentor the Duke of Wellington after Waterloo. To quote one historian: 'Chartism was a major threat to the British state, in the physical sense that the British ruling class was at times during the late 1830s and 1840s virtually in a state of siege as the people of this country protested, struck and armed against the Establishment.'[86] Severely disillusioned with the failure of the national petition and the 'sacred month' and most of all, angry and bitter with the leadership for all its bold talk that had come to nothing, extreme elements in the rank and file began to plan on their own, even daring to attempt a nationwide conspiracy. Among the most radical groups were the textile workers of Bradford, the coal miners of south Wales and the weavers of Ashton-under-Lyne.[87] How concrete these plans were is still a matter of dispute, but it seems clear they were kept from the leadership, and O'Connor in particular.[88] In the perfervid atmosphere of 1839 someone on either side was bound to snap sooner or later and accordingly, what everyone feared – a rerun of the Gordon riots – duly happened, though in Wales rather than London. On the night of 3–4 November 1839 a large crowd of Welsh Chartists assembled to force the authorities to disgorge some of their number held under arrest in the Westgate Hotel, Newport, and guarded by the army. They were led by three men: John Frost, a 54-year-old linen draper and defrocked magistrate, Zephaniah Williams, a free-thinking innkeeper, and William Jones, a travelling actor. As always on such occasions, there are disputes about the numbers involved. Most historians cite between 3–7,000 with 5,000 being a fair average, though *The Times* claimed 8,000 and contemporary Chartists spoke of 20,000.[89] The attack on Newport was supposed to be coordinated with similar uprisings in Brecon and Abergavenny, but the operation was badly botched at every level. Not only did the other two assaults fail to materialise, but cold, rainy weather detained the

Newport marchers, who did not reach the town until dawn. They found hundreds of troops and special constables waiting for them. Foolishly the attackers seem to have supposed that the soldiers would not open fire on them, but on approaching the Westgate Hotel they came under withering fire at close quarters. After twenty minutes of horrific scenes, with shouting, cursing and the screams of dying men in antiphonal counterpoint to the roll of musketry, the bloodbath was over. As at Peterloo, any estimate of the death toll must be impressionistic, as many badly wounded men made their escape to die later in bothies and hovels. Government sources admitted 24 rebels dead and 50 seriously wounded.[90]

Even granted the raised temperatures and high emotions of the time, something of a puzzle still hovers over the Newport affair. Was it simply an incompetent attempt to trigger a general uprising? Certainly no Chartists in other localities acted in sympathy, though there were two more attempted risings in early 1840 in Sheffield and Bradford. Was it a disastrous attempt at class solidarity, with workers convinced that troops recruited from the same lowly background would not open fire on their 'kith and kin'? Was it simply a show of Chartist strength that went disastrously wrong? Or was it perhaps an attempt to create martyrs, so that a conflagration would be ignited, rather like John Brown's raid on Harper's Ferry in 1859? Worst of all, was it a failure of leadership, yet another betrayal by the upper echelons of the movement? Although O'Connor can be acquitted of foreknowledge, not all the Chartist leaders can, for John Frost made a tour of northern England just before heading the march on Newport, where he met a senior Chartist official, described as 'a tall working man' to whom he divulged his plans. This has led the most recent historian of Chartism to a sombre verdict: 'What happened at Newport was no spontaneous outburst of fury or despair, nor a peaceful demonstration that went tragically wrong: it was the culmination of careful preparation.'[91] Whatever its causes and motivations, the tragedy evoked a furious backlash from the government: 125 Chartists were arrested, and 21 were charged with high treason, including Frost, Williams and Jones. Altogether between June 1839 and early 1840 no fewer than 543 Chartists were imprisoned, some for a few weeks, others for several years. The conditions in which they were held were appalling, except in O'Connor's case, and the prominent Chartists Samuel Holberry and John Clayton both died in captivity.[92] The government made a virtual clean sweep of the movement's leaders, with O'Connor and O'Brien both being sentenced to 18 months. Too late Joseph Rayner Stephens realised what a serious business he was now involved in. He had enjoyed his reckless and irresponsible oratory almost as if he was involved in an elaborate game, but as the spectre of the prison house loomed, he made desperate attempts to avoid his fate, abjuring his Chartist faith and offering a quite mendacious account of his activities. At his trial he pleaded thus:

> I am dragged here, my lord . . . as though I were a party to the Convention, and to the disturbances of Birmingham, to the Charter, to annual parliaments, vote by ballot, universal suffrage and all the rest of that rigmarole, in which I never had a share . . . I declared my detestation of the doctrines of Chartism, and declared that if Radicals were in power . . . my head would be brought first to the block and my blood would be the first blood that would have to flow.[93]

The judge remained unimpressed by this special pleading and Stephens too was sentenced to 18 months. He held fast to his recantation, except that he continued to preach against the Poor Law, on the grounds that this was an imperative of his Christian conscience. Many of those who had been spellbound by his oratory simply refused to believe that their hero had recanted and regarded the news as government propaganda or disinformation.

The decision to try O'Connor for seditious libel, get a verdict of guilty from a tame jury, and then imprison him for 18 months in York Castle seems an egregious example of broad-brush government injustice. O'Connor was accused of inciting the Newport disaster despite the absence of any 'smoking gun' linking him to the affair and despite the fact that he had actually been in Ireland at the time, trying to shore up his precarious finances.[94] When the government was determined to secure a conviction, inconvenient facts likc alibis counted for very little. To his credit General Napier protested to the government about the pointlessness of imprisoning O'Connor; it would make him a martyr and do nothing to retard the general Chartist movement.[95] O'Connor himself confessed that he felt guilty about the Newport disaster even though it was not his fault. To his critics he again revealed himself as 'flaky', at once urging caution in public while declaring in private that blood would flow if the sentence of execution was pronounced on any of the men who came to trial.[96] Ironically, the government's attempt to silence O'Connor and leave the Chartist movement rudderless was stymied by its own bloodthirstiness. Frost, Williams and Jones were found guilty of treason and sentenced to death, which in 1840 still meant a barbarous execution by the medieval ritual of being hanged, drawn and quartered. This overreaction from the Melbourne government in turn triggered a nationwide backlash. At first Melbourne remained adamant that the sentence should be carried out and ranted and raved about the 'softness' of most judges and juries. More sober-minded colleagues pointed out to the prime minister that such an execution would be the talk of Europe and would take place at the very moment (February 1840) that the country would be celebrating Queen Victoria's marriage to Prince Albert. Nonetheless Melbourne appeared implacable until the chief justice, Sir Nicholas Tindal, took him aside and pointed out some of the legal and political implications of the move, ending by solemnly warning him against the execution.[97] The sentence was commuted to transportation for life. Frost, Williams and Jones, together with seven other 'ringleaders' began the long journey to the penal colony in Australia. O'Connor saw the chance to revive a movement that seemed in a terminal state. Many Chartists withdrew from political activity altogether, fearful and abashed by the violence at Newport and thinking it the prelude to many more such outbreaks, which promised massive loss of life. Others went into denial and pretended that petitioning was the way forward, even after the government's contemptuous thumbs down. Even thoughtful Chartists were perplexed. They had tried petitioning, and that had got nowhere, they had opted for a general strike, but the leadership had called it off, and now the final option – armed violence – seemed also to have failed. What other options were there? The general despair after Newport is well conveyed in the outpourings of Chartist poetry in 1839–40, reminiscent in its doleful lamentations of the verses of the Gaelic bards after Culloden.[98] O'Connor, though, headed a persistent and effective campaign to get the sentence of transportation on the Newport Chartists rescinded. Once again, as before the threatened execution, O'Connor displayed great statesmanship, shrewdly pitching his appeal at the right position between the already converted and those he hoped to win over. The petition he organised for John Frost's pardon from the conviction for high treason gathered nearly 1.5 million votes. It was presented to the House of Commons in May 1841 by Thomas Slingsby Duncombe, radical MP and the only consistent supporter of Chartism in the House in the 1840s.[99] Such was the sympathy for Frost that the vote by members was tied, and thwarted only by the casting vote of the speaker, who voted against, arguing that the petition infringed the royal prerogative of mercy. Frost had to wait for his pardon until a general amnesty was declared in 1865. Nonetheless, O'Connor's bold stand consolidated his followers when the entire movement might have imploded or melted away in the aftermath of Newport.[100]

1840 saw Chartism at its lowest ebb. With every single one of its leading lights in jail except Harney and the Scottish leaders, James Leach, a Manchester mill-owner and trade union activist assumed command. In the spring of 1840 he helped to found the National Charter Association (NCA), which aimed to build on branch organisations rather than mass meetings. This represented 'right-wing' Chartism, dedicated to achieving the Six Points by peaceful means, reformist rather than revolutionary in character, to Harney's disgust. However, he accepted that it was probably the right stopgap solution for the times; he still believed in physical force, but recognised that a long period of reorganisation and preparation was now necessary before violence could again be considered.[101] By some indices the NCA could be considered the first modern political party and from 1840 to 1842 at the organisational level it achieved great success. By December 1841 it had 282 branches and 13,000 card-carrying members; a year later this had increased to 401 branches and 50,000 members. Its great achievement was to emphasise Chartism's protean character and to demonstrate to the government that mere repression could not bring it to an end, that the movement was bigger than its famous leaders and could not be extirpated or even intimidated by prison or transportation. Yet if at this level it flourished, with O'Connor, O'Brien and Harney all removed from centre-stage, its ideological and intellectual content was scarcely glittering. Impressive-sounding debates were held, for instance, as to whether Chartism should target the big bourgeoisie as their principal enemy rather than the landed aristocracy, the gentry and the Church, or it should ally itself with the bourgeoisie initially to smash the aristocracy. One such debate ended with the limp conclusion that the working class should deprive *both* of power but, as in the old fable about belling the cat, nobody had any real idea how this could be done.[102] Another debate concerned itself with whether Chartism should declare itself overtly republican or find a place in its ideal arrangements for the monarchy and the House of Lords. There was something deeply pathetic about the way right-wing Chartists clung to the idea that the queen and her husband were secretly on their side, when the reality was that both Victoria and Albert loathed and detested the Chartists. More clear-sighted analysts, from Left and Right, from Engels to Bagehot, saw clearly that the monarchy was simply a sham institution whose aim was mystification and the bamboozlement of the working classes.[103] The other weakness about Chartism in 1840–1 was that it began to splinter into factions: so-called 'Knowledge Chartism', trying to ground the movement in reason; Christian Chartism, attempting to align it with organised religion; and 'Teetotal Chartism' arguing, to the disgust of O'Connor and other hedonists, that abstinence from alcohol was a core aspect of the workers' struggle.[104] Also, as part of its movement away from radicalism in general, the NCA started to softpedal on the feministic aspects of its agenda. It granted women the same voting rights as men within the movement but campaigned only for universal *male* suffrage, on the grounds that public opinion was not yet ready for female emancipation. The feminist view is that this not only betrayed women but condemned them to more than a century of impotence. Women's support for and interest in Chartism began to fade, not only because of these disappointed hopes but because of the considerable impact on the female population of 'Teetotal Chartism' and the temperance movement in general.[105] However, not all women were natural converts for temperance, non-violence and sweetness and light. One female Chartist, Elizabeth Creswell of Mansfield, was arrested for carrying a loaded revolver and a spare clip of bullets.

To set against these losses in 1840–1 all Chartism had on the credit side were encouraging signs that the movement was beginning to make inroads in rural areas and to recruit supporters in the country-side.[106] In his cell in York Castle O'Connor chafed at some of the developments. Lovett, who had won admirers through his refusal to be bound over for good behaviour in order to secure an early release – on the grounds that this would be an admission of guilt – split definitively with both O'Connor and the NCA, published his own manifesto and threatened to start his own national movement. Lovett had by then become disillusioned with the old politics of campaigning and saw the future as the steady education of the working class, in particular weaning them off drinking and gambling. Not only did this make Lovett a de facto supporter of Teetotal Chartism but, as O'Connor pointed out, Lovett's programme was in effect a return to Bentham's idea of intellectual qualifications for the franchise.[107] Yet O'Connor had even more pressing problems in his own backyard. The jewel of his northern political empire was Leeds, more broadly based economically than Manchester or Sheffield, less inclined to boom and bust, and more politically sophisticated. Removed from the Irishman's aegis, Leeds Chartists grew increasingly attracted to Samuel Smiles and his doctrine of self-help and gravitated to a new body that was Smilesian in outlook. Smiles, editor of the *Leeds Times* from 1838 to 1842, had not yet fully developed the influential ideas that would make him famous and, theoretically, accepted the Six Points, but from the moment of his joining the Leeds Parliamentary Reform Association (LPRA), his deviationism into 'Knowledge Chartism' was evident, as in one of his 1840s pronouncements: 'Knowledge is of itself one of the highest enjoyments. The ignorant man passes through life dead to all pleasures, save those of his senses.'[108] The LPRA was a classic of trans-class coalition, containing as it did disillusioned Chartists, textile magnates and Anti-Corn Law activists. Under the banner of class cooperation the LPRA proposed jettisoning the Charter and universal suffrage and working instead for *household* suffrage (where the male head of the household alone had the vote) and triennial parliaments. O'Connor was right to be suspicious of the 'transforming' effect of middle-class culture in the LPRA, for after 1850 Smiles totally abandoned all his previous political beliefs and became, in effect, a propagandist for capitalism. One of his statements in an 1875 volume shows how far he eventually travelled from the Chartists: he described the infamous 1834 Poor Law as 'one of the most valuable that has been put on the statute book in modern times'.[109] Not surprisingly, one of O'Connor's first objectives when released from jail was to destroy this cuckoo in his nest (that is, the LPRA, not Smiles) –

something he achieved remarkably quickly. With the winter of 1840–1 spent largely by the NCA in preparing a second petition and supporting the families of their imprisoned brethren, O'Connor set the tone for the new year by announcing (to O'Brien's furious protests) that the Chartists should vote tactically and support the Tories in the forthcoming election, since the Tories had a certain tradition of radicalism exemplified by men like Disraeli – who in 1839–40 was sympathetic to their aims while voting against the petition in the house. If he expected the favour to be returned, O'Connor was soon disappointed, for in an address in 1841 Disraeli lumped together 'Jesuits and infidels' with 'Chartists and socialists' as revolutionary dangers to the State.[110]

A new chapter in Chartism opened when O'Connor was freed from jail on health grounds slightly before his term ended, on 30 August 1841. He struck the right note by emerging from prison dressed in a fustian jacket, the classic symbol of the nineteenth-century working man and, as such, 'a statement of class without words'. A younger radical Chartist, Ernest Jones, hailed the almost simultaneous release of O'Connor and O'Brien as the return of the movement's lions.[111] O'Connor's first task was to arrest the rightward drift of the movement which he, somewhat speciously, claimed to have founded. Lovett had faded, but a new threat appeared on the horizon in the shape of Joseph Sturge and the Complete Suffrage Movement. Sturge, a Quaker banker, grain merchant and importer, advocated an alliance with the Anti-Corn Law League (ACLL), the flagship of the industrial bourgeoisie and thus wanted to head the Labour movement in exactly the opposite direction from that proposed by O'Connor in the general election of 1841 (tactical support for the Tories). Given that the Tory Party under Sir Robert Peel went on to win a great victory, with 56.94 per cent of the votes, as against the Whigs' 41.08 per cent,[112] O'Connor's strategy seemed vindicated, but it was highly controversial. Sturge's movement, renamed the National Complete Suffrage Union (NCSU), tried to steal Chartist thunder by adopting the Six Points and did indeed win over large numbers of right-wing Chartists and those who, like Lovett, simply hated O'Connor.[113] The fallacy of the NCSU, for O'Connor, was, first, the alliance with the ACLL and, secondly, its proposal to turn Chartism into a more narrowly focused pressure group for electoral reform instead of a mass movement with a polygon of aims and intentions. Additionally, it became clear that Sturge was not interested so much in a genuine trans-class coalition as in cajoling Chartists away from O'Connor and into his own movement.[114] Even at a personal level most Chartists and NCSU men did not get on, with the Chartist perception that they were at root despised by the Suffragists, and the Suffragists clearly viewing the Chartists as wild men and crypto-revolutionaries. Possibly a handful of men might have been able to bridge the gap but they were all, like Lovett, individuals who loathed O'Connor and had (real or imaginary) scores to settle with him.

Accordingly 1842, which saw Chartism engaged in a titanic struggle with Peel's government, also saw the movement rending itself apart in a battle between the NCA and the NCSU. In answer to those right-wing Chartists who parroted the perennially popular mantra 'there is no alternative' (to support for the NCSU), O'Connor tried to build up the Celtic fringes as a countervailing source of support. This proved extremely difficult. In these years before the Great Famine in Ireland, a political alliance with John Bull's Other Island might have been very effective, but in his hatred of O'Connor O'Connell was second only to Lovett. O'Connor made a valiant appeal to the Irish, committing Chartism to repeal of the Act of Union, but there was no reply nor any form of reciprocity from O'Connell.[115] In any case, O'Connor's overture was not popular in England, where the attitude, among all but the most sophisticated Chartists, was that Ireland was a thing apart, in a separate sphere; the Irish should stick to Irish affairs and the English to English. Scottish Presbyterians, in particular, seemed likely to lose their taste for Chartism if there was an 'intrusion' by large numbers of Irish Catholics. One must never forget the deep-running anti-Irish bigotry among all classes in England in this era. Richard Carlile, a radical publisher from the Peterloo era who had courageously supported Orator Hunt then, made an unhelpful intervention in 1839, fuelled by his suspicions about O'Connor:

> I dislike the sound of these Irish O's, in connection with the question of English reform, and look upon an Irish Protestant as a base and bastard Irishman, a traitor to his persecuted country, without the apology of philosophical dissent from the Romish Church. If this be a unsound prejudice of mine, I feel, express and submit it to

> correction. I count such men obstacles to the public good of this country, and that the temper of an Irishman is best suited to the state of Ireland. I wish them all at home and happy, reforming themselves and Ireland. They are not solid and steady enough, not sufficiently philosophical, for the necessities of English reform. I dislike the mixture and think it does not work well.[116]

As for the other Celtic enclaves, Wales had never recovered from the trauma of Newport in 1839, while Scotland, particularly in the west, had been particularly badly hit by economic depression. The price of bread was an urgent issue, and for this reason the Anti-Corn Law League, with its promise of lower wheat prices in the event of repeal, had an obvious attraction. All O'Connor's vociferous opposition to the ACLL did there was to alienate Scottish Chartists.

There was nothing for it then but to engage the NCSU on ground of its own choosing. Four hundred delegates assembled in Birmingham in April 1842 for the annual conference of the NCSU. O'Connor denounced Sturge and his followers as the running dogs of the ACLL, but sent O'Brien to the conference as the official Chartist delegate; Lovett was also there as a peevish presence, in full support of Sturge. Meanwhile O'Connor staged his own official Chartist conference simultaneously in the same city.[117] When this failed to halt the Suffragists in their tracks, O'Connor decided he would have to lend a hand himself. He travelled through the north of England on another whirlwind tour, denouncing both the NCSU and the ACLL and pointing up the fallacies in their programmes. He had often boasted of his prowess in fistic encounters and this time he had to be as good as his word, for there was a violent confrontation in Manchester between supporters of the ACLL and O'Connor's supporters; the 'lion' of Chartism had his mane tugged, was knocked down in a brawl and sustained seven wounds.[118] He and Sturge momentarily collaborated to highlight the farce of the English electoral system when they 'contested' the Nottingham by-election in 1842. Sturge and his Chartist allies won a clear victory at the hustings by a show of hands, but were disqualified from voting in the 'real' election. In fury at this demonstration of their fraudulent position, the Tories hired bully boys to beat up the opposition. Sturge and his Suffragists prudently fled but O'Connor and Thomas Cooper, the Chartist poet and the flower of

Midlands Chartism, remained to face the thugs and gave as good as they got. Cooper related O'Connor's pugilistic talents with awe and described him as fighting like a dragon: 'it was no trifle to receive a blow from O'Connor's fists'.[119] It is worth noting that O'Connor had to use his fists on several occasions in 1842, both against the Tories and the ACLL. He was thus under attack on two fronts even within one of the two larger fronts he was fighting on during this one year (the other is described below). For all that he enhanced his personal reputation, however, O'Connor's fine rhetoric scarcely made a dent in the solid support for the ACLL. But, in December, he managed to give the coup de grâce to the struggling NCSU. A second conference was held, at which Sturge made the tactical mistake of trying to hijack the conference into adopting a reformist, middle-class programme. Even Lovett was alienated by this and swung his support over to mainline Chartism. When O'Connor won a cleverly timed motion to retain the Charter as an integral part of the NCSU, Sturge and his faction stormed out in dudgeon, leaving the field clear for O'Connor. Little more was heard from Sturge. The only setback for O'Connor at the ideological and organisational level was that O'Brien decided he had had enough and quit to plough his own furrow.[120]

Some of the stress O'Connor was under can be appreciated when it is realised that while all this was going on, Chartism was engaged in a deadly struggle with the government. Some historians regard 1842 as the most dangerous conjuncture of all, when revolution might have happened.[121] The Hungarian revolutionary Lajos Kossuth thought 1842 especially dangerous for the English elite, since it faced crises in China, Afghanistan and the Indies as well as potential conflict with both France and the USA at the very time Chartism again asserted itself at maximum force.[122] The Chartists collected signatures for a second national petition against an ominous background of economic depression; the 'hungry forties' became a byword for an era when factory workers had to choose between employment on any terms and starvation.[123] Many anxious observers used the image of an erupting volcano to convey the desperate state of affairs in the nation. Lord Francis Egerton, a Lancashire landowner, had this to say about his county: 'In living in it all, I always feel as if I were toasting muffins at a volcano.'[124] The atmosphere of crisis was exacerbated by the murder of Peel's private secretary (though not by Chartists) and three separate attempts on Queen Victoria's life. Such was the ambience in which the Chartists produced the new petition. 3,317,752 people signed it – two and a half times the signatures on the first petition of 1839 – or roughly one-third of the adult population in a nation of about 18.5 million souls. The Chartist leviathan presented to Parliament contained six miles of paper and represented a stupendous feat of organisation by O'Connor. It would have been deeply impressive if he had been doing nothing else, instead of battling with Sturge and the NCSU, Cobden and Bright and the Anti-Corn Law League, and the sullen O'Connell and his Irish party. Peel's government responded to the clearly expressed will of the people with the contempt that habitually characterises British governments when faced with real democracy; they like to prate about it rhetorically and even to try to export it, but never accept it. Hopes had been expressed, after the narrowness of defeat of the petition for pardon of the Newport rioters, that Parliament was getting closer to embracing the Six Points, but a rejection by 287 votes to 49 showed that the gap between the people and its so-called representatives was as wide as ever.[125] Particularly unsavoury was the intervention in the house by the historian Lord Macaulay, who served up the following galimaufry of nonsense, in which he chose to ignore the content of the Six Points and entered a dystopia of his own imagination:

> The government would rest upon spoliation . . . What must be the effect of such a sweeping confiscation of property? No experience enables us to guess at it. All I can say is, that it seems to me to be something more horrid than can be imagined. A great community of human beings – a vast people would be called into existence in a new position; there would be a depression, if not an utter stoppage of trade, and of all those vast engagements of the country by which our people were supported, and how is it possible to doubt that famine and pestilence would come before long to wind up the effects of such a state of things? The best thing which I can expect, and which I think everyone must see as a result, is, that in some of the desperate struggles which must take place in such a state of things, some strong military despot must arise, and give some sort of protection – some security to the property which may remain.[126]

The result of the rejection of the second petition was a wave of strikes in June–July 1842, beginning in Manchester and spreading across the Pennines to Yorkshire and thence to Scotland. Most of these seem to have been spontaneous outbursts of anger and frustration, but some local Chartists fomented and encouraged them. Coal miners and textile workers were especially prominent, with serious strikes in coalfields and mills in Staffordshire, Lancashire, Cheshire, the East Midlands, Tyneside, Yorkshire, South Wales and the Scottish Lowlands, especially Lanarkshire. Altogether there were strikes in fourteen English counties, eight Scottish and one Welsh.[127] The movement was in chaos, with the leadership caught off balance and unable to give a lead, and local activists the real decision-makers. The NCA, taken unawares, did no more than express vague sympathy for the strikers. Caught between a visceral desire to support the strikers and a secret fear that matters would get out of hand, producing mass violence and bloodshed, O'Connor dithered before finally denouncing them to demonstrate his 'soundness' to the authorities.[128] He and the other Chartist grandees lost caste by their ineffectual stance and seeming paralysis. Confusion was the order of the day. Local Chartist leaders did not know whether to concentrate on encouraging the unrest or keeping it peaceful. The gap between the leadership and the rank and file was strikingly evinced by the enrolment of some right-wing Chartists as special constables to contain the violence, thus acting as a fifth column against the movement's shock troops.[129] Other Chartists urged circumspection, on the grounds that the strikes were being manipulated by the hated ACLL – allegedly encouraging the strikes to give their friends the mill-owners the excuse to close the mills down; this seems to have been a mere canard.[130] Ominously, the industrial unrest of June–July 1842 produced much greater violence than the wave of strikes in 1839, largely because the government decided to make extensive use of the military to crack down hard. There was a nasty incident at Salterhebble in Yorkshire when workers attacked a troop of cavalry that had arrested some of their comrades. At Halifax on 16 August soldiers fixed bayonets and fired rounds to disperse a crowd; there were three deaths, including one of the troops. Manchester was the epicentre of the troubles, but most media attention went to Yorkshire, where gangs of striking workers pulled out the boiler plugs to put out furnaces and bring factories to a halt. The 'Plug Riots' seemed at first successful.

By mid-August more than a 100 cotton factories, many machine shops, dyeworks and other installations had been closed down and at least 50,000 workers had downed tools.[131]

In view of O'Connor's advice in the 1841 general election, it was ironic that the Peel administration proved even more repressive and hard line than the widely hated Whigs had in 1839. Not only was Sir James Graham at the Home Office much more of a 'hawk' than Russell had been, but there are signs that he panicked seriously.[132] He fulminated at the 'weak and supine' posture of local magistrates, but the truth was that many of them supported the ACLL and were quite happy to exploit industrial discontent for their own purposes; in any case, until August they did not have enough troops.[133] Graham committed the army extensively in August but this was dangerous, for this time there was no solomonic General Napier to restrain the excesses of gung-ho young officers. Peel's government decided to risk all on a no-holds-barred policy of repression, and the strategy worked.[134] By the end of August the strike wave was losing its pulse and ebbing; a steady drift back to work was evident.

There were many reasons for the failure of what some have termed a 'general strike', but the most important was the element of hunger: the strikers were starving and could afford only a short-term effort, whereas the government could play the long game. Moreover, the strike failed to be general, as the important centres of London, Tyneside, Birmingham and Monmouthshire were untouched by it; for a general strike a much more vigorous and organised NCA would have been needed. Once the government recovered from its initial dismay, the military preparations were highly efficient and organised.[135] Trans-class coalition revealed itself as the illusion O'Connor had always claimed it was when shopkeepers refused to extend credit to the strikers and the middle classes refused to contribute to the strike fund. Finally, once again in the realm of luck or contingency, the summer harvest of 1842 was the most abundant for a decade and grain prices began to fall rapidly. Not to be discounted either is the sheer scale and extent of government repression. There were mass arrests – 174 in Staffordshire alone – followed by trials and draconian punishment. Whereas in 1839 only 10 men had been transported to the Australian penal colonies, this time 100 were, including 54 from Staffordshire.[136] The government wanted to charge the Chartist leaders with conspiracy and high treason after the wave of strikes (Graham was convinced the seemingly 'spontaneous' industrial outbreaks were really part of a cunning conspiracy) but simply could not obtain the necessary evidence. He postponed the trials of the leaders to the spring of 1843, but to no avail. O'Connor was tried for sedition but acquitted, causing fury in elite circles.[137] But, as O'Connor himself realised, this was a pyrrhic victory. The Chartist movement had been more comprehensively routed even than in 1839, and the only question now was whether it could survive at all.

11

Chartism's Decline and Fall

By 1843 Chartism was at its nadir, seemingly in a political cul-de-sac. Increasingly the movement splintered into factions no longer controlled by the NCA. Many Chartists gave up the wider struggle and concentrated on special-interest activities: trade unions, friendly societies, local solidarity committees. In some quarters this was greeted with relief: Joseph Sturge told his friends that the final breach with the Chartists meant he no longer had to deal with such uncongenial bedfellows.[1] Others concluded that a purely political and constitutional movement was no longer adequate to deal with the blatantly class-based politics of early Victorian England. Typical was George Julian Harney, who in 1844 founded the Democratic Friends of All Nations, stressing international socialism and with Marx and Engels as members. Curiously, as Chartist fortunes dipped, Engels became more and more certain that revolution was imminent. He based this on his perception that capitalists were blind to the lurking danger to their position from the wretched of the earth in their slums and hovels. In remarkably upbeat mood he declared that the Six Points looked like meek and mild reformism but were actually dynamite, since the clear implication that the monarchy and House of Lords would be abolished would start an unstoppable momentum towards the euthanasia of the bourgeoisie.[2] In so arguing, of course, he reinforced the prejudices of the Russells, Disraelis and Macaulays who had long prophesied precisely that outcome. O'Brien, meanwhile, after his split with O'Connor, was thought likely to form a new party, but instead drifted to the margins of Chartism and went to live on the Isle of Man. There he made a scornful and splenetic attack on O'Connor's ideas for land reform, precipitating a virulent riposte, in which O'Connor accused his erstwhile lieutenant of malice, dishonesty, cowardice and desertion in the face of the enemy.[3] Some reformists continued to place their faith in constitutionalism and looked to the American constitution for guidance, arguing, for example, that since the British government was as much a tyranny as it had been in 1775–83, it should likewise be opposed by a citizen militia, as prescribed in the Second Amendment to the US Constitution.[4] O'Connor was increasingly preoccupied with land reform (see p. 321). In what seemed to be a new reformist mood he persuaded the NCA to jettison parts of the Charter when it published its new constitution in 1843, so that the manifesto referred merely to general hopes for social amelioration. He seemed to lose interest in the NCA, though he continued to finance it from his own pocket when it ran into financial difficulties. There are clear signs of the great leader losing his touch in the middle 1840s. In one flurry of intemperate activity he sacked the reliable editor of the *Northern Star*, William Hill, adding yet another disgruntled opponent to the long list of men who hated him.[5] The NCA itself, without O'Connor at the helm, was riven by personal and ideological factionalism at the highest levels and no longer had national authority, with local Chartist organisations operating virtually independently from it; the breach with Scotland was almost total. As a gesture of its own autonomy from O'Connor, in 1844 it reintroduced the Charter as a centrepiece in its constitution. Embattled on all fronts, O'Connor came under further pressure when mainstream newspapers began attacking him for his womanising. In a signal instance of *tu quoque*, O'Connor hit back by suggesting that the real reason the Reverend Joseph Rayner Stephens left the Chartist movement was to save himself from the details of a sexual scandal the media were about to divulge.[6] One of O'Connor's few consolations in the dreary period 1843–4 was the knowledge that, whereas he and fifty-eight others had been tried for treason at Lancaster in March 1843, not a single one of the accused had been found guilty.

Chartism was in the doldrums and, to add to its woes, its support was being nibbled away by the more dynamic and successful Anti-Corn Law League. Originating at roughly the same time as Chartism, the Anti-Corn Law League was fortunate to have as its leaders two distinguished politicians who were also friends, Richard Cobden and John Bright, and thus avoided the personal feuds and vendettas that disfigured Chartism. The ACLL was the elite corps in the struggle of the English bourgeoisie against the landed aristocracy. Cobden and

Bright understood that international trade had its own modalities, that the British manufacturing interests could increase their exports, and thus their profits, only if the primary producers to whom they exported factory articles had a tariff-free market for their goods – and this was prevented by the Corn Laws.[7] The ACLL was eager to recruit working-class support for its cause, but strictly on its own terms, without any quid pro quo. For the wider aims of Chartism the ACLL had only contempt, which was reciprocated. From the very earliest days the two sides had broken up each other's meetings, and this process came to a head in 1842.[8] In that year the tensions between the two sides peaked, especially on the issue of the famous 'Plug Riots' (when workers put out the fires beneath boilers and drew out the plugs to make factory work impossible). Many Chartists not in Yorkshire believed that the Plug Riots had been fomented and engineered by the ACLL simply to discredit the workers. This belief probably derived from the known fact that at one time Cobden and Bright had threatened to get all ACLL members to refuse taxes and close down workshops and factories to force repeal of the Corn Laws.[9] The National Complete Suffrage Movement of 1842, in its attempt to build a bridge between the middle and working classes, originally tried to fuse the aims of Chartism and the ACLL but by the end of that year Cobden and Bright concluded that working-class support could not be won. One of the factors was that Sturge, originally keen on a trans-class coalition, returned from a trip to the USA radicalised in abolitionist ideas. Advocating prohibitive tariffs to keep out slave-produced goods from England, he found that this collided head-on with the ACLL demand for free trade. More particularly, Manchester depended on cotton from the slave-owing southern states for its livelihood.[10]

Cobden lamented that the Chartists attacked capital, machinery, manufacture and trade, the basis of democracy, while ignoring the aristocracy (largely true) and the State itself (palpably false in light of the events of 1839 and 1842). There was, in the speeches of Cobden and Bright, an unacceptable attitude of intellectual superiority towards the Chartists and also the implication that in any alliance between the two sides the Chartists would have to be the junior partners. In their wider propaganda Cobden and Bright insinuated that if the demands of the ACLL were not met, the people at large would swing left into Chartism.[11] It should be clear that there was very little common ground between the two movements and that their aims were fundamentally antagonistic. The Chartists took it for granted, surely reasonably, that the interests of employers and workers were irreconcilable, whereas the ACLL raised the siren song that both would benefit from repeal. The ACLL stance was fundamentally cynical. They wanted proletarian support to scare the aristocracy and backed the Complete Suffrage Movement in 1841–2 purely on the grounds that more voters of the conservative type (under household suffrage) would mean more ACLL supporters. Some ACLL members thought courting the Chartists was always a waste of time as such people did not have the vote anyway. Moreover, the charge of snobbery is sustained, since the ACLL regarded all 'physical force' Chartists as hooligans.[12] For their part, the Chartists were sceptical about the benefits of an alliance with the ACLL. Even those right-wing Chartists who *were* sympathetic to Cobden and Bright considered that their own struggle must have priority, that repeal of the Corn Laws was irrelevant as long as the working class did not have the vote. Adherents of the Ten Hour Movement were especially hostile to the ACLL. They thought that repeal would simply diminish the acreage under wheat, reduce agricultural employment and swell the numbers of those dependent on the New Poor Law. They doubted that increased exports would lead to fuller employment and thought it would simply mean greater mechanisation. Further, without the kinds of pro-working-class measures the Chartists were proposing, any decrease in food prices would simply produce corresponding wage cuts.[13] Once again the perennial clash of personalities manifested itself. At a personal level Cobden detested O'Connor. In his view O'Connor had given hostages to fortune by his ill-advised recommendation that Chartists back the Tories in the 1841 general election. It was the Whigs who stood for Free Trade and the Tories for protectionism. Repeal of the Corn Laws would mean the irrevocable triumph of industrial capitalism over the aristocracy of land, and Tories derived most of their power from the land. The price of food, the principal determinant of land rents, was kept artificially high by the Corn Laws; their repeal would bring down the price of food, and thus rents, and thus the power of the Tory aristocracy.[14] Cobden hammered away at these points during a famous debate with O'Connor in Northampton on 5 August 1844. Although O'Connor drew blood, he was systematically outpointed by a superior dialectician; he later grudgingly conceded that Cobden had had the better of the verbal duel. A great streetfighter but never a superb debater in closely argued exchanges, O'Connor was mainly reduced to spluttering about the impact on factories of technology and machinery.[15] Cobden convinced his audience that repeal would mean greater economic prosperity, and certainly greater profits, but not that it would produce higher wages or even the same wages; on subsequent occasions neither he nor Bright could breach this adamantine part of the Chartist carapace. The charge that the grandees of the ACLL were primarily concerned with industrialists' profits could scarcely be refuted; after all, both Cobden and Bright opposed the Ten Hour Movement, working from the generally held axiom among manufacturers that all the real profits were made from the last hour of work.[16]

At the deepest level any thought of cooperation between Chartism and the ACLL made no sense. Chartists could see clearly that repeal would almost certainly lead to a worsening of conditions for factory workers, since employers would use the excuse of cheaper food to cut wages. The Chartist–ACLL failure to communicate was really because the two sides represented, respectively, employees and employers. For the ACLL free trade was a fetish and laissez-faire sacrosanct, but the Chartists always believed in the primacy of politics: economic considerations should always be subject to political objectives, and this meant political control of the economy and the 'market'.[17] Some even suspected the ACLL doctrine of the market to be mere camouflage – a bourgeois device to take the steam out of the Chartist movement. Two very different thinkers on the Left, one a contemporary, the other a twentieth-century observer have underlined the fundamental incompatibility of the two movements. Here is Marx on the ACLL: 'If the aristocracy is their vanishing opponent, the working class is their rising enemy. They prefer to compromise with the vanishing opponent rather than to strengthen the arising enemy, to whom the future belongs, by concessions of a more than apparent importance.'[18] And this is G. D. H. Cole: 'The League was embryonic liberalism, based on the collaboration of classes to get the best out of capitalism; the Chartist movement was embryonic socialism, based on class struggle, and hostile above all, to the newly dominant middle-class industrialists.'[19] O'Connor and O'Brien were united on this one issue at least, for both opposed repeal until 1846, when Peel accepted its inevitability and thus consigned himself to political oblivion. In any case, after 1843, with Chartism in decline, the ACLL abandoned its attempt to recruit the working class and changed its strategy. It switched its campaign from towns to the rural districts and from the population as a whole to known electors. Moreover, the good harvests of 1842–4 made the proletariat less interested in abstract arguments about the price of bread.[20] It would not be an exaggeration to say that by 1844 the mutual interest of the ACLL and Chartism was zero. One ominous development which O'Connor did not spot was that the triumph of the industrial bourgeoisie in 1846 would have other effects, such as blocking a return to the countryside or any agricultural solutions of the 'back to the land' kind, which by then had become of consuming interest to him.[21]

The middle years of Chartism (1843–7) were dominated by O'Connor's ambitious and Promethean Land Plan. This has attracted almost more opprobrium than the author himself. Indeed some say he was not the author, and attribute this role to Bronterre O'Brien. It is true that in 1842 O'Brien adumbrated *a* land plan, but it was a very different animal from O'Connor's conception, and indeed O'Brien was virtually the first critic out of the traps to condemn it as 'a nonsense'.[22] The usual line of criticism is to say that, whereas the British proletariat stood at a crossroads, desperate for an ideology that would take them forward into the future (with Harney and later Ernest Jones exhorting them to opt for Marxism), O'Brien now proposed to retreat into the past, to seek salvation in a mythical golden age of self-sufficient agricultural communities. As one historian has remarked harshly: 'His movement was just as hopeless and retrograde a phenomenon as if a hand loom weaver had wanted to compete with the power loom.[23] It is true that some of O'Connor's thinking on this subject was bizarre, if not downright eccentric, such as his notion that his Land Plan would ease the path towards general acceptance of the Charter. This has led his harshest critics to claim that the entire Land Plan project was an early sign of the insanity that would disable him after 1850 and lead to his early death. Yet, in another sense, all that O'Connor was doing was responding to the zeitgeist. Utopian thinking and utopian thought reached their zenith in the nineteenth century. In the United States, widely regarded in the 1840s as a promised land or tabula rasa on which new ideas could be imprinted, a number of would-be self-sufficient utopian and agricultural colonies sprang up, notably those of the Shakers, the Rappite, the Omana and the Oneida and Brook Farm communities.[24] Among utopian thinkers were Charles Henri, Comte de Saint-Simon, Charles Fourier, Etienne Cabet, Wilhelm Weitling and, most relevantly for O'Connor's case, Robert Owen. O'Connor was accused of repeating history, this time as farce – for the failure of the Levellers to secure manhood suffrage had been followed by the Diggers' attempt to return to the land. Yet from the Irishman's point of view he was filling a credibility gap that had opened up alarmingly in the Chartist movement. All the obvious options, petitioning, demonstrations, strikes and even violence had been tried without success; there was no increase of Chartist members of Parliament, Peel and the Tories had failed them. Chartist newspapers were folding, and funds were drying up. Unless he came up with something quickly, the movement would atrophy and die. It was this which lay behind the (at first sight puzzling) development whereby in 1843 the NCA dropped the Charter. The real explanation for this was in O'Connor's simultaneous 'talking up' of the Land Plan.[25]

O'Connor's basic idea was to enfranchise more and more Chartists by making them men of property and thus eligible to vote. The scheme would begin by raising £5,000 to buy an estate that would provide the livelihood for fifty men and give them the necessary property qualification. A mortgage on the existing real estate would then be raised with which a second estate would be purchased and then, by this process of piggy-backing, a third and a fourth, and so on.[26] Yet O'Connor also had *moral* aims with his Land Plan. He argued that it would mitigate poverty, lead to self-reliance and moral regeneration, and give the cultivator pride and self-respect. It would also enable the working man to become the master of machines rather than vice versa, to make technology 'man's holiday instead of man's curse'.[27] The years of the Land Plan were also the years of the Great Famine in Ireland, in which a million people died of starvation, and O'Connor sometimes claimed that his plan was his personal refutation of Malthusianism. Hard-hearted Benthamite 'market theorists' claimed that the famine in Ireland was not due to the incompetence of the British government or the poverty of its economic theory, but simply an appalling demonstration of the essential truth of Malthus's famous thesis: that in all societies the means of subsistence increases by arithmetical progress but the population by *geometric* progression. No less an authority than John Stuart Mill, for one, thought that O'Connor's Land Plan was feasible, and a possible way to avoid famine and make the country independent of foreign food supplies.[28] O'Connor originally intended to make his plan an integral part of the NCA, but when the NCA was refused legal registration as a friendly society (on the grounds that it was an obviously political one), O'Connor detached the plan from any association with the NCA. Despite the jeremiahs, at first everything went well. The Land Plan proved more popular than the NCA itself, with over 70,000 shareholders at its peak and more than 600 local branches. O'Connor had hit a nerve and struck the right note for the 1840s, when the idea of moral regeneration through agriculture and smallholdings was highly popular. Even some of the 'deviant' sects such as 'Teetotal Chartism' – previously denounced vociferously by the bibulous O'Connor for its petit-bourgeois and chapel 'temperancing' – embraced the Land Plan, seeing in it a potent weapon against drunkenness.[29]

Nothing infuriated O'Connor more than the accusation that his Land Plan was a feeble copy of ideas already put into practice by Robert Owen (1771–1858). Of all the nineteenth-century utopian socialists (Saint-Simon, Fourier, Cabet, Weitling, et al.) Owen was possibly the most interesting, since he was no mere dreamer and visionary but a factory owner with sustained and direct contact with working-class life for many years before he set down his theories. From 1800, as manager and co-owner of a large textile works at New Lanark, he carried out educational and social experiments designed to lift the working classes out of squalor and misery. These included the refusal to employ children younger than ten years of age, working hours set at ten and a half hours' a day maximum, free primary education and relatively hygienic working conditions. He aimed to eliminate theft and drunkenness by persuasion, not punishment, and amazed contemporaries by achieving higher productivity than the slave drivers in the satanic mills.[30] His great achievement was to secure (in 1819) a Factory Act, which for the first time outlawed child labour in the textile industry. Always courageous, he attacked the Anglican Church for its cynical and craven 'opium of the people' collusion with the ruling elite. The first great organiser of the British proletariat in its economic struggles, he promoted trade union and cooperative movements and spread his ideas abroad, principally in the United States.[31] Owen's great weakness was that he was a utilitarian and, as it were, paid-up member of the Benthamite brotherhood. He had a simple formula: the source of all social evils is ignorance, and this can be remedied by education. Mankind, he thought, had hitherto lived in a cloud of ignorance, but education would soon dispel that and reveal the obvious truth of socialism. As he grew older Owen became more radical.[32] In his *New View of Society* he argued for a modified capitalism and posited that the existing organisation of capitalist economy was self-defeating, since poverty and low wages led to overproduction. In his later years he opted for communistic settlements as the nucleus of a future society and preached socialism as a heaven-sent discovery – the key to future liberation and a doctrine so obviously true that humanity would embrace it as soon as it was proclaimed. Marx famously criticised Owenite socialism as seriously intellectually defective. Marx was convinced that his studies in Hegelian philosophy gave him, a priori, a greater insight into socialism than Owen, who was essentially a practical man. For Marx the key to human misery was not poverty but alienation. It was not enough to daydream like the utopian socialists, and contrast what was with what ought to be. One had to probe deeply the issues of class consciousness and class struggle. What would happen if the ruling classes refused to see the 'self-evident' truth of socialism? What was Owen's advice then?[33]

O'Connor always tried to distance himself from Owen and Owenism and resented any comparison. As far as he was concerned, his ideas had come to him during his imprisonment in York Castle in 1840–1. In 1843 he had published *The Management of Small Farms* – a down-to-earth guide to the mundane problems of planting potatoes and cabbages, in no way concerned with irrelevant abstract theory.[34] To accuse Owen of abstract theorising was of course a travesty – clearly O'Connor had never read the work of Marx and Engels, though it is true that Owen did have general things to say about human nature and the fundamentals of human society; for instance, he often declared his belief in the perfectibility of man, implicit in his view of the transformative possibilities of education. O'Connor never even went that far; it would be impossible to talk about him in terms of the Enlightenment or Benthamite ideology. Moreover, with his Land Plan, O'Connor was determined to press home the point that Chartism was no longer radical but gradualist. Cooperation, he stressed, did not mean communalism; land ownership under his scheme would be individual not common.[35] His plan was no threat either to private property or to any other established institution. He declared that he was no communist, no radical and not even a republican: he claimed he was for 'the altar, the throne and the cottage'.[36] He made it clear that he bitterly opposed Owen's deism and enmity to organised religion. Where Owen thought the nuclear family was the enemy of human happiness, O'Connor praised it and went out of his way to eulogise family values. There was considerable irony in the spectacle of a man who had fathered eight children in thirty-two years of stable marriage excoriating the family, while O'Connor, a womanising bachelor, extolled the family as the ideal social unit.[37] All of O'Connor's pronouncements were hostile to socialism: 'My Plan has no more to do with socialism than it has with the comet' was one of his sayings.[38] How far from socialism he was can be appreciated from his pro-bourgeois argument for smallholdings – that a small proprietary class would form the backbone of a citizen militia.[39] He pointed up the motivations of the skilled workers who took the opportunity to become agriculturalists: they disliked town life, they had increased security as the owners of property, and they were ideally suited to the new way of life since the craftsman and artisan was already used to the combination of agriculture and domestic industry that would be needed on the O'Connor estates. Above all, O'Connor stressed that he was a gentle utopian, as opposed to the frothing socialists on the continent: 'If those with money to lend would lend it, I would change the whole face of society in twelve months from this day. I would make a paradise of England in less than five years.'[40]

At first the Land Plan seemed to be working well. Ultimately 70,000 subscribers contributed £100,000 to the scheme. In March 1846 the Chartist Co-operative Land Society purchased its first estate of 103 acres in O'Connor's name, since the society was denied official registration. Lots were drawn to decide who would farm the lots of two, three and four acres, depending on shareholding. The grandiloquently named O'Connorville was made available for public inspection in August 1846 and officially opened in May 1847.[41] Eventually six agricultural colonies were founded with 250 tenants on 1,700 acres. O'Connor took an obsessive and even pedantic interest in his pet project, to the point of writing a homily on the correct relations between employers and employees in the form of a dialogue.[42] From the very start O'Connor's colonies were controversial. His plan was assailed both in a frenzied newspaper campaign by pro-Establishment organs and (in the early stages) by paid agents of the ACLL, all of them asserting much the same thing – that the Land Plan was a mere stalking horse for the eventual nationalisation and expropriation of *all* property.[43] Such hostility could have been expected, but much more alarming was the virulent criticism from within the Chartist movement. Bronterre O'Brien claimed that the plan would at best introduce landlordism and at worst would produce an elite who could be detached from the main body of Chartists. O'Brien could be discredited on the grounds that he was now an isolated, marginal figure sniping from the sidelines, but more serious was the critique mounted from within the core of Chartism by the ex-editor of the *Northern Star*, Joshua Hobson (whom O'Connor had sacked), accusing O'Connor of peculation and defalcation.[44] In this context O'Brien welcomed the sudden appearance of a new radical figure, Ernest Jones, who hailed the Land Plan in ecstatic terms as the dawn of a golden age.[45] Jones (1819–69), who became a major figure in the movement from 1846, was yet another of the gentleman radicals the nineteenth century produced in such profusion. Born in Berlin, the son of a British army major who was equerry to the Duke of Cumberland, Jones came to England in 1839, had his first novel published two years later and was called to the bar at Middle Temple in 1844, before seeing the light and throwing in his lot with the Chartists. Some say his conversion was rather like that of Tom Paine, in that he came to radicalism after bankruptcy and personal misfortune.[46] The author of the poems *Chartist Songs* (1846), he quickly displaced Thomas Cooper as the poet laureate of the movement; Cooper fell foul of O'Connor by, so to speak, letting the cat out of the bag and declaring that Chartists would never use violence, even in self-defence.[47] A skilful orator, Jones lacked O'Connor's magnetism and charisma and could never have been the leader of the movement. Though a failure as gentleman demagogue, he was always very popular and was at first hailed by O'Connor as his heir apparent. Needless to say, the honeymoon did not last, and O'Connor quarrelled with Jones, as he had previously with O'Connell, Stephens, Lovett, Sturge, Hobson, Harney and a host of others.

O'Connor was one of those individuals – one can think of analogies among great actors – who cannot bear even the second or third lead to shine, albeit in a subsidiary role. In Jones's case the parting of the ways came with international socialism. Increasingly friendly with Marx, Engels and the European socialists, Jones was publicly disowned by O'Connor in July 1847 when he declared emphatically against liaisons with European socialists in a famous, ripsnorting and xenophobic article in the *Northern Star*.[48]

The Land Plan was meant to revive Chartism through increasing its parliamentary representation under the existing electoral system, once the successful proprietors of the allotments became men of property. Yet, despite its promising start, the plan soon encountered massive problems, which made O'Brien charge that O'Connor had abandoned real political action for pointless tinkering, which was a bagatelle by comparison. In the first place, O'Connor was no businessman. He set up a Land and Labour Bank to finance the project at the end of 1846, but by August of the following year legal complications obliged him to separate the bank from the company, with O'Brien as sole proprietor of the bank. A glaring weakness of the bank was that the only security for depositors was the land owned by the company, but this was already mortgaged to the shareholders. The Land and Labour Bank was in the precarious position of having O'Connor's personal money as its only real security and O'Connor's shaky reputation as its only collateral.[49] The project of leapfrogging from estate to estate with successive mortgages meant that there was always a wild, speculative element about the scheme. The fact that O'Connor was the sole proprietor of the bank left him wide open to charges of peculation and financial dishonesty. These were later clearly proven to be false but, as has been well said: 'the Land Plan's directors faced a recurrent problem in preventing critics from drawing lurid conclusions from the fact that purchases of estates were made in O'Connor's name'.[50] Although O'Connor was personally honest, he encouraged his critics and gave hostages to fortune by keeping no proper accounts, employing no orthodox methods of bookkeeping and no minutes of directors' meetings. The confusion over rents was almost total and never solved: should all the allottees pay the same? How should the rents be collected? How much credit should be extended, etc? It was never even clear whether the holders of allotments were freeholders or tenants of the company.[51] There were too many applicants for the available lots, and this caused resentment and discontent. When the fortunate colonists arrived on their plots, all too often they found that the soil was barren and unproductive. The colonists themselves proved incompetent in agricultural technique. The small plots of 2–4 acres were insufficient to feed a family, given that a surplus was needed to pay the ground rent.[52] Worst of all, from the viewpoint of social amelioration, there was that perennial barrier to socialism or any form of the 'new man': human nature. The lucky 250 chosen ones took advantage of the chaos. Some simply did not pay their rents; others sublet their lots at a profit against the entire spirit of the enterprise, or went in for profiteering from the sale of shares.[53] From the public-relations viewpoint, the way O'Connor used his plan as part of his cult of personality led to disillusionment: 'he cast Chartism in a supporting role in the drama of Feargus O'Connor'.[54] By 1849 investors had had enough. Neither subscriptions nor investment from the bank were arriving in sufficient quantities to buy further estates; the fifth and final colony was set up in 1849. In a final acknowledgement of the 'original sin' component of human nature, evictions were started for non-payment of rent; 68 such orders were issued in 1850.[55]

Even while the Land Company was foundering, the government was waging a sustained war of legal attrition against it. Four separate stages may be discerned. When O'Connor discovered that the NCA itself could not be registered as a friendly society, he detached the Land Company from the NCA and tried to register it as such, but John Tidd Pratt, the registrar-general, with the backing of the attorney-general, made it clear that this was not acceptable because the Land Company had clear political aims. O'Connor next tried a change of nomenclature and set up the National Cooperative Land Society, using lottery money. Tidd declared that this too was illegal, even though a large number of building societies and friendly societies used lotteries. It soon became clear that, whatever device O'Connor used to achieve registration, Pratt would veto it, and that this was a pan-Establishment plot, with Pratt backed by the attorney-general and he in turn by the prime minister.[56] Accordingly, O'Connor tried a third tack: an attempt at registration under the Joint Stock Companies Act. After a ten-month delay, the Board of Trade ruled that this would not be allowed, unless the new legal entity paid stamp duty – which it had been O'Connor's purpose from the very beginning to avoid. The government was ingenious in finding legal obstacles to thwart O'Connor, but it must be conceded that even within Chartism there were doubts about the legal status of such a body, and uncertainty about payment to managers and their accountability. It is not surprising that O'Connor was frequently ill in these years.[57] He hit back with an eighteen-month legal campaign to overthrow the Board of Trade's decision, but the courts decided against him on the grounds that no profit from shareholders to the new entity could be foreseen, and therefore it had no bona fide status as a joint-stock company. Finally the dauntless O'Connor tried to enrol his plan under an act of Parliament and moved a first reading of this in the House of Commons. Unable to stymie him this time by the legal system, the government hit back by appointing a Select Committee. Sixteen MPs – not all of them inherently hostile to O'Connor – sat twice weekly for two months, starting work on 23 May 1848 and completing their 390-page report on 1 August (a work rate that puts to shame today's interminable committees and tribunals).[58] They found that there had been no personal dishonesty on O'Connor's part – indeed he had put in £3,000–4,000 of his own money – but that there was sloppy record and account keeping and no proper capitalisation of the bank, which was personally owned by O'Connor. Trying to establish who exactly had contributed and in what numbers was almost impossible, and it was clear that most rents had not been paid. The overall conclusion was that the plan did not remotely meet the criteria for a viable friendly society, that it was an illegal scheme which did not satisfy the legitimate expectations of shareholders and which did not make the directors accountable to them. A government actuary estimated that it would take 150 years to satisfy the legitimate aspirations of the shareholders and that the entire scheme thus came close to being fraudulent. That was a death sentence. As one student of the scheme has said: 'The Land Company petered out rather than burst like the speculative bubble which many of its critics declared it to be.'[59] A parliamentary petition to wind up the scheme was presented in 1850 and in August 1851 the company was formally dissolved but, as a result of litigation reminiscent of Jarndyce v. Jarndyce in Dickens's *Bleak House*, the entire ramshackle structure was not finally wound up until 1857. The moral most observers drew from the fiasco was that it was hubris followed by nemesis, that O'Connor had overreached himself in his Promethean ambitions and that he would have done better to set up a string of small building societies.[60]

During the halcyon years of 1845–7, when O'Connor still dreamed that he would transform England with his agricultural colonies, the wider Chartist movement went into steep decline. Apart from the failure and repression of 1842–3, there were many other reasons for the waning of working-class activism. For two years after 1845 there was a return to economic prosperity; many disillusioned proletarians, despairing of a future in England, joined the gathering exodus to the Americas. The People's International League, founded in November 1847 and supposedly Chartism's window to the outside world, directed the attention of radicals and the middle classes to foreign affairs.[61] Most of all, the repeal of the Corn Laws and Peel's consequent departure from the premiership meant not only that all chance of an alliance with the middle classes was lost but also that they no longer had any use for working-class agitation, thus proving that the attitude of the ACLL towards Chartism had always been deeply cynical. Three significant events in 1847–8, however, led to a significant revival of Chartism, if never at the level of the peak period 1839–42. First, 1847 saw a sharp reverse in prosperity, with the price of staples rising rapidly. In 1843–5 wheat prices never rose higher than 51s 3d per quarter, as against the crisis years of 1838–41 when Chartism was at its apogee and the average price was 64s 4d. But in 1847 the price per quarter suddenly soared to 69s 9d.[62] At the same time there was a crisis in the cotton industry of Manchester, with only one-third of the 1841 factory labour force in the city still in work in 1847, and also in the textile trade in the Midlands. Abdundant US harvests in 1845–6 came to an end just when there was a general downturn in demand. Storm clouds were evident when bank rate shot up from 5 per cent to 8 per cent. Those industries hit by the trade cycle or under pressure from mass production elsewhere were disproportionately represented in Chartism, so militancy increased.[63] Secondly, the 1847 general election took place without significant Chartist gains or, in some cases, involvement. Between 1839 and 1848 eighteen different Chartist candidates actually contested parliamentary elections, but the usual tactic of the National Central Registration and Election Committee (NCREC), apart from enfranchising a few

Chartists or paying election candidates' expenses, was to put up hustings candidates to demonstrate the farce of the electoral system. Such candidates would easily win a majority by public acclaim and then withdraw just before the real election, held under the limited franchise. The Chartists always won on the show of hands, and then the candidates who had lost democratically won on the restricted formal poll.[64] Yet there were many complaints that the O'Connorites had lost interest in the election since they had become so obsessed with the Land Plan. The exiguous resources of the NCREC were contrasted with what seemed like the lavish funding available for the Land Plan. This was certainly true of O'Connor, who had been entered as a formal candidate at Nottingham, but by a fluke he emerged the winner there and so, after twelve years, was again an MP with a platform in Parliament.[65] Otherwise the results of the 1847 election were very much a mixed bag. Nine radical or liberal candidates endorsed by the NCREC were elected, but this was just nine out of the hoped-for (and expected) thirty. There were none at all in Scotland, showing that the movement was virtually extinct there.

The third factor in the Chartist revival was probably the most important of all. In 1847 Daniel O'Connell died, opening up an opportunity for new leadership and a change of direction in the Irish party. The Liberator's last years had not been happy. In October 1843 he called for a mass meeting at Clontarf, one of the sacred sites of Irish history, to demand repeal of the Act of Union; it was expected that millions would attend. The authorities banned the meeting and announced they would use force to break it up if it was held. To avoid bloodshed O'Connell called it off, but was rewarded for this signal act of loyalty to the English Establishment by being charged with conspiracy to alter the constitution by force. He was found guilty, but the sentence was quashed on appeal. The debacle at Clontarf, followed by seeing their leader hauled before the courts, was too much for the Irish. O'Connell lost caste and by his death was a discredited figure.[66] His demise opened up the possibility for new alignments in Irish politics, and particularly for an Irish–Chartist alliance; O'Connell had often boasted that he had 'saved' England by holding the detested Chartists at arm's length. All O'Connell's methods were a demonstrable failure: loyalty to the British Crown, non-violence and especially (in the light of the famine) deference to the 'market'. Here surely was an opportunity for O'Connor to bid for the Irish leadership and bring about the alliance of the English proletariat and the Irish so dreaded by the English authorities. The English media were sufficiently alarmed to run frequent articles talking scathingly of the 'nuptials of Chartism and Repeal'.[67] But the marriage of convenience never happened. O'Connor was too busy with his Land Plan to turn his attention to Irish affairs and, in any case, he had nothing to offer. The dreadful tragedy of the Great Famine was by this time devastating Ireland. The dying O'Connell had no solutions to this catastrophe and neither had O'Connor. The power vacuum in Ireland was quickly filled by the anti-O'Connellite faction known as Young Ireland. These men detested O'Connell at a personal level as a weak and ineffective leader but, until the year of revolution in Europe in 1848 gave them other ideas, were committed to pacific solutions to Ireland's problems.[68] They were opposed to the entire tradition of republican, ultra-democratic, insurrectionary nationalism, as typified by the United Irishmen and the great revolt of 1798. O'Connor by contrast was an admirer of the 'martyrs' Wolfe Tone and Robert Emmet. Besides, an alliance with the Chartists would bring Irishmen in England to the fore, and these, mainly based in Liverpool, Manchester and Birmingham, were the most fire-eating and insurrectionist of the Chartists.[69] Ireland in 1847 was pulled in at least three different directions: towards Young Ireland; towards O'Connor and Chartism; and, not insignificantly, towards the temperance movement headed by Father Theobald Matthew (signing the pledge), which by the mid-1840s had signed up some 3 million people (more than half the adult population). Although some Irishmen deserted the O'Connellites for Chartism, attracted by O'Connor's frequent assertion that Ireland's problems lay deeper than repeal and that the issues of Eire and Chartism were really two horns on the same ram, others inclined to political quietism, since neither O'Connell nor Young Ireland seemed to have a clue what to do about the island's most pressing crisis: the famine. Still others saw that a union of Chartism and Ireland would be fissiparous, since Chartism was essentially a movement of the industrial proletariat while the key social class in Ireland was the peasantry.[70]

Nevertheless, although the new bearings in Ireland would eventually come to nothing, the absence of O'Connell seemed to open up myriad possibilities and gave the Chartists heart. Meanwhile the economic downturn in England accelerated discontent, and this was raised to a new pitch during the particularly harsh winter of 1847–8, when influenza, bronchitis, pneumonia, typhus, measles and scarlatina were all at near-epidemic levels.[71] The working class was already in a combustible state when a match was thrown onto the pyre in the form of an outbreak of revolution in Paris in February 1848, which ousted Louis Philippe and set the tone for what would be a famous year of revolutions in Europe. Despite the scepticism of the Hungarian nationalist leader Lajos Kossuth, who regarded the events of February 1848 in France as a mere intra-elite transfer of power as against a 'real' revolution such as the one in 1789, most historians since have seen February 1848 as the inchoate form of a potentially seismic transformation in France, and certainly light years ahead of 1830, which merely replaced 'a Bourbon with a baboon.'[72] The Chartist leadership were already collecting signatures for a third petition to be presented to Parliament, having judged that the change in circumstances in 1847 justified another change of tactics. They were particularly encouraged by what seemed to be, from the evidence of the 1847 election, a renewed middle-class interest in Chartism, though the truth was that any favourable signs in that election represented the misinterpetation of an anti-Tory protest vote. Nevertheless, the February revolution in Paris seemed at once to add urgency to Chartist endeavours and to suggest that there was a new spirit abroad which might waft its way to England. It is unquestionable that while the ruling classes were momentarily stunned by events across the Channel, the Chartists were euphoric, convinced that their hour was about to come.[73] Once again the rank and file and the leadership were out of step. Although most Chartist meetings held to congratulate the French revolutionaries passed off peacefully, in Glasgow city centre there were serious riots and clashes between looters and cavalry which left two rioters dead. More ominously, there were serious disturbances in London on 6 and 13 March. A three-day riot followed a reform meeting in Trafalgar Square, which was hijacked by 'physical force' Chartists on the 6th, and a week later there was a violent outbreak in Camberwell.[74] Chartist rhetoric became more insurrectionary. The ruling classes were warned that a third petition was about to be presented and it was broadly hinted that if this one received the contemptuous treatment of its two predecessors, armed rebellion and civil war would be the consequence. The date set for handing in the petition to Parliament was 10 April 1848. The plan was for a mass demonstration on Kennington Common followed by a procession to Downing Street.[75]

The government hit back by introducing a new law making seditious speech a felony. This time, unlike in 1839 and 1842, the police invoked moribund statutes to turn the screw on the demonstrators. It was declared illegal for more than twenty people to present a petition to the House of Commons or to hold a meeting within one mile of Westminster Hall; additionally the meeting on Kennington Common was declared illegal. The Whigs intended to call O'Connor's bluff as spectacularly as they had called O'Connell's at Clontarf five years earlier.[76] The Chartists at first appeared unfazed. There was a kind of dress rehearsal on Kennington Common in March 1848, and on 4 April a series of militant speeches threatened an armed reponse to any attempt at government repression. It was announced that if the third petition was rejected, the NCA would call on the queen to dissolve Parliament, with any new government pledged to implement the Charter.[77] The item in these speeches that most alarmed the government was the appeal to all Irish in London to support the third petition and thus to secure reforms which would have prevented the deaths of at least a million souls in the Great Famine.[78] The participation of the Irish, enraged and vengeful after the famine, particularly alarmed the elite. They knew from their spies that Chartism was now closely linked to the situation in Ireland (the palmy days of the deferential and collaborationist O'Connell were over) and that Young Ireland now viewed a rising in England as essential to its own plans. What they most feared was a 'perfect storm' of a Chartist revival, a radicalised Ireland and the revolutionary example of Paris in February.[79] They had some grounds for their fears. The Irish made up 5 per cent of the industrial proletariat in England and, given that by no means all workers were Chartists whereas the Irish were rock solid behind the Chartists, this made them an important element. Moreover, as it turned out, the Irish played a significant role in the great demonstration on 10 April 1848.[80] The combination of both realistic and unrealistic fears led some people, even those highly placed, to panic. Queen Victoria, unpersuaded by her ministers that they had the situation in hand, decamped to her eyrie on the Isle of Wight on 8 April.[81] The novelist William Makepeace Thackeray thought that revolution was imminent, and he was by no means the only one.[82]

Shrewder observers, however, and those in the know at the highest reaches of government, were confident that the Whig administration could see off any Chartist challenge, even an armed one. The composer Hector Berlioz, visiting London, expressed a typically Gallic contempt for the Chartists' potential as revolutionaries; the would-be insurgents, he said, knew 'as much about starting a riot as the Italians about writing a symphony'.[83] Lord John Russell, the prime minister, was supremely confident that he could handle any set of emergency contingencies and had so much aplomb that he originally wanted to allow the Chartist procession to cross the Thames and present the petition to the House of Commons, but he was argued, or more properly, nagged and chivvied, out of this stance. The 'nervous Nellies' wanting a blanket ban on 10 April included Sir James Graham, C. E. Trevelyan at the Treasury, *The Times* and the Duke of Wellington.[84] By this time the hero of Waterloo was in his late seventies, in the early stages of dementia and a veritable Jekyll and Hyde figure, notorious at this stage for his violently volatile moods. Wellington always portrayed himself as the man who had stood virtually alone against the Chartists in 1848, a latter-day Horatio on the bridge: 'I was ready,' he declared. 'I could have stopped them whenever you liked, and if they had been armed it would have been all the same.' The government humoured him and allowed him to think he was the supreme director of operations while getting quietly on with the job without him. As has been well said: 'The Duke, in these last years of his life, tended towards a highly coloured view of the risks confronting the realm.'[85] Russell's real secret weapon was not the Iron Duke but a highly efficient police and espionage system, which kept him informed of every nuance of Chartist intentions until 10 April. He was tipped off the day before the meeting that the Chartists wanted at all costs to avoid a flat-out confrontation with the government.[86] Russell's only worry was what the public reaction to massive civilian casualties would be if his troops were forced to open fire. As one of the most sober and realistic observers of April 1848 remembered it: 'There were no arms in London in April 1848, no persons were drilled, no war organisation existed, and no intention of rising anywhere. The government knew it, for they had spies everywhere. They knew it as well or better than in 1839.'[87]

By April 1848 the London proletariat, which in previous confrontations with the government had played almost no part, finally came out unambiguously for the Charter. The irony about the plans for Kennington Common was that on this occasion the Chartist leadership did not coordinate them with demonstrations of risings elsewhere in the country. Having previously neglected the capital, the leaders now neglected the provinces. Nevertheless, at a convention held on 4 April to make final arrangements for Kennington Common, there was euphoria mixed with sober-sided realism. O'Connell's debacle at Clontarf was in the forefront of minds, and speaker after speaker urged the importance of avoiding another dismal rerun of the Liberator's most humiliating hour. There was the usual chasm between 'moral force' and 'physical force' advocates, with Ernest Jones urging armed confrontation with the authorities, O'Brien recommending bowing the head and accepting the government's demands 100 per cent, and O'Connor, as usual, the man in the middle. Worried about bloodshed, O'Connor felt he had signalled his pacific intentions clearly enough to the ruling class, since if he had intended violent revolution, he would not have held a mass meeting south of the river, allowing government troops to hold all the bridges and deny them access to central London; on the other hand, a venue at Trafalgar Square or Hyde Park might have hinted at an attempt at revolution.[88] O'Connor was certainly wise to tread carefully, for in April 1848, even more than in 1839 and 1842, the government brought all its massive resources to bear on the problem. The Russell administration enjoyed at least two major strokes of good fortune. Several regiments of crack troops happened to be on home leave from imperial service at this very moment. This meant that, all told, the government had 33,738 soldiers on hand in Great Britain and another 28,942 in Ireland, as against, respectively, 26,345 and 13,112 in 1839–40.[89] Technology too was on the side of the forces of law and order. The railway network had expanded considerably in the 1840s – the great boom period (which Dickens's *Dombey and Son* pays eloquent testimony to) – and this increased the efficiency of the army exponentially. Whereas in 1839–40 a battalion of troops would take seventeen days' marching to get from London to Manchester (or vice versa) and would arrive exhausted, by 1848 it would take just nine hours by train and the men would arrive fresh and ready for action.[90] Early in April Russell stationed 7,122 troops in

London and brought in another 500 on the morning of 10 April; 12 heavy guns were transported from Woolwich and put on emplacements guarding the bridges. Having learned from the uprising in Paris in February, the government was determined that no buildings should be occupied by demonstrators, as these could serve as rallying points or oases for rest and recreation, allowing insurgents to fight in relays. In this regard the British Museum became something of an obsession for the government, since its researchers informed it that if the museum fell into Chartist hands it could be turned into a fortress capable of housing 10,000 armed defenders.[91]

In addition to the troops, the government deployed 4,000 officers of the Metropolitan Police – the new law-enforcement body founded by Peel less than twenty years earlier. Loathed and detested as class traitors by the Chartists, the 'Peelers' were an altogether new element in riot control – something the Chartist insurgents in the provinces had never had to face. By late summer police numbers had risen to 5,500.[92] Over and above all this the government recruited able-bodied members of the middle classes as 'special constables'. Bankers, merchants, shopkeepers, clerks and a host of 'white-collar' workers took an oath to defend property and uphold law and order and were issued with a badge and a truncheon. One of them was the future French emperor, Louis Napoleon (Napoleon III), on the eve of his rise to power, and whose periods in England bracketed his imperial years.[93] Even more egregious examples of class treachery seemed to be provided by those members of the London working class who enrolled as 'specials', but it has been convincingly demonstrated that they joined up because their employers told them that otherwise they would lose their jobs.[94] It is estimated that there was roughly one 'special' for every one-and-a-half demonstrators in London on 10 April, but this depends on a figure of about 85,000 specials on duty and 150,000 Chartists on Kennington Common.[95] The numbers of specials has (implausibly) been put even higher, at 175,000–200,000 and some Chartist historian put the numbers of demonstrators higher, at 170,000–250,000.[96] The final point of absurdity is reached if we take the official figures for demonstrators provided by the Metropolitan Police – a risible 15,000 – but this represents what has been well described as 'the occupational tendency of the police to underestimate the size of popular gatherings. This is a bias shared by all in authority.'[97]

If we were to take seriously the police figures for the Chartists and the wilder figures for the specials we would have a ludicrous and hilarious situation where 15,000 marchers were opposed by 200,000 specials, providing a crushing ratio of 13:1 for the government, even when leaving the regular police and the military out of the picture. It is perhaps hardly surprising that so much confusion has arisen over numbers on 10 April 1848 since even the government was at a loss. Lord John Russell reported in his private correspondence that 170,000 'specials' had been on duty on the 'day of days'.[98]

The actual 'confrontation' on 10 April turned out the dampest of damp squibs. After all his rhetoric (the temptation to use the word 'fustian' in both senses is overwhelming), O'Connor essentially bowed his head and conceded that the government held all the cards. Before the meeting he met the Metropolitan Police Commissioner Sir Richard Mayne (who had headed the Met since its foundation). Mayne told him that although the meeting on Kennington Common was technically an illegal assembly, the police would make no attempt to break it up; on the other hand, a mass procession to Westminster would be resisted with all the police and military power at the government's disposal. Mayne later spread the canard that O'Connor seemed shaken and scared by the scale of the police preparations, but the truth is that the valetudinarian O'Connor, always under great stress, was ill again that day.[99] He proceeded to Kennington Common, where he addressed a crowd acknowledged even by the Chartists themselves to be disappointingly small; some thought government intimidation had done its work well. A survey of 'no shows' later revealed three main categories: those who stayed at home because they were genuinely fearful of violence; 'moral force' Chartists, who thought the government ban had to be respected so that Chartism could retain the high moral ground; and those who took the pragmatic line that, since the threat of violence had not worked in 1839 or 1842, the government would simply call O'Connor's bluff once again. The meeting dispersed peacefully; heavy rain in the early afternoon dissuaded any who might have been thinking of violence. The petition was then taken in three cabs to Westminster. There was no mass procession, but some Chartists drifted north of the river in dribs and drabs to view the outcome at the House of Commons.[100] A massive petition, which O'Connor claimed had 5.5 million signatures, was presented to the House. All

England waited tensely to see what Parliament's response would be, for the Chartists had proclaimed often enough that the rejection of a third petition would trigger civil war. Next day a parliamentary committee reported that there were nowhere near 5 million authentic signatures on the petition, that the true figure was around 2 million (an allegedly exact count of 1,975,496). Something of a sensation was created when the committee reported that the House of Commons clerks had uncovered forgery on a massive scale, dozens of identical signatures purporting to be by different people, and hundreds of thousands of bogus signatures, some of them purporting to be by the Duke of Wellington, Victoria Rex (*sic*), Sir Robert Peel, etc. Not only were there large numbers of obviously fictitious names but there were also some obscene ones.[101] The press took up the idea of Chartism as farce and this undoubtedly had a considerable propaganda effect. Yet several comments are in order. It is quite clear that some of the fictitious names had been added to the petition by spies and agents provocateurs. This obvious fact was pointed out by O'Connor, but his words were drowned in a cascade of Establishment derision.[102] The Commons clerks had also discounted the 'signature' of anyone illiterate who got a proxy to sign for him and *all* signatures by women – which alone accounted for 8 per cent of the total. Moreover, as O'Connor pointed out, the 'downsizing' from 5.7 million to under 2 million could only have been an impressionistic hunch by the clerks. Only 13 of them had counted the signatures and for only 17 hours – which meant that they would have had to complete the impossible task of vetting the names of signatories at an average of 150 a minute.[103] It was clear that, as had been shown over the Land Scheme, the ingenuity of the ruling class at finding dubious ways to discredit Chartism was almost inexhaustible. In any case, even if the clerks' absurdly low figures were accepted, it still meant (with 2 million out of an adult population of 17 million) that Chartist support was double the size of the electorate and quadruple the number of the total votes cast in the general election of 1847.[104]

O'Connor reacted to the debacle of 10 April with a mixture of depression and fury. He had no answer to those who claimed that his advocacy of 'physical force' was always a sham, that he had been exposed as the emperor in his new clothes. He had done no better at Kennington Common than the much-derided O'Connell had done at Clontarf. One of O'Connor's more maddening characteristics was an abstract insistence on the need to use violence as a reserve weapon, coupled with such a reluctance to employ it that in the end it was doubted that 'physical force' had any real meaning for him: the time was not right, he reiterated, but almost ex hypothesi it was never right and never could be.[105] His rage manifested itself in an ill-judged challenging of a fellow MP to a duel and refusing to accept his apology in the House. In a fit of pique he also withdrew his motion to force the House to hold a committee of inquiry into the clerks' alleged figures for the number of signatures on the petition. Some say this was the first clear sign of the dementia that would increasingly afflict him.[106] The depression was surely indicated by O'Connor's withdrawal from Chartist affairs and absence from the next national convention in May. In a classic case of closing the stable door after the horse had bolted, he went on a mission in Ireland to establish Chartism there at the very moment when both Chartism and Irish militancy were almost defunct.[107] While O'Connor slunk away defeated, the euphoria of the ruling classes was boundless. Palmerston wrote to Clarendon on 11 April: 'Things passed off beautifully yesterday, but the snake is scotched not killed.' Prince Albert wrote to Baron Stockmar: 'We had our revolution yesterday, and it ended in smoke.' And to his equerry he wrote: 'What a glorious day was yesterday for England: how mightily will this tell all over the world.'[108] The middle classes spread a triumphalist and quite false view of 10 April, that middle England had rallied against the extremists and seen them off, and that the special constables, unaided by any police or troops, had 'put down' the rising. Just as with hindsight everyone is omniscient, in the aftermath of a failed revolution every cowardly pipsqueak becomes a hero. The publisher, journalist and oenophile Henry Vizetelly (1820–94), a shrewd observer and eyewitness, more sapiently wrote: 'The very people who had been almost prostrated with terror in the morning plucked up courage and laughed at what they described as their neighbours' fears; pretending that they themselves had never for a moment believed there was reason for apprehending the faintest danger.'[109] Probably the most profound reason for the failure of 10 April 1848, however it had been conducted and whoever had led it, was that London, by then a megalopolis of 3 million people was too large and too heterogeneous for a revolution to catch fire by mere rioting; a coup d'état by a dedicated cabal would have had to accompany it.[110]

It is the conventional view that Chartism was dead in the water by the evening of 10 April. Here is one view by a contemporary: 'Chartism was practically at an end on the night of 10 April, and all attempts to resuscitate it were only the old story of flogging a dead horse.'[111] All the evidence, however, suggests that, far from decreasing revolutionary fervour, the disappointment led to increased militancy. Lord John Russell agreed with Palmerston's quote from *Macbeth* and, to extend the serpentine imagery, thought that Chartism was a movement with many heads, that a setback in London would by no means be the end of the story in the industrial north.[112] In the aftermath of Kennington Common the government decided to take a 'softly, softly' attitude to the Chartist leaders, but were spurred into action four months later when the levels of ferment and agitation, especially in the northern cities, showed no signs of dying down. With O'Connor's and Harney's withdrawal from the Convention in May, the official leadership baton passed to Ernest Jones, but he was soon eclipsed by a revived figure from the past, the radical physician Peter McDouall. He had fled to France after the 1842 strike, with a £100 bounty for his capture hanging over his head, but he slipped back into the country surreptitiously in 1844 and continued to work for the movement.[113] In the vacuum created by O'Connor's and Harney's withdrawal, he moved to centre-stage and called for the 'final struggle' – code for an armed uprising. Palmerston's prediction was soon proved correct when there was serious rioting in Bradford, where there was a large Irish population. There were more grave outbreaks in London, at Clerkenwell for three days from 29 May to 1 June, and at Bishop Bonner's Field, Bethnal Green, on 4 June. These outbreaks were scarred by ugly scenes, characterised by genuine and undeniable police brutality.[114] McDouall now called for a monster demonstration followed by a national uprising; the signal for action was to be another rally in Bishop Bonner's Field. Tensions again rose in the capital, and some thought both the atmosphere and the objective situation worse than on 10 April: 'It was the events of Monday 12 June rather than of 10 April which proved the sterner test of the government's resolve and capacity to subdue discontent, and led it to impose the most draconian legal and physical measures.'[115] The idea of a national uprising on Whit Monday was bold, but once again depended on a level of discipline and organisation that had never been the Chartists' strong suit; it did not help that O'Connor weighed in from the sidelines, opposing the idea of simultaneous nationwide action. McDouall pressed on with his idea of a giant rally despite a government ban, but on the day found a huge force of police and troops (4,300 officers of the Met and 5,500 soldiers, backed up with 6 big guns) awaiting him. Faced with this, McDouall could do no better than O'Connor and ordered the meeting cancelled.[116] Infuriated, McDouall returned home and began plotting another uprising, this time for 18 June. The nervous strain soon told on him. He learned that his own organisation was deeply penetrated by government spies and, besides, he dared not divulge his plans in time for proper organisation lest O'Connor publicly denounce them again. Finally he admitted defeat and ordered the conspiracy postponed indefinitely.[117]

Further hammer blows were dealt to Chartism from the two quarters which had originally seemed to offer them much hope. Any expectations from Ireland were dashed when Young Ireland sustained a crushing debacle – the biggest flop in all the flops of 1848, the so-called turning point which failed to turn. A famous 'battle' in a cabbage patch on 29 July between 100 Confederates of Young Ireland and 40 police ended in something more like a traditional Saturday-night Donnybrook than a revolution. Chartism's putative allies in the Emerald Isle ended their bid more as a laughing stock than a genuine threat, though the British ruling classes were taking no chances and continued nervous of an uprising, perhaps subsidised by sympathisers in the USA. They remembered how they had breathed a sigh of relief in 1798 at the passing of the threat from French Generals Hoche and Humbert, only to be overtaken by the far more serious indigenous rising.[118] Meanwhile in France the 'June Days' had a demoralising effect on Chartism, for this seemed to be the Thermidorean reaction to the hopeful leftward turning taken in the February revolution. The bloodshed in Paris was indicative of what might have happened in London on 10 April or 14 June. More people were killed in the bloodbath of 24–8 June than in the entire period 1793–4; 15,000 were slain, many more perished afterwards and 20,000 were imprisoned either in France or the penal colonies overseas in what has been called 'the greatest slave wars of modern times', with the working class pitifully ranged against the combined weight of army, bourgeoisie and peasantry.[119] In despair McDouall quit the arena, but his place in turn was taken by two other firebrands: an Irishman named David Donovan and a sixty-year-old black man, William Cufay, only five feet tall, with both legs and spine deformed from birth, and the son of an African slave. Donovan and Cufay laid plans for a joint rising in London and Manchester on 16 August, but by this time Chartist ranks were honeycombed by secret agents and informers. Police raids in Manchester nipped this attempted insurgency in the bud. Although the Cufay–Donovan plot has often been portrayed as opéra bouffe, it was far more serious than this; there was more backing for it in London than has usually been realised.[120] The police coup was only just in time, for the situation in the north of England was extremely grave, with armed Chartists in Bolton, Oldham, Ashton-under-Lyne, Halifax and Bradford all waiting for the signal for a general rising which never came. The police fought pitched battles with Chartists in Halifax, Leeds and Bradford. The authorities now struck back with calculated venom. Mass arrests followed, with denial of bail terms, trials and draconian punishment. Fifteen ringleaders were handed sentences of between fifteen and twenty-four months; McDouall and Ernest Jones got two years' jail apiece. There were sixteen sentences of transportation to Australia, including Cufay, who was transported to Tasmania. Paroled in 1856, he elected to stay on under Capricorn and died in 1870, aged eighty-two.[121]

By all reasonable indices the outward form of Chartism perished in 1848. The combination of troops and firepower, the determination to use force, mass arrests, the suspension of Habeas Corpus and the huge volume of spies and paid agents who infiltrated Chartist ranks made most parties to the movement despair by the end of the year. Chartism ceased to be a viable mass movement and became merely another pressure group. The leaders fell out among themselves spectacularly. Harney launched a violent verbal fusillade on O'Connor in 1849, but by then the Irishman's increasingly erratic behaviour was common knowledge. A fourth Chartist petition in 1849 mustered only 53,816 signatures, and a Commons motion for the petition was defeated by the humiliating margin of 222–13. Sales of the *Northern Star* declined from the high point of 40,000 in 1839 to just 5,000 in 1849.[122] In retrospect Chartist defeat in 1848 looks inevitable. The government held practically all the cards: physical force, money, the support of the media, the bureaucracy and most significant sections of the intellectual 'clerisy'; they were in possession of all the sources of power, enjoyed a perceived political legitimacy, suffered no elite divisions and no fear of foreign invasion. Against this all Chartism could bring to bear was numbers, and not even highly organised numbers at that. Nevertheless, it was quite clear that 1848 was a decisive revolutionary moment, for one has only to imagine the scenario if a McDouall on one side or a Duke of Wellington on the other had been given their head. Most scholarly argument about 1848 reduces to whether it was a more serious threat to the political system than the Chartist incursions in 1839–40 and 1842 or a lesser one.[123] Particularly noticeable in 1848 was the ferocious repression visited on both Chartists and the Irish via the new Treason Felony Act, introduced to buttress the existing laws of sedition and unlawful assembly. Harney commented ruefully on the government's overt class warfare: 'Place *Fustian* in the dock, let *Silk Gown* charge the culprit with being a "physical force" Chartist, and insinuate that he is not exactly free from the taint of "Communism", and forthwith *Broad Cloth* in the jury box will bellow out: GUILTY.'[124] One of the profound reasons for Chartist failure in 1848 was precisely this division of the nation along class lines. The importance of middle-class support for Chartism has long been disputed, with some seeing the movement as almost entirely proletarian and others viewing the middle-class contribution as 'vanguard' as of supreme importance. The truth seems to be that some members of the middle class were initially sympathetic, that without Chartist ideology they would never have campaigned on behalf of the working class, and that this was demonstrated by total bourgeois indifference once the movement declined after 1848.[125] Yet even the most sympathetic members of the middle class sympathised with only a small and select part of the working class and its aspirations. In 1848 the choice was stark: back the government or support revolution. It was at this point that the entire middle class deserted Chartism, for 1848 showed 'the closing of ranks among all those with a property stake in the country, however small that stake was'. The entire propertied sector of society – anyone with *any* property to defend, in a spectrum running from the 'high' wealthy bourgeoisie to the shopkeepers of the bourgeois variety – rallied to the government and the status quo.[126]

Chartism was now in terminal decline and, as if to provide a personal dimension to the sociological debacle, the later history of most Chartist leaders was not a happy one. O'Connor rapidly plummeted into dementia – the result of tertiary syphilis or general paralysis of the insane and spent his remaining few years in an asylum.[127] With the great leader off the scene, what was left of Chartism splintered into many segments, but basically the divide was between those who moved left into socialism and those who opted for mild reformism, still with dreams of a trans-coalition. In the latter category were Lovett and O'Brien. Lovett tried to devote himself to the education of the working class and founded a movement called the New Move, but this was a dismal failure, with membership never topping 5,000. He gave up in 1857, opened a bookshop, which likewise did not prosper, wrote an autobiography and died in poverty.[128] Bronterre O'Brien tried his hand at newspaper publishing after his break with O'Connor and produced two short-lived organs: the *Poor Man's Guardian* in 1843 and the *National Reformer* in 1844. Neither was a financial success and both had ceased publication by 1847. O'Brien then essayed some desultory journalism and gave adult education classes. Despite his reputation as an intellectual, most observers found his writings rambling, inaccurate and incoherent, and as he got older he added peevish rancorousness to his defects as a politician. From 1850 his health was in decline with chronic bronchitis, though he lingered until 1864, sustained by financial subsidies from well-wishers.[129]

The fortunes of those on the Left were more mixed. After two harsh years in Kirkdale jail from 1848 to 1850, Peter McDouall tried to establish a medical practice to provide for his growing family, but this failed abysmally. He and his family emigrated to Australia in 1854 but he died soon after arrival at the age of forty.[130] George Julian Harney, who became close friends with Marx and Engels, spent a frustrating three years on unsuccessful and shortlived newspapers before finding a more stable position as editor of the *Jersey Independent*. However, in 1861–2 he fell out with the proprietor Joseph Cowen because Harney supported the North in the American Civil War; it should be remembered that, at least until the Battle of Antietam in 1862, British opinion was overwhelmingly in favour of the southern Confederacy. Harney resigned and emigrated to the USA, where he worked for fourteen years as a clerk in the Massachusetts State House. On his retirement he returned to England, wrote some part-time journalism, and died in 1897, aged eighty.[131] Perhaps the most interesting later Chartist career was that of Ernest Jones. After his sulphurous rhetoric in 1848, Jones was a marked man by the authorities, and they did not even need to deploy their ultimate legal weapon, the Treason Felony Act, against him, easily convicting him instead under the heading of sedition. Imprisoned in Tothillfields jail, the Alcatraz of Victorian England (off Victoria Street at the junction with the Vauxhall Bridge Road), Jones endured far harsher conditions than O'Connor had in 1840–1 in York Castle. Although we can discount the more lurid stories about his captivity – such as that he was denied pen and paper and had to write his epic poem *The Revolt of Hindoostan* in his own blood – his experience in jail was no picnic. Jones was treated as a common criminal rather than a political prisoner, still less a martyred poet, and spent much of his two years in solitary confinement because he refused to pick oakum like other common criminals. To show who was master, the warden put him on bread and water and placed him in a cell recently occupied by a cholera victim.[132] Promised an early release if he would abjure politics for the future, he refused and at the end of his sentence could no longer stand upright. On his release he was pressurised by a rich uncle to give up politics on pain of being disinherited from a large estate, but again refused, returned to his early calling as a lawyer and defended the Fenians in the 1860s. Like Harney, he had close contacts with Marx and Engels, though Marx gradually became disillusioned with him.[133] He continued with a prolific output of poems and novels, and was about to contest a parliamentary seat in Manchester which he was certain to win, when he suddenly died the day after his fiftieth birthday. Jones was a man of absolute integrity and dauntless courage but, like many 'sea-green incorruptibles' he was not a very attractive human being. Even his biographer calls him 'duplicitous and unpleasant: in short, a liar, a cheat, an anti-Semite, a racist bigot, and absent father, and a neglectful husband'.[134]

Two issues require further investigation: the deeper reasons for Chartism's failure in 1848, and the separate but allied question of why the movement declined thereafter. One salient consideration about 1848 is that England, with a repressive apparatus apparently lagging far behind those of continental ruling elites, yet managed one of the greatest police/demonstrator ratios in all history. This alerts us to the fact that large sections of the working class and the city of London, with a population of 3 million, simply absented themselves. By contrast Paris in February saw about 5,000 police and national guardsmen trying to contain a population of 700,000 and being overwhelmed. It is usually considered that a police/public ratio of about 1:200 is adequate for containing normal crime (in most US cities in the 1960s this was the ratio; Paris in 1968 had 1:187).[135] Yet such numbers cannot deal with an entire population driven by hunger and anger. In Paris in 1848 regular troops were not trusted, as they were both ill-paid and suspected of sympathising with the rioters. In France the loyalty of the army in revolutionary times was always suspect: Louis XVI feared to put them to the test in 1789, which was one of the factors that allowed the revolution to escalate.[136] In England there were never such fears, as General Napier's eupeptic comments in 1839–40 make clear. With a small turnout (relative to population) of 150,000 on Kennington Common on 10 April 1848, and an army loyal to the government, the result of a call to arms could only have been a bloodbath, as O'Connor concluded. The Chartists, meanwhile, were not united. Different people pursued different agendas in different places at different times, with O'Connor, McDouall and Cufay successively at the helm, and the focus shifting from London to the industrial north. Another view of 1848 was that the Chartists had, so to speak, already missed the revolutionary boat, that the ideal time for revolution was 1830–2, not 1838–9 or 1842, and still less 1848.[137] Allegedly, there was a greater revolutionary 'window' in 1830–42 for four main reasons: the 'Captain Swing' agitation in the countryside, sometimes called the last peasants' revolt in England, was cutting a swathe through the rural areas; there was industrial unrest involving miners, handloom weavers, spinners, artisans and factory workers; the Irish problem was acute, with a plethora of food riots; and the middle classes were involved in a movement for parliamentary reform. Certainly in some areas there was greater militancy than in the Chartist period, with the mini-Gordon riots in Bristol in 1831 featuring as the last great urban revolt. These arguments have a certain force, but the only really telling one concerns the middle classes. Chartism could only have succeeded with their support, but they had largely got what they wanted with the 1832 Reform Bill and, even more, with the repeal of the Corn Laws in 1846. It was quite clear that middle-class pressure groups sought what they wanted for themselves, not for the proletariat.[138] Besides, by 1848 their political consciousness had deepened, and they were aware that the gap between capital and labour was greater than in 1830. It followed that tinkering with revolution in 1848 was likely to have far more serious consequences than it would have done a dozen or so years earlier. The reason why 1838–48 was a more serious threat to the state than 1830–2 was because the demand for universal suffrage was a far more radical demand than anything the Establishment had had to confront at the time of the Great Reform Bill.[139]

The decline of Chartism after 1848 has invited many interpretations and speculations, ranging from the somewhat flippant and impressionistic to profound exegesis at the interface of history and sociology. Among the former we would classify the idea that Chartist supporters became cynical because of the fiasco over the bogus names allegedly contained in the third petition; no one in the movement ever took this seriously. A facile attempt to explain the fall of Chartism via the 'three Rs' – ridicule, repression and reactive indifference – will not take us very far. A famous attempt at the superficial explanation of 'decline and fall' was given by the journalist, novelist and Parnellite MP, Justin McCarthy (1830–1912): 'English Chartism died of publicity; the exposure to the air; of the Anti-Corn Law League; of the evident tendencies of the time to settle all questions by reason, argument and majorities; of growing education; of a strengthening sense of duty among all the more influential classes.'[140] More sophisticated views are that Chartism was trying to solve by political methods problems that were essentially economic, or to use reformism to achieve the kind of socio-economic change that could only be accomplished by revolution. Others say that in the 1850s and 1860s the ruling classes cleverly bamboozled the working classes by bombarding them with a number of sensations, one rapidly succeeding another, most drawn from the Empire or foreign affairs: the Great Exhibition of 1851, the Crimean War of 1854–6, the Indian Mutiny of 1857, the Volunteer Movement of 1859, Garibaldi and the Italian crisis in 1860, the American Civil War of 1861–5. More solidly based interpretations point to the growth of the British economy in the 1850s as against the depression and relative stagnation of the 1840s, so that 'hunger Chartism' lost its appeal. The repeal of the Corn Laws did lead to lower food prices. The burgeoning cotton industry soaked up previous unemployment;

the 262,000 employees in cotton factories in 1840 had become 427,000 by 1860.[141] The Chartist decade had also convinced the British elite that reforms were urgently needed to head off revolution. It took the ruling classes a long time to take in that they had defeated the quarter-century-long threat from France, first via the Revolution and then in the form of Napoleon, and could therefore relax; once they did, they were increasingly inclined to take off the repressive brakes.[142] The repeal of the Corn Laws, the Bank Charter Act of 1844, the passage of the Ten Hour Act in 1847, the Public Health Act of 1848, were all signs of the times. Additionally, class lines in England were not rigid but relatively fluid. In nineteenth-century Germany a coalition of Junkers, peasants and industrialists, backed by a programme of reaction and imperialism, had disastrous results for the working classes and, ultimately, for twentieth-century democracy. No such coalition appeared in England. And although it would be naive to put too much emphasis on individual personalities – which might result in the absurdity whereby the Duke of Wellington could genuinely, and with a straight face, believe that without him, there would have been a revolution in 1830[143] – it is worth underlining the way that Peel, Russell and others were prepared to bend to the wind and better the conditions of the working classes, albeit solely in ways they approved. Russell, for instance, said that the failure of the British people to support revolution in 1848 made him willing to work for genuine suffrage reform.[144]

After 1848 the English working class moved decisively away from thoughts of revolution. The workers embraced trade unions, cooperative societies, friendly societies – what Lenin would later call 'trade union consciousness' or mere 'economism', and in politics gradually attached themselves to the new Liberal Party, which would arise from the ashes of the Whigs. Conveniently for the elite, most proletarian riots and violence after 1850 tended to be directed against the Irish.[145] This led some observers to conclude that Chartism had only ever been a comfortable crutch for the workers, the default position for an unrevolutionary working class, the exact role that would later be fulfilled by the Labour Party.[146] The Chartists, for all their failures, had convinced the governing classes that something had to be done about their woes, the message had gone home, and even voting rights gradually returned to the liberal agenda. Of their two great opponents in the ACLL, Cobden never came round to working for an extension of the franchise, but his partner John Bright did.[147] The implosion of the British proletariat after 1850 has always puzzled observers, and some say the historiographical conundrum arises because historians have assumed the existence of a monolithic and persistent working class but that its segmented nature was temporarily masked by Chartism. A huge gulf separates the artisan of the early nineteenth century (the typical Chartist supporter) from the much more class-conscious factory worker at the end of the century. One theory is that the decline of working-class activism after 1848 is predicated on a monolithic proletariat with a continuity of aspirations and interests, so that if in the 1840s it was radical but in the 1850s quiescent this immediately generates a puzzle. Yet it could simply be that different sections of the working class were dominant at different times and that they evolved differently.[148] This would make sense of the lack of nationwide organisation among the Chartists, which is usually set down to inept leadership. To take two obvious examples, there was no real attempt made to integrate Scotland into the wider movement, and the same was the case in Wales. The Rebecca riots in Wales from 1839 targeted tollgates as a symbol of oppression of the Welsh working classes, but O'Connor and the other leaders proved incapable of utilising the riots for their own ends.[149] A fissiparous, heterogeneous proletariat, on the other hand, would do much to explain the failure.

Yet another explanation for Chartist decline insinuates the notion that the movement was an anachronism or, at any rate, that it did not have an 'organic' relationship with the highly industrialised society of the 1840s. Here are two statements of this idea, both from sympathetic historians: 'Chartism's tragic predicament as a political movement was its historical placement between pre-industrial and industrial modes of action.'[150] The idea is that Chartism was a hybrid of the 'spontaneous combustion' riots of the eighteenth century – most notably the Gordon riots – and the control and discipline of a modern Labour movement. While Chartism was still over-reliant on the older rhetoric and ideology directed at 'Old Corruption', the nature of the State had changed: the elite had both woken up to the potential danger of the social volcano on which they sat and had taken appropriate reformist measures to assuage the threat (the deluge of legislation mentioned above). Too much Chartist energy was used up in barging at open doors, and not enough in thinking through 'what if?' strategies – the most obvious one was what was to happen if the government continued to reject national petitions.[151] 'And here is another statement of the 'anachronism' thesis:

> The ethos of Chartism anyway may not have survived into the great urban centres of the later nineteenth century. It needed small communities, the slack religious and moral supervision, the unpoliced street and meeting place . . . As society in Britain became increasingly polarised between a depopulated countryside and large urban centres, the unifying influence of a common living area and shared institutions lessened.[152]

When the Labour movement became almost overwhelmingly a phenomenon of the great industrial cities, many important groups ceased to be part of it – especially women, immigrants, unskilled and semi-skilled workers, home-based artisans, radical lay preachers. And there can be no doubt about the unstoppable surge in urbanism. By 1840 only 22 per cent of England's labour force worked in agriculture, which accounted for just one-fifth of the Gross National Product of the United Kingdom.[153] The relationship of Chartism to increasing industrialisation is a fascinating one, for the nineteenth-century Industrial Revolution was itself Janus-faced. Some say that overpopulation or even rapid population growth are prime triggers for revolution. If so, industrialisation was the Chartists' enemy in more senses than one for, while on the one hand the huge growth in population after 1815 kept wages low and unemployment high for twenty years after Waterloo, the population increase was absorbed by industrialisation and did not subject English society to impossible stresses. As one authority has written: 'Without industrialisation, there might have been a social catastrophe.'[154]

The two most original attempts to account for the rapid decline of Chartism after 1850 involve the concepts of hegemony and the aristocracy of labour. Repeatedly, scholarly studies of the English working class in the second half of Victoria's reign emphasise notions such as deference, respectability, Smilesian self-help, 'incorporation', 'transformation' and 'embourgeoisement'.[155] This emphasises the crucial and sometimes underestimated role of culture and ideologies in history. While *revolutions* cannot occur simply as a result of a change of sensibilities in society – people thinking differently, looking at life differently, having a different world view, etc – such a process can often explain the otherwise inexplicable in non-revolutionary process. According to the Marxist theorist Antonio Gramsci, capitalism achieves its greatest success when it persuades the working class that the values, standards, ideals, images and ideologies embraced by the ruling class are truly universal values, and thus persuades the proletariat to subscribe to them; conversely, Gramsci thought that it was a necessary condition for proletarian revolution that the working class evolve its own, unique and distinctive culture and ideology.[156] Certainly after 1850 one can discern a social harmony in which the workers seem to have accepted 'bourgeois' modes of thought and absorbed them as the only sensible way of looking at society. The thesis is even more attractive if one conjoins to it the idea of an aristocracy of labour emerging among the proletariat. The phrase 'aristocracy of labour' has to an extent been discredited by Lenin's glib use of it – for instance, he alleged that the British Empire engendered super-profits with which the ruling class could buy off the more affluent sections of the working class – but is by no means self-evidently false as an intrinsic idea. It is not suggested that Chartism itself was anything other than an authentic working-class movement during the halcyon days of 1838–48, but what is proposed is that as part of the splintering process after 1850 potentialities that were always endemically present in Chartism – and which O'Connor himself noticed – allowed the detachment of a proletarian elite to occur.[157] This would make sense of some enduring historical puzzles. For example, if it is true, as Engels vociferously alleged, and he was backed up by many 'bourgeois' critics, that England hovered on the brink of revolution in the 1840s, what sense are we to make of certain economic statistics that seem to point the other way? By 1840 Great Britain had 72 per cent of Europe's total steam horsepower: 620,000 units of horsepower as against 90,000 in France. Britain was in the 1840s thirty years ahead of France and forty years ahead of Germany in industrial output. Her textile mills consumed 100,000 tons of raw cotton per year in 1830; France reached this level only in 1860 and Germany in 1871. Britain produced one million tons of pig iron in 1835; France reached this level in 1862, and Germany in 1867.[158] All this seems in flat contradiction to the situation reported by Engels in his famous *The Condition of the Working Class in England*. A possible explanation might be that the benefits of industrialisation were seen mainly in London and the south. Although it is sometimes alleged that Chartism's greatest mistake was to neglect the workers of London, perhaps it is rather that London proletarians saw no real need of Chartism but were lured into a radical posture in 1848 by the sheer euphoria of events in Europe and the expectation of continent-wide revolution.[159]

Superficially Chartism seems to have been as signal a failure as the Peasants' Revolt, the Jack Cade rebellion, the Pilgrimage of Grace, the campaigns by Levellers and Diggers and the Jacobite Risings. The deferential working class after 1850 was a disappointing outcome for those who had looked for so much from the People's Charter in 1838. In time, most of the famous Six Points were conceded by the ruling class, though usually grudgingly and on its own terms. The property qualification for MPs was removed in 1858 as no longer being relevant, but some anomalies, such as university voting, were not finally phased out until 1948. The secret ballot was granted in 1872 by Gladstone and his first government; Gladstone in many ways, most notably on Ireland, inherited the acceptable and transmogrified aspects of O'Connorism. Universal male suffrage was a long time coming. The Second Reform Bill added a million men to the electorate and the Third Reform Bill of 1884 another 2.5 million, though it still left one-tenth of adult males ineligible to vote.[160] The real breakthrough came only in 1918 with the Representation of the People Act, which in adding 13 million people to an existing electorate of just 8 million created the 'evolutionary gap' or breakthrough which enabled the Labour Party to displace the Liberals as the second party in a two-party system. The Chartist demand for equal constituencies was aimed at the multi-seat constituencies of the rotten borough type, so that in one sense it was a demand successfully accomplished. But if we mean by equal constituencies *equal-sized* constituencies, this has still not been attained. The same is the case for annual parliaments, whose prospect seems further away than ever, and even more utopian today than in 1838. With a first-past-the-post electoral system and wasted votes, the consequent two-party system has led to party machines making a mockery of democratic representation and the bizarre phenomenon of prime ministers with more formal powers than Roman emperors. Payment for members of parliament was achieved in 1911, and in those golden days the MP's salary was six times the average wage. Nowadays it is just two and a half times, but there are twice as many members as in Chartist days, with the Commons top-heavy by at least a third in the view of the best authorities. Against such a mixed picture of success can be set the undoubted fact that Chartism, and especially organs like the *Northern Star*, did a huge amount to increase working-class consciousness long-term, giving a medium for the articulation of hopes and aspirations nowhere else available in the world of the media.[161] Even the much-maligned Land Plan, which seemed a flight from reality, takes on a different hue when viewed from the perspective of early twenty-first-century green concerns and the emphasis on ecology, smallholdings and the world population crisis, thus fulfilling the hopes of those at the time, who saw the plan as the harbinger of great possibilities.[162] Others trace Gladstonian liberalism and the suffragettes to the Chartists. The saddest comment on the movement is perhaps this. In an account of his life given to his brother, O'Connor played up his athletic feats, his duels, his courtroom dramas and his victories over O'Connell, but barely mentioned the Chartists.[163] Perhaps the most wondrous thing about the movement was that, with uncertain and lacklustre leadership, and governments holding all the cards against them, these reluctant revolutionaries did so well.

12

The General Strike: Prelude

The General Strike of 1926 presents peculiar problems of interpretation, and needs even more nuanced treatment than previous revolutionary episodes. While there can be no doubt that it was a 'revolutionary moment' – in that the opportunity to overthrow an entire political and economic system did, however fleetingly, exist – almost none of the radical actors had revolutionary aims. Yet the government paranoia about 'red insurrection', even if deliberately exaggerated, did contain some rationality, since the general strike was the hottest of topics in the early twentieth century. If we return to our trusty trio of revolutionary stages – preconditions, triggers and precipitants – it is clear that part of the deep-seated causality we have to deal with relates to Marxist ideology about the general strike. It should be stated straight away that the concept 'general strike' by no means implies revolution. One study at the theoretical level finds four types: the radical, anarchist, syndicalist and socialist conceptions.[1] The basic notion is almost as old as history itself, for in ancient Rome in 449 BC the plebeian order used the threat of it to secure reforms and concessions from the patricians: this was the so-called *secession plebis*.[2] Indeed, if one was purely interested in taxonomy, one could extend the classifications manyfold, since it was a popular tactic in the early twentieth century to use the threat of a general strike to try to prevent war: both Jean Jaurès in France and Keir Hardie in England were advocates of this kind of strong-arm pacifism.[3] This approach was also attempted to try to salve wounded nationalism and to wring concessions from the occupying power in Japan after 1945, but the 'American Caesar' General Douglas MacArthur outlawed it in 1947.[4] The term 'general strike' is also used loosely to denote a total work stoppage in a given city or community – the 'general strike' in Naples, say. Cutting through the luxuriant thicket of usage, we may say that there are really only two kinds of authentic general strike: the total cessation of work within a given nation-state to achieve purely economic and political ends – higher wages, new labour laws, the reform of the voting system, etc; and the general strike used as the prelude to root-and-branch socio-economic revolution. The economic or reformist general strike is really a large-scale sympathy strike. In a sense it can be perceived as a purely negative or defensive phenomenon – what has been termed the 'general strike of protest'. In British labour history until 1926 there had never been any serious talk of the revolutionary general strike; it was always the reformist variety that was at issue, and even that was in a lukewarm way. The first glimmerings of the idea came in the 1830s when William Benbow, a radical cobbler and lay preacher, came up with the notion of a 'Grand National Holiday'.[5] The Chartists certainly considered the idea, especially in 1842, but they were both too disorganised and ideologically primitive to get a proper handle on it; Robert Owen, on the other hand, opposed what he saw as a manifestation of blatant class warfare.[6] Thereafter the idea languished until the 1889 dock strike; once again it was threatened but never seriously entertained.[7]

If the rulers of the British political elite had paid closer attention to the rising Labour movement in their own country, they would have realised that revolutionary aspirations for the general strike did not exist there. Instead, they worried about the power and influence of Marxism on the continent and its supposedly baneful influence on the proletariat in their own island. In so doing they proved themselves woefully inadequate as psychologists of human nature. Yet even if they had attended carefully to the ideological debates between continental Marxists, they would have found profound rifts and divisions. Marxism was probably at its high-water mark in the period 1848–1914, with all the following (apart from Marx and Engels) well to the fore in the impassioned doctrinal debates that raged about the best tactics to bring about the 'inevitable' demise of capitalism: Proudhon, Blanqui, Bakunin, Kautsky, Bernstein, Rosa Luxemburg, Lenin and Trotsky. Marx himself had little to say about the general strike, but his arch-collaborator Engels did, and found it both irrelevant to the question of revolution and a prime example of 'false consciousness'. His violent opposition to the idea of the general strike found expression in some splenetic animadversions. On the Belgian national strike in 1891 he had this to say: 'I almost wish the Walloon coal workers, who have provoked the general strike nonsense this time, will put it into practice in Belgium to try to win universal suffrage. They will be mercilessly cut up, and the nonsense will be buried.'[8] Here Engels made the elementary mistake of failing to distinguish between the revolutionary general strike and the reformist variety; the elite might well yield to demands articulated under the latter heading, but never to the former. As it turned out, the Belgian national strike that year *did* secure universal suffrage, even though the Catholic party in Parliament gerrymandered the outcome in favour of the bourgeoisie. Even more vociferous was Engels's denunciation of the threatened general strike during the London dock strike of 1889, which he saw as a mindless gesture of despair:

> Now this was playing *va banque*, staking £1,000 to win, possibly, £10; it was threatening more than they could carry out; it was creating millions of hungry mouths . . . they could not feed; it was casting away wilfully all the sympathies of the shopkeepers and even the great mass of the bourgeoisie who hated the dock monopolists, but who would now turn against the workers.[9]

The outcome of that strike enabled Engels to breathe again, for the unions sympathetic to the dockworkers concluded that a general strike would be counterproductive; in any case, before the issue could be exhaustively debated within the Labour movement, the shipyard workers caved in.[10] In general, the more orthodox the Marxist, the more scepticism there was about the general strike, and the more maverick the 'Marxist' the more popular the idea was. Lenin, too, saw no value in the general strike unless it was the immediate prelude to an armed insurrection which had been meticulously planned by a workers' party. Employing his favourite 'put down' for workers' movements not directed by a 'vanguard' Communist Party, Lenin stated that the general strike was merely another example of the limited 'trade union consciousness' which the proletariat unaided by the Communist Party could never transcend.[11] Kautsky, who tried to avoid the 'bourgeois deviationism' of Bernstein on the right and the anarchism of Rosa Luxemburg on the left, argued that a general strike was obviously useless, since the workers would either end up starving before obtaining their demands or, if they used violence, would find themselves machine-gunned by repressive regimes backed with all the power of modern technology.[12] Here Kautsky was faithfully echoing Engels's line that the age of the barricades and street revolts was over; to succeed in revolution you had first to win over the proletarian elements in the police and the army.[13]

Yet within Marxism's broad church there were many dissenters and heterodox opinions. Eduard Bernstein, a 'right-wing' Marxist, argued that it was the traditional Marxist notion of revolution that was dangerous folly, and that the gradualism implicit in a reformist general strike was a valuable exercise in consciousness-raising. So far from being 'general nonsense', as its critics alleged, the general strike was actually the logical corollary of universal suffrage, since attempts to dilute, vitiate or nullify universal suffrage (through gerrymandering, plural votes for the rich, etc) had to be resisted by extra-parliamentary means.[14] Echoing the century-long bifurcation between French and German radical thought, the French Marxist Jules Guesde argued that the general strike was not a revolutionary weapon at all but a tool of capitalism, since it handed employers a pretext to stage lockouts, starve strikers into surrender and generally place the workers on the defensive.[15] In sum, there was a wide spectrum of attitudes among Marxists towards a general strike. Some thought, like Bernstein, that the mere threat of it would scare governments into making concessions; others, like Lenin, thought it would work only as a prelude to an armed insurrection; still others that it would spontaneously generate a revolution. The most famous apologist for 'spontaneous revolution' was Rosa Luxemburg. She criticised both the social-democrat *and* the anarchist reading of the general strike, and (albeit implicitly) the Leninist view. According to the social-democrats, the workers were mere tools, to be ordered out by unions or party at their whim. According to the anarchists, all that was needed for success in a general strike was that workers should be ready and willing to strike when called on. According to the Bolsheviks, the proletariat need the guidance of a vanguard party. For Luxemburg, however, the general strike was always an inchoate form of 'spontaneous combustion' (the form in which she expected the revolution to occur). Communist parties had a role to play in the process, but simply to *educate* the workers about the realities of class struggle not to *direct* them from above.[16] Particularly after the Russian Revolution of 1905, she saw the general strike as a key element in the revolutionary struggle – the proletariat's battering ram, as it were. An educated and class-conscious proletariat would know instinctively when the time was right to launch the strike 'spontaneously' – just as an apple falls from the tree of its own accord. For her – and this aligned her closely to anarcho-syndicalism – it did not matter so much whether this or that general strike was contingently successful (though critics said this in itself made nonsense of 'spontaneous combustion'). Consciousness-raising was all important, and one day all the hard work would pay off in a general strike that broke through to the revolution. Although she was critical of most other elements within the mainstream of Marxism, her most withering scorn was reserved for people like Eduard Bernstein and the gradualists, who preached the benefits of the reformist strike. As she put it: 'A general strike forged in advance within the fetters of legality is like a war demonstration with cannons dumped into a river within the very sight of the enemy.'[17] For her the reformist national strike and the revolutionary general strike had no connection with each other at all and were inherently in conflict, just as much as contradictory propositions in logic were ruled out by the law of excluded middle.[18]

The two Marxists who devoted most attention to the concept of the general strike were Leon Trotsky and the French thinker Georges Sorel (though many dispute that Sorel justifies such an epithet). Sorel came to political philosophy in his forties after a career as an engineer and an early 'formation' in Jansenism. Sorel's thought is turbid, apocalyptic and bewilderingly eclectic, and he comes close to the definition of 'crank'. On any strict interpretation of Marxism, Sorel could not really be thought to have much connection with that dispensation, and it is significant that he was a major influence in Mussolini's Italy.[19] Sorel's interpretation of Marxism was partial and selective. He liked the economic and realistic side of Marxism, not the philosophical or Hegelian one, but considered Marx himself just one in a polygon of important thinkers, not the infallible oracle of Engels, Lenin and Trotsky. Other major influences were Nietzsche, Proudhon, Tocqueville and Bergson.[20] Sorel was a voluminous and expansive writer, so it is peculiarly difficult to offer a thumbnail sketch of his thinking, but half a dozen topics seem salient. First, there was his emphasis on heroic endeavour, which recalls Carlyle or Nietzsche's 'moral strenuousness'. Sorel was a very 'masculine' theorist, for all his most favoured societies are ones where martial valour, self-reliance, the cult of the individual and what Machiavelli called civic *virtù* are uppermost: the Swiss communes, the pre-1745 Scottish clans, the primitive peasant societies of Corsica, Sardinia and Sicily, the world of Homer's heroes, the Norse legends, etc. Greatness and heroism, plus anything that can energise or revive mankind, and a disdain for money and materialism, are his supreme values. The liking for heroic societies easily shades into primitivism. What Sorel liked about the Bolshevik Revolution of 1917 was precisely what repelled most Westerners: what seemed to him an abandonment of the cult of St Petersburg and Peter the Great, with its associated modernism and 'window' to the West, in favour of Moscow, the traditions of Ivan the Terrible and, beyond him, the Mongol legacy. Secondly, there is his anti-rationalism.[21] The philosophy of the Enlightenment, the notion of human perfectibility, Benthamite utilitarianism and English empiricism are all objects of contempt; even Marxism is 'true' only in a pragmatic sense, not the 'scientific' one urged by Marx's most loyal disciples, and it would be far better if Marxists stopped trying to imagine life under a Marxist utopia and instead confronted the neglected (by them) topic of metaphysical evil. Socialism, for him, should be 'a revaluation of all values'.[22] That 'utopianism' is a dirty word in Sorel's vocabulary brings us to the third salient point of his thought: his pessimism. He likes the pessimistic side of Marxism, Calvinism, Jansenism and the culture of the early Christians (for Sorel, in the teeth of historical evidence, argues that the early Christians were pessimists who withdrew from ordinary life to await the Second Coming). The villains in his portrait gallery were Socrates, the Jesuits, the eighteenth-century *philosophes* and utopians and ameliorist socialists, all of them tainted with the disease of optimism. The fourth significant aspect of Sorelianism was his anarcho-syndicalism. Sorel shared the anarchist hatred of the State and thought the proper units for a healthful organisation of society were the cooperative syndicates of craftsmen. Social life should simply be aggregates of production units, and the object of socialism should be to apply the workshop system to the whole of political life. Class itself was simply 'a collection of families'.[23] Perhaps reflecting his engineering background, Sorel always placed great value on the social therapy of work; what he most detested about the Marxist 'blueprint' for communist society was the breakdown of division of labour in order to generate a surplus of leisure; to him this was merely bourgeois hedonism in another form. Anarcho-syndicalism also had a messianic flavour. It wanted no truck with bourgeois society, whereas orthodox Marxists thought that there were valuable aspects of that culture which could be retained in the new society. The anarcho-syndicalists also despised organised religion, trade unions and political parties (even Communist parties), parliaments and all aspects of the 'indirect democracy' involving representation.[24]

The fifth core element of Sorel's thought was his treatment of 'myth' and his consequent views on revolution. For Sorel the greatest of modern ideas was the general strike, but by this he meant, not the actual national strikes taking place in, say, Sweden, Belgium or England, but an apocalyptic myth of the general strike, involving the holocaust of existing society and the apotheosis of the proletariat. Sorel defined myth as any set of ideas which would lead to a call for *action*: the myth of the general strike, then, was meant to inspire solidarity, heroism and self-sacrifice and to make the proletariat aware of its awesome power. In contrast to Lenin, Trotsky and Rosa Luxemburg, the myth of the general strike in Sorel's thought was purely destructive: it was not meant to usher in communist revolution but simply to destroy existing society at a stroke. At times Sorel came close to Trotsky's notion of 'permanent revolution', for in his view it did not matter whether this or that contingent general strike was successful or not; the education of the proletariat would go on. In line with his admiration for heroic conquerors, insofar as Sorel thought seriously about revolution at all, he conceived of it as something like the process whereby Cortés destroyed the mighty Aztec Empire almost overnight but put nothing worthwhile in its place. It can thus be seen that, in Sorel's thinking, the general strike was not an adjunct or prelude to revolution but really had nothing to do with it at all, or, as he expressed it delphically, myth is an act of creation, not prediction, and the whole point of socialism can be subsumed in the myth of the general strike.[25] The aim of the general strike, if it has one besides heroic gigantism, is the rejection of any future hierarchy.[26] This was why Sorel was violently opposed to the idea of the 'dictatorship of the proletariat' as famously promulgated by Lenin. Not only would this end by simply replacing one elite with another instead of generating an egalitarian society, but the involvement of the middle classes always spelt death for the proletariat, which had to remain clean and uncontaminated by intellectualism. Yet the dizzying combination of Marxist historical realism, Bergsonian intuitionism, Nietzschean heroism, anarcho-syndicalism and – a key aspect – revolutionary voluntarism[27] does not exhaust Sorel's theoretical panoply. There remains the sixth factor: his emphasis on violence. All revolutions have to envisage violence, if only because no socio-economic elite ever goes gently into the night, but in Sorel violence acquires a new dimension. Sorel actually believed that violence acted as a moral educator for the working class, as it exposed the hidden violence of bourgeois society, with its sham 'pseudo-democracy'. Far more honest than the system of judges and law courts operating a bogus system masquerading as 'the rule of law' was the lynch law of frontier societies or the vendetta of Corsica and Sicily, which had an authenticity not possessed by the violence of police and the military in 'civilised' societies'.[28] This was all part of the 'myth' of the general strike as an apocalyptic event which would purify and renew mankind. Yet the alleged distinction between police and military violence on the one hand and 'authentic' primitive violence on the other was a very fine one. It is not surprising that Sorel was popular in fascist societies. As has been well said: 'A morality that regards violence in itself as a source of heroism or greatness is very near to being an instrument of despotism.'[29]

Theoretical debates in Marxism and bastardised Marxism may seem a long way from the mundane world of national strikes, but they were significant. The British ruling class in the 1920s was largely educated and sophisticated, and many of these ideas had been absorbed, albeit at second or third hand, fuelling what looks like absurd paranoia in the 1920s. And there was nothing theoretical about the upsurge of syndicalism in Britain in 1910–14, promoted by the great labour organiser Tom Mann, a veteran along with John Burns and Ben Tillett of the 1889 dock strike. Despairing of revolution in England, Mann departed for Australia in the first decade of the twentieth century but returned in 1910 to spread the gospel of anarcho-syndicalism. In 1912 he was convicted under the 1797 Incitement to Mutiny Act for publishing an article in his organ the *Syndicalist* – 'An Open Letter to

British Soldiers' – urging them to refuse to shoot at strikers. Sentenced to a long term of imprisonment, he was released after public pressure led to the quashing of the sentence.[30] If Sorel's legacy and influence were mixed, the mainstream Marxists fared better. There could hardly be any mistake about the importance of Trotsky's thinking to the universe of the 1926 General Strike in Britain, as he devoted a major essay expressly to that very subject. Trotsky and Sorel ran along the same lines in advocating the importance of the general strike for building up the confidence of the proletariat but thereafter they diverged sharply, for Trotsky laid great emphasis on the 'soviets' as the embryonic form of a future workers' government.[31] Although Trotsky would have little time for Sorel's unfocused apocalyptic violence, he agreed with Engels and Lenin that the age of street barricades was over, that the key element in any general strike was to win over the proletarian elements in the police and the military. This would happen only if the working class displayed a fearless face, seemingly unafraid of death and determined to do whatever it took and to bear any sacrifice to prevail: 'One may undertake a general strike only when the working class, and, in the first place, its advance guard, are prepared to carry the struggle through to the end.'[32] In such circumstances, Trotsky thought, the rankers overwhelmingly drawn from the working class would be bound to question their role. He certainly had more than a glimmering of a case here: the British government admitted that in 1919–20 it had tried to bribe the military with enhanced pay and perks, fearful that returning servicemen might turn their triumphal guns against the Establishment itself.[33] For Trotsky, unlike Sorel, a general strike had no meaning unless it was the prelude to armed insurrection; a genuine general strike was *bound* to end in violence. 'If arms are not resorted to, it is impossible to organise a general strike; if the general strike is renounced, there can be no thought of any serious struggle.' And again: 'The General Strike is one of the most acute forms of class warfare. It is only one step from the General Strike to armed insurrection.'[34]

If Trotsky and Sorel typified the thoughts on the general strike that were swirling around in the zeitgeist of the 1920s, in a British context they were certainly not operating in a vacuum, as the years 1910–14 and 1919–21 saw the most serious industrial unrest in the nation's history; only the interruption of World War One in 1914–18 prevented this from being a non-stop decade of turbulence. After the failure of Chartism, for sixty years the British Labour movement was quiescent, with occasional exceptions such as its success in the 1889 London Dock Strike. But in 1910–14 the country was rocked by industrial turbulence of a kind not seen since the 1830s and 1840s. Some statistics are eloquent. Between 1900 and 1909 an average of 3.5 million working days were lost each year through strikes and lockouts. In 1910 the figure was 12 million days and in 1912 over 38 million. Miners, seamen, dockers and carters were particularly to the fore, and at one time or another in 1911–12 every port, coalfield and railway in the country was on strike. Nine per cent of the total industrial population was involved in strikes in 1911 as against an average of 2.9 per cent for the period 1902–10. In 1904, 67,653 persons were involved in strikes but this number shot up to 1,232,116 by 1912.[35] Even more worrying was that, by British standards, the new strike wave was marked by an unprecedented violence. There was widespread looting in the Tonypandy riots of 1910, and the firing of the dockyards at Hull conjured uncomfortable memories of the Newport rising. Historians dispute the causes. Some attribute it to the failure of wages to keep pace with prices and profits after 1900.[36] Others say that Edwardian England saw a reduced rate of economic growth, stagnant productivity and, above all, failure to invest in new technology: by 1900 this made the railways and the steel industry dinosaurs when compared with the sharpest competitors in Germany and the USA.[37] Still others, inferring from the fact that many workers in 1910–14 who on paper should not have been striking nevertheless *were* striking, speak of a 'syndicalist uprising', with syndicalism a spontaneous challenge from workers tired and disillusioned with the 'softly, softly' approach of the Trades Union Congress and the reformist and collaborationist stance of the Labour Party, which was in the doldrums in these years.[38] Certainly some 'mixed' causal approach seems most likely to untangle this complicated skein. One fruitful suggestion is that these years saw both a resurgence of *old* unionism, typified by the strikes in the coal, cotton and building trades and the appearance of a new unionism, associated with transport workers and particularly linked to the docks and railways; the locus classicus was the nationwide strike on the railways in 1911.[39] Yet another interpretation, dating from a classic study in the 1930s, is that 1910–14 saw a 'systemic crisis' as Edwardian England lurched into the social equivalent of a 'hole in the ocean'. Not only was there continual international tension, as Germany challenged the Royal Navy's superriority at sea, and with crises in Morocco and the Balkans, but Britain itself was beset by a threefold internal challenge: from the Unionists in Northern Ireland as the Liberal government promised Home Rule to a united Ireland; from the suffragettes, whose campaign reached its zenith in these years; and from labour unions, at the very time the country tore itself apart with the constitutional crisis over the reform of the House of Lords – an issue which necessitated two general elections in 1910 before the bill curbing the Lords' power was passed the following year.[40] Some historians have tried to deny that these phenomena were interconnected and claim that they each have separate causes, but the best recent scholarship sustains the older view. Even more ingeniously, there is yet another thesis in the field, purporting to show that 1910–14 was another of those periods of 'general crisis', with workers manifesting a new rebelliousness not just in Britain but also in Germany, France, USA, Canada, Russia, Italy and Spain.[41]

The years 1910–14, then, saw strikes in every significant industry and every corner of the United Kingdom, and this pattern was picked up in 1919–21 immediately after the war.[42] In 1919 35 million working days were lost to strikes, and on average every day there were 100,000 workers on strike – this was six times the 1918 rate. There were stoppages in the coal mines, in the printing industry, among transport workers, and in the cotton industry, where 450,000 workers were on strike for eighteen days, and among iron-moulders, throwing 150,00 men out of work. More worrying to the elite were the mutinies in the military and the two separate police strikes in London and Liverpool over union recognition. Altogether 6,000 officers struck in August 1918 when called out by the National Union of Police and Prison Officers. In August 1919, after being forbidden union membership, the police came out again, but this time the response was patchy. In London, out of 19,000 policemen only 1,083 stopped work; in Liverpoool, however, the figures were 932 out of 2,100, and the shortage was such that the army had to be called in to quell riots. Altogether around 3,000 strikers were dismissed. The elite had learned its lesson, and thereafter made sure that adequate pay and conditions secured the loyalty of the 'thin blue line'.[43] In Glasgow in January the army was called in to deal with riots and protests against high rents in Glasgow which, together with the official mass strike in the city, combined to form the fearsome image of 'Red Clydeside'.[44] There was another serious strike in another part of the Celtic fringe, this time in Belfast. The spirit of revolution was truly in the air, fostered by the uprisings in Germany and Hungary that year and the continuing Bolshevik success in Russia. The British elite meanwhile was not just immersed in the Big Four negotiations for what would become the disastrous Treaty of Versailles, but was also preoccupied with major troubles in Ireland and India. The prime minister, Lloyd George, confessed that a revolution was likely and that he had few resources to pit against the putative revolutionaries.[45] His opinion was shared by many later analysts, who considered that the working class missed its best chance in 1919 when elite opposition was divided and fragmented and technology had not swung decisively in the government's favour, as it would do by 1926. Lloyd George's doubts did not put an end to his reflex Machiavellianism: a railway strike in the same year was thought to have been deliberately provoked by him.[46] 1919 was also the year in which the miners entered definitively into the political frame. The crisis in the coal industry was the trigger that would nudge the nation decisively in the direction of a national strike; such an eventuality was not inevitable, but lamentable failures by successive prime ministers to deal methodically and coherently with the problem meant that already by 1919 the country was headed in a dangerous direction. Sometimes a revolutionary situation is brought about not so much by repression and reaction but sheer laziness, short-termism and incompetence, and so it proved in the early 1920s. Paradoxically, the leftist impetus of these years catapulted the Labour Party to power, though the party was the least revolutionary body conceivable.[47]

The problems in the British coal industry were cultural, structural and, above all, financial. Pre-World War One Britain had relied heavily on the export trade in coal, iron and steel and textiles, and these 'traditional' industries were located in regions (Lancashire, Yorkshire, Clydeside and the Lowlands of Scotland, South Wales) with their own distinctive customs, traditions, mores, folkways and ethos, at odds with and remote from the general hegemonic culture of the wider nation. This was particularly the case with the coal industry, for miners were geographically and culturally isolated even from their brethren in the wider trade union movement. Miners were accustomed to long and bitter strikes, lasting three, six, nine, even twelve, months, but other members of the working class were not.[48] Structurally the mining industry was wildly heterogeneous, with conditions varying enormously from county to county, colliery to colliery and sometimes even varying between different pits in the same coalfield. This produced a nightmare, since most pay agreements were local, not national, so that district federations rather than the national union were the important factor; this was why delegates to the national conference of the union came with binding mandates. The local pay agreements produced startlingly different results in miners' pay. Between 1921 and 1925 skilled miners in Nottinghamshire received 17s 3d per shift, and unskilled ones 13s 7d. By contrast in Durham the rate was, respectively, 8s and 5s 10d and in Bristol 7s 4d and 6s 4d.[49] Worst of all problems was the economic crisis afflicting coal. The industry was huge – by 1914 coalmining employed one-tenth of the labour force – but output per man had been declining since 1880 (199 tonnes per man in 1920–4 as against 247 tonnes in 1910–14 and 310 tons in the 1880s). Declining productivity was largely the fault of poor management, with little technical innovation or farsighted investment in evidence, so that by 1926 the Ruhr coalfields in Germany produced 80 per cent of its coal by mechanical means while Britain produced just 25 per cent. The result was that labour costs in mining accounted for 65–75 per cent of the total costs of production.[50] The dangers of work in the coalfields were terrific. In the 1920s the average life expectancy of a miner was fifty. In 1922–4 3,603 miners were killed in pit accidents and 597,198 injured – and this was in a context where injuries which did not keep a man off work for more than seven days were not recorded.[51] Hardly surprisingly, the miners were both heavily unionised and inclined to be militant. By the 1920s more than a million of them were members of the national union, the Miners' Federation of Great Britain (MFGB). Founded with 36,000 members in 1888, it had acquired 200,000 by 1893 and 360,000 by the turn of the century.[52] This was in line with the wide rise of trade unionism. The Trades Union Congress (TUC) was founded in 1868, and by 1920 some 45 per cent of Britain's workforce belonged to a union. The Miners' Federation was the giant that straddled the scene, but other powerful bodies were beginning to make their presence felt in the early 1920s, especially the

Transport and General Workers' Union (established in 1922), the Amalgamated Engineering Union (founded 1921) and the National Union of General and Municipal Workers (1924), each with over 0.25 million members. By 1926 the TUC represented 6.5 million workers.[53]

The results of the First World War would eventually bring the British coal industry to near-terminal crisis, although the implications took a long time to percolate, both in objective terms and subjective perceptions. Total coal output fell after 1914, and the heavy use of coal in wartime severely curbed British exports, with Germany, Poland and the USA the particular beneficiaries. In 1919 Lloyd George proposed to return the mines, under government control and direction during the war, to private hands but was threatened with a general strike on the issue by a new and powerful combination of unions, the so-called Triple Alliance of mine workers, railwaymen and transport workers. The alliance had been formed before the war and in 1914 threatened Prime Minister Asquith with a general stoppage – a threat overtaken by the outbreak of war. Now reformed and stronger than ever, the Triple Alliance warned Lloyd George that renewed privatisation, with its concomitant pay cuts, would lead to a national strike. The miners wanted a pay rise of 30 per cent, a six-hour working day and nationalisation of the mines, and voted 6–1 in favour of a strike to secure these terms.[54] Beset by industrial and international problems on all sides, Lloyd George got the Triple Alliance to suspend the threat until a royal commission on mining had reported. But he cunningly chose the composition of the commission so that paralysis would result. Heading the commission was the lawyer John Sankey (1866–1948). Working with him were three miners' representatives, three mine owners, three industrialists and three economists. Best known to the general public were the two leftist economists Sidney Webb and R. H. Tawney and their liberal colleague, the aptly named Leo Chiozza Money.[55] Hardly surprisingly, this diverse group produced three separate reports. The phalanx of economists and unionists recommended that the miners' claim on pay and hours be met in full. The owners offered 1s 6d a day pay increase and a seven-hour working day, while Sankey and the industrialists opted for a middle course of a seven-hour day and 2s a day pay rise, plus some fringe benefits. The issue of nationalisation engendered four reports. The economists and unionists broadly agreed on this, the mine owners took the line that only reprivatisation would do, while the industrialists tried to find a third way between nationalisation and private ownership. On this issue Sankey cast the deciding vote for nationalisation, giving a narrow 7–6 majority.[56] Lloyd George seized on the lack of unanimity to reject nationalisation, and opted instead for fudge and short-termism – a decision for which Stanley Baldwin would ever afterwards blame him, as this one measure more than any other was to precipitate the General Strike of 1926.[57] While he dithered on the other recommendations, and with the mines still under government control, the miners struck in October 1920. Lloyd George rushed an Emergency Powers Act through Parliament, allowing for imprisonment without trial and the deployment of the military in an emergency ('emergency' to be defined, naturally, by the government), but meanwhile settled on the miners' terms, privately vowing that there would be a return match when he would settle decisively with them.

Peace in the coalfields did not last long. In 1921 the mines were handed back to private ownership. The owners at once announced wage cuts, and when the miners refused to accept this they were locked out. It was time for the Triple Alliance to spring into decisive action, but both the miners' leader, Frank Hodges, and the railwaymen's general secretary, J. H. Thomas, were moderates (trimmers, their critics said) who had no taste for nationwide confrontation. Hodges was prepared to accept a wages freeze while negotiations to secure a national wages board went on. He argued that the situation was unlike that a year ago, for now the miners had not just the government to deal with but a plethora of owners also. Most miners, however, wanted a fight to the finish and heeded the radical oratory of the rising star in the MFGB, the Yorkshireman Herbert Smith. The miners' executive rejected Hodges's proposals by one vote. At this Thomas and the transport workers pulled the rug out from under the miners by abandoning their own strike a few hours before it was due to begin. This was 'Black Friday' (15 April 1921) – the end of the Triple Alliance and a dark day for radical trade unionism.[58] Hodges and Thomas argued, with some justification, that the year 1921 was no time for a general strike, with unemployment in the country running at over 2 million and exports having declined by a massive 47.9 per cent.[59] But it was the abrupt manner of the railwaymen's 'betrayal' that most upset the miners, and it seemed to many of them that Hodges, having been rejected at the front door, had simply gone round to the back door and used his close friendship with Thomas to get his own way. Black Friday was the beginning of acute radicalism in the MFGB. Hodges was out of step with the overall mining culture. He represented a new breed of collaborationist, compromising union leader, concerned only with pay and conditions and not at all with the evils of capitalism or the class struggle. In many ways Black Friday represented the head-on collision of revolutionary and reformist ideologies. The miners stayed out until June then returned to work, beaten as always by hunger and shortage of money. They did not get their national wages board and had to accept the cuts. This was a bitter pill for them, since in 1910–14 and 1917–20 the MFGB had always managed to secure increases in real wages. Increasingly, both sides in the mining industry saw the other as the devil; both capital and labour had their own demonology.[60] It is sometimes overlooked that the left-wing unionists had more than the ghost of a case, for the other sides in 1921 also saw the issue in stark terms. Lloyd George called up volunteers for a Special Defence Force in 1921 – he raised 75,000 men – and was generally provocative, as well as secretly inveigling Hodges. 'There were the makings of civil war' is the mild comment of one historian.[61] Here is just one comment of the time from an upper-middle-class reactionary: 'We must get the working classes back to their kennels. Back to cheap labour. Back to discipline. Otherwise we're done.'[62]

Herbert Smith and A. J. Cook (see pp. 392–7) have often been criticised for leading the miners into disaster in 1926, but it was Hodges's failures as a union leader that sowed the seeds. He had had a meteoric rise in the movement and had been the favourite son of his union, pampered and promoted as a young man when he posed as a champion of the Left. Groomed for leadership at Ruskin College, Oxford, he was a full-time official in the MFGB at twenty-five and general secretary at thirty-one. Like Thomas, he requited this indulgence by trying as hard as he could to use his position as a stepping-stone to society's glittering prizes, and this meant playing the Establishment game.[63] Herbert Smith saw his game at an early stage and warned his confidants: 'You must not trust him. He is always playing about with the coalowners . . . the men won't stand that too long. He will burn his fingers badly some time.'[64] Like Thomas too,

Hodges was fanatically hostile to communism, and fancied himself as something of an intellectual; he wrote books on the problems of the mining industry.[65] What impressed most observers were his 'bourgeois' aspirations. John Paton of the Independent Labour Party pointed out that, even when general secretary, Hodges always dressed as though an invitation to the aristocratic fleshpots was no pipe dream: he wore 'an impressively well-cut suit with carefully creased trousers. His wide-winged, glossy-white collar was encircled by a spotted bow-tie, which lay neatly above his buttoned, double-breasted jacket. A silk handkerchief, coloured like the tie, exposed an artistic triangle from his breast pocket.'[66] Hodges achieved the first step in his ambitions when he was elected Labour MP for Lichfield in 1923. Under MFGB rules this meant he could not continue as the miners' general secretary. Hodges initially defied the ruling and for a while the union seemed inclined to let him get away with it. But he was eventually displaced as general secretary by A. J. Cook and 'kicked upstairs' to become secretary of the Miners' International Federation. His ouster rankled with him and, like Thomas in similar circumstances, when things did not go his way he played the 'red card' as a kind of reflex action. He dubbed Cook and the left-wing miners 'communists' and called them 'the intellectual slaves of Moscow, unthinking, unheeding, accepting decrees and decisions without criticism or comment, taking orders from the Asiatic mind'.[67] Hodges later achieved his ambitions. He received a sinecure on the Central Electricity Generating Board, became a director of several coal, steel and iron companies and left more than £100,000 when he died in 1947. The historian A. J. P. Taylor memorably described him as 'an interesting example of how THE THING, as Cobbett called the entrenched English system, looks after its own. What discredited Hodges with the miners was his making in other circles.'[68]

Since the beginning of George V's reign in 1910 there had been persistent voices crying that Britain was 'finished', and the general despondency of 1910–14 found expression in emigration levels of 300,000 a year before 1914.[69] The gloom was particularly acute in the working class in the 1920s, for unemployment consistently remained above one million throughout the decade. Real wages in the mining industry fell sharply in 1921–4. The issue of nationalisation continued to be raised from time to time, but never with energy and vigour. Even the short-lived Labour government of 1924, which might have been thought sympathetic to labour rather than capital, seemed more interested in proving its credentials as an alternative manager of capitalism than in doing much for its own people, even though the enthusiasm of the masses for the first Labour government could not be denied.[70] Successive prime ministers – Lloyd George, Bonar Law, Ramsay MacDonald – accepted the anti-nationalisation line of the mine owners. This tended to follow a twin track: everything was at root satisfactory, the industry was merely suffering a blip, and everything would work out successfully if the government simply held aloof; and the alleged incompatibility of managing an industry while being subject to democratic control. The incompetence of both governments and owners in the period 1921–5 was abject. Yet the industry limped along for a few years without severe wages cuts for a number of contingent reasons. All Britain's chief competitors suffered unexpected jolts of one kind or another. The real halcyon period had been 1918–19, when the devastation of French mines in the war and the immobilisation of German ones gave Britain for a short time a virtual monopoly in European markets. By the time of Black Friday in 1921 the rivals were all back in the saddle and prospects for Britain seemed grim. Poland, though, reconstituted by the Treaty of Versailles, took an unconscionable time getting launched again, with a Bolshevik invasion and the Battle of the Vistula supervening. In 1922 the USA was hit by a six-month coal strike. In 1923 German production ceased when French troops occupied the Ruhr coalfields in retaliation for the non-payment of war reparations. Even trade union membership picked up after the debacle of 1921, with a halt in the declining membership by 1923 and a growing willingness to strike.[71]

All these events gave the British mining industry a considerable boost and postponed the inevitable day of reckoning. Yet once Poland, Germany and the USA returned to normal production, the result was clear for everyone to see. Although by 1925 the overall British economy had recovered, with total industrial production 10 per cent higher than in 1913 and more working people in jobs than ever before, most of this upsurge was in new sectors of the economy. The old industries producing for export – coal, iron and steel, textiles – were by now producing goods for which demand was not expanding; primary producers could not buy them because of the changing terms of trade. Whereas imports were up by 10 per cent in volume from 1913, exports were 25 per cent down.[72] Of the more than one million unemployed in 1925, three-quarters were in coalmining, shipbuilding, engineering and textiles. The crisis was particularly acute in the mining industry when the production in the Ruhr coalfields resumed. In 1923–4 the British coalmining industry was making about £1 million a month profit but by 1925–6 this had become a £1 million loss. Coal exports declined from 79.5 million tons in 1923 to 50.8 million tons in 1925. Sixty per cent of all coal mined in Britain was being produced at a loss.[73] Unemployment was running at 16 per cent, and by the beginning of 1925 300,000 miners were out of work.[74] All this was in a social context where a quarter of the population owned about three-quarters of the capital, and one-tenth of them enjoyed 42 per cent of national income (with just 1.5 per cent taking 20 per cent of it).[75] It is not surprising that people on all sides prophesied revolution. As Ernest Bevin, most able of the new breed of pragmatic trade unionists, put it:

> The struggle for economic possession is bound to come. How will it come? Will public opinion welcome an expansion of possession and with it the extension of responsibility among the workers in industry? Or will public opinion, especially among the employing classes, be negative at best, at worst retrogressive and obstinate . . . Experience has driven me to the conclusion that we shall be drifting in the next five years towards a great upheaval.[76]

With an undercapitalised industry losing on all fronts against its competitors, British coal prices unable to compete with those from Germany, Poland and the USA, and with general demand anyway drying up as nations switched to oil or hydroelectricity (even the Royal Navy powered its ships on oil), there wanted only one further straw to break this particular dromedary's back. This duly arrived when the incoming Conservative government under Stanley Baldwin elected to return to the gold standard. This was a classic instance (of which there have been many more in British history) of finance capitalism trumping the industrial and commercial varieties, of bankers dictating the terms on which the economy should be run and determining the living standards of ordinary people. The City, the Treasury and the Bank of England in effect colluded to force down the wages of workers in pursuit of a will-o'-the-wisp – giving the City of London the same clout as Wall Street. Those pushing hardest for a return to gold, which meant sterling parity with the dollar at $4.86, were Montagu Norman, governor of the Bank of England, Sir Otto Niemeyer and Lord Bradbury at the Treasury. Since the great economist John Maynard Keynes opposed the return, while this egregious trio proselytised for it, it is worth underlining their credentials. Montagu Norman (1871–1950), who liked to dress and pose as an artist, in raffish clothes and long beard, was a classic neurotic who had consulted the famous Swiss psychologist C. G. Jung about his problems. In the 1930s he was extremely close to the Nazis, had an almost sibling-like relationship with the president of the German Central Bank, Hjalmar Schacht, and, after Hitler's liquidation of Czechoslovakia in 1938, notoriously returned £6 million of Czech gold to the Führer, in effect depositing Czech money in the coffers of the Third Reich.[77] Sir Otto Niemeyer (1883–1971), his intimate collaborator, was financial controller at the Treasury and a director of the Bank of England. He too became notorious in the 1930s. Asked by the Australian premier to compile a report on his country's economy, Niemeyer stated in all seriousness that Australia's only function was to supply Britain with goods at preferential rates.[78] John, Lord Bradbury (1872–1950), though taken seriously in high finance circles in the 1920s and 1930s, was a nonentity as an economist. Yet it was these men that the lethargic and intellectually undistinguished prime minister Stanley Baldwin heeded.[79] Winston Churchill, then chancellor of the exchequer, accepted the 'necessity' to return to gold reluctantly; Keynes did not blame him personally, as he felt he had been misled by his advisers.[80] The arguments Keynes marshalled against the new gold standard parity were as devastating as those he had unleashed on Lloyd George six years earlier in *The Economic Consequences of the Peace* and, in his mind, were linked with them. Referring to the Treaty of Versailles, he said: 'the rulers of Europe had destroyed a delicate social and economic equilibrium in their pursuit of "victory at any price". Now they expected the workers to bear the costs of trying to restore it.'[81] Moreover, British rulers were once again trailing on the coat tails of US policy, for the essence of the Montagu Norman project was to make the City the handmaiden of Wall Street: 'The whole object is to link rigidly the City and Wall Street.' The correct value of the pound in 1925, Keynes argued, was \$4.40 not \$4.86, since the discrepancy between US and UK prices was of the order of 4.5 per cent, not then the 10 per cent alleged by the pro-gold lobby. The return to gold was an unnecessary gamble on a rise in US prices *and* it took no account of prices in other countries, yet a moment's consideration would have revealed that the coal industry's problems were a direct result of the high exchange rate of the pound in relation to the German mark; the dollar was a sideshow.

Keynes initially developed his arguments in three articles in the *Evening Standard* on 22, 23, 24 July 1925 and, a week later, published them in pamphlet form as *The Economic Consequences of Mr Churchill* – an obvious reference to his earlier attack on the Versailles Treaty.[82] He attacked the return to the gold standard on three different levels. First, the obvious economic one: that sterling was overvalued by 10 per cent did not guarantee that the cost of producing a tonne of UK goods would fall by 10 per cent, but Montagu Norman and his ilk assumed an automatic adjustment. Secondly, the more sophisticated macroeconomic argument – that to use bank rate to maintain the restored parity would lead to large-scale borrowing rather than exporting and would thus inevitably push up the rate of unemployment. Thirdly there was the political economy argument: that assuming domestic costs could automatically adjust to the new rate of exchange was to live in an unreal world of economics textbooks, whereas people actually lived in a political world, where trade unions were a major factor.[83] If the aim of the bankers was to restore the City of London to its position as the world's leading banker and sterling as the leading currency, the return to gold should have been carried out when British prices were actually competitive internationally at a parity of \$4.86, not before. In other words, the international value of sterling should have been adjusted to domestic costs of production, not vice versa. The determination to press on regardless was, Keynes thought, ample evidence of 'a sadistic desire by bankers to inflict pain on the working class'.[84] Britain in 1925 could be seen, Keynes said, as poised between two economic conceptions: wages fixed by what was fair and reasonable; and wages fixed by the 'economic juggernaut' aka the world of Gradgrind and 'hard facts'. The return to gold marked a triumph for the latter persuasion, whereas Keynes favoured the former, which meant he was on the side of the workers. Later studies show that in 1925 the exchange rate of $4.30 would have been about right, and this would have produced higher exports, lower imports and lower interest rates.[85] At $4.86, exports would plummet, and this would mean a choice between maintaining parity or endangering the balance of payments. The bankers' way to cut the Gordian knot was to force wages down. This put the miners firmly in the firing line, since it was widely known that their wages made up two-thirds of the costs of coal production. It was therefore obvious that restoring parity would mean wage cuts and much greater unemployment. Keynes's target in his attack was always the bankers, not Churchill, whom he regarded as, in economic terms, an innocent abroad. Keynes even dealt gently with Churchill's more egregious absurdities, as when he declared that the return to gold had no more connection with the problems of the coal industry than had the Gulf Stream. After showing incontrovertibly that there was a direct causal relationship, Keynes asked rhetorically: what were the miners supposed to do? Change trades? To traditional industries that were also declining? And why did the miners have to suffer more than any other group? Although his pamphlet did not sell well, the overwhelming consensus of economists has been that Keynes won this debate, and history's verdict is that sterling *was* severely overvalued between 1925 and 1931.[86]

The effects of the return to gold were dramatic, and exactly as Keynes had predicted. Although in 1921–4 the miners had clawed back some of their losses because of the serendipity of the French occupation of the Ruhr and the 1922 coal strike in the USA, they now collided with the bankers' ramp. On 30 June 1925 the mine owners announced that they were terminating all previous agreements and henceforth would pay only the standard wage, with no profit-related additions. This, it was clear, would produce savage pay cuts in the industry, in some cases as high as 50 per cent. Additionally the employers demanded a return to an eight-hour day. The MFGB hit back with some biting statistics, showing that mine owners' profits between 1921 and March 1925 had been £58.4 million, while shift-working miners were earning only between 9s 4d and 12s 8d (45–60p) a day. Moreover, in the years 1913–25 the total profits in mining amounted to £259 millions and, in addition, the owners paid out £6 million a year in royalties to the owners of the subsoil rights.[87] A hastily convened tribunal, the Macmillan Court of Inquiry, found in July that this was unacceptable treatment of the miners. Baldwin and his government now hoped that the mine owners would withdraw their proposals for lower wages and 'protected' (i.e. not shared with the workforce) profits, but, to their consternation and Baldwin's fury, they refused. The TUC then intervened and announced a total embargo on coal from 31 July, when the employers' new rules were supposed to come into force. By this time the TUC had a leftward tinge, since many of the leading right-wing unionists had abandoned their posts for office during the Labour government of 1924, especially Alonzo Swales and J. H. Thomas. The TUC let it be known that the obvious way forward was a subsidy to delay any wages cuts until there was a complete review of the mining industry; when Baldwin refused these terms, they let him know that the coal embargo would continue indefinitely. With the other unions apparently solidly behind the miners, the stage was set for a general strike but, at the last moment, just twenty-six hours before the employers were due to begin their lockout of the miners, Baldwin climbed down and announced a subsidy of £10 million (in the event it grew to £23 million). He saved face by saying that this did not mean that in the future the miners might not have to accept cuts and announced to the House of Commons that he had 'bought peace at the price of a subsidy of £10 million'.[88] The employers were arm-twisted by the government into withdrawing the lockout notices.

This was the so-called 'Red Friday' when revolutionary socialism was supposed to have beaten the government to its knees. In fact it was just a breathing space, as both sides realised. Herbert Smith, now president of the MFGB, announced: 'we have no need to glorify [*sic*] about victory. It is only an armistice. The recent crisis was an affair of outposts. It was a mere skirmish. The main battle has still to be fought and won.'[89] Right-wing and centrist opinion was largely appalled by the settlement. Churchill took it better than most, telling A. J. Cook, general secretary of the MFGB: 'It's a good job it's over but you have done it over my bloodstained corpse. I have got to find the money for it now.'[90] But Lloyd George, who liked to think of himself as a radical, characterised the climdown as 'cowardice in the face of A. J. Cook'.[91] Ramsay MacDonald, the ex-Labour prime minister, believed the settlement would strengthen the hands of the revolutionaries and extremists in the Labour movement and claimed that Baldwin 'has sided with the wildest Bolsheviks'.[92] Ernest Bevin, the organisational genius of the Transport and General Workers' Union, quite rightly scouted such extreme reactions as nonsense; TUC support for the miners was a purely sympathetic action and talk of revolution was an irrelevance introduced by right-wing propagandists.[93] Right-wingers tended towards incandescent rage. Lord Salisbury argued that if the subsidy was to continue until the complete reorganisation of the mining industry, knowing the difficulties and the obstructionism of both sides in the dispute, the process would drag on so long that Baldwin might just as well proceed to nationalisation now.[94] There was much talk in the press about how the miners had been unfairly subsidised – why not other workers, was the predictable cry, and this was just a cushion or a crutch to enable the miners to escape reality. This view did not make much impression for, as has been pointed out: 'The subsidy has usually been described as a subsidy in aid of wages, it was just as much a subsidy in aid of profits.[95] In fact, on a cold, utilitarian calculation, the chief beneficiaries may have been overseas buyers, since the subsidy was used to finance competitive price reductions by exporters.[96] Red Friday probably did the Labour movement a disservice also. It did nothing to create the conditions for success in the long run – in this sense Herbert Smith was quite right – it encouraged an undue faith in last-minute 'quick-draw' action by the TUC, and it seemed to create a precedent whereby the miners, if not quite able to dictate policy to the TUC, were justified in making all the running.

The general feeling was that Baldwin had backed away from conflict because the government was not yet ready to deal with the consequences of a national strike. Some say he was a ruthless operator, now more than ever determined to settle accounts with the miners but at a time and in conditions of his own choosing. Others say that he was a ditherer, a Micawberish figure who believed in 'wait and see', who somehow imagined that the mining crisis, if postponed, might not recur. The most convincing interpretation is, not that he was unready, but that he was nervous because he did not yet have public opinion on his side. The Macmillan Court of Inquiry seemed to indicate that all neutral and middle-of-the-road opinion favoured the miners. If Baldwin wanted to defeat them, he would somehow have to contrive it so that he and his government stood for common sense, rationality and moderation while the TUC and the miners were dangerous revolutionaries bent on confrontation.[97] Meanwhile he played for time in the tradition-hallowed manner by appointing a royal commission. He was determined to avoid Lloyd George's mistakes with the Hankey Commission, one of which, in Baldwin's view, was to allow a pro-miner consensus to emerge. He therefore elected not just for a 'safe pair of hands' but a quartet of the same, making sure they were all pro-Establishment figures. One was Kenneth Lee, a Lancashire cotton manufacturer who had a certain reputation in Manchester commercial circles but no national profile. Another cautious choice was General Sir Herbert Lawrence (1861–1943), a soldier-banker. Lawrence was a fast-track Sandhurst product groomed for top military roles. He served in South Africa with the infamous Douglas Haig, but left the army when Haig was preferred for promotion instead of him and made a successful career in banking. In World War One he served in Gallipoli, Palestine and (1917–18) on the Western Front, where fate contrived to make him Haig's Chief of Staff. He then returned to the City and became chairman of Vickers in 1926. Sir William Beveridge, the third appointee, was director of the London School of Economics and still two decades away from his greatest fame as author of the wartime Beveridge Report, establishing the post-1945 welfare state. Heading the commission was Herbert (later Viscount) Samuel (1870–1963), who was not, however, Baldwin's first choice. That had been Viscount Grey of Falloden (formerly Sir Edward Grey, 1862–1933), who turned the job down on grounds of ill health. For this very reason, and because the appointment was widely perceived as a poisoned chalice, Samuel was initially reluctant to take up the challenge.[98] Samuel was in many ways a very odd fish: the waspish Lloyd George remarked that when his Jewish elders circumcised him, they threw the wrong piece away.[99] A liberal of eclectic leanings, he was another of the statesmen-cum-amateur philosophers in which the 1920s abounded – others of the breed were A. J. (Earl) Balfour, Lord Haldane and General J. C. Smuts. An ardent Zionist, Samuel had been controversially appointed high commissioner of the mandated territory of Palestine in 1920, in a move seemingly calculated to insult the Arabs. Samuel tried hard to be fair to both sides but, as so often happens in such cases, ended up by alienating and disappointing both sides.[100] Now, faced with entirely new problems, he leaned heavily on the expertise of Beveridge, but the truth was that none of the four Commissioners really knew anything significant about the coal industry (and perhaps Baldwin had designed things that way).[101] Certainly Baldwin had made it a point of principle that no representatives of miners or mine owners should serve on the commission as part of his quest for 'new minds'. A. J. Cook, the secretary of the MFGB, was particularly scathing about the amateurism of those who would decide the fate of his members: 'What would they say if *I* appointed a commission on the Stock Exchange out of a plate-layer, a shop assistant and an engine driver?'[102]

Despite the misgivings on all sides, Samuel and his colleagues went to work with gusto. Samuel described the royal commission as 'the most strenuous six months' work I have ever done'.[103] The principal fact he had to deal with was that, between 1914 and 1926, coal exports had fallen by 25 per cent but the numbers of miners had increased by 10 per cent. Immensely complicating his task were not just the implications of the return to the gold standard but the recently adopted Dawes Plan, allowing Germany to export 'free coal' to France and Italy as part of her wartime reparations package.[104] The commission examined 76 witnesses in 33 public settings, read a mass of written evidence and visited 25 mines, even going underground in some of them, as well as commissioning HM Inspector of Mines to report on another 40. The most arduous task for Samuel was to chair the public proceedings, for when miners and owners testified together, the predictable result was 'a dogfight'. There were particularly ferocious clashes between Herbert Smith and A. J. Cook on the one hand and Evan Williams, most reactionary of the mine owners, on the other. Cook was in his element and proved he could have been an outstanding barrister, subjecting the Duke of Northumberland, representing the royalty owners, to a relentless cross-examination.[105] Tempers rose so high that one of the moderate mine owners, David Davies, told Samuel in private that he deplored the truculent attitude of his fellow employers. The four chief issues Samuel and his comrades had to resolve were the level of wage cuts (for all agreed there would have to be some), the constitution of a national wages council to end the anomaly of the multitudinous local agreements, the repeal of the Seven Hours Act, and whether to nationalise the industry. After six months a 300-page report was ready. To general surprise it became a bestseller: 100,000 copies were sold, making it the most widely read and purchased report of a royal commission ever, only to be eclipsed in 1943 by the Beveridge Report.[106] While rejecting outright nationalisation of the industry, the commission agreed to the public ownership of subsoil rights and royalties. Samuel and *confrères* repudiated the idea of longer hours but stressed that there had to be wage cuts. Above all, the structure of the industry had to be changed, and it behoved the government to adopt a reform programme with urgency; the pill of wage cuts could thus be sweetened. Once again, as in Palestine, Samuel found that a liberal, middle-of-the road solution satisfied no one. Herbert Smith and A. J. Cook said they would go over the report line by line, not ruling anything in or out, though Smith could not resist the taunt that the commission's findings were smug conclusions by prosperous individuals who had never known a day's hard work in their lives.[107] Cook, who had more of a public reputation as a firebrand (unjustifiably), was more conciliatory; he remarked that the the report gave the miners three-quarters of what they wanted. For the employers Sir Adam Nimmo said that the report was totally negative and unsympathetic.[108] On the government side the secretary for mines, G. R. Lane-Fox urged Baldwin to accept the report in its entirety, but he was ignored. Baldwin was particularly reluctant to give a categorical assurance that reorganisation of the industry would take place immediately and alongside the wage cuts. Eventually, realising that he was losing the battle for public opinion and thus in a corner, Baldwin grudgingly declared that he would accept the report provided there were *no* quibbles from either side.[109] The TUC said that it accepted the commission's findings but would back the miners if they found them unacceptable. This gave Baldwin his opportunity. By not accepting the report wholeheartedly, he tacitly invited both sides to the dispute to veto Samuel. Whereas progress would have been possible if he had declared unequivocally that restructuring of the mining industry would take place *pari passu* with temporary wage cuts, it was evident that he wanted to appease the employers by getting the pay cuts accepted and then stalling on the rest of the deal. Faced with this intransigence, A. J. Cook repeated his famous mantra: 'Not a minute on the day, not a penny off the pay.' On 15 April the mine owners showed their contempt for Samuel by posting lockout notices, to come into operation at the end of the month, as well as requiring an eight-hour day *and* reduction of wages to 1921 levels – far lower than the Samuel Commission had recommended. Even Baldwin declared that this was 'not an offer but an ultimatum'.[110] With the mine owners intransigent, Baldwin's government unwilling to restrain them, and the TUC committed, albeit reluctantly, to back the miners through thick and thin, the spectre of a general strike now loomed as an inevitability.

13

The General Strike and Its Enemies

Much of what happened in the General Strike of 1926 is unintelligible without an understanding of the human personalities involved. Social historians and sociologists dislike interpretations which lay stress on individuals, preferring instead to explain key revolutionary moments in terms of grand socio-economic causes, religious and ideological conflicts, population increases and all the other non-human historical agencies. Yet in the final analysis what determines whether historical process takes one fork in the road rather than another depends on individual actors. The classic case is that of Lenin, who in early 1917 said that, judged by all objective factors, the revolution was many years away yet contrived it himself in the very same year. 1926 in Britain was a time when most of the objective building blocks constituting a revolutionary moment were present, yet the human actors determined that this was not the path that would be followed. The conflict in 1926 was not even that between Left and Right but between the forces of reason and moderate gradualism on one side and right-wing extremism on the other. That the forces of extremism were able, so to speak, to steal the clothes of the other side, can be attributed to the political skills of one man: Prime Minister Stanley Baldwin, who was yet another demonstration that the most successful politicians are rarely gifted intellectually but have an overplus of peasant cunning. Baldwin always liked to pose as a simple country gentleman, interested only in pig farming. In fact he was systematically two-faced, a serpentine political operator rated by Lloyd George as his most formidable antagonist. Baldwin was a wealthy ironmaster with literary connections (Rudyard Kipling was his first cousin).[1] His basic personality was that of an old-fashioned patriarch and paternalist, but he liked to appear as the pipe-smoking and kindly uncle. The first clear political master of the radio 'fireside chat', he invited the public to trust him on the basis that he was the custodian of 'one nation' Britain.[2] What he neglected to say was that this was strictly on the understanding that Labour should come to heel and obey the dictates of capital. Moreover, the reality was that Baldwin in his own quiet way was just as much a prima donna as the more obviously histrionic Churchill or Lloyd George. In Washington in 1922–3 to discuss Britain's war debts, he had foolishly agreed to repay UK debt to the USA without securing as a corollary debt payment to the United Kingdom from her European allies. Baldwin not only accepted Washington's harsh terms but did so without consulting the cabinet and then used the threat of a split in the government to force the prime minister, Bonar Law, to yield to the fait accompli.[3] Some observers thought his laziness and fecklessness ('fatal inertia') when in office recalled the similar posture of Sir Robert Walpole in the eighteenth century. Others thought his dislike of hard work meant he had chosen the wrong career,[4] but his wiliness as a politican made up for any lack of energy or statesmanship. It was said of him that he displayed real attack on only two occasions: during the General Strike and later when forcing the abdication of Edward VIII. He has also been judged one of the 'guilty men' who failed to discern the Nazi threat in the 1930s and did not rearm in time.[5] Baldwin also displayed traces of paranoia, most notably in his permanent obsession with and hatred of Lloyd George.[6]

All these facets of Baldwin's psychology can be observed during the critical period 1925–6. His explanation for the climbdown at 'Red Friday' and the granting of the subsidy was: 'We were not ready.'[7] This has usually been interpreted to mean that his government had not yet assembled the necessary administrative machinery for dealing with a national strike, but it is more likely to mean that Baldwin refused to be rushed into a snap decision, that he needed time, as a good chess-player, to ponder all the options and to work through counterfactual scenarios on a step-by-step 'what if?' basis. The financial repercussions of an immediate strike were far from obvious, in a year already fraught with economic menace. Moreover, public opinion was still running strongly in favour of the miners. And Baldwin felt that he had been 'bounced' by the employers' sudden announcement of a lockout; for this reason he had tried in vain to convene a joint meeting of management and labour on 24 July 1925.[8] His decision to grant a subsidy had been bitterly fought in cabinet, principally by Lord Salisbury, Sir William Joynson-Hicks and W. C. Bridgeman, but he prevailed, partly by unveiling his ideas for national organisation to combat the threat of a national strike next time around. Moreover, a cabinet split so early in the government and a return to the country would mean that the Conservatives had formed a circular firing squad. The general election in 1924 had produced 419 Tory MPs out of 615 members, even though the Conservatives secured only 48.3 per cent of the vote (the ludicrous inequities of the British electoral system are, sadly, still with us).[9] For almost a year Baldwin ran true to form, displaying no statesmanship whatever while the Samuel Commission sat, but immediately making difficulties once Samuel had presented his report. Baldwin liked the fact that Samuel had disapproved of the subsidy and had pointed out that three-quarters of the coal produced in the last quarter of 1925 cost more to extract than it would fetch on the open market. He could even agree that the mine owners' demand for an eight-hour day was an absurdity, as supply of coal was already exceeding demand. But he was unhappy with Samuel's recommendation of pit closures, amalgamations and general reorganisation of the mining industry. And he particularly disliked the call to nationalise mineral rights as this offended his feeling that private property was sacred; his loathing of socialism was always pronounced. Even some of the firebrand members of his cabinet were prepared to concede on this, as the situation was obviously anomalous. Owners of the land on which these subsoil rights existed had to be paid a royalty regardless of the profitability of the pit concerned. For example, the Duke of Northumberland received an annual royalty of £73,000 – which Churchill described as like having an allotment.[10] To abolish royalties was too rich for the blood of one of the most right-wing governments of the century, but Baldwin would have been prepared to concede this if *all* parts of the commission's report were accepted by all sides. His essentially reactionary nature emerged with his insistence that the miners would have to accept pay cuts *before* he would proceed with reorganisation of the industry – but with no guarantees, of course. The disingenuousness of this fooled nobody. Baldwin would not even budge on this point when the liberal industrialist Sir Alfred Mond, founder of ICI, begged him to intervene and conciliate the two sides. Yet for all his slipperiness, Baldwin had given hostages to fortune, as indeed had the TUC. When Baldwin said the mining dispute was nothing to do with the government, he ex hypothesi accepted the TUC case that a general strike was not a revolutionary act but simply a sympathy action. By the same token, the TUC's demand that the government intervene in the dispute was, in the days before Harold Wilson and beer and sandwiches at Number 10, when governments tried not to involve themselves in industrial relations, also an attempt to make the dispute political.[11]

The real Baldwin was hard line and uncompromising right through 1925–6. When Keynes proposed that sacrifices in a recession had to be equally shared by all strata of society and that Baldwin should introduce a 5 per cent levy on *all* income plus a 1s increase in income tax, this was pointedly ignored. Even industrialists got short shrift from Baldwin, who listened only to the City. Keynes made his contempt clear: 'There was an attraction at first that Mr Baldwin should not be clever. But when he forever sentimentalises about his own stupidity, the charm is broken.'[12] Yet Baldwin was a wily enough politician to know that to pursue overtly reactionary policies would not play with the voting public, so he liked to pose as the man of moderation surrounded in his cabinet by foaming crackpots. While his own self-assigned credentials might be suspect, he was right about his colleagues, for the Conservative government of 1924–9 was one of the most right-wing on record. As a Christian who prayed daily and someone who held himself out as a man of the people, Baldwin attracted a lot of contempt in his own party and in his own cabinet; he was referred to out of earshot as 'the little dud'.[13] Among his critics was Winston Churchill, Chancellor of the Exchequer, whose reactionary posture on everything from Ireland to India was well known. Indeed his inclusion in the cabinet was something of a mystery, for he had characterised Baldwin's 1924 government as 'brainless, spineless and dangerous'. In a pre-echo of Lyndon Johnson's famous explanation (though in more refined language), Baldwin explained that 'he would be more under control inside than out'.[14] Other notorious right-wingers were Lord Salisbury, Lord Privy Seal, and Leo Amery, the Colonial Secretary, an imperialist who did all in all as Churchill did.[15] Neville Chamberlain, Minister of Health, and William Clive Bridgeman, First Lord of the Admiralty, had opposed both the 1925 subsidy and the setting up of the Samuel Commission.[16] Sir Samuel Hoare, Secretary of State for

Air, would become well-known in the 1930s as a notorious appeaser of the fascist dictators, while Sir Arthur Steel-Maitland, Minister of Labour, and another vehement opponent of trade unions, was widely regarded as unimpressive and incompetent. Here is a charitable assessment of him by a later historian: 'A tall, athletic-looking dark man who came into the house with a tremendous reputation and promise which he never fulfilled.'[17] Yet Tom Jones, Baldwin's indispensable cabinet secretary, assessed him more harshly: 'the total impression is one of weakness and cloudiness'.[18] Yet another right-wing ultra was F. E. Smith, Ist Earl of Birkenhead, whom Baldwin had appointed as Secretary of State for India. Widely (though inaccurately) hailed as 'the cleverest man in England', Birkenhead was yet another of Churchill's cronies, and he shared his reactionary views on Ireland. Smith was a rich and successful barrister with a reputation for forensic brilliance and wit, legendarily exercised at the expense of mediocre judges and dishonest litigants. Smith was a friend, college chum and legal rival of the future Home Secretary Sir John Simon, who sailed under liberal colours until he finally threw off the mask and joined Ramsay MacDonald's National Government of 1931. Smith was also a notorious alcoholic, who became steadily more right-wing as he grew older, and died in 1930 at the age of fifty-eight from cirrhosis of the liver.[19] Even at the bureaucratic level the colour was true blue. The influential permanent secretary at the Ministry of Labour was Sir Horace Wilson, later an ill-starred appeaser of dictators and collaborator with Neville Chamberlain. An arch-manipulator, Wilson was finally forced to admit at the end of his career that he was out of his depth when dealing with the Nazis.[20]

Yet the worst of all Baldwin's reactionaries was the Home Secretary, Sir William Joynson-Hicks, affectionately known to his cronies as 'Jix' but to his many critics and enemies as 'Mussolini minor'. Jix's purblind fanaticism made him little more than a crank. To crack down on unlicensed drinking and drug dealing was one thing, but to prosecute D. H. Lawrence for 'obscene' paintings and to lead a fervent campaign against the Book of Common Prayer suggests a man not quite in command of his faculties.[21] Habitually discovering Reds under the bed, Jix also wanted to outlaw the Communist Party, but liberal opinion found him more of a menace than any Marxist ever could be, as he was 'the gravest of existing menaces to law and order. For many months the rather scrubby little cause of British Communism had had no such public crier to advertise it as he.'[22] While absurdly lenient on the growing menace of fascist hooliganism, Jix brought the full force of the law down even on abstract advocacy of the doctrines of Marx and Lenin.[23] In October 1925 twelve members of the Communist Party were found guilty of sedition at his urging. Even though the Communist Party was an entirely legal organisation, a tame judge sentenced Marx's twelve apostles to six to twelve months in jail, but added that they could walk free if they there and then resigned from the party. Nothing like that had been seen since the Romans required the early Christians to recant their beliefs. Even Ramsay MacDonald, whose reflex action was to back the Establishment at all points, spoke out, calling the prosecution a political trial with directly political aims which was both fatuous and self-defeating as it would play into the hands of the communists.[24] Jix was also close to the British fascists and to the more ultramontane elements in the British intelligence services, where paranoia and tall stories about Red revolution were a daily staple. From this arose the later canard that 'Mussolini minor' sympathised with the Nazi doctrines on racial purity and the Jews; this was a bridge too far, but Jix had only himself to blame for the inference.[25] To keep Jix quiet while the Samuel Commission did its work, Baldwin put him in charge of a major aspect of contingency preparations for a national strike and set up the Organisation for the Maintenance of Supplies (OMS), designed to provide alternative manpower and transport if the worst came to the worst. Intended to train volunteer labour, OMS soon became notorious for recruiting fascists and right-wing cranks, and its extremist colouring meant that even chief constables of the more responsible kind held it at arm's length.[26] Nevertheless, by early 1926 Jix was able to report that he had requisitioned 25,000 lorries and had also recruited drivers for the vehicles. The administrative side of government preparations was put in the hands of J. C. C. Davidson, who held the title chief civil commissioner. He divided the country into sixteen regions (later reduced to twelve), each with a deputy civil commissioner (usually an ex-general or brigadier) responsible for running transport, distributing food and ensuring the maintenance of light and power.[27] The scheme was criticised as inherently undemocratic. Whereas in the shires the deputy civil commissoners might reflect the political complexion of elected local government, in the industrial heartlands of the country they certainly did not. On 22 April 1926 Jix reported to the cabinet that his Supply and Transport Committee had approved 98 volunteer service sub-committees, 147 haulage committees, and 331 local food offices. He boasted that arrangements for food convoys, maintenance of London's milk supply and emergency electricity generation were at or near completion.[28]

Yet criticism of the commissioners was always mild alongside the invective expended on OMS. So bad was its reputation that it could not raise the funds it needed even from putative allies, for most industrial firms, bankers, manufacturers and shipping companies refused to contribute.[29] Ramsay MacDonald was led to protest about some of OMS's activities: 'Private enterprise is being entrusted to maintain order in such a way as to make a breach of order inevitable.'[30] Even the BBC under John Reith, in this era excessively fearful of upsetting government, refused to broadcast an inflammatory speech by an OMS representative on the grounds that it would ruin its reputation for being non-political.[31] It seemed to sober, middle-of-the-road opinion that OMS was inflaming the very passions Baldwin claimed to be dousing down. It is hard to recapture the virulence of anti-communist feeling in right-wing circles in 1925–6, always rationalised as hatred of a creed that was subservient to Soviet Russia, and which aimed to expropriate all private property. It was also, its critics said (truthfully), atheistic and (not just falsely but absurdly so) aimed at 'nationalising women for sexual purposes'.[32] Alongside right-wing loathing of communism, there was also discernible that distaste for trade unionism that has characterised so many political radicals in England, from Richard Cobden to Enoch Powell; Cobden was alleged to have said that he would rather live under the rule of the Bey of Algiers than under the thumb of trade unionists.[33] Moderate trade unionists reacted to all this with scorn. Bevin commented on the government's energetic preparations for a showdown: 'If it had shown anything like the same initiative in approaching the problems of the coal industry, the emergency need never have arisen.' It was indicative of the poor and supine showing of the Labour Party during the entire crisis that for this very mild criticism of Baldwin, Ramsay MacDonald riposted by calling Bevin 'a swine'.[34] So, far from being concerned about the living standards of miners and the working class in general, MacDonald and his followers were much more concerned with maintaining their cosy relationship with the Establishment. Hand in hand with this went a contempt for left-wing thought and intellectuals in general. It is an authentic curiosity that the men of the Labour Right between the wars genuinely thought that their political stance was the only rational one and that opposition to it must come from ignorance. It was the old either/or: either Leftists were stupid or they were evil, morally vicious or crypto-communists. The long roll-call of right-wing Labourites in this era reveals the same syndrome: cocksure arrogance, a pretension to omniscience and a conviction that they knew better than experts or thinkers. Ramsay MacDonald, Philip Snowden, Herbert Morrison, Emanuel Shinwell – the list is potentially endless – of those who dispensed truisms and bromides about national strikes while suggesting no concrete proposals in return which might alleviate the plight of the social groups they were supposed to be representing.[35] It is hard not to see all this as guilty conscience. There was truth in Trotsky's observation: 'Men who did not wish for the General Strike, who fear nothing so much as the consequences of a victorious strike, must inevitably direct all their efforts towards keeping the strike within the scope of a political half-strike, i.e. depriving it of power.'[36]

If the Conservative government of 1924–9 was the most right-wing ever, even they seemed like bien-pensant liberals alongside the mine owners. As F. E. Smith (Birkenhead) expressed it: 'It would be possible to say without exaggeration that the miners' leaders were the stupidest men in England if we had not frequent occasion to meet the owners.'[37] Smith was right: the employers were blockheads, but unfortunately blockheads with power and influence. One of them told the Samuel Commission, in all seriousness, that all miners spent ten shillings a week going to the cinema.[38] Their leading lights were Lord Gainsford, a Durham coal owner who in 1927–8 became president of the Federation of British Industries, Arthur Balfour – not to be confused with Earl (A. J.) Balfour – later Lord Riverdale, a Sheffield steelmaker and Chairman of the National Federation of Iron and Steel Manufacturers, Sir Allan Smith, director of the Engineering Employers' Federation and, especially Evan Williams and Sir Adam Nimmo, lay preacher, boss of the Fife Coal Company and Chairman of the Scottish Coal Owners Association.[39] Here is Nimmo in action at the National Liberal Club in 1925: 'The wages of those engaged in industry cannot permanently rest upon considerations of the cost of living or what the men may call a living wage . . . British coal has to compete with coal produced in other countries . . . It is of no avail to suggest that the wages received do not permit of miners having a proper standard of living.'[40] Nimmo did not explain how miners were supposed to summon the physical strength to hew coal if they were not paid a living wage. His comments and those of other owners sound more like extracts from Zola's *Germinal* than from people living in the twentieth century. Needless to say, whenever these worthies were cross-examined before the Samuel Commission by A. J. Cook and others and asked to reveal details of their own income, they blustered and bellowed about 'impertinence' and 'irrelevance'. Baldwin's aide Tom Jones, who probably saw the owners at close quarters more often than most, was full of contempt for them.[41] Williams and Nimmo were particularly hawkish and hard line. Jones noted in his diary: 'Evan Williams . . . has not made a single positive contribution towards the solution of the problem. One would feel inclined to dissociate oneself officially and in every other way from the vapourings of these people.'[42] The greatest criticism of Baldwin is that he consistently allowed the mine owners a veto on any proposal not to their liking; it was almost as though he was afraid of them. Or perhaps the truth is that the real Baldwin was at heart every bit as reactionary as the fire-eaters (Birkenhead, Churchill, Jix, etc) he claimed to be restraining. When the influential industrialist Sir Alfred Mond wrote to him asking him to repudiate the ultramontanes like Evan Williams, to bring real pressure to bear on them and get their agreement to settle on the basis of the Samuel Report, Baldwin did not deign to answer. When those interested in a solution pressed him to do something about the intransigence of Nimmo and Evan Williams, Baldwin abruptly changed the subject and switched the conversation to cricket.[43]

Faced with such attitudes from the owners, the miners' representatives became super-obstinate in turn. The two dominant figures in the MFGB in 1925–6 were its president, Herbert Smith, and its secretary, Arthur Cook. The two became anathema to the Labour Party, right-wing unionists, the government and even so-called socialist intellectuals. Beatrice Webb, from her self-assigned lofty perch as the doyenne of Fabian socialism, despised them both: 'It is a tragedy to think that this inspired idiot [Cook], coupled with poor old Herbert

Smith, with his senile obstinacy, are the dominant figures in so great and powerful and organisation as the Miners Federation.'[44] A wartime patriot, and the kind of blunt-spoken working-class man invariably referred to by contemporaries as 'the salt of the earth', Herbert Smith, in his sixties, was almost the stereotypical Yorkshireman whose utterances became legendary in the 1920s. Deriding the timidity of the TUC and its reluctance to back the miners to the hilt, Smith exhorted them thus: 'Get on t'field. That's t'place.'[45] His response of 'nowt' when asked what concessions the MFGB was prepared to make likewise placed him as an almost Old Testament figure in his righteousness and inflexibility. 'Nowt. Nowt doin'. We've nowt to offer,' became almost a mantra from Smith's lips. When Baldwin urged him to accept the report of the Samuel Commission in its entirety, Smith hit back at once that he needed to go through the report line by line: 'I want to see the horse I'm going to mount.'[46] Walter Citrine, the TUC general secretary was inordinately fond of him – 'straight as a die. I liked his calm way of looking at things. Always cool and steady, he never got flustered.' But Citrine was always inclined to patronise Smith and, fatally, to underrate him and his tenacity. 'There he sat in his blue suit and soft collar, with his little moustache turning grey and his high balding forehead, with his spectacles resting on the end of his nose.'[47] It sounds like the portrait of a doddery old uncle, but Smithy was really adamantine steel. The received opinion early in 1926 was that Arthur Cook was the demon agitator, irrational, crazed, a communist stooge and that Smith was the old-fashioned unionist, perhaps slightly out of his depth. But by the end of the year most observers had seen the truth. The alleged demon, Cook, turned out to be moderate and accommodating, but Smith was a rock that the elements could not shake. One by one the sophisticated commentators changed their mind and concluded that, on the union side, Smith, not Cook, was the real obstacle to peace in the coalfields. Acknowledging that he had been wrong in identifying Cook as the problem instead of Smith, Ramsay MacDonald remarked: 'If Cook is a feather, Smith is a monolith.' His apostasy was the signal for a general about-turn by Labour intellectuals, with even Beatrice Webb falling into line.[48]

Yet, partly because Cook was more intelligent than Herbert Smith, he was loathed and detested by virtually all sides in 1926: by the government, the right-wing members of the TUC and the Labour intelligentsia. He was the central figure in the demonology of the newspapers during 1926. He makes a fascinating psychological study, much more interesting than men on whom vast tomes have been expended. A soldier's son, he was given a basic education in army schools before starting work as a farmhand in Somerset at the age of twelve. He was originally an Anglican, but the combination of a narrow-minded vicar and a sympathetic employer made him a Baptist. Attracted to radical ideas from an early age, at sixteen he was horsewhipped for his views by an irascible local grandee. When his employer fell on hard times and could no longer pay him a living wage, he migrated to the South Wales coalfields and worked in the pits. He experienced all the trials and tribulations of life as a miner and learned the craft of oratory from the preachers of the Welsh Revival of 1904–5.[49] With a thirst for learning, he borrowed £50 to enrol at Ruskin College, Oxford, but was diverted into the breakaway movement that founded the Central Labour College in Earls Court. During his year there his most memorable encounter was with the famous novelist and socialist Jack London, then in England's capital to research his book *The People of the Abyss*.[50] Cook was an eyewitness to London's well-known fistic prowess in rough-house brawls. Cook abandoned his studies after a year and returned to the pits, where he continued to make his name in the Labour movement. Expelled from the pits for his work as a union organiser ('agitator' to the owners), he took part in the Tonypandy riots of 1910–11, where the calculated brutality of the police disgusted him, as it disgusted Keir Hardie (who raised the issue in Parliament). The hatred of the police was so intense that a saying became common in the coalfields: 'When a copper dies, he's so low in the fiery pit that he has to climb up a ladder to get into Hell. Even then he's not welcome.'[51] In 1912 Cook wrote a syndicalist pamphlet as a member of the Miners' Unofficial Reform Committee and the same year was made a delegate for the South Wales miners during the 1912 national coal strike. A pacifist in World War One, he was imprisoned for sedition for three months in 1918 under the Defence of the Realm Act. Yet it was his incarceration in 1921 for incitement and unlawful assembly that most embittered him. He told Walter Citrine that the memory of being handcuffed and then led in chains from one end of a train to the other, both on boarding in Swansea and alighting in Cardiff had been seared into him.[52] The experience led him into brief membership of the Communist Party, but he quit by the end of the year, unable to accept the party's discipline. He had also realised that membership would preclude his becoming general secretary of the miners' union, on which his ambitions were now fixed. When Frank Hodges's moderate stance proved unacceptable to the MFGB, Cook's chance came and he was elected to the position. This caused alarm in the TUC. Fred Bramley, the right-winger said to Citrine: 'Have you seen who has been elected secretary of the Miners' Federation? Cook, a raving, tearing Communist. Now the miners are in for a bad time.'[53]

The canard that Cook was a crypto-communist was embraced with avidity by the media and his legion of enemies but has no substance. Like many on the Left, Cook inevitably found himself at one with the communists on certain issues, but he had no interest in abstract Marxism and disliked the whole notion of the party line. The CP, for its part, always disliked and distrusted Cook; the communist hierarchy was prepared to exploit him when useful but generally classed him as one of the 'useful idiots', to use Lenin's phrase.[54] Yet there was no question but that Cook was intemperate and he seemed almost to go out of his way to earn himself a bad press. In August 1925 he declared: 'I don't give a hang for any government, or Army or Navy. They can come along with their bayonets. Bayonets don't cut coal. We have already beaten, not only the employers, but the strongest government in modern times.'[55] When, in the great period of crisis in 1925–6, King George V expressed anxiety about where the nation was heading and asked to see Cook at Buckingham Palace, the miners' secretary made a point of snubbing the invitation: 'Why the hell should I go to see the king? . . . I'll show them that they have a different man from Frank Hodges to deal with now.'[56] Yet in private Cook was tactful, courteous, diplomatic, reasonable and pragmatic; he was the classic case of the bark being worse than the bite, or, to put it another way, 'a calculator of feasibilities more judicious than his platform rhetoric might suggest'.[57] The truth was that Cook was a man of the utmost integrity who could articulate the hopes, fears and aspirations of the miners better than any other man. Completely sincere, as general secretary he did not take the line beloved of so many political leaders, that they are representatives, not delegates, and therefore can do whatever they like, regardless of the wishes of those who voted them into office.

Cook saw his role as doing what pithead resolutions bound him to do.[58] His greatest strength was his rhetoric. The 1920s was an era of great orators, invariably political outsiders with limited access to the mass media – James Maxton, Oswald Mosley – but arguably the greatest of them was A. J. Cook. He was a total master of the craft of platform oratory, beloved of the miners. No figure in the history of the Labour movement, not even Keir Hardie, ever inspired such passionate partisanship. Testimonies to his rhetorical power are legion, so a few must suffice. The radical politician David Kirkwood, one of the great figures of 'Red Clydeside', had this to say: 'Mr Arthur Cook, who talked from a platform like a Salvation Army preacher, had swept over the industrial districts like a hurricane . . . He was utterly sincere, in deadly earnest and wore himself out in the agitation.'[59] Arthur Horner, Cook's deputy and a former South Wales communist, said that Cook represented 'a time for new ideas – an agitator, a man with a sense of adventure'. Even when tired, Cook on the platform could electrify a meeting. Horner wondered why he could not achieve the same effects himself, until he realised that he was speaking *to* the miners but Cook was speaking *for* them: 'He was the burning expression of their anger.'[60] Lest it be thought that Cook's powers as an orator could sway only impressionable miners or socialists already converted to the sermon being preached, it is worth remembering that Lord Sankey, he of the Sankey Commission, once listened to one of Cook's speeches about the plight of the miners and found himself in tears at the end of it.[61]

None of this impressed the panjandrums of the Labour Party or socialist intellectuals of the Fabian variety. Beatrice Webb, who basically despised everyone not of Oxbridge provenance or similar, recorded the following impressions of Cook:

> He is a loosely-built, ugly-featured man – looks low-caste – not at all the skilled artisan type, more the agricultural labourer. He is oddly remarkable in appearance because of his excitability of gesture, mobility of expression in his large-lipped mouth, glittering china-blue eyes, set close together in a narrow head with lanky yellow hair – altogether a man you watch with a certain admiring curiosity . . . it is clear that he has no intellect and not much intelligence – he is a quivering mass of emotions, a mediumistic magnetic sort of creature – not

> without personal attractiveness – an inspired idiot, drunk with his own words, dominated by his slogans. I doubt whether he even knows what he is going to say or what he has just said.[62]

And on the eve of the General Strike Kingsley Martin entered the following in his diary:

> Cook made a most interesting study – worn out, strung on wires, carried in the rush of the tidal wave, afraid of the struggle, afraid, above all, though, of betraying his cause and showing signs of weakness. He'll break down for certain, but I fear not in time. He's not big enough, and in an awful muddle about everything. Poor devil and poor England. A man more unable to conduct a negotiation I never saw. Many Trade Union leaders are letting the men down; he won't, but he'll lose. And socialism in England will be right back again.[63]

But this was mild stuff alongside the positive hatred Ramsay MacDonald felt for Cook. He would later accuse Cook of incompetence and, when Cook challenged this, reiterated: 'In all my experience of trade union leadership, I have never known one so incompetent as yourself.' Cook replied that the only 'incompetence' that could be demonstrated was that the MFGB would now allow a reduction in the living standards of its members. Moreover, MacDonald's personalising of complex issues was simplistic, since the entire Miners' Committee and Conference endorsed the policy Cook, as general secretary, carried out, including some of MacDonald's own colleagues, who must therefore presumably also be incompetent. 'I think it abominable that leaders of the Labour Party should attack trade union representatives who did nothing more than protect their members.'[64] In some ways the most balanced view of Cook comes not from the 'Guilty Men' of the Labour Party or the impassioned advocates in the South Wales valleys but from a middle-of-the-road bureaucrat, Walter Citrine, long-time general secretary of the TUC. Citrine thought Cook unstable, over-emotional and too close to the Communist Party, but was very fond of him at a personal level and found him to be man of absolute integrity. Citrine was only acting secretary of the TUC until confirmed in September 1926 and, despite earlier promises of support from Ernest Bevin and Cook, thought he would not get the job in the aftermath of the general bitterness in 1926; in particular, that Cook would be constrained by the miners, who regarded Citrine and the TUC as traitors. But Cook proved most loyal and delivered his support as promised. Cook's main blemishes, for Citrine, were that he was not good in committee rooms or in the detailed negotiations in smoke-filled rooms. So often his spellbinding oratory, so effective on the miners, was used on the TUC to nil effect, and he tended to lose his audience with his rhetorical tropes. Moreover, he was emotional to a high degree and liable to pour out a cascade of words, almost as though his brain worked too fast for his tongue to do justice to it. Cook often 'worked himself up into a state bordering on hysterics, his face was flushed and tears were standing in his eyes while he was speaking. He apologised for coming so repeatedly to the Trade Union movement for support. It was not the fault of the miners, it was the fault of a derelict industry, ruined by private enterprise.'[65]

By 1926 Cook and Smith were isolated figures within the general trade union movement. Red Friday marked the high point of leftist influence in the TUC. Hopes among rank-and-file workers that they might finally be getting leaders who reflected their views rose with the simultaneous prominence of three figures thought to be on the Left, Alfred Purcell of the Furniture Workers Union, George Hicks of the Building Trade Workers and Alonzo Swales of the powerful Amalgamated Engineering Union. Purcell was Chairman of the TUC General Council in 1924 and Swales in 1925. The acme of their influence was at the TUC Congress in Scarborough in September 1925, where Swales made a powerful fighting speech and motions were passed condemning both the Dawes Plan and the British Empire.[66] Yet already by 1926 this trio was on the wane and the newer breed of bureaucratic, pragmatic, compromising leader on the rise. Long-term the most significant new face was Ernest Bevin, in his mid-forties and general secretary of the Transport and General Workers' Union, founded in 1922. An administrator of very high talent, he made his name as an organiser in Bristol and was originally deputy to the legendary trade unionist Ben Tillett. He soon became the driving force and the power in the union, while the venerable Tillett, still retaining his seat on the TUC General Council until 1932, was 'kicked upstairs' to hold the post of international and political secretary of the TGWU.[67] Squared-jawed, swarthy of countenance, with the shoulders and chest of a heavyweight all-in wrestler, Bevin made a formidable physical impact, as befitted a natural fighter. He proved his mettle in the unofficial dock strike of 1923 and had proved his credentials by getting tough with Ramsay MacDonald when he was prime minister in 1924, refusing to call off strikes in the name of 'labour solidarity'.[68] Bevin had a strong West Country accent which flummoxed many of his listeners (a bottle of Nuits St George, for example, became 'Newts Saint George') but, more significantly, he had an inordinate estimate of his own abilities. His favourite method of blunting views contrary to his own was a curt: 'I've 'eard different.' Some day a study should be made to discover why the early leaders of the Labour Party all had such a hypertrophied view of their own abilities, for MacDonald, Snowden, Herbert Morrison, Bevin and J. H. Thomas all shared this trait. Bevin despised intellectuals and, even more so, Ramsay MacDonald and his coterie of political trimmers.[69] It has sometimes been said that Bevin approached the General Strike as a lukewarm supporter. It is true that he had misgivings about the miners' inflexible approach, but his record was a creditable one and there is no reason to dissent from his own opinion that he gave his all for the cause. What he did *not* believe in was the General Strike as a revolutionary opportunity, and he condemned all talk of taking up arms to form a labour defence corps against fascism. Armed revolt, he thought, would play Baldwin's game and give the government the excuse they needed to smash the Labour movement: 'Resorting to physical force is the way to set the clock back half a century.'[70] At the same time he thought the attitudes of Ramsay MacDonald and his acolytes were so treacherous that the trade union movement might have to detach itself from the Labour Party and go its own way.[71] He particularly despised J. H. Thomas, and the feeling was reciprocated with the hatred Thomas felt for anyone in the movement he suspected might be his intellectual or moral superior (unfortunately for him their name was legion). Citrine, always a meticulous observer, noted several occasions when Thomas's attitude to Bevin simply had to be set down to pure jealousy.[72]

The figure in the higher echelons closest to Bevin in outlook and ideology, though they were never personally close, was Walter Citrine, who became one of the enduring monuments of the TUC. Born in poverty to a nurse and an alcoholic sailor, he left school at twelve and, incredibly, had a position as a full-time union official by the age of fifteen. Beatrice Webb described him as follows with her typical snobbishness: 'Tall, broad-shouldered, with the manners and clothes and way of speaking of a superior bank clerk, black hair growing low on his forehead, large pointed ears, bright grey eyes set close together, big nose, long chin and tiny, rather "pretty", mouth, it is difficult to say whether or not he is good looking. In profile he is; in full face he is not.' He came across as loquacious, disputatious, vain and self-conscious. Webb went on to say he had 'the integrity and loyalty of the better type of British mechanic', but that his main flaw was that he 'expects too much relative to his faculties'.[73] La Webb did not care for Citrine, but it should be borne in mind that she was piqued because he did not show her the deference she expected and put his feet up on her window seat. Some of her portrait of Citrine is accurate. He was inordinately ambitious and was the nearest thing to Cromwell's Puritans in the twentieth-century Labour movement. He had no 'silly pleasures', did not believe in small talk, neither drank nor smoked, ate slowly and always plain food, took a daily cold bath, slept with the windows open, and was still exercising at eighty. His sole interest outside his trade union duties was devouring books or, as he put it in his inimitable self-congratulatory way in his autobiography: 'Hobbies? Practically none except reading. My work has been my hobby since my early trade union days.'[74] Webb described him as the first intellectual in the Labour movement, but in reality he despised intellectuals and abstract theories. He described Sir Stafford Cripps's leftist ideas as 'drivel' and took a de haut en bas attitude to the Labour intellectuals G. D. H. Cole, R. H. Tawney, Kingsley Martin and Harold Laski, while admitting that at a pinch he preferred Laski to Cole.[75] Citrine was a familiar type in politics, the dispassionate lover of power, privilege and the company of the powerful. His overweening personal vanity and conceit may have derived, as Webb suggested, from mixing too much on a daily basis with the uneducated, but some of it seems to be the familiar 1920s Labour Party arrogance already noted; certainly he was witheringly contemptuous in 1926 not just of the miners but of his own colleagues in the TUC. Originally an electrician, Citrine had made his name in the Electrical Trades Unions (ETU) before beginning his ascendancy at the TUC.[76] Essentially a careerist, he was regarded on the Left as an Establishment stooge, and in 1935 Low attacked him in an *Evening Standard* cartoon as a capitalist toady.[77] A more unlikely candidate to foment a social revolution it is difficult to imagine; his presence at the centre of the TUC alone refutes the absurd canard that the 1926 General Strike had *revolutionary* aims. Hobnobbing with the great and the good was Citrine's idea of the purpose of life. Like J. H. Thomas, he spent a lot of his career travelling the world on expenses-paid trips, none of which seem in any way essential to his duties.[78] Citrine's most congenial bedfellows were his comrades on the centre-right. Although he could see through J. H. Thomas, he was always prepared to enter special pleading on his behalf. His most natural ally was Bevin, but he and Citrine were essentially in competition for the same space. Their personal relations were always distant and formal, even when they were at one on many issues: as for instance, on the absurdity of a trade union movement providing the Labour Party with the bulk of its funds while being systematically ignored and swatted aside by the party hierarchy. Occasionally, though, Citrine could not resist sideswipes at the man who would go further than him in the Labour movement. Bevin, he said, was ill-read and intellectually incurious, but he had greater energy, drive and ruthlessness. He infuriated Citrine by always, as it were, playing the man rather than the ball, consistently arguing ad hominem instead of addressing the issue.[79]

By far the most controversial personality in the entire apparatus of top TUC officialdom was the secretary of the National Union of Railwaymen, J. H. ('Jimmy') Thomas. He did all in all as Ramsay MacDonald did, perhaps not surprisingly, as both men were born illegitimate and thus, as Celts, doubly 'outsiders'. Their abiding ambition was to be the most insiderish of insiders, to be accepted by the Establishment and appear in polite society. Their natural home was the Conservative Party – to which they would eventually gravitate (in 1931) under the guise of a National Government. But since the Conservative Party of the early twentieth century would not have accepted such 'low lives' in their ranks, their only option was to use the trade union movement and the Labour Party as ladders for their entirely personal ambitions. Part of the problem with both MacDonald and Thomas was that they were self-deluding: even as they betrayed their 'brothers', in their own minds they were doing (in that tiresome modern mantra) 'nothing wrong' but were acting as genuine friends of the proletariat.[80] Born in 1874 as John Henry Thomas, the Welshman was educated at an elementary school and became an engine driver (by all accounts not a very good one) on the Great Western Railway. In 1917 he became general secretary of the NUR – a post he retained for forty years. He was already a member of parliament, having been elected for Derby in 1910. He was colonial secretary in MacDonald's 1924 cabinet. Everything about Thomas was inauthentic, starting with his accent. Although he was a Welshman, he acquired a Cockney accent and, when asked who would be the first prime minister, inaccurately forecast: 'Me or 'Enderson.'[81] His accent occasioned even more levity than Bevin's. F. E. Smith (Birkenhead) and he were on exceptionally friendly terms and addressed each other as 'Jimmy and Freddy'. Although Birkenhead admired him, he was distressed by his unrefined accent and, being F. E. Smith, sometimes allowed his penchant for wit to transcend his friendship. On one occasion Thomas complained in the Garrick Club that he had an ''orrible 'eadache'. Birkenhead at once riposted: 'Why not try a couple of aspirates?'[82] Nirvana for Thomas was a dinner in London's clubland or a reception at Buckingham Palace. Low the cartoonist, habitually referred to 'champagne and cigars' Thomas as 'The Right Honourable Dress Shirt, MP'.[83] His political ally Philip Snowden disapproved of Thomas's hedonism and relish for the fleshpots. He claimed that Thomas in an average year attended 150 high society lunches and dinners, smoked 320 cigars and drank 9 gallons of champagne, as well as running up a laundry bill of £18 a year just for starched shirts.[84] 'Jimmy' disgusted even some of the Establishment figures who should have been his staunchest allies. Lord Sankey (of the 1919 Sankey Commission) commented: 'He would like to appear at a dinner in trousers and coat made out of a Union Jack and shout for Empire.' Even his latter-day apologists find it hard to make out a convincing case for him. Here is one (charitable) assessment: 'His negotiating skills had always been flavoured with sentimentality and showmanship.'[85] His fellow Welshmen could see right through him. Lloyd George remarked caustically in 1921, even when Thomas was effectively doing the government's work for him by his stance on Black Friday: 'He wants no revolution. He wants to be Prime Minister. He does not want to be a commissary for Bevin . . . I have complete confidence in Thomas's selfishness.'[86]

Thomas was one of the earliest recorded practitioners of the (now tiresomely ubiquitous) habit of rejecting another person's ideas vehemently, only to serve them up a week later as original insights of his own. Citrine recorded an allied Thomas tactic. Not only would he arrive late for meetings of the TUC General Council and start blathering about matters that were not on the agenda or irrelevant but, when this was pointed out, would adopt the following tactic: 'Thomas would look pityingly at the interrupter for a second or so and then observe, "Isn't that exactly what I am telling you?" Everyone would fall into a stupefied silence, with Thomas immediately changing his line of argument.'[87] Thomas also frequently wearied the General Council with his boasting about the royal receptions he had attended and his aristocratic connections. He and MacDonald particularly treasured their entrée to the social circle at Londonderry House on Park Lane. This was the ancestral home of Charles, Marquess of Londonderry, both a well-known Rightist and later Nazi sympathiser and the most celebrated society host in the country. His wife Edith enjoyed a close friendship with Ramsay MacDonald which, even though platonic, caused scandal.[88] Another connection was with Sir Henry 'Chips' Channon, Conservative politician and renowned anti-American (albeit born in Chicago to an Anglo-American family), though this was complicated by Channon's visceral loathing for MacDonald.[89] Thomas's history of opposition to trade union militancy was no secret. He confessed that he always regretted the Triple Alliance had ever come into being. He told American reporters after Red Friday that he was unhappy about the miners' victory. He tried to ensure that the NUR was not involved in a national strike, only to be overruled by his own executive. He was frequently on record as saying that he was vehemently opposed to the mere idea of a general strike. He tried to get the miners' dispute stifled by involving the Labour Party in anti-union legislation in the House of Commons.[90] That such a man should not only have had access to the inner councils of the TUC but had even been appointed their de facto chief negotiator with the government seems well-nigh incredible. It was as though Baldwin had had an agent of the Soviet government in his cabinet in the period 1925–6. Much of Trotsky's analysis of politics in the 1920s and 1930s was inaccurate, but on J. H. Thomas he hit the nail on the head. The only way the attitude of the mainstream Labour movement to the looming general strike was explicable was on the assumption that Ramsay MacDonald, J. H. Thomas and their ilk were systematically counter-revolutionary. In other words, *pace* Sorel, their aim was not to paralyse the bourgeois state with a general strike but to paralyse the General Strike with the help of the bourgeois state. Trotsky shrewdly pointed out that for Thomas and MacDonald to dress up in court regalia and other finery while posing as representatives of the working class was as if Cromwell and the Roundheads had suddenly decided to ape the Cavaliers. Not surprisingly, much of Trotsky's prime invective was reserved for Thomas personally. After pointing out that Thomas was the classic historical avatar of reformism – 'the labour representative who is always in his place when it is necessary for someone to make a gesture of lackeyism' – he characterised Thomas as 'this absolutely unprecedented lackey' and concluded: 'Men who did not wish for the General Strike, who deny the political character of the General Strike, who fear nothing so much as the consequences of a victorious strike, must inevitably direct all their efforts towards keeping the strike within the scope of a political half-strike i.e. depriving it of power.'[91]

It is hardly surprising that between A. J. Cook, avid for a general strike as the means of gaining the miners' demands, and Thomas, equally keen to see a national strike fail, there should have existed the most bitter and rancorous relations. This was partly ideological difference, partly personal distaste, but it should be remembered that the miners had detested Thomas ever since Black Friday, long before they elected Cook as their general secretary, and that Thomas was already a byword for a betrayer and seller-out.[92] This is scarcely to be wondered at in the light of Thomas's many hostile comments. Typical was this when the Samuel Commission's report was published: 'Never mind what the miners or anybody else say, we [the TUC] accept it.'[93] The almost continual clashes between Cook and Thomas in themselves point to the weakness of the Left vis-à-vis the government; there are no similar reports of clashes between Baldwin and, say, Sir Adam Nimmo. Some of the passages of arms between the two were mild, as when Cook urged the TUC to lay in emergency provisions against a protracted strike. 'My own mother-in-law has been taking in an extra tin of salmon for weeks past,' Cook remarked ingenuously. 'My God, a British revolution based on a tin of salmon,' Thomas shot back.[94] Most of the passages of arms were, however, more vicious. In January 1926 Thomas wrote a letter to the *Daily Herald*, regretting that 'a great organisation like the Miners' Federation should day after day have its case ruined by the childish outbursts of its secretary'. Cook replied that he could not

> claim to be a leader of fashion, especially of the evening dress variety, but I do claim to be a class conscious fighter for the workers . . . It is true I do not possess a dress suit, and I do not attend dinners and banquets given by enemies of the working class and make alleged witty after-dinner speeches there. Thomas may think that comes within the province of a trade union leader, but if it is one of the 'elemental' principles of leadership, I am not going to adopt it. Thomas is giving vent to his personal spite because I have remained true to the cause of the workers. Along with other noble lords, dukes and gentlemen, he has long wished me in a warm place.[95]

Cook despised Thomas both for his cosy relationship with Britain's oligarchy – he lived on the Astor estate and often shared Lord Derby's box on Grand National day – and for his humbug. Thomas was notorious for having announced, at a lavish banquet given by railway magnates, that his soul belonged, not to the working class but to the 'truth'.[96] The animosity between Thomas and Cook really requires a lengthy study. It is tempting to see Thomas's animadversions as the product of a guilty conscience. A son of South Wales, he had abandoned its cause for life with the rich and famous, while Cook, an adopted son of the coalfields, had remained loyal and four square. Needless to say, as in so many cases when a right-wing figure is confronted with home truths by a leftist, Thomas described Cook as 'mad' – the epithet always applied to difficult radicals.[97]

That Thomas was the evil genius of the Labour movement in 1926 becomes clear once we examine the attitude of the TUC towards likely future conflict with the government after Red Friday. While Baldwin and his cabinet made active preparations for the next round in the struggle, the TUC did virtually nothing. 'This failure has never been satisfactorily explained,' one student of 1926 has written.[98] Actually the riddle of the TUC's inertia can be explained by reference to J. H. Thomas, but then another riddle replaces it: why did the egregious 'Jimmy' have so much power and influence? Essentially the TUC never wanted a general strike, thought it could be avoided, pinned most of its hopes on the Samuel Commission, was committed to the miners only very reluctantly, and seemed almost to go out of its way to make sure that any contingency plans of its own were inept.[99] Also, one needs an awareness of month-by-month chronology, for the TUC of the 1925 Scarborough Conference was a very different animal from the one in existence when the Samuel Commission reported. The seeming leftward drift of 1925 was abruptly reversed in late 1925 when Arthur Pugh replaced Alonzo Swales as chairman of the TUC General Council and the right-wing figures Thomas, Bevin and Margaret Bondfield were elected to it; in October 1925, additionally, Citrine took over as general secretary. The hopes that had earlier been reposed in the supposedly leftist triumvirate of Purcell, Hicks and Swales swiftly evaporated. After late 1925 only Swales held on to a leftward course, while Hicks and Purcell became tame creatures of the Citrine/Thomas axis.[100] The key TUC body in 1925–6 was the Special Industrial Committee (SIC), charged with finding ways to assist the miners in their struggle against Baldwin and the mine owners. The original membership of the SIC was Swales, Citrine, Ben Tillett, Hicks, John Bromley, secretary of the Associated Society of Locomotive Engineers and Firemen (ASLEF), John Marchbank of the NUR , Edward Poulton of the National Union of Boot and Shoe Operatives (NUBSO), Arthur Hayday of the National Union of General Workers and Alexander Walkden, general secretary of the Railway Clerks Association – supposedly a cross-section of the entire union movement.[101] But at the end of 1925 three crucial changes occurred. Arthur Pugh, a right-winger from the Steelworkers' Union replaced Swales as chairman, Poulton and Marchbank were dropped and J. H. Thomas came in. This gave the Right a vital majority on the all-important SIC. Although the SIC's remit was to find ways to support the miners, the astonishing upshot was that between the Scarborough Conference and 27 April 1926 it *never discussed the mining crisis once*. As has been well remarked: 'The inactivity of the SIC during the period between July 1925 and May 1926 is quite remarkable, and of course stands in marked contrast to the preparations made on the government side.'[102] Bromley, Pugh and Thomas utterly dominated proceedings and spent most of their time criticising Cook, Herbert Smith and the MFGB, complaining about how the TUC was being 'blackmailed' by the miners.[103]

J. H. Thomas's influence on the SIC during the four crucial months of January–April 1926 was entirely negative and destructive. A conspiracy theorist might well use the term 'sabotage', except that that would imply something clandestine. The astonishing thing about 'Jimmy' was that his opposition to and dislike of the miners was overt, yet he was the prime figure in a body supposed to be doing its utmost for them. The real riddle about the TUC was not so much their lack of any real preparations for a confrontation with the government as their supine and almost deferential attitude to Thomas. Writing up his accounts of the SIC, Citrine often says simply that Thomas opposed something and that was an end of it. Did he have much greater ambition and energy than his colleagues? Or were they simply irremediably defeatist from Day One? Can any apology be offered for the TUC? Their inert posture did contain some elements of rationality. The General Council was torn between a morbid terror of a revolutionary general strike and scepticism about the utility of a national sympathy strike. To an extent history was on their side in the latter case. The Swedish general strike of 1909, a classic of a reformist national strike, was a failure because the unions were too timid in their dealings with blacklegs, were overawed by an aggressive employers' lockout and their tactic of bringing agrarian workers into the city as strike-breakers, to say nothing of the lack of support from Labour elsewhere in Europe.[104] The debacle in Sweden led many orthodox Marxists, like Karl Kautsky, to argue that the general strike had no future as a revolutionary weapon and should be abandoned in favour of a long-term campaign of attrition against bourgeois society. It was true that national strikes in Belgium in 1893 and Holland in 1903 had been successful, but only because the governments had been taken by surprise. In the mildest of reformist national strikes, in Belgium in 1913, to achieve universal suffrage and genuine one man, one vote, the railways and public services had continued to function during the strike, so the result was fiasco.[105] The TUC was very impressed by the argument that if you announced the intention of a general strike ahead of time, the government had ample time to prepare countermeasures (as Baldwin was then doing) so that it was a foregone conclusion that the strike would fail. As Herbert Morrison put it, you should never start anything you could not finish, and a general strike was a demonstration of weakness not strength.[106] There was also the awful example of France where Prime Minister Aristide Briand, himself a one-time revolutionary, had dealt with a national rail strike by conscripting all striking workers, thus in effect placing them under martial law.[107] In other words the corollary was that a national organisation like the TUC would have to be densely layered and cell-like so that a government could not stymie it simply by arresting the leaders, yet the TUC was almost laughably transparent and open. More sophisticated arguments, with which Citrine was sympathetic, were that ideally the TUC should lay in a year's provisions and a year's worth of funds, so that the workers could not be starved into submission, but this would require resources well beyond the TUC's capacity. Moreover, a successful general strike, capable of beating a government in a long-drawn-out battle, would require the organisation of the entire working class at a pitch of implausible efficiency. If such a capability existed, by definition the unions would already be in lotusland and could get all they required from the government without any strikes at all. Yet Thomas and his acolytes were impatient even with such down-to-earth speculations. One of the SIC members told Citrine: 'Walter, you are too logical. You look too far ahead. Don't worry. Let things develop.'[108]

To reiterate, if all this was the rational side of the TUC, the irrational side was the way Thomas was given carte blanche. Citrine proved totally incapable of dealing with him. At the very beginning of the SIC deliberations Citrine sought clarification on the TUC's attitude to continuing the subsidy to the mining industry, but Thomas successfully inveigled the committee onto a different tack. Next Citrine proposed coopting miners' representatives onto the SIC, which was the only sensible way forward given that the committee was supposed to be discussing how best to help them. Again Thomas objected, this time with a rhetorical (and totally irrelevant) flourish: 'Had they reached a stage when an industrial dispute affecting the largest union in the country was now handed over to someone else [ignoring the obvious fact that the MFGB had done precisely that by co-opting the TUC]. If the SIC was dealing with the rail situation, *he* would decide it was time he cleared out.'[109] Instead, Thomas encouraged the grousing of John Bromley and joined him in bitter criticism of the MFGB leadership; he agreed with Bromley that the miners should be told to 'pull their weight' (whatever that meant). The other members of the SIC seemed either too much under Thomas's thumb or too lethargic to oppose his many interventions. Citrine next raised the issue of the Cooperative Union, which wanted to know what would happen in the event of a national stoppage. Many local co-operative societies had still not recovered from the miners money they had advanced as loans during the 1921 dispute. The Cooperative Union wanted the TUC to guarantee them against further losses or to suggest some way of collaboration. The SIC turned down the suggestion that the TUC should guarantee loans but made no suggestions of its own.[110] Despite Citrine's efforts, the SIC did nothing to organise general union support for the miners or prepare any contingency plans for a national strike; once again Thomas was the culprit.[111] Thomas and Bromley made determined efforts to uncouple the TUC from its commitment to the miners; Bromley indeed said he would be quite happy to accept wage reductions for the miners. It was not surprising that when the SIC finally deigned to hold a meeting with the MFGB on 26 February 1926, tempers rose. Thomas declared that no statement should be made to the press assuring the miners of TUC backing, but A. J. Cook pointed out, correctly, that such a statement had already been issued. There followed a heated verbal collision between Cook and Thomas, which ended with Cook calling Thomas a gutless wonder.[112] At the next meeting between the miners and the SIC (on 11 March) Thomas tried a new disingenuous refinement. This time he stated that the SIC could not get involved in any discussions with Herbert Samuel and his Royal Commission on the grounds that the committee were mere amateurs in the intricacies of the coal industry; only the miners themselves were competent to do that.[113]

What Thomas most feared was that Ernest Bevin, with his proven powers of military-style organisation, would be drafted onto the SIC and would lick it into shape as a proper body. Once again, in retrospect it seems incredible that the TUC should have sidelined their most brilliant administrative talent, but Bevin was well known to be critical of the gradualists, like Thomas and Ramsay MacDonald, whom he criticised bitterly for failing to raise the mining issue in the House of Commons. The absence of Bevin from the SIC was, so to speak, the elephant in the room in early 1926.[114] Thomas loathed A. J. Cook for his integrity but what he hated about Bevin was the man's manifest intellectual superiority. He played on the big man's weaknesses, knowing him to be a 'short fuse' individual who could be gulled into storming out of meetings if provoked sufficiently, and therefore deployed the full range of sarcasm on him. Bevin usually took the bait, on one occasion erupting and charging from the room 'to the accompaniment of rude noises from Jimmy Thomas', as Citrine recorded the scene.[115] Meanwhile Thomas encouraged the Labour Party's intellectuals to hold meetings with Cook and Herbert Smith, hoping they would provide him with propaganda ammunition on the 'hopelessness' of the miners. They duly obliged. R. H. Tawney said of Herbert Smith that he suffered from tunnel vision: he seemed to see England as 'a coal-pit with some grass growing on top'.[116] Beveridge dined with Cook and Smith and was distinctly unimpressed: 'Herbert Smith's mind was granite. Cook's mind . . . [had] the motions of a drunken dragon-fly.'[117] With strong support from chairman Arthur Pugh and John Bromley, Thomas had a virtually free run on the SIC until April. In his memoirs Citrine dealt very mildly with Thomas, but to have revealed the full extent of his Machiavellianism would have been a self-indictment for his (Citrine's) own weakness. As the dutiful committee man he produced lengthy position papers and memoranda for the SIC but did nothing to impede Thomas.[118] The TUC General Council, for its part, seems to have adopted a 'wait and see' approach, hoping in Micawberish fashion that something would turn up. Citrine described the atmosphere on the council: 'Swales beams over his glasses, but looks doubtful about Jimmy. Poulton looks sad but resolute, and Maggie Bondfield calmly goes on with her knitting.'[119] Even simple matters like the exact definition of the respective powers of the MFGB and the TUC in the event of a national strike – which Citrine repeatedly tried to resolve – were pushed aside on the *mañana* principle. There was a curious feeling abroad that a general strike would never happen, that the government would cave in at the last moment, as it had done on Red Friday. Even if it did not, many TUC officials took the line that the strength of trade unionism was not in negotiation, compromise and arbitration (the Citrine path), but in surprise, ambuscade and blitzkrieg. They had bluffed Baldwin once and they could do it again. As Bevin wryly commented: 'As usual there was a lot of talk on the General Council by people who thought they were not going to be involved.'[120] Some, absurdly, put their bets on intervention by the monarch, despite the fact that such a scenario would have triggered a constitutional crisis. George V was known to be unhappy with Baldwin's hard line and had actually made a speech from the throne in the House of Lords in February, urging moderation and conciliation on both sides.[121] Disappointed by Cook's refusal to come to Buckingham Palace to talk to him, the king, thinking Baldwin not conciliatory enough, urged restraint on him, but received the same contemptuous response.[122]

Hoping that the Samuel Commission would provide the desired deus ex machina, the TUC continued to let J. H. Thomas have a free run on the SIC. His stranglehold there was complete. Only Swales and (on the rare occasions when he was co-opted as an ex officio member) Ben Tillett spoke up for the miners. Hicks was by this time completely at one with Pugh, Thomas and Bromley, with Bromley continuing to be vociferous on the theme that the miners had the SIC 'over a barrel'.[123] Any pretence that the SIC had the miners' interests at heart had to be abandoned when the Samuel Commission published its report on 10 March, and those who wanted to bow their heads to Baldwin were flushed out. Predictably, Thomas, Pugh, Ramsay MacDonald and Frank Hodges declared that the Samuel Report provided an acceptable basis for settlement as it stood. Pugh thought the miners should at once accept the report unconditionally: 'It was a profound mistake to think that the whole trade union movement could be brought out to support a subsidy.' He wanted the TUC to back the miners only if Baldwin rejected the Samuel Report and tried to impose a pro-owners' deal.[124] Baldwin, characteristically, made an evasive reply to Samuel on 24 March, then did nothing for a month. On the same day the SIC managed to secure an interview with the prime minister, who promptly ducked his responsibility and said that the entire affair was the responsibility of the miners and the owners. Next day the SIC met to discuss the implications of this meeting. Tillett saw at once the gravity of the situation and suggested that the TUC General Council should be alerted to how serious the crisis had now become; above all, the respective powers of the MFGB and the TUC to negotiate with Baldwin and the mine owners had to be defined. This did not suit Jimmy Thomas; once again he got his way and no action was taken, even though Citrine, for once bestirring himself, pointed out that Pugh and Thomas were now working directly against the declared policy of the TUC. He added, waspishly, that if the Pugh/Thomas line was now official policy, the MFGB should be so informed, as they were unaware of it.[125]

April 1926 was certainly the cruellest month, for there was little sign of compromise from Baldwin and the TUC was in disarray. Bevin, deliberately kept in the dark by Thomas, was reduced to contacting A. J. Cook to enquire what exactly was going on. His analysis of the mining industry was sound. It was abundantly clear that the mining industry would never be able to pay a proper wage until it had been thoroughly reorganised, with the closure of pits and the reduction in the total number of miners employed.[126] The key to the entire mess was a commitment from Baldwin to oblige the owners to accept a mandatory reorganisation of the industry, including a national wages council, as the quid pro quo for wages cuts. Yet the owners made it quite clear they wanted no reorganisation; in particular they objected to a national wages council and insisted on wage negotiations purely at the local level.[127] Even Thomas and Pugh drew back when faced with this level of intransigence. The spectre of a general strike drew nearer. At all levels there was impasse: the government would not accept the Samuel Commission's report unconditionally; the mine owners would not accept reorganisation; and the miners would not accept pay cuts. The only glimmer of hope came from A. J. Cook. Despite his famous slogan, he told the government that the miners would accept some pay cuts *provided* reorganisation of the industry had already got under way.[128] They would not accept Baldwin's selective response to the report, which was that wage cuts should be immediate but the reforms postponed to the future. Even Samuel himself agreed with this: a vague promise of future reorganisation was simply 'sometime or perhaps never' as he put it.[129] The general atmosphere of chaos in April 1926 was well conveyed by a trivial incident in the world of the media. The well-known Catholic apologist Monsignor Ronald Knox, anticipating Orson Welles's 'War of the Worlds' broadcast in the USA twelve years later, put out a radio programme on 16 April which purported to be live coverage of a riot of the unemployed in central London. Even though the 'live report' contained the sensational item of a well-known philanthropist being roasted alive, and was thus an obvious spoof, more than 2,000 people phoned the BBC in alarm.[130]

On 15 April the mine owners gave notice that existing wage contracts would be terminated on 30 April and wage cuts implemented the following day. The proposed wage scales were far lower than those recommended by the Samuel Commission and in some pits in South

Wales had the effect of reducing miners' pay packets by 50 per cent.[131] The TUC was thus in a position where, unless it was to lose all credibility, it *had* to support the miners. A general strike loomed in two weeks, and the spectre which everyone hoped would never materialise had now done so. Both the government and the TUC were in danger of becoming a laughing stock unless prompt evasive action was taken. Baldwin, who had buried his head in the sand for a month ever since the Samuel Commission reported, reluctantly bestirred himself. On 21 April he called a meeting with the owners to see if there was any chance of compromise, but they remained adamant: the wage cuts must not be made contingent on reforms in the industry and, in particular, there must be no national wages council; all wage bargaining must be at local level. They were quite happy with the prospect of a strike, and greeted Baldwin's warnings with an insouciance that dismayed the prime minister's *fidus Achates*, assistant secretary Tom Jones.[132] The owners thus effectively torpedoed Thomas's strategy of sapping the TUC from inside; even he and Pugh were forced to concede that in the face of such intransigence there would have to be a national strike. Even with such dire and unpredictable consequences looming, Baldwin refused to put any pressure on the owners. The Tory Party of Peel, Disraeli and Salisbury would not have been so weak, but by 1926 the Conservatives had swung sharply right and were effectively in thrall to business, with no moderating influence from the old landowning aristocracy. In the entire cabinet only Bridgeman was a county landowner and the rest were businessmen or their backers.[133] Baldwin's pusillanimous behaviour was disastrous for, by rolling over before the mine owners, he lost any chance of being able to persuade the miners' leaders to compromise. Once Herbert Smith realised that Baldwin intended to bring no pressure at all to bear on the owners, he gently rebuked A. J. Cook for his overtures linking some pay cuts with industry reorganisation, stressing instead that all members of the MFGB were *mandated* by their district association.[134] In the TUC meanwhile all was confusion. Citrine and the other centrist unionists had all along accepted Thomas's assurances that he had the social contacts and political clout to avoid disaster and to prevent the TUC from being sucked into a general strike. Now it became obvious that he had miscalculated. Even worse, trusting this emperor in his new clothes, they had given him carte blanche to pursue his sabotage on the SIC, with the consequence that that body emerged from all its deliberations with nothing accomplished. 'Six months had elapsed since the 1925 Trades Union Congress and a week remained before lockout notices took effect, yet the SIC did not know what its policy was!'[135] The committee had neither worked out a TUC policy on the coal industry nor made any preparations for the nationwide stoppage which now loomed. In alarm at the SIC's hopeless record of achievement, a Ways and Means Sub-Committee was set up by the General Council on 27 April, with a remit to improvise hurriedly. The unkindest cut of all for Thomas was that this would be headed by the man he most disliked (as a manifestly superior talent), Ernest Bevin.[136]

Baldwin's next step was to call a joint meeting of mine owners and the MFGB on 23 April, though what he hoped to achieve from this is unclear, unless it was the propaganda advantage that Herbert Smith unwittingly handed him. The meeting of men like Evan Williams and Herbert Smith was always likely to be a dialogue of the deaf, and so it proved. Baldwin appalled the miners by having so little grasp of the Samuel Commission that he suggested longer hours, already expressly rejected by the commission.[137] Herbert Smith chided him with having no knowledge whatsoever of the working class and the conditions they lived and worked in, and it is true that 1925 marked the very first time Baldwin had even seen a slum (in Dundee).[138] This vision had somehow given Baldwin an idea of himself as a godlike figure, above class and party faction, guided only by the Almighty or, as he put it: 'The longing to help the bewildered multitude of common folk is the only motive power to make me face the things I loathe so much. And the longing only comes from love and pity.'[139] How he squared this with his overwhelming partiality for the mine owners he did not reveal. The miners pressed him to implement the desired reforms and reorganisation in the industry, after which they would discuss pay cuts, but Baldwin insisted the cuts had to come first and the reorganisation later (but how much later?) Even J. H. Thomas's biographer was moved to protest: 'In other words the miners must give up their aces before the card game could begin.'[140] The fact that the miners would have accepted some pay cuts if Baldwin had committed irrevocably to reorganisation was a point that was lost in the repeated mantra of 'Nowt doin' from Herbert Smith, which allowed Baldwin, successfully, to portray the miners as intransigent hard liners and all other parties to the dispute as paragons of sweetness and light. Herbert Smith's correct strategy would have been for the MFGB to commit openly and unequivocally to the Samuel Commission report, somehow ride out the pay cuts Samuel recommended (far less harsh than those the owners were now committed to a lockout to achieve), and thus put Baldwin on the spot. If he in turn did not then accept the report, thus committing himself to reorganisation, he would be publicly revealed as a fraud and hypocrite. In the heat of the moment Smith and Cook could not see where their best interests lay and let Baldwin off the hook.[141] Baldwin reiterated that he would implement the commission's findings if all parties signed up to them, but he was being disingenuous as he knew the mine owners would not agree to this, and therefore neither would the miners' leaders. In retrospect it is clear that he always wanted a strike, a decisive confrontation with Labour, so that he could smash it once and for all. Yet the media colluded with his version of events, presenting a scenario where only the miners' incredible obduracy prevented a settlement.[142]

Baldwin was well aware of the reluctance of the TUC to be sucked into a general strike and dithered between trying to manoeuvre them into a showdown alongside the miners, so as to drag down the wide Labour movement, and a countervailing desire to pull off another Black Friday by detaching the other unions from the MFGB. Accordingly, his next move, on 25 April was to summon Arthur Pugh for a private meeting. Baldwin always had a soft spot for Pugh, a countryman from Herefordshire who had become a steelworker and who, off duty, could be a genial companion, his incompetence as chairman of the SIC notwithstanding.[143] Sufficiently encouraged by Pugh, Baldwin then met the full complement of the SIC, but lost interest once he realised the SIC had absolutely no influence on the miners. However he did agree to the setting up of a negotiating committee, much derided by A. J. Cook on the grounds that there was nothing to negotiate given the government's stance. On the TUC side this consisted of Pugh, Thomas, Citrine and Swales and on the government side of Baldwin, Birkenhead, Steel-Maitland and Horace Wilson. It was thus a meeting of moderates on one side and right-wingers on the other, with the Left unrepresented (except for Swales, who was ineffective). There was particular matiness between old friends F. E. Smith (Birkenhead) and Jimmy Thomas. When Swales mentioned that Herbert Smith had been a prize-fighter in his younger days, Birkenhead chimed in with his pet theme that mining and fighting went together; he claimed to have a great-grandfather who was both.[144] Horace Wilson tended to act as the go-between for Baldwin and the TUC men when they were not meeting together. Citrine noticed that Thomas on such occasions liked to be rude to Horace Wilson; doubtless as a power-worshipper he calculated that Smith, a mere civil servant, did not have to be deferred to and could therefore be kicked.[145] Baldwin was asked why, if he was now so opposed to a subsidy for the mining industry, he had granted one in 1925. Baldwin declared that he was frightened of encouraging fascism if class tensions were ratcheted up too tightly.[146] Inferring from this that Baldwin was now unconcerned about the threat from the extreme Right, Thomas tried to frighten his colleagues by lurid scenarios about fascist thugs on shooting rampages.[147] While using the right-wing bogeyman to scare his comrades, Thomas simultaneously tried to use a left-wing bugbear on Baldwin and his cabinet, insinuating that the proletariat was now in a revolutionary fever pitch, and that only the valiant efforts of the TUC were holding them in check.[148] Yet events were by this time evolving beyond the ambit of Thomas's scheming. A delegate conference of miners' leaders was held on 28 April, which backed Cook and Smith and reiterated 'no surrender'. Perhaps more significantly, on Thursday 29 April a conference of trade union leaders met and stayed in session at the Memorial Hall in Faringdon Street until Friday, constantly adjourning, remeeting and readjourning as they awaited the latest developments. 1,300 representatives of 141 unions were expected to hand plenipotentiary powers to the TUC. Ernest Bevin was the star of the day. He told the delegates that a titanic struggle was coming in twenty-four hours and that all unions would have to become one union to counter the threat. His message of 'all power to the TUC General Council' was heeded. All 141 unions voted to cede full powers to the TUC.[149] It seemed now that a general strike was inevitable. Yet there were still optimists who thought that Baldwin, Thomas or the full negotiating committee could pull an eleventh-hour rabbit out of the hat. The last two days of the month were to be both action-packed and crucial.

14

Towards the Abyss

After his tortoise-like performance until the last week of April, Baldwin was now involved in negotiations at white heat. The tourbillon of events began at 5.45 p.m. on 29 April when the SIC, flushed with the rousing endorsement just given to the TUC in the Memorial Hall, went to 10 Downing Street. There was a tripartite meeting with Baldwin and the miners' leaders, which began with a long, embarrassed silence. Finally Herbert Smith broke the deadlock. 'Are you waiting for us to speak, Mr Prime Minister? Do you think our people are likely to go back to longer hours? Ah don't think you can expect us to do it, and we're not going to.'[1] Baldwin replied to this by adjourning the meeting until 10.30 p.m. when he expected the coal owners to join them. While they waited, Jimmy Thomas tried more of his scare tactics on Citrine. He asserted in all seriousness that the country was honeycombed with Reds, that Baldwin was bent on a showdown and there would soon be bloodshed. He expected the entire General Council to be arrested and the strikers to be mown down by gunfire, not from the military but from the fascists, whom the government were secretly encouraging but who were 'deniable'. Thomas went on to say that from Baldwin's perspective such violence would be understandable: 'Who is this strike against? It is not against the coal-owners, it must be against the State. The money is not in the industry, so the strike is against the State. Well, Baldwin says that the State must be supreme, and he is right. Churchill is the man who will play the big part in all this.'[2] Citrine then spoke to Swales and said what had often been said before, that Thomas was a born scaremonger whose true metier was as a fireside teller of ghost stories. When he reported the gist of Thomas's remarks, Swales said defiantly: 'I hope they do arrest us. It will be just the thing for our movement.' At this point Pugh, who had been listening to the conversation, expressed the reservations entertained towards 'Jimmy' even by right-wing unionists: 'You know, Thomas is an enigma. I can't make him out.'[3] The evening came to a dismal end when Baldwin's aide came to tell them that there would, after all, be no further talks that night. The SIC members traipsed back to the Memorial Hall to find the delegates singing folk songs. They reported that Baldwin had preferred an early night to getting down to serious business – and there was truth in this. Thomas melodramatically claimed that he 'never begged and pleaded like I begged and pleaded today'.[4] Herbert Smith told his friends that the stumbling block was that Baldwin would not commit to reforms *before* wage cuts were imposed, but merely stated in a vague way that they would be 'initiated' (whatever that meant).

On Friday 30 April the SIC went to the House of Commons and kicked their collective heels all morning, waiting for the result of Baldwin's talks with the coal owners. At last word arrived of the owners' latest offer. They wanted a 13 per cent cut in wage rates, an eight-hour day, guaranteed until 1929 and no significant reorganisation until that date. The only concession they were prepared to make was to accept a national wages board. This 'generous' offer was clearly always going to be unacceptable to the MFGB. The mine owners were delivering impossible terms impossibly late.[5] Again Baldwin made an excuse to delay detailed talks, and it was 7 p.m. before both sides got down to serious business. Swales, Thomas and Pugh were the chief SIC negotiators, with Baldwin, Birkenhead and Steel-Maitland facing them, and Citrine and Sir Horace Wilson taking minutes. The meeting soon bogged down in an impasse about reform of the mining industry, with Baldwin steadfastly refusing to go beyond a pledge to 'initiate' restructuring. The SIC delegates became more and more impatient, increasingly convinced that Baldwin had no serious intention of implementing the Samuel Report, even if Herbert Smith and A. J. Cook could be brought to accept it. Baldwin was uncomfortable, not daring to admit to the union men that Birkenhead and Steel-Maitland had threatened a cabinet revolt if he made any concessions. Eventually Thomas produced a bombshell in the form of a poster printed by Odhams Press in which the government announced a state of emergency. What was the meaning of this, he asked sharply. Baldwin shuffled uneasily in his chair and said it was merely part of the government's contingency plans and the poster had not yet been printed. Citrine described the atmosphere: 'The silence was ominous. Every one of us concluded that we had been badly tricked. We felt we could no longer trust either Baldwin or anyone else and that they were simply playing for time to complete the arrangements which the Government had in hand.'[6] Citrine accused Baldwin of bad faith, and Thomas weighed in to say that the government seemed unaware of the dangerous, revolutionary situation which now existed. Baldwin *was* being disingenuous. That very day the government had sent Circular 99 out to the local authorities, in effect implementing the emergency procedures which had been planned since the previous November. The duplicity of the government could scarcely be denied, as the entire communication was published in the press next day.[7] The SIC went through the formality of consulting the miners once again about their position and returned to meet Baldwin at 9.45 p.m. How seriously the government took their efforts can perhaps be gauged from the sequel. They found Baldwin with Steel-Maitland (Birkenhead had departed), but present also were Neville Chamberlain, Lord Salisbury, Bridgeman and Lane-Fox, all in dinner jackets. The SIC men delivered another of Herbert Smith's 'Nowt doin' messages and took their leave. Just outside Baldwin's room Thomas ran into Churchill, who said: 'Is it over?' When Thomas nodded, Churchill went on: 'Well, it is over as far as we are concerned. I have given you twenty-four millions, and that is all you are going to get. You can't have another bob.'[8] By 11 p.m. all parties to the farce were on their way home.

May 1st was the most gloomy May Day Citrine could remember. At the special TUC conference a roll-call of all unions present was held. The miners confirmed (or seemed to) that they would hand over the dispute entirely to the General Council provided they could be present at any negotiations. The SIC was reappointed as a negotiating committee. Further evidence that Baldwin was determined on a showdown seemed to come from the revelation that just before he had met the SIC the previous evening, Baldwin had been at Buckingham Palace for a meeting of the Privy Council, with George V present. This had arranged for the proclamation of a state of emergency under the Emergency Powers Act, even though it was still conceivable that there would be no General Strike and, in particular, that the NUR would defect at the last moment and produce another Black Friday.

Given that the only actual emergency on 30 April was the expiration of the mine owners' notices to their workers and the beginning of their lockout, this and Baldwin's other actions looked more and more like deliberate provocation.[9] Depending on their political hue, trade unionists prepared for the coming struggle with despondency or elation. The General Council announced some vague plans for food distribution but left it to the individual unions to call out their members, contenting itself with setting the exact time for a national strike: 11.59 p.m. on Monday 3 May.[10] Meanwhile Citrine sent a letter to Baldwin saying that, despite the critical pass events had reached, the General Council was still available for last-minute talks. This received an immediate reply: Baldwin's secretary came on the phone to arrange a meeting for 8.45 p.m. that evening. Talks continued until 1 a.m. and, though neither side gave ground, Baldwin was sufficiently encouraged to set out a 'formula' which ran as follows: 'The Prime Minister has satisfied himself as a result of the conversations . . . that if negotiations are continued (it being understood that the notices cease to operate) the representatives of the TUC are confident that a settlement can be reached on the lines of the Report within a fortnight.'[11] Some government ministers seriously thought this was the end of the threatened General Strike. Steel-Maitland passed Birkenhead a slip of paper on which he had written the words: 'A taper had been lit this day in England.' The irrepressible F. E. scribbled back: 'If it's a taper without a wages agreement, not even God's help will enable it to be put out.'[12] Next day, Sunday 2 May, the General Council met at its headquarters in Eccleston Square. Now it was A. J. Cook's turn to be alarmed. He had heard about the talks and was surprised by them, scenting a sell-out. He joined the General Council in its deliberations but, when asked for the miners' response to it, replied that all members of the miners' executive had already left London for their various coalfields – naturally, since the coal strike had already begun. Cook, rightly, said he could take no responsibility for any meaningful reply to the formula until the hastily recalled delegates were back in London, which would not be until some time on Monday.[13] Painful combing through the small print of Herbert Smith's statements to the TUC conference on 28–9 April, and the caveats and qualifications Cook had urged him to make, revealed that the MFGB had not, after all, given the TUC carte blanche but only a provisional mandate to manage their affairs vis-à-vis the government, and that they retained the right to a veto; incredibly, this cardinal issue had never been cleared up unequivocally. The TUC was now in an impossible situation: on the one hand they had signed up to Baldwin's 'formula' as men of honour; on the other, they were also committed by honour to the miners and could not ditch them, for yet another Black Friday might destroy the TUC's credibility for all time.[14]

While Cook cabled his colleagues to return to London, the General Council took its eye off the ball and forgot to inform Baldwin of the latest developments. Baldwin had called a cabinet meeting for noon, expecting to hear back from the General Council around 1 p.m. at the latest. When nothing happened, and there was no sign of the negotiating committee nor any telephone message, the cabinet members ('naturally disgruntled and perhaps a few of them inwardly elated')[15] dispersed, after agreeing to keep in touch so that they could hurriedly reassemble. It was 7 p.m. before Citrine rang 10 Downing Street and by this time, the mood among Baldwin's cabinet was black: 'they did not seem particularly anxious to see us,' as Citrine put it mildly.[16] The cabinet had remet and had adjourned a second time, and the hard liners particularly were in no mood to rush their dinners and hasten back to the conference table. There were even rumours that the 'hawks' were so disgusted with the TUC that they were planning a coup against the prime minister himself. This would replace Baldwin with an interim triumvirate of Churchill, Birkenhead and Neville Chamberlain; all talks with the TUC would then cease forthwith.[17] Finally a meeting was organised for 9 p.m. This time the negotiating committee was joined by Ramsay MacDonald and 'Uncle' Henderson, with Baldwin, Birkenhead and Steel-Maitland as the principal spokesmen for the government. Birkenhead said in his best charmless manner (in which he could excel) that a very unfavourable impression had been left in the government's mind at the General Council's inability to recall the miners' delegates after a gap of nearly twenty-four hours. Citrine apologised profusely, and this seemed to soften Baldwin at least. Birkenhead then announced that he had devised what he called the 'Samuel formula', which read as follows: 'We will urge the miners to authorise us to enter upon a discussion with the understanding that they and we accept the Report as a basis for settlement, and we approach it with the knowledge that it may involve some reduction in wages.'[18] Both sides then agreed that two weeks was too short a time in which to reach a settlement: even Birkenhead conceded that the pestiferous owners were so difficult that they would require every one of their 'paltry pits' considered individually and separately. The negotiating committee then asked leave to withdraw and confer among themselves. They went next door to 11 Downing Street through an upstairs connecting door. Some inconclusive debate about the Birkenhead formula then ensued, with Thomas declaring that he was going to accept it, and was indifferent to the miners' attitude.[19] Suddenly it was announced that the Miners' Executive had arrived. By now it was almost midnight. Herbert Smith reminded his 'brothers' that the miners were now locked out and scouted the notion that any settlement could be cobbled together in a fortnight. Before any really serious horse-trading could begin, a message was brought from Baldwin that he wanted to see the negotiating committee. Pugh, Swales, Citrine and Thomas went through to Number 10 and down, leaving the miners behind.[20] Seeing Tom Jones, Baldwin's éminence grise, at the door, Thomas could not resist a hit at A. J. Cook, telling Jones that Cook was 'a bloody swine'.[21] When they encountered Baldwin, his face was described as either ashen or thunderous, depending on the eyewitness. He handed the committee a formal note and then spoke as follows: 'The task of the peacemakers is hard. Since we were here an hour ago an incident has happened which the British Cabinet takes such a serious view upon that they have instructed me to break off negotiations and convey their decision in this letter which I now hand to you. But I felt, having regard to all that you gentlemen have done to try and effect an honourable peace, courtesy demanded that I should tell you personally. Goodbye. This is the end.'[22]

What had happened? It seems that the hawks did not trust Baldwin not to appear as the deus ex machina last-minute peacemaker and hatched a plot to force him to throw in the towel and accept a general strike and its consequences. Their stalking horse was Thomas Marlowe, right-wing editor of the *Daily Mail*.[23] He knew that the printers were not hard-line left-wingers – after all they had printed the government's state of emergency notices – so devised something that was *bound* to provoke them. On this fateful evening he prepared a leader which read: 'A general strike is not an industrial dispute. It is a revolutionary move which can only succeed by destroying the government and subverting the rights and liberties of the people.'[24] This was blatant nonsense, and Marlowe knew it, but he was prepared to do the bidding of the conspirators. Who were they exactly, and who was the true author of the *Daily Mail* incident? Fingers have been pointed variously at Churchill, Birkenhead and Joynson-Hicks, but the most ingenious suggestion is that Jimmy Thomas was playing an elaborate game. He had already shown that he was a master of duplicity, at once frightening his comrades with lurid tales of fascist atrocities to come and terrifying Baldwin by telling him that if a settlement was not reached short of a national strike, the rank and file of the proletariat, much further to the left than their leaders in the union movement, would quickly get out of hand and foment red revolution.[25] Kingsley Martin, the left-wing intellectual, directly accused Thomas of 'winding up' Baldwin so that he would object to the *Daily Mail* affair with outrage.[26] Certainly there was something very odd about Thomas's behaviour that night. Citrine recorded that after the final breakdown of talks Thomas lost his head. When Baldwin's letter was read to the full General Council, Purcell said he was glad it had come to a fight but Thomas rounded furiously on him. 'Some of those who have been talking have now got their will . . . We should inform the government that we regret any incidents that have happened and which have rendered the task of the peacemakers more difficult, but we cannot accept responsibility for them. You must control this thing, you who are on top, or you will not be able to control it at all. You won't have the opportunity to issue instructions very long, I know.' When he repeated these words, some of those present smiled but, in Citrine's words, 'Thomas turned viciously on them.'[27] The obvious reading is that he was piqued because his much-trumpeted prophecy that there would be a settlement had turned out to be wrong, but it may be that he was playing an even more devious game.[28] Baldwin's duplicity was soon afterwards accidentally revealed when it was learned that he had sent his letter of 'shocked disillusionment' about the *Daily Mail* incident *before* his very first meeting with the negotiating committee that day.[29] Certainly by this time even moderates in the Labour movement were beginning to get the measure of Baldwin. When the meeting of the Privy Council at Buckingham Palace announced the state of emergency, Bevin remarked that the proclamation was 'equal in stupidity to the actions of the well-remembered Lord North and George III combined'.[30] Always suspicious of Thomas, he surmised that he and Baldwin might be colluding and that the four-man committee was making unjustified promises to Baldwin and concealing things from the General Council. He proposed, sensibly, that the General Council simply disown the action at the *Daily Mail* by the NATSOPA operatives and send a letter of apology to the government. This was done, and the trade union leaders returned to the conference room only to find that all the lights were out and Baldwin had gone to bed, almost as though he had anticipated the General Council's next move and trumped it with his non-availability.[31] Bevin always believed a settlement of the *Daily Mail* affair could have been reached, but the villain in his demonology was Churchill.[32] It is interesting that George V, never happy with Baldwin's conduct of industrial affairs and his indulgence of the hard liners in his own cabinet and the mining industry, repudiated Thomas Marlowe's analysis of the General Strike, and said of the *Daily Mail* article and its attitude to the miners: 'Try living on their wages before you judge them.'[33]

Monday 3 May was a day of forlorn hopes and eyebrow-raising rationalisations. Desperate to avoid accusations that the TUC had sat on its hands until the strike officially began at 11.59. p.m., the negotiating committee again met Ramsay MacDonald (and the Labour Party Executive) to see if there was any way out of the imbroglio. Pugh suggested a mining board, with equal representation for employers and unions but MacDonald objected that Baldwin would 'spin' this as the Board 'giving laws' to an elected government.[34] MacDonald's behaviour both during the General Strike and in the few days previous was odd. In his diary for 2 May he noted: 'It really looks tonight as though there is to be a general strike to save Mr Cook's face. Important man! The election of this fool as miners' secretary looks as though it might be the most calamitous thing that has ever happened to the trade union movement.'[35] This fatuous statement ignored the fact that Cook had never been on the SIC or the negotiating committee, had expressed pragmatic moderation if only the mine owners would meet him halfway (they would not) and acted entirely correctly (as even MacDonald conceded) when he said he could take no decisions on his own but would have to recall the mining delegates. The idea that the strike took place to save the miners' faces was a travesty of events but, even if total culpability could be laid at the door of the MFGB, the unbudgeable mule of the piece was Herbert Smith, not A. J. Cook. MacDonald's talents as an observer of the events of 2 May have been seriously questioned by scholars, as when he claimed that Bevin had tried to 'bully' Herbert Smith, and his description of Pugh's bored and offhand manner.[36] There was not a breath of criticism of Jimmy Thomas (always something of a sacred cow in MacDonald's eyes) for his erratic antics or of the General Council for their woeful failure to make contingency plans for the General Strike. Much shrewder was Trotsky's comment that the so-called British Left was so only as long as it had to accept no practical obligations. Even 'leftists' on the General Council like Alonzo Swales were disposed 'either to direct betrayal or compromise, or else to a policy of wait and see with reference to compromises and complaints against traitors'.[37] While MacDonald doused any faint embers in the TUC's fire, his future collaborator in government, Stanley Baldwin, was giving another of his 'appalling frankness' speeches in the House of Commons. He expressed disappointment and disillusionment that his hopes for peace had come to nothing and said he looked forward to the time when 'the angel of peace with healing in his wings will be among us again'. He reiterated that the General Strike was a revolutionary threat to the constitution.[38] Curiously, his faithful acolyte Tom Jones saw nothing amiss in Baldwin's clichéd gush, but instead criticised the speeches by Ramsay MacDonald (which was generally conceded to be lame), Lloyd George (in which he accurately nailed the lie that the strike was the work of revolutionaries) and J. H. Thomas, who colluded with Baldwin in the myth of revolutionary intent: 'I have never disguised,' said Thomas, 'that in a challenge to the constitution, God help us unless the government won.'[39] Even neutral observers were unconvinced by Baldwin's effusions. The *Manchester Guardian* commented: 'Mr Baldwin spoke his piece, but one had the feeling that the militants in his cabinet had taught it to him.'[40]

The psychology and intentions of the enigmatic and devious Baldwin still arouse controversy. Was he really, as he insinuated, a man of peace, with only Steel-Maitland on his side, surrounded by the ring of fire that was Churchill, Neville Chamberlain, Joynson-Hicks, Bridgeman and Amery, and suffering grievously from the late defection of Birkenhead, who was a dove in 1925 but now, on the very eve of the strike, had turned ultra-hawkish? Was he genuinely looking for a way out even at this late hour? Or, in his pious hopes of trans-class collaboration in 'one nation', was he systematically deceptive and even self-deceiving? The reasons he gave for breaking off negotiations do not inspire confidence in his good faith. The letter he handed the TUC negotiating committee in the small hours of 3 May explained his apparent disgust: 'It has come to the knowledge of the Government not only that specific instructions have been sent . . . directing their members . . . to carry out a general strike on Tuesday next, but that overt acts have already taken place, including gross interference with the freedom of the press.'[41] The first point was nonsense: the same call for a general strike had preceded Red Friday, but Baldwin, so far from declaring it a revolutionary and unconstitutional act, had climbed down. What was the qualitative difference this time? It was doubtless Tom Jones's fury at Lloyd George's impeccable logic on this point that led him to dismiss the House of Commons speech by 'the goat' as 'bad'. As for 'overt acts', there was only *one* act: the refusal of NATSOPA to print the provocative editorial in the *Daily Mail*. This hardly constituted 'gross interference in the freedom of the press' – a phrase that would have characterised the complete shutdown of Fleet Street. Moreover, this was a unilateral action by NATSOPA which the General Council, that body allegedly chock-full of howling revolutionaries, had instantly repudiated. Furthermore, this statement had been prepared *before* the NATSOPA men took their action.[42] Additionally, circumstantial evidence favours a conspiracy or 'set-up'. It was Thomas Marlowe who had effectively brought down the Labour government in 1924 by publishing the famous 'Zinoviev letter' which purported to show the MacDonald administration as Soviet stooges. The only possible defence for Baldwin is that he issued the statement when tired and exhausted and that the alleged 'issue' on which he fought was 'a triviality, ludicrous if its consequences were not so serious'.[43] Baldwin sometimes hinted that he had been 'ambushed' by the 'hard men' on the evening of 2 May, but this is not really any more convincing than his constant lament to Tom Jones that the entire crisis over the coal industry was a bed of nails bequeathed to him by the incompetence and cowardice of Lloyd George.[44] The charitable view on Baldwin has been expressed thus: 'At a late hour a silly argument may sound as good as a sane one, and on one of those points where tired and irritated men dig in their toes – points of pride, of supposed principle, of constitutional rights – the "wild men" were able to stand and win.'[45] This view of the prime minister as 'peacemaker' ignored the fact that Baldwin, as an ideologically pure man of business, would never have browbeaten the mine owners, so all hopes of a peace were a priori vain. In the end even wishful thinkers like Citrine, who really wanted to believe in Baldwin, had to give up. 'I sometimes wonder whether Baldwin is as honest, plain and straightforward as he appears to be, or whether he is a hypocrite and a humbug. When in personal contact with him he conveys feelings of sincerity, but his subsequent actions can only be justified by the assumption that he is dominated by his cabinet.'[46] Citrine was too genteel to draw the entailment if he was *not* dominated by his cabinet but simply using them as a shield in an elaborate 'good cop, bad cop' charade.

Any million-to-one hopes of a last-minute miracle were dashed when Arthur Henderson and Ramsay MacDonald went to Number 10 on the evening of the 3 May; they attended, since Baldwin had already branded the negotiating committee disingenuous revolutionaries. Citrine had been tipped off by Sir Horace Wilson and Tom Jones that Baldwin still entertained a glimmer of hope that a deal could be stitched together, though this was almost certainly Baldwin in another of his moods of self-deception. To use modern terminology, it often seems that Baldwin was 'in denial' about his own actions. When MacDonald and Henderson arrived, they were confronted by Baldwin, Churchill and Steel-Maitland. A tense and sometimes turbulent meeting ensued. Churchill was in gung-ho mood or, as Kingsley Martin put it, 'Churchill revelled in the chance to smash what he considered as an incipient revolution.'[47] 'You [meaning the Left],' Churchill said, 'tried it in Italy and failed, and you are not going to be successful in Great Britain.' Steel-Maitland, too, was in aggressive form: 'It's about time you [the Labour movement] were put in your places.' Henderson managed a cutting jibe at Churchill, referring to his over-the-top hyper-belligerent personal appearance at an anarchist siege in 1911: 'It seems to me, Winston, that you are trying to give us a dose of Sidney Street.'[48] The meeting proved an utter waste of time, and in any case by this time attitudes were hardening on both sides. On the Left were those joyful and jubilant that the gradualist, stalling tactics of the TUC were at an end and they could finally engage with the Great Beast, Capital.

One of them said, in delighted stupefaction: 'It is like asking for an elephant or dragon. And, lo, here it is, walking up the garden path.'[49] The labour leader David Kirkwood said: 'I was heartily in favour of the General Strike. I believed we should see such an uprising of the people that the government would be forced to grant our demands.'[50] But the more reflective and moderate Labour Party supporters could see only disaster looming ahead. Beatrice Webb thought that a general strike was intrinsically revolutionary and to be deplored, no matter how justified the demands of the strikers. All governments, even a Labour one, would have to fight tooth and nail against it: 'A General Strike aims at coercing the whole community and is only successful *if it does so* and in so far as it does. Further, if it succeded in coercing the whole community it would mean that a militant minority were starving the majority into submission to their will, and that would be the end of democracy, industrial as well as political.'[51] She deprecated the rhetoric of the left-wingers, inevitably working demon-king Cook into her equation: 'A. J. Cook on behalf of the T. U. C. Left, and Maxton and Wheately on account of the Clyde, talk about immediate revolution – whilst George Lansbury thunders threats of the immediate dissolution of "capitalist civilisation".'[52]

And so the minutes ticked away, midnight, 3 May came, and the General Strike was finally a reality. On Tuesday morning there was an eerie stillness and silence all over the land, with the docks at a standstill, few trains running and virtually no buses. As the day wore on, the hum of traffic increased as thousands of cars, taxis and bicycles took to the road, producing spectacular jams and gridlocks in urban areas, especially London.[53] The government's preparations had been well laid. Its main aims were to provide volunteer labour, especially drivers for trains and buses, to ensure food supplies and to maintain law and order. The Emergency Powers Act allowed it to requisition whatever it liked and to use the police in any capacity without a warrant. Unlike the TUC, it had access to all the latest technology, had a system of intelligence and information far in advance of the unions', quite apart from basking in the aplomb natural to a class 'born to rule'. Sir John Anderson, the permanent secretary at the Home Office charged with nationwide preparations had done his job well, eventually whittling down the areas under Civil Commissioners to just ten. The military were on standby, with warships anchored in the Mersey, Tyne, Clyde, Humber and at Cardiff, Swansea, Barrow, Middlesbrough and Harwich. There was a particular show of force on Merseyside, with the battleships *Ramillies* and *Barham*, recalled from the Atlantic fleet, training their guns menacingly on Liverpool. Two battalions of infantry landed from a troopship and paraded ominously through the city, in full kit, with steel helmets and rifles at the ready.[54] The government's call for volunteers had been successful, even if more in the quantity than quality of the recruits it attracted. Exact statistics are difficult to come by, but estimates range from a low of 300,000 to a high of 500,000 – mainly elderly and middle-aged people of right-wing persuasion, employees in small businesses with paternalistic employers, blacklegs and students. Most of these became special constables, of whom there were 51,807 in London and more than 200,000 elsewhere in England and Wales.[55] Undergraduates from the older universities became notorious as strike-breakers. Cambridge University alumni were employed as follows: 137 on the London Tube, 100 on the buses, 36 on trams, 99 as car and lorry drivers, 63 as railway workers, 64 in the Air Ministry, 460 as dockworkers, 710 special constables in London and 308 employed as 'general labour'.[56]

Many hilarious stories were told about the incompetence of the volunteers and the sheer amateurism of their method of recruitment. Admiral Lord Jellicoe, who had commanded the fleet at Jutland in 1916, went to a police station to volunteer, where the following conversation took place:

'Name?'

'Jellicoe.'

'Ever done anything?'

'I commanded the Grand Fleet.'

'Fleet of what?'[57]

The one big government failure was the much-touted OMS. Only 30,000 volunteers were raised under its auspices, and most of these were rabid extremists. The government, rightly fearing an outbreak of fascism, used very few of them.[58]

The TUC, on the other hand, put up a dismal showing throughout the strike. It was a classic instance of the British working class being prepared to make sacrifices for a better world only to be betrayed by its leaders. Citrine, a natural pessimist, was taken aback by the sheer solidity of the strike and the unexpected solidarity of the workers.

The loyalty of the working class in 1926 closed the gap between revolutionary fantasy and reality, for the proletariat on this occasion closely resembled the mythical 'class for itself' that had so exercised Marx.[59] One million striking miners were joined by another 1.5 million in the railways, docks, road transport, iron and steel, chemical, building and power industries. Of 15,062 London, Midland and Scottish railway engine drivers, only 207 reported for work on the first day of the strike; of 14,143 firemen only 62; of 9,979 train guards, only 153. The LMS railway ran only 3.8 per cent of its normal passenger service on the first day of the strike, though nine days later this was up to 12.2 per cent with the aid of volunteer crews. Altogether at the beginning of the strike only 3–5 per cent of passenger trains and 2–3 per cent of goods trains were running.[60] Because of the expertise required, volunteer labour was a total failure on the railways (though the government tried to 'spin' the facts otherwise). In London not one of the General Omnibus Company's 3,293 buses left the garage, though by 11 May 526 of them were on the road. Nothing at all was unloaded at the docks for the first four days of the strike.[61] For obvious reasons, it was more difficult for the strikers to interdict Tube trains, so that by Saturday 8 May 71 out of 315 trains on the London Underground were running. The General Strike was, however, as has often been remarked, a very British affair in that almost the only trains running were bringing milk to the towns and cities. The unions communicated with their districts in the usual way and drew money for strike pay from the banks. In general, strike-breaking lorries were not attacked.[62] Yet the overwhelming impression left by the first day of the strike was the chaotic organisation of the TUC, especially when contrasted with the government's meticulous preparations. The members of the General Council had entered the strike with extreme reluctance, relying on the threat of a national strike as a deterrent, and, like most deterrents, not supposed to be actually used. They were now terrified of the genie they had released from the bottle. In a curious paradox, whereas the government did not really believe the strike was a revolutionary threat to the constitution, but said so repeatedly for propaganda effect, many members of the General Council thought, with more insight, that a genuinely revolutionary situation was objectively present. As one student of the strike has commented: '[they were] feebly timid; they hoped for the collaboration of their opponents and never wholly trusted the mass of their supporters; they feared the consequences of complete victory more than those of a negotiated defeat.'[63]

The errors of the General Council were legion. In a panic that no real preparations for a general strike had ever been made, they allowed Bevin, their best administrator to improvise with the Strike Organisation Committee – essentially a retreading of the old Ways and Means Committee – but drew the line at making him the strike supremo; J. H. Thomas was particularly insistent that his great rival not be given such powers and, as usual, Thomas got his way.[64] Bevin then took the disastrous decision not to go for an all-out, no holds barred, nationwide stoppage but to call out the workers in waves. The first wave consisted of the transport, railway, iron and steel, building, chemical and power workers – to which was absurdly added the printers, which meant that the government could print propaganda but none of the usual newspapers could rebut it. Even pro-strike newspapers like the *Manchester Guardian* were affected and, despite the pleading from that organ's editor, the TUC remained adamant.[65] The second wave, to be brought out a week later, comprised the Post Office, engineering, textiles and shipbuilding workers; the seamen were outside the TUC's ambit, as their union was the only significant one to refuse to heed the strike call.[66] Bevin's thinking was deeply flawed: given the exiguous strike funds available to the TUC, he had go for a 'quick kill'. The idea of increasing the power and severity of the strike week by week made sense only if the General Council had amassed a six-month strike fund. Even Thomas and Citrine disagreed with Bevin's strategy, but lacked the commitment or killer instinct to come up with an alternative.[67] Bevin's thinking was that the strike would be a long-drawn-out affair that would last at least a month, and that the 'two-front' approach he favoured would be an incentive to the government to be reasonable and come to terms; after all, a truly revolutionary strike would undoubtedly go for the jugular from day one.

Bevin's mistake was to assume that Baldwin wanted compromise rather than the crushing victory he sought in reality. For all that, Bevin was the only TUC grandee to emerge from the strike with his reputation enhanced.[68] Yet the decision to go for a two-stage strike was only the most cardinal of the TUC's errors. There was no real mind overseeing the entire operation. The chaotic management of the

General Council found expression in the unsatisfactory division of power between TUC and individual unions, and *within* unions at local and national levels, and the overlapping functions of many trade union committees. The General Council was anxious to maintain the supply of food and power, to prove conclusively that they did not have revolutionary aims, and so initiated a system of permits and licences exempting certain entities from blockades and picketing. It was decreed that the movement of 'essential' goods be permitted, but nobody understood what was essential and what inessential. What, for example, was the meaning of calling out 'all workers on buildings except such as are employed definitely on housing and hospital work'?[69] Power workers continued to supply electricity since the TUC never issued an explicit order to all power workers; how was an electrician supposed to differentiate between lighting and power?[70] Different unions drew different conclusions from the selfsame instructions, and there was chaos at TUC headquarters in Eccleston Square as officials tried to make sense of the instructions or reconcile orders that cancelled each other out. Moreover, the TUC had laid no general plans for the strike or thought through its implications at any level, whether these were administrative, financial or constitutional. Individual unions were left to organise strike pay, picketing and food distribution on a local level, and meanwhile a flood of puzzled enquiries about how best to proceed threatened to inundate Eccleston Square. For example, it became clear that moving food around the country effectively would end up with the return to work of 75 per cent of the railwaymen.[71] As for supporting the miners, the General Strike, unless it was to be a revolutionary one, was too blunt an instrument to support them, always assuming that was the General Council's real intention. The mine owners had stockpiled vast quantities of coal and had contingency plans to buy from the USA and elsewhere. The General Council (and the SIC) might have been better advised to order a general embargo on the movement of coal by the dockers and railwaymen. But the truth was that the top TUC grandees had blundered into a crisis they never imagined they would have to confront. Terrified of devolving power to local strike committees, which might have returned genuinely democratic decisions, they preferred to play dog-in-the-manger, reserving for themselves direction of the strike while doing nothing significant to promote it.[72]

The second day of the strike (5 May) found the working class as solid as ever. Meanwhile there was an increasing perception of Baldwin as a 'flaky' personality, by no means the bluff, honest man he pretended to be. In the House of Commons J. H. Thomas forced him to admit that he had (on the evening of 2 May) instituted his own personal 'lockout' when he went to bed while the negotiating committee was still talking to the miners.[73] According to Tom Jones, Baldwin was behaving oddly and displaying a strange turn of mind, at one moment lucidly and correctly identifying Bevin as the most able man in the TUC and then immediately branching off into a kind of academic speculation, in which he dubbed Ramsay MacDonald the 'Kerensky' of the Labour movement but without identifying a Lenin and then, by a kind of weird association of ideas, wondering if Bevin would emerge as the 'Napoleon' of industrial relations.[74] Beatrice Webb, who loathed left-wing politics, trade unions and communism and thought the General Strike a catastrophic mistake for the Labour movement, nonetheless saw clearly that Baldwin's failure to bring the coal owners to heel was *the* root cause of the strike. Writing on 3 May she declared: 'It is that mean wriggling of the Baldwin Cabinet, to some extent justified by the wriggles of the Liberal Commission of Herbert Samuel and Beveridge – typical Liberals – that has brought about the General Strike of tonight.'[75] Yet even though emotion and reason inclined Webb against the government, she was always more comfortable adopting a position of superiority towards the trade unions and soon she found a new excuse for her lofty attitudinising: the allegedly unhealthy life-style of the General Council.

> Those fifty or sixty men who were directing the General Council were living a thoroughly unwholesome life – smoking, drinking, eating wrong meals at wrong times, rushing about in motor-cars, getting little or no sleep and talking aimlessly one with another . . . sitting in groups singing songs and telling stories, soothed and enlightened by a plentiful supply of tobacco and alcohol . . . After a Council meeting some of the members would adjourn to a neighbouring public house and discuss matters at the bar with reporters present.[76]

Webb always found experience of mundane living and quotidian lives tiresome, but the General Council members at least understood everyday reality, as Webb did not. Her attitude is most reminiscent of Churchill's, who, as his wife Clementine pointed out, lived largely in a wonderland of his own imagination. 'He knows nothing of the life of the ordinary people. He's never been on a bus, and only once on the Underground. This was during the General Strike, when I deposited him at South Kensington. He went round and round (on the Circle Line) not knowing where to get out and had to be rescued eventually.'[77]

Wednesday 5 May also saw the appearance of a government newspaper, the *British Gazette*, an organ of the most hysterical and mendacious propaganda, 'edited' by Winston Churchill. Baldwin decided that he would never win the battle for public opinion if the facts and arguments concerning the General Strike were published objectively and dispassionately; in a word, he would have to go for the big lie. After importing newsprint from Holland and commandeering the offices of the *Morning Post*, the government made its appearance in the media world on the second day of the strike. 232,000 copies of its newspaper were printed, with the kind of blatantly over-the-top affirmations that were to become the *Gazette*'s hallmark. 'The General Strike is . . . a direct challenge to ordered government . . . an effort to force upon some 42,000,000 British citizens the will of less than 4,000,000 others.' Baldwin himself entered the fray next day with this: 'Constitutional government is being attacked . . . Stand behind the government . . . The laws are in your keeping. You have made Parliament your guardian. The General Strike is a challenge to Parliament and is the road to anarchy and ruin.'[78] Government propaganda liked to concentrate on the idea that public transport had not been impeded and that there had been a steady drift back to work by the strikers. Both assertions were untrue: only 3 per cent of railwaymen returned to work before the end of the strike. On 6 May the *Gazette* claimed that 200 buses were running in London when the true figure was 86 – actually a dismal performance by the government, for almost anyone could drive a vehicle, as against the difficulties of being a train driver.[79] The lies of the *British Gazette* were so poisonous that even moderates like Ramsay MacDonald and Arthur Henderson were led to vociferous protest in the House of Commons. The sole consolation for the TUC and the strikers was that the *Gazette* was widely regarded as an embarrassment. Thousands of copies were dumped, jettisoned or even ejected from aeroplanes; almost nobody read it. Yet it was a sinister and dangerous excrescence in political life. It openly supported fascism and by falsely preaching imminent red revolution it came perilously close to self-fulfilling prophecy, whipping up passions to the kind of fever pitch where extremists on both sides actually would turn to revolution.[80] Lloyd George viewed the *British Gazette* as 'a first-class indiscretion clothed in the tawdry garb of third rate-journalism', while the *New Statesman* described it as 'a disgrace alike to the British government and to British journalism . . . it made no pretence of impartiality; it exaggerated, distorted and suppressed news, speeches and opinions for propagandist purposes'.[81]

Quite the most disgraceful aspect of the *British Gazette* was the light it shed on the personality of its editor Winston Churchill. As Churchill's own books on the Second World War would demonstrate, he was no respecter of truth, which he always seemed to regard as an optional extra. Such a trait can be defended in a peerless wartime leader, where image and propaganda must necessarily triumph over objective fact, but in 1926 this attribute was undesirable, irresponsible and dangerous. One of the problems was that Baldwin had given Churchill the job to absorb his energies, to keep him quiet and shut him up. As he later boasted: 'Don't forget the cleverest thing I ever did. I put Winston in a corner and told him to edit the *British Gazette*.'[82] A notoriously bad editor, more yellow than W. R. Hearst's yellow press, Churchill was at odds with everyone: other editors, journalists, printers, politicians, churchmen, even the king himself, although the impressionable George V was worked up by the *Gazette*'s sensational reporting of the 'intimidation' employed by pickets.[83] Churchill's critics dubbed him 'the British Mussolini' and it was widely remarked that Winston on the crest of a wave was the stuff of which tyrants were made.[84] Lloyd George said his actions were 'like a chauffeur who is apparently perfectly sane and drives with great skill for months but . . . suddenly takes you over a precipice'.[85] Hamilton Fyfe, the editor of the official Trade Union organ, *British Worker*, remarked of his opposite number: 'He sees the whole affair as a film producer would see it, with this difference. Film producers do not act; Winston intends to appear as the hero of the story himself.'[86] Yet Churchill's activities were not confined to lying propaganda of the most grotesque kind. By restricting the supply of newsprint, he also threw the entire newspaper industry into turmoil.

Only forty of 1,870 national, regional and local newsapers were unaffected. Most provincial newspapers were reduced to turning out editions on roneo'd sheets. *The Times* was given government protection and rewarded Baldwin with nuanced support. The Rothermere press was also a 'teacher's pet', since it abandoned its earlier reservations and praised Baldwin as the hero of the hour. The *Daily Mail* was printed in Paris and flown over.[87] Yet even the favoured publications had to appear in truncated editions as Churchill commandeered all supplies of paper, both at the docks and in the paper mills. Geoffrey Dawson, editor of *The Times*, was furious about this, but Churchill told him that the *Gazette* had to have priority as it was 'defending civilisation'.[88] Newspapers were also affected by the sometimes hostile attitude of printers though in one such case, that of the *Manchester Guardian*, the organ had only itself to blame. Supposedly sympathetic to the Left, the *Guardian* announced on 5 May that it could not understand what the TUC's objectives in the strike were.[89] Yet the government's main target was always the TUC's publication, the *British Worker*, edited by Hamilton Fyfe, a far superior product to the *Gazette*. Although Fyfe was driven to distraction by the permanent presence of a team of TUC censors, neurotically anxious to prevent the appearance of *anything* that could be construed as communist or revolutionary, he did a very good job of counter-propaganda, in particular hammering away at the theme that 'the nation' did not simply mean the non-striking middle class.[90] Churchill especially targeted the *British Worker*, requisitioning newsprint to make it difficult, if not impossible, for the *Worker* to be published. The TUC newspaper got smaller and smaller, eventually ending up as a four-page publication, but it struggled through until 16 May. Fyfe got his revenge for Churchill's vindictiveness by ridiculing him for his defence of 'freedom', in particular pointing to the contradiction between a government which had supposedly started a strike on the issue of freedom of the press (the *Daily Mail* incident) but was now trying to stifle the press freedom of the opposition.[91] The issue of the press was always acrimonious and came close to generating violence, especially when anti-government demonstrators tried to torch the offices of *The Times*.[92] In the provinces the editor of the *Birmingham Worker*, a communist news-sheet, was arrested and the journalist John Strachey (ironically later to become a right-wing apologist) was threatened with a trial for treason.[93] Yet the incident that left the nastiest taste in TUC mouths was Baldwin's attempt (on 5 May) to close down the pro-TUC *Daily Herald* – an attempt only thwarted when the attorney-general advised Baldwin that the proposed action was illegal.[94]

By day three of the strike the general public was becoming used to the new routine and was relieved to find that life went on much as usual, with food in the shops and people managing to get to work by driving cars and thumbing lifts. The only departure from normality was the absence of some of the newspapers and the closure of some rail stations such as Victoria.[95] The Oxbridge undergraduates were enjoying the sheer 'lark' of their time as strike-breakers – it seemed an even better jape than their 'silly ass' drinking parties – though the more serious, intelligent and high-minded students and dons tended to sympathise with the strikers: typical were such men as the 20-year-old A. J. P. Taylor, the 21-year-old Hugh Gaitskell, A. D. Lindsay, the master of Balliol, and the libertine and dilettante, Tom Driberg.[96] On the TUC side Jimmy Thomas continued to play the gadfly, irritating Herbert Smith with his would-be role as conciliator and his tendency to promise Baldwin far more than he could deliver. Butterfly as well as gadfly, Thomas, who had previously prophesied confidently that the entire General Council would be arrested, now backtracked and declared this unlikely. As usual, he amused himself by hobnobbing with cabinet ministers. He breezily accosted Jix only to find the home secretary in no mood for Thomas's levity. When he told Jimmy that he was seriously worried, Thomas riposted: 'Yes – and you see where your Mussolini is driving you.' At this obvious hit at Churchill, Joynson-Hicks simply shook his head dolefully.[97] Thomas continued his usual policy of running with both the hare and the hounds, at one time bizarrely asking Baldwin for police protection – but whether from the government or his own colleagues he did not say.[98] Amid the general atmosphere of stasis if not opéra bouffe observable on General Strike day three, there were two significant developments. Sir John Simon announced in the House of Commons that the strike was illegal, using the following legalistic casuistry: 'A strike was a strike against employers to compel employers to do something. A general strike was a strike against the general public to make the public, Parliament and government do something.' All taking part in such a stoppage were therefore engaged in illegal activity and could be sued for damages. The protection of the 1906 Trade Disputes Act was, he argued, made null and void by a general strike and 'every trade union leader who has advised and promoted that course of action is liable in damages to the utmost farthing of his personal possessions'.[99] A few days later (10 May) Mr Justice Astbury concurred with Simon. Giving judgement in a case brought by Havelock Ellis, general secretary of the National Sailors and Firemen Union to prevent any of his members being called out by the TUC, Ellis argued that it was against his union's rules to strike if no ballot had been held to decide the issue, and there had been no ballot. Astbury granted the injunction but then took it upon himself to declare that the General Strike was illegal on the grounds that it was not an industrial dispute and therefore did not fall within the terms of the 1906 Trade Disputes Act.[100] The former Labour Attorney-General Sir Henry Slesser subjected Astbury's claims to withering criticism, citing ample authorities that sympathetic strikes were legal and therefore gave immunity to financial damages. Yet for a while the combined onslaught of Simon and Astbury put the TUC on the back foot. Simon was essentially an overpromoted nonentity who liked to put himself on a footing of legal equality with Birkenhead, seemingly on the basis that both had been at Wadham College, Oxford, and were both lawyers. Deeply unpopular and widely despised, Simon was an object of particular contempt for Lloyd George who remarked: 'He has sat so long on the fence, the iron has entered his soul.'[101] As for his legal expertise, his arguments were soon taken apart in devastating fashion by A. L. Goodhart, then editor of the *Law Quarterly Review* and later professor of jurisprudence at Oxford. A far superior lawyer to Simon, Goodhart demonstrated that the General Strike *was* a sympathy strike, that pressure on a third party was implicit in such a strike, and the fact that the government was the third party was irrelevant. To prove that the TUC was acting against the State and the constitution, one would have to prove that its leaders were guilty of treason, felony, seditious libel or seditious conspiracy, which was clearly 'idiotic'.[102] Baldwin's government later tacitly conceded that Simon and Astbury were hopelessly wrong by bringing in a new act of Parliament in 1927 explicitly to outlaw sympathetic strikes – which by definition they would not have needed to do if the General Strike had in fact been illegal.[103]

The other salient development was the re-entry of Herbert Samuel into the fray. Disgusted at Baldwin's response to his hard work and statesmanship (as he saw it) on the Royal Commission, Samuel washed his hands of the government before the strike and took himself off to his villa on Lake Como in northern Italy, where he lolled by the pool and read his beloved Pliny the Younger. Stirred by various informal appeals, Samuel decided when the strike broke out that his place was back in England. He harnessed his considerable financial muscle to getting himself back through France and across the Channel at speed. On the early afternoon of 6 May he arrived at Folkestone, where he was met by the famous racing driver Major Henry Segrave in a powerful Sunbeam. Segrave took just one hour and ten minutes to whisk Samuel from Folkestone harbour to the Reform Club in Pall Mall, driving with speed and skill. Since the roads in Kent were almost clear of traffic because of the strike, Segrave often touched 85 mph on the open road, but was more cautious in villages and the suburbs.[104] Once in London Samuel gathered his contacts for a conference, buoyed by his golden dream of being the peacemaker and determined to have the last word after Baldwin's insouciant and cavalier treatment of his commission. His arrival was greeted by neutral observers as being the proverbial breath of fresh air.[105] The venue for the talks was the house of Samuel's friend Sir Abe Bailey, the South African magnate, in Bryanston Square. Almost inevitably, his principal transmission belt to the TUC General Council was the egregious Jimmy Thomas, who heartily agreed with Samuel that three points were cardinal: there must be nationally agreed wages, not district rates, and a national wages board; the lockout notices must be withdrawn; and the subsidy should be temporarily extended. Thomas was glad to be once more the focus of attention; he was piqued at being dislodged from pole position at the TUC by Bevin and Alf Purcell, who formed a kind of duumvirate, running the strike on quasi-military lines.[106] But Samuel was brought bumpily down to earth at his first meeting with Steel-Maitland, who impressed on him that he would be merely a private negotiator on his own initiative and the government would not be bound by one of the accords he concluded with the TUC. Samuel thought that the response was churlish, ungrateful and lacking in any form of statesmanship.[107] For a couple of days he concentrated on the miners. At a personal level he liked Herbert Smith, and they established a kind of intimacy jokingly based on the fact that they shared the same first name. But he admitted that Smith, not Cook, was the real barrier to a breakthrough on the union side and described Smith as 'a burly Yorkshireman full of courage . . . when his mind was made up he was not to be moved. Three hours of argument in our conference left Herbert Smith's attitude on every point precisely what it had been at the beginning.'[108] Samuel then switched back to Baldwin. He found him just as adamantly determined as ever not to pressurise the mine owners but seemingly more accommodating in principle.[109] The truth was that Baldwin found Samuel's return deeply embarrassing and inconvenient. Having, as he thought, snubbed him into retirement to Italy, the turbulent Samuel had reappeared, once again putting him on the spot. He dared not be too distant lest he undo all the propaganda advantage he had secured in middle-class minds.[110] He therefore made some encouraging sounds to Samuel and various ideas were kicked around and memoranda presented, whether with much sincerity on the prime minister's part is doubtful.[111] But even if he had wanted to make concessions he had two main problems. If he conceded anything that could have been conceded before the strike, he would be accused of being responsible for an unnecessary strike. And even if he had wanted to give ground, the hard liners in his cabinet – Joynson-Hicks, Neville Chamberlain, Steel-Maitland and Birkenhead – would not have allowed him.[112] The worst problem of all was Churchill. Tom Jones tried to talk him round to a more moderate position, but made the mistake of saying that Arthur Pugh and Thomas were just as loyal to the constitution as he (Churchill) was. At this there was a veritable explosion from Churchill. 'This infuriated him,' wrote Jones, 'and he broke out into a fresh tempest in the corridor, and I felt tossed about like a small boat in an angry sea.'[113]

Friday 7 May found the TUC still dithering and uncertain about what to do next. Bevin proposed, and the General Council accepted, that no minutes should thenceforth be kept of their proceedings, which would prevent the government charging them with conspiracy and treason; clearly John Simon's threats had had an effect. Citrine noted that Bevin seemed to be receding in forcefulness while Thomas increased in self-satisfaction and, as a corollary, that Thomas was becoming increasingly pessimistic and Bevin, in compensation, was more optimistic. The bad blood between the two continued but, since Thomas continually boasted of his contacts with the Lords

Londonderry and Mansfield (vice-president of the Federation of British Industry) the General Council let him have his head rather than admit that it was totally at a loss.[114] That afternoon Thomas and the negotiating committee met Samuel and, after the meeting, Thomas announced that he was now totally committed to the Samuel Commission as the way forward towards a settlement.[115] Citrine continued to be bemused by 'Jimmy's' Machiavellian ways, finding him naturally secretive and more a figure in an Alexandre Dumas intrigue than a trade union negotiator: he was 'always discovering new situations, with mysterious side glances and knowing looks, endowed with facile entry into the innermost circles of government. If only we knew what he knew!'[116] And now it turned out that Baldwin had been right to fear Samuel's return to the arena, for influential centrist and liberal figures began to take up the idea that Samuel's tripartite solution – the immediate cessation of the strike, a temporary renewal of the mining subsidy and the acceptance of a national wages agreement *simultaneously and concurrently* – was the only conceivable solution. Samuel's idea was backed by Ramsay MacDonald, Maynard Keynes, Lloyd George and many other people of middle-range opinion. Even the novelist Arnold Bennett, who opposed the strike, signed an appeal to Baldwin couched in these terms.[117] It was a promising bid for compromise but there was one major obstacle. Baldwin absolutely refused to countenance this tripartite solution. It meant he would have to dragoon the mine owners, which he had always declined to do, it would alienate the hawks in his cabinet and most of all it let the miners off the hook, since they did not have to agree to immediate wage cuts. Baldwin's position was that the miners had to accept wage cuts *before* anything else could even be talked about and he was prepared to tough matters out even in defiance of public opinion, which, it was clear, would have welcomed such a solution.[118] Besides, he was beginning to scent the possibility of a devastating victory over the unions without having to make *any* concessions. The longer the strike went on, the more hard line Baldwin became.

The issue soon sucked in the British Broadcasting Corporation, which had tried to remain aloof from the conflict. On 7 May Randall Davidson, the Archbishop of Canterbury, called for a settlement on the basis of Samuel's three points and demanded the right to broadcast on the BBC, setting out his thoughts.[119] This was instantly denied him by the young Director-General of the BBC, John Reith. To make sense of this development we have to retrace our steps to the period immediately before the outbreak of the strike. Realising the importance of the media in the moulding of public opinion, Baldwin had ordered the BBC to be turned into an auditory version of the *British Gazette*, pumping out pro-government and anti-union propaganda. His principal agent of control was J. C. C. Davidson, deputy civil commissioner, a veritable Pooh bear of the intellect who thought that the *Gazette* was a better newspaper than all mainstream newspapers.[120] The calibre of Davidson's mind may perhaps be gauged from his eulogy of Baldwin: '[He] had complete faith in the common sense and sanity of the working classes. Many of the talks we used to have during the coal strike and the months which preceded the General Strike always resulted in our agreement that the British would reject dictatorship, whether from the right or the left.'[121] Evidently Davidson considered Neville Chamberlain, Birkenhead, Joynson-Hicks and Churchill were moderates. He and Baldwin ordered Reith to come to heel and turn the BBC into a government puppet on pain of being taken over and 'commandeered'. A genuinely courageous man might have resisted or resigned, but that was not Reith's way. On the Saturday before the strike he collaborated with Baldwin in an embarrassing charade. Baldwin planned to 'make over' the public with a series of 'fireside chats' in which he would pose as an avuncular peacemaker beset by wild extremists. To set the scene Reith himself came on the air incognito, with consequences described by Beatrice Webb:

> Then in a stentorian voice some other person [i.e. not the announcer] gave this message, two or three times, each time with louder and more pompous emphasis 'Be steady, be steady' – pause – 'Remember that peace on earth comes to men of good will.' Perhaps if Baldwin himself, in his kindly and common sense accent, had spoken his own words the effect would have been different. But in the emissary's melodramatic shout it sounded not a little absurd. What is wanted is to face the facts with knowledge and determination. *Goodness* – i.e. diffused sympathy – is beside the mark. In a great crisis these sloppy emotions rouse irritation or contempt in the listeners to wireless – even to a far greater extent than readers – there is no contagious enthusiasm at the end of

> the 'phone; you listen coldly and critically to all that comes, and bathos is easily detected in the silence of your own sitting-room.[122]

Webb's critique was almost universally endorsed by intelligent listeners. The novelist Virginia Woolf complained that the BBC broadcast only absurdity, nonsense or trivia.[123]

When the strike began, Baldwin became a regular fixture on the airwaves. He told the nation that the strike was a revolutionary threat to the constitution and distinguished sharply between the miners' strike, which was legitimate if misguided, and the General Strike, which was illegal and unconstitutional: 'I am a man of peace . . . but I will not surrender the dignity of the constitution.'[124] Reith had always made much of the supposed independence of the BBC, from which it followed that the views of the other side should have been heard. Yet not only were the TUC and the miners denied airspace but so were middle-of-the-roaders and liberals such as Lloyd George and Ramsay MacDonald.[125] The greatest scandal arose over the Archbishop of Canterbury on 7 May. It was Davidson who told Reith that the archbishop's appeal could not be broadcast and ordered that there was to be no mention of it in the *British Gazette*.[126] The archbishop was angry and sent off an irate letter to Reith: 'Are we to understand that if the Churches desire to put something forth, their grave utterance must be subject to the approval of its wording by the Broadcasting Committee?'[127] The two Davidsons cordially loathed and despised each other, so that it is not surprising that the commissioner scoffed at his namesake's attempt to be 'statesmanlike', considered him a political meddler and described the archbishop's proposed broadcast message as 'weak and waffly.'[128] This was supremely disingenuous, since if the prelate's words really were so pathetic and inadequate, the smart move by the government would have been to give him the go-ahead so that he could discredit himself. The truth was that Archbishop Davidson's broadcast was supremely just, poised and rational, and it was just this which Baldwin and his henchmen could not abide. When Lloyd George raised the issue in the House of Commons and asked why the words of the leading cleric of the Church of England had not even been deemed worthy of inclusion in the *British Gazette*, Churchill replied to general guffaws that this was due to shortage of newsprint.[129] The real casualty from the incident was Reith. Although he swore up and down that he had done his best to be neutral and impartial during the strike, the reality was that he had bowed his head and done Baldwin's bidding. He was a frighteningly ambitious man, who had already set his sights on becoming viceroy of India, and there are those who have suggested that Baldwin encouraged him to think that such a reward might be his if he toed the line. In the privacy of his diaries Reith complained bitterly that Commissioner Davidson made all the decisions on censorship and he then had to carry them out and take the flak. He particularly objected to being the 'bad guy' when it was hawks like Churchill who would not allow him to be impartial.[130] He took his revenge by writing privately to Archbishop Davidson to tell him that he personally would have welcomed the broadcast but he was under orders from Commissioner Davidson. In the end, he ruefully admitted to his diary that he would have done better to let the BBC be 'commandeered'.[131] Reith received little gratitude from Baldwin. In return for writing and editing Baldwin's speeches, advising him on microphone technique and much else, he suffered the indignity of having Churchill unleashed on him, together with Baldwin's admonition that he should strive to make the BBC as much like the *British Gazette* as possible. When Reith demurred at this final indignity, Churchill suggested that an old war wound (in Reith's head) was affecting his reason.[132] Yet Reith cannot be absolved of all guilt for the poor showing of the BBC during the General Strike. As has been pointed out: 'In the privacy of his diary Reith railed against the bind he was in, without acknowledging that he had conspired with the government to achieve it.'[133] He also tried to justify his stance by saying he was unable to be more sympathetic to the strikers since the High Court had declared the strike illegal, but omitted to mention that this declaration did not come until the penultimate day of the strike.[134]

The entire Randall Davidson episode did far more harm, short-term, to the BBC's reputation than many historians have been prepared to admit. Even those Christians who thought the strikers mistaken thought them honest and sincere and were scandalised at the shabby treatment of the archbishop. Lord Astor told all who would listen that it was a grievous mistake to gag churchmen, since the government would need their full support in the anticipated future struggles with Mussolini and Stalin.[135] Even some sections of the Tory press became to grow disillusioned with Baldwin and his intransigence after the BBC affair.[136] There was a volume of middle-class protest, and the disgust evinced by Virginia Woolf in her diaries was an accurate barometer of intellectual opinion.[137] The cartoonist Low produced a memorable satire on the government, showing his contempt for the BBC's coverage with the following caption, burlesquing a BBC news broadcast: 'Mr Baldwin has eaten a good lunch and is hopeful . . . it is denied that the Albert Memorial has been wrecked. There will be several trains and the other six million of you can walk.'[138] Modern authorities have been just as severe on Reith and the network over which he presided. Here is Asa Briggs, doyen of broadcasting history: 'the low-water mark of the power and influence of the BBC'. And this is A. J. P. Taylor: 'The vaunted independence of the BBC was secure so long as it was not exercised.'[139] So appalled have most historians been by the bullying by Baldwin, Davidson and Churchill and the supine attitude of Reith that there has been, perhaps by a kind of compensation, a tendency to overplay the role of radio in the General Strike. It is often said that it was the second most crucial technological factor in 1926, after the motor car. This attitude may perhaps be traced to Beatrice Webb, who remarked on the first day of the strike that 'the sensation of a General Strike . . . centres round the headphones of the general set . . . One reiterated communication over the wireless is a solemn undertaking by the cabinet that all who return to work or accept work in these days of the community's peril will be permanently "protected and secured" in their employment – which implies "at the expense of the strikers".'[140] What can be safely said is that for those with radios the General Strike was the first major event in British history to make a real impact over the airwaves. But to make it a salient factor or in any way to attribute Baldwin's eventual victory to his skill (anticipating Franklin Roosevelt) at cosy 'one nation' chats is to overstate the influence of this medium at this juncture in British history. For one thing, only 2 million wireless sets existed in a population of 43 million.

15

Revolution's Last Chance

Saturday 8 May was the day when the government gained the upper hand in the strike. Already on the back foot from the legal threat announced by John Simon and the hostility of the BBC, the TUC was dealt a hammer blow when Baldwin deployed the army to break the four-day blockade of the London docks. All that week the government had been massing troops. Observers reported the roads and country lanes of Surrey choked with military vehicles, and there was a particular concentration in Hyde Park, which had been an unofficial army camp since the beginning of the strike. At 4.30 a.m. the operation to secure the London docks began. Baldwin claimed he had to order the operation as there were food shortages in London, with only forty-eight hours' supply of flour left, but the unions saw the action as gross provocation and an intimidating display of armed force.[1] A hundred and five army lorries sped to the Victoria Docks in the East End, all of them full of grenadier guards who had been issued with 150 rounds each. Accompanying them were twenty armoured cars. Once at the docks, the grenadiers dismounted to form a defence in depth while the lorries were loaded with food. By 7 a.m. the dock gates were secured and by 11.30 the entire convoy was on its way back to Hyde Park, which was converted into a gigantic food storage depot.[2] That afternoon a much larger convoy of 170 lorries made the same trip, and next day the entire docklands area was opened up by 267 trucks loaded with troops in an armed demonstration. There was no resistance from the pickets or the locals except for jeering and booing. Churchill exacerbated the situation by announcing that the military now had enough artillery assembled to kill every living soul in every single street in the capital and that troops had carte blanche to open fire; in effect they would have a licence to kill.[3] It was through his influence that the soldiers at the dockside trained machine guns on the watching crowd. This was too much for George V, who protested to Baldwin. Churchill was quietly reprimanded, and word went out that there were no 'shoot to kill' orders.[4] Nevertheless, the smashing of the blockade of the docks convinced many that the TUC was a paper tiger. Members of the General Council were despondent. It was now obvious that the 'short, sharp shock' strategy of a brief strike had failed, and that the TUC would have to settle in for a protracted struggle. This they manifestly lacked both the stomach and the necessary funds to undertake. Not only did morale sag badly over the weekend, but there were clear signs that the strike, if prolonged, might soon turn very ugly indeed.[5] The General Council did make a few lame attempts to respond to the government's coup de main. Electricians cut off all power to the London docks on Monday 10 May, imperilling both frozen meat and the water level in the docks, but after just twenty minutes power had been restored, being generated by batteries of six interconnected submarines.[6] Trotsky exulted that the unions' defeat at the docks was a classic of bourgeois perfidy. The restraint of the TUC, and their repeated demonstration that they did not have revolutionary aims, simply encouraged the government to act in a brutal way redolent of the role of the State as portrayed in the most far-fetched Red propaganda. Baldwin had made a poor requital for the General Council's moderation and showed that he would stop at nothing, and use any methods, to win the struggle.[7]

However, that Saturday was not without its lighter moments. How committed J. H. Thomas was to the cause of the Left was clearly shown by the lavish lunch party he attended at Wimborne House on 8 May, along with Osbert Sitwell, Lord Londonderry, Lord Gainsford (the Chairman of the BBC), ex-Viceroy Lord Reading and Philip Snowden's wife Ethel, whose activities so incensed Trotsky. According to Sitwell, the talk was so reactionary and inflammatory that the guests had to ask the servants to leave the room.[8] Meanwhile those members of the General Council who had chosen to remain at their desks prided themselves on taking decisive action when they turned down an offer of £26,247 from the trade unions of the Soviet Union, the first tranche in payments that were expected to reach £300,000. Their motive was obvious: to accept would be to hand the Tories a wonderful propaganda weapon and would allow the *British Gazette* to portray them as revolutionaries.[9] The serious aspect of this was that, as part of their general crackdown, the government had used its powers under emergency regulations to interrupt bank transfers by organisations deemed to be a danger to the constitution. This meant blocking cheques to the TUC. Lloyds Bank told Citrine that morning that £100,000 paid in by its supporters could not be credited.[10] If this was a grave development, the next item the General Council dealt with was closer to farce. Its members had earlier been approached by an army veteran who, for a payment of £1,000, offered to raise 100 armed men, all disgruntled veterans like himself, who would storm the cabinet rooms and assassinate all the cabinet. Pugh had at once dismissed the man as an obvious lunatic. It later transpired that he was a well-known fraudster and conman, specialising in getting money advances on wild promises.[11] Yet another incident that day seemed to some to take the General Strike closer to the world of opéra bouffe. In Plymouth a football match was arranged between strikers and police, which the strikers won 2–1. A French socialist reacted to the news in disgust: 'The British are not a nation – they are a circus.'[12] It is interesting that both sides in the conflict regarded the football match – reminiscent of the fraternisation of German and British troops in the trenches at Christmas 1914 – as a mistake. Churchill thought it undermined the *Gazette*'s daily message about fighting revolutionary forces and refused to print a report of the match. On the Left there was a feeling that such antics ran the risk of turning the struggle into farce or a Bank Holiday Punch and Judy show. The Labourite David Kirkwood thought that 'mateyness' of the police–striker kind insidiously weakened any notion of class struggle. 'A trifling inconvenience is resented because it usually only affects a few, but the dislocation caused by the General Strike was so universal that people laughed at each other's difficulties and their own. When I saw car-loads of girls driving through the streets of London looking upon the experience as if it were a picnic, I knew that we were beaten.'[13]

Yet in general the weekend saw the strike enter a new phase, with a much more hawkish attitude from the government in evidence and the TUC, partly as a consequence, flustered and at sea. It is one of the great, consoling myths of the General Strike that it was a peaceful affair. It is true that there was no loss of life but, from 8 May onwards, there were almost continual clashes between strikers and police. In the working-class ghettos of London, Glasgow and Edinburgh there was vicious and sustained rioting. In London the first major clash came at the Elephant and Castle, but there were ferocious riots in the East End. The police drew batons and charged on two successive nights in Poplar and Canning Town and at the Blackwall Tunnel. On Saturday 8 May there were baton charges in Battersea, Lambeth, Deptford, Paddington and Camden Town. At New Cross tram depot a vast crowd gathered to prevent the running of blackleg trams, and the demonstration was so successful that the would-be drivers never got onto the tracks. At Hammersmith there was a running battle between strikers and fascists.[14] In some ways the violence in the provinces and Scotland was even more dramatic. In Edinburgh and Glasgow there were violent scenes for five nights with hundreds of arrests; Aberdeen also saw trouble. The north-east was another black spot, with serious riots in Middlesbrough, Newcastle, Darlington, Gateshead, York (where the crowd tried to release a prisoner), Leeds (an ugly confrontation between police and 5,000 rioters) and Hull. Other outbreaks occurred in Barnsley, Burnley, Wolverhampton, Ipswich, Plymouth (perhaps significantly, on the very day of the famous police v. strikers' football match), Southsea, Swansea, Cardiff, Newark, Mansfield and Nottingham. In Preston 5,000 people charged the police station to release an arrested striker and were beaten back only after repeated baton charges. In Doncaster a thousand-strong crowd took to stopping the traffic and had to be cleared away by a baton charge.[15] The attempt to run buses caused a lot of trouble from stone-throwing mobs, though such incidents were inevitably written up by government propaganda. Virginia Woolf took a bus journey, expecting the experience to resemble travelling by stage coach in the frontier period of the Wild West, but was disappointed to find that it passed without incident.[16] Shots were fired at a train at Crewe, and on the line between Durham and Newcastle there occurred the only act of sabotage when the locomotive *Merry Hampton*, drawing the Flying Scotsman train service, was derailed. The *British Gazette*, sensing a propaganda coup, took advantage of the confusion between the Flying Scotsman service and the famous record-breaking locomotive of that name, and claimed that it was the loco, a national treasure, that had been crippled.[17] In general, government disinformation liked to stress that the increasing incidence of train crashes, the natural consequence of the inexperience of the engine drivers, was always due to sabotage. In light of Merseyside's reputation for industrial unrest, it is perhaps curious that Liverpool had a poor record of militancy during the strike, but this was mainly a consequence of the dominant seamen's union's having refused to join the action.[18]

The violence that occurred was largely (though not exclusively) caused by the government crackdown, beginning on the weekend on 8–9 May, occasioned by the (correct) belief that the Baldwin administration was winning the struggle. The government could draw on almost infinite powers under the Emergency Powers Act. Although the Orders in Council, especially the notorious Order 13A denying the unions access to their own money, had to be given parliamentary approval, this was a formality with the government's huge majority. The result was that Baldwin and his cabinet could do all of the following: seize land, buildings and food; commandeer all vehicles and issue special licences to allow buses and trains to be driven by volunteer labour; take over the docks, railways, shipping, mines, power stations, petrol; control the supply of electricity, gas and water; prohibit public meetings; declare any overtures to police and soldiers by the strikers ipso facto criminal acts; undertake the most sweeping searches and seizures.[19] In effect the rule of law had broken down: the definition of legality was whatever the government said it was, and this was in a context where judges and lawyers were still solemnly giving particular reasons as to why the General Strike was illegal. The rationale for all this was supposed to be that the TUC was mounting a revolutionary threat to the constitution; the palpable falsity of this was such that even pro-government newspapers started deriding the claim as nonsense.[20] Yet the government by the weekend had the bit between its teeth and seemed to be going out of its way to produce the very revolutionary situation it was denouncing. There was talk among the hawks that the best thing to do was to engineer the ascendancy of the hard Left and the eclipse of Thomas, Citrine, Bevin and the other right-wing unionists so that armed force could be used to crush the 'revolution' decisively. Recruitment of the Special Constabulary rocketed from 98,000 at the beginning of the strike to 226,000 by the end.[21] Joynson-Hicks made a broadcast appealing for another 50,000 special constables, then produced a sabre-rattling exhortation in the *British Gazette*: 'Protection is the one thing which will kill the strike and restore England to its normal life . . . Give the government enough Special Constables to enable me to allot two to every vehicle . . . thus releasing the regular police for perhaps sterner work. Give us men in numbers that we may have mobile forces of young and vigorous Special Constables available in any London area where trouble is anticipated.'[22] A new paramilitary body, the Civil Constabulary Reserve (CCS), was recruited, with 18,000 steel-helmeted members. OMS instructions gave its recruits to understand that any deaths they meted out in the course of their duties would be regarded as 'justifiable homicide'. Jix was prepared to pay all his myrmidons – whether special constables, CCS or (yet another body of irregulars) the Metropolitan Emergency Constables – 5s a day as a constable and 10s a day as an officer, a sum well above the daily pay for a miner even in the pre-cuts halcyon days.[23]

Without question policing became noticeably more heavy-handed from 8 May onwards, in contrast to the first four days of the strike, when such tension as there was between constables and strikers was largely engineered by police brought in from the outside and thus new to a locality and its folkways. In the early days it was frequently asserted that the shared experience in the trenches in 1914–18 enabled police and unionists tacitly to make common cause, and ex-servicemen wearing medals was said to be a shibboleth, protecting them from any possibility of police brutality.[24] This was no longer the case after the weekend of 8–9 May, when the police seemed to go out of their way to be harsh and provocative. Part of the problem was that weak and indecisive regional commissioners tended to call them in at the first sign of difficulty instead of sorting out the problem themselves. The correct way to proceed was demonstrated in Lincoln, where the sympathetic chief constable refused the help of troops or mounted police and cooperated with the strike committee, which provided all the special constables.[25] This of course infuriated the hard liners in Baldwin's cabinet, as in their minds such cooperation implied that the government had lost control and the TUC was running things. The more usual pattern was that evinced in Brighton and Edinburgh, where the chief constables were outrageously provocative.[26] Sometimes well-meaning but inept commissioners began by acting dovishly, and then switched to asperity when things did not work out as they had planned.

In Northumberland and Durham the communist strike committee organiser Robin Page Arnot initially worked in a friendly, harmonious way with Sir Kingsley Wood, a protégé of Neville Chamberlain and the region's special commissioner (later to be a chancellor of the exchequer).[27] However, Wood soon lost control of the situation, largely because he would not accede to the strikers' demand that he refrain from using blackleg labour. There was also the complication of lack of liaison between civil and military authorities. The Royal Navy (whether or not at the government's behest is not clear) had decided to station two destroyers and submarines in the Tyne, and the unions declared that in no circumstances would they unload ships, even if the blacklegs were removed, unless the warships put to sea. Affronted, Wood worked himself into a lather and unleashed calculated police brutality, intending to show Arnot that what he could not get by consensus he would get by force.[28] Naturally strikers did not take kindly to this high-handed attitude by the police, struck back, and as a consequence swelled the growing number of arrests. Altogether around 4,000 arrests were made out of 3 million strikers, 1,000 of the arrests being of communists. There were daily raids on 'Reds', either at the Communist Party's headquarters in King Street or at private addresses. The first arrest of a member of parliament occurred when the communist Shapurji Saklatvala refused to be bound over to keep the peace and was sentenced to two months in Wormwood Scrubs for sedition.[29] There were 3,149 prosecutions for incitement to sedition, violence and incitement to violence, though the flimsy nature of the charges contrasted with the cavalier attitude displayed by the authorities to the rule of law, with 604 of the 4,000 arrests being made without a warrant. In Glasgow some 230 men were arrested for 'impeding traffic' and 100 of them sentenced to an average of three months' imprisonment.[30] Arrests and sentencing tended to be particularly draconian in the trouble spots of Scotland and north-eastern England, which accounted for 1,760 of the 4,000 arrests.[31] But there was rough justice everywhere. The disturbances at Doncaster were little more than a brawl, yet 84 brawlers got three-month sentences. In Birmingham the entire strike committee was arrested, while in Aberavon three men were jailed for two months simply for having communist literature in their possession.[32]

The upper hand gained by the government over the weekend was all the more pronounced since the General Council continued to turn in its usual lacklustre performance, playing dog in the manger, doing little except wring its hands at the police crackdown, but being much more exercised by the possible loss of its own powers in the localities as its credibility with the workers lessened. It was the besetting fault of all Labour Party executives and all bureaucratised Labour institutions: obsession with the far Left at the expense of collaboration against the common enemy. Jimmy Thomas characteristically identified 400 trade councils where he feared communist influence; particular attention was drawn to the 5 communists on the 12-strong executive of the London Trades Council.[33] Unwilling to allow Bevin to act as strike supremo – for that might imply that the TUC was an enthusiastic rather than a reluctant participant in the strike – the General Council fussed neurotically over 'Red' influence while local strike committees got on with the real work of organising the strike. Another problem was the multiplicity of committees, some of them overlapping. Nomenclature was considered important. Fifty-four towns boasted councils of action; seventy-seven others had strike committees or emergency committees. These were usually complex organisations embracing the local trade council executive committees, representatives of the various unions and members of the Labour Party, with the detailed work of issuing permits, picketing, arranging publicity, a courier service and liaison with London devolved to subcommittees.[34] The most important task of the strike committees was issuing permits for the movement of food and other essential items, and to the fury of government supporters in the regions lorries and cars were driven around with 'By Permission of the TUC' prominently displayed where modern vehicles would exhibit a tax disc. The General Council's decision to grant permits for essential services was controversial, as it was too dependent on subjective perception. Granting food permits to delivery drivers was a prized perk, but there was an obvious opportunity for corruption.[35] Moreover, there were no checks on the transport of goods once the permits were granted, so that many of those granted the necessary licence transported luxury and inessential items instead.[36] Instead of clarifying matters, the General Council further muddied the waters by deciding (on 7 May) to revoke the permits. Their decree to this effect was widely disregarded, and in any event it exacerbated the already dreadful relations between the TUC and the Cooperative Wholesale Society. On the eve of the strike the CWS had urged its retail societies to withhold credit from the miners because of their previous debts but, like all centrally issued decrees in 1926, this one was widely disregarded. Those local coops which had collaborated with the strikers by providing credit vouchers for food or advancing 'subs' in advance of strike pay felt that the General Council had slapped them in the face.[37]

Although the received opinion is that the General Strike was all a bit of a lark, that it showed the British inability to take anything seriously and that the would-be general stoppage was nothing more than, in Beatrice Webb's words, 'a cricket match . . . a batch of compulsory Bank Holidays without any opportunity for recreation and a lot of dreary walking to and fro',[38] it seems clear that by the weekend of 8–9 May something like a pre-revolutionary situation had been reached. The threat of major violence and loss of life hung heavily in the air, a consequence both of the government crackdown and the lack of leadership by the General Council. Lunching at the Reform Club and sounding the opinions of members, Arnold Bennett reported: 'General opinion that fight will be short but violent. Bloodshed anticipated next week.'[39] J. H. Thomas told his TUC colleagues with a kind of grim satisfaction that the hotheads were going to have their way and there would soon be blood on the streets. He painted an apocalyptic scenario, with a serious police–striker clash going badly wrong, the TUC totally losing control of the situation, troops being called in, strikers machine-gunned, union leaders imprisoned, punitive legislation, expropriation of trade-union assets and, with the General Council all in jail, leaderless workers generating spontaneous risings in the provinces.[40] Thomas was disregarded because he had cried wolf so often before, but this did not mean his analysis was necessarily wrong. Some observers thought that sheer boredom and frustration would lead the workers to find some way to arm themselves. Another factor was that the knock-on effects of the strike were causing unemployment even in small industries and businesses supposedly unconcerned with the strike; by 10 May unemployment had risen in the city of York from 1,363 to 4,301 in just a week among non-strikers.[41] Dissatisfaction with TUC leadership was certainly general, with water and electricity workers threatening to join the strike whatever the General Council ordered. Worries about spontaneous combustion were entertained on both sides of the divide. Churchill's deputy Ronald

McNeil, financial secretary to the Treasury, said the country was nearer to civil war than for centuries.[42] Harold Laski was certain that serious violence with loss of life would be an inevitable concomitant once the second wave of strikers was called out.[43] The deliberate escalation of police activity was a very risky, and even reckless, strategy on Baldwin's part. And what would happen if soldiers took seriously Churchill's words that they had a licence to kill? Would not any loss of life from military gunfire in itself ignite a major conflagration? Conversely, what would happen if troops were ordered to open fire but refused to execute their kith and kin? The possibility of an army mutiny was the government's ultimate nightmare. The real danger in the General Strike was that nobody had a real grip on the situation and there was no real mind at work on either side, thinking five or six steps ahead in a counterfactual way. Most thoughtful obervers took an 'a plague on both your houses' attitude to both the TUC and the government, viewing them as equally responsible for the mess the country was in after almost a week of the strike. Yaffle of the *Daily Mail* summed up a general attitude of contempt for the General Council on all sides when he remarked scathingly that Britain would never have a revolution for, as soon as Baldwin said the strike was illegal, the TUC folded its tents and went home.[44] The influential Catholic journalist and writer G. K. Chesterton, always plugging his pet notion of distributism, a third way between capitalism and socialism, put the blame for the General Strike entirely at Baldwin's door and accused him of being deliberately confrontational.[45] His *The Return of Don Quixote* dealt with the strike allegorically, but in his publication *Chesterton's Weekly* he named Baldwin as the guilty man. In *Quixote* he portrayed Baldwin witheringly as Michael Herne and said of him: 'Everything is too simple to him . . . He will succeed . . . a new sort of history will have begun . . . (with) a sword that divides. It is not England.'[46]

The world looked on in amazement as Britain seemed paralysed, deadlocked between the irresistible force of Baldwin's government demanding unconditional surrender and the immovable object of the miners, with their slogan 'Not a penny off the pay, not a minute on the day'. In France the General Strike swamped all other international news and most national reporting as well. Whereas French correspondents based in Britain were remarkably impartial in their copy, opinion in France itself was more critical, with financiers particularly upset about the tumbling value of the franc as the run on sterling manifested 'spin-off' effects, and government sources solemnly declaring that this was the most dangerous crisis for Europe since the Great War.[47] German trade unions pointedly offered their British brethren no help – a move generally interpreted as tit-for-tat, as the TUC had remained inactive when the French invaded the Ruhr in 1923. The Italians were more jubilant. Mussolini announced that the strike meant the end not just for that sham creation, parliamentary democracy, but for the British Empire itself, which would soon be supplanted by an Italian one.[48] American newspaper reporting tended towards the sensational with (inaccurate) headlines such as these: 'Dictator Rule in Britain in Strike' and 'Martial Law Status Proclaimed in Britain'. Insofar as the strike was taken seriously, it was taken to be a sign of the inevitable decline of the deeply unpopular British Empire. Eyebrows were raised at the closing of so many British offices and the departure of their middle-class employees for continental holidays, evincing a most unPuritan work ethic. The *New York Times* backed Baldwin 100 per cent, claiming that Wall Street was alarmed by the declining value of sterling on the markets.[49] Intriguingly, the British media seemed increasingly to lose interest even as the strike reached crisis point. Attention was diverted to other big news of the day: the touring Australian cricketers, in England to win the Ashes (they lost), had matches against Essex, Surrey and Hampshire during the nine days of the strike. But the most fascinating non-strike news story was Amundsen's flight in the airship *Norge* from Spitzbergen to Alaska on 10–13 May, making Amundsen the first man to have reached both North and South Poles.[50] Back at home, Sunday 9 May was a typical British Sunday, with little attempt made by anyone except the indefatigable Herbert Samuel to find a solution to the strike. Baldwin visited the zoo in Regent's Park, which was thought by some to show contempt for the strikers and to denote a frivolous attitude to his responsibilities.[51] Yet the truly sensational development was the sermon delivered in Westminster Cathedral by the leader of the Catholic Church in Britain, Cardinal Francis Bourne, Archbishop of Westminster. Bourne, who had been elevated to the purple at the age of fifty in 1911 and enjoyed a 32-year reign over the archdiocese of Westminster was a protégé of Pope Pius XI (1922–39), who had a reputation as a reactionary pope.[52] The truth is more complex. It is true that he signed the concordat with Mussolini in the 1929 Lateran treaties, but in 1937 he would issue a blistering condemnation of Nazism in his encyclical *Mit Brennender Sorge*. Attempting to steer a middle course between the great competing ideologies, in his famous encyclical *Quadragesimo Anno* (1931) Pius denounced both Marxism and revolutionary socialism on one hand and unbridled capitalism on the other. Unfortunately Bourne, and his acolyte Bishop Peter Amigo of Southwark, were far more right-wing than the pope (Amigo was a notorious supporter of General Franco in the Spanish Civil War), ignored his strictures on capitalism, but took up with relish Pius's statement that no one could be both a Catholic and a socialist (as opposed to a social democrat). In a truly shameful effusion from the pulpit Bourne announced that the current strike was 'a sin against the obedience which we owe to God' and that Baldwin's government was 'the lawfully constituted authority of the country and represents . . . in its own appointed sphere the authority of God himself'.[53] Needless to say, these remarks were reported in full in the *British Gazette* and on the BBC. The contrast with the treatment meted out to the Archbishop of Canterbury could hardly have been more glaring.

By the morning of Monday 10 May the General Council had reached the point of being desperate to call off the strike, if they could only find a way to do it without sacrificing their credibility, abandoning the miners and incurring the charge of having presided over another Red Friday. There were alarming rumours about government intentions: calling up army reservists, arresting the members of the General Council and the local strike committees, impounding and expropriating *all* union funds.[54] It was known that Baldwin was under extreme pressure from the hawks, with Neville Chamberlain foremost. 'The best and kindest thing,' said Chamberlain, 'is to strike hard and quickly.'[55] The government did intend to move decisively against the TUC but via the law, through making all sympathetic strikes illegal. Most of 10 May was spent in detailed discussions about the precise wording of the bill to be rushed through Parliament, but by late afternoon there was a complete about-turn. Baldwin told his colleagues that the king had vetoed the proposal in the strongest possible terms, fearing it would fan the flames of revolution.[56] Meanwhile on the General Council Thomas and John Bromley were pressing hard for the miners to be cut adrift. Bromley declared: 'I am willing to fight right along with them [the miners] and to suffer as a consequence, but I am not going to be strangled by my friends.' When he heard this, an exasperated Herbert Smith replied: 'If he wants to get out of this fight, well, I am not going to stop him.'[57] The defeatist triumvirate of Thomas, Bromley and Pugh continued to utter warnings of the dire consequences if a settlement was not reached soon, but Citrine comforted himself with the generally good humour induced by the weather, which had been bright and sunny except for a curious patch on the afternoon of 5 May when a thick brown fog enveloped London.[58] Great hopes were set on Samuel, but his early reports were not encouraging. When Herbert Smith and A. J. Cook met him on 10 May, they found him spluttering with fury at the mine owners' reaction to his intervention. Far from making concessions, they were demanding much steeper wage reductions than recommended by the Royal Commission, and this at a time when Samuel was seeking for further compromise. Once again the two Herberts (Smith and Samuel) engaged in a lot of friendly badinage, but Samuel made it clear that he thought Smith, not Cook, was the real obstacle to peace when he remarked: 'When it is a case of Herbert versus Herbert, then there is bound to be a tug of war.'[59] From these talks emerged the famous Samuel memorandum, later the subject of bitter disputation. It proposed a renewal of the subsidy pending further negotiations; a national wages board under an impartial chairman; and no revision of wages until the new board was satisfied that the government would 'effectively adopt' reorganisation in the mining industry. To humour Smith, Samuel added that it would be a fixed condition that the wages of the lowest-paid miners would not be lowered. The inevitable issue of wage cuts in general was fudged at this stage, as Samuel wanted the miners to sign up to the memorandum. With their agreement to the document he could put Baldwin on the spot. Smith agreed to consider the memorandum once he had called a delegate meeting of the MFGB.[60]

The irrepressible Thomas found all this too good an opportunity to miss and jumped the gun in spectacular fashion. Either with a mandate from the negotiating committee or on his own initiative (it is not entirely clear which) he used his entrée into government circles and held man-to-man talks with Baldwin. While conceding nothing, Baldwin was happy to have this unique insight into thinking on the General Council. Thomas surpassed himself in duplicity this time, playing both sides against the middle. He told Baldwin that the miners would accept wage cuts if the government in turn accepted the rest of the Samuel memorandum. He then told the General Council that Samuel was making proposals at the behest of the government, even though Samuel had already told Arthur Pugh that he was acting entirely on his own initiative. Both statements were flat lies. But Thomas was determined to brazen it out, hoping that he could somehow 'bounce' both sides into compromise and he could then don the halo of peacemaker. Under questioning by the General Council he stated categorically that the negotiating committee had secured withdrawal of the lockout notices and the resumption of work at the old wages.[61] He and Bromley meanwhile started a campaign of disinformation to the effect that there had been a significant drift back to work by the strikers – another grotesque falsehood. His Machiavellianism was in vain. On 11 May the MFGB finally and categorically rejected the Samuel memorandum. Smith pointed out (correctly) that the issue of wage cuts had been fudged, that the memorandum did not contain clear and explicit guarantees on reorganisation and the withdrawal of lockout notices. He was scathing about Thomas's secret meetings with Samuel and Baldwin: 'I don't understand what has been going on in these conversations. I don't believe in these methods and I protest about the miners not being consulted. Why should a decision be taken tonight? Have you committed us to anything?'[62] Thomas exhorted the miners to change their mind but they were adamant, and he was reduced to the somewhat piteous pleas with reference to Samuel: 'You may not trust my word, but will you not accept the word of a British gentleman who has been Governor of Palestine?'[63] Smith and Cook replied that a gentleman's word was irrelevant; what mattered was binding guarantees that Baldwin would *have* to carry out. The miners' inflexibility was understandable but was a tactical mistake. Their scepticism was warranted, as even the General Council was sceptical that Samuel could deliver the goods.[64] But the miners' refusal to countenance the Samuel memorandum once again let Baldwin off the hook. If they had accepted it, the prime minister would have been in an almost impossible position, faced with either risking the wrath of public opinion through intransigence or precipitating a cabinet revolt in which Birkenhead, Churchill, Chamberlain, Salisbury, Joynson-Hicks and Steel-Maitland would all have taken part. Acceptance of the memorandum would certainly have secured the MFGB better terms than it eventually gained.[65] And it handed the propaganda advantage to the other side, enabling both the government and the TUC to say that the miners' obstinacy was the only real obstacle to peace. As Harold Laski wrote to the eminent American jurist Felix Frankfurter about the 'impossibility' of the miners: 'They never budged an inch throughout. They have no plans, and if they had their way, the TUC would be out until Domesday. Even now they have nothing to say except that they won't budge. I have certainly never seen more hopeless (though more courageous) leadership than theirs.'[66] Blaming the miners also allowed Thomas to indulge in more of his eccentric behaviour – sometimes so bizarre that Citrine seriously thought he was cracking up. Thomas and Bromley said openly that the miners were selfish and solipsistic, with no regard for the wider union movement. Histrionically he declared that he had had enough and that he was going back to 'his own people' (the railwaymen).[67] Bromley cried out that he and Thomas intended to take their men back to work unilaterally if the strike was not called off. 'Take them back,' shouted Herbert Smith defiantly. Bevin made a futile final intervention with what some considered an attempt to bully Smith, but the burly West Countryman met his match in the burly Yorkshireman.[68]

The General Council originally wanted to call off the strike on the evening of 11 May, partly to forestall the emergence of the second wave which Bevin had instituted; now that the TUC was determined to cut its losses and accept whatever terms it could secure, escalation of the dispute was the last thing they needed. But the miners insisted there had to be further talks between the MFGB and the General Council, even though it was difficult to see what the two sides had to talk about any longer.[69] Bevin and Thomas were both vehement that their members had suffered grievous losses on the miners' behalf, that the miners were ingrates who seemed to think they had a divine right to be supported through thick and thin, and that enough was enough. In both the NUR and the TGWU the issue of superannuation rights had suddenly come to the fore, as the strikers realised that their actions might have serious pension implications.[70] The

General Council was now determined to use the Samuel memorandum as the fig-leaf with which to clothe their humiliation. If they could go to Baldwin and get his agreement to proceed on the basis of the memorandum, they hoped they could still the increasingly vociferous taunts from the miners that they were being sold out.[71] The General Council held a plenary session at 6 p.m. on Tuesday 11 May to decide the details of their approach to Baldwin, but were forced to postpone an actual visit to Downing Street when Smith and the miners requested yet another meeting, which was held at 8 p.m. At the meeting Smith waved a copy of the Samuel memorandum in the air and said his executive would retire to make its final decision on it.[72] But before leaving, he fired this Parthian shot: 'Do you people realise the serious position you are putting yourselves in? Are you going back without any consideration for the men who are going to be victimised in this movement? Are you not going to consider that at all?'[73] While they were gone, Bevin began to express doubts about the direction in which Thomas was nudging the General Council. Suppose the miners returned to say they accepted the memorandum, but Baldwin then refused to accept it? What guarantees were there from the government? And if the strike was called off, who would guarantee that there would be no workplace victimisation? Even Citrine began to be convinced for, as he put it: 'I do not feel that we should hand ourselves over body and soul to Baldwin.'[74] All this seemed somewhat academic when Smith and the miners returned just before midnight to give their final veto. Smith said they could not accept the document as it stood, and if the General Council wanted to do so, they must accept full responsibility and state this in writing. Citrine recorded that this made 'a nasty impression', but it was quite clear that the MFGB wanted to cast all the blame onto the TUC so that they would not face censure from their own delegates.[75] Amazingly, Bevin proposed yet another meeting with the miners next morning, claiming that an eleventh-hour breakthrough was still not impossible. As the talk went on, with the clock creeping up to 1 a.m., a phone message came through from 10 Downing Street. The prime minister's secretary spoke to Citrine and said that Baldwin had been sitting up long past his usual bedtime, hoping for some tidings from the TUC. Did the General Council have any news for him?[76] The reality was that Thomas had primed Baldwin about the TUC's imminent abject surrender, but not about the postponement, so the prime minister was mystified that the expected white flag had not appeared. Citrine rang off, went upstairs to the council room at Eccleston Square, consulted with his colleagues, then rang Number 10 back with word that the General Council would go to see the prime minister at noon the next day. This was accepted as a firm commitment by both sides. As Citrine went to bed at 2 a.m., he reflected that his phone call effectively signalled the end of the General Strike.[77]

Next morning, after another predictably futile meeting between Bevin, plus a six-man TUC delegation, and the miners, when they adamantly refused to change their stance, the members of the negotiating committee made their way to Downing Street. Bevin was slightly late for the colloquy with Baldwin and had to make a fast cab journey from the MFGB headquarters at Russell Square to Number 10. He caught up with his colleagues (Ben Turner, Pugh, Swales, Citrine and Thomas) in an ante-room, where it became apparent that Baldwin was determined on his pound of flesh. Sir Horace Wilson told the deputation that they would not be admitted to the prime minister's presence unless they gave a cast-iron guarantee that the only reason for their presence was to call off the strike. Bevin was angry at this contemptuous treatment and exclaimed: 'For Christ's sake let's call it on again if this is the position.'[78] Jimmy Thomas replied emolliently that the committee had come to call the strike off and should not be diverted from their objective by rudeness from Wilson and or Baldwin. The hapless delegation was then ushered into Baldwin's presence to announce the surrender. With Baldwin were most of the hard liners – Birkenhead, Neville Chamberlain, Steel-Maitland, Bridgeman, Worthington-Evans – determined to squeeze the last drop of pleasure from the humiliation of their humbled foe.[79] As Birkenhead later noted: 'It was so humiliating that some instinctive breeding made one unwilling even to look at them. I thought of the burghers of Calais approaching their interview with Edward III, haltered on the neck.'[80] Arthur Pugh then made a long, rambling statement which wound up with the following: 'We are here today, sir, to say that this general strike is to be terminated forthwith in order that negotiations may proceed, and we can only hope may proceed in a manner which will bring about a satisfactory settlement.' Baldwin replied with a statement that in the light of his subsequent actions cannot be regarded as other than the purest humbug: 'All I would say in answer to this is that I thank God for your decision . . . I shall lose no time in using every endeavour to get the two contending parties together and do all I can to ensure a just and lasting settlement.'[81] Thomas said he needed the prime minister's help to prevent what he called 'guerrilla warfare' – his abiding fear that the strikers would ignore the TUC's treachery and carry on regardless. It was clear that he was desperate to end the strike on almost any terms and to that end was willing to waive all talk about the Samuel memorandum, lockout notices, miners' pay and protection against victimisation of workers returning to their jobs. It is often said that in the face of a terrible emergency, a plane crash, say, only 10 per cent of those involved can react with anything other than panic. The atmosphere that day was like that, with all the members of the negotiating committee except Bevin seemingly paralysed by the enormity of the situation they now found themselves in.[82] The only person on the TUC side who kept his head and pressed Baldwin for some genuine guarantees on his intentions was Bevin. Sharply he posed the question of positive reassurances on reinstatement for the strikers and resumption of negotiations with the miners. Baldwin brushed this aside with bromides and, when Bevin persisted, bridled and replied pompously: 'You know my record. I think it may be that whatever decision I come to, the House of Commons may be the best place in which to say it.'[83]

Almost before they could recover their wits, the members of the negotiating committee were out in the corridor. For the first time Bevin realised the extent of Thomas's knavery. The negotiating committee had agreed a threefold programme: call off the strike, negotiate on the Samuel memorandum, and resume work in an orderly manner with no victimisation. To his stupefaction it now transpired that the other members of the committee had lamely allowed Baldwin to cherrypick the single issue of the ending of the strike without the other matters which were supposed to be its corollary.[84] It seemed to Bevin that without a guarantee on victimisation the TUC had effectively committed suicide. He told his colleagues before leaving: 'Thousands of men will be victimised as a result of this day's work.' Later that day, as he realised how deeply the General Council had been duped by Thomas's oft-repeated assertion that Samuel was acting as the government's unofficial agent, he told all who would listen that he had been 'sold a bill of goods' and had voted to end the strike on the basis of wholly false information.[85] The naivety of the other members of the negotiating committee and their inability to see through Jimmy Thomas were evinced by the correspondence published in the *British Worker* next day – including the full text of the Samuel memorandum and the letters exchanged between Samuel and Pugh on the subject – which concluded with the following ingenuous declaration: 'They (the General Council) assume that during the resumed negotiations the subsidy will be renewed and the lockout notices to the miners will be immediatedly withdrawn.' Incredible as it may sound, all the committee but Bevin still trusted Baldwin.[86] How treacherous Baldwin was became clear late that afternoon when he issued the following communiqué: 'His Majesty's Government have no power to compel employers to take back every man who has been on strike, nor have they entered any obligation of any kind on this matter.'[87] Few members of the public would have read this obscure pronouncement but millions heard the bogus avuncular Baldwin on the radio when he announced: 'Our business is not to triumph over those who failed in a mistaken attempt.' The public was also reassured when the king appealed for an end to all bitterness on 13 May.[88] Baldwin craftily left it until 14 May before expressly repudiating the Samuel memorandum – the first clear indication of the direction he really meant to take. Meanwhile in his circle triumphalism was the order of the day – and, sadly, that circle included the reformist trio of the Labour Party, Thomas, Snowden and Ramsay MacDonald. Thomas openly praised the 'settlement' (he refrained from calling it unconditional surrender), and MacDonald noted in his diary: 'Thomas rang me and spoke through tears. He has been photographed with the railway managers and feels that the old happy world has returned.'[89] Birkenhead, Thomas's trans-class chum, was especially delighted about the turn of events. He declared that the failure of the strike proved once again that 'old England' could always defeat all enemies: it had seen off the pope in the sixteenth century, the Jacobites in the eighteenth, Napoleon in the nineteenth and now revolutionary socialism in the twentieth.[90]

Among the proletariat the news that the strike had been called off was greeted with stupefaction, incredulity and then anger. The broadcast information that strikers should stay out until their individual unions told them to return to work also had people scratching their heads. The truth was that the TUC was so keen to end the strike on any terms that it had made no contingency plans for a resumption of working, sketched out no administrative plans for the post-strike period or indeed sent out any instructions whatsoever. That evening telegrams flooded into Citrine's office asking to know the terms of the settlement. Citrine could not tell them that there were none so opted for being incommunicado.[91] The General Council disingenuously implied that it had secured terms from the government and nowhere admitted that the miners had rejected the Samuel memorandum, which might have alerted the nation's labour force to what was really going on. That Thomas and his colleagues should have capitulated unconditionally seemed so incredible that at first such an idea was discounted. After all, the strike was still rock solid, with little signs of the drift back to work claimed both by the government and Thomas and his henchmen.[92] Gradually it was realised that the TUC had betrayed not just the miners but the entire body of strikers. The result was what has sometimes been called 'the second general strike', beginning on 13 May, when working-class anger manifested itself in a second round of stoppages, including ones by people who had not previously been on strike: 100,000 more employees were on strike than had been out during the 'Nine Days' themselves.[93] For a day or two the possibility of civil war or revolution was probably higher than it had ever been. Baldwin's government, like the Bourbons, seemed to have learned nothing and forgotten nothing. Onto this tinder box they heaped petrol, in the form of a long food convoy sent through the streets of London on the 13th, flanked by armoured cars and soldiers. That evening in Poplar the police went one better by breaking up a peaceful protest meeting with savage baton charges.[94] For two or three days the strike was resumed under the direction of local strike committees. The Cardiff committee cabled the General Council to call the strike back on but received the ludicrous general statement: 'Stand together' – whatever that meant in the present context, and despite the fact that this was precisely what the General Council had not done.[95] Citrine contented himself with bromides – the General Strike had been 'the most magnificent effort of rank-and-file solidarity that the British movement has ever displayed' – and tried to put all the blame on the miners. He disingenuously implied that the TUC had negotiated a cancellation of the lockout notices but that the miners had refused to accept the deal Samuel proposed, so it was not after all the case that the General Council had sustained a terrible defeat. From now on, he averred, any large-scale stoppage would have to be conducted by the TUC without the veto power the miners had claimed in this one.[96] A moment's consideration ought to have told him that, after the debacle of the Nine Days, no credible union would ever be able to trust the TUC again.

The extent of the General Council's failure can scarcely be exaggerated. Its members were involved in a double betrayal, for while the council betrayed the working class, Jimmy Thomas betrayed them. As one writer summed the situation up: 'The strikers numbered among themselves several mules and fools but only one traitor.'[97] There was at every level in the TUC a quite staggering inability to think through the implications of a general strike. The General Council seemed to rely wholly on a mixture of bluff and primitive deterrence theory. As in all such theories, the weapons were not supposed to be used but, whereas the theory might work in a context of mutually assured destruction, what was supposed to be the Armageddon the government was terrified of? Since the TUC went out of its way to reiterate that it had no revolutionary aims, it should never have become involved in a collective action whose logic pointed remorselessly in that direction. Herbert Morrison summed up the situation in a way Trotsky might have approved (save for his concluding seventeen words):

> A General Strike beginning as an industrial struggle, if carried to the bitter end, and if it is to be successful, must become a physical force, revolutionary struggle aiming at the forcible overthrow of the constitutional government and the seizing of power by the General Council of the TUC. Nobody believes that the General Council contemplated or wished any such thing, and nobody with half a brain believes that in Great Britain such a policy could be successful.[98]

A general strike's best chance of victory over a modern government lay in the paralysing of all transport. Twenty years earlier such a strategy might have worked, but the advent of the automobile meant that transport was not dependent merely on public, union-controlled modalities like the railways and buses. The motor car was Baldwin's secret weapon, and, given its existence an intelligent General Council should have seen that not even a non-revolutionary 'national strike' (to use the TUC's preferred nomenclature) would be able to bring the government to its knees. No such thinking went on and insofar as there was risk assessment, the General Council all seemed bewitched by the myth of Red Friday and to regard it as a shibboleth. As Beatrice Webb scathingly remarked: 'They play at revolution and they run away from the consequences with equal alacrity.'[99] Moreover, the TUC repudiated its own 'inflexible' resolution of 1 May that there would be no victimisation or, as the wording of their communiqué ran: 'in the event of any action being taken and Trade Union agreeements being placed in jeopardy, it will be definitely agreed that there will be no general resumption of work until those agreeements are fully recognised'.[100] The irony of Jimmy Thomas's betrayal over victimisation was that, the miners excepted, the railwaymen bore the brunt of employers' post-strike vindictive actions. The stoppage of trains was the most successful part of the General Strike, which was both why it routinely attracted grotesque lies from the *British Gazette* about the number of trains running and why the owners were so vindictive when the railwaymen returned to work. Despite its boast that it could keep services running with volunteers, the Great Western Railway never managed to use more than 40 per cent of its amateur recruits (most of these company pensioners or managerial staff) and these usually proved incompetent.[101] Almost all dockers and railway workers were forced to concede in writing that the strike had been illegal before being re-employed and then had to take pay reductions. Nearly a quarter of the NUR members had still not gone back to work by October. By autumn 1926 45,000 striking railwaymen had still not been re-employed and normality would not be restored on the railways until 1931. Thomas lost caste with his own NUR and eroded his own power base by his absurd boast that he had secured assurances from the government about his members' jobs. The real flavour of the man was conveyed by his response in the immediate aftermath of the strike. Instead of staying to fight things out with the employers, he departed on a tropical cruise.[102]

The plight of the miners was even more horrendous. Baldwin once again proved unwilling to exert maximum pressure on the mine owners. He tried to introduce some of the milder reforms recommended by the Samuel Commission only to be sharply rebuffed. The owners declared that the Samuel proposals for reorganisation were a monstrous impertinence and charged Baldwin with making it impossible for them to run the industry in the true manner of private enterprise; why were they singled out for special government interference and why could they not have the freedom enjoyed by other industries? Baldwin replied sharply that he regretted this uncompromising attitude; as for 'government interference' this had occurred only because of the egregious incompetence of the owners who, unlike other industries, had proved incapable of putting their own house in order.[103] This was brave talk, but talk was all Baldwin seemed capable of with the owners. So far from being singled out for interference, they were allowed far more rope than any middle-of-the-road government would have permitted them; only the ultra-right government of 1924–9 with its massive parliamentary majority could have been so indulgent. With the miners there was no such indulgence. In June 1926 Baldwin passed legislation ending the seven-hour day and allowing an eight-hour one, 'equipping the owners with knuckledusters', as Ramsay MacDonald put it.[104] They proved supremely ungrateful. In July a deputation of Christian divines led by William Temple went to see Baldwin to try to press for a four-month subsidy while the mining industry was reorganised.[105] Baldwin predictably turned the subsidy idea down flat and said the owners and the miners had to get together between themselves to sort out the mess. Taking up this cue, A. J. Cook wrote to Churchill to ask him to convene a meeting of the MFGB and the owners. Churchill was willing and asked to see the owners. At a meeting with them on 6 September Evan Williams told Churchill not only that the Mining Association would not enter into any national negotiations but claimed it was illegal for it to do so, as all power was vested in the district associations. Churchill lost his temper at this and told the owners that if the government had been aware of the depth of their intransigence, it would never have humoured them by suspending the seven-hour day.[106] Baldwin returned to the fray using parliamentary privilege, denouncing the owners in the House of Commons as 'discourteous and stupid'.[107] But to Labour's queries about what he intended to *do* about it, the predictable answer was as usual: nothing. Faced with Baldwin's refusal to turn the screws on the owners, the miners for their part refused to make any sacrifices. Even when both Cook and Herbert Smith declared that the time had come to negotiate, the national delegate conference in August refused to endorse this, albeit by a narrow majority.[108] With money dwindling and hunger in miners' families increasing, the adamant attitude of the delegates' conference was eventually overborne by individual miners voting with their feet and drifting back to work. The drift back was particularly noticeable in Nottinghamshire and Derbyshire, always the mining unions' weak spot (as would be shown again in the 1984 miners' strike). Finally realising the need to legitimise a fait accompli, another delegates' conference in November agreed that miners could conclude agreements with the owners in each district. Between 29 November and 23 December a multiplicity of such agreements was concluded and the men all returned to work. The six-month struggle had been heroic but had yielded no concrete results. The terms of the return to work varied but usually included an eight-hour day and the wage conditions as at 1921 rather than 1924. The owners scored a total victory. The miners had to work longer hours for lower wages (in 1927 an average of 7d loss per shift).[109]

Nobody, apart from the strikers themselves, emerged from the General Strike with much credit. Bevin and Thomas seemed to the workers to have added to their 'traitorous' credentials when they refused to impose a coal-handling embargo during the last six months of 1926 when the miners stayed out. Nor would the TUC agree to raise additional funds for their struggling 'brothers' through an ad hoc compulsory levy. Baldwin gained much kudos in the immediate aftermath of the strike but threw all this political capital and goodwill away when, in 1927, in reponse to pressure from his hawks, he brought in the Trade Disputes and Trade Union Act. This banned sympathetic strikes, restricted the areas and occupations where unionism was permitted and required trade unionists to 'contract in' to the unions' political levy paid to the Labour Party, instead of having expressly to 'contract out' as previously.[110] This unnecessary legislation (its clauses banning sympathetic or general strikes were never invoked) caused great and continuing bitterness on the Left[111] – it was habitually regarded as both stupid and egregiously wicked – and would be triumphantly revoked by the Attlee government in 1946. From having been at the top of the popularity poll in 1926, Baldwin and his reputation slumped disastrously as a result of this folly. In public perception the strikers were finally proved right in their assertion that Baldwin had waged class war on them in 1926 and this perception was instrumental in securing the Labour Party its electoral victory in 1929.[112] Yet it cannot be denied that the Labour movement suffered also in the years after 1926. Trade union membership fell from around 5.5 million in 1925 to 4.8 million in 1928; the TGWU lost one-tenth of its members. Total cash reserves of all unions fell from around £12.5 million to £8.5 million. Strike pay alone cost the NUR and the TGWU one million pounds apiece.[113] These sums were dwarfed by the hits sustained by the nation (in lost trade) and the government itself. Lost coal production alone amounted to £97 million plus a further £42 million on imports of coal, but the overall trade loss amounted to some £400 million.[114] In addition the government spent an extra £80 million on troop movements, the organisation of food supplies, extra policing, special constables, enhanced intelligence activity and much else. So embarrassed was Baldwin by government expenditure that he had Birkenhead compile a set of bogus figures totting the bill up to no more than £30 million, but few were taken in.[115] It would have made far more sense to renew the £23 million subsidy to the coal industry, especially since the government had to pay £26 million out of public funds on poor relief to families of strikers. Baldwin thus took a net loss of £3 million for obstinately refusing to renew the subsidy, and that for purely doctrinaire, ideological reasons.[116] The only consolation the Conservative government could draw from the entire episode was that it heralded an era of relative industrial peace. In the years before 1926 strikes involved an average of more than a million workers a year, but in 1926–36 the average was never more than 300,000. The contrast between 1921 and 1927 was particularly striking, for whereas in the former year 85,872,000 working days had been lost, the figure for 1927 was only 1,174,000.[117] Additionally, productivity in the mines increased from 200 tons per miner in 1925 to 300 tons by 1939.[118]

The General Strike also lit a fuse that would eventually detonate the Labour Party in the 1930s. Although in the short term Baldwin's vindictiveness handed the party the narrow electoral victory that would enable it to form the minority government of 1929, the traumatic events of 1931, when MacDonald, Thomas and Philip Snowden dumped it for the spurious solution of a National Government, were already adumbrated by the trio's right-wing attitudes in 1926. Whereas MacDonald's and Thomas's reactionary form was fully exposed, Snowden played a very clever hand and kept his head down; Churchill scathingly commented that he had been 'as mum as a mouse'.[119] Snowden was secretly just as hostile to the strike as MacDonald and Thomas but kept his thoughts for his diary: 'If the Trade Unionists had fully realised the forces that would be ranged against them, they would never have embarked upon the strike.'[120] By common consent his finest hour came in 1927 when he denounced the Trade Disputes Bill in a ninety-minute speech in the House that Lloyd George considered easily his best ever. The absurdities of the bill, Snowden pointed out, were manifold. Outlawing general strikes made no sense for only time would tell whether the strikers were in tune with the rest of the country or out of it; if enough people wanted a general stoppage, fifty acts of Parliament could not stop it and, in any case, how do you bring 5 million people before the courts? Moreover, the act was 'so ridiculously worded that nobody understands it. No lawyer in the House of Commons will venture an opinion as to what it means.'[121] Curiously, the greatest casualty of the General Strike was probably the Liberal Party, for the long-standing strife between old rivals Herbert Asquith and Lloyd George finally tore the stricken party apart.[122] Asquith, backed by John Simon and other right-wing Liberals, vehemently denounced the General Strike on many occasions, most notably in the House of Commons on 4 May. On that occasion he underlined the contradiction between a nation supposedly striving for international disarmament at the very time it was waging a civil war, and said it was a conflict in which only the innocent suffered. He differentiated between the miners' dispute, which was legitimate, and the General Strike, which was 'an offence of the gravest kind against both law and morals. It was an attempt to coerce the whole community and to substitute for the authority of Parliament that of a class dictatorship.'[123] After the strike he reinforced this view: 'There is a tendency, I regret to see, to look back upon the General Strike as a trivial and transient incident – a shortlived and more or less picturesque adventure. There could not be a worse example of distorted political perspective.'[124] Lloyd George considered this view wholly erroneous. He thought he knew all about the coal industry, having published his own proposals for reorganisation in *Coal and Power* (1924) and thought the government should implement them. It followed that for him the Samuel Commission was a waste of time since he himself had already 'solved' the problems. As one close student of the period has written: 'Lloyd George's pose of moderation during the General Strike is one of those things, like the première of an Ibsen play, which aroused in contemporaries a degree of shock and outrage incomprehensible fifty years later.'[125] Matters came to a head with a speech Lloyd George made in Cambridge on 1 May, where he vehemently attacked the idea that the threatened strike had anything to do with revolution. 'It has nothing to do with Zinoviev or Bolshevism. It is an honest trade dispute where the parties have been unable to come to an agreement.'[126]

From Asquith's viewpoint this was fighting talk, and matters escalated when Lloyd George refused to attend a Liberal shadow cabinet meeting on 10 May, and instead sent a letter which contained the following:

> I . . . cannot see my way to join in declarations which condemn the General Strike while refraining from criticism of the government, who are equally, if not more, responsible; and I certainly think that if we support the government in an absolute refusal to negotiate until the General Strike is called off, the struggle may be a prolonged one and the damage to the nation may well be irreparable . . . I prefer the liberal policy of trusting to conciliation rather than to force.[127]

The letter caused a sensation. Asquith in reply in effect accused Lloyd George of sulking and of having cast in his lot with 'the clericals', and an acrimonious correspondence ensued.[128] Asquith's supporters started a whispering campaign to the effect that the Welsh wizard was a hypocrite and humbug, and it is true that his attitude was puzzling. In July 1925, at the time of Red Friday, he had taunted the Baldwin government with 'being afraid of cold steel . . . running away from the Reds'.[129] Moreover, his cryptic remark to Sir Hugh Trenchard, Chief of the Air Staff, in 1921 when he himself was still prime minister – 'How many airmen are available for the revolution?' – seemed to imply that the preponderance of military force would always be with the government of the day.[130] He it was, also, who first passed an Emergency Powers Act enabling the government to deploy the military at will and imprison at will. So what was his game in 1926? Some say that the mutual loathing between him and Baldwin had got out of hand; Baldwin was incandescent that the man who could have solved the entire problem of the coal industry in 1921 at the time of the Sankey Commission, but had ducked the responsibility, should now be trying to occupy the high moral ground over the General Strike. Lloyd George's answer was that he had not gone looking for trouble in 1921, but Baldwin had deliberately courted confrontation five years later (in this he was correct). Others say that his long-term aim was to unite the large numbers of discontented liberals and disillusioned Labourites in a new party under his leadership.[131] Another view is that Lloyd George was schizoid: he was a power worshipper when he had his hands on the levers of government but sympathised with the underdog when he did not: 'He had a highly dialectical cast of mind which liked to see a balance of forces.'[132] Yet others say he was deliberately baiting a trap for Asquith and the Asquithians. At any rate, his next step was to write an article on the General Strike to be syndicated in US newspapers. Because the article was nuanced and not outright condemnation of the strike, it caused a furore when reprinted in the UK media.[133] Asquith, furious about Lloyd George's behaviour, sent him a letter of rebuke on 20 May, which 'the goat' chose to interpret as expulsion from the Liberal Party. His mild reply wrongfooted Asquith. The wrangle over whether Lloyd George should be formally expelled backfired badly, with many liberals feeling that the aged Asquith had lost his touch. A student of the incident has written: 'Having taken so much from Lloyd George, his [Asquith's] ageing patience snapped suddenly in 1926; but he acted impetuously, badly misjudged his moment, and achieved the opposite of his purpose.'[134] Lloyd George enjoyed the powerful support of J. M. Keynes, whose particular bêtes noires were Birkenhead and Simon. Sympathetic to the miners and particularly contemptuous of the idea that the General Strike was red revolution, Keynes agreed with Lloyd George that the root cause of the strike was the lethargy and stupidity of Baldwin and his government. Predictably, he was accused of 'betrayal' by the Asquithians. But his support was important for swinging the party behind Lloyd George and seeing him once again confirmed as Liberal leader in 1927.[135]

An interesting study could be done on the later careers of all the principals in the General Strike, with some surprising results. Ramsay

MacDonald became Labour prime minister in 1929 and then, in 1931, at the height of a financial crisis committed his 'great act of betrayal' by forming a National Government with the Conservatives, then holding a general election which reduced Labour to fifty-four seats. Ironically the issue which caused the crisis was the very same gold standard (abandoned that year), which Keynes had warned against and which precipitated the General Strike.[136] MacDonald retired, broken and discredited in 1935. Baldwin took over once more as prime minister, made a terrible hash of dealing with the Nazi menace and also retired, discredited in 1937. The third premier of the National Government, Neville Chamberlain, one of the principal hawks in 1926, was also discredited, and his career has been memorably described thus: 'Chamberlain sinned against Napoleon's rule: he was a man of No Luck. The cards always ran against him. He was humiliated by Lloyd George at the beginning of his political career, and cheated by Hitler at the end. Baldwin kept him in second place, almost without trying.'[137] Two of Baldwin's hard liners enjoyed the most bizarrely contrasting fortunes, for Birkenhead died of alcoholism at fifty-eight in 1930 while Churchill, no mean drinker himself, survived a miserable period in the political wilderness in the 1930s before emerging as Britain's saviour and inspiration in 1940. Jimmy Thomas, after a political career dishonestly trying to keep the Ulster issue alive, when Ireland had already become a republic and accepted the separate existence of the North as part of the UK, finally met his comeuppance in 1936. Not surprisingly, the issue was money, specifically 'insider dealing' or leaking budget secrets so that he and his business accomplices could benefit.[138] Herbert Samuel devoted much of his later life to Zionism but remained bitter about his treatment by Baldwin. He brusquely turned down later suggestions from both Thomas (end of May 1926) and Ramsay MacDonald (September 1926) that he should again intervene in the coal industry. Although he regarded the Tories as ingrates, he had the satisfaction of being held in the highest regard in liberal and intellectual circles. In October 1926 Beatrice Webb claimed that Samuel and Keynes would make infinitely better leaders of the Labour Party than MacDonald and Thomas.[139] On the union side, Citrine enjoyed a long life and career as a super-bureaucrat, while Bevin became Attlee's foreign secretary in 1945, a doughty anti-communist and Cold War Warrior. A. J. Cook enjoyed the most dismal fortunes. Despite his reputation as a rabble-rouser he was actually a pragmatist with an acute sense of what was industrially feasible.[140] Thomas's ally John Bromley, who loathed Cook, tried to criticise him from the platform at the TUC Conference in late 1926, but was howled down by the miners' delegates; Arthur Pugh in the chair could not restore order and had to adjourn the meeting for half an hour.[141] Snowden, too, tried to make Cook personally responsible for the General Strike, while his other enemies were animated by such hatred that they started a canard that Cook had secretly negotiated with the coal owners in July 1926. The Communist Party, displaying the usual sin of factionalism on the Left, absurdly accused him of being a renegade who was secretly in collusion with Ramsay MacDonald and the reformists, even though it was widely known that MacDonald detested Cook.[142] A Robespierrean figure, Cook particularly disliked the creeping corporatism of the late 1920s and attacked the 'trans-class' talks of Ben Turner and Sir Alfred Mond, only to be himself repudiated by the MFGB.[143] By 1928 he was attacked from both Left and Right: 'I am blamed for everything which is wrong. I am made the scapegoat . . . a kind of evil genius going around the Districts making trouble,' he lamented. Finding himself, in trade union terms, virtually an analogue of the Independent Labour Party, for a short while he allied himself with Jimmy Maxton in the ILP. The following year, with Labour once more in power, he became so disgusted with the rejection of Oswald Mosley's imaginative plans for public works to revive the economy (a kind of pre-echo of Keynes's later famous ideas) that he resigned from the Labour Party and joined Mosley in his New Party.[144] Before he could witness Mosley's swing hard right into black-shirted fascism, Cook died in 1931 at the age of forty-seven from sarcoma. Around the bedside of the dying man were grouped Citrine, Mosley and the South Wales communist Arthur Horner. As Citrine noted: 'Rather an odd group: an embryo Fascist, a Communist – and Citrine.'[145]

The General Strike was one of the most clear-cut revolutionary moments in British history. It did not matter that neither the TUC nor the participating unions were revolutionary and that they were indeed the very mildest of reformists. Both Baldwin and the General Council had dived into waters where they were out of their depth. It only needed a shot from a trigger-happy or frightened soldier or a death resulting from an over-zealous police baton charge to pitch the entire process into a void whose outcome was uncertain or, if eventually certain, only obtained after massive bloodshed. More thoughtful eyewitnesses such as Virginia Woolf continually lamented the provocative and habitual shows of strength by the military, most of them irresponsibly engineered by Churchill.[146] The early surrender by the TUC allowed the strike to end without loss of life. Neither the General Council nor the government acted towards the working class with decency and morality, but at least the TUC had the sense to see what loomed ahead; for all the loose talk about 'revolution', Baldwin and his colleagues showed no understanding of the phenomenon of revolution and to this extent were living in cloud cuckoo land. The peaceful outcome of the strike allowed observers to see it in retrospect as little more than the petty pique of the middle class versus the working class and vice versa. As G. K. Chesterton remarked, the strike simply illustrated a truism, that people who dress as gentlemen will instinctively band together against people working in shirtsleeves and with their coats off.[147] This rather shallow interpretation of class conflict was echoed in many contemporary sources. The more thoughtful reflected that what had seemed praiseworthy at the time, enthusiastic undergraduates manning buses, looked on cold reflection more like Flashman, the bully in *Tom Brown's Schooldays*.[148] Even Baldwin's supporters recognised that he had overreacted in his determination to defeat the strikers at all costs.[149] Commentators on the Left reflected ruefully on the selfishness of the middle class. As Kingsley Martin reported:

> The great middle class has returned to business as usual, with nothing settled except its character, content with the achievement of an exciting victory over those on whom its prosperity depends, congratulating itself that Englishmen are not as other men, excitable and given to thought, that they are not vindictive . . . [the General Strike] meant . . . that there was no serious resistance to the Tory policy of deflation in the 1930s: that, apart from hunger marching, the divided and disillusioned workers had no reply to poverty and unemployment. England remained a crudely class society.[150]

David Kirkwood scoffed at those middle-class intellectuals who had been all in favour of the strike at the outset but, when it failed, denounced it as though they had always opposed it.[151] Yet there was not much rejoicing among the 'victorious' classes. Even middle-class sympathisers took a cynical view of the way Baldwin had exploited them: the Establishment would always mobilise the middle class when it was in danger itself but otherwise ignored it or looked on it simply as a source of tax revenue.[152] When Beatrice Webb's patronising Fabian attitudes became known, she was regarded in the working class as a class enemy, a classic wolf in sheep's clothing. Particular objection was taken to this statement: 'Future generations will, I think, regard it [the General Strike] as the death-gasp of that pernicious doctrine of "workers' control" of public affairs through trade unions and by the method of direct action.'[153] More and more people on the Left came forward to denounce Mrs Webb for her supercilious view of the workers and her arrogant condescension in instructing Labour leaders' wives in the fine points of social etiquette.[154] Some observers felt that what had begun as high tragedy had ended in something close to farce. There are always great souls in all eras with a keen sense of the absurd who can see the humour even in unpromising situations. One of these, evidently 'born with the gift of laughter and the sense that the world was mad', was the leftist David Kirkwood, who was even able to see the poisonous Jix as 'a character'. He described a moment of high pantomime in the House of Commons when Churchill was being barracked and catcalled by Labour members. Churchill got up and began: 'If ever this happens again . . . (pause for dramatic effect) then I will publish another *British Gazette*.' The house collapsed into guffaws, in which even Labour joined. As Kirkwood said: 'No one can be serious when the victims treat their victimisers as a joke.'[155] That was the way the General Strike ended: not with a bang but a belly laugh.

CONCLUSION

Revolutions

It is often said that the absence of revolution in Britain's history is an example of 'exceptionalism' and rather like the issue of why socialism never took a hold in the USA. Yet devotees of British (and especially English) uniqueness like to riposte that there is particular exceptionalism even within the general exceptionalism. For example, the Peasants' Revolt of 1381 was not passive or conservative, as most peasant revolts are held to be.[1] And the Jacobite Rising of 1745 was like a meteorite from a clear blue sky, occurring as it did in the midst of an era of Augustan calm, when all indices of demography, economics and political stability suggested that on paper it was 'impossible' (in contrast to the situation from about 1770 onwards), with all potential popular forces in England astonishingly inert – one reason why some scholars prefer to see the '45 as a Scottish invasion.[2] All this suggests that to seek a general explanation for the absence of revolution is to quest for a Holy Grail. Nevertheless, one can see why the temptation to do so is overwhelming. Usually analysts have tried to locate some essential feature of the English character and then 'read off' political consequences from this. Some see the mere fact of being an island as crucial. Unquestionably the psychic significance of islands in the British collective unconscious is considerable. In literature it surfaces in Defoe's *Robinson Crusoe*, Stevenson's *Treasure Island*, Ballantyne's *Coral Island*, Swift's floating island of Laputa in *Gulliver's Travels*, H. G. Wells's *The Island of Dr Moreau*, the half dozen islands in J. M. Barrie's *oeuvre*, to say nothing of its presence in children's classics like Ransome's *Swallows and Amazons* and Enid Blyton's *Famous Five*. Then there are the modern examples like Golding's *Lord of the Flies*, John Fowles's *The Magus*: one could go on and on.[3] Others think that Britain's seafaring role and the production of a nation of sailors and navigators is crucial. This was always a major motif with Winston Churchill. As he boasted to the House of Commons in 1901: 'Whereas any European nation has to support a vast army first of all, we in this fortunate, happy island, relieved by our insular position of a double burden, may turn our undivided efforts and attention to the Fleet. Why should we sacrifice a game in which we are to win to play a game in which we are bound to lose?'[4] Modern writers as various as George Orwell, G. K. Chesterton, J. B. Priestley, D. H. Lawrence and George Santayana have all sought the golden key that would unlock the secrets of the island nation, variously seeking the answer in climate, landscape, xenophobia, atavism and urbanisation.[5] Often these writers insinuate the dubious view that revolution is more to do with a change of *sensibilities* in society – the historical change where people think differently, look at life differently, have a different world-view.

The basic problem with such interpretations is simply that the zeitgeist changes over time. For example, the British were notorious for mindless violence and hooliganism in the eighteenth century, transformed themselves in the reign of William IV to emerge as the relatively polite and deferential masses of the Victorian era, then underwent another sea-change in the 1960s to return to something like the eighteenth-century position. Certainly the idea that the absence of revolution links with a pacific people will not hold water. England alone experienced 162 violent rebellions of one kind or another – what sociologists call 'internal disturbances in intra-group relationships' – between the years 656 and 1921, or roughly one every eight years.[6] Yet another problem is that attempts to pierce to the heart of the matter usually assume a homogeneous political and social culture – a thesis which, if it was ever true, is certainly so no longer in the era of multiculturalism. But the attempts continue to be made.[7] In general, searchers for the 'open sesame' of British (and particularly English) culture underrate the considerable ambiguity in Anglo-Saxon attitudes. For example: the English were philistines yet created a cult of the countryside; had a State religion but are largely unbelievers; always despised intellectuals, but were at the forefront of intellectual inquiry. Nonetheless, certain recurring motifs tempt one to wonder if some of the more astute critics are not 'on to something'. André Maurois, noting that in the eternal struggle between liberty and equality the French preferred the latter and the British the former (albeit usually confusing liberty with licence), concluded that the British were less intelligent than the French. This was harsh, and perhaps Tocqueville put it better when he said that the French prized equality but the British always needed social inferiors.[8] It has been frequently asserted that the British would rather have a society of great inequality in which there is an infinitesimal chance of winning the national lottery or the football pools than one based on fairness, justice and equity. This would tie in with the national mania for sports and for gambling. This was a phenomenon that Orwell and his close friend the sociologist Geoffrey Gorer paid particular attention to. Without putting it in so many words, they and other critics have agreed with the Marxist tenet that in England the State is mystified so that it appears, not as the instrument of oppression by the ruling classes, but as the impartial umpire guaranteeing fair play and 'playing the game'.[9] Orwell's jaundiced view of sport is well known: 'Serious sport has nothing to do with fair play. It is bound up with hatred, jealousy, boastfulness, disregard of all rules and sadistic pleasure in witnessing violence. In other words, it is war minus the shooting.'[10] As for the wider counter-revolutionary role of sport, it is not without significance that the most famous British conservative political theorist of the twentieth century, Michael Oakeshott (see below p. 493) once wrote a book entitled *A Guide to the Classics, or How to Pick the Derby Winner*, published in 1936.

None of this really takes us very close to the core issue: why has there been no true revolution in British history? It goes without saying that Britain never approached anything like the socio-economic convulsions of the Russian, Chinese or Cuban Revolutions. The nearest the nation came to something like the upheavals in the French and Mexican varieties was in the aftermath of the English Civil War, but Cromwell slammed the brakes on hard and turned abruptly right. So opposed were his acolytes like Generals Monk and Lambert to real social change that they acquiesced in the Restoration in 1660. With a few further tweaks in 1688–9 the British constitution and the system for which it stands have remained unchanged in their essentials, with the main concession to pressure from below being the grudging and protracted granting of universal franchise, not finally achieved until 1928. How can we account for this? The only realistic comparison is with other European countries. The sceptic says that other nation-states have been revolution-free, but these turn out to be societies either of recent creation (Norway, Ireland, Finland) or those blessed with a small population and with an adamantine commitment to consensus, co-optation and local democracy (Switzerland, Sweden, Holland). The true comparison, therefore, must be with those nations which in the past 400 years have challenged Britain for European and global hegemony: Spain, France, Germany, Russia. All four societies have undergone almost endless turbulence. France was racked by wars and rebellions even before the French Revolution of 1789.[11] There were further revolutions in 1830, 1848 and 1871, and a state of near civil war during the 1930s, when the Popular Front was under pressure from the extreme Right, and in 1958–62 on the issue of Algeria. Russia was similarly afflicted, largely as a result of the supreme autocracy of the tsars, and there is no need to labour the incidence of the revolutions of 1905 and 1917. Germany suffered the Spartacist rising in 1919, the abortive Munich putsch in 1923 and the Nazi seizure of power in 1933, which by any standards was a revolution, and can only be dismissed as such if we take the simplistic notion that revolutions can only ever move in a leftward direction and involve the working class as primary agent.[12] Italy, too, albeit a nation-state united only since the 1860s, sustained a right-wing revolution in 1922 when Mussolini came to power. Although Francesco Nitti, the Italian Prime Minister, told Austen Chamberlain in 1925 that Italy was the least revolutionary country in the world, such a view is treated with contempt by scholars, who point to a history before unification positively studded with riots, tumults, coups, rebellions, insurrections and peasants' revolts. One leading authority goes further and alleges that Italy had a propensity towards *counter-revolution*, as evinced by Cavour's reactionary machinations to neutralise Garibaldi. The only reason the events of 1922 came as a surprise to leading Italian thinkers like Benedetto Croce was that conservative factions and their tame historians had lied about the unpalatable reactionary truth about the Risorgimento.[13] One is almost tempted to accept Jack Goldstone's thesis about overpopulation (see above, pp. 513–4) since all European countries with a significant population, Britain excepted, have been visited by the spectre of revolution.

The phenomenon of European revolution translates into another, also noted below (pp. 495–6) whereby revolutions, revolutionary situations and revolutionary potential engender dictatorship or the phenomenon of Caesarism. The Marxist theorist Antonio Gramsci explicitly linked Caesarism to revolution, for he saw the 'man on horseback' as the inevitable 'solution' for societies faced with the problem of an equilibrium of forces heading towards catastrophe.[14] France has certainly had its share of Caesars. Even if we exclude Louis XIV and Louis XV, who were absolute rulers as absolute as one could conceive, complete with *lettres de cachet* with which to punish anyone who displeased them for whatever reason, from the time of the Revolution in 1789 there has been a long succession of French 'strong men': Napoleon, Louis Napoleon (Napoleon III), General Boulanger, Clemenceau, Poincaré, Pétain, de Gaulle.[15] Germany had Frederick the Great, Bismarck, Kaiser Wilhelm and Hitler. Spain had a long tradition of *caudillos* culminating in General Franco, spent much of the nineteenth century in civil war (the Carlist wars), lurched into chaos in the twentieth century, suffered three years of civil war and then thirty-six years of fascist dictatorship.[16] Russia's record for autocracy is even worse, with Ivan the Terrible, Peter the Great, Catherine the Great and the Romanovs well to the fore, and ending with Stalin, Yeltsin and Putin. Echoing the psychologist C. G. Jung, who saw Hitler as an introjection of Wotan and the ancient German forest gods, some Russian specialists speculate that two centuries under the yoke of the Mongols – Batu, Berke, the Golden Horde, the Blue Horde, Toktamish, Tamerlane – has left a permanent scar, that Russia has aborbed despotism and autocracy into its collective unconscious.[17] Britain, by contrast, has experienced just one dictator since the despotism of the Tudors – Cromwell, memorably described by Trotsky (a grudging admirer) as a fusion of Luther and Robespierre.[18] Cromwell turned down the offer of a crown, thought his son Richard incapable of carrying on his work, and all but confessed that in the British context dictatorship was a dead end. Just as sociologists try to find a master-key explanation for revolution, so they attempt to explain Caesarism. Various studies have appeared, claiming organic linkages between dictators, but unable to agree on the causal lines; with one author Napoleon leads logically to Hitler (doubtless partly because both were foolish enough to invade Russia and made abortive attempts to invade Britain); with others the line leads from Napoleon to Stalin or, even more ingeniously, from Rousseau through Napoleon to Stalin.[19] The only common factor sociological studies of Caesarism identify convincingly (apart from Gramsci's very broad-brush analysis) is that most dictators come to power at a relatively young age and tend to hail from the provinces or marginal areas, never from the capital or metropolis. Hence Napoleon (from Corsica, coming to power at 30); Hitler (from Austria, coming to power at 44); Mussolini (Emilia Romagna, 39); Franco (Galicia, 44); Cromwell (Huntingdon, 46) and Mao Tse-tung (from Hunan province but slightly letting the side down by taking until the age of 56 to ascend to supreme power).[20] Other than fitting into this 'young outsider' schema, Cromwell has little in common with the others and is but one more example of 'English exceptionalism'.

In trying to analyse why Britain has escaped serious revolution (defined as those of ranks two and three), there are basically four approaches that can be adopted. One can try to find an overarching theory explaining *all* revolutions; for the reasons mentioned in the Introduction this seems a forlorn hope.[21] One can try to find an explanation for all attempted revolutions in *Britain* (England before 1603). Or one can admit that this too is an implausible objective and aim instead for convincing causality for a single 'near miss'. Or one can abandon hope entirely and concede that the causes of even a single revolution remain beyond our grasp. It must be admitted that the last, defeatist scenario is the one most in line with current thinking. Gradually all the 'grand theories' purporting to explain the seismic events of the past have been abandoned. Until the end of the 1950s it was still commonplace to describe the English and French Revolutions in Marxist terms as part of the transition from feudalism to capitalism. The objections to this thesis multiplied to the point where the attempt was eventually abandoned.[22] Similarly, the American Civil War was often seen as the irreconcilable conflict between primary and secondary production systems, between an industrial North requiring protectionism and an agrarian South needing free trade. Even slavery is no longer considered a key issue, with most recent writers opting for the idea of the State cracking under the competing demands, political and economic, of two powerful political cultures.[23] The origins of the English Civil War, the French Revolution and the American Civil War, to name just three of history's 'great events' are increasingly sought in the misperceptions, miscalculations and mistakes of individual actors, in unintended consequences, in contingency of the most aleatory kind, even in what would be called the demotic 'cock-up theory'.

Many historians have retreated into the study of accident and circumstance of the most adventitious kind. Roughly speaking, one can say that mainstream liberal and conservative historians believe in contingency and discontinuity, while those of a leftist or sociological orientation still maintain a structural approach implying continuity and commonality of historical phenomena. The latter believe that there are patterns in history, the former that history never repeats itself. Two good examples of the latter view may be given. Here is Crane Brinton on why general studies of revolution are needed: 'We shall have to be content with the crude assertion that the doctrine of the absolute uniqueness of events in history seems a nonsense. History is essentially an account of the behaviour of men, and if the behaviour of Man is not subject to any kind of systematisation, this world is even more cockeyed than the seers would have it. History at least gives us case studies, is at least material for the clinician.'[24] And here is Trotsky on why the Chartist movement denoted an essential continuity in the British revolutionary tradition:

> The Chartist epoch is immortal by reason of the fact that for the space of ten years it gave us in a compressed and diagrammatic form apparently the whole gamut of proletarian struggle – from petitions in Parliament to armed insurrection . . . one may say that the Chartist movement is like a prelude which gives us in an undeveloped form the musical theme of the whole opera . . . Chartism was unsuccessful not because its methods were incorrect, but because it came too early. It was only an historical overture.[25]

Devotees of historical uniqueness or adventitious contingency, on the other hand, look for support from the physical sciences. They argue that since each human being is radically different, it follows that their collision and interpenetration in history will never produce the same or even similar results. As for the radical difference, the noted physicist Carl Sagan pointed out that the number of permutations in the human brain, based on the count of neurones or synapses connecting them, is greater than the whole number of elementary particles (electrons and protons) in the entire universe.[26] A word of caution is in order. David Hume long ago pointed out that virtually everything we hold to be 'knowledge' can be devastated by the method of philosophical scepticism, but that the sane philosopher will retire with a good book and a good bottle after he has completed his lucubrations. Insistence on the absolute uniqueness of everything and the denial of the validity of universals is a project that cannot really be carried out in good faith, especially in historical study. Radical empiricism, nominalism and its analogues would prevent us not just from using the word 'revolution' but absolutely basic concepts such as 'war', 'rebellion', 'society', 'system', etc.

It seems clear that there are certain basics about Britain which, while not in themselves *guarantees* of a revolution-free existence, are at least pointers to the factors likely to be involved. Most fundamental is the fact that Britain is an island, and Shakespeare's famous paean to 'this England' underlines the importance of the 'sea girt' element in national culture. Britain (and especially England) has never been successfully invaded since 1066, though serious attempts were made in 1588 by Spain, in 1692, 1759, 1779 and 1803–5 (by France) and in 1940 (by Germany).[27] The main reason is that the Royal Navy was in a successful alliance with the elements themselves. Historians notoriously dislike determinism, which is why they systematically underrate weather as a factor in human history. Characteristic accounts of the Spanish Armada, for example, wildly overrate the personality of Elizabeth I, her 'sea dogs' and the inconclusive Battle of Gravelines and play down the storms that ravaged the Spanish fleet on its perilous journey home, into the Atlantic off the west coast of Ireland.[28] One of the principal reasons these islands have not been successfully invaded since 1066 is that they are surrounded by dangerous, gale-lashed seas, and only recently has it been realised just how terrifying oceanic elements can be. Tales of 100-foot waves were usually dismissed as the tall stories of old salts who had spent too many years before the mast, but modern science has demonstrated that such seas are an ever-present danger and that no ship yet built is designed to withstand them. It is a moral certainty that so-called freak waves were responsible for some of the most famous maritime losses of the twentieth century, including those of the ships *Waratah*, *Derbyshire* and *München*.[29] 'Near misses' in the past few years after encounters with 100-foot waves featured the *Caledonian Star*, *Bremen* and *QE2*. Oceanographers now accept that 'rogue waves', sheer walls of water one hundred feet high, are a relatively frequent occurrence. The turning point in the scientific debate occurred on New Year's Day 1995 when the Draupner oil rig in the North Sea was hit by an eighty-foot monster, which was clearly recorded on instrumentation and profoundly shook those previously sceptical that such watery leviathans could exist. Radar satellites from the German Aerospace Centre were trained on the problem and identified ten such giants in just three weeks. The German study, while locating some of these monsters off South Africa and in the North Pacific, also found 100-foot waves in the North Sea, in the Atlantic Ocean north of Scotland, near the Fastnet Lighthouse off the south-west coast of Ireland[30] and in the Bay of Biscay; significantly all of the last four named regions featured in historical attempts to invade the British Isles. The latest scientific thinking, using the Schrodinger equation derived from quantum physics, is that there are both linear and non-linear waves, and that the non-linear type becomes a monster by sucking in energy from other waves in a storm.[31]

Every week at least one ship is lost at sea in unexplained circumstances, which the shipping industry is, naturally, disposed to attribute to human error or poor maintenance; to face the genuine problem of freak waves would mean scrapping the entire merchant fleet and building vessels capable of dealing with these sea monsters. We can, therefore, be confident in asserting that in the great maritime duels between France and Britain in the 'Second Hundred Years War' (1689–1815), both sides faced a terrifying common enemy.[32] Hurricanes destroyed the elaborate French preparations to invade England in early 1744 and the attempt to land a huge army in Ireland in 1796. Those who portray the Royal Navy as an indomitable barrier to invasion often forget that in 1796 General Hoche got 15,000 men plus the Irish patriot Theobald Wolfe Tone safely to Bantry Bay, evading the Royal Navy, only to be dispersed by a force-twelve tempest. Tone remarked: 'England has had its luckiest escape since the Armada.'[33] In the fight against Napoleon in the period 1803–15, out of a total Royal Navy loss of 317 ships, calamitous seas accounted for 223 vessels; an educated guess would be that freak waves played more than a small part here.[34] Pytheas of Massilia (Marseilles), the Greek sailor who circumnavigated the British Isles at the very time Alexander the Great was conquering the Persian Empire (in the 320s BC), reported 100-foot waves in Pentland Firth and has always been laughed to scorn for his hyperbole.[35] But now we know the ancient wisdom was right after all.

In fact the British authorities have known it longer than the scientific community but chose to hush it up. In 1943, while on Atlantic troop-carrying duty, the liner *Queen Elizabeth* was hit by two eighty-foot waves in quick succession, ploughing into the 'hole in the ocean' after the first one and nearly being engulfed by the second. In December 1942, the *Queen Mary*, carrying 15,000 troops from America to Britain, was hit broadside by a 92-foot wall of water north of Scotland, rolled at an angle of more than forty-five degrees and came within a few feet of capsizing. This would have been the greatest maritime disaster in history, involving ten times the fatalities of the *Titanic*.[36] Conceivably, it could have altered the course of world history, for the effect on Allied morale at this crucial stage of World War Two might have been catastrophic. Hitler would have claimed that God (or the gods or Wotan) was on his side. The little-known story of the *Queen Mary*, therefore, illustrates two constants in British history: the culture of secrecy and the perilous nature of the seas that wash these islands.

The dislocating impact of invasion on a nation-state can hardly be exaggerated. In the twentieth century Germany was invaded and occupied (1945); the potential revolutionary situation thus engendered was avoided because Germany was divided and then immediately subsumed in the Cold War. Much the same happened in Italy, and the occupation and disruption of 1943–5 came close to returning a communist government in 1948. Spain suffered invasion and occupation in the Napoleonic era. Since the early nineteenth century Russia has suffered two major invasions, by Napoleon and Hitler, and a number of minor ones from Poles, Swedes and Turks. France was invaded three times between 1870 and 1940. Britain, protected by the seas and the Royal Navy, escaped all of this. In Britain the navy has always been the senior service, with the army relatively unimportant; in continental nations the army is necessarily one of the engines of power. A continental position also means involvement in almost permanent warfare, and wars on land are another of the major precipitants of revolution, especially if a nation-state has been unsuccessful.[37] It is no accident that Britain's only movement in the direction of a revolution of rank two was in the aftermath of the English Civil War. In Russia the debacle of the Russo-Japanese war of 1904–5 triggered the Russian Revolution of 1905, and the much greater collapse on the Eastern Front in early 1917 precipitated the Russian Revolution of 1917 (which in turn led to civil war between Reds and Whites). French failure in the Franco-Prussian War of 1870–1 produced the Paris Commune of 1871. Chinese failure against Japan in World War Two led directly to the triumph of the communists in the Chinese Revolution of 1949. In the Russian case, some scholars have tried to extend the argument by seeing the sequence war–revolution–civil war as a manifestation of a single phenomenon.[38] It is sometimes objected captiously that not all wars lead to revolution and that sometimes the sequence is reversed, as with the French Revolution, leading to the wars of 1792–1815.[39] This is a statement of the obvious: if war *always* produced revolution, the entire debate about the causality of revolutions would be otiose; we would know a priori that revolution would follow war as night follows day. War is not a sufficient condition for revolution nor even a necessary one, but it is often a key factor. The other important point about warfare is that it generates serious economic and financial consequences and can often ruin national treasuries.[40] The locus classicus of this process was the way French participation in the War of American Independence led to financial crisis in the 1780s, the consequent summoning of the Estates-General in 1789, and all the momentous events that flowed from that. Again, this thesis is sometimes queried on the grounds that French expenses in the American war were 1.3 billion livres, which compared favourably with an expenditure of 1.2 billions in the War of Austrian Succession (1740–8) and the higher costs of 1.8 billions in the Seven Years War (1756–63).[41] Yet the objections depend on seeing each war as a discrete entity; the salient point surely is that, because of the weakness of its taxation system and its accumulated debts, France could not really afford its intervention in the American War; in short, objections to the 'French financial crisis triggered the French Revolution' thesis depend on ignoring the *cumulative* wartime expenses of France in the eighteenth century.

The other relevant consideration, helping to show how the avoidance of land warfare on native soil helps to ward off revolutionary situations, is that, since Britain always depended for its defence overwhelmingly on the Royal Navy, the role of the army was significantly reduced. Almost by definition a navy cannot stage coups d'état or intervene significantly in domestic politics. Barracks-based military are another matter entirely, as the history of Latin America reveals vividly.[42] Even in Europe the army has been an omnipresent political factor. Ever since Napoleon's invasion of Spain, the Spanish military has been a major factor, first in the Carlist wars of the nineteenth century, then most dramatically in 1930–6, precipitating the Spanish Civil War, and a reliable menace to political stability as late as 1981. The Romanovs relied heavily on the military during their long period of despotism, and it was the collapse of the military that led directly to the Russian Revolution. The most striking case is that of France. In the seventeenth century it was racked by civil war, not just during the period of the Fronde but also in the long-running military duel between 'the great Condé' (Louis de Bourbon, Prince de Condé) and Turenne (Henri de la Tour d'Auvergne, Vicomte de Turenne).[43] Some scholars speculate that the 'Second Hundred Years War' represented an attempt by the Bourbons, conscious or unconscious, to export endemic military violence onto an international stage. The rise of Napoleon's Grande Armée, for the first time introducing a meritocratic and even proletarian officer class, immensely complicated nineteenth-century French politics, and this baneful legacy surfaced most menacingly at the end of the nineteenth century in the crises involving General Boulanger and the Dreyfus case.[44] Yet the most disturbing manifestations of the military probably came in the twentieth century, especially in the great crisis over Algeria in 1958–62. France in these years hovered close to civil war. In Algeria there was particular intra-military tension, both between units of the regular army and national servicemen drafted to North Africa and between regular army regiments and the French Foreign Legion.[45] Nothing like this has ever occurred in Britain, and the military is generally considered thoroughly socialised and non-political. Yet even here the exclusion of the military has not been absolute. One should always beware when it is asserted that the military 'never would' intervene in politics; the same was said of the army in Chile before General Pinochet's bloody coup in 1973.[46] When Ian Smith and his party made a Unilateral Declaration of Independence in Rhodesia in 1965, it was widely considered that the British army could not be used against the rebels as they were 'kith and kin', much to the general fury of Black Africa.[47] Even more serious was the insufficiently known 'Curragh Mutiny' of 1914. When the Liberal government under Asquith passed the Third Home Rule Bill, envisaging a united Ireland in which the Catholic south would predominate, Sir Edward Carson raised the paramilitary Ulster Volunteers to oppose Home Rule by force; 'Ulster will fight and Ulster will be right' was his watchword. British army units in southern Ireland were ordered north to deal with the Ulster Volunteers but, in a notorious incident, fifty-seven out of seventy army officers based at the Curragh barracks in Kildare resigned rather than constrain their fellow Protestants. Technically, they avoided outright mutiny by resigning before announcing that they would never use force against Ulster, but it was clear to everyone that this was a case of the army refusing to obey the orders of a civilian government.[48] On paper it created the most catastrophic crisis. Asquith ducked the issue by claiming that he had been 'misunderstood' and the rebellious fifty-seven were reinstated. The Curragh Mutiny is regarded by some historians as the key to an ongoing mystery: why did the Asquith government give such ambiguous and misleading signals to Kaiser Wilhelm's Germany in the run-up to the Great War of 1914–18? While it is conceded that Germany might have drawn back had it been certain that Britain would enter the war on the side of France, the idea is that Asquith and his cabinet preferred to fight a bloody war in Europe, with all the bloodshed that involved, rather than face the implications of the army revolt in Northern Ireland.[49]

Because of the relative marginality of the army in British life, the central apparatus of government repression has always been weaker in these islands than in continental countries. Unable in normal circumstances to deploy overwhelming military force against rioters, rebels, demonstrators and other dissidents, the British Establishment has had to use extreme cunning to keep the lid on simmering discontents. Even the most vehement critics of the British power elite concede that the timing of its concessions and its handling of revolutionary situations have usually been impeccable. Whereas the French, Russian and Chinese Revolutions, once again exhibiting those common features that have so beguiled sociologists, took place after the elite carried out reforms that were too little, too late, the British State always acted just in time, especially during the critical period of Chartism in the 1830s and 1840s.[50] Here is one Marxist critic on the astuteness of the elite in these years: 'An attack by the authorities on a large demonstration, or the kind of harassment of the common people that had been practised in Ireland before the rising of 1798, might have goaded a desperate population into armed resistance. No such provocation occurred.'[51] Trotsky, grudgingly conceding that the ruling classes always granted 'timely concessions, always very niggardly', thought that the English avoidance of revolution was highly dependent on their perception of revolution elsewhere: the spectacle of France after 1789, for example, awoke the rulers of Britain from their dogmatic slumbers and made them institute nick-of-time reforms.[52] Another perennial tactic of the ruling class has always been a clever use of political camouflage, mystification and obfuscation. Over the years ploys as various as the Official Secrets Act, D-Notices and a draconian law of libel (still in existence) have been used to this end. The culture of secrecy – so ingrained that there is even secrecy about the use of secrecy, as the modern phenomenon of judicial 'superinjunctions' shows clearly – makes it difficult for dissidents to target the enemy properly or to see the shape of the opposition in full focus; one frequent result is the splintering of revolt, with a number of riots or disturbances aiming at different targets instead of concerted efforts on a single one that might be vulnerable to concentrated force.[53] Another frequently used agent of camouflage is the cult of the amateur, which insinuates that everything is a matter of well-meaning semi-incompetents muddling through, instead of the cold-eyed and ruthless calculations of an inner circle. Many observers have pointed to the paradox that England was the pioneer of professionalism in medicine, the law, architecture, etc, but is anti-professional in ethos. The Elizabethan age, with characteristic figures like Raleigh and Sir Philip Sidney, is sometimes seen as the dawn of amateurism in English life. It is asserted, variously, that Cromwell was self-taught and not a professional soldier like Napoleon, that Gladstone was an amateur classical scholar, Churchill an amateur historian, and so on. Some claim that amateurism promotes a tendency to see the humorous or absurd side of everything, so that resentments and hatreds are dissolved in laughter. Others aver that amateurism makes society less brittle. 'A society with an amateur quality is a society with a good circulation, less liable to clots and seizures' is one estimate.[54] One of the most lauded historians of the first half of the twentieth century, Sir Lewis Namier, had this to say about the cult of the amateur:

> We prefer to make it appear as if our ideas came to us casually – like the Empire – in a fit of absence of mind . . . specialisation necessarily involves distortion of mind and loss of balance, and the characteristically English attempt to appear unscientific springs from a desire to remain human . . . What is not valued in England is abstract knowledge as a profession, because the tradition of English culture is that professions should be practical and culture should be the work of the leisured classes.[55]

Yet perhaps the pièce de résistance in the entire gallimaufry of mystification and obfuscation is the use of the monarchy. Walter Bagehot, the Victorian critic, long ago pointed out the vagaries of the unwritten British constitution, which used the 'dignified' element of the system to bamboozle and mesmerise the masses while Parliament, the 'efficient' part of the system, did the real work.[56] Defenders of monarchy have argued that the institution gives the ship of state an inherent buoyancy, since governments can totally lose credibility while the regime or system itself does not. The argument is that a scandal like that of Watergate in the USA triggers a constitutional crisis and impeachment proceedings where a rough analogue in the UK, the 1963 Profumo scandal, say, discredits the government but leaves the regime intact because it is symbolised by the monarchy. Naturally critics riposte that this is simply another layer of the general mystification, yet another veil that has to be lifted in the dance of the veils connoted by the Privy Council, the royal prerogative, the principle of Crown-in-Parliament, and so on. Meanwhile the monarchy continues to devalue intellect and meritocracy in favour of tradition and inherited privilege, effectively infantilises society and reinforces hierarchy and deference; even Bagehot, a supporter of the status quo, made the point about deference.[57] Vulgar Marxists have tended to dismiss the monarchy as a mere sideshow alongside the core issue of class struggle, but more thoughtful opinions on the Left have pointed up just how crucial, albeit baneful, the institution has been historically. As one critic has written, the reverence for monarchy suggests that Britain is more a nation of butlers than of shopkeepers and that royalism 'may express something deeply and incorrigibly archaic about the society whose institution it is'.[58] One view of the British monarchy describes it as 'surrogacy', taking the role that in other nation-states would be played by crude nationalism, and an appanage of finance capitalism, always the favoured modality of capitalism in Britain – for the interests of the City have always been placed ahead of those of manufacturing industry.[59] Indeed, the more the British monarchy is studied, the more protean and multi-faceted it appears, suggesting that serious discourse about royalty is very much above the intellectual salt.[60] We should remember that the monarchy was used as one of privileged society's 'big guns' after the Chartist challenge. The Treason Felony Act of 1848 made advocacy of republicanism a criminal offence attracting transportation to Australia (later life imprisonment). Only in 2003 did the Law Lords formally rule that the act did not cover the mere abstract advocacy of republicanism.[61]

Yet, as the phenomenon of monarchy illustrates, in politics there is always a very fine line between subjective perception and objective reality – necessarily so since most people are more influenced by myth than fact. One clear objective aid to the elite in its bid to ward off revolution is the entire intellectual culture of empiricism. 'Fog in Channel. Continent Isolated' is a famous joke illustrating British insularity but it helps to illustrate the gulf between the island nation and its continental neighbours. 'Too clever by half' is another adage with no equivalent in any of the continental languages. The usual interpretation is that the British (and especially the English) distrust and despise intellectuals because, though they will allow differences of rank based on hereditary aristocracy or inherited wealth, they will not tolerate any suggestion of intellectual differences or rankings of intellect.[62] This in turn has been traced to the mere fact of living on an invasion-free island. The British live in what was (at least until recently) a remarkably homogeneous society.[63] With few significant upheavals, there was no need for reinventing oneself. Intellectuals, on the other hand, flourish in more fluid and changeable societies where anything is possible. Some have even brought the weather into the picture and argued that the brute facts of climate preclude in Britain the kind of cafe society where general ideas can be discussed with gusto over coffee or alcohol. Whatever the ultimate reasons, the crevasse between the continental ethos of a priori rationalism and British empiricism is a gaping one. Leftists frequently deplore English separateness, backwardness and traditionalism, fact-worshipping empiricism and the instinctive trust of reason, which produces a coagulated conservatism suffused with philistinism, with the bourgeoisie supine and the proletariat subordinate, plus 'a dilettante literary culture descended from the aristocracy and the crudest of lumpen-bourgeois utilitarian ethics'.[64] One can understand the frustration and impatience. Where continental Europe has produced the epic theories of Marx and Freud, to say nothing of Rousseau, Nietzsche, Schopenhauer, Kant, Hegel, Kierkegaard, Heidegger, etc, etc, Britain has turned out a philosophical tradition vacuous in its sterile conservatism and blinkered empiricism. The reactionary politics of Edmund Burke and his famous political duel with Tom Paine are well known, but even Britain's greatest philosopher, David Hume, could not ground his theories in anything more ground-breaking than 'custom and habit' – a duo Hume tends to use with mantra-like effect.[65] Two examples may be cited from the twentieth century to show the profound conservatism of mainstream British political and philosophical thought. Here is Michael Oakeshott, famous for his definition of politics as 'the pursuit of intimations'. The ship of state, he says, has 'neither starting place nor appointed destination . . . the enterprise is to keep afloat on an even keel . . . To be conservative, then, is to prefer the familiar to the unknown, to prefer the tried to the untried, fact to mystery, the actual to the possible, the limited to the unbounded, the near to the distant, the sufficient to the superabundant, the convenient to the perfect, *present laughter* [italics mine] to utopian bliss.'[66] And this is J. L. Austin, another deeply conservative figure, doyen of the school of 'ordinary language philosophy', the dominant dogma at Oxford University at the mid-century:

> Our common stock of words embodies all the distinctions men have found worth drawing, and the connections they have found worth making, in the lifetime of many generations: these surely are likely to be more numerous, more sound, since they have stood up to the long test of the survival of the fittest, and more subtle, at least in all ordinary and reasonable practical matters, than any that you or I are likely to think up in our armchair of an afternoon – the most favoured alternative method.[67]

It is not surprising that 'ordinary language philosophy' was finally buried under a blizzard of criticism, but the salient point is that to continental philosophers it was like listening to the talk of Martians.[68]

When we have discounted the arguments from the peculiarity of the English, the power of anti-intellectualism and the entire quasi-philistine nature of British empiricism, certainly as primary factors in the entire revolutionary debate, four main theories remain to explain the British avoidance of revolution. The first is the key factor that Britain developed earlier and faster than the continental countries: it had its civil war and 'revolution' earlier; it industrialised earlier; it embraced capitalism earlier; it solved its peasant problem earlier. Some would extend the argument to conclude that Britain was the first real nation-state.[69] The Civil War of the 1640s swept away the potential for an absolutist monarchy that would have left Britain as brittle and ossified a society as France was under the Ancien Régime. The 'dialectic' established thereafter between a constitutional monarch and a sovereign parliament has sometimes been hailed as the final triumph of the fusion of Norman and Anglo-Saxon elements, with the Norman tradition working in favour of strong monarchy and the Anglo-Saxon emphasising the collegiality of the old *witan* or primitive assembly of the 'Ancient Constitution'. Some scholars, however, maintain that regal absolutism had shallow roots and that the Tudor despotism of Henry VIII and Elizabeth I was only possible because the nation temporarily 'ran for cover' after the turmoil and exhaustion of the Wars of the Roses.[70] At all events, having jettisoned royalist, ecclesiastical and feudal residues, Cromwell's successors hastened to solve the problem of the peasantry through enclosure. The way was now clear, since the move towards enclosure had been stoutly resisted before the Civil War by Charles I's Star Chamber. There is no need to posit a master plan to introduce new types of capitalism, for the main impetus for the changes came from the wool industry. Simply put, the profits to be made from wool encouraged sheep pasturing, and this in turn led the yeomanry to deprive the peasants of their commons and strips of agricultural land.[71] Moreover, this process took place over time. The 'hidden violence' whereby capitalism destroyed the peasantry through enclosures was a gradual process, and achieved by parliamentary and legal means rather than brutal immediate expropriation, thus avoiding the worst social tensions. Gradualism manifested itself elsewhere too. The rural elites, who traditionally and in most societies have relied on a combination of strong monarchy and the peasantry to maintain their position, were sucked into the power elite by a 'bourgeois impulse'. An alliance or symbiosis between bourgeoisie and landed aristocracy, which some have claimed was unique to Britain, was consolidated in the eighteenth century. From 1650 onwards a streamlined modern system emerged – a political coalition of landlords and merchants, cohesive, financially efficient and self-confident.[72] Insofar as there was conflict, this took the form of competition between manufacturing and agrarian interests for the support of the have-nots, and the equilibrium thus engendered knocked out all the more selfish and thus dangerous repressive measures which might have triggered a revolution.[73] The euthanasia of the peasantry was possible in England because of the country's small size. In geographically vast nations the peasants were cocooned in rural hinterlands and backwoods and thus the impact of modernising trends in the market was considerably diffused; for example, rural isolation meant that the French peasantry was not reached by Enlightenment thought before 1789.

It is now that the beauty of the Skocpol model of revolution can be appreciated. In the French, Russian and Chinese Revolutions, as we have seen, three overarching factors obtained. A powerful peasantry was the key social class; there was acute intra-elite conflict; and the nation-state was defensive, vulnerable, paranoid and under acute strain because of the competition of more powerful nations. None of this was the case in Britain after 1640. The road to parliamentary democracy was thus clearly open, since the survival of the peasantry into the modern era is a virtual guarantee of social turmoil and eventual dictatorship. The more heterogeneous the society (with the survival of peasants, rural elites and feudal residues from earlier eras) and the more resistance there is to capitalism and modernisation, the more likely is revolution. The timing of industrialisation and the social structure at the time of the transition from primitive society seem to be the key factors that determine the emergence of communism and fascism.[74] The survival of a peasant economy into a modern industrial society without a revolution is a virtual guarantee of fascism. The other salient factor in all this is urbanisation. Since the seventeenth century Britain has been a predominatly urban society. Although the literary conceit of 'city bad, countryside good' and the disdain for the 'city slicker' is a notion that goes back to the Romans – and from its association with Cato the Elder is sometimes called Catonism – the glorification of traditional or peasant society is bound to produce an ideology of conservatism.[75] In its harmless manifestations, as in the American Midwest, it produces extremes of support for the Republican Party, but in less advanced societies it is apt to produce the great despots: Stalin, Mao, Pol Pot, etc. To sum up, then, Britain got rid of its worst social tensions *before* the tsunami of the Industrial Revolution hit her. Yet instead of the expected process whereby the bourgeoisie displaced the landed aristocracy as the hegemonic class, what happened was a symbiosis of the two lasting roughly 200 years from 1640 to 1832. This was bad news for the proletariat since, from its point of view, the civil war of the 1640s happened too soon, and the working-class movement was premature because, of necessity, it was formed in the Industrial Revolution of the late eighteenth century before proper revolutionary consciousness had dawned.[76] Historians have proposed that two main consequences flowed from this. The alliance of aristocracy and bourgeoisie meant, by definition, that there was no middle-class revolution. When the working class began to organise itself seriously in the early nineteenth century, there was thus no model of bourgeois revolutionaries that proletarians could follow. There was no preceding ideological clash which could have sharpened the working class's own critique of society. The result was a climate of compromise in which the proletariat was forever on the defensive and reactive.[77] Naturally, this theory has been criticised on the obvious ground that it assumes the proletariat needed a pre-existing code of bourgeois ideology and practice before it could itself function effectively, yet the experience of the German socialist parties in the nineteenth century, similarly placed but much more vigorous and incisive, proves that it was not necessarily so.[78] The second deduction from the early onset of the Industrial Revolution is that it left the working class fragmented, unable to draw on either the support of an international proletariat or solidarity within the entire British proletariat itself. Industries were isolated, with little interconnection. Miners knew little of textile workers, coal heavers were ignorant of weavers. The consequent divisions by skill, locality and trade died very hard. Indeed, some sociologists have gone so far as to suggest that this workplace isolation and lack of more general solidarity is the true explanation for the phenomenon of working-class conservatism, so notable a feature of the British political scene, and usually attributed to deference.[79]

The second theory of the avoidance of revolution stresses the importance of the British Empire. The possession of empire automatically excluded Britain from that class of nations identified by Skocpol as under severe strain from conflicts with much more powerful international competitors. There are several aspects to this. It was a staple of J. A. Hobhouse's critique of economic imperialism that it was motivated mainly by the export of surplus capital. The dispersal of economic surpluses throughout the 'Empire on which the sun never sets' generated the idea that other surpluses too were being exported, the main candidate for consideration being sexuality, since it was a commonplace that, especially in India, men could enjoy a climate of sexual licence unthinkable in Britain.[80] The number, level, degree and ferocity of Britain's colonial wars also soaked up a great mass of proletarian energy which at home might have been expended on revolutionary designs.[81] Trotsky remarked that the British ruling classes were able to avoid war at home more easily the more successful they were in increasing their own power overseas through imperial exploitation. Instancing the British record in India, Egypt, South Africa and Ireland, he scoffed at the idea that this was a nation averse to violent change: 'the greater success with which Britain applied force to other peoples, the greater was the degree of gradualness she was able to realise within her own borders.'[82] Distraction from notions like the class struggle was another motif. Disraeli thought that the great benefit of empire was that it enabled Britain to transcend European limitations and all the baleful European ideologies such as socialism and communism: 'The abstention of England from any unnecessary interference in the affairs of Europe is the consequence, not of her decline of power but of her increased strength. England is no longer a mere European power; she is the metropolis of a great metropolitan Empire . . . she is really more an Asiatic power than a European.'[83] All the evidence suggests that the tactic of diversion was largely successful: the British working class was turned away from ideas of class struggle by a patriotic nationalism deriving from pride in empire.[84] Lenin hypothesised that the Empire was *the* great barrier to revolution in England, since the super-profits generated in the colonies enabled the elite in effect to bribe the upper strata of the working class to break class ranks; this was his famous 'aristocracy of labour' argument.[85] At the same time he was aware of the immense complications caused for the proletariat by the existence of empire, if only because the workers themselves (or at any rate some of them) were now benefiting from 'surplus labour':

> Only the proletarian class, which maintains the whole of society, can bring about the social revolution. However, as a result of the extensive colonial policy, the European proletarian party member finds himself in a position where it is not his labour, but the labour of the practically enslaved natives in the colonies, that maintains the whole of society . . . In certain countries this provides the material and economic basis for infecting the proletariat with colonial chauvinism. Of course this may be only a temporary phenomenon, but the evil must nonetheless be clearly realised and its causes understood.[86]

The final two explanations for avoidance of revolution relate to the period after 1760. Some have sought the answer in religion, specifically Methodism. The followers of John Wesley, it is alleged, played a vital role in taming the British proletariat: by repressing discontent or diverting it into politically harmless conduits; by allowing ordinary folk to subscribe to equality and reform without becoming revolutionaries; but mainly by giving working-class people a new sense of identity and hence self-confidence. Methodism, in short, produced a conformist and reformist working-class elite and thus headed off revolution. Given that the bourgeoisie was until 1832 in alliance with the aristocracy, Methodism provided the only sliver of middle-class leadership, without which the working class was sunk in endless night. This is the famous 'Halévy thesis' often thought discredited but as often revived and given a new coat of paint.[87] The strange thing about the French historian Elie Halévy was that he seemed to have worked entirely independently of the great German sociologist Max Weber, whose work linking Protestantism and capitalism was so influential; it has been speculated that this was because Halévy, as a French historian, worked entirely within a very different French intellectual tradition hailing from the nineteenth century and typified by Taine and Guizot.[88] Supporters of the thesis argue that Methodism was able to suggest a way to accommodate the change from traditional to modern modalities without revolution or violence, and may even have transformed British culture so as to produce the atypical Victorian society, whose nature so fascinates historians and social critics.[89] Unquestionably Wesleyanism itself prescribed strict respect for hierarchy and authority, as well as condemning political dissent and social unrest. It implicitly rejected class conflict and all dialectical notions by preaching an avoidance of either/or and instead recommending pragamatism and compromise. Further than this one cannot go, for the thesis is beset with problems and riddled with objections from a number of quarters. The most basic is that the Halévy thesis is a circular argument. Halévy claims that Methodism found a fertile seedbed in the English character, which he described as serious, reserved, melancholic and puritanical, as against the hedonistic, extroverted and irreligious French, but then claims that the Victorian mindset (serious, reserved, melancholic and puritanical) was produced by Methodism.[90] More generally, critics allege that Halévy assumed that the primary meaning of religion was social, and discounted the variety of meanings Methodism might have had both for an individual proletarian or even a putative working-class elite; religion, on this view, has a personal meaning for people, whatever their social position. Most Methodists were moderate radicals but did not carry their views over into political activism; most of all they were *socially* deviant, not politically; moral regeneration not political revolution was their aim.[91]

More seriously, Halévy seems to have assumed that Methodism was monolithic, whereas in fact there were many strands and offshoots encompassing a range of doctrine. The Kilhamites, for example, expelled in 1796, did advocate violent revolution.[92] Moreover, what has been termed 'popular religion' (i.e. anything other than Catholicism or Anglicanism – the Baptists, Methodists, Plymouth Brethren and other sects) had a variety of manifestations, most of them a long way from Wesley's tenets. Some stress the importance of radical evangelical cottage religions, with female preachers as a core element.[93] In sum, there were many creeds just as important as Methodism in the era when radicalism and religion advanced together. Not surprisingly, the Halévy thesis has particularly exercised Marxists. E. P. Thompson, the best-known exponent of the New Left, influential from the 1960s to the 1980s, particularly excoriated Methodism as a detestable doctrine, plugging the oldest Christian pro-Establishment idea of all:

accept your miserable lot in this life in exchange for glory in the next. Even more despicably, it did not pre-empt radical action but followed parasitically in its wake. He described it as 'a chiliasm of despair . . . psychic exploitation . . . the desolate inner landscape of utilitarianism'.[94] As for the Halévy thesis itself, this was mere broad-brush a priori; not enough was known about the minutiae of Methodism to make the thesis plausible and 'we should know more about, not the years of revivalism but the months, not the counties, but the towns and villages'.[95] However, it is worth pointing out that, whereas mainstream historians tend to accept Halévy's hypothesis in its entirety, even some Marxists give it grudging acceptance.[96] Yet by and large the Marxist view is sceptical. It seems unlikely that Methodism, on its own, really could have done all its proponents claim for it and set such a block on the development of the working-class world. It was too patchy in membership, too vulnerable to lukewarm supporters who drifted away and too multi-faceted and eclectic in its political interpretations for that to be feasible. Most fundamentally, there were not enough committed Methodists – an estimated 90,000 in England in 1800 – to be able to wield the influence claimed.[97] Probably the most that can be said is that Methodism heightened elements in English culture that were already there. If it had an influence, this was largely confined to its leaders, for there is no evidence of a groundswell of moderation among ordinary workers. It did increase social mobility – this has been termed the 'Methodist escalator',[98] but that is a different matter. The alleged effects of Methodism can be independently attributed to other and larger factors, and Methodism could not have averted revolution if these other factors, favourable to stifling revolutionary influences, had not been present. The doctrines of John Wesley, then, can be seen as icing on a non-revolutionary cake.

The final explanation for the enigma of 'the dog that barked in the night' is the failure of Marxism to take hold in Britain – yet another example of 'English exceptionalism', since the doctrine made great strides in Europe until the mid-twentieth century. On paper Britain from 1848 to 1919 had all the objective conditions propitious for socialism: 15 per cent of the working class were members of a trade union in 1901, and the figure rose to 25.8 per cent by 1914.[99] Yet British trade unions never evolved in sensibility beyond what Lenin contemptuously called 'economism' or 'trade union consciousness'. Since 1848 was the date when Marxism first made a significant impact in Europe but 1919 was probably the last date at which revolution could realistically have been attempted in Britain, there was thus a very narrow 'window' in which the revolutionary moment could appear. These were precisely the high days of Victorian and Edwardian triumphalism when no overwhelming grievances united the working class against civil society.[100] One convincing study finds a threefold explanation for the failure of Marxism to inspire a revolutionary proletariat: the fragmented nature of the workforce; the presence of a rich, varied but apolitical culture; and the integration of workers into the institutions of the State.[101] Only the last really calls for comment. As trade unions and cooperative societies acquired funds and assets, they necessarily depended on the stability of the capitalist system and its institutions, since no one had devised a way of inventing a non-capitalist bank.[102] In other respects the failure of Marxism to make a showing in Great Britain is to a remarkable extent explicable in terms of the arguments already considered. Tensions within the working class, with acute factionalism between (and sometimes within) industries, and numerous coteries jostling for supremacy in the trade union movement, increased rather than diminished. Religion played an important role, not only because some leaders of the infant Labour Party, such as Arthur Henderson, really were Methodists but because Catholics joined the new party in large numbers; the negative attitude of the Catholic Church has already been noted, especially in reference to the General Strike. The fact that women were always in the majority of churchgoers was also not unconnected with their non-radical attitudes.[103] The already-mentioned importance of sport in British life was particularly important in the years 1848–1919, with working-class culture having regressed since the days of the Chartists into an inward-looking ethos obsessed with sport, gambling and the music hall.[104] There was one give-away remark from a socialist thinker when he declared that socialism implied democracy just as cricket implied batting.[105] So: the working class was highly dispersed by occupation, with a low level of communitarian solidarity, seam-burstingly pluralistic in its pursuit of a number of different competing activities and implicitly accepting of the 'play the game' ideology which saw the State not as the instrument of the class enemy but as a benign ringmaster. One commentator says that the mentality and temperament of the typical worker at the weekend was not far from that on the Conservative back benches.[106] Meanwhile the elite had become ever more sophisticated in its methods of social control, clever enough to emphasise fairness rather than coercion, playing up the way the empire distinguished Britain from the rest of Europe and binding the working class to imperial pride with themes of silken sentimentality. How much more astute the elite was in its ability to play the social balancing game was indicated by Bertrand Russell the philosopher when he wrote to Elie Halévy: 'I wish the [House of] Lords would reject the Trade Disputes Bill: that might give a real chance of getting them abolished, as it would rouse fury. But I fear they have too much sense.'[107] Finally, and not insignificantly, Marx himself (and Engels later) believed socialism could be reached by parliamentary means in Britain, so even committed Marxists did not feel the revolutionary pressure of their continental counterparts.[108]

After 1919 the dominance of the Labour Party on the left-centre of British politics gave the coup de grâce to any lingering hope of revolution still entertained on the Left. One expert commentator has put it like this: 'Two of the prime assumptions of any Marxist party – a rejection by much of the working class of existing political institutions and a belief in the unity of "economics" and "politics" – did not hold. The Labour Party, therefore, was not free to choose between Marxism and reformism but only between varieties of reformism.'[109] That rather makes it sound as though the Labour Party was reluctant not to have that choice. But by 1919 its 'counter-revolutionary' character was clear, and this would be seen to devastating effect in the General Strike. Both by background, temperament and ideology, the leaders of the Labour Party were the least imaginable candidates as revolutionaries. The performance of MacDonald, Snowden and Thomas in the 'great betrayal' of 1931 was so dispiriting that from his prison cell in Italy Antonio Gramsci suggested that this trio had performed the historical role usually reserved for Caesarism.[110] Defenders of MacDonald point out that he was convinced that, should a left-wing party ever take command without a huge electoral mandate (unlikely), it would simply propel the extreme Right into fascist reaction.[111] Since this is precisely what happened in Chile in 1970–3, there is a case for giving him the benefit of the doubt. MacDonald's supporters make the further point that the interwar Labour Party knew its limitations and thus acted as the most effective defence against extreme action by either the Left or the Right.[112] Revolutionaries and socialists of all stripes have suffered more than 100 years of disappointment with the Labour Party, which, apart from a brief leftward lacuna in 1945–51, has drifted ever more to the right, first from an ostensibly socialist party to a social-democratic one and finally, under the impact of Thatcherism and transmogrifying itself as 'New Labour', from a social-democratic to a neo-liberal party.[113] It was always the Labour Party which, in the twentieth century, made the formation of a genuinely left-wing party very difficult almost to the point of impossibility. As for revolution, that was beyond the pale, for even left-wing members of the party like Sir Stafford Cripps thought that socialism could only ever emerge by consent not revolution.[114] In defence of these Labour Party stalwarts it can perhaps be entered as a plea that some kind of psychic factor was at work, that they feared that socialism would usher in the void and the chaos world. Given that revolution means sailing into the unknown, and it is precisely this which is so alien to the entire British culture, perhaps we should leave the last word to Arthur Henderson:

> Revolution is a word of evil omen. It calls up a vision of barricades in the street and blood in the gutters. No responsible person . . . can contemplate such a possibility without horror . . . Revolution . . . will be veritable civil war. The prospect of social convulsions on this scale is enough to appal the stoutest heart. Yet this is the alternative that unmistakeably confronts us, if we turn aside from the path of ordered social change by constitutional methods.[115]

APPENDIX

Revolution is a concept with an interesting provenance. As used in Aristotle's classic work *Politics*, it indicates a mere change of constitution resulting from intra-elite (i.e. not class-based) 'stasis' or strife. When employed by scientists such as Copernicus, it denoted a circularity, whereby the wheel (whether celestial or terrestrial) returned to its original location after an orbit. In this sense it is indistinguishable from the circular notion of history found in Schopenhauer, Nietzsche and their modern analogues.[1] The modern notion of revolution can be dated fairly precisely to the French Revolution of 1789 and its most distinguished theorist, Alexis de Tocqueville. The most famous thesis in his work is that revolutions tend to occur not when social conditions are deteriorating but when they start improving both objectively and in the sense that the government of the day starts to relax oppression.[2] Tyrants and despots have often defended their unblinking resistance to all change by citing Tocqueville's brilliant observation that concessions and liberal reforms are a slippery slope, that they are the start of an inexorable process that cannot be halted. As he put it: 'Those parts of France in which the improvement of living standards was the most pronounced were the chief centres of the revolutionary movement.'[3] Against the Tocquevillian thesis of rising expectations can be set the contrary notion promoted by Karl Marx. It is well known that the core of Marxist theory is historical materialism – the notion that socio-economic structures (and the class systems they engender) are the engine of history. Marx conceded that revolution was not an inevitable or logical entailment of the process whereby one system of production was replaced by another – slavery by feudalism and feudalism by capitalism – but argued that the transition from capitalism to socialism would have to be attended by violent revolution simply because of consciousness: ruling elites knew that their privileges were at stake and would fight to maintain them, which meant that his designated historical agent – the proletariat (not the actual working class but a mythically conceived 'class for itself') – would in turn have to use violence. As for the precipitants towards revolution, Marx though these would be the declining rate of profit under capitalism and the consequent increasing immiseration of those who possessed nothing and had only their labour power to sell.[4] Some specialists argue that Engels diverged from Marx in thinking that the revolution could be achieved by peaceful means, through parliamentary democracy and the rise of socialist parties, though he did not rule out the change-by-violence scenario. Marx, according to his critics, was more hard line and considered violence and violent revolution to be imbricated in the very process of historical materialism. One of the much-cited aphorisms from *Capital* is: 'Force is the midwife of every old society pregnant with the new one. It is itself an economic power.'[5] Because Tocqueville took a more broad-based view of revolution – his definition was tripartite, embracing merely political revolutions, violent socio-economic convulsions and the profound changes wrought by, for example, the Reformation and the Industrial Revolution (significantly so called), it is Tocqueville who has had more influence on modern *thinking* about revolution, though it would be foolish to deny Marx the palm when it comes to the practice and motivation of actual revolutionaries.[6]

The twentieth century saw many attempts by historians and social scientists to refine the concept of revolution. According to one influential typology, theories of revolution came in four waves, roughly emphasising psychological, sociological, political and cultural/ideological perspectives respectively.[7] Yet this attempt at hermeneusis via four waves was unsatisfactory. The fourth wave in many respects returned to the first, except that Third World dimensions were emphasised in place of Western ones. In any case, to interpret revolution by psychology meant entering the minefield of academic psychology itself, with everything from crowd theory to psychoanalysis jostling for attention. At least four main theories arose. One suggested, in quasi-Freudian terms, that revolutionaries were guilty of neurotic behaviour, that dissidents threatened the essential business of society, which was to arrest mankind's perennial impulses towards violence.[8] The notion that all societies skated on remarkably thin ice and that it was remarkably easy to fall into an ontological void or chaos world was particularly popular with theorists of a conservative inclination. Another theory took up the Tocquevillian theme that the selfishness of elites was largely responsible for lighting the revolutionary fuse that detonated societies. A very popular idea at one time was that of 'relative deprivation', which emphasised the middle-class genesis of many revolutions. In this model the middle class was thrown into revolutionary turmoil by being taxed while the elite classes systematically evaded tax and at the very time the middle class was losing its status vis-à-vis the proletariat and other groups below. Others criticised 'relative deprivation' as an empty concept that could be applied in almost any historical situation; as an explanation it was therefore vacuous.[9] A fourth psychological theory, influenced by psychoanalysis, stressed the notion of psychological alienation (a very different concept from alienation in the Marxist sense) and emphasised the conflict between an individual's values and the general values of society.[10] Meanwhile, the allegedly sociological wave fractured into several wavelets, as did the third. Moreover, some important insights could not be categorised under any of the four headings. For example, the noted thinker Hannah Arendt proposed the idea that revolution was a category that applied only to secular phenomena and excluded religion, which many had seen as a kind of passepartout to pre-1789 revolutions.[11] And notable attempts were made to fuse the Marxist and Tocquevillian perspectives, positing rising expectations that are suddenly thwarted, and thus in effect sidestepping the issues raised in the 'waves'.[12] The political approach via the study of the State seemed at first sight the most promising avenue, but again there was little agreement even on basic premises. Some saw the State as the key construct or institution in the revolutionary crossover, but Marxists tended to define it as that which will wither away as a result of revolution.[13] Even within liberal theory there was a collision between those who asserted that revolution was impossible without the modern State and those who, on the contrary, thought that the power of the modern State ruled out revolution which, in the Western world at least, remained a mere 'academic pipe dream'.[14]

Underlying all the contradictions and disagreements was the ineluctable fact of the writers' political affiliations. Naturally those who welcomed revolution saw it very differently from those who were repelled and horrified by it. Revolution has always had an ambiguous aspect, and one analyst summed up its Janus face as follows: 'One is an elegant, abstract and humanitarian face, an idyllic face, the dream of revolution, its meaning under the calm distance of eternity. The other is crude, violent and very concrete, rather nightmarish, with the hypnotic power of nightmare and the loss of perspective and breadth of understanding which you might expect to go with this.'[15]

Rather than work through the myriad interpretations of revolution in general and in its particular manifestations (the French Revolution, the English Revolution, etc), it seems more fruitful to rehearse four of the most influential works that have appeared on the subject. Crane Brinton's *The Anatomy of Revolution* is usually considered the first modern classic on the subject. Brinton's approach is heavily dependent on taxonomy: he likes to present lists. His schedule of features present in all revolutions includes government deficits, complaints over taxation, governments favouring one set of interests over another, administrative inefficiency, loss of self-confidence in the ruling class, the desertion of intellectuals, loss of self-confidence within the elite, and conversion of significant numbers of the rulers to the perception that their privileges are unjust, blocking of careers open to talents, the separation of economic power from political power and general social prestige. In the case of the intellectuals' desertion, Brinton uses the example of the French Revolution, instancing the alienation from the Ancien Régime of Voltaire, Rousseau, Diderot, Raynal, d'Holbach, Volney, Helvetius, Rousseau, d'Alembert, Condorcet, Bernardin de St Pierre and Beaumarchais.[16] Brinton's ideas – such as that six seventeenth-century 'revolutions', in England, France, Spain, Portugal, the Netherlands and Naples all had their origin in protests against taxation – are always interesting, but what he says essentially amounts to the proposition that revolutions occur when relations between rulers and ruled become impossibly brittle.[17] Yet is there not something pleonastic or tautological here? By definition, revolutions would not occur unless this had happened. Another criticism of Brinton's approach is that it is overly psychological. Aping Jung and his psychological types, Brinton attempts a similar typology of revolutionaries. So, for example, there are the gentleman revolutionist, the frustrated intellectual, the contrarian, the transmogrified criminal, the utopian fanatic, the idealist, the demagogue.[18] Since this list covers such a wide spectrum of human beings, it is unclear how it advances one's understanding of revolution. A more serious criticism of Brinton is that he can be naive, and not just in his unintentionally risible (at least to non-American readers) description of Clement Attlee's 1945–51 government as a 'socialist revolution'.[19] Methodologically, the analogy he constantly draws between revolution and disease is unsound. Diseases have a generally agreed aetiology, diagnosis and prognosis; to assume the same with revolutions is absurd, quite apart from the intrinsic absurdity of imagining that the structure of viruses and social phenomena are homologous. More seriously, Brinton assumes what has to be proved, that the French Revolution really was the template for all true revolutions.[20] His over-identification with 1789–94 comes across not just in his generally Tocquevillian analysis of revolutions, but in his assumption that 'Thermidorean reaction' is a constant in all of them. He claims (incorrectly) that all revolutions have a life-cycle involving the old order, a moderate regime, a radical regime, and a counter-revolutionary 'Thermidorean' phase. Inevitably, perhaps, the 1794 coup in the revolutionary month of Thermidor that ended the rule of Robespierre and the Jacobin Republic is described as a 'convalescence from the fever'.[21] Yet the worst of all Brinton's many faults is his inability to distinguish revolutions of different types (see below pp. 515–17) He lumps together the English Revolution of the 1640s, the American 'Revolution' of 1776, the French Revolution of 1789 and the Russian Revolution of 1917 as phenomena of the same kind. In fact they are representatives of three very different violent manifestations. Even Edmund Burke, notable reactionary though he was, was acute and sophisticated enough to see that the American rebellion of 1776 and the post-1789 events in France were very different matters. The first was concerned to return to a (half true, half fantastic) notion of an earlier era of 'no taxation without representation'. The second was a leap into the unknown, an attempt to reconstruct society from abstract, a priori principles.[22]

The next seminal work on revolution was by Chalmers Johnson, a disciple of Talcott Parsons, the Harvard-based sociologist associated with 'structural-functionalism'. Deeply imbued with the notion of society as a system and with notions of homeostasis and equilibrium, Johnson's work is often turbid because of the heavy use of sociological jargon, an unfortunate by-product of the quasi-Teutonic approach of the influential Talcott Parsons Harvard school of sociology. Since the key to social stability for Johnson is 'equilbrium', revolution is perceived as something pathological and an example of severe 'disequilibrium'. Revolution was to riot what a hurricane or typhoon was to a gale, not an entirely different phenomenon but a more serious and dangerous one. Revolutions, in short, were merely the most important events in a scale of violence that ran the gamut from riots through rebellions to 'grave disequilibrium'. Gradual change can be absorbed within a 'system', but revolution means 'multiple dysfunctions' because of the inability of the system to deal with it. Using his peculiar jargon, Johnson suggested that revolutions occur when two or more of the following occur: exogenous value-changing sources, endogenous value-changing sources, exogenous environment-changing sources and endogenous environment-changing sources.[23] To put this in plain English, an example of the first of the four might be the influence that the French and Russian Revolutions had on other nations; an example of the second would be the way Enlightenment thinkers changed people's attitudes to religion; an example of the third would be the impact of the West on the Third World through military conquest, trade, investment, imported technology, migration or modern medical knowledge; and the fourth would be exemplified by such things as the invention of the wheel or the coming of the railways. All of these drastic changes constitute the *necessary* conditions for revolution; the *sufficient* conditions are supplied by what Johnson calls 'accelerators'. These accelerators typically occur when the political elite can no longer operate the State as the 'monopolist of violence' (to use Max Weber's famous phrase), when the opposition knows this and is thus confident of being able to overthrow it, and when the elite responds incompetently or (more usually) with intransigence.[24] The main criticism of all this is that, with the jargon stripped away, Johnson is simply telling us what is blindingly obvious. Many writers have pessimistically concluded that only contingency, mere chance or aleatory circumstance can explain revolution. Clearly if there is subversion of a society's armed forces, a politically conscious revolutionary class employing the correct strategy for the circumstances (e.g. guerrilla warfare), and an incompetent or intransigent elite, the conditions for revolution are present, and one scarcely needs the entire gallimaufry of 'systems', 'homeostasis' and 'disequilibrium' to buttress the explanation. Chalmers Johnson partly rescues himself from the charge of banality by providing a typology of revolution which, though ultimately unconvincing, is nonetheless stimulating. He proposes six types.[25] There is *jacquerie*, when a government is overthrown by a peasantry with limited aims. There is millenarian revolution (usually occurring in societies subject to external stresses such as industrialisation, colonialism or imperialism), of which good examples would be the Pugachev rising in eighteenth-century Russia and the great Taiping revolt in China in the middle of the nineteenth century. 'Anarchistic revolution' is Johnson's somewhat eccentric term for revolutions caused by 'dysfunction' perceived by an oppressed majority; this is particularly relevant for British history, since both the Pilgrimage of Grace and the Jacobite Rising of 1745 (discussed below) fit into this category. Jacobin Communist Revolution is the nomenclature used by Johnson to describe the root-and-branch transformation of society, as in the Russian Revolution of 1917. Then there are two final categories relating to the post-1945 experience of the Third World: the conspiratorial coup d'état, as in Egypt in 1952, and the militarised mass insurrection, as in the Chinese Communist Revolution and the Algerian War of 1945–62.[26]

Probably the most influential of all academic work written on the theory of revolutions is that by Theda Skocpol, a political sociologist with a keen sense of the particularities of historical research and thus not given to unthinking broad-brush theorising. Her work is nuanced, reflective, intellectually sophisticated and a clear advance on Brinton and Chalmers Johnson. Aware that any cogent analysis of revolution must be multi-causal on one hand but not just omnium gatherum (as with Chalmers Johnson and Brinton) on the other, she analyses the French, Russian and Chinese Revolutions and finds a common tripartite thread: threats against the State by a strong peasantry; a conflict between the State and autonomous elites; and the impact of international relations, specifically economic and military competition from stronger nation-states. In all three societies the peasantry was powerful and could mobilise quickly to attack landlords; this was particularly the case in China.[27] In the case of France, the entire wealth of the nation could not be harnessed, and the national treasury was dependent mainly on direct taxes levied on land, which fell on the modest cultivators, not the big landowners. As Skocpol points out: 'Rentier agrarian systems, where smallholder peasant families possess and work the land on their own, are notoriously susceptible to peasant revolts.'[28] The case of the State was more complex. According to Marxist theory, the State was 'nothing but' the interests of the ruling class masquerading as the common good, but many studies made it clear that a bureaucracy, put in place to guarantee the interests of a ruling elite, could develop its own interests and ideology which put it in conflict with the ruling class. In Ancien Régime France the entire aristocracy, supposedly committed to Bourbon absolutism, was systematically treacherous to the State of Louis XV and Louis XVI by its systematic tax evasion and demands for special financial perquisites and privileges. Lack of financial muscle makes it extraordinarily difficult for certain states to deal with their international competitors and when they attempt to do so, the domestic problems of a divided elite and a restless peasantry vitiate their efforts.[29] In Russia during World War One it proved impossible to extract a sufficient surplus from the peasantry to finance and equip a modern army. When Russian armies were humiliated by Germany in the field, the military in effect threw in the towel and were thus unavailable to deal with domestic revolt. This was a classic instance of the perennial truth that in trying to deal with international threats, a ruling class may leave itself vulnerable to threats from below; in Russia, additionally, the elite had shot itself in the foot by blocking the modernisation of agriculture.[30] In China the combination of a backward agrarian society and the impact of Western imperialism had already made the situation perilous when Chiang Kai-shek and his Kuomintang compounded the problem with 'liberal' decentralisation, which led to chaos, the dominance of the provincial gentry and finally warlordism – all factors preparing the ground for the eventual communist takeover.[31] The strength of Skocpol's work is the way she dovetails all the complex elements involved in the run-up to revolution. She is particularly good on France, showing how the bread riots of 1788 coincided with elite factionalism, the Tocquevillian factor of rising aspirations, the declining capacity of the regime to use force against internal opposition and the steady decline of the nobility as the urban bourgeoisie and city proletariat made their presences felt.[32]

Skocpol displays interdisciplinary sophistication in emphasising that revolutions arise from a number of factors – State crises, popular uprisings, elite actions – all of which have different causes and have to be explained separately. Her work is studded with insights, such as the perception that socialism is most likely to emerge when economic interests are concentrated in a few capital-intensive centres, when mass mobilisation is extensive, and when external pressures from powerful capitalist countries are modest. Her analysis is in line with that of other specialists, for here is a very similar estimate: 'States crack when they are hit simultaneously by three sorts of crisis: a state financial emergency, elite divisions, and a potential and propensity for popular groups to mobilise.'[33] The analytical approach she adopts incidentally throws up a convincing narrative, showing the convergence of French, Russian and Chinese experiences. So: the competition between states drives forward centralisation, and bureaucratisation, and strengthens the State in both military and economic ways; but some states fall behind in the international race and consequently try to extract resources beyond the point the society will tolerate; this breaks up the balance of power between the rural nobility and the peasantry, which in turn leads to general crisis; previously marginal urban elites then assume the helm but cannot unite all the fissiparous elements in the society; and the end of the road is the 'man on horseback'. This is convincing, for the turmoil caused by any revolution that attempts socio-economic transformation seems inevitably to lead to dictatorship, either to arrest such progress or to further it, as the examples of Cromwell, Napoleon, Stalin and Mao clearly show. Yet for all the brilliance of Skocpol's work, it has been subjected to criticism on a number of fronts, some of it devastating. The objection – made by Sinologists and Kremlinologists – that she is more convincing on the French Revolution than the Russian and Chinese ones is probably valid, but it must be remembered that academic specialists always object to wide-ranging and cross-cultural speculation. More soundly based is the criticism that she neglects the role of ideology in culture in her analysis.[34] A variant of this is that her analysis is entirely an 'objective conditions' piece of work and that consequently she neglects human agency, 'subjective conditions', and, in particular, discounts revolutionary voluntarism as a powerful agent. Her defenders say that her emphasis on the State as a pro-active factor is a necessary corrective to the view of it as simply a target for revolutionaries. But there is no denying that sometimes she seems to edge uneasily towards something like the conservative view of Brinton, who famously asserted that top-down reforms – such as those of Kemal Atatürk in Turkey, Japan under the Meiji restoration or even General Douglas MacArthur in his proconsular period (1945–51) – invariably achieve more than revolutions.[35] Much stronger criticism is that in her work the State sometimes seems to be hypostasised or to attain a Hegelian stature. The ex-revolutionary turned reformist Regis Debray seemed to have had her in mind when he accused certain sociologists of committing the Feuerbachian fallacy. Where Feuerbach had burlesqued Christians for making a subject–predicate mistake – they preached that God made Man whereas the reality was that Man invented God – Debray claimed American sociology often made the same mistake. Revolution, capitalism, democracy and other universals were all assumed to be independent entities, but the truth was that they came to life only when embraced by individuals, classes or nations.[36] Finally, it might be observed that Skocpol does not take enough care to dissociate herself from Brinton's 'Thermidorean fallacy' outlined above. It is true that the French, Russian and Chinese Revolutions all ended with the man on horseback, but in no sense are they similar in having a Thermidorean stage. There was no Thermidor in Mao's China and, though Trotsky famously 'placed' Stalin as the man of Thermidor, this was inexact. Stalin was very different from Cromwell and Napoleon. They slammed the brakes on, but he took the revolution in a new direction – admittedly a direction that was heresy both according to the doctrine of Marx and of Marxism–Leninism. Stalin took Russia into the unknown territory of 'socialism in one country', an experiment doomed to failure in hindsight. Whereas in both classical Marxism and Marxism–Leninism socialism is the system that replaces capitalism as part of an inevitable process of historical change, Stalin postulated a battle of socialism versus capitalism – according to the orthodoxy a solecism as extraordinary as a writer of science fiction having dinosaurs and cavemen living in the same era.[37]

The final attempt at a theory of revolution that commands attention is that by Jack Goldstone, like Skocpol a scholar of great erudition and sophistication. His principal innovation was to point to population increase as a principal trigger for revolution. He scores some palpable hits and opens up new dimensions for study. For instance, having established that population in England grew from about 2 million at the time of the Pilgrimage of Grace to 5 million at the outbreak of the Civil War in 1640, he points out that this explosion created an army of squatters and landless who were the main causes of riots and disorders; the protests usually involved such displaced groups complaining vociferously about the loss of forest and commons to arable land, creating food scarcity and high prices.[38] To an extent one can see him following in the Skocpol tradition but putting icing on the cake. For example, he agrees with her that agrarian/bureaucratic states are particularly vulnerable to revolution but traces this in the main to population increase, which can place intolerable strains on an inflexible regime which relies on traditional systems of taxation, economic organisation and elite recruitment. Population explosions raise real costs and prices of staples simultaneously, crippling regimes like England under the early Stuarts or France under the Ancien Régime. Faced with an army of young men seeking employment and patronage, the government tended to solve the problem by enlarging its armies, thus further increasing its costs and creating a need for fresh revenue.[39] Since population increase automatically triggers inflation – with expenses rising faster than revenues, larger armies and mounting expenditure on the relief of indigence and poverty – and this is a phenomenon more noticeable in the cities than the countryside, Goldstone suggests that Skocpol might have overdone the emphasis on peasant revolt as central to revolution. He points out that the periodicity of peasant revolt in France can be correlated with demographic change and that Skocpol's model does not explain regional differences in the peasantry around the time of the French Revolution.[40] There is no question but that Goldstone's mastery of demography is impressive and he makes the interesting and original point that mortality in revolutions has increased significantly over the centuries. In the English Civil War 100,000 Englishmen died out of a population of 5 million – about one in fifty. In France in the turbulent war years of 1792–1815 he estimates the death tally at 1.3 million (many scholars would put the figure much higher) – one in twenty – while in the Mexican Revolution of 1910–20 the fatalities were 2 million out of a population of 17 millions – one in ten.[41] Many such sparkling insights cannot disguise a slightly mechanical schema of population growth, inflation, fiscal crisis, elite competition and mass mobilisation (as with Skocpol, revolutionary voluntarism is entirely absent). Nor does Goldstone deal adequately with some obvious objections to this thesis. For example, if demography was king, one would have expected England to have faced its worst revolutionary crisis around 1850, since the population had increased by 92 per cent since 1800.[42] Some would say, of course, that Chartist agitation was just such a crisis but, although Chartism certainly denoted a *revolutionary moment*, it lacked the power to ignite revolution. Goldstone on several occasions asserts that he is not advocating demographic determinism[43] but, if he is not, the space given to this factor seems excessive. In any case, if population increase is just one more variable in the revolutionary bouillabaisse, no more potent than any other, why should we accord it any kind of primacy? Goldstone seems to be caught in a fork of his own making: either population increase is a prime determinant in a kind of Marxist base / superstructure sense, in which case he must be committed to demographic determinism, or his entire argument must be circular.

These four theories, identifiable as the most influential to emerge since the Second World War, are of course just the tip of the theoretical iceberg. There are dozens of other explanations given by scholars for the phenomenon of revolution but these invariably subdivide into the psychological and the structural.[44] One stresses the common factor of rejection of tradition and consequent symbolic reconstruction; another says that revolutions are the political equivalent of the human hunger for exploration, that it is the thrill of venturing into the unknown that is salient.[45] Yet other psychologically oriented theories stress human irrationality and revolution as pathology:

'A revolution implies a deep schism within the state. It reveals a pathological condition of the political will which shows by contrast the normal nature of authority.'[46] It is a fair comment that all such psychological theories derive ultimately from the pioneering work of Crane Brinton and are vulnerable to the same objections. It will be remembered that Brinton at once likened the dynamics of revolution to the progress of a fever *and* argued that you can systematise revolutions, identify the causes and provide a convincing fourfold periodisation. But since fevers strike randomly, the analogy does not work, for, according to Brinton, this would have to mean that we can identify in advance the individuals who will be struck by disease – a manifest absurdity. Psychological theories can tell us why men rebel and what the motivations of revolutionaries are, but they cannot identify the objective circumstances surrounding revolutionary outbreaks or explain why they succeed and why they fail. Structural theories, on the other hand, too often look like formulaic presentations of the obvious or are ex post rationalisations. Another structural theory, popular in the 1970s, was that revolutions arose from the failure of states to modernise, that the gap between cutting-edge technology and the culture and institutions of a given society was the 'open sesame' to understanding.[47] Yet, since a modernising society would presumably, by definition, have solved its peasant problem, the 'failure to modernise' thesis looks remarkably like Skocpol's militant peasantry thesis in different clothes. It would be true to say that at the beginning of the twenty-first century, traditional historians, dedicated to archive-based study of the minute particulars of individual historical events, have gained the high ground, while political scientists and sociologists are in retreat or on the defensive. The main thrust of the straitlaced historians' case is that it is usually impossible to explain causation satisfactorily even in minute historical events, so that the hopes of providing general explanations of 'revolution' are even more chimerical.[48] The strongest card traditional historians have to play is the incontrovertible fact that only contingency separates successful from unsuccessful revolutions, which makes retrospective attempts to explain the success of this or that revolution inherently bogus.[49]

Nevertheless, we cannot dispense with universals like 'revolution' since we need them to explain how revolutions differ from rebellions, coups d'état or civil wars. One of the problems is the slapdash way military coups in Latin America are routinely described as 'revolutions' when they are no such thing. One wag indeed pilloried this common misconception by dubbing Latin America 'the land of the long-playing record – 33 revolutions per minute'. The main difference between true revolution and the other violent categories mentioned is that revolution aims to transform socio-economic structures as well as political institutions or, at the very least, to replace one elite with another differing in kind and nature. Some writers distinguish between 'great revolutions' which achieve or at least attempt socio-economic transformation, with 'little revolutions', which entirely change the orientation, direction, political culture and ideology of a society, as well as the elite membership, while stopping short of root-and-branch change.[50] The difference between rebellions, coups, civil wars and revolutions is easier to resolve. In a mere rebellion the dissidents are not strong enough to overthrow the State, in a coup they are, but simply replace one elite figurehead with another, Tweedledum with Tweedledee, while in a revolution the rebels *are* strong enough to overthrow the State and do so. Civil war marks the situation where there is no single ruling class strong enough to dominate the State, where two or more competing factions process their demands through a central authority or clearing house (a liberal government of compromise, say) which then cracks apart under the strain, leaving the factions to fight it out. Civil war essentially denotes a context of competing interest groups which cannot come to terms through the winnowing process of central government and have enough resources to be able to use force to pursue their aims. As one writer has put it, the most a rebellion can do is modify the system; it cannot displace it as a revolution does: 'revolution and rebellion differ in results but have like origins . . . revolution succeeds, rebellion fails and civil wars leave the question open'.[51] It should be stressed that the difference between revolution and civil war is often a very fine one. One definition of revolution by a leading theoretician makes it sound remarkably like civil war: 'A transfer of power over a State through armed struggle in the course of which at least two distinct power blocs make incompatible demands to control the State, and some significant portion of the population subject to the State's jurisdiction acquiesces in the claims of each bloc'.[52] This definition cleverly leaves open the question whether a 'little revolution' can be achieved without violence. For some specialists violence is imbricated in the very notion of revolution, though Engels and others have dissented from this view. Certainly the transformation brought about in Spain and Portugal since 1975 fits the criteria for 'little revolution' as no violence attended it (though it was threatened in the attempted coup by Antonio Tejero in 1981 – an opéra bouffe event only in the comfort of retrospect).[53] Other problems of interpretation arise when we consider the 'great revolutions'. Skocpol and others have conditioned us to believe that in all such enterprises the peasantry must play a major role, and it is true that this perception is usually accurate: it was the case in the French, Mexican, Russian and Chinese Revolutions. Yet Cuba ranks as a 'great revolution' in that Castro and his acolytes were able to achieve a total socio-economic transformation of the country. Although Castro and Che Guevara consistently claimed the Cuban

Revolution as a 'peasant revolution', so as to fit the tenets of Marxism–Leninism, the truth is that the dramatic events of 1958–9 were largely the work of the middle classes. Suffering from unemployment, underemployment and disguised unemployment, the middle classes used their muscle to throw out the corrupt Batista regime. Yet when Castro converted to Marxism–Leninism in 1961, he rewrote the legend of the Cuban Revolution to make it appear a second China, with the peasantry in the vanguard, making use of the incontestable fact that he had based himself among the peasants of the Sierra Maestra, but omitting to mention that the guerrilla activity there was a mere sideshow.[54]

The endless debate about revolutions, their causation, their alleged commonality or uniqueness, whether they are triggered primarily by human agency or social structures, whether the 'objective conditions' of socio-economic life are most salient or whether pride of place should go to 'subjective conditions' (revolutionary voluntarism), how to differentiate them from rebellions and civil wars, all this can to an extent be short-circuited if we concentrate instead on the *consequences* of revolution. If we judge revolutions by their outcome rather than by the intentions, perceptions, ideologies and neuroses of the actors, it is possible to narrow the range, so to speak, and achieve some kind of lucidity. Just as in tensor theory in higher mathematics, a scalar is a tensor of rank zero, a vector of rank one, and so on, so one can convincingly draw up a typology of revolutions based purely on their consequences and assign them a rank. In rank zero are the alleged revolutions which are really mere transfers of power within a given elite. Revolutions of rank one would roughly correspond with the 'little revolutions' identified above. The 'great revolutions' would correspond to a narrow definition of revolution and the 'little revolutions' to a broad interpretation of the term.[55] Revolutions of rank two are in some ways the most interesting of all, for in these cases the revolution begins with a moderate, liberal, reformist or what Marxists used to call a 'bourgeois' stage and then proceeds to a struggle for genuine socio-economic transformation; if this is successful the revolution ascends to rank three; if unsuccessful it remains in rank two. Rank three revolutions are rare: only the Russian of 1917, the Chinese of 1949 and the Cuban of 1959, involving root-and-branch socio-economic change can validly be described as Close Encounters of the Third Revolutionary Kind. Classic examples of rank zero revolutions are the 'Glorious Revolution' of 1688 and the alleged American Revolution of 1776. These were essentially intra-elite transfers of power.[56] Someone once described the events of 1775–83 as one set of nasty capitalists fighting another. Certainly, if we accept the thesis that violence is a *necessary* condition for revolution, the rather gruesome War for American Independence would qualify. As for 1688, there was minimal violence in England at the time of the Dutch invasion (the horrendous aftermath in Scotland and Ireland is another matter). But further than that the evidence will not go. The Convention of 1787 at Philadelphia, which drew up the US Constitution, explicitly refused any relief to debtors and made a point of stressing that the pre-1775 financial system, shorn of the 'exactions' previously demanded by London, had to remain. The hard line taken towards debtors was the principal cause of Shays's rebellion in 1787.[57] Devotees of 1688 and 1776 like to make large claims for their areas of specialisation but these are not really convincing. To take just one example, there was not even a significant change of elite in both cases, as the comfortable transition to the new regime of Benjamin Franklin and Marlborough respectively demonstrates. The 'Kossuth test' is a good one as a simple yardstick for revolution. The great Hungarian nationalist and hero of 1848 argued that the real test of revolution is always whether it benefits the majority. In his view, France in 1789–94 experienced a real revolution which liberated seven-eighths of the population, but the revolution of February 1848 was a mere intra-elite transfer of power, which is why France experienced a second (abortive revolution) in July that year.[58]

Revolutions of rank one, aimed at a significant change of elite personnel and some tinkering with the economic system stopping short of root-and-branch change, would include most of the revolutionary 'near misses' described in the following chapters: the Peasants' Revolt of 1381, the Jack Cade rising of 1450, the Pilgrimage of Grace of 1536–7 and the Jacobite Rising of 1745. How the changes demanded by the Chartists would have worked out remains imponderable, but it is worth remembering the quasi-Tocquevillian notion of rising expectations, whereby one demand, once satisfied, generates another, more radical one. The only 'road not taken' that might have led further, to rank two at least, was a successful General Strike. That leaves the English Civil War or English Revolution as the only possible candidate for rank two in English history. At this point it would be useful to review those revolutions clearly in this rank. The French Revolution and the Mexican Revolution show an initially reformist revolt against the Ancien Régime (respectively Louis XVI and Porfirio Diaz) developing into a more radical phenomenon: the Jacobin Republic of 1793–4 in the case of France and the Pancho Villa/Emiliano Zapata of 1914–15 in Mexico. In both cases the drive for a radical restructuring of society was arrested by 'reactionary' elements: the men of Thermidor in France, and the Carranza/Obregon alliance in Mexico.[59] For our purposes it is immaterial whether the liberal revolution transmogrified into the radical one or if both elements were present from the very beginning. Nor is it necessary to become involved in the arguments about the popular 'double revolution' model. According to this, all revolutions which have the potential to achieve rank three go through a twofold stage, separated by a chronological gap which can be months or years. Thus, Cromwell's victory in the English Civil War was the first stage, and the Leveller/Digger attempt to push the postwar settlement into genuine revolution was another. However, the radical party in England never constituted the kind of threat in England that Robespierre did in France or Villa and Zapata did in Mexico; pedants might therefore like to characterise the 'English Revolution' as a revolution of rank one and a half. In Russia, the Kerensky revolution which overthrew the Romanovs was stage one, and the Bolshevik revolution of 1917 was stage two. Even in China, stretching a point, one might sustain the argument, by claiming that the overthrow of the Manchus by Sun Yat-sen in 1911 was stage one and then, after nearly forty years of warlordism and the hegemony of Chiang Kai-shek, the Communist Revolution of 1949 was stage two.[60] Happy is the country that has no history, runs the old adage. Certainly in Britain's case, the nation can be thankful that it never had to endure the travails of rank two revolutions. Yet in comforting ourselves that Britain has never experienced a true revolution, we should not fall into the trap of imagining that the country has never trembled on the brink. Here it is necessary to distinguish between revolutionary *outcomes* and revolutionary *situations*. As has been well said, 'Few revolutionary situations have revolutionary *outcomes*.'[61] Whether this was all due to contingency in Britain's case it has been our task to discover.

Notes

Abbreviations

Add. MSS	Additional Manuscripts at the British Library
AHR	*American Historical Review*
BIHR	*Bulletin of the Institute of Historical Research*
DNB	(The original) *Dictionary of National Biography.*
EHR	*English Historical Review*
HMC	Reports of the Historical Manuscript Commission
NS	New Series
ODNB	*Oxford Dictionary of National Biography* (2004)
OS	Old Series
PP	*Past and Present*
TRHS	*Transactions of the Royal Historical Society*
YLS	*Yearbook of Langland Studies*

1 *The Origins of the Revolt of 1381*

1. Jean Froissart, *Chronicles*, ed. and trans. Geoffrey Brereton (1978), pp. 211, 213. See, in general H. M. Hansen, 'The Peasants' Revolt of 1381 and the Chronicles', *Journal of Medieval History*, 6 (1980), pp. 393–415. • **2**. Aristotle, of course, identified four elements in causality: material, formal, efficient and final causes. Aristotle, *Metaphysics*, I, iii–vii; 5, ii. • **3**. G. Christakos, *Interdisciplinary Public Health Reasoning and Epidemic Modelling: The Case of the Black Death* (2005), pp. 110–14. • **4**. S. Scott and C. J. Duncan, *Biology of Plagues: Evidence from Historical Populations* (Cambridge, 2001). • **5**. Norman F. Cantor, *In the Wake of Plague: The Black Death and the World it Made* (NY, 2001). • **6**. J. P. Byrne, *The Black Death* (2004), pp. 21–9. • **7**. David Herlihy, *The Black Death and the Transformation of the West* (Harvard, 1997), pp. 29–33. • **8**. For views additional to those mentioned see W. G. Napley, *The Black Death and the History of Plagues, 1345–1730* (Stroud, 2000); O. J. Benedictow, *The Black Death: The Complete History* (Woodbridge, 2004); Stuart Borsch, *The Black Death in Egypt and England: A Comparative Study* (Austin, Texas, 2005); John Hatcher, *The Black Death: An Intimate History* (2008); Benedict Gummer, *The Scourging Angel: The Black Death in the British Isles* (2009). • **9**. S. K. Kohn, *The Black Death Transformed: Disease and Culture in Early Renaissance Europe* (2002). • **10**. J. M. W. Bean, 'Plague, Population and Economic Decline in England in the Later Middle Ages', *Economic History Review*, 2nd series, 15 (1963), pp. 423–37; J. Horrox, ed., *The Black Death* (Manchester, 1994); A. F. Butcher, 'English Urban Society and the Revolt of 1381', in R. H. Hilton and T. H. Aston, eds, *The English Rising of 1381* (Cambridge, 1984), pp. 84–111 (at pp. 86, 93, 95); Christopher Dyer, 'Social and Economic Background to the Revolt of 1381', in ibid., pp. 9–42 (at p. 21). • **11**. John Taylor, Wendy R. Childs and Leslie Watkins, eds, *St Alban's Chronicle: The Chronica Majora of Thomas Walsingham*, 2 vols (Oxford, 2003), vol. 1, *1376–1394* (hereinafter *St Alban's Chronicle*) pp. 342, 894, 900, 912, 916, 944. • **12**. Butcher, 'English Urban Society'; R. B. Dobson, ed., *The Peasants' Revolt of 1381* (1970). • **13**. Dobson, ed., *Peasants' Revolt*, pp. 63–70; B. H. Putnam, *The Enforcement of the Statutes of Labourers During the First Decade after the Black Death, 1349–1359* (NY, 1908). • **14**. J. Bolton, 'The World Upside Down: Plague as an Agent of Economic and Social Change', in M. Ormrod and P. Lindley, eds, *The Black Death in England* (Stamford, 1996), pp. 26–32; Robert C. Palmer, *English Law in the Age of the Black Death* (Chapel Hill, NC, 1993). • **15**. Rosamund J. Faith, 'The Great Rumour and Peasant Ideology', in Hilton and Aston, eds, *English Rising*, pp. 43–73; R. H. Britnell, 'Feudal Reactions after the Black Death in the Palatinate of Durham', *PP* 128 (1990), pp. 28–47. For the sumptuary laws see Alan Hunt, *The Governance of the Consuming Passions: A History of Sumptuary Law* (Basingstoke, 1996); Alan Hunt, The Governance of Consumption: Sumptuary Laws and Shifting Forms of Regulation', *Economy and Society*, 25 (1996), pp. 410–27. • **16**. As Charles Oman commented about the Statute of Labourers: 'If legislation had not intervened, the period would have been a sort of golden age for the labourer, more especially the free labourer.' Charles Oman, *The Great Revolt of 1381* (1906). • **17**. Vast amounts have been written about all this. See Christopher Allmand, *The Hundred Years War* (Cambridge, 1989); A. Curry, *The Hundred Years War* (Basingstoke, 1993); E. Perroy, *The Hundred Years War* (1959); D. Green, *The Black Prince* (Stroud, 2001). • **18**. Jonathan Sumption, *Divided Houses: The Hundred Years War*, vol. 3 (2009), p. 75; David Nicolle, *Medieval Warfare Sourcebook: Warfare in Modern Christendom* (1999), p. 215. • **19**. V. H. Galbraith, ed., *The Anonimale Chronicle* (Manchester, 1927) – hereinafter *Anon. Chron.* – pp. 63–5. • **20**. See Anthony Goodman, *John of Gaunt:*

the Exercise of Princely Power in Fourteenth-Century Europe (NY, 1992); Sydney Armitage-Smith, *John of Gaunt, King of Castile and Leon, Duke of Lancaster* (1904). • **21**. G. A. Holmes, *The Good Parliament* (Oxford, 1975); W. M. Ormrod, *The Reign of Edward III: Crown and Political Society in England, 1322–1377* (Yale, 1990). • **22**. Simon Walker, *The Lancastrian Affinity, 1361–1399* (Oxford, 1990), pp. 237–40; Josiah Wedgwood, 'John of Gaunt and the Packing of Parliament', *EHR*, 45 (1930), pp. 623–5. • **23**. *St Alban's Chronicle*, pp. 301–7. • **24**. A. A. Ruddock, *Italian Merchants and Shipping in Southampton, 1270–1600* (Southampton, 1951), pp. 48–9. • **25**. *St Alban's Chronicle*, pp. 400–1. • **26**. Goodman, *John of Gaunt*, p. 77. • **27**. Alastair Dunn, *The Peasants' Revolt: England's Failed Revolution of 1381* (2004), p. 41. • **28**. Dobson, ed., *Peasants' Revolt*, pp. 103–5. • **29**. Oman, *Great Revolt*, p. 2. • **30**. Dobson, ed., *Peasants' Revolt*, pp. 105–11. • **31**. Ibid., p. 111. • **32**. G. H. Martin, ed. and trans., *Knighton's Chronicle 1337–1396* (Oxford, 1995) – hereinafter *Knighton's Chronicle* – pp. 206–7. • **33**. Dobson, ed., *Peasants' Revolt*, p. 113. • **34**. For the Northampton Parliament of November 1380 see HMC, XI, Appendix, part Seven. Some interesting details on the composition of the Parliament are available in N. B. Lewis, 'Re-election to Parliament in the Reign of Richard II', *EHR*, 48 (1933), pp. 364–94. The contribution of the clergy is assessed in A. K. McHardy, *The Church in London, 1375–1392* (1977), pp. 1–17. • **35**. Dobson, ed., *Peasants' Revolt*, pp. 111–18. • **36**. Ibid., p. 113. • **37**. For the scant detail avilable on Sudbury's career see E. B. Fryde, D. E. Greenway, S. Porter and I. Roy, *Handbook of British Chronology* (Cambridge, 1996), pp. 86, 233, 258. • **38**. Some of the older discussions on the collection and evasion of the Third Poll Tax are still valuable (e.g. Oman, *Great Revolt*, pp. 24–9, 162–3), but modern scholarship rests squarely on the definitive three-volume work by Carolyn C. Fenwick, *The Poll Tax Returns of 1377, 1379 and 1381* (Oxford, 2005). • **39**. T. F. Tout, *Chapters in the Administrative History of Medieval England*, 6 vols (Manchester, 1933), iii, pp. 359–63. • **40**. *Knighton's Chronicle*, pp. 208–9. • **41**. Pioneering work was done on the Essex revolt by J. A. Sparvel-Bayly in *Transactions of the Essex Archaeological Society*, 1 (Colchester, 1878). This has largely been superseded by W. H. Liddell and R. G. Wood, *Essex and the Great Revolt of 1381* (Chelmsford, 1982); see also Herbert Eiden, 'Joint Action Against "Bad" Lordship: The Peasants' Revolt in Essex and Norfolk', *History*, 83 (1998), pp. 5–30, and the miscellaneous essays by Eiden in Marie-Louise Heckmann and Jens Rohrkasten, eds, *Von Nowgorod bis London . . . Festschrift für Stuart Jenks* (Göttingen, 2008). • **42**. N. Brooks, 'The Organisation and Achievement of the Peasants of Kent and Essex in 1381', in M. Mayr-Harting and R. I. Moore, eds, *Studies in Medieval History Presented to R. H. C. Davis* (1985), pp. 247–70 (at pp. 247–50). • **43**. *Knighton's Chronicle*, pp. 208–9; *Anon. Chron.*, pp. 134–5. • **44**. Dan Jones, *Summer of Blood* (2009), p. 43. • **45**. Edward

Vallance, *A Radical History of Britain* (2009), pp. 55–6. • **46**. Brooks, 'Organisation and Achievement', pp. 252–4. • **47**. W. E. Flaherty, 'The Great Rebellion in Kent of 1381 Illustrated from the Public Records', *Archaeologia Cantiana*, 3 (1860), pp. 65–96. • **48**. P. E. Russell, *The English Intervention in Spain and Portugal in the Time of Edward III and Richard I* (Oxford, 1955). • **49**. Dobson, ed., *Peasants' Revolt*, pp. 132–3. • **50**. Frank McLynn, *Lionheart and Lackland* (2006), pp. 439–40. • **51**. Froissart, *Chronicles*, pp. 214–15. • **52**. Ibid., p. 218; 'Wat Tyler', *ODNB*, 55, pp. 770–2. • **53**. *Anon. Chron.*, pp. 135–8. • **54**. Alan Harding, 'The Revolt Against the Justices', in Hilton and Aston, eds, *English Rising*, pp. 165–93. • **55**. J. A. Tuck, 'Nobles, Commons and the Great Revolt of 1381', in ibid., pp. 195–8. • **56**. Dunn, *Peasants' Revolt*, p. 78. • **57**. Vallance, *Radical History*, p. 57. • **58**. Tyler continued to use Sir John Newton as go-between. Froissart, *Chronicles*, p. 216. • **59**. David Horspool, *The English Rebel* (2009), p. 127; A. Reville and C. Petit-Dutaillis, *Le Soulevement des travailleurs d'Angleterre en 1381* (Paris, 1898), pp. 216–39. • **60**. Froissart, *Chronicles*, p. 219. • **61**. See R. Bird, *The Turbulent London of Richard II* (1949); C. M. Barron, *Revolt in London, 11th to 15th June 1381* (1981). • **62**. *Anon. Chron.*, p. 137. • **63**. Froissart, *Chronicles*, p. 212. • **64**. *Knighton's Chronicle*, pp. 222–4. Ball's speeches have been imaginatively reconstructed by William Morris, *A Dream of John Ball* (1895), pp. 27–41. • **65**. The theory of the identity of Straw and Tyler is set out in F. W. D. Brie, 'Wat Tyler and Jack Straw', *EHR*, 21 (1906), pp. 106–11. The Chaucer reference is in *The Nun's Priest's Tale*, Nevill Coghill, trans. and ed., folio edn (1956), i, p. 275. Brie's theory has been decisively refuted in Dobson, ed., *Peasants' Revolt*, pp. 138, 147, 188–98, 206, 315, 360, 361. • **66**. Reville and Petit-Dutaillis, *Le Soulevement*, pp. 216–39. • **67**. Oman, *Great Revolt*, pp. 49–50. • **68**. Reville and Petit-Dutaillis, *Le Soulvement*, pp. 190–8. • **69**. *Anon. Chron.*, pp. 139–40; *Knighton's Chronicle*, pp. 215, 222–4; *St Alban's Chronicle*, pp. 418–19. • **70**. Froissart, *Chronicles*, p. 216. • **71**. *St Alban's Chronicle*, pp. 422–3; *Anon. Chron.*, p. 138; Oman, *Great Revolt*, pp. 15–17. • **72**. Froissart, *Chronicles*, p. 216. • **73**. There is material on Salisbury in W. M. Ormrod, 'The Peasants' Revolt and the Government of England', *Journal of British Studies*, 29 (1990), pp. 1–30. • **74**. *Anon. Chron.*, pp. 138–9. • **75**. Goodman, *John of Gaunt*, p. 73. • **76**. M. Aston, 'Corpus Christi and Corpus Regni: Heresy and the Peasants' Revolt', *PP* 143 (1994), pp. 1–47. • **77**. L. C. Hector and Barbara F. Harvey, eds and trans., *The Westminster Chronicle, 1381–1394* (Oxford, 1982) – hereinafter *Westminster Chronicle* – pp. 2–3. • **78**. Bird, *Turbulent London*; Derek Keene, 'Medieval London and Its Region', *London Journal*, 14 (1989), pp. 99–111; J. L. Bolton, 'London and the Peasants' Revolt', *London Journal*, 7 (1981), pp. 123–42; Robert Epstein, 'London, Southwark, Westminster: Gower's London Contexts', in Sian Echard, ed., *A Companion to Gower* (Cambridge, 2004), pp. 43–60. • **79**. Reville and Petit-Dutaillis, *Le Soulevement*, p. 198. • **80**. *Anon Chron.*,

p. 140; Reville and Petit-Dutaillis, *Le Soulevement*, p. 194. • **81**. *Knighton's Chronicle*, pp. 216–17. • **82**. Froissart, *Chronicles*, p. 217. • **83**. *Anon. Chron.*, p. 141. • **84**. Ibid., pp. 141, 143–4. • **85**. Jones, *Summer of Blood*, p. 94. • **86**. Dunn, *Peasants' Revolt*, pp. 107–9. • **87**. *St Alban's Chronicle*, pp. 418–19. • **88**. S. Walker, *The Lancastrian Affinity 1361–99* (Oxford, 1990), p. 96. • **89**. *Knighton's Chronicle*, pp. 216–17. • **90**. Dobson, ed., *Peasants' Revolt*, pp. 184–5. • **91**. Dunn, *Peasants' Revolt*, p. 88; Reville and Petit-Dutaillis, *Le Soulevement*, p. 202. • **92**. *Westminster Chronicle*, pp. 4–5. • **93**. Oman, *Great Revolt*, p. 18. • **94**. Dobson, ed., *Peasants' Revolt*, pp. 162, 210. • **95**. *St Alban's Chronicle*, pp. 288–93, 430–1; *Anon. Chron.*, pp. 145–6; *Westminster Chronicle*, pp. 6–8; Barron, *Revolt in London*, op. cit. • **96**. Quoted in A. Musson, *Medieval Law in Context: The Growth of Legal Consciousness from Magna Carta to the Peasants' Revolt* (Manchester, 2001) pp. 243–4. • **97**. Froissart, *Chronicles*, pp. 212–13; *St Alban's Chronicle*, pp. 542–9; R. F. Green, 'John Ball's Letters: Literary History and Historical Literature', in B. Hanwalt, ed., *Chaucer's England: Literature in Historical Context* (Minneapolis, 1992), pp. 180–90. • **98**. For those who think it was so influenced see M. Aston, 'Lollardy and Sedition, 1381–1431', *PP* 17, pp. 1–44 (esp. pp. 1–5); A. Hudson, *Premature Reformation: Wycliffite Texts and Lollard History* (Oxford, 1988), p. 69. • **99**. Hudson, *Premature Reformation*; A. Kenny, *Wycliff* (Oxford, 1985). • **100**. *St Alban's Chronicle*, pp. 500–3. • **101**. Ibid., pp. 74–99; Kenny, *Wycliff*, pp. 42–55; Walker, *Lancastrian Affinity*, pp. 100–10; Goodman, *John of Gaunt*, pp. 241–3. • **102**. William Langland, *Piers Plowman*, 23, ll, 274–5: 'They preach to men of Plato to prove it by Seneca That all things under Heaven ought to be in common.'

2 *Failure and Consequences of the Peasants' Revolt*

1. Reville and Petit-Dutaillis, *Le Soulevement*, p. 190. • **2**. Nigel Saul, *Richard II* (1999), p. 67. • **3**. *Westminster Chronicle*, pp. 68, 92, 116. • **4**. Froissart, *Chronicles*, pp. 218–19. • **5**. Dunn, *Peasants' Revolt*, p. 95 • **6**. Reville and Petit-Dutaillis, *Le Soulevement*, pp. 195–6. • **7**. *Anon. Chron.*, p. 144. • **8**. Saul, *Richard II*, p. 68. • **9**. Jones, *Summer of Blood*, p. 127. • **10**. St Albans was a locus classicus (*St Alban's Chronicle*, pp. 442–79). See in general R. Faith, 'The Class Struggle in Fourteenth Century England', in R. Raphael, ed., *People's History and Socialist Theory* (1981), pp. 50–80. • **11**. Oman, *Great Revolt*, pp. 13–19. • **12**. Reville and Petit-Dutaillis, *Le Soulevement*, pp. 160–9. • **13**. See, for example, C. Dyer, 'The Rising in 1381 in Suffolk', in C. Dyer, *Everyday Life in Medieval England* (1994), pp. 228–30. • **14**. Oman, *Great Revolt*, p. 10. • **15**. Dunn, *Peasants' Revolt*, p. 126; Musson, *Medieval Law*. • **16**. Alan Harding, 'The Revolt Against the Justices', in Hilton and Aston, *English*

Rising, pp. 165–93. • **17**. R. H. Hilton, *Bond Men Made Free: Medieval Peasant Movements and the Rising of 1381* (1973), pp. 186–207. • **18**. Barron, *Revolt in London*, p. 5. • **19**. For an estimate of Richard's ruthlessness see G. B. Stow, 'Richard II in Thomas Walsingham's Chronicles', *Speculum*, 59 (1984), pp. 68–102. • **20**. Dunn, *Peasants' Revolt*, pp. 91–5. • **21**. *Knighton's Chronicle*, p. 210; *Anon. Chron.*, p. 138; *St Alban's Chronicle*, pp. 422–3. • **22**. *Westminster Chronicle*, pp. 6–7; *St Alban's Chronicle*, pp. 424–31. • **23**. *St Alban's Chronicle*, pp. 424–5. • **24**. *Knighton's Chronicle*, pp. 216–17; Reville and Petit-Dutaillis, *Le Soulevement*, pp. 210–12. • **25**. For Lyons see A. R. Myers, 'The Wealth of Richard Lyons', in T. A. Sandquist and M. R. Powicke, eds, *Essays in Medieval History* (Toronto, 1969), pp. 301–29; Holmes, *Good Parliament*, pp. 108–14. • **26**. *Westminster Chronicle*, pp. 8–9; Reville and Petit-Dutaillis, *Le Soulevement*, p. 212. • **27**. *Anon. Chron.*, pp. 145–6; *Westminster Chronicle*, pp. 6–9; *St Alban's Chronicle*, pp. 288–93, 430–1. • **28**. Barron, *Revolt in London*, pp. 14–16. • **29**. Saul, *Richard II*, pp. 68–70. • **30**. *Anon. Chron.*, p. 147; *Knighton's Chronicle*, p. 147; Dobson, ed., *Peasants' Revolt*, pp. 164–5. • **31**. For example, Christopher Hill, 'The Norman Yoke', in Christopher Hill, *Puritanism and Revolution* (2001), pp. 44–6. • **32**. Rosamund Faith, 'The Great Rumour of 1377 and Peasant Ideology', in Hilton and Aston, *English Rising*, pp. 43–73. • **33**. G. Grauss, 'Social Utopias in the Middle Ages', *PP* 38 (1967), pp. 4–19 (at pp. 16–17). • **34**. Saul, *Richard II*, pp. 68–70. • **35**. Oman, *Great Revolt*, p. 73. • **36**. Jones, *Summer of Blood*, p. 139. • **37**. Froissart, *Chronicles*, pp. 224–5. • **38**. Ibid.; *Westminster Chronicle*, pp. 8–11. • **39**. *Anon. Chron.*, p. 147; *St Alban's Chronicle*, pp. 436–7; *Knighton's Chronicle*, p. 218. • **40**. Dobson, ed., *Peasants' Revolt*, pp. 164–6. • **41**. *Anon. Chron.*, p. 148; *Knighton's Chronicle*, p. 219. • **42**. *St Alban's Chronicle*, pp. 437–9; Froissart, *Chronicles*, p. 226. • **43**. *Anon. Chron.*, p. 148; *Knighton's Chronicle*, pp. 220–1. • **44**. Ralph Standish was from a Lancashire family. For full details see Thomas Cruddas Porteus, *A History of the Parish of Standish, Lancashire* (Wigan, 1927). Standish succeeded his father to the lordship of the manor in 1396 and died in 1418. • **45**. Saul, *Richard II*, pp. 70–1. • **46**. *St Alban's Chronicle*, pp. 438–9 • **47**. Ibid. • **48**. *Anon. Chron.*, p. 149. • **49**. *Westminster Chronicle*, pp. 12–13. • **50**. May McKisack, *The Fourteenth Century, 1307–1399* (Oxford, 1959), pp. 413–14. • **51**. Froissart, *Chronicles*, pp. 227–8. • **52**. The overall balance of forces is discussed in Eleanor Searle, 'The Defence of England and the Peasants' Revolt', *Viator*, 3 (1972), pp. 365–88. There are pointers too in Ormrod, 'The Peasants' Revolt'. • **53**. Some of these issues are discussed, inconclusively, in Dobson, ed., *Peasants' Revolt*, pp. 152–87. See also Barron, *Revolt in London*, pp. 6–8, and Saul, *Richard II*, pp. 70–1. • **54**. Jones, *Summer of Blood*, p. 162. • **55**. *Westminster Chronicle*, pp. 16–17. • **56**. Reville and Petit-Dutaillis, *Le Soulevement*, p. 193. • **57**. *Knighton's Chronicle*, pp. 240–1. • **58**. *St Alban's*

Chronicle, pp. 496–501. • **59**. Ibid., pp. 542–9. • **60**. Reville and Petit-Dutaillis, *Le Soulevement*, pp. 198–9. • **61**. A. J. Prescott, '"The Hand of God": The Suppression of the Peasants' Revolt in 1381', in Nigel J. Morgan, ed., *Prophecy, Apocalypse and the Day of Doom* (Donnington, 2004), pp. 317–41. • **62**. Dobson, ed., *Peasants' Revolt*, pp. 310–11. A slightly differently worded version is given in Horspool, *English Rebel*, p. 135. • **63**. *St Alban's Chronicle*, pp. 518–23. • **64**. Hilton, *Bond Men Made Free*, pp. 186–207; cf. Oman, *Great Revolt*, pp. 13–19. • **65**. R. B. Dobson, 'The Risings in York, Beverley and Scarborough, 1380–1381', in Hilton and Aston, *English Rising*, pp. 112–42 (at pp. 113–15); Reville and Petit-Dutaillis, *Le Soulevement*, pp. 160–9. • **66**. Oman, *Great Revolt*, p. 142. • **67**. Dobson, 'Risings in York', pp. 135, 140. • **68**. Reville and Petit-Dutaillis *Le Soulevement*, pp. 253–6. • **69**. Prescott, 'The Hand of God'. • **70**. Dunn, *Peasant's Revolt*, p. 125. • **71**. *St Alban's Chronicle*, pp. 442–77. • **72**. Oman, *Great Revolt*, pp. 104–10. • **73**. Exhaustive details about the risings in Suffolk are contained in E. Powell, *The Rising in East Anglia in 1381* (Cambridge, 1896). • **74**. C. Dyer, 'The Rising of 1381 in Suffolk', in C. Dyer, *Everyday Life in Medieval England* (1994), pp. 228–30. • **75**. Dobson, *Peasants' Revolt*, pp. 257–8; Eiden, 'Joint Action'. • **76**. Although Froissart has a tall story about a one-man defiance of the rebels by a knight he calls Sir Robert Salle (Froissart, *Chronicles*, pp. 222–4). • **77**. Powell, *Rising in East Anglia*, p. 30. • **78**. Dobson, *Peasants' Revolt*, p. 258. • **79**. D. R. Leader, *A History of the University of Cambridge*, vol. 1, *The University to 1546* (Cambridge, 1988), pp. 87–8. • **80**. Dunn, *Peasants' Revolt*, p. 129 • **81**. For full details of his controversial career see R. Allington-Smith, *Henry Despenser: The Fighting Bishop* (Dereham, 2003). • **82**. *St Alban's Chronicle*, pp. 490–4. • **83**. Dobson, *Peasants' Revolt*, pp. 260–1. • **84**. J. A. Tuck, 'Nobles, Commoners and the Great Revolt of 1381', in Hilton and Aston, eds, *English Rising*; pp. 194–212 (at pp. 196–7); cf. also Herbert Eiden, 'Norfolk 1382: A Sequel to the Peasants' Revolt', *EHR*, 114 (1999), pp. 370–7. • **85**. *St Alban's Chronicle*, pp. 494–5. • **86**. Prescott, 'Hand of God'. • **87**. *Westminster Chronicle*, pp. 18–19. • **88**. *St Alban's Chronicle*, pp. 516–19, 550–63; *Knighton's Chronicle*, pp. 240–1. • **89**. *St Alban's Chronicle*, pp. 518–23; C. D. Liddy, 'The Estate of Merchants in the Parliament of 1381', *Historical Research*, 74 (2001), pp. 331–45. • **90**. *Anon. Chron.*, pp. 151–6. • **91**. *St Alban's Chronicle*, pp. 562–73. • **92**. Goodman, *John of Gaunt*, pp. 80–90. • **93**. J. A. Tuck, 'Richard II', *ODNB*, 46, pp. 724–38. • **94**. A. J. Prescott, 'Judicial Records of the Rising of 1381', Ph.D. thesis, University of London (1984), passim. • **95**. Reville and Petit-Dutaillis, *Le Soulevement*, pp. 175–240. • **96**. Tuck, 'Nobles, Commons', pp. 194–212 (at p. 202); Ormrod, 'Peasants' Revolt'. • **97**. Dobson, *Peasants' Revolt*, pp. 9, 14. • **98**. Christopher Dyer, 'Social and Economic Background to the Revolt of 1381', in Hilton and Aston, *English Rising*, pp. 9–42 (esp. pp. 15–17).

• **99**. Ibid. • **100**. C. Dyer, 'A Redistribution of Incomes in 15th Century England?', *PP* 39 (1968), pp. 11–33. • **101**. Tuck, 'Nobles, Commons', p. 211. • **102**. J. J. N. Palmer, *England, France and Christendom, 1377–79* (1972), p. 11. • **103**. Aston, 'Lollardy and Sedition', pp. 1–5. • **104**. R. H. Jones, *The Royal Policy of Richard II* (Oxford, 1968), p. 19. • **105**. Dunn, Peasants' Revolt', p. 141. • **106**. Saul, *Richard II*, pp. 183–4, 193. • **107**. W. Stubbs, *The Constitutional History of England in Its Origin and Development* (Oxford, 1875), ii, p. 463. • **108**. David Aers, 'Vox Populi and the Literature of 1381', in David Wallace, ed., *The Cambridge History of Medieval English Literature* (Cambridge, 1999), p. 441. • **109**. Eric Stockton, *The Major Latin Works of John Gower* (Seattle, 1962), p. 65. • **110**. Ibid. • **111**. Derek Pearsall, *William Langland: Piers Plowman, a New Annotated Version of the 'C' Text* (Exeter, 2008), p. 2. • **112**. David Aers, *Chaucer, Langland and the Creative Imagination* (1980), p. 61. • **113**. C. Muskatine, *Poetry and Crisis in the Age of Chaucer* (Notre Dame, 1972), pp. 88, 106. • **114**. William Morris, *The Dream of John Ball*, pp. 17–20. • **115**. Linda Platt, ed., *Robert Southey: Poetical Works, 1793–1810* (2004), v, pp. 170–1. • **116**. Tom Paine, *The Rights of Man* (1915 edn), ii, pp. 236–7; cf. 1998 edn (Oxford), p. 284.

3 *Jack Cade*

1. For women, S. Federico, 'The Imaginary Society: Women in 1381', *Journal of British Studies*, 40 (2001), pp. 159–83. For freemasonry see John J. Robinson, *Born in Blood: The Lost Secrets of Freemasonry* (NY, 1989). • **2**. 'Although unique in its scale, geographical extent and the degree of violent energy that it released, the 1381 revolt must also be seen in the context of previous acts of disturbance and protest.' Alistair Dunn, *The Great Rising of 1381* (Stroud, 2002), p. 30. • **3**. For the 1640s see Trevor Aston, ed., *Crisis in Europe, 1560–1660* (NY, 1967). • **4**. William S. Atwell, 'A Seventeenth-Century "General Crisis" in East Asia?' in Geoffrey Parker and Lesley M. Smith, eds, *The General Crisis of the Seventeenth Century* (1997), p. 235. • **5**. For a general survey see Joseph Canning, Hartrunt Lehmann and J. M. Winter, eds, *Power, Violence and Mass Death in Pre-Modern and Modern Times* (2004). • **6**. Henry S. Lucan, 'The Great European Famine of 1315–17', *Speculum*, 5 (1930), pp. 343–77. • **7**. Wiliam Chester Jordan, *The Great Famine: Northern Europe in the Early Fourteenth Century* (Princeton, 1996), pp. 186–7. • **8**. Ian Kershaw, 'The Great Famine and Agrarian Crisis in England, 1315–1322', *PP* 59 (1973), pp. 3–50. • **9**. Carlo M. Cipolla, ed., *The Fontana Economic History of Europe*, vol. 1, *The Middle Ages* (1972), pp. 25–71; Peter Billen, *The Measure of Multitude:*

Population in Medieval Thought (NY, 2001). • **10**. *Piers Plowman*, vi, ll, 280–91; viii, ll, 168–91; cf. also R. W. Frank, 'The 'Hungry Gap'; Crop Failure and Famine: the 14th century Agricultural Crisis and Piers Plowman', *Yearbook of Langland Studies*, 4 (1990), pp. 87–104. • **11**. Emmanuel Le Roy Ladurie, *Times of Feast, Times of Famine: A History of Climate Since the Year 1000* (NY, 1971); Brian Fagan, *The Little Ice Age: How Climate Made History* (2000). • **12**. M. W. Blomfield, *Piers Plowman as a Fourteenth-Century Apocalypse* (New Brunswick, 1962), p. 114. • **13**. See especially A. F. Butcher, 'English Urban Society and the Revolt of 1381', in Hilton and Aston, eds, *English Rising*, pp. 84–111. • **14**. The classic defences of Edward III are in May McKisack, 'Edward III and the Historians', *History*, 45 (1960), pp. 1–15 and W. M. Ormrod, 'Edward III and the Recovery of Royal Authority in England, 1340–1360', *History*, 72 (1987), pp. 398–422. Hagiography is evident in Ian Mortimer, *The Perfect King: The Life of Edward III, Father of the Nation* (2006). See also C. J. Rogers, ed., *The Wars of Edward III: Sources and Interpretations* (Woodbridge, 1999). • **15**. For the negative comments see Norman Cantor, *In the Wake of the Plague* (2001), pp. 37, 39. • **16**. C. M. Reinhart and K. Rogoff, *This Time Is Different: Eight Centuries of Financial Folly* (Princeton, 2009), p. 87. • **17**. Ephraim Russell, 'The Societies of the Bardi and the Peruzzi and Their Dealings with Edward III, 1327–1345', in George Unwin, ed., *Finance and Trade under Edward III* (1962), pp. 93–135; Armando Sapori, *La crisi delle compagnie mercantile dei Bardi e dei Peruzzi* (Florence, 1926). • **18**. Herman Melville, *Moby-Dick*, Ch. 132. • **19**. John Holland Smith, *The Great Schism, 1378* (NY, 1970). • **20**. Walter Ullmann, *The Origins of the Great Schism: A Study in Fourteenth-Century Ecclesiastical History* (Hamden, CT, 1967). • **21**. Johann Huizinga, *The Waning of the Middle Ages* (1924), p. 14. • **22**. Derek Pearsall, *William Langland: Piers Plowman, a New Annotated Bibliography of the 'C' text* (Exeter, 2008), p. 7. • **23**. *Piers Plowman*, iii, 38–67; v, 175; vii, 105–7; viii, 147; x, 9; xi, 31–41; xii, 5–10, 276–93; xv, 29; xx, 113; xxii, 364–72, 383. • **24**. P. R. Szittya, *The Anticlerical Tradition in Medieval Literature* (Princeton, 1986), pp. 249–64; W. Scase, *Piers Plowman and the New Anticlericalism* (Cambridge, 1989); L. Clopper, *'Songs of Rechelesnesse': Langland and the Franciscans* (Ann Arbor, 1997). • **25**. *Piers Plowman*, ix, 27–64. • **26**. Coghill, ed. and trans., *The Canterbury Tales by Geoffrey Chaucer*. • **27**. *Piers Plowman*, xi, 199–203; xii, 60, 107–10. • **28**. C. Muskatine, *Poetry and Crisis in the Age of Chaucer* (Notre Dame, 1973), pp. 107, 122, 172. • **29**. V. H. Galbraith, 'Thoughts about the Peasants' Revolt', in F. R. H. Du Boulay and C. M. Barron, eds, *The Reign of Richard II* (1971), pp. 46–57. • **30**. G. Kriehn, 'Studies in the Sources of the Social Revolt in 1381', *AHR*, 7 (1902), pp. 254–85, 458–84. • **31**. See Michael Mollat, *The Poor in the Middle Ages: An Essay in Social*

History (Yale, 1986). • **32**. There are literally dozens of articles and sections of books devoted to this theme. A random sample might include R. H. Hilton and Christopher Hill, 'The Transition from Feudalism to Capitalism', *Science and Society*, 17 (1953), pp. 340–51; Robert Brenner, 'Dobb on the Transition from Feudalism to Capitalism', *Cambridge Journal of Economics*, 2 (1978), pp. 121–40; Stephan R. Epstein, 'Rodney Hilton, Marxism and the Transition from Feudalism to Capitalism', *PP* 195 (2007), Supplement 2, pp. 248–69. • **33**. Christopher Dyer, *Daily Life in Medieval England* (1994), pp. 36–141. Here might be the place to acknowledge my debt to Dr Dyer, surely the doyen of English social history in the fourteenth century. • **34**. Dyer, ibid., and additionally his *Lords and Peasants in a Changing Society* (Cambridge, 1980) and *Standards of Living in the Later Middle Ages: Social Change in England, c.1200–1520* (Cambridge, 1989). • **35**. Eileen White, 'The Great Feast', *Leeds Studies in English*, NS, 29 (1998), pp. 401–10. • **36**. Christopher Dyer, 'Did the Peasants Really Starve in Medieval England?', in Martha Carlin and Joel T. Rosenthal, eds, *Food and Eating in Medieval Europe* (1998), pp. 53–71. • **37**. *Piers Plowman*, viii, 329–38. • **38**. Christopher Dyer, 'Piers Plowman and Plowmen: A Historical Perspective', *Yearbook of Langland Studies*, 8 (1994), pp. 155–76. • **39**. This theme is particularly explored in K. B. McFarlane, *England in the Fifteenth Century: Collected Essays* (1981). • **40**. For Langland on beggars see *Piers Plowman*, viii, 28–35, 208–88; ix, 61–187. On minstrels, ibid., Prologue, 35; vii, 96, 108. On hermits, ix, 193, 241; xvii, 6–34. On the distinction between the deserving and the undeserving poor, viii, 228, 288; ix, 63, 176. • **41**. R. W. Frank, 'The 'Hungry Gap', *YLS*, 4 (1990), pp. 87–104; B. A. Hanawalt, 'Reading the Lives of the Illiterate London's poor', *Speculum*, 80 (2005), pp. 1067–86; Dobson, ed., *Peasants' Revolt*, pp. 59–74. • **42**. Richard W. Kaueper, *War, Justice and Public Order: England and France in the later Middle Ages* (Oxford, 1988), pp. 355–60, 366–76. Cf. the remark in M. Moffat and P. Wolff, *Ongles bleus: Jacques et Ciompi* (Paris, 1970): 'If there was a symphony, it was not at all played to time.' Ibid., p. 139. I would prefer to use the symphonic analogy in another way. A Beethoven symphony is very different from, say, a Prokofiev symphony in melody, tone, mood, harmonies, use of dissonance, etc, etc, yet both are clearly symphonies, utilising traditional sonata form. Historians perhaps concentrate too much on the content of rebellions while sociologists concentrate too much on their form. Here as elsewhere I am in favour of a 'dialectic' of the general and the specific. • **43**. See the discussion by Samuel K. Cohn, 'Florentine Insurrections, 1342–85, in Comparative Perspective', in Hilton and Aston, *English Rising*, pp. 143–64 (esp. p. 160) and the same author's *Popular Protest in Late Medieval Europe* (Manchester, 2004). • **44**. In addition to the Cohn works cited see also A. Brucker, *Florentine Politics and Society, 1343–1378* (Princeton, 1962). • **45**. Maurice Dommanget, *La Jacquerie* (Paris, 1971); Louis Raymond de Vericour, 'The Jacquerie', *TRHS*, 1 (1872), pp. 296–310. • **46**. Raymond Carelles, 'The Jacquerie', in Hilton and Aston, *English Rising*, pp. 74–83. • **47**. Froissart, *Chronicles*, pp. 151–2. • **48**. Ibid., pp. 153–5. In contrast to England, where not a single chronicler supported the peasants, in France Jean de Venette and Guillaume de Nauquis were sympathetic to the *jacquerie*. • **49**. A convenient thumbnail sketch of these events is provided in Horspool, *English Rebel*, pp. 140–60. • **50**. M. E. Aston, 'Lollardy and Sedition', *PP* 17 (1960), pp. 1–44. • **51**. I. M. W. Harvey, *Jack Cade's Rebellion of 1450* (Oxford, 1991), p. 24. • **52**. Ibid., pp. 29–30. • **53**. See Colin Richmond, ed., *The Paston Family in the Fifteenth Century*, 3 vols (2000); Helen Castor, *Blood and Roses: The Paston Family in the Fifteenth Century* (2004). • **54**. G. Harriss, *Shaping the Nation: England 1360–1461* (Oxford, 1998), p. 234. • **55**. Vallance, *Radical History*, p. 77. • **56**. P. B. Munche, *Gentlemen and Poachers: The English Game Laws, 1671–1831* (Cambridge, 1981), p. 11. • **57**. D. G. Watts, 'Popular Disorder in Southern England, 1250–1450', in B. Stapleton, ed., *Conflict and Community in Southern England* (1992), pp. 1–15. • **58**. E. F. Jacob, *The Fifteenth Century, 1399–1485* (Oxford, 1961), pp. 475–81. For Henry VI in the 1440s see B. P. Wolfe, *The Reign of Henry VI: The Exercise of Royal Authority 1422–1461* (1981). • **59**. C. A. J. Armstrong, 'Politics and the Battle of St Albans, 1455', *BIHR*, 33 (1960), pp. 1–72. • **60**. J. C. Wedgwood, *History of Parliament: Biographies of the Members of the Commons House, 1439–1509* (1936), pp. 253–5, 744–6, 873–4. • **61**. J. O. Halliwell, ed., *A Chronicle of the First Thirteen Years of the Reign of King Edward the Fourth by John Warkworth* (Camden Society, 1839), p. 11. East Anglia in this context has been exhaustively studied in P. C. Maddern, 'Violence, Crime and Public Disorder in East Anglia, 1422–1442', D.Phil. thesis, University of Oxford (1984). • **62**. M. G. A. Vale, *Charles VII* (1974), pp. 116–18; R. A. Griffiths, *The Reign of Henry VI* (2004), pp. 510–13; M. H. Keen, *England in the Later Middle Ages* (1973), pp. 401–3. • **63**. J. Ferguson, *English Diplomacy, 1422–1461* (Oxford, 1972), pp. 30–2, 100–1. • **64**. J. Stevenson, ed., *Narrative of the Expulsion of the English from Normandy, 1449–1450* (Rolls Series, 1863). • **65**. G. L. Harriss, 'Marmaduke Lumley and the Exchequer Crisis of 1446–9', in J. G. Rowe, ed., *Aspects of Late Medieval Government and Society* (Toronto, 1986), pp. 143–78; R. Virgoe, 'The Parliamentary Subsidy of 1450', *BIHR*, 55 (1982), pp. 125–38; M. H. Keen, 'The End of the Hundred Years War: Lancastrian France and Lancastrian England', in M. Jones and M. Vale, eds, *England and Her Neighbours, 1066–1453* (1989), pp. 297–311. • **66**. J. Gairdner, ed., *The Historical Collections of a Citizen of London in the Fifteenth Century*, Camden

Society, NS, 17 (1876) – hereinafter *Gregory's Chronicle* – p. 189; J. S. Davies, ed., *An English Chronicle of the Reigns of Richard I, Henry IV, Henry V and Henry VI*, Camden Society, OS, 64 (1856) – hereinafter *Davies Chronicle* – p. 64. • **67**. G. L. and M. A. Harriss, 'John Benet's Chronicle for the Years 1400 to 1462', *Camden Miscellany*, 24, Camden Society, 4th series, 9 (1972), pp. 151–233 (at p. 197). • **68**. R. Virgoe, 'The Death of William de la Pole, Duke of Suffolk', *Bulletin of the John Rylands Library*, 47 (1965), pp. 489–502. • **69**. Griffiths, *Reign of Henry VI*, pp. 610–65. • **70**. Harvey, *Jack Cade's Rebellion*, p. 77. • **71**. Ibid., p. 111. • **72**. M. Mate, 'The Economic and Social Roots of Medieval Popular Rebellion: Sussex in 1450 to 1451', *Economic History Review*, 45 (1992), pp. 661–76 (esp. p. 668). • **73**. Bertram Wolfe, *Henry VI* (2001), pp. 232–5. • **74**. Harvey, *Jack Cade's Rebellion*, pp. 78–9; Vallance, *Radical History*, pp. 87–8. • **75**. Griffiths, *Reign of Henry VI*, pp. 617–19. • **76**. A. H. Thomas and D. Thornley, eds, *The Great Chronicle of London* – hereinafter *Great Chronicle* – (Gloucester, 1983), p. 181; Alexander L. Kaufman, *The Historical Literature of the Jack Cade Rebellion* (Vermont 2009), p. 26. • **77**. Guy Forquin, *The Anatomy of Popular Rebellion in the Middle Ages* (Oxford, 1978), p. 71; R. M. Jeffs, The Poynings–Percy Dispute: An Example of the Interplay of Open Strife and Legal Action in the Fifteenth century', *BIHR*, 34 (1961), pp. 148–64; N. Davis, ed., *The Paston Letters, 1422–1509* (1976), I, no. 99. • **78**. G. L. and M. A. Harriss, eds, 'John Benet's Chronicle', p. 198; Griffiths, *Reign of Henry VI*, p. 619. • **79**. R. W. Kaueper, ed., *Violence in Medieval Society* (Woodbridge, 2000). • **80**. M. Bohna, 'Armed Force and Civic Legitimacy in Jack Cade's Revolt', *EHR*, 118 (2003), pp. 563–82 (at p. 576). • **81**. Ibid., p. 578. • **82**. Griffiths, *Reign of Henry VI*, pp. 423–33, 504–50. • **83**. Bohna, 'Armed Force', p. 574. • **84**. Vallance, *Radical History*, pp. 88–9. • **85**. *Great Chronicle*, p. 181; G. L. and M. A. Harriss, 'John Benet's Chronicle', p. 199. • **86**. G. L. and M. A. Harriss, 'John Benet's Chronicle', p. 199. • **87**. Mary Rose McLaren, ed., *The London Chronicles of the Fifteenth Century* (Cambridge, 2002), pp. 100–3. • **88**. Charles Petheridge Kingsford, ed., *Chronicles of London* (1905), pp. 159–60; Griffiths, *Reign of Henry VI*, pp. 612–13, 623–4. • **89**. R. Flenley, ed., *Six Town Chronicles* (1911), pp. 153–4; Robert Fabyan, *The New Chronicles of England and France, ed. Henry Ellis* (1811), pp. 622–5. • **90**. *Great Chronicle*, pp. 182–3. • **91**. Griffiths, *Reign of Henry VI*, p. 613; Harvey, *Jack Cade's Rebellion*, p. 86. • **92**. Kingsford, ed., *Chronicles of London*, p. 162. • **93**. 'Whether his conduct is egotism, bravado or megalomaniac behaviour we are unsure.' Kaufman, *Historical Literature of the Jack Cade Rebellion*, p. 130. • **94**. Flenley, ed., *Six Town Chronicles*, p. 54; *Great Chronicle*, p. 182. • **95**. Kaufman, *Historical Literature of the Jack Cade Rebellion*, p. 189. • **96**. Flenley, ed., *Six Town Chronicles*, p. 155. • **97**. Kaufman, *Historical Literature* *of the Jack Cade Rebellion*, p. 130. For the confusion between serious rebellion and the traditional carnivals held at this time of the year see Craig A. Benthal, 'Jack Cade's Legal Carnival', *Studies in English Literature*, 42 (2002), pp. 259–74; François Laroque, 'The Jack Cade Scenes Reconsidered: Popular Rebellion, Utopia or Carnival?' in Tetsuo Hishi et al., eds, *Shakespeare and Cultural Tradition* (Newark, Delaware, 1991) pp. 76–89. • **98**. *London Chronicles of the Fifteenth Century*, p. 68; *Six Town Chronicles*, pp. 132–3; James Gairdner, ed., *The Historical Collections of a Citizen of London in the Fifteenth Century*, Camden Society, NS, 17 (1876), p. 192. • **99**. 'John Benet's Chronicle', pp. 199–202; Flenley, ed., *Six Town Chronicles*, pp. 153–6; *Historical Collections of a Citizen of London*, pp. 190–3; Richard Jowlett, ed., 'The Chronicle of the Grey Friars in London', *Monumenta Franciscana*, Rolls Society, 4 (1982), ii, p. 173. • **100**. Vallance, *Radical History*, pp. 92–3. • **101**. 'John Benet's Chronicle', p. 201. • **102**. *New Chronicles of England and France*, pp. 624–5. • **103**. Elizabeth Hallam, ed., *The Chronicles of the Wars of the Roses* (Surrey, 1996), p. 205. • **104**. Harvey, *Jack Cade's Rebellion*, pp. 95–6. • **105**. Griffiths, *Reign of Henry VI*, pp. 615–16. • **106**. *New Chronicles of England and France*, p. 625; Flenley, ed., *Six Town Chronicles*, p. 134. • **107**. Harvey, *Jack Cade's Rebellion*, p. 97. • **108**. Flenley, ed., *Six Town Chronicles*, pp. 134–5. • **109**. Vallance, *Radical History*, pp. 95–6. • **110**. Y. M. Bercé, *Revolt and Revolution in Early Modern England* (Manchester, 1987), pp. 117–20. • **111**. Ronald Hutton, *The Rise and Fall of Merry England: The Ritual Year, 1400–1700* (Oxford, 1994), p. 89; Kaufman, *Historical Literature of the Jack Cade Rebellion*, pp. 92–3. • **112**. R. Virgoe, 'Some Ancient Indictments in the King's Bench referring to Kent, 1450–1452', in F. R. H. Du Boulay, ed., *Documents Illustrative of Medieval Kentish Society* (Ashford, 1964), p. 229; Wolfe, *Henry VI*, p. 233. For the legal situation on pardons in general see Naomi D. Hurnard, *The King's Pardon for Homicides* (Oxford, 1969). • **113**. Harvey, *Jack Cade's Rebellion*, pp. 176, 183–5. • **114**. See, e.g., J. R. Landor, *Conflict and Stability in Fifteenth Century England* (1969), p. 72; R. L. Storey, *The End of the House of Lancaster* (1967), pp. 61–8; John L. Watts, 'Polemic and Politics in the 1450s', in Margaret Lucille Kekewich, *The Politics of Fifteenth-Century England: John Vale's Books* (Phoenix Mill, 1995), pp. 3–42. • **115**. *2 Henry VI*, Act III, Scene 1, ll, 356–81. • **116**. Ibid., Act IV, Scene 2, ll, 61–6. • **117**. For a study of Shakespeare's Cade see Thomas Cartelli, 'Jack Cade in the Garden: Class Consciousness and Class Conflict in *Henry VI, Part 2*', in Richard Burt and John Milland Archer, eds, *Enclosure Act: Sexuality and Property and Culture in Early Modern England* (Ithaca, NY, 1994), pp. 48–67. • **118**. Watts, 'Polemic and Politics', pp. 3–42 (at pp. 7–17). • **119**. J. Day, 'The Great Bullion Famine in the Fifteenth Century', *PP* 79 (1978), pp. 3–54; P. Spufford and P. Woodhead,

'Calais and its Mint: Part One', in N. J. Mayhew, ed., *Coinage in the Low Countries, 880–1500* (Oxford, 1979), pp. 171–202; J. Munro, 'Bullion Flows and Monetary Contraction in Late Medieval England and the Low Countries', in J. F. Richards, ed., *Precious Metals in the Later Medieval and Early Modern World* (Durham, NC, 1985), pp. 97–158. • **120**. Moffat and Wolff, *Ongles Bleues*, pp. 276–7. • **121**. M. Mate, 'Pastoral farming in South-East England', *Economic History Review*, 40 (1987), pp. 523–36; Mate, 'Economic and Social Roots', pp. 661–76. • **122**. Dobson, *Peasants' Revolt*, p. 304. • **123**. Mate, 'Economic and Social Roots', pp. 663–4. • **124**. For this crucial point see Griffiths, *Reign of Henry VI*, pp. 628–40; Harvey, *Jack Cade's Rebellion*, pp. 186–91; P. Slack, *Rebellion, Popular Protest and Social Order in Early Modern England* (Cambridge, 1984), pp. 1–15; Y. M. Bercé, *Revolt and Revolution*, pp. 3–33; P. Zagorin, *Rebels and Rulers* (Cambridge, 1982), I, pp. 22–4; John L. Watts, 'Ideas, Principles and Politics', in A. J. Pollard, ed., *The Wars of the Roses* (NY, 1995), pp. 110–33 (esp. pp. 110–11). • **125**. For pre-industrial revolts see Eric Hobsbawm, *Primitive Rebels* (1959) and George Rudé, *The Crowd in History* (2005). Engels's animadversions are in his *The Peasant War in Germany* (Moscow, 1956), pp. 55–60. • **126**. Mark Twain, *A Connecticut Yankee at the Court of King Arthur*, Ch. 13.

4 *The Pilgrimage of Grace*

1. There have been numerous biographies of Henry VIII, but J. J. Scarisbrick, *Henry VIII* (1968), still holds the field. • **2**. The estimate in Robert Hutchinson, *The Last Days of Henry VIII* (2005). Christopher Haigh's estimate is mild: 'Henry VIII disposed of the Pope, the monasteries, four of his wives and two of his closest advisers'. Christopher Haigh, *English Reformations: Religion, Politics and Society under the Tudors* (1993), p. 295. • **3**. See Peter Gwynn, *The King's Cardinal: The Rise and Fall of Thomas Wolsey* (1992). • **4**. Robert Hutchinson, *Thomas Cromwell: The Rise and Fall of Henry VIII's Most Notorious Minister* (2007). • **5**. G. W. Bernard, *The King's Reformation: Henry VIII and the Remaking of the English Church* (2005). • **6**. G. W. Bernard, *Anne Boleyn: Fatal Attractions* (2005) argues for her probable guilt. Eric Ives, *The Life and Death of Anne Boleyn* (2004) and David Starkey, *The Six Wives of Henry VIII* (2003) believe the charges were trumped up. • **7**. For this view see A. G. Dickens, *The English Reformation* (1991), p. 13. Also, more generally, Ann Hudson, *The Premature Reformation: Wycliffe Texts and Lollard History* (1988); Margaret Aston, *Lollards and Reformers: Image and Literacy in Late Medieval England* (1984); Joseph R. Block, *Factional Politics and the English Reformation* (1993); J. F. Davis, *Henry* *and the Reformation in the South-East of England, 1520–1589* (1983); David Loads, *Revolution in England: The English Reformation, 1530–1570* (1992); Rosemary O'Day, *The Debate of the English Reformation* (1986). • **8**. Eamonn Duffy, *The Stripping of the Altars: Transitional Religion in England c.1400–c.1580* (Yale, 1992), pp. 479–81; Robert Whiting, *The Blind Devotion of the People: Popular Religion and the English Reformation* (1989). The ultimate in scepticism is expressed in Christopher Haigh, *English Reformation: Religion, Politics and Society under the Tudors* (1993): 'There may have been no Reformation; indeed, there barely was one', p. 455. • **9**. 'There is no evidence of a loss of confidence in the old ways, no mass disenchantment', J. J. Scarisbrick, *The Reformation and the English People* (1984), p. 12. For further exploration of the view that the Reformation was carried out by a small group of heretics – who succeeded purely because they controlled the government – and the vitality of the old religion, see Scarisbrick, *Henry VIII*, pp. 338–45. See also C. A. Haigh, *Reformation and the Resistance in Tudor Lancashire* (Cambridge, 1975); C. S. L. Davies, 'Popular Religion and the Pilgrimage of Grace', in A. Fletcher and J. Stevenson, eds, *Order and Disorder in Early Modern England* (Cambridge, 1985), pp. 58–91; C. S. L. Davies, 'The Pilgrimage of Grace Reconsidered', *PP* 41 (1968), pp. 54–75. • **10**. A. G. Dickens, 'Secular and Religious Motivation in the Pilgrimage of Grace', *Studies in Church History*, 4 (1967), pp. 39–64. • **11**. Stanford E. Lehmberg, *The Reformation Parliament, 1529–1536* (Cambridge, 1970). • **12**. Jasper Ridley, *Thomas Cranmer* (Oxford, 1962), pp. 113–15. • **13**. William Holdsworth, 'The Political Causes Which Shaped the Statute of Uses', *Harvard Law Review*, 26 (1912), pp. 108–29 ; E. W. Ives, 'The Genesis of the Statute of Uses', *EHR*, 82 (1967), pp. 673–97. • **14**. C. S. L. Davies, 'Popular Religion and the Pilgrimage of Grace', in A. Fletcher and J. Stevenson, eds, *Order and Disorder in Early Modern England* (1986), pp. 58–91 (at p. 90). • **15**. For full details see Anne Ward, *The Lincolnshire Rising, 1536* (1986). • **16**. Geoffrey Moorhouse, *The Pilgrimage of Grace, 1536–7; The Rebellion that Shook Henry VIII's Throne* (2003), p. 47. • **17**. M. E. James, 'Obedience and Dissent in Henrician England: The Lincolnshire rebellion, 1536', *PP* 48 (1970), pp. 3–78; S. J. Gunn, 'Peers, Commons and Gentry in the Lincolnshire Revolt of 1536', *PP* 123 (1989), pp. 52–79. • **18**. James Gairdner and R. H. Brodie, eds, *Letters and Papers, Foreign and Domestic, Henry VIII*, XI, *July–December 1536* (1888) – hereinafter *LP* – no. 585. • **19**. Eric Ives, 'Will the Real Henry VIII Please Stand Up?', *History Today*, 56 (2006), pp. 28–36. • **20**. As argued in James, 'Obedience'. • **21**. M. Bowker, 'Lincolnshire 1536: Heresy, Schism or Religious Discontent', *Studies in Church History*, 9 (1972), pp. 200–1. • **22**. Michael A. R. Graves, 'Howard, Thomas, 3rd Duke of Norfolk (1473–1554), Magnate and Soldier', *ODNB* (2004). • **23**. G. W. Bernard, *The Power of the Early Tudor Nobility: A Study of the Fourth and Fifth Earls of Shrewsbury* (Brighton, 1985);

see also A. F. Pollard, 'George Talbot, 4th Earl of Shrewsbury', *DNB* (1898), 55, pp. 313–14; J. A. Froude, *History of England from the Fall of Wolsey to the Defeat of the Spanish Armada*, 3 vols (1870), iii, p. 109. • **24**. David Starkey, *Rivals in Power: Lives and Letters of the Great Tudor Dynasties* (1990), p. 178. See also Steven J. Gunn, *Charles Brandon, Duke of Norfolk c.1485–1545* (Williston, 1988). • **25**. For the refusal to make concessions see M. E. James, *Politics and Culture* (1986), pp. 188–269 (at pp. 266–7). • **26**. A. Fletcher and B. McCulloch, *Tudor Rebellions* (1997), p. 31; M. L. Bush, '"Up for the Commonweal": The Significance of Tax Grievances in the English Rebellion of 1536', *EHR*, 106 (1991), pp. 299–318 (at p. 303). • **27**. *LP*, XI, no. 569. • **28**. R. W. Hoyle, *The Pilgrimage of Grace and the Politics of the 1530s* (Oxford, 2001), pp. 25, 67, 159, 407. • **29**. M. H. and R. Dodds, *The Pilgrimage of Grace, 1536–1537, and the Exeter Conspiracy, 1538*, 2 vols (1915), i, p. 98. • **30**. 'That Henry's scratch forces were never put to the test was their extreme good fortune.' Hoyle, *Pilgrimage*, p. 171. • **31**. M. Bush, *The Pilgrimage of Grace: A Study of the Rebel Armies of October 1536* (Manchester, 1996), p. 166. • **32**. Ibid., p. 172. • **33**. Ibid., p. 139. • **34**. R. B. Smith, *Land and Politics in the England of Henry VIII* (Oxford, 1970), p. 173; R. R. Reid, *The King's Council in the North* (1975), pp. 133–4. • **35** 'Aske, Robert', *ODNB* (2004), 2, pp. 707–12. • **36**. Respectively, Hoyle, *Pilgrimage*, pp. 192–5, and Mary Bateson, ed., 'The Pilgrimage of Grace and Aske's Examination', *EHR*, 5 (1890), pp. 330–48 and 550–78 (at pp. 333–4). • **37**. *LP*, XI, no. 750. • **38**. Bateson, 'Pilgrimage of Grace', pp. 559, 569. • **39**. Hoyle, *Pilgrimage*, pp. 47–50, 195–9, 414. • **40**. Reid, *King's Council*, p. 126. • **41**. G. R. Elton, 'Politics and the Pilgrimage of Grace', in G. R. Elton, *Studies in Tudor and Stuart Politics and Government*, 4 vols (1992), iii, pp. 183–215; G. R. Elton, *Reform and Reformation: England 1509–1558* (1977), pp. 260–70; Hoyle, *Pilgrimage*, p. 190. • **42**. James, 'Obedience'. • **43**. Bateson, 'Pilgrimage of Grace', pp. 558–9, 562–3; Scarisbrick, *Henry VIII*, p. 341. • **44**. M. Bush, 'Enhancement and Importunate Change: An analysis of the Tax Complaints of October 1536', *Albion*, 22 (1990), pp. 403–18. • **45**. Moorhouse, *Pilgrimage of Grace*, p. 108. • **46**. The king 'probably thought that if things came to the worst it would be better to lose a doubtful supporter than send arms to a possible rebel'. Dodds, *Pilgrimage of Grace*, i, p. 144. • **47**. Bush, 'Up for the Commonweal', p. 303; Bush, *Pilgrimage*, pp. 43–47. • **48**. J. C. Cox, 'William Stapulton and the Pilgrimage of Grace', *Transactions of the East Riding Antiquarian Society*, 10 (1903), pp. 82–98 (at pp. 82, 85). • **49**. Ibid. • **50**. Ibid., pp. 91–5. • **51**. H. J. Allison, *A History of the County of York* (1974), iii, pp. 138–42; cf. also Stephen Tobin, *The Cistercians: Monks and Monasteries in Europe, 1502–37* (1995). • **52**. Cox, 'William Stapulton', pp. 95–8. • **53**. A. Fletcher and D. MacCulloch, *Tudor Rebellions* (1997), p. 132. • **54**. *LP*, XI, no. 826. • **55**. Hoyle, *Pilgrimage*, p. 206. • **56**. *LP*, XI, no. 705. • **57**. For this aspect of the German rebellion see

E. Belfort Bax, *The Peasant War* (1899), pp. 108, 137–42. • **58**. Bush, *Pilgrimage*, p. 214. • **59**. Ibid., pp. 98–100. • **60**. *LP*, XI, no. 1086. See also Gairdner and Brodie, eds, *Letters and Papers, Henry VIII January–May 1537*, vol. 12, part one – hereinafter *LP*, XII, i – nos 783, 976, 899. • **61**. R. W. Hoyle, 'Thomas Master's Narrative of the Pilgrimage of Grace', *Northern History*, 21 (1985), pp. 53–79 (at p. 79); Hoyle, *Pilgrimage*, p. 417. • **62**. For the connections between Hussey and Darcy see Dodds, *Pilgrimage of Grace*, i, pp. 301–3. On the entire issue of Darcy's guilt, its extent, and the extenuating case that can be made for him see Hoyle, *Pilgrimage*, pp. 68–70, 256–81 (esp. pp. 257, 260–6, 271–3), 416–17. • **63**. *LP*, XII, i, nos 851, 891. • **64**. Bush, *Pilgrimage*, pp. 67–8; Cox, 'William Stapulton', Bateson, 'Pilgrimage of Grace', pp. 336–7. • **65**. Cox, 'William Stapulton', p. 82. For Bowes himself see C. Newman, *Robert Bowes and the Pilgrimage of Grace* (Teesside, 1997). • **66**. M. L. Bush, 'Captain Poverty and the Pilgrimage of Grace', *Historical Research*, 65 (1992), pp. 17–36 (at pp. 17–18); M. L. Bush, 'The Richmondshire Uprising of October 1536 and the Pilgrimage of Grace', *Northern History*, 39 (1993), pp. 88–95; Bush, *Pilgrimage*, pp. 72–6. • **67**. S. M. Harrison, *The Pilgrimage of Grace in the Lake Counties, 1536–7* (1981), pp. 47–56; Bush, *Pilgrimage*, p. 12. • **68**. Dodds, *Pilgrimage of Grace*, i, pp. 370–2. • **69**. The untenable notion of the Pilgrims as an aristocratic revolt manipulating the Commons to rise against an unpopular Thomas Cromwell is in G. R. Elton, 'Politics and the Pilgrimage of Grace', in B. Malament, ed., *After the Reformation* (Manchester, 1980), pp. 25–6. See also R. B. Smith, *Land and Politics in the England of Henry VIII* (Oxford, 1970), esp. Ch. 5. For the more convincing view that the Pilgrimage was always principally a popular revolt see Hoyle, 'Master's Narrative', and Reid, *King's Council*, pp. 136–9. • **70**. Bateson, 'Pilgrimage of Grace', pp. 336–7; Hoyle, 'Master's Narrative', pp. 70–1; Bush, 'Richmondshire uprising'. • **71**. *LP*, XI, no. 927. • **72**. R. W. Hoyle, 'The First Earl of Cumberland: A Reputation Reassessed', *Northern History*, 22 (1986), pp. 63–94; M. E. James, 'The First Earl of Cumberland (1493–1542) and the Decline of Northern Feudalism', *Northern History*, 1 (1966), pp. 63–94; Louis A. Knaffla, 'Stanley, Edward, 3rd Earl of Derby (1509–72), Magnate', *ODNB* (2004), pp. 175–7; Dodds, *Pilgrimage of Grace*, i, pp. 215–16. • **73**. Dodds, *Pilgrimage of Grace*, i, p. 238. • **74**. W. A. J. Archbold, 'Henry Percy, 6th Earl of Cumberland', *DNB* (1898), 44, pp. 416–17; Dodds, *Pilgrimage of Grace*, i, pp. 32–4. • **75**. *LP*, XI, no. 714. • **76**. Bush, *Pilgrimage*, pp. 41, 205; Dodds, *Pilgrimage of Grace*, i, p. 192. • **77**. *LP*, XII, i, no. 393; Dodds, *Pilgrimage of Grace*, i, pp. 198–9. • **78**. Bush, *Pilgrimage*, p. 376. • **79**. Hoyle, *Pilgrimage*, p. 294. • **80**. Ibid., p. 413. And, for another opinion: 'Central to the uprising, then, was an outraged, independent and self-conscious commons urgently demanding redress. Their presence influenced the behaviour of other aggrieved groups, clerical and aristocratic.' • **81**. Dodds, *Pilgrimage of Grace*, i, p. 54. • **82** *LP*, XI, no. 826; Dodds, *Pilgrimage of Grace*, i, pp. 228–30. • **83**. Bush, *Pilgrimage*, pp. 66–7. For the Ellerkers see B. English, *The Great Landowners and East Yorkshire* (NY, 1990), pp. 18–19. • **84**. Bateson, 'Pilgrimage of Grace', p. 39; Cox, 'William Stapulton', p. 94; Bush, *Pilgrimage*, pp. 56–8; Hoyle, *Pilgrimage*, pp. 437–9. • **85**. Bateson, Pilgrimage of Grace', pp. 554–5; Dodds, *Pilgrimage of Grace*, i, p. 239. • **86**. *LP*, XI, no. 786. • **87**. Moorhouse, *Pilgrimage of Grace*, p. 143. • **88**. *LP*, XI, nos 615, 621, 768, 803. • **89**. Dodds, *Pilgrimage of Grace*, i, p. 246. • **90**. *LP*, XI, nos 758, 845–6. • **91**. Dodds, *Pilgrimage of Grace*, i, p. 255. • **92**. *LP*, XI, no. 846; Cox 'Stapulton', p. 337. • **93**. Hoyle, 'Master's Narrative', pp. 50–1, 70–1; *LP*, XI, nos 846, 909. • **94**. *LP*, XI, nos 887, 909. • **95**. Cox 'Stapulton', p. 554; Dodds, *Pilgrimage of Grace*, i, pp. 253–4. • **96**. Cox 'Stapulton', p. 559. • **97**. Here one is irresistibly reminded of the words of Mao Tse-tung: 'A revolution is not a dinner party, or writing an essay, or painting a picture or doing embroidery; it cannot be so refined, so leisurely and gentle, so temperate, kind, courteous, restrained and magnanimous.' *Report on an Investigation of the Peasant Movement in Hunan*. • **98**. M. E. James, 'English Politics and the Concept of Honour, 1485–1642', in M. E. James, *Society, Politics and Culture in Early Modern England* (1986), pp. 380–415 (at pp. 350–4); Hoyle, *Pilgrimage*, p. 297; Dodds, *Pilgrimage of Grace*, i, p. 257. • **99**. *LP*, XI, no. 909. • **100**. *LP*, XI, nos 909, 1241. • **101**. *LP*, XI, no. 864. • **102**. Hoyle, *Pilgrimage*, p. 294. • **103**. Hoyle, 'Master's Narrative', pp. 70–1; Bush, *Pilgrimage*, pp. 390–1. • **104**. Hoyle, *Pilgrimage*, p. 297. • **105**. Dodds, *Pilgrimage of Grace*, i, p. 262. • **106**. Moorhouse, *Pilgrimage of Grace*, p. 151. • **107**. Bateson, 'Pilgrimage of Grace', p. 338; *LP*, XI, no. 1319. • **108**. *LP*, XI, no. 186. • **109**. Bateson, 'Pilgrimage of Grace', p. 338; *LP*, XI, no. 405; Dodds, *Pilgrimage of Grace*, i, p. 260. • **110**. *LP*, XI, no. 864. • **111**. Bateson, 'Pilgrimage of Grace', p. 338. • **112**. *LP*, XI, nos 928, 1045. • **113**. Bush, *Pilgrimage*, p. 394. • **114**. D. MacCulloch, *Thomas Cranmer: A Life* (1996), p. 178. • **115**. *LP*, XI, nos 1174–6. • **116**. *LP*, XI, nos 979, 1009. • **117**. Dodds, *Pilgrimage of Grace*, i, pp. 326–7. • **118**. *LP*, XI, nos 1138, 1175. • **119**. *LP*, XI, no. 1061. • **120**. *LP*, XI, no. 780. • **121**. Bateson, 'Pilgrimage of Grace', p. 555. • **122**. *LP*, XI, no. 957; Dodds, *Pilgrimage of Grace*, i, pp. 275–8. • **123**. *LP*, XI, nos 1027, 1077, 1120. • **124**. Dodds, *Pilgrimage of Grace*, i, pp. 321–2.

5 *Treachery and Debacle*

1. Dodds, *Pilgrimage of Grace*, i, pp. 51–3. • **2**. MacCulloch, *Thomas Cranmer*, p. 34. • **3**. *LP*, XII, i, no. 1022. • **4**. *LP*, XI, nos 1300, 1336; Dodds, *Pilgrimage of Grace*, i, p. 381. • **5**. *LP*, XI, no. 1136. • **6**. *LP*, XI, nos 1300, 1336; Dodds, *Pilgrimage of Grace*, i, pp. 342–3. • **7**. *LP*, XI, no. 1049. • **8**. *LP*, XI, no. 1058. • **9**. *LP*, XI, nos 1050, 1051, 1059, 1068, 1096, 1167. • **10**. *LP*, XII, i, no. 1013; *LP*, XI, no. 995.

• **11**. *LP*, XI, nos 1045, 1007. • **12**. Dodds, *Pilgrimage of Grace*, i, p. 293. • **13**. *LP*, XI, no. 1046. • **14**. Hoyle, *Pilgrimage*, p. 322. • **15**. *LP*, XI, no. 998; Dodds, *Pilgrimage of Grace*, i, p. 282. • **16**. Dodds, *Pilgrimage of Grace*, i, pp. 325, 340. • **17**. *LP*, XI, nos 826, 955, 1044, 1064, 1170. • **18**. Dodds, *Pilgrimage of Grace*, i, p. 340 • **19**. For these issues in general see Frank McLynn, *Invasion: From the Armada to Hitler* (1987). • **20**. For Pole see Martin Haile, *Life of Reginald Pole* (NY, 1910). • **21**. *LP*, XI, no. 1131. • **22**. Dodds, *Pilgrimage of Grace*, i, pp. 335–9. • **23**. Ibid., pp. 310, 341; Moorhouse, *Pilgrimage of Grace*, p. 185. • **24**. *LP*, XI, nos 1115–16. • **25**. Dodds, *Pilgrimage of Grace*, i, pp. 312–13. • **26**. *LP*, XI, no. 1032. • **27**. Hoyle, *Pilgrimage*, pp. 302–20. • **28**. *LP*, XI, no. 1120. • **29**. For Norfolk's advice see *LP*, XI, nos 884–6. Henry habitually reacted to this advice by accusing Norfolk of defeatism and of exaggerating Pilgrim numbers (*LP*, XI, no. 1271). • **30**. *LP*, XI, nos 1139, 1175; Bateson, 'Pilgrimage of Grace', p. 339. • **31**. Hoyle, *Pilgrimage*, p. 312. • **32**. Ibid., p. 326. • **33**. *LP*, XI, no. 1170; Dodds, *Pilgrimage of Grace*, i, pp. 379–80. • **34**. Moorhouse, *Pilgrimage of Grace*, p. 166. • **35**. Hoyle, 'Master's Narrative', p. 74. • **36**. Hoyle, *Pilgrimage*, pp. 326–8; Dodds, *Pilgrimage of Grace*, i, pp. 311–18. • **37**. *LP*, XI, no. 1170. • **38**. Hoyle, *Pilgrimage*, p. 341. • **39**. *LP*, XI, nos 1226–8. • **40**. *LP*, XI, nos 1209–10. • **41**. For a full list of participants in the Pontefract conference see Dodds, *Pilgrimage of Grace*, i, p. 345. • **42**. Ibid., pp. 48–53. • **43**. It is worth remarking, parenthetically, that Aske's apparently ingenious solution would have offered no answer to the conundrum of the divorce of Catherine of Aragon. Did this come under the heading of 'temporal' matters or the care of souls? The answer, depending on one's premises, is: both. • **44**. Dodds, *Pilgrimage of Grace*, i, pp. 351–2. • **45**. Ibid., pp. 357–8. • **46**. Ibid., pp. 355–6. • **47**. Ibid., pp. 359–60. • **48**. Bateson, 'Pilgrimage of Grace', pp. 559, 565, 570; cf. also *LP*, XI, no. 853. • **49**. Moorhouse, *Pilgrimage of Grace*, p. 173. • **50**. For gressoms see Bush, *Pilgrimage*, pp. 54–5, 170–3, 202–4, 277, 297, 302, 309–11, 336–40. • **51**. Ibid., pp. 311–14, 337: • **52**. Ibid., pp. 314–20. • **53**. ibid., pp. 170–3, 276–9, 297–8, 309–14, 322–4, 336–9, 408–9, 413–14. • **54**. M. L. Bush, 'Enhancement and Importunate Changes: An Analysis of the Tax Complaints of October 1536', *Albion*, 22 (1990), pp. 403–18. • **55**. Ibid., p. 406. • **56**. Moorhouse, *Pilgrimage of Grace*, p. 101; Cox, 'William Stapulton', p. 82. • **57**. Bush, *Pilgrimage*, pp. 364–73. • **58**. Ibid., p. 318. • **59**. *LP* XI, nos 1196, 1237, 1242. • **60**. *LP*, XI, no. 1226. • **61**. *LP*, XI, no. 1237. • **62**. Bateson, 'Pilgrimage of Grace', pp. 340–1. • **63**. Dodds, *Pilgrimage of Grace*, ii. p. 12. • **64**. Bateson, 'Pilgrimage of Grace', p. 341; *LP*, XI, no. 1271. • **65**. Bateson, 'Pilgrimage of Grace', pp. 341–2. • **66**. *LP*, XI, no. 1226; Hoyle, *Pilgrimage*, p. 366. • **67**. Hoyle, 'Master's Narrative', p. 75; Hoyle, *Pilgrimage*, p. 361. • **68**. *LP*, XI, no. 1271. • **69**. Hoyle, *Pilgrimage*, pp. 359–65. • **70**. Dodds, *Pilgrimage of Grace*, ii, pp. 17–18. • **71**. Hoyle, *Pilgrimage*, p. 419. • **72**. For some pointers in this area see Claire Cross, 'Monasticism and Society in the Diocese of York, 1520–1540', *TRHS*, 38 (1988), pp. 131–45; Christopher Haigh, *The Last Days of the Lancashire Monasteries and the Pilgrimage of Grace*, Chatham Society, 3rd series, 17 (1969); R. W. Hoyle, 'The Origins of the Dissolution of the Monasteries', *Historical Journal*, 38 (1995), pp. 275–305. • **73**. For Cumberland see S. M. Harrison, *The Pilgrimage of Grace in the Lake Counties, 1536–7* (1981). • **74**. Bush, *Pilgrimage*, p. 129. • **75**. Though this may have affected Henry's attitude later. See Hutchinson, *Thomas Cromwell*. • **76**. *LP*, XI, nos 1234, 1238, 1271; Bateson, 'Pilgrimage of Grace', p. 341. • **77**. *LP*, XII, i, no. 131. • **78**. Dodds, *Pilgrimage of Grace*, ii, p. 17. • **79**. *LP*, XI, nos 1337, 1339, 1368. • **80**. *LP*, XI, no. 1294. • **81**. *LP*, XI, nos 1358, 1369. • **82**. Moorhouse, *Pilgrimage of Grace*, pp. 217–20. • **83**. *LP*, XI, no. 1306. • **84**. Moorhouse, *Pilgrimage of Grace*, p. 221. • **85**. *LP* XI, nos 1337, 1365, 1380. • **86**. *LP*, XI, nos 1410, 1459, 1481–2. • **87**. For Scarborough see J. Binns, 'Scarborough and the Pilgrimage of Grace', *Scarborough Archaeological and Historical Society*, 33 (1997), pp. 23–39. • **88**. Hoyle, *Pilgrimage*, pp. 404–5. • **89**. M. L. Bush, 'The problem of the Far North: A Study of the Crisis of 1537 and Its Consequences', *Northern History*, 6 (1971), pp. 40–63. • **90**. Dodds, *Pilgrimage of Grace*, ii, pp. 89–90. • **91**. Ibid., ii, pp. 91–2. • **92**. *LP*, XII, i, no. 578. For the Bigod family in general see Dodds, *Pilgrimage of Grace*, i, pp. 40–4. • **93**. Dodds, *Pilgrimage of Grace*, ii, pp. 56–60. • **94**. *LP*, XII, i, nos 145, 1087. • **95**. *LP*, XII, i, no. 1087. • **96**. Hoyle, *Pilgrimage*, p. 384. • **97**. Dodds, *Pilgrimage of Grace*, ii, pp. 62–78. • **98**. *LP*, XI, no. 1410. • **99**. Dodds, *Pilgrimage of Grace*, ii, p. 53. • **100**. Ibid., ii, p. 93. • **101**. Ibid., ii, p. 97. • **102**. Ibid., ii, pp. 99–100. • **103**. Ibid., ii, p. 109. • **104**. Ibid., ii, p. 111. • **105**. Moorhouse, *Pilgrimage of Grace*, p. 278. • **106**. Hoyle, *Pilgrimage*, pp. 399–404. • **107**. For the Cliffords see Add. MSS. 48, 965. • **108**. Dodds, *Pilgrimage of Grace*, ii, pp. 116–20, 133. • **109**. K. J. Allison, 'The Sixteenth Century: Political Affairs Before 1542', in K. J. Allison, ed., *A History of the County of York East Riding*, vol. vi, *The Borough and Liberties of Beverley* (1989), pp. 70–3. • **110**. The entire macabre story is told in D. M. Bownes, *The Post-Pardon Revolts, December 1536–March 1537* (Manchester, 1995), and Michael Bush and David Bownes, *The Defeat of the Pilgrimage of Grace: A Study of the Postpardon Revolts of December 1536 to March 1537 and Their Effect* (Hull, 1999). • **111**. Dodds, *Pilgrimage of Grace*, ii, p. 226. • **112**. Hoyle, *Pilgrimage*, pp. 397–9. • **113**. Ibid., pp. 410–11. • **114**. Dodds, *Pilgrimage of Grace*, ii, pp. 186–95. • **115**. Bateson, 'Pilgrimage of Grace', pp. 550–73; Dodds, *Pilgrimage of Grace*, ii, pp. 207–25. • **116**. Dodds, *Pilgrimage of Grace*, ii, p. 221. • **117**. Ibid., ii, pp. 105, 216, 227. • **118**. Moorhouse, *Pilgrimage of Grace*, p. 308; cf. also P. Blickle, *The Revolution of 1525: The German Peasant War from a New Perspective* (1981). • **119**. Dodds, *Pilgrimage of Grace*, ii, pp. 278–89. • **120**. Ibid., ii, pp. 289–99, 307–27. • **121**. The whole story is told in Jesse Childs, *Henry VIII's Last Victim* (2008). • **122**. A. G. Dickens, *The English Reformation* (1989), pp. 74–9.

• **123**. Bush, 'Up for the Commonweal', pp. 314–15. • **124**. Bush, *Pilgrimage*, pp. 401–3. • **125**. See the interesting synoptic treatment in A. Wood, *The 1549 Rebellion and the Making of Early Modern England* (Cambridge, 2007). • **126**. R. B. Manning, 'The Rebellion of 1549 in England', *Sixteenth Century Journal*, 10 (1979), pp. 93–9. • **127**. See S. Hindle, *The State and Social Change c.1550–1640* (Basingstoke, 2000), pp. 44–8. • **128**. D. MacCulloch, 'Kett's Rebellion in Context', *PP* 84 (1981), pp. 36–59; J. D. Alsop, 'Latimer, the "Commonwealth of Kett" and the 1549 Rebellion', *Historical Journal*, 28 (1985), pp. 379–83. • **129**. B. L. Beer, 'The Commoyson in Norfolk, 1549: A Narrative of Popular Rebellion in Sixteenth-Century England', *Journal of Medieval and Renaissance Studies* 6 (1976), pp. 80–99. • **130**. Wood, *1549 Rebellion*, p. 71. • **131**. Andrew Graham-Dixon, *A History of British Art* (1996), pp. 22–3.

6 *Cromwell and the Levellers*

1. Geoffrey Parker and Lesley M. Smith, eds, *The General Crisis of the Seventeenth Century* (1997). • **2**. T. Ashton, ed., *Crisis in Europe, 1560–1660* (1965). • **3**. E. Hobsbawm, 'The Crisis of the Seventeenth Century', *PP* 6 (1954), pp. 44–65: H. Trevor-Roper, 'The General Crisis of the Seventeenth Century', *PP* 16 (1959), pp. 31–64. See also the discussion by half a dozen other notables in *PP* 18 (1960), pp. 8–42. • **4**. For this famous controversy see Christopher Hill, *Puritanism and Revolution* (1958); H. Trevor-Roper, *The Crisis of the Seventeenth Century: Religion, the Reformation, Social Change and Other Essays* (1967); H. Trevor-Roper, *Catholics, Anglicans and Puritans: Seventeenth-Century Essays* (1987). This was largely a debate between Marxists and non-Marxists, the former represented by Hill, Hobsbawm, R. H. Tawney and Laurence Stone, the latter by Trevor-Roper, G. R. Elton and J. H. Hexter. When the Marxists identified the gentry as the ascendant class, Trevor-Roper, with his love of paradox and pure disputation, asserted that the gentry were *declining*. Curiously, now that the dust has settled, historians have in effect returned to the very earliest interpretations: that the English Civil War was largely caused by a struggle between king and Parliament and the contingent mistakes of Charles I. • **5**. For the Elizabethan Poor Laws see A. L. Meier, *Masterless Men: The Vagrancy Problem in England, 1560–1640* (1985); N. Fellows, *Disorder and Rebellion in Tudor England* (2001); John F. Proud, *Poverty and Vagrancy in Early Modern England* (1971); Paul Slack, *Poverty and Policy in Tudor England* (1988). • **6**. For this point see Karl Marx, *Capital*, i, p. 773. • **7**. M. Poster, *Existential Marxism in Postwar France* (Princeton, 1975), p. 340. • **8**. John Spurr, *English Puritanism, 1603–1689* (1998). See also John Coffey and Paul C. H. Lim, eds, *The Cambridge Companion to Puritanism* (Cambridge, 2008). • **9**. Disraeli, *Sybil*,

Book 4, Ch. 6. • **10**. For Laud see Antony Milton, 'Laud, William', *ODNB* (2004), 32, pp. 655–70; H. Trevor-Roper, *Archbishop Laud, 1573–1645* (1940). • **11**. Kevin Sharpe, *The Personal Rule of Charles I* (1995). • **12**. Michael Mendle, 'The Ship Money Case: The Case of Ship Money and the Development of Henry Parker's Parliamentary Absolutism', *Historical Journal*, 32 (1989), pp. 513–36. There is a good popular account in David Gross, ed., *We Won't Pay! A Tax Resistance Reader* (2008), pp. 9–16. See also Michael Mendle, *Henry Parker and the English Civil War* (2003). • **13**. Pauline Gregg, *Freeborn John: A Biography of John Lilburne* (2001), pp. 56–63. • **14**. A. Sharp, ed., *The English Levellers* (Cambridge, 1998), pp. 38–9. • **15**. Austin Woolrych, *Britain in Revolution, 1625–1660* (2002), p. 134. For divine-right theory see Glenn Burgess, 'The Divine Right of Kings Reconsidered', *EHR*, 107 (1992), pp. 837–61. For Sir Edmund Coke see Catherine Drinker Bowen, *The Lion and the Throne* (1958). • **16**. Trevor Royle, *Civil War: The Wars of the Three Kingdoms* (2005), pp. 89–94. • **17**. For Pym see J. H. Hexter, *The Reign of King Pym* (1941). For the 16 April 1640 speech see J. P. Kenyon, *The Stuart Constitution, 1603–1688: Documents and Commentary* (1986), pp. 183–9. • **18**. D. Cressy, *England on the Edge: Crisis and Revolution, 1640–1642* (Oxford, 2006), p. 426. • **19**. For Strafford in Ireland see Hugh F. Kearney, *Strafford in Ireland, 1633–1641: A Study in Absolutism* (1989). • **20**. Ronald G. Asch, 'Thomas Wentworth, 1st Earl of Strafford', *ODNB* (2004), 58, pp. 142–57. • **21**. There is no better account of all this than C. V. Wedgwood, *Thomas Wentworth, 1st Earl of* Strafford (2000). For Charles's assent to the attainder see Woolrych, *Britain in Revolution*, p. 178. • **22**. C. V. Wedgwood, *The King's Peace* (1955) provides full details. • **23**. R. Fletcher, ed., *Prose Works of Milton* (Harvard, 1835), pp. 11–13. • **24**. Cressy, *England on the Edge*, p. 247. • **25**. J. Morrill, B. Manning and D. Underdown, 'What Was the English Revolution?', *History Today*, 34 (1984); Glenn Burgess and Matthew Festenstein, *English Radicalism* (Cambridge, 2011), p. 69. • **26**. For the Grand Remonstrance see S. R. Gardiner, ed., *The Constitutional Documents of the Puritan Revolution, 1625–1660* (1906), pp. 202–32. • **27**. Cressy, *England on the Edge*, p. 218. • **28**. J. P. Kenyon, *Stuart England* (1978), p. 136; David L. Smith, *The Stuart Parliaments, 1603–1689* (1999), p. 129. • **29**. David Starkey, *Monarchy* (2006), pp. 113–14. • **30**. Woolrych, *Britain in Revolution*, p. 291. • **31**. Antonia Fraser, *Cromwell: Our Chief of Men* (1973), pp. 120–9. • **32**. The details can be followed in John Morill, ed., *Oliver Cromwell and the English Revolution* (1990). • **33**. John Kenyon and Jane Ohlmeyer, eds, *The Civil Wars: A Military History of England, Scotland and Ireland* (Oxford, 2000), p. 141. • **34**. Charles Carlton, *The Experience of the English Civil War* (1992), pp. 211–14. • **35**. Ian Gentles, *The English Revolution and the Wars in the Three Kingdoms* (2007), pp. 433–9. • **36**. Carlton, *Experience*. • **37**. George Nelson Godwin, *The Civil War in Hampshire (1642–45)* (1904), pp. 314–17. • **38**. Spurr, *Puritanism*; Coffey and Lim, eds, *Cambridge Companion to Puritanism*.

The works of Weber and Tawney referred to are Max Weber, *The Protestant Ethic and the Spirit of Capitalism* (1905) and R. H. Tawney, *Religion and the Rise of Capitalism* (1926). • **39**. There is a very good discussion of all these points in Laurence Stone, *The Origins of the English Revolution* (1972). • **40**. Friedrich Engels, *Neue Zeit* (1892–3), i, pp. 43–4. • **41**. See George Williams, *The Radical Reformation* (Philadelphia, 1962). • **42**. Voltaire, *Essai sur les moeurs*, Ch. 136, 'Suite de la religion de l'Angleterre' (1756). • **43**. William C. Braithwaite, *The Beginnings of Quakerism* (1912). • **44**. Everyone knows that biblical exegesis is a minefield. For what it is worth, Antinomians often cited the following passages in St Paul: 2 Peter 3: 16; Galatians 2: 4; 3: 23–5, 4: 21–3; Colossians 1: 13–14; 1 Corinthians 3: 16–17; Romans 6: 14–15; 7: 1–7; Ephesians 2: 15 as well as the Acts of the Apostles 13: 39; 18: 12–16. • **45**. And so gave a literally true meaning to the experience of modern airline travellers of the 'six miles high' variety. • **46**. E. P. Thompson, *The Making of the English Working Class* (1963), p. 52. • **47**. Christopher Hill, *Milton and the English Revolution* (1977), pp. 70–6; John Coffey, 'Puritanism and Liberty Revisited: The Case for Toleration in the English Revolution', *Historical Journal*, 41 (1998), pp. 961–85. • **48**. There has been a scholarly debate about the Ranters. The extreme view is that they never existed but were simply bogeymen conjured up by the Presbyterians – see J. C. Davis, *Fear, Myth and History: The Ranters and the Historians* (1986). The more cogent view is that they did exist but, like the communists conjured up by Senator Joseph McCarthy in the USA in the 1950s, were too insignificant to be taken seriously – see the review of Davis's book by Richard L. Greave in *Church History*, 57 (1988), pp. 376–8 and by G. Aylmer in *PP* 117 (1987), pp. 208–19. • **49**. J. F. McGregor and B. Reay, eds, *Radical Religion and the English Revolution* (1984). • **50**. See Leo Miller, *John Milton Among the Polygamophiles* (NY, 1974); Annabel Patterson, 'Milton, Marriage and Divorce', in Thomas Corn, ed., *A Companion to Milton* (Oxford, 2003), pp. 279–93. • **51**. B. S. Capp, *The Fifth Monarchy Men: A Study in Seventeenth-Century Millenarianism* (1972). • **52**. Wallace Notestein, *A History of Witchcraft in England from 1558 to 1718* (NY, 1965), p. 195. See also Craig Cabell, *Witchfinder-General: The Biography of Matthew Hopkins* (2006); Malcolm Gaskill, *Witchfinders: A Seventeenth-Century Tragedy* (2005); Keith Thomas, *Religion and the Decline of Magic: Studies in Popular Beliefs in Sixteenth and Seventeenth Century England* (1971). • **53**. This is apparently not a genuine Chestertonism, but a distillation of his thought by Emile Cammaerts in his biography *The Laughing Prophet* (1937). • **54**. There is much detail on all this in D. L. Smith, *Oliver Cromwell, Politics and Religion in the English Revolution* (1991). • **55**. John Milton, 'On the New Forces of Conscience Under the Long Parliament' (1646) – the last line of the poem. • **56**. J. C. Davis, 'The Levellers and Democracy', *PP* 40 (1968), pp. 174–80. • **57**. John Milton, *Areopagitica* (1646). • **58**. T. Carlyle, ed., *Letters and Speeches* *of Oliver Cromwell* (1845), i, p. 205. • **59**. 'According to some conservative contemporary observers, the mental atmosphere in the Army resembled (in modern terms) something like a mixture of a revivalist religious congress and an extreme left-wing debating society.' G. E. Aylmer, *The Levellers in the English Revolution* (Cornell, 1975), p. 11. • **60**. Blair Worden, 'The Levellers in History and Memory *c*.1660–1960', in Michael Mendle, ed., *The Putney Debates of 1647* (Cambridge, 2001), pp. 256–82 (esp. pp. 280–2). • **61**. See the discussion in Colin Davis, 'Religion and the Struggle for Freedom in the English Revolution', *Historical Journal*, 35 (1972), pp. 507–31; J. C. Davis, 'The Levellers and Christianity', in B. Manning, ed., *Politics, Religion and the English Civil War* (1973), pp. 225–50. • **62**. H. N. Brailsford, *The Levellers and the English Constitution* (1961), pp. 9, 30–4. • **63**. From a mountain of material on the Levellers, their beliefs and ideology see: G. E. Aylmer, 'Gentlemen Levellers', *PP* 49 (1970), pp. 120–5; D. E. Brewster and R. Howell, 'Reconsidering the Levellers: The Evidence of the "Moderate"', *PP* 46 (1970), pp. 68–86; K. Thomas, 'Another Digger Broadside', *PP* 42 (1969), pp. 57–61. • **64**. The work of J. C. Davis is particularly stimulating. See 'Levellers and Democracy' 'General Winstanley and the Restoration of True Magistracy', *PP* 70 (1976), pp. 76–93; 'Fear, Myth and Furore', *PP* 129 (1990), pp. 79–103. • **65**. Brailsford, *Levellers*, p. 309. • **66**. Gregg, *Freeborn John*, pp. 102–3. • **67**. D. M. Masson, ed., *The Quarrel between the Earl of Manchester and Oliver Cromwell: Documents Collected by J. Bruce, with a Historical Preface*, Camden Society, NS, 12 (1875). • **68**. For Blanqui see L. Kolakowski, *The Mainstream of Marxism* (2005), pp. 176–7. • **69**. Gregg, *Freeborn John*, pp. 111, 120, 135. • **70**. Ibid., pp. 170–4. • **71**. Brailsford, *Levellers*, p. 74. • **72**. Ibid., pp. 237–8. • **73**. Ibid., p. 77. • **74**. Aylmer, *Levellers in the English Revolution*, pp. 56–62. • **75**. A. L. Morton, *Freedom in Arms* (1975), pp. 87–99. • **76**. J. T. Peacey, 'John Lilburne and the Long Parliament', *Historical Journal*, 43 (2000), pp. 625–45. • **77**. Rachel Foxley, 'John Lilburne and the Citizenship of "Freeborn Englishmen"', *Historical Journal*, 47 (2004), pp. 849–74; cf. also Brailsford, *Levellers*, pp. 122–5. • **78**. See William Godwin, *History of the Commonwealth* (1824). • **79**. Christopher Hill, *The World Turned Upside Down: Radical Ideas During the English Revolution* (1972), pp. 91–9. The preference for Walwyn over Lilburne is evident in Brailsford, *Levellers*, esp. pp. 59–71. • **80**. Jack R. McMichael and Barbara Taft, eds, *The Writings of William Walwyn* (Athens, Georgia, 1989), pp. 143–53. For the 'mess of pottage' see Aylmer, *Levellers in the English Revolution*, pp. 63–7. • **81**. Barbara Taft, 'William Walwyn', *ODNB* (2004), 57, pp. 225–31. • **82**. McMichael and Taft, eds, *Writings of William Walwyn*, pp. 236–44. • **83**. William Haller and Godfrey Davies, eds, *The Leveller Tracts, 1647–1653* (Gloucester, Mass., 1964), pp. 350–98; McMichael and Taft, eds, *Writings of William Walwyn*, pp. 383–432. • **84**. McMichael and Taft, eds, *Writings of William Walwyn*, pp. 433–45, 446–52. • **85**. B. J. Gibbons, 'Richard Overton',

ODNB (2004), 42, pp. 166–71. • **86**. Hill, *World Turned Upside Down*, pp. 91–9. His brilliant pupil, David W. Petegorsky, *Left-Wing Democracy in the English Civil War* (Stroud, 1999), likewise characterises Overton. • **87**. D. Como, 'Secret Printing, the Crisis of 1640 and the Origins of Civil War Radicalism', *PP* 196 (2007), pp. 37–82 (at p. 69). • **88**. Don M. Wolfe, *Leveller Manifestos of the Puritan Revolution* (1967), pp. 154–95. • **89**. Brailsford, *Levellers*, pp. 49–57, 233. • **90**. Sharp, *English Levellers*, pp. 20–3. • **91**. Aylmer, *Levellers in the English Revolution*, pp. 82–7. • **92**. M. A. Gibb, *John Lilburne the Leveller: A Christian Democrat* (1947), pp. 215–16. • **93**. S. Barber, *A Revolutionary Rogue: Henry Marten and the English Republic* (Stroud, 2000), p. 30. • **94**. Gregg, *Freeborn John*, pp. 167, 191, 193–5, 199. • **95**. M. A. Kishlansky, 'The Army and the Levellers: The Roads to Putney', *Historical Journal*, 22 (1979), pp. 795–824. • **96**. Brailsford, *Levellers*, p. 181. • **97**. Gregg, *Freeborn John*, pp. 170–1. • **98**. Barry Coward, *The Stuart Age, 1603–1714* (2003), pp. 188–95. • **99**. Ian Gentles, 'Thomas Fairfax, 3rd Lord Fairfax of Cameron', *ODNB* (2004), 18, pp. 933–41. • **100**. There has been an impassioned debate on the authorship of this manifesto. See John Adamson, 'The English Nobility and the Projected Settlement of 1647', *Historical Journal*, 30 (1987), pp. 567–702; Mark Kishlansky, 'Saye What?', *Historical Journal*, 33 (1990), pp. 919–37. • **101**. For details see Geoffrey Robertson, ed., *The Putney Debates: The Levellers* (2007), pp. 25–30. • **102**. A. S. P. Woodhouse, *Introduction to Puritanism and Liberty: The Army Debates 1647–49* (1992), p. 24; Brailsford, *Levellers*, pp. 241–4, 252. • **103**. D. Farr, *Henry Ireton and the English Revolution* (Woodbridge, 2006), pp. 86–9. • **104**. Brailsford, *Levellers*, p. 247. • **105**. Wolfe, *Leveller Manifestos*, pp. 196–222; Haller and Davies, eds, *Leveller Tracts*, pp. 64–87. • **106**. Brailsford, *Levellers*, pp. 142, 183–4. For Sexby's authorship of *The Case of the Army Truly Stated*, see Mendle, ed., *Putney Debates*, pp. 103–24. • **107**. Wolfe, *Leveller Manifestos*, pp. 223–34; Morton, *Freedom in Arms*, pp. 134–49. • **108**. In yet another example of Protestant schism, the Arminians were a seventeenth-century break-away movement from Calvinism. Although every aspect of their doctrine is hotly disputed, they had a distaste for the hard-line version of original sin and were to the Calvinists roughly what Pelagius had been to St Augustine. They were a major influence on John Wesley and Methodism. See Roger Olson, *Arminian Theology: Myth and Realities* (2006). • **109**. Brailsford, *Levellers*, pp. 203, 216. • **110**. M. Ashley, *John Wildman: Plotter and Postmaster; A Study of the English Republican Movement in the Seventeenth Century* (1947). • **111**. Disraeli, *Sybil*, ed. T. Braun (1980), p. 40. • **112**. Brailsford, *Levellers*, pp. 270–1. • **113**. See W. R. D. Jones, *Thomas Rainborowe (c.1610–1648): Civil War Seaman, Siegemaster and Radical* (Woodbridge, 2005). • **114**. Brailsford describes Ireton as 'by far the ablest debater at Putney' (*Levellers*, p. 269) and, contrasting him with Rainsborough, adds: 'Henry Ireton was, at all events on the theoretical plane, by far the abler and honester man of the two, but he had none of the tact and none of the intuitive understanding of other men's feelings which a good leader must possess.' Ibid., p. 229. Such a view can hardly be sustained by a close reading of the Putney Debates, which show Cromwell and Ireton curtailing the meeting after they had been worsted in argument. But there seems a general inclination to underrate Rainsborough. Another scholar opines that in the Putney Debates Wildman was intellectually more formidable than Rainsborough or Sexby but a less powerful speaker. Aylmer, *Levellers in the English Revolution*, pp. 100–1. • **115**. Sharp, *English Levellers*, p. 120. • **116**. Robertson, *Putney Debates*, pp. 61–8. • **117**. Ian Gentles, 'Henry Ireton', *ODNB* (2004), 29, pp. 344–52. See also Alex Craven, *Henry Ireton and the English Revolution* (2000). • **118**. Much of the debate at Putney was a rehash of arguments already made in *The Agreement* (Aylmer, *Levellers in the English Revolution*, pp. 88–96). • **119**. 'For God's sake! Why do you have to bring God into everything!' (Evelyn Waugh, *Brideshead Revisited*, Book 1, Ch. 5). • **120**. Brailsford, *Levellers*, p. 217. • **121**. Ibid., p. 202. • **122**. For Robert (or William?) Everard see Nigel Smith, *Literature and Revolution in England, 1640–1660* (1994), p. 336. As to the identity of Everard and the conflation of the Leveller figure of that name and a later Digger see Hill, *World Turned Upside Down*, pp. 284–6; Hill, *Experience of Defeat*, pp. 18, 207; Hill, *Puritanism and Revolution*, p. 305. • **123**. Brailsford, *Levellers*, p. 267. • **124**. Aylmer, *Levellers in the English Revolution*, pp. 112, 115. • **125**. Alexander Pope, *Essay on Man*, iii, II, 303–4. • **126**. Brailsford, *Levellers*, pp. 286–7, 365; R. C. Richardson and G. M. Ridden, eds, *Freedom and the English Revolution: Essays in History and Literature* (1986), pp. 25–44 (including, on p. 26, a direct accusation of hypocrisy). • **127**. Philip Baker, 'A Despicable Contemptible Generation of Men: Cromwell and the Levellers', in Patrick Little, ed., *Oliver Cromwell: New Perspectives* (2009), pp. 90–115 (at p. 110). • **128**. Robertson, *Putney Debates*, p. 69. • **129**. For a full discussion of this eighteenth-century refinement see H. T. Dickinson, *Liberty and Property* (1977). • **130**. Robertson, *Putney Debates*, p. 70. • **131**. C. B. MacPherson, *The Theory of Possessive Individualism* (1962), pp. 107–59. • **132**. Aylmer, *Levellers in the English Revolution*, p. 102. • **133**. This is the first full-blooded appearance in Leveller thought of the 'Norman yoke' thesis that would figure so largely in Digger ideology. Brailsford, *Levellers*, pp. 129–30. • **134**. Many have considered that 'Why should I obey the government?' is the key issue in all pre-twentieth-century political theory and that all the 'great books' of Hobbes, Locke, Rousseau, et al., are simply different answers to the same question. A. J. Ayer, *Metaphysics and Commonsense* (1969), pp. 240–60. • **135**. This is a reference to the rumoured conscription for a campaign in Ireland. • **136**. The entire Rainsborough–Ireton clash can be followed in detail in Sharp, *English Levellers*, pp. 103–16. • **137**. Ibid. • **138**. Robertson, *Putney Debates*, p. 75. • **139**. Ibid., p. 76. • **140**. Brailsford, *Levellers*, pp. 278–9. • **141**. J. and J. A. Venn, *Alumni Cantabrigienses*, 10 vols (Cambridge, 1958), I, iii, p. 35, cf. Brailsford, *Levellers*,

p. 217. • **142**. Robertson, *Putney Debates*, p. 93. • **143**. Woodhouse, *Puritanism*, p. 452. • **144**. Austin Woolrych, *Soldiers and Statesmen: The General Council of the Army and Its Debates* (Oxford, 1987), p. 250. • **145**. A. J. Hopper, *'Black Tom': Sir Thomas Fairfax and the English Revolution* (Manchester, 2007). • **146**. David Farr, *Henry Ireton* (Woodbridge, 2006), p. 114. • **147**. Woolrych, *Soldiers*, p. 255. • **148**. Brailsford, *Levellers*, p. 290. • **149**. Mendle, ed., *Putney Debates*, pp. 73–5, 138–9. • **150**. John Ashburnham, *A Narrative of John Ashburnham on His Attendance on King Charles I from Oxford to the Scottish Army and from Hampton Court to the Isle of Wight*, 2 vols (1830), ii, pp. 117–36; Anton Bantock, *Ashton Court* (2004). • **151**. For a full account of these events see Alan Thompson, *The Ware Mutiny: Order Restored or Revolution Defeated?* (1996). • **152**. Brailsford, *Levellers*, p. 297. • **153**. Ibid., p. 300. • **154**. Hopper, *'Black Tom'*, p. 99.

7 *England's Revolution Manqué*

1. Keith Lindley, *The English Civil War and Revolution* (1998), p. 167. • **2**. Stephen Bull and Mike Sead, *Bloody Preston: The Battle of Preston, 1648* (Lancaster, 1998), pp. 100–1. • **3**. W. Haller and G. Davies, *The Leveller Tracts, 1647–53* (NY, 1944), pp. 97–101. • **4**. A. Woolrych, *Britain in Revolution, 1625–60* (Oxford, 2002), p. 397. • **5**. Brailsford, *Levellers*, p. 241. • **6**. Norah Carlin, 'The Leveller Organisation in London', *Historical Journal*, 27 (1984), pp. 955–60; Brailsford, *Levellers*, p. 328. • **7**. Brailsford, *Levellers*, p. 326, Gregg, *Freeborn John*, pp. 244–5. • **8**. Haller and Davies, eds, *Leveller Tracts*, pp. 147–55; Wolfe, *Leveller Manifestos*, pp. 279–90; Morton, *Freedom in Arms*, pp. 181–94; Aylmer, *Levellers in the English Revolution*, pp. 131–8. • **9**. Woolrych, *Britain in Revolution*, p. 424. • **10**. Gregg, *Freeborn John*, pp. 203–5, 259; Brailsford, *Levellers*, pp. 366–7, 457–8. • **11**. Jones, *Rainsborowe*, p. 123. • **12**. Ibid. • **13**. The sequence of events can be followed in detail in David Underdown, *Pride's Purge: Politics in the Puritan Revolution* (Oxford, 1971). • **14**. Woolrych, *Britain in Revolution*, p. 428. • **15**. Wolfe, *Leveller Manifestos*, pp. 291–310; Aylmer, *Levellers in the English Revolution*, pp. 139–41. • **16**. Gardiner, ed., *Constitutional Documents*. • **17**. There is a huge literature on the trial and execution of Charles I. See Clive Holmes, *Why Was Charles I Executed?* (2006); Graham Edwards, *The Last Days of Charles I* (Stroud, 1999); C. V. Wedgwood, *The Trial of Charles I* (1964). Amazingly, new light has been shed on all of this by Sean Kelsey, 'The Trial of Charles I', *EHR*, 118 (2003), pp. 583–616. For the regicides see Geoffrey Robertson, *The Tyrannicide Brief: The Men who Sent Charles I to the Scaffold* (2005); Jason Peachey, ed., *The Regicides and the Execution of Charles I* (Basingstoke, 2001). • **18**. James Alsop, 'A High Road to Radicalism? Gerrard Winstanley's Youth', *Seventeenth Century*, 9 (1994), pp. 11–24; James Alsop, 'Gerrard Winstanley: What Do We Know of His Life?' in Andrew Bradstock, ed., *Winstanley and the Diggers, 1649–1999*

(2000), pp. 19–36. • **19**. Mark Kishlansky, *A Monarchy Transformed: Britain, 1603–1714* (1996), p. 196. • **20**. Olivier Lustand, *Winstanley: socialisme et christianisme sous Cromwell* (Paris, 1976), pp. 39–42. • **21**. Gerrard Winstanley, *The Law of Freedom* (Cambridge, 1983), pp. 128, 216, 232. • **22**. Richardson and Ridden, *Freedom and the English Revolution*, pp. 157–8; Brailsford, *Levellers*, pp. 666–9. • **23**. Thomas N. Corns, Anne Hughes and David Loewenstein, eds, *The Complete Works of Gerrard Winstanley*, 2 vols (Oxford, 2009) – hereinafter Winstanley, *CW* – i, pp. 51–65. • **24**. Andrew Bradstock, *Faith in the Revolution: The Political Theologies of Munster and Winstanley* (1976). For the influential passage in the Acts of the Apostles, see Acts 2: 42–7. • **25**. 'The law in its majestic equality forbids the rich and poor alike to sleep under bridges, to beg in the strets, and to steal bread.' Anatole France, *Le Lys rouge*. • **26**. Winstanley, *CW*, ii, pp. 291–2. • **27**. Ibid., p. 13. • **28**. Ibid., pp. 10, 224, 302. • **29**. Wallace Stevens, *Esthétique du mal* (poem): 'Revolution is the affair of logical lunatics.' • **30**. Quoted in John Gurney, *Brave Community: The Digger Movement in the Revolution* (Manchester, 2007), p. 180; cf. also Winstanley, *CW*, i, p. 523. • **31**. Steve Hindle, 'Dearth and the English Revolution: The Harvest Crisis of 1647–50,' *Economic History Review*, 61 (2008), pp. 1–21 (at pp. 4–5). • **32**. Christopher Hill, 'Winstanley and Freedom', in Richardson and Ridden, eds, *Freedom and the English Revolution*, pp. 151–68; Keith Thomas, 'Another Digger Broadside', *PP* 42 (1969), pp. 57–68 (at p. 58). • **33**. J. Thirk, ed., *The Agrarian History of England and Wales* (Cambridge 1967), iv, pp. 95–7, 107–8, 224–5, 409–12, 445–6. • **34**. Winstanley, *CW*, i, p. 67. • **35**. Winstanley, *CW*, i, pp. 422–600 (esp. pp. 508–17). • **36**. George Juretic, 'Digger No Millenarian: The Revolutionising of Gerrard Winstanley', *Journal of the History of Ideas*, 36 (1975), pp. 263–80; C. Robert Cole and Michael Moody, eds, *The Dissenting Tradition* (Athens, Ohio, 1975), pp. 191–225; Christopher Hill, 'The Religion of Gerrard Winstanley', *PP* Supplement 5 (1978), pp. 1–56; see also *PP* 89 (1980), pp. 147–51. • **37**. For the offending passages see Winstanley, *CW*, ii, pp. 312–13, 326–9. For the proto-feminism see *CW*, ii, pp. 188, 378. • **38**. Frank McLynn, *C. G. Jung: A Biography* (1996), pp. 409–12. • **39**. J. C. Davis, *Utopia and the Ideal Society* (Cambridge, 1983), pp. 183–4; Christopher Hill, *Liberty Against the Law: Some Seventeenth-Century Controversies* (1996), pp. 285–6, 289, 295. • **40**. Winstanley, *CW*, ii, p. 130. • **41**. For the Norman yoke see Winstanley, *CW*, ii, pp. 65–78; cf. also Hill, 'The Norman Yoke', in Hill, *Puritanism and Revolution*, pp. 58–125. Hill points out that the signatories of the Digger manifestos all bore Saxon names. Ibid., p. 69. • **42**. Gurney, *Brave Community*, p. 13. • **43**. Winstanley, *CW*, ii, pp. 57–64. • **44**. To the City of London and the Army (*CW*, ii, pp. 79–106); to the Commons (ibid., ii, pp. 65–78); to Fairfax (ibid., ii, pp. 32–58). • **45**. Charles Firth, ed., *The Clarke Papers*, 4 vols (1901), ii, pp. 210–11. For Everard see Petegorsky, *Left-Wing Democracy*, p. 167; Ariel

Hessayon, 'William Everard', *ODNB* (2004), 17, pp. 789–90. • **46**. Brailsford, *Levellers*, pp. 657–8. • **47**. Thomas, 'Another Digger Broadside', pp. 58–9. • **48**. Hill, *World Turned Upside Down*, pp. 91–9; Brian Manning, *The Far Left in the English Revolution, 1640–1660* (1999), pp. 33, 36, 52, 78. • **49**. Winstanley, *CW*, ii, pp. 108–9, 113–19, 283, 295. • **50**. Joan Thirsk, 'Agrarian Problems and the English Revolution', in R. C. Richardson, ed., *Town and Countryside in the English Revolution* (Manchester, 1992), pp. 169–97. • **51**. Gurney, *Brave Community*, p. 123. • **52**. Winstanley, *CW*, ii, pp. 235–42. • **53**. Brailsford, *Levellers*, p. 525. • **54**. For a detailed narrative see Brian Manning, *1649: The Crisis of the English Revolution* (1992). • **55**. François Guizot, *History of Oliver Cromwell and the English Commonwealth: From the Execution of Charles I to the Death of Cromwell* (1854), pp. 61–4. • **56**. Haller and Davies, *Leveller Tracts*, pp. 156–70; Aylmer, *Levellers in the English Revolution*, pp. 142–8; Gregg, *Freeborn John*, pp. 266–9; Brailsford, *Levellers*, p. 472. • **57**. Aylmer, *Levellers in the English Revolution*, p. 149. • **58**. Brailsford, *Levellers*, p. 481. • **59**. Ibid., p. 317. • **60**. Ian Gentles, 'Katherine Chidley', *ODNB* (2004), 11, pp. 410–12 and, also by Gentles and at greater length, 'London Levellers and the English Revolution: The Chidleys and Their Circle', *Journal of Ecclesiastical History*, 29 (1978), pp. 281–309; cf. also George Ballard, *Memoirs of British Ladies* (1752). • **61**. Aylmer, *Levellers in the English Revolution*, pp. 150–8, Morton, *Freedom in Arms*, pp. 245–9; Haller and Davies, eds, *Leveller Tracts*, pp. 276–84; McMichael and Taft, eds, *Writings of William Walwyn*, pp. 334–43. • **62**. McMichael and Taft, eds, *Writings of William Walwyn*, pp. 383–432; Haller and Davies, eds, *Leveller Tracts*, pp. 350–98. • **63**. Aylmer, *Levellers in the English Revolution*, pp. 159–68; McMichael and Taft, eds, *Writings of William Walwyn*, pp. 344–7; Haller and Davies, eds, *Leveller Tracts*, pp. 31–328; Morton, *Freedom in Arms*, pp. 397–410. • **64**. Brailsford, *Levellers*, p. 515. For a lengthier examination of this theme see Brian Manning, *Aristocrats, Plebeians and Revolution in England, 1640–1660* (1996). • **65**. Brailsford, *Levellers*. • **66**. Keith Lindley, *The English Civil War and Revolution: A Sourcebook* (1998), pp. 173–4. • **67**. Precisely who were Cromwell's political commissars and who were the army officers who lost confidence in him in 1645–9 is a ticklish question. Exhaustive research would be needed in, e.g., A. Woolrych, *Soldiers, Writers and Statesmen in the English Revolution* (Cambridge, 1998), and C. H. Firth and G. Davies, *The Regimental History of Cromwell's Army*, 2 vols (1940). It is quite clear that some of the rebels were minor gentry, see G. Aylmer, 'Gentlemen Levellers', *PP* 49 (1970), pp. 120–5. • **68**. Manning, *1649*, pp. 173–7. • **69**. Firth, ed., *Clarke Papers*, i, p. 419. • **70**. Paul H. Hardacre, 'Eyre, William fl. 1634–1675', *ODNB* (2004), 18, p. 860. See also William Eyre, *The Serious Representations of William Eyre* (1649). • **71**. Michael T. Vann, 'Quakerism and the Social Structure in the Interregnum', *PP* 43 (1969), pp. 71–91; Brailsford, *Levellers*, pp. 632, 637–40. • **72**. Gregg, *Freeborn John*, pp. 270–1,

294–301; Brailsford, *Levellers*, pp. 582–615. • **73**. John Morill, *Oliver Cromwell and the English Revolution* (1990), p. 155; S. R. Gardiner, *Oliver Cromwell* (1901), p. 155. For the loathing of the Irish see Padraig Lenihan, *Confederate Catholics at War* (Cork, 2000), p. 115. • **74**. See Malcolm Atkin, *Cromwell's Crowning Mercy: The Battle of Worcester, 1651* (Stroud, 1998). • **75**. Thomas Salmon, *Chronological Historian* (1723), p. 106; W. C. Gaunt, ed., *Writings and Speeches of Oliver Cromwell* (1947), pp. 642–3. • **76**. Peter Gaunt, *Oliver Cromwell* (1996), pp. 155–6. • **77**. McMichael and Taft, eds, *Writings of William Walwyn*, pp. 433–52. • **78**. Brailsford, *Levellers*, p. 616. • **79**. Richard T. Vann, 'The Later Life of Gerrard Winstanley', *Journal of the History of Ideas*, 26 (1965), pp. 133–6. • **80**. M. Ashley, *John Wildman: Plotter and Postmaster: A study of the English Republican Movement in the Seventeenth Century* (1947), p. 90. • **81**. Alan Marshall, 'Edward Sexby', *ODNB* (2004), 49, pp. 847–9. See also Alan Marshall, 'Killing No Murder', *History Today* (February 2003). • **82**. Gregg, *Freeborn John*, pp. 312–31; Brailsford, *Levellers*, pp. 611–19. • **83**. Gregg, *Freeborn John*, p. 332. • **84**. Ibid., pp. 336–46. • **85**. 'If this (seizure of power) never happened or came near to happening, in spite of the two attempts at Ware and Burford, part of the explanation was that Lilburne in his vanity must needs give Cromwell warning of what he meant to do.' Brailsford, *Levellers*, p. 240. • **86**. Davis, 'Levellers and Democracy', • **87**. Kolakowski, *Main Currents of Marxism*, pp. 179–84. • **88**. 'The England of the *Agreement*, if ever it had come into existence, would never have grown rich by the slave trade, nor could it have conquered India.' Brailsford, *Levellers*, p. 491. • **89**. Ibid., pp. 504–5. • **90**. Blair Worden, *The Rump Parliament* (1973), pp. 274–5. • **91**. Philip Baker, '"A Despicable Contemptible Generation of Men": Cromwell and the Levellers', in Patrick Little, ed. *Oliver Cromwell: New Perspectives* (2009), pp. 90–115. • **92**. This idea is developed at some length by the revisionist Marxist Edward Bernstein in *Cromwell and Communism* (1963). For Bernstein in general see Kolakowski, *Main Currents of Marxism*, pp. 433–46.

8 *The Jacobite Rising of 1745*

1. For examples of the Jacobite diaspora see Rebecca Wills, *The Jacobites in Russia* (2002); Steve Murdoch, *Network North* (2006). • **2**. The complexity of the movement can be gauged by a reading of four entirely different approaches to the phenomenon: Paul Monod, *Jacobitism and the English People, 1688–1788* (Cambridge, 1989); Jonathan Clark, *English Society, 1688–1832* (1985); Alan MacInnes, *Clanship, Commerce and the House of Stuart, 1603–1788* (1996); Eamonn O'Ciardha, *An Unfortunate Attachment: Ireland and the Jacobite Cause, 1685–1766* (2002). • **3**. Again, it is instructive to contrast Daniel Szechi,

Jacobitism and Tory Politics, 1710–1714 (Edinburgh, 1984) with Paul S. Fritz, *The English Ministers and Jacobitism between the Rebellions of 1715 and 1745* (1975) and Doron Zimmermann, *The Jacobite Movement in Scotland and Exile, 1746–1759* (Basingstoke, 2003). • **4**. The moving court has been dealt with admirably in four volumes by Edward Corp, *A Court In Exile: The Stuarts in France, 1689–1718* (Cambridge, 2004); *The Jacobites at Urbino: An Exiled Court in Transition* (2008); *The Stuart Court in Rome: The Legacy of Exile* (Aldershot, 2003) and with Eveline Cruickshanks, eds, *The Stuart Court in Exile and the Jacobites* (1995). • **5**. See John S. Gibson, *Playing the Scottish Card: The Franco-Jacobite Invasion of 1708* (Edinburgh, 1988). • **6**. Edward Gregg, 'The Jacobite Career of John, Earl of Mar', in Eveline Cruickshanks, ed., *Ideology and Conspiracy: Aspects of Jacobitism, 1689–1759* (1982), pp. 179–200. • **7**. For an excellent account of the disastrous '15 see Daniel Szechi, *1715: The Great Jacobite Rebellion* (Yale, 2006). • **8**. W. H. Dickson, *The Jacobite Attempt of 1719* (Edinburgh, 1896). • **9**. See Peggy Miller, *A Wife for the Pretender* (1965). • **10**. For a complete biography of the prince see Frank McLynn, *Charles Edward Stuart: A Tragedy in Many Acts* (1988). • **11**. Erik Eriksson, *Young Man Luther* (NY, 1958) pp. 95–121. • **12**. McLynn, *Charles Edward*, pp. 348–9, 428–9, 453–4. • **13**. The entire plan is dealt with in comprehensive detail in Jean Colin, *Louis XV et les Jacobites: Le projet de débarquement en Angleterre en 1743–44* (Paris, 1901). • **14**. McLynn, *Charles Edward*, pp. 80–3. • **15**. W. S. Lewis, ed., *The Yale Edition of Horace Walpole's Correspondence*, 48 vols (1983), 18, pp. 373–9. • **16**. McLynn, *Charles Edward*, pp. 88–91. • **17**. Eveline Cruickshanks, *Political Untouchables: The Tories and the '45* (1979), pp. 53–8. • **18**. McLynn, *Charles Edward*, pp. 92–3. • **19**. Ibid., pp. 94–5. • **20**. Ibid., pp. 96–115. • **21**. The great proponents of 'subjective conditions' in the twentieth century were Mao Tse-tung and Che Guevara. See Mao, *On Guerrilla Warfare*, ed. Samuel B. Griffith (Ill., 2000); Ernesto 'Che' Guevara, *Guerrilla Warfare* (2002). See also J. M. Maravell, 'Subjective Conditions and Revolutionary Conflict: Some Remarks', *British Journal of Sociology*, 27 (1976), pp. 21–34 ; José Moreno, 'Che Guevara on Guerrilla Warfare: Doctrine, Practice and Evaluation', *Comparative Studies in Society and History*, 12 (1970), pp. 114–33. • **22**. For Lenin's thinking on this subject see V. I. Lenin, *Collected Works* (1962), 10, pp. 333–4. Trotsky agreed with him on this issue. See R. Knei-Par, *The Social and Political Thought of Leon Trotsky* (1978), p. 140. For a lucid summary of this aspect of Leninism vis-à-vis the theory of Marx and Engels see Steve Paxton, 'The Communist Manifesto, Marx's Theory of History and the Russian Revolution', in Mark Cowling, ed., *The Communist Manifesto: New Interpretations* (1998), pp. 86–96; cf. also A. J. P. Taylor's introduction to John Reed, *Ten Days that Shook the World* (1977), p. xviii. • **23**. These men are examined in detail in a number of books: Charles de la Trémoille, *Une*

Famille royaliste, irlandaise et française (Paris, 1901); Gaston Martin, *Nantes au dix-huitième siècle* (Toulouse, 1928); Henri Malo, *Les Derniers Corsairs, 1715–1815* (Paris, 1925). • **24**. For character portraits see McLynn, *Charles Edward*, pp. 119–20. • **25**. A. and H. Tayler, *1745 and After* (1938), pp. 46–7. • **26**. The sea battle is examined in detail in Henry Paton, ed., *The Lyon in Mourning*, 3 vols (Edinburgh, 1895) – hereinafter *LM* – i, pp. 285–8. • **27**. *LM*, i, p. 205. • **28**. McLynn, *Charles Edward*, pp. 130–1. • **29**. Ibid., pp. 131–4. • **30**. For full details of this intricate operation see Christopher Duffy, *The Forty-Five* (2003), pp. 175–84. • **31**. For the highly complex politics of the Atholl sept and the divisions between the two eldest brothers (which later inspired R. L. Stevenson's *The Master of Ballantrae*) see 7th Duke of Atholl, *Chronicles of the Families of Atholl and Tullibardine*, 5 vols (1908). For Cluny MacPherson see Tayler, *1745 and After*, pp. 66–7, and Bruce Lenman, *The Jacobite Clans of the Great Glen, 1650–1784* (1984), pp. 155–6. • **32**. Elcho's account of his (distinguished) role in the '45 is in E. Charteris, ed., *A Short Account of the Affairs of Scotland in 1744, 1745 and 1746* (1907) – hereinafter Elcho. • **33**. Murray's own account of the '45 is in R. Chambers, ed., *Jacobite Memoirs of the Rising of 1745* (1834), which contains Murray's 'Marches of the Highland Army' – hereinafter Murray, 'Marches'. Lord George continues to be a controversial figure. A highly favourable account is provided in Katherine Tomasson, *The Jacobite General* (Edinburgh, 1958). Far less favourable and even at times highly critical is Duffy, *The Forty-Five*, pp. 102–3. • **34**. The issue of Scots–Irish rivalry and the clashes between the prince and Lord George Murrray form a good deal of the substance of two important primary sources for the '45: James Maxwell of Kirkconnell, *Narrative of Charles, Prince of Wales's Expedition to Scotland in the Year 1745* (Edinburgh, 1841) – hereinafter Maxwell – and Chevalier de Johnstone, *A Memoir of the Forty-Five* (1820) – hereinafter Johnstone. • **35**. Duffy, *Forty-Five*, pp. 102–5. • **36**. Andrew McKillop, 'Jacobitism', in Michael Lynch, ed., *The Oxford Companion to Scottish History* (Oxford, 2001), pp. 349–52. • **37**. McLynn, 'Sea Power and the Jacobite Rising of 1745', *Mariners' Mirror*, 67 (1981), pp. 163–72. • **38**. Duffy, *Forty-Five*, pp. 193–8. • **39**. McLynn, *Charles Edward*, pp. 145–9. • **40**. K. Tomasson and F. Buist, *Battles of the '45* (1962), pp. 42–61; Murray, 'Marches', p. 36; John Murray of Broughton, *Memorials*, ed. R. F. Bell (Edinburgh, 1898), pp. 198–205. • **41**. For a full analysis of English reactions to Prestonpans see W. A. Speck, *The Butcher: The Duke of Cumberland and the Suppression of the Forty-Five* (Oxford, 1981), pp. 55–87. • **42**. McLynn, *Charles Edward*, pp. 160–4. • **43**. The entire subject is discussed in detail in Frank McLynn, *France and the Jacobite Rising of 1745* (Edinburgh, 1981). • **44**. Michel Antoine, *Louis XV* (Paris, 1989), passim. • **45**. For Steuart see Andrew S. Skinner, 'Steuart, Sir James of Coltness and Westshield, 3rd baronet (1713–70)', *ODNB* (2004), 52, pp. 550–5.

• **46**. McLynn, *France*, pp. 85–116. • **47**. See A. and H. Tayler, *Jacobites of Aberdeenshire and Banffshire in the '45* (Aberdeen, 1928); A. and H. Tayler, *Jacobite Letters to Lord Pitsligo, 1745–46* (Aberdeen, 1930); Sir James Fergusson, *Lowland Lairds* (1949). • **48**. For the background to these men see Lenman, *Jacobite Clans*. • **49**. Frank McLynn, 'Issues and Motives in the Jacobite Rising of 1745', *Eighteenth Century: Theory and Interpretation*, 23 (1982), pp. 97–133. • **50**. Jeffrey Stephen, 'Scottish Nationalism and Stuart Unionism: The Edinburgh Council, 1745', *Journal of British Studies*, 49 (2010), pp. 47–72. • **51**. Tomasson, *Jacobite General*, p. 66; Henrietta Tayler, *Jacobite Epilogue* (1941), pp. 252–4. • **52**. For the prince's arguments see Frank McLynn, *The Jacobite Army in England, 1745* (1983) pp. 8–10. • **53**. Ibid. • **54**. For this important subject see Rupert C. Jarvis, *Collected Papers on the Jacobite Risings*, 2 vols (Manchester, 1972), i, pp. 175–97. • **55**. For Lord George's arguments see Elcho, pp. 303–5; McLynn, *Jacobite Army*, pp. 11–12. • **56**. Jarvis, *Collected Papers*, i, pp. 175–97. • **57**. McLynn, *France*, p. 109. • **58**. Duffy, *Forty-Five*, pp. 56–72. • **59**. *Chronicles of Atholl*, iii, pp. 81–2. • **60**. The siege of Carlisle is treated in great detail in G. C. Mounsey, *Carlisle in 1745* (1846). • **61**. McLynn, *Jacobite Army*, pp. 60–75. • **62**. 'John Daniel's Account', in W. B. Blaikie, *Origins of the Forty-Five* (Edinburgh, 1916), p. 168. • **63**. McLynn, *Jacobite Army*, pp. 80–1. • **64**. Ibid., pp. 98–9. • **65**. Murray, 'Marches', in Chambers, ed., *Jacobite Memoirs*, pp. 52–3; Speck, *Butcher*, pp. 87–8. • **66**. McLynn, *Jacobite Army*, pp. 113–19. • **67**. There are many detailed accounts of the council at Derby: L. Eardley-Simpson, *Derby and the Forty-Five* (1933); McLynn, *Jacobite Army*, pp. 124–32; Duffy, *Forty-Five*, pp. 300–13. • **68**. Jarvis, *Jacobite Risings*, ii, pp. 100–1. • **69**. Ibid. • **70**. Tomasson, *Jacobite General*, p. 114. • **71**. *The Life and Adventures of Captain Dudley Bradstreet* (1755), pp. 126–7. • **72**. Sir John Clapham, *The Bank of England* (Cambridge 1945), i, pp. 233–4; W. Marston Acres, *The Bank of England from Within*, 2 vols (Oxford, 1931), i, p. 181. • **73**. Duc de Choiseul, *Mémoires, 1719–1785* (Paris, 1904), p. 55. • **74**. Murray, 'Marches', p. 57. • **75**. *The Allardyce Papers*, 2 vols (Aberdeen, 1896), i, pp. 287–93. • **76**. Maxwell, pp. 78–9. • **77**. McLynn, *Jacobite Army*, p. 148. • **78**. Johnstone, p. 84. • **79**. Duffy, *Forty-Five*, pp. 330–8. • **80**. Elcho, pp. 348–9. • **81**. McLynn, *Jacobite Army*, pp. 187–9; Speck, *Butcher*, p. 99. • **82**. 'O'Sullivan's Account', in A. and H. Tayler, *1745 and After*, p. 110; Johnstone, pp. 95–7; Maxwell, p. 87; Speck, *Butcher*, pp. 99–102. • **83**. Elcho, p. 379; Johnstone, p. 76; Maxwell, p. 90. • **84**. *LM*, ii, p. 344; iii, p. 55; McLynn, *France*, p. 133. • **85**. Ibid. • **86**. Elcho, pp. 361–2. • **87**. McLynn, *Charles Edward*, pp. 203–4, 232–3. • **88**. W. B. Blaikie, *Itinerary of Prince Charles Edward from His Landing in Scotland, July 1745, to His Departure in September 1746* (Edinburgh, 1897), pp. 73–4. • **89**. Tomasson and Buist, *Battles of the '45*, pp. 105–26. • **90**. Falkirk is particularly rich in eyewitness accounts. See O'Sullivan's account in Tayler, *1745 and After*, pp. 118–19; Elcho, pp. 370–84; Maxwell, pp. 99–111; Johnstone; Murray, 'Marches', pp. 79–96; cf. also Tomasson, *Jacobite General*, pp. 142–56. • **91**. An exhaustive account is provided by Geoff B. Bailey, *Falkirk or Paradise: The Battle of Falkirk Muir* (Edinburgh, 1996); cf. also Stuart Reid, *Battles of the Scottish Lowlands* (Barnsley, 2004). • **92**. McLynn, *Charles Edward*, p. 215. • **93**. Ibid., p. 217. • **94**. 'John Daniel's Account', in Blaikie, *Origins*, p. 203. • **95**. These campaigns are explored in great detail in Duffy, *Forty-Five*, pp. 442–82. • **96**. *LM*, i, p. 356; ii, p. 270; Elcho, p. 398; Johnstone, p. 70; Maxwell, p. 121; 'O'Sullivan's Account', in Tayler, *1745 and After*, p. 114. • **97**. 'O'Sullivan's Account', pp. 255–6; Maxwell, p. 135; *LM*, i, p. 350; ii, pp. 271–5. • **98**. Murray, 'Marches', p. 118; *LM*, i, p. 359; ii, p. 273. • **99**. Blaikie, *Origins*, p. 415; *LM*, ii, p. 275. • **100**. 'O'Sullivan's Account', pp. 155–7; *LM*, i, pp. 258–64; ii, pp. 275–6; Tomasson, *Jacobite General*, pp. 206–11. • **101**. There are many accounts of Culloden extant but the two best are John Prebble, *Culloden* (1961), a gripping and impressionistic account of the battle, and Jeremy Black's massively researched *Culloden and the '45* (1990). See also Stuart Reid, *Culloden Moor, 1746: the Death of the Jacobite Cause* (2002). • **102**. McLynn, *Charles Edward*, pp. 259–60. • **103**. Prebble, *Culloden*, pp. 88–91. • **104**. Ibid., pp. 92–106; Elcho, pp. 432–3. • **105**. Duffy, *Forty-Five*, pp. 521–4. • **106**. Johnstone, p. 148. • **107**. The encyclopaedist and doyen of the Enlightenment Denis Diderot regarded this refusal to sell out the prince as one of the most signal proofs of his belief in the innate goodness of Man – Diderot, *Correspondance*, ed. Georges Roth (Paris, 1957), iii, p. 228. • **108**. McLynn, *Charles Edward*, pp. 308–557. • **109**. Annette M. Smith, *Jacobite Estates of the Forty-Five* (Edinburgh, 1982). • **110**. A. J. Youngson, *The Prince and the Pretender* (1985), p. 22. • **111**. Duffy, *Forty-Five*, p. 313.

9 *Evolutionary Jacobitism*

1. J. C. D. Clark, 'British America: What if There Had Been no American Revolution?' in Niall Ferguson, ed., *Virtual History* (1997), pp. 125–74 (at p. 130). See also Paul Monod, 'Whatever Happened to Divine Right? Jacobite Political Argument, 1689–1753', in Gordon J. Schochet and N. T. Phillipson, eds, *Politics, Politeness and Patriotism* (Washington, 1993), pp. 209–28. • **2**. This vast subject is best approached initially via two books by Bruce Lenman, *The Jacobite Risings in Britain* (1980) and *The Jacobite Clans of the Great Glen* (1984). • **3**. For a brief analysis see McLynn, *Charles Edward*, pp. 176–81 and, for more extended treatment, Murray Pittock, *The Myth of the Jacobite Clans* (Edinburgh, 1996). • **4**. Nonetheless, much good work has been done along these lines: Nicholas Rogers, 'Popular Protest in Early Hanoverian London', *PP* 89 (1978), pp. 70–100; Douglas Hay, 'Staffordshire Jacobitism', *Staffordshire*

Studies, 14 (2002), pp. 53–88; Leo Gooch, *The Desperate Faction: The Jacobites of North-East England, 1688–1745* (Hull, 1995). • **5**. For this see Paul S. Fritz, *The English Ministers and Jacobitism Between the Rebellions of 1715 and 1745* (Toronto, 1975), passim, and Paul Langford, *The Excise Crisis* (1975). • **6**. For the classic statement of the Tory Party as crypto-Jacobite in this era see Eveline Cruickshanks, *Political Untouchables: The Tories and the Forty-Five* (1979). • **7**. It will be recalled that Disraeli viewed Charles I as a man who positioned himself as a protector between the common people and their exploiters among the Parliamentarians and thus became 'the holocaust of direct taxation'. *Sybil*, Book 4, Ch. 1. Yet those who maintain that Disraeli looked back to the Jacobites as his model for Tory democracy have to contend with the considerable difficulty that Disraeli's eighteenth-century hero was Bolingbroke. *Sybil*, Book 4, Ch. 14. Bolingbroke, after his disastrous flirtation with 'the Pretender' in 1715–16, was a dedicated anti-Jacobite, and it is usually set down to his credit that he freed the Tory Party from the shackles of Jacobitism, so that the party was able to re-emerge in 1761 under George III. A thorough examination of this point would of course involve a critical examination of Disraeli's famous distinction, drawn in *Sybil*, between Tories and Conservatives. • **8**. Langford, *Excise Crisis*, p. 153. • **9**. Romney Sedgwick, ed., *The History of Parliament: The House of Commons, 1715–54*, (1970), 2 vols, ii, p. 200; i, p. 483. • **10**. Royal Archives, Windsor Castle. The Stuart Papers – hereinafter RA Stuart – 216/111 D-E. • **11**. RA Stuart, 253/51. • **12**. Colin, *Louis XV et les Jacobites*, p. 23. • **13**. RA Stuart, 248/111. • **14**. Sedgwick, *History of Parliament*, i, p. 599; RA Stuart, 204/151. • **15**. RA Stuart, 204/144. • **16**. Carte's assertions were backed during the '45 not just by Jacobite agents in England but by some staunchly Whig observers like Lady Jane Nimmo. RA Stuart, 272/92; G. F. C. Hepburne Scott, ed., 'Marchmont Correspondence Relating to the '45', *Scottish History Society*, 3rd series 12, Miscellany (Edinburgh, 1933), p. 343. • **17**. Murray Pittock, *The Social Composition of the Jacobite Army in Scotland in the '45*, Royal Stuart Papers, 48 (1996). • **18**. For a detailed analysis see Bruce Gordon and Jean Gordon Arnot, *The Prisoners of the '45*, 3 vols (Edinburgh, 1929). • **19**. Adam Rounce, 'Wilkes, Churchill and Anti-Scottishness', *Eighteenth-Century Life*, 29 (2005), pp. 20–43. • **20**. Gooch, *Desperate Faction*. • **21**. Jean-Jacques Rousseau, *Confessions* (Paris, 1964 – Pléiade edition), p. 596. • **22**. Eardley-Simpson, *Derby and the Forty-Five*, p. 18. • **23**. W. R. Ward, *Georgian Oxford* (Oxford, 1958), p. 182. • **24**. Caroline Robbins, *The Eighteenth-Century Commonwealthman* (Harvard, 1959), p. 31. • **25**. For the (often confused) reaction of Jacobites to republicanism see RA Stuart, 142/141, 160/1, 205/73, 240/65. • **26**. For the pamphlet warfare see State Papers, Domestic, George II, 72 ff., 348–50, and 'The Sequel to the Arms and the Man: A New Historical Ballad' (1746); 'Considerations addressed to the Public'

(Edinburgh, 1745); 'The Chronicles of Charles the Young Man' (Edinburgh, 1745). • **27**. For this see the various essays in Douglas Hay, Peter Linebaugh, E. P. Thompson et al., eds, *Albion's Fatal Tree* (1975). • **28**. For highwaymen see Frank McLynn, *Crime and Punishment in Eighteenth Century England* (1989), pp. 56–82. • **29**. For Gay and his work see Vinton A. Dearing, ed., *Poetry and Prose of John Gay*, 2 vols (Oxford, 1974); cf. also W. E. Schultz, *Gay's Beggar's Opera* (1923). • **30**. RA Stuart, 158/69. • **31**. RA Stuart, 123/59. • **32**. William Beaumont, ed., *The Jacobite Trials at Manchester in 1694*, Chatham Society, 28 (1853), pp. 22, 81; Narcissus Nuttrell, *A Brief Historical Relation of State Affairs from September 1678 to April 1714*, 6 vols (Oxford, 1857), i, pp. 494–5, 505; ii, pp. 124, 135, 252; iii, pp. 26–7, 537. • **33**. *New Newgate Calendar* (1818) – hereinafter *NNC* – i, pp. 252–4. • **34**. *NNC*, iii, p. 236. • **35**. Andrew Michael Ramsay, *An Essay on Civil Government* (1732), p. 69; cf. also RA Stuart, 123/59. • **36**. John Bromley, 'Les Corsairs Jacobites dans la guerre de neuf ans', *Revue de la société dunkerquoise d'histoire et d'archéologie*, 31 (1997), pp. 123–42; David Bracken, 'Pirates and Poverty: Aspects of Irish Jacobite Experience in France, 1691–1720', in Thomas O'Connor, ed., *The Irish in Europe, 1580–1815* (Dublin, 2001), pp. 127–42; cf. C. R. Rennell, *Bandits at Sea: A Pirate Reader* (2001). • **37**. Joel H. Baer, 'The Complicated Plot of Piracy', *Eighteenth Century: Theory and Interpretation*, 23 (1982), pp. 3–26; John Biddulph, *The Pirates of Malabar* (1907); Anne Perotin, 'The Pirate and the Emperor: Power and Law on the Seas, 1450–1850', in Rennell, *Bandits at Sea*. • **38**. RA Stuart, 101/34, 111/2, 119/26, 122/31, 133/180, 193/141. Cf. also Louis Dermigny, *La Chine et l'Occident: le commerce à Canton au XVIIIe siècle, 1719–1833* (Paris, 1964), pp. 92–103. • **39**. Adam Smith, *An Inquiry into the Nature and Causes of the Wealth of Nations*, 2 vols, ed. R. H. Campbell and A. S. Skinner (Oxford, 1976), ii, pp. 553, 881–2, 898. • **40**. RA Stuart, 88/98, 91/79. • **41**. RA Stuart, 111/2. • **42**. Paul Monod, 'Dangerous Mechandise: Smuggling, Jacobitism and Commercial Culture in South-East England, 1690–1760', *Journal of British Studies*, 30 (1991), pp. 150–82. • **43**. Cruickshanks, *Political Untouchables*, pp. 62–3, 90, 96, 99, 102; Cal Winslow, 'Sussex Smugglers', in Hay et al., eds, *Albion's Fatal Tree*, pp. 119–66 (at p. 147). • **44**. Add. MSS 28, 231, ff. 19–31. • **45**. Robertson of Struan to Edgar, 4 September 1755, RA Stuart, 358/16. • **46**. *NNC*, iii, pp. 188–98; *The Complete Newgate Calendar*, ed. J. L. Rayner and G. T. Crook (1926), iii, pp. 155–8; *Gentleman's Magazine* (1747), p. 397; (1748), p. 475; (1749). p. 359; Anon, *A Full and Genuine History of the Unparalleled Murders . . . by Fourteen Notorious Smugglers* (1749). • **47**. The Duke of Richmond's involvement in this case requires a study to itself. Some preliminary pointers can be obtained from a reading of his papers for this period, especially his correspondence with the Duke of Newcastle. Add. MSS 32, 711–18. • **48**. See Pelham's remarks in Add. MSS 32, 709, ff. 273–4; 32, 711, f. 211. For further confirmation of Jacobitism as the hidden factor see Winslow, 'Sussex Smugglers', pp. 150–7, 166. • **49**. Lewis, *Walpole's Correspondence*, 35, p. 141. • **50**. RA Stuart, 301/5; Monod, 'Dangerous Merchandise'. • **51**. Respectively Pat Rogers, 'The Waltham Blacks and the Waltham Black Act', *Historical Journal*, 17 (1974), pp. 465–86; E. P. Thompson, *Whigs and Hunters* (1975); E. Cruickshanks and H. Erskine-Hill, 'The Waltham Black Act and Jacobitism', *Journal of British Studies*, 24 (1985), pp. 358–65. • **52**. Thompson, *Whigs and Hunters*, pp. 63–6, 68–75. • **53**. Ibid., pp. 163–4. • **54**. Ibid., pp. 90–3; RA Stuart, 67/16. • **55**. Paul Monod, *Jacobitism and the English People* (Cambridge, 1989), p. 118. • **56**. McLynn, *Crime and Punishment*, pp. 240–1. • **57**. Monod, *Jacobitism*, pp. 161–94; Nicholas Rogers, 'Riots and Popular Jacobitism', in Cruickshanks, ed., *Ideology and Conspiracy*, pp. 70–88. • **58**. Abel Boyer, *The Political State of Great Britain*, 40 vols (1740), 18, pp. 44–7. • **59**. Monod, *Jacobitism*, p. 225. • **60**. Ibid., p. 225. • **61**. Ibid., pp. 198–9. • **62**. Ibid., pp. 205–9. • **63**. State Papers, Domestic, George II, 135 f. 272; Add. MSS 32, 867, ff. 3–4. • **64**. Add. MSS 32, 874, ff. 222, 274–5; 32, 884, f. 283; Egerton MSS 3346, ff. 153–5, 159; J. R. Western, *The English Militia in the Eighteenth Century* (1965), pp. 290–302. • **65**. T. S. Ashton and J. Sykes, *The Coal Industry in the Eighteenth Century* (Manchester, 1929), p. 130. • **66**. E. W. Hughes, *North Country Life in the Eighteenth Century*, 2 vols (Oxford, 1952), i, pp. 251–2. • **67**. State Papers, Domestic, George II, 112, ff. 331–3. • **68**. Sedgwick, *History of Parliament*, i, p. 464. • **69**. State Papers, Domestic, George II, 83, ff. 46–7, 70–1, 145–57. • **70**. Ibid., 85, f. 38; Edward Charlton, 'Jacobite Relics, 1715 and 1745', *Archaeologia Aeliana*, NS, 6 (1865), pp. 29–34; Frank McLynn, 'Newcastle and the Jacobite Rising of 1745', *Journal of Local Studies*, 2 (1982), pp. 95–105. • **71**. For the rise of the textile industry see Alfred P. Wadsworth and Julia de Lacy Mann, *Cotton Trades and Industrial Lancashire, 1600–1780* (Manchester, 1965). For Manchester Jacobitism see Monod, *Jacobitism*, pp. 331–41. • **72**. C. D. A. Leighton, 'The Non-Jurors and Their History', *Journal of Religious History*, 29 (2005), pp. 241–57. • **73**. G. Rudé, *Hanoverian Society* (1971), pp. 149–51. • **74**. This conventional view is expounded in J. Doran, *London in the Jacobite Times* (1877), vol. 2; A. A. Mitchell, 'London and the Forty-Five', *History Today*, 15 (1965), pp. 719–26. A neutral position is taken up by Jarvis, *Jacobite Risings*, ii, pp. 212–34. The thesis of London as Jacobite in 1745 has been attacked by Nicholas Rogers, 'Popular Disaffection in London during the Forty-Five', *London Journal*, 1 (1975), pp. 1–26. • **75**. *The Life and Uncommon Adventures of Dudley Bradstreet* (1755), p. 124. • **76**. R. Sharpe, *London and the Kingdom*, 3 vols (1895), iii, pp. 50–6. • **77**. McLynn, *Jacobite Army*, pp. 1–8. • **78**. Western, *English Militia*, pp. 72–3. • **79**. Ibid., p. 210. • **80**. Jarvis, *Collected Papers on the Jacobite Risings*, i, passim. • **81**. Staffordshire County Record Office, MSS D/798/3/1/1. • **82**. Add. MSS 29, 913, f. 14. • **83**. See, for example *An Address to that Honest Part of the Nation Called the Lower Sort of*

People on the Subject of Popery and the Pretender (1745); *Gentleman's Magazine*, 15 (1745), pp. 522–6. • **84**. Reprinted in James Ray, *History of the Rebellion* (1749), pp. 72–6. • **85**. For the (convincing) thesis that Jacobitism did not really die until 1759 see Doron Zimmermann, *The Jacobite Movement in Scotland and Exile, 1746–1759* (Basingstoke, 2003). • **86**. Monod, *Jacobitism*, pp. 269–71. • **87**. For a very negative view of this trio see Cruickshanks, *Political Untouchables*, pp. 60–1; cf. also Linda Colley, *In Defiance of Oligarchy: The Tory Party, 1714–1760* (Cambridge, 1982), p. 34; Sedgwick, *History of Parliament*, i, pp. 441, 585; ii, p. 445; Gabriel Glickman, 'The Career of Sir John Hynde Cotton', *Historical Journal*, 46 (2003), pp. 817–41. • **88**. Monod, *Jacobitism*, p. 295. • **89**. Horspool, *English Rebel*, p. 302. • **90**. RA Stuart, 310/139. • **91**. Monod, *Jacobitism*, pp. 271–306. • **92**. This was particularly a feature of the thinking of George Keith, 9th Earl Marischal: see Edith Cuthell, *The Scottish Friend of Frederick the Great*, 2 vols (1915), passim. See also James Francis Stuart (the Pretender)'s manifestos at RA Stuart, 161/3–13 and 162/47–58. • **93**. McLynn, *Crime and Punishment*, pp. 156–71. For James's disdain for coining see RA Stuart, 101/110. • **94**. Frank McLynn, *Jews, Radicals and Americans in the Jacobite World-View* (Royal Stuart Papers, 1987). • **95**. For Jacobites and the world of espionage see Frank McLynn, *The Jacobites* (1985), pp. 171–87 and, at greater length, Hugh Douglas, *Jacobite Spy Wars: Moles, Rogues and Treachery* (1999). • **96**. 'The eighteenth century was developing towards a society in which politicisation was possible, and Jacobitism definitely promoted this trend; but it took the economic changes of the period after 1760, and the effects of the long and arduous conflict between 1792 and 1815, to mobilise huge segments of the population.' Monod, *Jacobitism*, p. 264. • **97**. A. Remond, *John Holker* (Paris, 1944); Albert Nicholson, 'Lieutenant John Holker', *Transactions of the Lancashire and Cheshire Antiquarian Society*, 9 (1891), pp. 147–54. • **98**. RA Stuart, Box 1/454. • **99**. In principle, there can be no definitive answer to this vexed question. For the issues involved see A. G. Hopkins, 'Back to the Future: From National History to Imperial History', *PP* 164 (1999), pp. 198–243; Natasha Glaisyer, 'Networking: Trade and Exchange in the Eighteenth Century British Empire', *Historical Journal*, 47 (2004), pp. 451–76. For some other pointers see Nicholas P. Canning, *The Origins of Empire* (Oxford, 2001) and P. J. Marshall, *The Eighteenth Century* (Oxford, 1998). • **100**. Robert A. Ferguson, 'The Commonalities of Common Sense', *William and Mary Quarterly*, 57 (2000), pp. 465–504. See also 'Commonsense', one of Bernard Bailyn's essays in Bernard Bailyn, *Faces of Revolution: Personalities and Themes in the Struggle for American Independence* (NY, 1990). • **101**. See McLynn, *France*, passim. • **102**. Rosalind Mitchison, *Essays in Eighteenth-Century History* (1966), p. 263; Gerald B. Hertz, 'England and the Ostend Company', *EHR*, 22 (1907), pp. 255–79. • **103**. John Miller, *Charles II* (1991) pp. 93, 99; Phyllis S. Lachs, 'Parliament and Foreign Policy under the Later Stuarts', *Albion*, 7 (1975), pp. 41–54. • **104**. Jeremy Black, *Natural and Necessary Enemies: Anglo-French Relations in the Eighteenth Century* (1986); H. Leclerq, *Histoire de la Régence pendant la minorité de Louis XV*, 3 vols (Paris, 1922); James Brock Perkins, *France Under the Regency* (1892). • **105**. Pierre André O'Heguerty to Maurepas, 30 October 1745, Maurepas Papers, Cornell University, Ithaca, NY; O'Heguerty to Comte d'Argenson, 4 October 1745, ibid. • **106**. RA Stuart, 93/20, 189/95. • **107**. *The Calm Address to All Parties, Whether Protestant or Catholick, on the Score of the Present Rebellion* (1745). • **108**. T. B. Howells, *A Complete Collection of State Trials*, 34 vols (1828), 18, p. 499. • **109**. Ministry of Foreign Affairs France, Quai d'Orsay, Archives Etrangères, Mémoires et Documents, Angleterre, 52, f. 38. • **110**. Rohan Butler, *Choiseul* (1981), p. 624. • **111**. Sir William Blackstone, *Commentaries on the Laws of England*, 4 vols (1783), iv, pp. 115–16. • **112**. For Sir William Temple (1628–99) see Pierre Marambaud, *Sir William Temple, sa vie, son oeuvre* (Paris, 1968). For Sir James Harrington (1611–77) see J. G. A. Pocock, *The Political Works of James Harrington* (Cambridge, 1977). Harrington famously argued (in pre-Marxist fashion) in his *Oceana* that property was the cause of political power, not vice versa. • **113**. For his apologia for James II, including this point, see Nathaniel Johnston, *The King's Visitorial Power Asserted* (1688). • **114**. HMC, v. pp. 188–9. • **115**. RA Stuart, 253/51. • **116**. Jarvis, *Jacobite Risings*, ii, pp. 169–88. • **117**. Walpole to Mann, 27 September 1745, in Lewis, ed., *Walpole's Correspondence*, 19, p. 116. • **118**. Carl L. Klose, *Memoirs of Prince Charles Stuart, Count of Albany* (1845), p. 238. • **119**. C. Haydon, *Anti-Catholicism in Eighteenth-Century England* (Manchester, 1993). • **120**. RA Stuart, 78/181. • **121**. For Shippen (1673–1743) see Stephen W. Baskerville, 'Shippen, William', *ODNB* (Oxford, 2004), 50, pp. 381–3. • **122**. Frank McLynn, 'Ireland and the Jacobite Rising of 1745', *Irish Sword*, 13 (1979), pp. 339–52. • **123**. A. A. Luce and T. E. Jessop, eds, *The Works of George Berkeley* (1957), vi, pp. 229–30. • **124**. John Wells and Douglas Wills, 'Revolution, Restoration and Debt Repudiation', *Journal of Economic History*, 60 (2000), pp. 418–41 (at p. 424). • **125**. P. G. M. Dickson, *The Financial Revolution in England: A Study in the Development of Public Credit, 1688–1756* (1967). • **126**. Wells and Wills, 'Revolution, Restoration and Debt Repudiation', p. 423. • **127**. *Calm Address*; cf. also RA Stuart, 169/19. • **128**. *A Full Collection of the Proclamations and Order issued by Order of Charles, Prince of Wales* (Glasgow 1746) p. 29. • **129**. O'Heguerty in Maurepas Papers. • **130**. RA Stuart, 278/129. • **131**. Frank O'Gorman, *The Long Eighteenth Century* (1997), p. 154. • **132**. HMC, 15, vii, p. 333. • **133**. Sedgwick, *History of Parliament*, i, pp. 515–17. • **134**. K. G. Feiling, *The Second Tory Party, 1714–1832* (1959), p. 17. • **135**. A. F. Steuart, ed., *The Woodhouseless MSS* (Edinburgh, 1907), p. 89; *British Magazine*, 1746, p. 192. • **136**. Add. MSS 35, 886, f. 60. For acknowledgement of the correlation between Jacobitism and financial ruin by a hostile observer see G. C. Mounsey, *Carlisle in 1745* (1846), p. 232. • **137**. Hughes, *North Country Life*, i, p. xvii. • **138**. RA Stuart, 130/133. • **139**. RA Stuart, 205/16. • **140**. Daniel Defoe, 'The Fears and Sentiments of All True Britons with respect to Public Credit', in Walter Scott, ed., *The Somers Collection of Tracts* (NY, 1965), pp. 8–9; David Hume, 'Of Public Credit', in Hume, *Philosophical Works* (1826), pp. 196–203. See also Eugene Rotwein, ed., *Writings on Economics by David Hume* (Madison, 1955), pp. 207–14; Stephen Copley and Andrew Eiger, eds, *Hume: Selected Essays* (NY, 1993); John Christian Lanssen and Greg Coolidge, 'David Hume and Public Debt: Crying Wolf?', *Hume Studies*, 20 (1994), pp. 143–9. • **141**. Wells and Wills, 'Revolution, Restoration', esp. pp. 430–4. See also R. B. Ekelund and R. D. Tollison, *Political Economies: Monarchy, Monopoly Mercantilism* (Texas, 1997); Larry Neal, 'Integration of International Capital Markets: Quantitative Evidence from the Eighteenth to the Twentieth Centuries', *Journal of Economic History*, 45 (1985), pp. 219–26; Larry Neal, *The Rise of Financial Capitalism: International Capital Markets in the Age of Reason* (Cambridge, 1990). • **142**. C. Douglas North and Barry Weingart, 'Constitutions and Commitments: The Evolution of Institutions Governing Public Choice in Seventeenth-Century England', *Journal of Economic History*, 49 (1989), pp. 803–32. • **143**. Pittock, *Myth of the Jacobite Clans*, pp. 2, 64.

10 *The Advent of the Chartists*

1. For some very different estimates of Wilkes and his movement see George Rudé, *Wilkes and Liberty: A Social Study of 1763 to 1774* (1982); D. G. Thomas, *John Wilkes: A Friend to Liberty* (1996); Arthur H. Cash, *John Wilkes: The Scandalous Father of Liberty* (Yale, 2006). • **2**. John Nicholson, *The Great Liberty Riot of 1780* (1985); George Rudé, 'The Gordon Riots: A Study of the Rioters and Their Victims', *TRHS*, 5th series, 6 (1956), pp. 93–114. • **3**. There have been almost as many answers to this question as there are books on the French Revolution. A good starting point is George Rudé, *The French Revolution* (1988). • **4**. See Clive Emsley, 'Repression, Terror and the Rule of Law in England During the Decade of the French Revolution', *EHR*, 100 (1985), pp. 801–26. • **5**. Robert Reid, *The Peterloo Massacre* (1989), pp. 186–7; Joyce Marlow, *The Peterloo Massacre* (1969); pp. 150–1; Michael Bush, *The Casualties of Peterloo* (2005), passim. • **6**. Bush, *Casualties*, pp. 31, 73, 103–5. • **7**. Reid, *Peterloo Massacre*, p. 78. • **8**. Eric J. Evans, *The Great Reform Act of 1832* (1983). There is superb background information on the rotten boroughs and much else in Frank O'Gorman, *Voters, Patrons and Parties: The Unreformed Elector System of Hanoverian England, 1734–1832* (Oxford, 1989). • **9**. D. Hirst, *The Representatives of the*

People? Voters and Voting in England under the Early Stuarts (Cambridge, 1975), p. 105. • **10**. O'Gorman, *Voters, Patrons and Parties*, p. 217. • **11**. See, for example, Norman Gash, *Politics in the Age of Peel* (1951), p. xii; E. A. Smith, *Reform or Revolution? A Diary of Reform in England, 1830–1832* (Stroud, 1992), p. 141. The quote from Giuseppe di Lampedusa is from *The Leopard* (1960), trans. Archibald Colquhoun, p. 40. • **12**. N. C. Edsall, *The Anti-Poor Law Movement, 1834–44* (Manchester, 1971); G. C. and E. O. A. Checkland, eds, *The Poor Law Report of 1834* (1970); M. Blang, 'The Myth of the Old Poor Law and the Making of the New', *Journal of Economic History*, 23 (1963), pp. 151–84. • **13**. E. P. Thompson, *The Making of the English Working Class* (1963), p. 567. • **14**. J. V. Orthro, *Combination and Conspiracy: A Legal History of Trade Unionism, 1721–1906* (Oxford, 1991); M. Chase, *Early Trade Unionism: Fraternity, Skill and the Politics of Labour* (Aldershot, 2000). • **15**. J. Marlow, *The Tolpuddle Martyrs* (1971). • **16**. Patricia Hollis, *The Pauper Press: A Study of Working-Class Radicalism of the 1830s* (Oxford, 1970); Joel Wiener, *The War of the Unstamped: The Movement to Repeal the British Newspaper Tax, 1830–1836* (Ithaca, NY, 1969). • **17**. P. Richards, 'State and Early Industrial Capitalism: The Case of the Handloom Weavers', *PP* 83 (1979), pp. 91–111; Malcolm Chase, *Chartism: A New History* (Manchester, 2007), pp. 20–2; Dorothy Thompson, *The Chartists* (1984), p. 19. • **18**. George Howell, *A History of the Working Men's Association from 1836 to 1850* (Newcastle, 1973); D. J. Rowe, 'The LWMA and the People's Charter', *PP* 36 (1967), pp. 73–86. • **19**. See Joel Wiener, *William Lovett* (Manchester, 1989). • **20**. Gregory Claeys, ed., *The Chartist Movement in Britain, 1838–1850*, 6 vols (2001), i, pp. 110–33. • **21**. Asa Briggs, ed., *Chartist Studies* (1959), pp. 291–2. • **22**. For a more modern analysis see Donald Read, 'Chartism in Manchester', in Briggs, *Chartist Studies*, pp. 29–64; J. F. C. Harrison, 'Chartism in Leeds', in ibid., pp. 65–98; Alex Wilson, 'Chartism in Glasgow', in ibid., pp. 249–87. • **23**. David Goodway, *London Chartism, 1838–1848* (1982), pp. 159–218. • **24**. See A. Clark, *Struggle for the Breeches: Gender and the Making of the British Working Class* (1995), pp. 220–47; E. J. Yeo, ed., *Radical Femininity* (Manchester, 1998), pp. 108–26; H. Rogers, *Authority, Authorship and the Radical Tradition in Nineteenth-Century England* (Aldershot 2000), pp. 80–123. • **25**. Gareth Stedman Jones, 'Rethinking Chartism', in Stedman Jones, *Language of Class: Studies in English Working Class History, 1832–1982* (Cambridge, 1983), pp. 90–183. • **26**. D. Hay and N. Rogers, *Eighteenth-Century Society: Shuttles and Swords* (Oxford, 1997), p. 9. • **27**. Claeys, ed., *Chartist Movement*, ii, pp. 205–95, 369–77; iv, pp. 49–70, 233–7, 287–92; v, pp. 47–53, 77–82. • **28**. For Lovett's view of his feud with O'Connor see W. Lovett, *Life and Struggles of William Lovett* (1876), pp. 158–67. • **29**. Eva Haraszti, *Chartism* (1978), pp. 78–90; Goodway, *London Chartism*, p. 41. • **30**. Goodway,

London Chartism, p. 57; Claeys, ed., *Chartist Movement*, iii, pp. 197–200. • **31**. See R. G. Gammage, *History of the Chartist Movement* (1854), pp. 55–62 and, especially, Haraszti, *Chartism*, pp. 19–40. • **32**. For Stephens's speeches see Claeys, ed., *Chartist Movement*, i, pp. 175–356. • **33**. Quoted in P. A. Pickering, 'The Hearts of Millions: Chartism and Popular Monarchism in the 1840s', *History*, 88 (2003), pp. 227–48 (at p. 238). • **34**. Claeys, ed., *Chartist Movement*, i, p. 214. • **35**. Thompson, *Chartists*, p. 75. • **36**. Edward Vallance, *A Radical History of Britain* (2009), p. 375. Cf. also M. S. Edwards, *Purge This Realm: A Life of Joseph Rayner Stephens* (1994). • **37**. The three most significant biographies of O'Connor are Donald Reid and Eric Glasgow, *Feargus O'Connor: Irishman and Chartist* (1961); James Epstein, *The Lion of Freedom: Feargus O'Connor and the Chartist Movement, 1832–1842* (1982), and Paul Pickering, *Feargus O'Connor* (2009). • **38**. Epstein, *Lion of Freedom*, pp. 39–53. • **39**. H. Rickard, *Memoirs of Joseph Sturge* (1864), p. 313. • **40**. Claeys, ed., *Chartist Movement*, ii, pp. 335–55; Reid and Glasgow, *Feargus O'Connor*, p. 35. • **41**. W. J. Fitzpatrick, ed., *Correspondence of Daniel O'Connell, the Liberator*, 2 vols (1888), ii, pp. 215, 222–3. • **42**. Gammage, *History of the Chartist Movement*, pp. 45, 52, 246–7. The damning quote is from E. L. Woodward, *The Age of Reform* (1949), p. 130. • **43**. G. D. H. Cole, *Chartist Portraits* (1941) pp. 300–36. • **44**. Max Beer, *History of British Socialism* (1920), 2 vols, ii, pp. 9–11. • **45**. Pickering, *Feargus O'Connor*, p. 30–1. • **46**. Ibid., p. 29. • **47**. Chase, *Chartism*, p. 14. • **48**. Claeys, ed., *Chartist Movement*, v, pp. 1–18; Haraszti, *Chartism*, pp. 97–100. • **49**. For his biography see A. Plummer, *Bronterre: A Political Biography of Bronterre O'Brien, 1804–1864* (1971). • **50**. Claeys, ed., *Chartist Movement*, v, pp. 299–442; Haraszti, *Chartism*, pp. 68–77. • **51**. W. J. Linton, *Memories* (1895), p. 42. • **52**. Whether this was mental illness or alcoholism is discussed in Plummer, *Bronterre*. For the eccentric political thinking see Cole, *Chartist Portraits*, p. 262; Thompson, *Chartists*, pp. 101–4. • **53**. Tristram Hunt, *The Revolutionary Life of Friedrich Engels* (2009), p. 90. • **54**. Haraszti, *Chartism*, pp. 90–7. • **55**. F. G. and R. M. Black, eds, *The Harney Papers* (1969), pp. 241–2; A. R. Schoyen, *The Chartist Challenge: A Portrait of George Julian Harney* (1958); Epstein, *Lion of Freedom*, p. 90; John Bedford Leno, *The Aftermath: With Autobiography of the Author* (1892). • **56**. Lovett, *Life and Struggles*, pp. 201–2; Thompson, *Chartists*, pp. 64–70; Haraszti, *Chartism*, pp. 105–21. • **57**. Briggs, ed., *Chartist Studies*, p. 302. • **58**. Thompson, *Chartists*, p. 68. • **59**. Edward Hoyle, *Chartism* (1986), p. 97. • **60**. Haraszti, *Chartism*, p. 46. • **61**. Goodway, *London Chartism*, pp. 24–37. • **62**. F. C. Mather, 'The Government and the Chartists', in Briggs, ed., *Chartist Studies*, pp. 372–405 (at pp. 379–80). • **63**. Claeys, ed., *Chartist Movement*, i, p. 264. • **64**. Chase, *Chartism*, pp. 75–84; cf. also P. A. Pickering, '"And your Petitions" etc: Chartist Petitioning in Popular Politics,

1838–1848', *EHR*, 116 (2001), pp. 386–8. • **65**. Thompson, *Chartists*, p. 60. • **66**. Ibid., pp. 57–8. • **67**. Chase, *Chartism*, pp. 63, 67. • **68**. For the 'sacred month' see ibid., pp. 63–108 passim. • **69**. Boyd Hilton, *A Mad, Bad and Dangerous People? England, 1783–1846* (Oxford, 2000), p. 500. • **70**. There are many biographies of Melbourne extant: Philip Ziegler, *A Life of William Lamb, 2nd Viscount Melbourne* (1976); L. G. Mitchell, *Lord Melbourne* (1997); Dorothy Marshall, *Lord Melbourne* (1976). The hatred of Queen Victoria for the Chartists is in Cecil Woodham-Smith, *Queen Victoria: Her Life and Times*, 2 vols, (1972), i, pp. 190–1. • **71**. Haraszti, *Chartism*, p. 143. • **72**. Mather, 'The Government and the Chartists', p. 378. For a full portrait of Russell see John Prest, *Lord John Russell* (S. Carolina, 1972). • **73**. Chase, *Chartism*, pp. 95–6. • **74**. Thompson, *Chartists*, p. 67. • **75**. J. C. Hobhouse (Lord Broughton), *Recollections of a Long Life*, ed. Lady Dorchester (1909), v, p. 240. • **76**. Chase, *Chartism*, pp. 100–6. • **77**. A. R. Schoyen, *The Chartist Challenge: A Portrait of G. J. Harney* (1958), pp. 80–1. • **78**. Chase, *Chartism*, pp. 105–6. • **79**. Byron Farwell, *Queen Victoria's Little Wars* (1972), pp. 27–31. • **80**. For the connection with Byron see William Napier Bruce, *The Life of General Sir Charles Napier* (1885), p. 94. For that with Burton: see Frank McLynn, *Burton. Snow Upon the Desert* (1990), pp. 35–6. • **81**. W. Napier, *The Life and Opinions of General Sir Charles Napier*, 2 vols (1857), ii, pp. 48–9. • **82**. Ibid., ii, pp. 5–6, 8. • **83**. Ibid., ii, pp. 7–15, 23–8, 32–3, 36, 39, 42–3, 45. • **84**. Ibid., ii, pp. 42, 59, 89. • **85**. Farwell, *Queen Victoria's Little Wars*. • **86**. M. Taylor, 'The Six Points: Chartism and the Reform of Parliament', in O. Aston, R. Fyson and S. Roberts, eds, *The Chartist Legacy* (1999), pp. 1–19. • **87**. David Williams, 'Chartism in Wales', in Briggs, ed., *Chartist Studies*, pp. 220–48; Thompson, *Chartists*, p. 133; A. J. Peacock, *Chartism in Bradford* (York, 1969). • **88**. Chase, *Chartism*, pp. 106–10; Haraszti, *Chartism*, p. 148 • **89**. Since the Newport attack occasioned the most serious loss of life in the Chartist years, it is not surprising that every single major study of the movement has something to say about it. See, for example, Chase, *Chartism*, pp. 106–10; Gammage, *History of the Chartist Movement*, pp. 16–63; J. West, *The Chartist Movement* (1920), pp. 143–4; F. W. Slosson, *The Decline of the Chartist Movement* (1916), pp. 195–200; R. P. Groves, *A Narrative History of Chartism* (1938), pp. 93–9. • **90**. The best estimate of casualties is in D. J. V. Jones, *The Last Rising: the Newport Insurrection of 1839* (1985), which is generally acknowledged as the classic work on the subject (at pp. 154–6). See also John Humphries, *The Man from the Alamo: Why the Welsh Chartist Uprising of 1839 ended in a Massacre* (St Athan, 2004). • **91**. Chase, *Chartism*, p. 110. • **92**. Gammage, *History of the Chartist Movement*, pp. 214–15. • **93**. G. J. Holyoake, *The Life of Joseph Rayner Stephens* (1881), p. 165; see also Claeys, ed., *Chartist Movement*, i, pp. 357–82. • **94**. Pickering, *Feargus O'Connor*, pp. 80–2. • **95**. Napier, *Life*, ii, pp. 82, 88–9. • **96**. Pickering, *Feargus O'Connor*, pp. 80–1. • **97**. Hobhouse, *Recollections*, v, pp. 242–4. • **98**. See Mike Saunders, *The Poetry of Chartism: Aesthetics, Politics, History* (Cambridge 2009). • **99**. Matthew Lee, 'Duncombe, Thomas Slingsby', in *ODNB* (Oxford, 2004), 17, pp. 261–3; Thomas H. Duncombe, *The Life and Correspondence of Thomas Slingsby Duncombe, Late MP for Finsbury* (1868); Ann Mitchel Pfaum, 'The Parliamentary Career of Thomas S. Duncombe, 1826–1861', Ph.D. thesis, University of Minnesota, 1975. • **100**. Chase, *Chartism*, p. 158. • **101**. Schoyen, *Chartist Challenge*, p. 96. • **102**. Haraszti, *Chartism*, pp. 162–3. • **103**. Tom Nairn, *The Enchanted Glass: Britain and its Monarchy* (1994), pp. 205, 327; P. A. Pickering, '"The Hearts of Millions": Chartism and Popular Monarchism in the 1840s', *History*, 88 (2003), pp. 227–48; Friedrich Engels, *The Condition of the English Working Class in 1844* (NY, 1892), p. 259. • **104**. Brian Harrison, 'Teetotal Chartism', *History*, 58 (1993), pp. 193–217. • **105**. Jutta Schwarzkopf, *Women in the Chartist Movement* (1991), pp. 256–8; cf. also Claeys, ed., *Chartist Movement*, ii, pp. 299–313. • **106**. See Hugh Fearns, 'Chartism in Suffolk', in Briggs, ed., *Chartist Studies*, pp. 147–93; R. B. Pugh, 'Chartism in Somerset and Wiltshire', in ibid., pp. 174–219. • **107**. Claeys, ed., *Chartist Movement*, i, p. 244; Chase, *Chartism*, pp. 168–71. • **108**. Aileen Smiles, *Samuel Smiles and His Surroundings* (1956), pp. 70–1. • **109**. Samuel Smiles, *Thrift* (1875), p. 330. • **110**. J. A. Phillips, *The Great Reform Bill in the Boroughs* (Oxford, 1992), pp. 155–6. • **111**. P. A. Pickering, 'Class Without Words: Symbolic Communication in the Chartist Movement', *PP* 112 (1986), pp. 144–62; Claeys, ed., *Chartist Movement*, ii, pp. 359–68. • **112**. Figures taken from Colin Rallings and Michael Thrasher, *British Electoral Facts, 1832–1999* (Ashgate, 2000). • **113**. For Sturge himself see Alex Tyrell, *Joseph Sturge and the Moral Radical Party in Early Victorian England* (1987); Cole, *Chartist Portraits*, pp. 163–86. • **114**. For Sturge's programme see Claeys, ed., *Chartist Movement*, ii, pp. 381–450. • **115**. For O'Connor on Ireland at this time see ibid., pp. 335–55. • **116**. Quoted in Vallance, *Radical History*, p. 399. • **117**. Henry Richard, ed., *Memoirs of Joseph Sturge* (1864), pp. 315–16; Haraszti, *Chartism*, p. 173; Claeys, ed., *Chartist Movement*, iii, pp. 3–102. • **118**. Chase, *Chartism*, p. 197. • **119**. Thomas Cooper, *The Life of Thomas Cooper Written by Himself* (1872), p. 157. • **120**. For the prolonged battle between O'Connor/Chartists and Sturge/NCSU in 1842 see Lovett, *Life*, pp. 283–5; Tyrell, *Sturge*, pp. 129–31; S. Hobhouse, *Joseph Sturge* (1919), p. 78; Cooper, *Life*, pp. 221–7; Thompson, *Chartists*, pp. 268–9. • **121**. See, for example, Haraszti, who rates the 1839 and 1842 agitation as far more serious than that of 1848, in contrast to, say, John Savile in *1848: The British State and the Chartist Movement* (Cambridge, 1987). • **122**. Haraszti, *Chartism*, p. 234. • **123**. John Stevenson, *Popular Disturbances* *in England, 1700–1870* (1979), p. 262. • **124**. Chase, *Chartism*, p. 192. • **125**. Ibid., pp. 203–5. • **126**. Ibid., p. 206. • **127**. F. C. Mather, 'The General Strike of 1842: A Study in Leadership, Organisation and the Threat of Revolution During the Plug Plot Disturbances', in J. Stevenson and R. Quinault, eds, *Popular Protest and Public Order* (1974), pp. 115–35. • **128**. Mather, 'Government', in Briggs, ed., *Chartist Studies*, p. 386. • **129**. Chase, *Chartism*, pp. 223–4. • **130**. Thompson, *Chartists*, pp. 289–90. • **131**. Chase, *Chartism*, pp. 209–27, 229–30, 232–4. • **132**. C. S. Packer, *Life and Letters of Sir James Graham* (1907), i, p. 323. • **133**. Mather, 'Government', pp. 387–9. • **134**. Chase, *Chartism*, pp. 225–6. • **135**. Mather, 'Government', p. 389. • **136**. Robert Fyson, 'The Transported Chartist: The Case of William Ellis', in Owen Ashton, Robert Fyson and Stephen Roberts, eds, *The Chartist Legacy* (1999), pp. 80–101 (at p. 80). • **137**. Mather, 'Government', pp. 390–3.

11 *Chartism's Decline and Fall*

1. H. Richard, *The Memoirs of Joseph Sturge* (1864), p. 318. • **2**. Engels, *Condition of the English Working Class*. • **3**. Plummer, *Bronterre*, p. 177; Claeys, ed., *Chartist Movement*, ii, pp. 427–59; Chase, *Chartism*, pp. 255–6. • **4**. Claeys, ed., *Chartist Movement*, i, pp. 340–1; ii, p. 13. • **5**. J. A. Epstein, 'Feargus O'Connor and the *Northern Star*', *International Review of Social History*, 21 (1976), pp. 51–97 (at pp. 96–7). • **6**. Chase, *Chartism*, pp. 255–6. • **7**. Eric Hobsbawm, *The Age of Revolution* (1962) pp. 41, 48. • **8**. N. McCord, *The Anti-Corn Law League, 1838–1846* (1958), pp. 102–3. • **9**. Cooper, *Life*, p. 178; R. P. Groves, *A Narrative History of Chartism* (1938), p. 126. • **10**. Lucy Brown, 'The Chartists and the Anti-Corn Law League', in Briggs, ed., *Chartist Studies*, pp. 342–71 (at pp. 363–6). • **11**. Thompson, *Chartists*, p. 97. • **12**. Brown, 'Chartists and the Anti-Corn Law League', p. 346. • **13**. Thompson, *Chartists*, p. 97. • **14**. Brown, 'Chartists and the Anti-Corn Law League'; Gammage, *History*, pp. 253–5. • **15**. Pickering, *Feargus O'Connor*, pp. 104–5. • **16**. These points are admirably dealt with in P. A. Pickering and Alex Tyrell, *The People's Bread: A History of the Anti-Corn Law League* (2000). • **17**. Thompson, *Chartists*, pp. 273–6. • **18**. *NY Daily Tribune* (25 August 1872). • **19**. G. D. H. Cole, *A Short History of the British Working Class Movement, 1789–1947* (1948), p. 109. • **20**. Brown, 'Chartists and the Anti-Corn Law League', pp. 366–70. • **21**. Haraszti, *Chartism*, p. 181. • **22**. For O'Brien's 1842 conception see Claeys, ed., *Chartist Movement*, ii, pp. 427–59. For the repudiation of O'Connor's notions see Haraszti, *Chartism*, p. 196. The idea of O'Brien as the brains behind the Land Plan was an idea particularly associated with the volume by Julius West, *A History of the Chartist Movement* (1918). • **23**. Haraszti, *Chartism*, p. 193. • **24**. There are many fine books on this subject. Mark Holloway, *Heaven on Earth: Utopian Communities in America, 1680–1880* (1960); Delores Hayden, *Seven American Utopias: The Architecture of Communitarian Socialism, 1790–1975* (Cambridge, Mass., 1975); William Alfred Hines, *American Communities and Comparative Colonies in America, 1680–1880* (1966); J. F. C. Harrison, *The Second Coming: Popular Millenarianism, 1780–1850* (1979). • **25**. Chase, *Chartism*, p. 248; Thompson, *Chartists*, p. 306. • **26**. For a detailed explanation of O'Connor's scheme see Alice Mary Hadfield, *The Chartist Land Company* (Newton Abbot, 1970). • **27**. Thompson, *Chartists*, pp. 305–6. • **28**. J. S. Mill, *Principles of Political Economy*, Book II, Ch. 10, Section 7. • **29**. J. Bronstein, 'The Homestead and the Garden Plot: Cultural Pressures on Land Reform in Nineteenth-Century Britain and the USA', *European Legacy*, 6 (2001), pp. 159–75 (at p. 168). • **30**. There is a huge bibliography on Owen. Representative titles include G. D. H. Cole, *The Life of Robert Owen* (1930); M. I. Cole, *Robert Owen of New Lanark* (1953); R. H. Harvey, *Robert Owen: Social Idealist* (1949); S. Pollard and J. Salt, eds, *Robert Owen: Prophet of the Poor* (1971). • **31**. J. F. C. Harrison, *Robert Owen and the Owenites in Britain and America* (1969). • **32**. See A. L. Morton, *The Life and Ideas of Robert Owen* (1962). • **33**. L. Kolakowksi, *Main Currents of Marxism* (2005), pp. 150–91. • **34**. Claeys, ed., *Chartist Movement*, iv, pp. 89–232. • **35**. Edward Royle, 'Chartists and Owenites – Many Parts but One Body', *Labour History Review*, 65 (2000), pp. 2–21; Haraszti, *Chartism*, pp. 191–3. • **36**. Claeys, ed., *Chartist Movement*, i, p. xxxv. • **37**. Harrison, *Robert Owen*, pp. 159–60. Cf. also E. Royle, *Robert Owen and the Commencement of the Millennium* (Manchester, 1998). • **38**. Joy MacAskill, 'The Chartist Land Plan', in Briggs, ed., *Chartist Studies*, pp. 304–41 (at p. 339). • **39**. Ibid., p. 339. • **40**. Ibid., p. 323. • **41**. Malcolm Chase, 'The Concept of Jubilee', *PP* 129 (1990), pp. 132–47. • **42**. Claeys, ed., *Chartist Movement*, iii, pp. 407–75. • **43**. Benjamin Wilson, *The Struggles of an Old Chartist* (1887), p. 14; Thompson, *Chartists*, p. 305. • **44**. MacAskill, 'Chartist Land Plan', p. 339; Chase, *Chartism*, p. 275. • **45**. Claeys, ed., *Chartist Movement*, iii, pp. 407–75. • **46**. See the biography by Miles Taylor, *Ernest Jones, Chartism and the Romance of Politics, 1819–1869* (Oxford, 2003). Cf. also Cole, *Chartist Portraits*. • **47**. Taylor, *Ernest Jones*, pp. 77–107. • **48**. Chase, *Chartism*, pp. 276–7. • **49**. MacAskill, 'Chartist Land Plan', p. 324. • **50**. Chase, *Chartism*, p. 275. • **51**. MacAskill, 'Chartist Land Plan', pp. 314, 331–2. • **52**. Bronstein, 'Homestead', pp. 168–71. • **53**. Chase, *Chartism*, p. 331. • **54**. Ibid., p. 273. • **55**. MacAskill, 'Chartist Land Plan', pp. 336–8; Bronstein, 'Homestead and Garden Plot'. • **56**. Eileen Yeo, 'Some Problems of Chartist Democracy', in J. Epstein and D. Thompson, eds, *The Chartist Experience: Studies in Working Class Radicalism and Culture, 1830–60* (1982), pp. 345–80; Chase, *Chartism*, pp. 256–7. • **57**. Pickering, *Feargus O'Connor*. • **58**. Bronstein, 'Homestead', pp. 168–71; Chase, *Chartism*, pp. 328–9.

• **59**. MacAskill, 'Chartist Land Plan', p. 313. • **60**. Gregory Claeys, *Citizens and Saints: Politics and Anti-Politics in Early British Socialism* (Cambridge, 1989), pp. 208–60. • **61**. For the People's International League see Henry Weisser, *British Working Class Movements and Europe, 1815–1848* (Manchester, 1975). • **62**. H. M. Boot, *The Commercial Crisis of 1847* (Hull, 1984). • **63**. Chase, *Chartism*, p. 290. • **64**. Ibid., pp. 282–5. • **65**. Stephen Roberts, 'Feargus O'Connor in the House of Commons 1847–1852', in Ashton, Roberts and Fyson, eds, *Chartist Legacy*, pp. 102–18 (at pp. 105–7). • **66**. Kathleen Quigley, 'Daniel O'Connell and the Leadership Crisis Within the Irish Repeal Party', *Albion*, 2 (1970), pp. 99–107. • **67**. Chase, *Chartism*, pp. 292–4. • **68**. Dennis Gwynn, *Young Ireland and 1848* (Cork, 1949). • **69**. D. Thompson, 'Ireland and the Irish in English Radicalism before 1850', in Epstein and Thompson, *Chartist Experience*, pp. 120–51; see also G. Davis, *The Irish in Britain, 1815–1914* (Dublin, 1991). • **70**. J. H. Treble, 'O'Connor, O'Connell and the Attitude of Irish Immigrants towards Chartism in the North of England, 1838–48', in J. Butt and P. F. Clarke, eds, *The Victorians and Social Protest* (Newton Abbot, 1973), pp. 33–70. See also D. Goodman, *London Chartism, 1838–1848* (Cambridge, 1982), pp. 64–5. • **71**. Benjamin Wilson, *Struggles*, p. 10; Goodway, *London Chartism*, p. 69. • **72**. For the Kossuth analysis see Haraszti, *Chartism*, p. 244. For the 'baboon' remark see Thompson, *Chartists*, p. 311. For 1848 in general there is a huge literature. Jonathan Sperber, *The European Revolutions 1848–1851* (2005), is a good survey. • **73**. Chase, *Chartism*, pp. 294–7. • **74**. Savile, *1848*, pp. 88–9. • **75**. Goodway, *London Chartism*, pp. 70–2. • **76**. John Belchem, 'Feargus O'Connor and the Collapse of the Mass Platform', in Epstein and Thompson, eds, *Chartist Experience*, pp. 269–310. • **77**. Savile, *1848*, pp. 90–1, 103–4. • **78**. Thompson, *Chartists*, p. 311. • **79**. Gwynn, *Young Ireland*, pp. 167–8. • **80**. Mather, 'Government and the Chartists', pp. 394–5. • **81**. A. C. Benson and Viscount Esher, eds, *The Letters of Queen Victoria*, vol. 2, *1837–61* (1907), pp. 198–200. • **82**. Gordon M. Ray, ed., *The Letters and Private Papers of W. M. Thackeray* (1946), ii, p. 364. • **83**. D. Cairns, *Berlioz: Servitude and Greatness* (1999), p. 412. • **84**. Lord John Russell, *Recollections and Suggestions, 1813–73* (1875), pp. 252–3; Mather, 'Government', p. 396. • **85**. L. Strachey and R. Fulford, eds, *The Greville Memoirs* (1938), ii, p. 198; Savile, *1848*, p. 81. • **86**. Spencer Walpole, *The Life of Lord John Russell*, 2 vols (1889), ii, p. 69. • **87**. George Jacob Holyoake, *Bygones Worth Remembering*, 2 vols (1905), i, p. 375. • **88**. For O'Connor in early April see Pickering, *Feargus O'Connor*, p. 133. • **89**. Savile, *1848*, pp. 24, 238–9. • **90**. Ibid., p. 25. • **91**. Goodway, *London Chartism*, pp. 72–4; Savile, *1848*, p. 111. • **92**. Goodway, *London Chartism*, pp. 100–5. • **93**. Mark Almond, *The Springtime of Peoples' Revolutions: Five Hundred Years of Struggle for Change* (1996), p. 96; Haraszti, *Chartism*, p. 226. • **94**. Goodway, *London Chartism*, pp. 131–3. • **95**. The sanest and most convincing estimate, as provided by Goodway, ibid., 130–1. • **96**. The high figure for Chartists is provided in Mark Hovell, *The Chartist Movement* (Manchester, 1966), p. 290; cf. also Elie Halévy, *A History of the English People in the Nineteenth Century*, 6 vols (1961), iv, p. 245. The figure of 175,000 specials is given in Jasper Ridley, *Lord Palmerston* (1970), p. 339 and is raised to 200,000 in T. A. Critchley, *A History of Police in England and Wales* (1978), p. 99 and Elizabeth Longford, *Wellington: Pillar of State* (1972), p. 379. For a good overall summary see R. E. Swift, 'Policing Chartism, 1839–1848: The Role of the "Specials" Reconsidered', *EHR*, 122 (2007), pp. 669–99. • **97**. Goodway, *London Chartism*, p. 139. • **98**. G. P. Gooch, ed., *The Later Correspondence of Lord John Russell, 1840–1878*, 2 vols (1925), i, p. 174. • **99**. For O'Connor as 'yellow' see T. A. Critchley, *The Conquest of Violence: Order and Liberty in Britain* (1970), p. 140. For the correct interpretation see Roberts, 'Feargus O'Connor', pp. 102–18 (at pp. 105–7) and Pickering, *Feargus O'Connor*, pp. 134–5. • **100**. There have been many studies of 10 April 1848 apart from those in Savile, *1848*, pp. 102–20 and Goodway, *London Chartism*, pp. 129–42. The most comprehensive is Henry Weisser, *April 10: Challenge and Response in England 1848* (1983). See also David Large, 'London in the Year of Revolution', in J. Stevenson, ed., *London in the Age of Reform* (Oxford, 1977), pp. 177–211; Stanley Palmer, *Police and Protest in England and Ireland, 1780–1850* (Cambridge, 1988) pp. 484–90. • **101**. Pickering, '"And your petitions"', pp. 383–6. • **102**. Chase, *Chartism*, pp. 312–13, says it was a bad error on O'Connor's part to make this allegation – surely a statement of the blindingly obvious – but does not explain why he thinks that. • **103**. Roberts, 'Feargus O'Connor', p. 113; Pickering, '"And your petitions"', pp. 383–6. • **104**. Chase, *Chartism*, pp. 313–14. • **105**. Here is a (perhaps fanciful) analogy from my own experience. In the Hitchcock film *Rope* (1948), the Nietzschean professor played by James Stewart tells his students that the 'superman' is beyond good and evil, and to him all things are permitted. When two of his students take him at his word and commit the 'perfect murder', he tells them that they have misinterpreted his meaning. But what other meaning *could* his words have had? Similarly, O'Connor advocated a revolutionary violence which was never supposed to be actualised and if anyone – Jones, Harney, McDouall et al. – tried to actualise it, they were immediately denounced and disowned. • **106**. Again, being speculative, one wonders if O'Connor turned to the (by now almost outmoded) process of duelling because of an unconscious association of ideas with O'Connell. Chartists were jeering at O'Connor, saying that he had flopped as badly at Kensington as O'Connell had at Clontarf. Now in some eyes O'Connell's greatest claim to fame was that he had killed John D'Esterre in a duel (1815), and D'Esterre at the time had the reputation as the nation's premier duellist. It is also well known that O'Connell in a fit of remorse thereafter renounced duelling for all time. Might not O'Connor, by issuing the duel challenge, have been trying to go 'one better' than the Liberator? • **107**. P. A. Pickering, 'Repeal and the Suffrage: Feargus O'Connor's Irish Mission, 1849–50', in Ashton, Roberts and Fyson, eds, *Chartist Legacy*, pp. 119–46. • **108**. All quotes are from Savile, *1848*, pp. 120, 126. • **109**. Henry Vizetelly, *Glances Back through Seventy Years: Autobiographical and Other Reminiscences*, 2 vols (1893), i, p. 334. • **110**. Eric Hobsbawm, *Labouring Men* (1964), pp. 297–300; Iorwerth Prothero, 'Chartism in London', *PP* 44 (1969), pp. 76–105; George Rudé, 'Why Was There No Revolution in England in 1830 or 1848?', *Studien über Revolution* (Berlin, 1969), pp. 231–44; Goodway, *London Chartism*, pp. 223–4. • **111**. Henry Solly, *These Eighty Years*, 2 vols (1893), ii, p. 59. • **112**. Thompson, *Chartists*, p. 327; Edward Royle, *Robert Owen and the Commencent of the Millenium* (Manchester, 1998), p. 45. • **113**. P. A. Pickering and S. Roberts, 'Pills, Pamphlets and Politics: The Career of Peter Murray McDouall (1814–54)', *Manchester Region Historical Review*, 11 (1997), pp. 34–83; cf. also Claeys, ed., *Chartist Movement*, v, pp. 1–8. • **114**. Goodway, *London Chartism*, p. 123; Chase, *Chartism*, pp. 317–20. • **115**. Chase, *Chartism*, p. 320. • **116**. Goodway, *London Chartism*, pp. 85–7. • **117**. Chase, *Chartism*, p. 322. • **118**. J. Belchem, 'Britishness and the UK Revolutions of 1848', *Labour History Review*, 64 (1999), pp. 143–58. • **119**. See Armand Coutant, *Quand la République combattait la démocratie* (Paris, 2009); Ines Murat, *La Deuxième République* (Paris, 1987). See also *Collected Works of Marx and Engels* (Moscow, 1969) 7, pp. 130–61. The quote is from A. J. P. Taylor, *Revolutions and Revolutionaries* (1980), p. 80. • **120**. Goodway, *London Chartism*, pp. 93–5. • **121**. Savile, *1848*, pp. 166–9; Fyson, 'The Transported Chartist', p. 80; Chase, *Chartism*, pp. 322–6. For Cufay's biography see Chase, *Chartism*, pp. 303–11. • **122**. Ibid., pp. 332–3. • **123**. For example, Savile, *1848*, inclines to the former view and Haraszti, *Chartism*, to the later. Goodway, *London Chartism*, strongly supports Savile's view: 'It was in 1848 that the English ruling class regarded Chartism as a serious threat *for the first time* [italics mine].' • **124**. Quoted in John Belchem, *Popular Radicalism in Nineteenth-Century Britain* (1996), pp. 93–4. • **125**. Thompson, *Chartists*, pp. 237–70; R. N. Soffer, 'Attitudes and Allegiances in the Unskilled North, 1830–1850', *International Review of Social History*, 10 (1965), pp. 429–54; D. J. Rowe, 'The London Working Men's Association and the "People's Charter"', *PP* 36 (1967), pp. 73–86. • **126**. Savile, *1848*, p. 227; Henry Weisser, 'Chartism in 1848: Reflections on a Non-Revolution', *Albion*, 13 (1981), pp. 12–26. • **127**. Pickering, *Feargus O'Connor*, p. 153–4. See also Pickering, 'The Chartist Rites of Passage Commemorating Feargus O'Connor', in P. A. Pickering and A. Tyrell, eds, *Contested Sites: Commemoration, Memorial and Popular Politics in Nineteenth-Century Britain* (Basingstoke, 2004), pp. 116–17; L. M. Geary, 'O'Connorite Bedlam', *Medical History*, 34 (1990), pp. 125–43. • **128**. Goodway, *London*

Chartism, p. 40. • **129**. Plummer, *Bronterre*. See also Ben Maw, 'The Democratic Anti-Capitalism of Bronterre O'Brien', *Journal of Political Ideologies*, 13 (2008), pp. 201–26. • **130**. Pickering and Roberts, 'Pills, Pamphlets and Politics'. • **131**. There is a huge volume of material on Harney in R. M. Black, *The Harney Papers* (1969). For his time in the USA see Schoyen, *Chartist Challenge*, p. 268; Holyoake, *Bygones Worth Remembering*, p. 111; Ray Boston, *British Chartists in America, 1839–1900* (Manchester, 1971), p.33. Harney was always the most internationally minded of the Chartists. See Iorwerth Prothero, 'Chartists and Political Refugees', in Sabine Freitas, ed., *Exiles from European Revolutions: Refugees in Mid-Victorian England* (2003), pp. 209–33. • **132**. Taylor, *Ernest Jones*, pp. 20–1, 116–28. • **133**. Ibid., pp. 137–255. • **134**. Ibid., p. 258. • **135**. A. Williams, *The Police of Paris, 1718–1789* (Baton Rouge, 1979), pp. 63–4. • **136**. For the army in 1789 see Samuel F. Scott, *The Response of the Royal Army to the French Revolution: The Role and Development of the Line Army, 1787–1793* (Oxford, 1978), pp. 60–1. For the difference between Paris and London in 1848 see C. J. Calhoun, 'Classical Social Theory and the French Revolution of 1848', *Sociological Theory*, 7 (1989), pp. 210–25. • **137**. This is a view argued for in Goldstone, *Revolution and Rebellion*, pp. 332–4. • **138**. Gareth Stedman Jones, *Languages of Class: Studies in English Working Class History, 1832–1882* (Cambridge, 1983), p. 178. • **139**. G. Rudé, 'Why Was There No Revolution in England in 1830 or 1848?' in Harvey J. Kaye, ed., *The Face of the Crowd: Selected Essays of George Rudé* (1988), pp. 148–63. • **140**. Justin McCarthy, 7 vols, *A History of Our Own Times* (1887), i, p. 242. • **141**. Savile, *1848*, p. 207. • **142**. Mather, 'Government'. • **143**. W. H. Maehl, ed., *The Reform Bill of 1832: Why not Revolution?* (NY, 1967), pp. 71–6. • **144**. Mather, 'Government', p. 399. • **145**. John Foster, *Class Struggle and the Industrial Revolution* (1974), pp. 243–6; N. Kirk, *The Growth of Working Class Reformism* (Urbana, Ill., 1985). • **146**. Henry Mayhew, *London Labour and the London Poor* (1861), i, p. 20. • **147**. G. M. Trevelyan, *The Life of John Bright* (1913), p. 185. • **148**. This is the idea elaborated in C. J. Calhoun, *The Question of Class Struggle: Social Foundations of Popular Radicalism During the Industrial Revolution* (Chicago, 1982). The one criticism one can make of the otherwise excellent *The Making of the English Working Class* (1963) by E. P. Thompson is that it assumes a homogeneous monolithic identity of the proletariat and thus comes close to Marx's Hegel-influenced mythical view of the proletariat as 'class for itself'. Perhaps it is significant that Thompson's study ends in 1832, before the Chartists. • **149**. D. Williams, *The Rebecca Riots* (Cardiff, 1955), pp. 150–1, 212–13, 265–93. • **150**. Goodway, *London Chartism*, p. 125. • **151**. Savile, *1848*, p. 121. • **152**. Thompson, *Chartism*, p. 338. • **153**. E. Evans, *The Forging of the Modern State: Early Industrial Britain, 1783–1870* (1983), p. 412. • **154**. Norman Gash, *Aristocracy and the People: Britain, 1815–1865* (1979), p. 3. • **155**. P. Joyce,

Work, Society and Politics (1980); Joyce, 'The Factory Politics of Lancashire in the Late Nineteenth Century', *Historical Journal*, 18 (1975), pp. 525–33; Theodore Koditschek, *Class Formation and Urban Industrial Society: Bradford, 1750–1850* (Cambridge, 1990); Jonathan Sperber, 'Reforms, Movements for Reforms and Possibilities of Reforms: Comparing Britain and Continental Europe', in Arthur Burnes and Joanna Innes, eds, *Rethinking the Age of Reform: Britain, 1780–1850* (Cambridge, 2003), pp. 312–30; Miles Taylor, *The Decline of British Radicalism, 1847–1860* (Oxford, 1995). • **156**. There are numerous excellent surveys of Gramsci's thought in English: T. Bottomore, *A Dictionary of Marxist Thought* (1983), pp. 201–3; Kolakowski, *Main Currents of Marxism*, pp. 963–88; James Joll, *Gramsci* (1977). For a wide-ranging discussion of 'hegemony' see Francis Hearn, *Domination, Legitimation and Resistance* (1978). • **157**. Epstein and Thompson, *The Chartist Experience*, p. 285. • **158**. T. S. Hamerow, *Restoration, Revolution and Reaction: Economics and Politics in Germany, 1815–1871* (Princeton, 1983), pp. 4–6. • **159**. A 'grand slam' argument, uniting 'hegemony' with the 'aristocracy of labour' has been provided for France in 1848: M. Trangoff, *Armies of the Poor: Determinants of Working Class Participation in the Parisian Insurrection of 1848* (Princeton, 1985). • **160**. D. G. Wright, *Democracy and Reform, 1815–1885* (1991), p. 105. • **161**. Ben Brierley, *Home Memories and Out of Work*, ed. Roy Westall, (Bramhall, 2002), p. 23. • **162**. D. Vincent, ed., *Testaments of Radicalism: Memoirs of Working-Class Politicians, 1790–1885* (1977), pp. 141, 211. • **163**. Pickering, *Feargus O'Connor*, pp. 5, 147–51.

12 *The General Strike: Prelude*

1. Phil H. Goodstein, *The Theory of the General Strike from the French Revolution to Poland* (NY, 1984), pp. 2–3. • **2**. H. G. Wells, *An Outline of History* (1920), pp. 225–6. • **3**. Milovad M. Drakhovic, *The Revolutionary Internationals, 1864–1943* (Stanford, 1966) pp. 81–3. • **4**. D. Clayton James, *The Years of MacArthur*, vol. 3, *Triumph and Disaster, 1945–1964* (Boston, 1985), pp. 177–83. • **5**. Iorwerth Prothero, 'William Benbow and the Origins of the General Strike', *PP* 63 (1974), pp. 132–71. • **6**. For detail on the specific issue of the Chartists and the General Strike see Julian West, *A History of Chartism* (Boston, 1920), pp. 53–4, 92–4, 153–69; R. G. Gammage, *History of the Chartist Movement* (NY, 1969), pp. 105–9, 127–30, 144–57; J. T. Ward, *Chartism* (NY, 1973), pp. 113–19, 129–32, 161–73. For Robert Owen see G. D. H. Cole, *The Life of Robert Owen* (1966), pp. 22–31, 253–70. • **7**. Sidney and Beatrice Webb, *The History of Trade Unionism* (1920), pp. 415–17. • **8**. Engels to Friedrich Sorge, 18 April 1891, in Karl Marx and Friedrich Engels, *Werke*, 42 vols (Berlin, 1968), vol. 38, p. 81. • **9**. Engels, *Correspondence*, 3 vols (Moscow, 1959), ii, p. 306. • **10**. T. McCarthy, *The Great*

Dock Strike, 1889 (1988). See also Ben Tillett, *Memories and Reflections* (1931). • **11**. For Lenin on the General Strike, see V. I. Lenin, *Collected Works*, 45 vols (Moscow, 1974), vol. 10, pp. 139–42; 2, pp. 113–15, 213–23; 13, pp. 100–8. • **12**. Goodstein, *Theory of the General Strike*, pp. 120–1. • **13**. Marx and Engels, *Selected Works*, 3 vols (Moscow, 1969), pp. 187–207. • **14**. For Bernstein's thinking on the General Strike see Peter Gay, *The Dilemma of Democratic Socialism* (NY, 1962), pp. 237–9. • **15**. For the many doctrinal twists and turns of Guesde and his followers see Goodstein, *Theory of the General Strike*, pp. 57–60, 64–5, 139–40. • **16**. Rosa Luxemburg, *The Mass Strike and the Junius Movement* (NY, 1971). • **17**. Paul Frohlich, *Rosa Luxemburg, Ideas in Action* (1994), p. 41. • **18**. Milovad Drakhovich, *The Revolutionary Internationals, 1864–1963* (Stanford, 1966) pp. 99–100. • **19**. There is considerable dramatic irony here. The government hard liners in the 1926 General Strike – Joynson-Hicks, Churchill, F. E. Smith (Lord Birkenhead) – were in the mid-1920s admirers of fascism (it has often been observed that Churchill's anti-fascist credentials are really only *anti-Nazi* ones) yet the most famous ideologue of the General Strike was Sorel, himself admired by Mussolini. • **20**. Sorel has attracted a lot of attention. See Richard Humphrey, *Georges Sorel* (NY, 1974); Jeremy Jennings, *Georges Sorel: The Character and Development of His Thought* (NY, 1985); James H. Meisel, *Georges Sorel* (1985). • **21**. For this see Irving L. Horowitz, *Radicalism and the Revolt against Reason* (Carbondale, Ill., 1961), pp. 1–95. • **22**. Georges Sorel, *Matériaux d'une théorie du prolétariat* (Paris, 1919), p. 170. • **23**. Ibid., pp. 70, 184. Perhaps curiously for a revolutionary, Sorel valued the family unit, condemned free love and promiscuity and preached sexual restraint and chastity. Ibid., p. 199. • **24**. For anarcho-syndicalism in its various manifestations see Eugene Pyziur, *The Doctrine of Anarchy of Michael Bakunin* (Marquette, Milwaukee, 1955); F. F. Ridley, *Revolutionary Syndicalism in France* (Cambridge, 1970); David D. Roberts, *The Syndicalist Tradition and Italian Fascism* (Chapel Hill, NC, 1979). • **25**. See especially Sorel, *Reflections on Violence* (1908), Ch. 4. • **26**. Sorel, *Matériaux*, pp. 59–60. • **27**. Isaiah Berlin, *Against the Current: Essays in the History of Ideas*, 2 vols (1997), i, pp. 301–28. • **28**. Jack J. Roth, *The Cult of Violence: Sorel and the Sorelians* (Berkeley, 1980), pp. 1–82. • **29**. Kolakowski, *Main Currents of Marxism*, p. 494. • **30**. For Tom Mann (1856–1941) see Donna Torr, *Tom Mann and His Times* (1956). • **31**. This is a repeated motif in Leon Trotsky, *1905* (NY, 1971). • **32**. Leon Trotsky, *Where is Britain Going?* (1926), p. 82. • **33**. *The Times* (10 March 1925). • **34**. Trotsky, *Where is Britain Going?*, pp. vii, 85. • **35**. Ronald V. Sires, 'Labour Unrest in England, 1910–1914', *Journal of Economic History*, 15 (1955), pp. 246–66. • **36**. Alan Bullock, *Ernest Bevin* (2002), p. 10. • **37**. Joe White, '1910–1914 Revisited', in J. Cronin and J. Schneer, eds, *Social Conflict and Political Order in Modern Britain* (1982), pp. 73–95 (at p. 75). • **38**. Bob Holton, *British Syndicalism, 1900–1914: Myths and*

Realities (1976); R. Douglas, 'Labour in Decline, 1910–1914', in K. D. Browne, ed., *Essays in Anti-Labour History* (1974), pp. 116–23; cf. Keith Laybourne, ed., *Modern Britain since 1906: A Reader* (1999). • **39**. White, '1910–1914 Revisited', p. 80. • **40**. This classic thesis was set out in George Dangerfield, *The Strange Death of Liberal England, 1910–1914* (1936). See also S. Meecham, 'The Sense of an Impending Clash: English Working-Class Unrest Before the First World War', *AHR*, 77 (1972), pp. 1343–64. • **41**. For an attempt to refute the notion that the three internal crises were interconnected see R. Pelling, *Politics and Society in Later Victorian Britain* (1968). White, '1910–1914 Revisited', convincingly demolishes this (see esp. p. 89). For the international 'general crisis' see Leonard H. Haimson and Charles Tilly, eds, *Strikes, Wars and Revolutions in an International Context: Strike Waves in the Late Nineteenth and Early Twentieth Centuries* (Cambridge, 1989). • **42**. For the geographical spread and heterogeneity of the phenomenon the following are indicative: W. Corpi and M. Shalev, 'Strikes, Industrial Relations and Class Conflict in Capitalist Societies', *British Journal of Sociology*, 30 (1979), pp. 164–87; J. E. Cronin, 'Strikes and Power in Britain, 1870–1920', *International Review of Social History*, 32 (1987), pp. 144–67; Charles Wrigley, *A History of British Industrial Relations, 1875–1914* (Brighton, 1982); William Kenefik and Arthur McIvor, eds, *Roots of Red Clydeside, 1910–1914* (Edinburgh, 1996); J. L. White, *The Limits of Trade Union Militancy: The Lancashire Textile Workers, 1910–1914* (1978); Roy Gregory, *The Miners in British Politics, 1906–1914* (Oxford, 1969). • **43**. G. Dilmot, *The Story of Scotland Yard* (1926), pp. 130–48. • **44**. Chris Howell, 'Constructing British Industrial Relations', *British Journal of Politics and International Relations*, 2 (2000), pp. 205–36. • **45**. Thomas Jones, *Whitehall Diaries*, 3 vols (1969), i, pp. 97–103. • **46**. Margaret I. Cole, ed., *The Diaries of Beatrice Webb, 1912–24* (1952), pp. 167–9. • **47**. Maurice Cowling, *The Impact of Labour, 1920–1924: The Beginning of Modern British Politics* (Cambridge, 1971). • **48**. Walter Citrine, *Men and Work* (1964), pp. 130–2. • **49**. G. D. H. Cole, *Labour in the Coal-Mining Industry* (Oxford, 1923), pp. 162–3. • **50**. W. M. Kirby, *The British Coalmining Industry, 1870–1946. A Political and Economic History* (1977), pp. 12–13, 67. • **51**. J. T. Murphy, *The Political Meaning of the Great Strike* (1924), p. 38. • **52**. Patrick Renshaw, *The General Strike* (1975), p. 41. • **53**. D. G. Butler, *Twentieth-Century Political Facts* (2000) • **54**. For the rise of the Triple Alliance see R. P. Arnot, *The Miners: Years of Struggle: A History of the Miners' Federation of Great Britain* (1953); R. A. S. Redmayne, *Men, Mines and Memories* (1942). • **55**. The miners' representatives were Smillie, Hodges and Herbert Smith, then president of the Yorkshire Miners' Federation. The three industrialists were Sir Arthur Balfour, Sir Thomas Royden and Sir Arthur Dukham. Leo Chiozza Money (1870–1944) was later involved in two sexual scandals. In the first, which involved a 'conversation' with a secretary, Miss Irene Savidge, in Hyde Park in 1928, Money and Savidge were acquitted at a trial for indecency, questions were raised in the House of Commons and the police were criticised for excessive zeal by a tribunal of inquiry. In the second, in 1933, Money was not so lucky. Another 'conversation' ensued, this time in a railway carriage, and this time Money was found guilty of public indecency. A. J. P. Taylor, *English History, 1914–1945* (1965), p. 261. • **56**. C. L. Mowat, *Britain between the Wars* (1955), pp. 31–5. • **57**. Jones, *Whitehall Diaries*, ii, *1926–1930*, p. 19. • **58**. Cole, *Labour in the Coal-Mining Industry*, p. 217. • **59**. Mowat, *Britain Between the Wars*, p. 125. • **60**. For a broad survey see A. Campbell, N. Fishman and D. Howell, eds, *Miners, Unions and Politics* (Aldershot, 1996). • **61**. Cole, *Labour in the Coal-Mining Industry*, pp. 212–13. The comment on civil war is from Mowat, *Britain Between the Wars*, p. 121. • **62**. Philip Gibbs, *Middle of the Road* (1923), p. 132. • **63**. For a survey of Hodges's career see Chris Williams, 'The Odyssey of Frank Hodges', *Transactions of the Honourable Society of Cymmrodorion* (1998), pp. 110–30. • **64**. Quoted in David Howell, *MacDonald's Party: Labour Identities and Crisis, 1922–1931* (Oxford, 2002), p. 116. • **65**. Frank Hodges, *Nationalisation of the Mines* (1920); *My Adventures as a Labour Leader* (1924); cf. Kenneth O. Morgan, *Rebirth of a Nation* (Oxford, 1982). • **66**. John Paton, *Left Turn* (1936), p. 101. • **67**. Quoted in Anne Perkins, *The General Strike: A Very British Strike* (2007), p. 69. • **68**. Taylor, *English History*, p. 240. • **69**. Ibid., p. 120. • **70**. David Marquand, *Ramsay MacDonald* (1977), pp. 378–81. • **71**. H. A. Clegg, *A History of British Trade Unions since 1889*, vol. ii, *1911–1933* (Oxford, 1985), p. 568. • **72**. E. J. Hobsbawm, *Industry and Empire* (1967), pp. 175–6. • **73**. Barry Supple, *The History of the British Coal Industry* (Oxford, 1987), p. 223. • **74**. Citrine, *Men and Work*, p. 132. • **75**. Perkins, *General Strike*, p. 23. • **76**. Bullock, *Ernest Bevin*, p. 252. • **77**. For Montagu Norman see Philip Williamson, 'Norman, Montagu Collet, Baron Norman (1871–1950)', *ODNB* (Oxford, 2004), 41, pp. 18–21. For his appalling behaviour over the Czech gold see David Blaazer, 'Finance and the End of Appeasement: The Bank of England, the National Government and the Czech Gold', *Journal of Contemporary History*, 40 (2005), pp. 25–39. For the treatment by Jung see Frank McLynn, *C. G. Jung* (1996), p. 214. For the more general context in which the British financial establishment played footsie with the Nazis see Neil Forbes, *Doing Business with the Nazis: Britain's Economic and Financial Relations with Germany, 1931–1939* (2000). • **78**. Bernard Attard, *The Bank of England and the Origins of the Niemeyer Mission, 1921–1930* (1989). • **79**. For the trio of Norman, Niemeyer and Bradbury and the context in which they operated see Liaquat Ahamed, *Lords of Finance: 1929, the Great Depression and the Bankers Who Broke the World* (2009). • **80**. Robert Skidelsky, *John Maynard Keynes: The Economist as Saviour, 1920–1937* (1992), p. 203. • **81**. Ibid., p. 188. • **82**. See the entire volume dealing with the genesis of the pamphlet in Donald Moggridge, ed., *The Collected Papers of John Maynard Keynes,* 19 (Cambridge, 1981), i, pp. 357–453. • **83**. For the entire argument see Donald Moggridge, *The Return to Gold, 1925* (Cambridge, 1969). • **84**. Skidelsky, *John Maynard Keynes,* p. 188. • **85**. John L. Halstead, 'The Return to Gold: A Moment of Truth', *Bulletin of the Society for the Study of Labour History,* 21 (1970), pp. 35–40; Skidelsky, *John Maynard Keynes*, p. 207. • **86**. Skidelsky, *John Maynard Keynes*, pp. 187–207 (esp. pp. 203–4, 206). For a dissenting view see K. C. P. Matthews, 'Was Sterling Overvalued in 1925?', *Economic History Review,* 2nd series, 31 (1986), pp. 572–87. For some other views see Barry J. Eichengreen, *Globalizing Capital: A History of the International Monetary System* (Princeton, 2008); Eichengreen, *Golden Fetters: The Gold Standard and the Great Depression, 1919–1939* (NY, 1995). • **87**. John Gilbert Murray, *The General Strike of 1926* (1951), pp. 68–9. • **88**. *Daily Herald* (31 July 1925); Arthur Pugh, *Men of Steel* (1951), pp. 389–90. • **89**. G. A. Phillips, *The General Strike: The Politics of Industrial Conflict* (1976), p. 69. • **90**. Citrine, *Men and Work,* p. 142. • **91**. Phillips, *General Strike,* p. 67. • **92**. Marquand, *Ramsay MacDonald,* p. 424. • **93**. Bullock, *Bevin,* i, p. 274. • **94**. Renshaw, *General Strike,* pp. 128–9. • **95**. Taylor, *English History,* p. 241. • **96**. M. Kirby, *The British Coalmining Industry, 1870–1946: A Political and Economic History* (1977), p. 78. • **97**. More will be said about Baldwin later. The standard biography is Keith Middlemas and John Barnes, *Baldwin* (1969). • **98**. John Bowle, *Viscount Samuel* (1957), p. 240. • **99**. Quoted in Skidelsky, *John Maynard Keynes,* p. 704. • **100**. Bernard Wasserstein, 'Herbert Samuel and the Palestine Problem', *EHR*, 91 (1976), pp. 753–75. • **101**. John Harris, *William Beveridge: A Biography* (Oxford, 1977), pp. 34–41. • **102**. Michael Hughes, *Cartoons from the General Strike* (1968), pp. 21–2. • **103**. Herbert Samuel, *Memoirs* (1945), p. 184. • **104**. Stephen A. Schuker, *The End of French Predominance in Europe: The Financial Crisis of 1924 and the Adoption of the Dawes Plan* (Chapel Hill, NC, 1976). • **105**. Herbert Wasserstein, *Herbert Samuel: A Political Life* (Oxford, 1992), pp. 276–8. • **106**. Samuel, *Memoirs,* p. 184. • **107**. Pugh, *Men of Steel,* pp. 397–9; Kirby, *British Coalmining Industry,* p. 76. • **108**. Robert Skidelsky, *Politicians and the Slump: The Labour Government of 1929–1931* (1970), p. 24. • **109**. Supple, *History of the British Coal Industry,* p. 240. • **110**. Kirby, *British Coalmining Industry,* p. 86; Middlemas and Barnes, *Baldwin*, p. 397.

13 *The General Strike and Its Enemies*

1. The massive work by Keith Middlemas and John Barnes, *Baldwin: A Biography* (1969), is a sustained case for the defence. More sceptical views are found in Taylor, *English History*, and Mowat, *Britain Between the Wars.* • **2**. Philip Williamson, *Stanley Baldwin: Conservative Leadership and National*

Values (Cambridge, 1999). • **3**. Robert Blake, *The Unknown Prime Minister: The Life and Times of Andrew Bonar Law, 1858–1923* (1955), pp. 491–4. • **4**. Alfred F. Havighurst, *Britain in Transition: The Twentieth Century* (1985), p. 188. • **5**. For Baldwin in the abdication crisis see Middlemas and Barnes, *Baldwin*, pp. 979–1008. These authors defend Baldwin on the rearmament issue on the grounds that public opinion at the time was not ready for rearmament (ibid., p. 772). • **6**. Jones, *Whitehall Diaries*, passim; cf. also C. L. Mowat, 'Baldwin Restored?', *Journal of Modern History*, 27 (1955), pp. 169–74. • **7**. G. M. Young, *Stanley Baldwin* (1952), p. 99. • **8**. *The Times* (25 July 1925). • **9**. F. W. S. Craig, *British Electoral Facts, 1832–1987* (Aldershot, 1989). • **10**. Perkins, *General Strike*, p. 84. • **11**. Taylor, *English History*, pp. 240–1. • **12**. Skidelsky, *Keynes*, p. 232. • **13**. Middlemas and Barnes, *Baldwin*, pp. 168, 260. • **14**. Havighurst, *Britain in Transition*, pp. 188–9. • **15**. The 4th Marquess of Salisbury (1861–1947) was notable mainly for his longevity. As lord privy seal and leader of the House of Lords he was a valuable Baldwin ally, though his natural partner was Churchill, whom he supported especially over Indian Home Rule. Leo Amery was an altogether more substantial political figure. See L. S. Amery, *My Political Life*, 3 vols (1955); John Barnes and David Nicolson, eds, *The Leo Amery Diaries, 1896–1929* (1980); Philip Williamson, *National Crisis and National Government: British Politics, the Economy and Empire 1929–1932* (Cambridge, 1992); David Faber, *Speaking for England; Leo, Julian and John Amery. The Tragedy of a Politial Family Tree* (2005). • **16**. Bridgeman was an ex-Home Secretary (1922–4) with a reputation for harshness. He was notable mainly for being a steadfast Baldwin supporter; see Venn, eds, *Alumni Cantabrigienses*, II, i, p. 376. Just as some politicians are obsessed with foreign affairs to the detriment of matters at home, Neville Chamberlain was always more interested in domestic affairs, and it may have been his lack of interest in foreign affairs that finally brought him to grief. David Dutton, *Neville Chamberlain* (2001); Robert Self, *Neville Chamberlain. A Biography* (2006). • **17**. Robert Rhodes James, *Memoirs of a Conservative: J. C. C. Davidson's Memoirs and Papers, 1910–1937* (1969), p. 255. • **18**. Jones, *Whitehall Diaries*, ii, p. 12. • **19**. The fullest study is by John Campbell, *F. E. Smith: First Earl of Birkenhead* (1983). • **20**. See Rodney Lowe and Richard Roberts, 'Sir Horace Wilson, 1900–1935: The Making of a Mandarin', *Historical Journal*, 30 (1987), pp. 641–62; Leonard Mosley, *On Borrowed Time* (1969); R. J. Câputi, *Neville Chamberlain and Appeasement* (2000). Cato (M. Foot, P. Howard, F. Owen), *Guilty Men* (1940), Martin Gilbert, 'Horace Wilson, Man of Munich', *History Today*, 32 (1982). • **21**. Sir Wyndham Childs, *Episodes and Reflections* (1930). • **22**. *Manchester Guardian* (26 October 1925). • **23**. Robert Benewick, *The Fascist Movement in Britain* (1972), p. 38. • **24**. Margaret Morris, *The General Strike* (1980), p. 381. • **25**. An uncritical biography of Joynson-Hicks is W. A. Taylor, *Jix* (1933). Much better is David Cesarini, 'Joynson-Hicks and the

Radical Right in England after the First World War', in Tony Kusher and Kenneth Lunn, eds, *Traditions of Intolerance: Historical Perspectives on Fascism and Race Discourse in Britain* (Manchester, 1989), pp. 118–39. On the more complex question of Jix's relationship to Nazism see W. D. Rubinstein, 'Recent Anglo-Jewish Historiography and the Myth of Jix's Anti-Semitism', *Australian Journal of Jewish Studies*, 7 (1993), pp. 24–5. For the Red mania in the security services see Perkins, *General Strike*, pp. 63–6. • **26**. Perkins, *General Strike*, pp. 71–2. • **27**. Rhodes James, *Memoirs, of a Conservative*, pp. 169–70. • **28**. Phillips, *General Strike*, p. 98. • **29**. Ibid., p. 97. • **30**. *The Times* (5, 8 October 1925). • **31**. Asa Briggs, *The History of Broadcasting in the United Kingdom* (1961), i, p. 367. • **32**. Robert Graves and Alan Hodge, *The Long Weekend* (1940), p. 148. • **33**. Quoted in Trotsky, *Where is Britain Going?*, p. 136. • **34**. Bullock, *Bevin*, pp. 78, 280. • **35**. See, for example Howell, *MacDonald's Party*, pp. 59, 75; Herbert Morrison, *Autobiography* (1960), p. 111; Bernard O'Donoghue and G. W. Jones, *Herbert Morrison: Portrait of a Politician* (1973), p. 79. • **36**. Trotsky, *Where is Britain Going?*, p. viii. For his devastatingly withering view of Ramsay MacDonald see ibid., pp. 53–70. • **37**. Mowat, *Britain between the Wars*, p. 300. • **38**. Citrine, *Men and Work*, p. 194. • **39**. Morris, *General Strike*, p. 259; Mike Hughes, *Spies at Work* (1994), Ch. 4. • **40**. Ibid. • **41**. Jones, *Whitehall Diaries*, pp. 12–13 • **42**. Ibid. • **43**. Christopher Farman, *General Strike* (1972), p. 73; Perkins, *General Strike*, pp. 86–7. • **44**. Renshaw, *General Strike*, pp. 82, 87. • **45**. Cole, ed., *Diaries of Beatrice Webb* (under 10 September 1926). • **46**. For Smith and his sayings see Jack Lawson, *The Man in the Cap* (1941). • **47**. Citrine, *Men and Work*, pp. 133–4. • **48**. Howell, *MacDonald's Party*, p. 134; Farman, *General Strike*, p. 257. • **49**. See J. Gwynfor Jones, 'Reflections on the Religious Revival in Wales 1904–05', *Journal of the United Reformed Church History Society*, 7 (2005), pp. 427–55. • **50**. For this period in London's career see Alex Kershaw, *Jack London: A Life* (1997), pp. 119–20. • **51**. Gwyn Evans and David Maddox, eds, *The Tonypandy Riots, 1910–11* (Plymouth, 2010). • **52**. Citrine, *Men and Work*, p. 139. • **53**. Ibid., p. 77. • **54**. Howell, *MacDonald's Party*, p. 121. • **55**. W. H. Crook, *The General Strike: A Study of Labor's Tragic Weapon in Theory and Practice* (NC, 1931), pp. 236–7. • **56**. Citrine, *Men and Work*, p. 139. • **57**. Howell, *MacDonald's Party*, p. 120. • **58**. For favourable views of Cook see Paul Davies, *A. J. Cook* (Manchester, 1987), and Paul Foot, *Agitator of the Worst Kind: A Portrait of Miners' Leader A. J. Cook* (1986). • **59**. David Kirkwood, *My Life of Revolt* (1935), p. 231. • **60**. Arthur Horner, *Incorrigible Rebel* (1961), p. 72; cf. also the testimony from Will Paynter, another famous Welsh miner (who led hunger strikes in the 1930s) in *My Generation* (1972). • **61**. Citrine *Men and Work*, p. 210. • **62**. Cole, ed., *Diaries of Beatrice Webb*, p. 116. • **63**. Kingsley Martin, *Father Figures* (1966), p. 162. • **64**. 'Howell, *MacDonald's Party*, pp. 120–1, 134. • **65**. Citrine, *Men and Work*, pp. 155, 209–10, 235–6. • **66**. For this trio see Alan Clinton, *The Trade Union*

Rank and File: Trades Councils in Britain, 1900–1940 (1977), pp. 111–12; A. Hutt, *The Postwar History of the Working Class* (1937), p. 114; *The Times* (24 March 1926). • **67**. For the career of Ben Tillett (1860–1943) see Jonathan Schneer, *Ben Tillett: Portrait of a Labour Leader* (1982). • **68**. Peter Weiler, *Ernest Bevin* (Manchester, 1993), pp. 36–8; Bullock, *Bevin*, p. 236. • **69**. Bullock, *Bevin*, 1, p. 260; Howell, *MacDonald's Party*, p. 187. 'Bevin viewed many senior Labour politicians with a prickliness that degenerated into contempt and hatred.' Ibid., p. 183. • **70**. Hugh Dalton, *Call Back Yesterday* (1953), pp. 273–4; Bullock, *Bevin*, p. 79. • **71**. Cole, ed., *Diaries of Beatrice Webb*, pp. 61, 178. • **72**. Citrine, *Men and Work*, pp. 189, 191. • **73**. Cole, ed., *Diaries of Beatrice Webb*, pp. 146–7. • **74**. Walter Citrine, *Two Careers* (1967), pp. 864–5. • **75**. Citrine, *Men and Work*, pp. 270, 293, 300; Cole, ed., *Diaries of Beatrice Webb*, p. 147. • **76**. John Lloyd, *Light and Liberty: A History of the EEPTU* (1990), pp. 146–53. • **77**. Citrine, *Men and Work*, pp. 314–15. • **78**. For the incessant globetrotting see *Men and Work*, pp. 95–128, 262–6, 274–8, 306–9, 329–44; *Two Careers*, pp. 35–40, 64–87, 97–115, 139–75, 181–91, 206–18, 223–8, 231–8, 318–28, 370. • **79**. Howell, *MacDonald's Party*, p. 194 Citrine, *Men and Work*, pp. 238–40. • **80**. One wag pointed out that whereas most men were either bastards through an accident of birth or were self-made men, Thomas and MacDonald managed to be both. • **81**. Taylor, *English History*, p. 141. Arthur Henderson (1863–1935), 'Uncle Arthur' to the Labour movement, was a member of Lloyd George's War Cabinet in 1916–17 and home secretary in MacDonald's 1924 government. • **82**. Campbell, *F. E. Smith*, pp. 258, 769–70. • **83**. Gregory Blaxland, *J. H. Thomas: A Life for Unity* (1964), p. 211. • **84**. Ibid., p. 212. • **85**. Howell, *MacDonald's Party*, pp. 9–10. • **86**. Jones, *Whitehall Diaries*, i, pp. 133–6. • **87**. Citrine, *Men and Work*, p. 216. • **88**. Ian Kershaw, *Making Friends with Hitler: Lord Londonderry and the British Road to War* (2004), pp. 17–19, 65–6, 108, 128. • **89**. For Channon see Robert Rhodes James, *The Diaries of Sir Henry Channon* (1967). • **90**. J. H. Thomas, *My Story* (1937), p. 63; *New York Times* (9 August 1925); *The Times* (10 May 1926); *Manchester Guardian* (10 May 1926); Citrine, *Men and Work*, pp. 139–40. • **91**. Trotsky, *Where is Britain Going?*, pp. viii, 6–7, 39, 143. • **92**. For the miners' detestation of Thomas and his reputation as a Judas see Citrine, *Men and Work*, pp. 102–3, 130, 153. For the personal dislike see Thomas, *My Story*, p. 111. • **93**. Julian Symons, *The General Strike: A Historical Portrait* (1959), p. 64. • **94**. Thomas, *My Story*, pp. 105–6. • **95**. Blaxland, *J. H. Thomas*, p. 184; cf. Farman, *General Strike*, p. 49. In view of Cook's emergence as the victor in every single recorded debate with Thomas, it seems bizarre to read this comment in an otherwise sound account of the General Strike: 'the contrasting dialectical skills of Bevin, Thomas and Citrine far excelled those of Smithy and Cook' (Phillips, *General Strike*, p. 270). If, however, one means by 'dialectical skills' evasion, prevarication, *suggestio falsi, suppressio veri*, deliberate obfuscation and general double-talk, the statement may be allowed to stand. • **96**. Blaxland, *Thomas*, pp. 152, 161; Trotsky, *Where is Britain Going?*, pp. 152–3. Lord Derby was Edward George Villiers (1865–1948), 17th Earl of Derby, former secretary of state for war and ambassador to France. Lord Astor was Waldorf Astor, 2nd Viscount Astor – see R. Q. J. Adams, 'Astor, Waldorf', *ODNB* (Oxford, 2004), 2, p. 801. • **97**. For the accusation of insanity, made by Thomas to a disbelieving Citrine, see Howell, *MacDonald's Party*, p. 134. Similarly, Huey Long in Louisiana was 'mad', as were Tony Benn and Arthur Scargill in the 1980s. It is curious how the West, which prided itself on its manifest superiority to the Soviet Union during the Cold War, should have adopted the selfsame stance made notorious by the USSR: dissident = insane. • **98**. Renshaw, *General Strike*, p. 134. • **99**. Keith Laybourne, *The General Strike: Day by Day* (1996), p. 30. • **100**. A. J. Cook, *The Nine Days* (1926), pp. 18–24. • **101**. John Lovell, 'The TUC Special Industrial Committee: January–April 1926', in Asa Briggs and John Savile, eds, *Essays in Labour History, 1918–1939* (1977), pp. 36–56. • **102**. Ibid., p. 138. • **103**. Allen Hutt, *The Postwar History of the British Working Class* (1937), p. 153. • **104**. W. H. Crook, *The General Strike; A Study of Labour's Tragic Weapon in Theory and Practice* (1931), pp. 120–44. • **105**. Ibid., pp. 67–102. • **106**. Herbert Morrison, *Autobiography* (1960), p. 111; B. Donoghue and G. W. Jones, *Herbert Morrison, Portrait of a Politician* (1973), p. 79. • **107**. For Briand's machinations see Jean-Marie Mayeur and J. R. Foster, *The Third Republic from its Origins to the Great War 1871–1914* (Cambridge, 1984). • **108**. Citrine, *Men and Work*, p. 138. • **109**. Lovell, 'TUC Special Industrial Committee', pp. 38–9. • **110**. Farman, *General Strike*, p. 50. • **111**. Lovell, 'TUC Special Industrial Committee', p. 39. • **112**. Ibid, p. 42. • **113**. Ibid., p. 43. • **114**. Robert Taylor, *The TUC from the General Strike to the New Unionism* (2000), p. 34. • **115**. Citrine, *Men and Work*, pp. 178, 235. • **116**. Martin, *Father Figures*, p. 162; Jones, *Whitehall Diaries*, ii, pp. 2–3. • **117**. William Beveridge, *Power and Influence* (1953), p. 220. • **118**. For the memoranda see Citrine, *Men and Work*, pp. 143–53. • **119**. Ibid., p. 191. • **120**. Bullock, *Bevin*, p. 300. • **121**. *Hansard* (2 February 1926). • **122**. Jones, *Whitehall Diaries*, ii, p. 5. • **123**. Lovell, 'TUC Special Industrial Committee', pp. 46–9. • **124**. Ibid., p. 45; *The Times* (13 March 1926). • **125**. Lovell, 'TUC Special Industrial Committee', pp. 45–6. • **126**. Ibid., p. 50. • **127**. Samuel, *Memoirs*, pp. 185–6. • **128**, Farman, *General Strike*, p. 63. • **129**. Samuel, *Memoirs*, p. 189. • **130**. Briggs, *History of Broadcasting*, i, p. 374. • **131**. Samuel, *Memoirs*, p. 186. • **132**. Jones, *Whitehall Diaries*, ii, p. 19. • **133**. Taylor, *English History*, p. 236. • **134**. Citrine, *Men and Work*, p. 195. • **135**. Lovell, 'TUC Special Industrial Committee', p. 53. • **136**. Ibid., pp. 37–8. • **137**. Farman, *General Strike*, p. 73. • **138**. Rhodes James, *Memoirs of a Conservative*, pp. 105–7. • **139**. Ibid., p. 193. • **140**. Blaxland, *J. H. Thomas*, p. 186. • **141**. Farman, *General Strike*, p. 246. • **142**. Geoffrey McDonald, 'The Defeat of the General Strike', in Gillian Peale and Chris Cook, eds, *The Politics of Reappraisal, 1918–1939* (1975), pp. 64–87. • **143**. Lovell, 'TUC Special Industrial Committee', pp. 52–3. • **144**. Citrine, *Men and Work*, p. 165 • **145**. Ibid. • **146**. Middlemas and Barnes, *Baldwin*, p. 387. • **147**. Citrine, *Men and Work*, p. 157. • **148**. Keith Feiling, *The Life of Neville Chamberlain* (1946), p. 157. • **149**. Bullock, *Ernest Bevin*, p. 302.

14 *Towards the Abyss*

1. Citrine, *Men and Work*, p. 156. • **2**. Ibid., p. 157. • **3**. Ibid., p. 158. • **4**. Hamilton Fyfe, *Behind the Scenes of the General Strike* (1926), pp. 12–13. • **5**. Pugh, *Men of Steel*, p. 399. • **6**. Citrine, *Men and Work*, p. 159; Thomas, *My Story*, pp. 114–120. • **7**. *The Times* (1 May 1926). Circular 699, giving effect to Circular 636 of 20 November 1925, is reproduced virtually in its entirety in George Glasgow, *General Strikes and Road Transport* (1926), pp. 112, 137–8. • **8**. Citrine, *Men and Work*, p. 160 • **9**. W. H. Crook, *The General Strike: A Study of Labor's Tragic Weapons in Theory and Practice* (North Carolina, 1931), pp. 370–2; R. Page Arnot, *General Strike* (1926), pp. 110–32; see also R. Page Arnot, *The Miners: A History of the Miners' Federation of Great Britain* (1953), pp. 408–16. • **10**. Crook, *General Strike*, pp. 349–51; W. Milne-Bailey, *Trade Unions and the State* (1934), p. 63; W. Milne-Bailey, *Trade Union Documents* (1929), pp. 342–4. • **11**. Citrine, *Men and Work*, pp. 165–6; Crook, *General Strike*, pp. 361–2. • **12**. Jones, *Whitehall Diaries*, ii, p. 27. • **13**. Pugh, *Men of Steel*, pp. 399–400. • **14**. Citrine, *Men and Work*, pp. 166–7. • **15**. Mowat, *Britain Between the Wars*, p. 306. • **16**. Citrine, *Men and Work*, p. 167. • **17**. Rhodes James, *Memoirs of a Conservative*, p. 231. • **18**. Fyfe, *Behind the Scenes*, p. 23. • **19**. Blaxland, *J. H. Thomas*, p. 192. • **20**. Jones, *Whitehall Diaries*, ii, pp. 32–3. • **21**. Farman, *General Strike*, p. 107. • **22**. Thomas, *My Story*, pp. 125–6. • **23**. Thomas Marlowe was a Tory of the extreme Right, notorious for his eager participation in the 1924 Zinoviev Letter fraud (Farman, *General Strike*, p. 162). For his falling out with Lord Rothermere and resignation from the editorship later in 1926 see *Time* (27 September 1926). • **24**. Pugh, *Men of Steel*, pp. 400–1; Citrine, *Men and Work*, p. 171. • **25**. Feiling, *Life of Neville Chamberlain*, p. 157. • **26**. Kingsley Martin, *Father Figures* (1966), p. 162. See also L. S. Amery, *My Political Life* (1953), ii, p. 483; Middlemas and Barnes, *Baldwin*, pp. 408–9. • **27**. Citrine, *Men and Work*, p. 172. • **28**. Thomas, *My Story*, p. 102. • **29**. Citrine, *Men and Work*, p. 172. • **30**. Bullock, *Ernest Bevin*, p. 97. • **31**. The General Council's letter was published next day. It is reproduced in Milne-Bailey, *Trade Unions and the State*, p. 67 and Milne-Bailey, *Trade Union Documents*,

p. 340. • **32**. Citrine, *Men and Work*, p. 218; Bullock, *Bevin*, i, p. 309. • **33**. David Sinclair, *Two Georges: The Making of the Modern Monarchy* (1988), p. 105. • **34**. Citrine, *Men and Work*, p. 173. • **35**. Marquand, *Ramsay MacDonald*, p. 425. • **36**. Marquand, *Ramsay MacDonald*, p. 439, upholds his hero but Bullock, in his assertion that Bevin a) could not have 'bullied' a granite block like Smith and b) in fact did not do so, is more convincing. Bullock, *Ernest Bevin*, pp. 330–1. • **37**. L. J. MacFarlane, *The British Communist Party: Its Origin and Development until 1929* (1966), pp. 156–7. • **38**. *Hansard* (3 May 1926). • **39**. Jones, *Whitehall Diaries*, ii, p. 36. • **40**. Quoted in Perkins, *General Strike*, p. 113. For other views, linking the speech with the *Daily Mail* incident, see *Daily Herald* (3 May 1926); *The Times* (3 May 1926). • **41**. Crook, *General Strike*, pp. 364–5. • **42**. Feiling, *Neville Chamberlain*, p. 157; G. M. Young, *Baldwin* (1952), p. 114. • **43**. Mowat, *Britain Between the Wars*, p. 308. • **44**. For Baldwin's obsession with Lloyd George see Jones, *Whitehall Diaries*, ii, pp. 190–2. • **45**. Mowat, *Britain Between the Wars*, p. 309. • **46**. Citrine, *Men and Work*, p. 184. • **47**. Martin, *Father Figures*, p. 162. • **48**. Citrine, *Men and Work*, p. 175. • **49**. Julian Symons, *The General Strike: A Historical Portrait* (1959), p. 44. • **50**. David Kirkwood, *My Life of Revolt* (1935), p. 231. • **51**. Cole, ed., *Diaries of Beatrice Webb*, p. 91. • **52**. Ibid., pp. 71–2 • **53**. Crook, *General Strike*, p. 425. • **54**. *Liverpoool Echo* (5 May 1926). • **55**. Phillips, *General Strike*, p. 161. • **56**. Ibid., p. 154. • **57**. H. Montgomery Hyde, *Baldwin: The Unexpected Prime Minister* (1973), pp. 270–1. • **58**. R. A. Florey, *The General Strike of 1926: Economic, Political and Social Causes of the Class War* (1981), pp. 100–2, 111–12. • **59**. Arnot, *General Strike*, p. 175. • **60**. The subject of the railways in the General Strike is dealt with in a number of studies: A. J. Mullay, *London's Scottish Railways: LMS and LNER* (2005); Michael R. Bonavia, *The Four Great Railways* (Newton Abbot, 1980); Norman McKillop, *The Lighted Flame* (1950). • **61**. Bullock, *Bevin*, i, p. 317. • **62**. Taylor, *English History*, p. 245. • **63**. Symons, *General Strike*, pp. 52, 143. • **64**. Citrine, *Men and Work*, p. 178. • **65**. Ibid., p. 177. • **66**. Crook, *General Strike*, pp. 373–7; R. W. Postgate et al., *Workers' History of the Great Strike* (1927), pp. 17–32. • **67**. Citrine, *Men and Work*, p. 180. • **68**. *Yorkshire Evening Post* (27 May 1926). • **69**. Perkins, *General Strike*, p. 118. • **70**. Citrine, *Men and Work*, p. 180. • **71**. Ibid. • **72**. Mowat, *Britain Between the Wars*, p. 313. • **73**. Citrine, *Men and Work*, p. 179; Jones, *Whitehall Diaries*, ii, p. 39. • **74**. Ibid., p. 38. • **75**. Cole, ed., *Diaries of Beatrice Webb*, p. 90. • **76**. Ibid., p. 100. • **77**. Lord Moran, *Winston Churchill: The Struggle for Survival, 1940–1965* (1965), p. 247. • **78**. Crook, *General Strike*, pp. 383, 400–1; Milne-Bailey, *Trade Unions and the State*, p. 71. • **79**. Symons, *General Strike*, p. 58; Perkins, *General Strike*, p. 203.

• **80**. For an overall analysis of the *British Gazette* see Fyfe, *Behind the Scenes*, pp. 25–38; Kingsley Martin, *The British Public and the General Strike* (1926), pp. 69–95; Farman, *General Strike*, pp. 125–33. For its encouragement of fascism see R. H. Haigh, D. S. Morris and Anthony R. Peters, eds, *The Guardian Book of the General Strike* (1988), pp. 141–2; cf. also Citrine, *Men and Work*, p. 183. • **81**. Farman, *General Strike*, p. 131; Perkins, *General Strike*, p. 251. • **82**. Hyde, *Baldwin*, p. 270. • **83**. Renshaw, *General Strike*, p. 132. • **84**. Robert Rhodes James, *Churchill: A Study in Failure, 1900–1939* (1970), p. 244. • **85**. Jones, *Whitehall Diaries*, II, p. 36. • **86**. Fyfe, *Behind the Scenes*, p. 25. • **87**. S. J. Taylor, *The Great Outsiders: Northcliffe, Rothermere and the Daily Mail* (1996), p. 249; cf. also J. H. Porter, *Devon and the General Strike* (1926). • **88**. Perkins, *General Strike*, pp. 171–2. • **89**. *Manchester Guardian* (5 May 1926). • **90**. Hamilton Fyfe (1869–1951) was a star journalist, who had covered Blériot's 1909 maiden flight across the English Channel, the overthrow of General Huerta in the Mexican Revolution (1914) and the retreat from Mons in World War One, as well as covering turbulent events in Spain, Portugal and Russia. H. B. Grisditch and A. J. A. Morris, 'Fyfe, Henry Hamilton', *ODNB* (Oxford, 2004), 21, pp. 222–3. For his editorship of the *British Worker* see Farman, *General Strike*, pp. 133–8. • **91**. Fyfe, *Behind the Scenes*, pp. 25–38. • **92**. Perkins, *General Strike*, p. 142. • **93**. Hugh Thomas, *John Strachey* (1973), pp. 57–8. • **94**. Citrine, *Men and Work*, pp. 181–2. • **95**. A. E. Bell, ed., *The Diary of Virginia Woolf*, 5 vols (1980), iii, p. 78; N. Flower, ed., *The Journal of Arnold Bennett*, 3 vols (1933), iii, p. 132. • **96**. Francis Wheen, *Tom Driberg: The Soul of Indiscretion* (2001), pp. 44–5. • **97**. Citrine, *Man and Work*, pp. 182–3. • **98**. Jones, *Whitehall Diaries*, ii, p. 38. • **99**. *Hansard* (6 May 1926); Crook, *General Strike*, pp. 470–1; Keith Laybourne, *The General Strike: day by day* (Stroud 1996) p. 75. • **100**. Crook, *General Strike*, pp. 471–2. For Astbury see P. A. Landon, 'Astbury, Sir John Meir (1860–1939)', *ODNB* (Oxford, 2004), 2, pp. 764–5. • **101**. Cited in Skidelsky, *Keynes*, ii, p. 105. • **102**. A. L. Goodhart, 'The Legality of the General Strike in England', *Yale Law Review*, 36 (1927), pp. 464–85. • **103**. Crook, *General Strike*, pp. 472–3; Martin, *British Public*, pp. 96–109. • **104**. Samuel, *Memoirs*, p. 187. Henry Segrave (1896–1930) was one of the most famous figures of the day. He set three land-speed records, plus the water-speed record, and held land- and water-speed records simultaneously. He was the first person to travel at over 200 mph (in 1927 at Daytona Beach, Florida) and set a land-speed record of 231.45 mph at Daytona Beach in 1929. He was knighted in 1930, but died shortly afterwards while capturing the world water-speed record. He published his autobiography as *The Lure of Speed* (1928). • **105**. *Manchester Guardian* (13 May 1926).

• **106**. Citrine, *Men and Work*, p. 179. • **107**. John Bowle, *Viscount Samuel: A Biography* (1957), pp. 250–1; Citrine, *Men and Work*, pp. 186–7. • **108**. Wasserstein, *Samuel*, p. 286. • **109**. Citrine, *Men and Work*, p. 187. • **110**. Wasserstein, *Samuel*, pp. 289–90. • **111**. Jones, *Whitehall Diaries*, ii, p. 40. • **112**. Wasserstein, *Samuel*, p. 42. • **113**. Ibid., p. 41. • **114**. Citrine, *Men and Work*, pp. 184, 191. • **115**. Ibid., pp. 185–6. • **116**. Ibid., p. 190. • **117**. *Journal of Arnold Bennett*, iii, pp. 133–4. • **118**. Phillips, *General Strike*, p. 223. • **119**. J. K. A. Bell, *Randall Davidson, Archbishop of Canterbury* (1938), pp. 1306–7; Briggs, *History of Broadcasting*, i., pp. 362–77. • **120**. Rhodes James, *Memoirs of a Conservative*, p. 245. • **121**. Ibid., p. 231. • **122**. Cole, ed., *Diaries of Beatrice Webb*, pp. 90–1. • **123**. Bell, ed., *Diary of Virginia Woolf*, iii, p. 77. • **124**. Charles Stuart, ed., *The Reith Diaries* (1975), pp. 94–5. • **125**. John Reith, *Into the Wind* (1949), pp. 108–9; Briggs, *History of Broadcasting*, i, pp. 362–77. • **126**. Rhodes James, *Memoirs of a Conservative*, p. 248. • **127**. Bell, *Randall Davidson*, pp. 1306–7. • **128**. Rhodes James, *Memoirs of a Conservative*, p. 249. • **129**. *Guardian Book of the General Strike*, p. 95. • **130**. *Reith Diaries*, pp. 93, 96; Reith, *Into the Wind*, pp. 108–9. • **131**. Briggs, *History of Broadcasting*, i, pp. 363, 369, 376. • **132**. Reith, *Into the Wind*, pp. 111–12. • **133**. Perkins, *General Strike*, p. 213. • **134**. Briggs, *History of Broadcasting*, i, p. 365. • **135**. Fyfe, *Behind the Scenes*, pp. 63, 75. • **136**. *Spectator* (8 May 1926). • **137**. Bell, ed., *Diary of Virginia Woolf*, iii, p. 80. • **138**. S. Usherwood, 'The BBC and the General Strike', *History Today*, 22 (1972). • **139**. Briggs, *History of Broadcasting*, i, p. 369; A. J. P. Taylor, *English History*, p. 246 • **140**. Cole, ed., *Diaries of Beatrice Webb*, pp. 91–2.

15 *Revolution's Last Chance*

1. Crook, *General Strike*, pp. 387–8, 417–19. • **2**. *Guardian Book*, pp. 82–3. • **3**. Fyfe, *Behind the Scenes*, pp. 58, 68; Scott Nearing, *The British General Strike: An Economic Interpretation of Its Background and Significance* (NY, 1926), pp. 45–6. • **4**. Harold Nicolson, *King George V: His Life and Reign* (1952), p. 418. • **5**. Martin, *British Public*, pp. 90–1. • **6**. Perkins, *General Strike*, p. 206. • **7**. MacFarlane, *British Communist Party*, pp. 156–7, 162. • **8**. Osbert Sitwell, *Laughter in the Next Room* (1958), p. 236. • **9**. Donoghue and Jones, *Herbert Morrison* (1973), p. 80; Citrine, *Men and Work*, p. 186. • **10**. Phillips, *General Strike*, p. 146. • **11**. Citrine, *Men and Work*, pp. 192–3. • **12**. Renshaw, *General Strike*, p. 271. • **13**. Kirkwood, *My Life of Revolt*, p. 232. • **14**. Crook, *General Strike*, pp. 411–12, 415–17. • **15**. *Guardian Book*, pp. 59–60, 65–6, 72–3, 81–2. • **16**. Bell, ed., *Diary of Virginia Woolf*, iii, p. 82. • **17**. For a thorough study of the entire incident and its aftermath see Margaret Hutcheson, *Let No Wheels Turn: The Wrecking of the Flying Scotsman* (2006). • **18**. Phillips, *General*

Strike, pp. 212–13. • **19**. Nearing, *British General Strike*, pp. 71–3. • **20**. *The Times* (12 May 1926). • **21**. Crook, *General Strike*, p. 387. • **22**. Quoted in Mowat, *Britain Between the Wars*, p. 316. • **23**. Milne-Bailey, *Trade Unions and the State*, p. 73; Fyfe, *Behind the Scenes*, p. 60; Perkins, *General Strike*, p. 80. • **24**. Postgate, *Workers' History*, pp. 58–60; E. Burns, *The General Strike 1926: Trades Councils in Action* (1926), pp. 70–2. • **25**. Farman, *General Strike*, p. 184. • **26**. Phillips, *General Strike*, p. 203. For a general survey of the problems in policing strikes in the interwar period see Jane Morgan, *Conflict and Order: The Police and Labour Disputes in England and Wales, 1900–1939* (Oxford, 1987). • **27**. G. C. Peden, 'Wood, Sir Kingsley', *ODNB* (Oxford, 2004), 55, pp. 124–7; Roy Jenkins, *The Chancellors* (1998), pp. 394–400. • **28**. Crook, *General Strike*, pp. 406–10; Postgate, *Workers' History*, pp. 67–8; Nearing, *British General Strike*, pp. 148–65; Arnot, *Miners*, pp. 436–43; Farman, *General Strike*, pp. 172–82. • **29**. For his colourful career see Michael Squires, *Saklatvala: A Political Biography* (1990). • **30**. *Guardian Book*, p. 81. • **31**. Phillips, *General Strike*, pp. 203–4. • **32**. Martin, *British Public*, pp. 52–67; J. T. Murphy, *The Political Meaning of the General Strike* (1926), pp. 89, 120–1. • **33**. MacFarlane, *British Communist Party*, p. 158. • **34**. Nearing, *British General Strike*, pp. 83–97; Burns, *General Strike*. • **35**. Postgate, *Workers' History*, pp. 34–5; Crook, *General Strike*, pp. 402–12. • **36**. Farman, *General Strike*, pp. 162–3. • **37**. Ibid., pp. 165–6; Jones, *Whitehall Diaries*, ii, p. 38. • **38**. Cole, ed., *Diaries of Beatrice Webb*, p. 92. • **39**. *Journal of Arnold Bennett*, iii, p. 148. • **40**. Citrine, *Men and Work*, p. 190. • **41**. For a full analysis see R. I. Hills, *The General Strike in York* (1980). • **42**. Perkins, *General Strike*, p. 160. • **43**. Kingsley Martin, *Harold Laski* (1953), p. 66. • **44**. Symons, *General Strike*, p. 218. • **45**. Alzina Stone Dale, *Outline of Sanity: A Biography of G. K. Chesterton* (Grand Rapids, Mich., 1983), pp. 255–7. • **46**. G. K. Chesterton, *The Return of Don Quixote* (1927), p. 263. • **47**. *Guardian Book*, pp. 62, 68; Bowle, *Viscount Samuel*, p. 257. • **48**. *Guardian Book*, p. 69. • **49**. Ibid., pp. 30, 37, 49, 149. • **50**. Bowle, *Viscount Samuel*, p. 52; *Guardian Book*, p. 76. Peary, Cook and Byrd had all claimed to have reached the North Pole earlier, but the best modern scholarship rejects their claims. • **51**. Robin Page Arnot, *The General Strike, May 1926: Its Origin and History* (1926), p. 201. • **52**. Ernest J. Oldmaster, *Francis, Cardinal Bourne*, 2 vols (1944); Michael J. Walsh, *The Westminster Cardinals: The Past and the Future* (2008), pp. 85–109. • **53**. Fyfe, *Behind the Scenes*, p. 60. • **54**. Ibid., p. 69; Crook, *General Strike*, p. 421; Arnot, *General Strike*, p. 201. • **55**. Feiling, *Neville Chamberlain*, pp. 157–8. • **56**. Jones, *Whitehall Diaries*, ii, pp. 45–7; Nicolson, *George V*, pp. 418–19; Kenneth Rose, *King George V* (1983), p. 341. • **57**. Citrine, *Men and Work*, p. 186. • **58**. Ibid., p. 189; Perkins, *General Strike*, pp. 139–40. • **59**. Citrine, *Men and Work*, pp. 193–4; Samuel, *Memoirs*, p. 190; Wasserstein, *Samuel*, p. 286. • **60**. Crook, *General Strike*, pp. 429–30, 602–3; Arnot, *General Strike*, pp. 225–6; Milne-Bailey, *Trade Union*

Documents, pp. 348–50. • **61**. Farman, *General Strike*, pp. 222–7; Symons, *General Strike*, pp. 241–7. • **62**. Citrine, *Men and Work*, p. 198; Nearing, *British General Strike*, pp. 49–53. • **63**. Thomas, *My Story*, pp. 131–4; A. J. Cook, *The Nine Days* (1926), pp. 20–2 • **64**. Citrine, *Men and Work*, p. 196. • **65**. *The Times* (15 May 1926), (21 January 1927); Sitwell, *Laughter*, p. 242; Wasserstein, *Samuel*, pp. 289–90; Jones, *Whitehall Diaries*, ii, p. 42. • **66**. Martin, *Laski*, p. 66. • **67**. Citrine, *Men and Work*, pp. 197, 199–200. • **68**. Marquand, *Ramsay MacDonald*, p. 439. • **69**. Nearing, *British General Strike*, pp. 49–53. • **70**. Citrine, *Men and Work*, pp. 196–7. • **71**. Ben Turner, *About Myself* (1930), pp. 311– 13. • **72**. Citrine, *Men and Work*, pp. 197–8. • **73**. Bullock, *Ernest Bevin*, p. 117. • **74**. Citrine, *Men and Work*, p. 199. • **75**. Ibid. • **76**. Sitwell, *Laughter*, pp. 237–8. • **77**. Citrine, *Men and Work*, pp. 200–1. • **78**. Bullock, *Bevin*, i, p. 334. • **79**. Citrine, *Men and Work*, p. 202. • **80**. Frederick Winston Birkenhead, *The Life of F. E. Smith, 1st Earl of Birkenhead* (1959), p. 533. • **81**. Turner, *About Myself*, p. 298. • **82**. Crook, *General Strike*, pp. 604–8. • **83**. Hyde, *Baldwin*, p. 273. • **84**. Arnot, *General Strike*, pp. 221–4. • **85**. Bullock, *Bevin*, i., pp. 230, 337. • **86**. Turner, *About Myself*, p. 314. • **87**. Arnot, *Miners*, pp. 446–9. • **88**. *The Times* (13 May 1926). • **89**. *The Times* (15 May 1926); Marquand, *Ramsay MacDonald*, p. 440. • **90**. Campbell, *F. E. Smith*, p. 775. • **91**. Citrine, *Men and Work*, p. 203. • **92**. Crook, *General Strike*, pp. 436–46. • **93**. Perkins, *General Strike*, pp. 246–7. • **94**. Crook, *General Strike*, pp. 441–4. • **95**. Arnot, *General Strike*, pp. 230–9. • **96**. Citrine, *Men and Work*, pp. 204–5. • **97**. Symons, *General Strike*, p. 231. • **98**. Donoghue and Jones, *Herbert Morrison*, p. 80. • **99**. Cole, ed., *Diaries of Beatrice Webb*, p. 98. • **100**. Crook, *General Strike*, p. 601. • **101**. Philip S. Bagwell, *The Railwaymen* (1963), pp. 479–97. For a detailed analysis of the situation on the GWR see C. R. Potts, *The Great Western Railway and the General Strike* (1996). • **102**. Cook, *Nine Days*, p. 20; Thomas, *My Story*, p. 135; Crook, *General Strike*, pp. 452–65, 609–12. • **103**. Mowat, *Britain Between the Wars*, p. 332. • **104**. *Hansard* (26 July 1926). • **105**. F. A. Iremonger, *William Temple* (1948), pp. 337–43. • **106**. Mowat, *Britain Between the Wars*, p. 334. • **107**. *Hansard* (27 September 1926). • **108**. J. R. Raynes, *Coal and Its Conflicts* (1928), pp. 247–82. • **109**. Arnot, *Miners*, pp. 457–506. • **110**. Crook, *General Strike*, pp. 614–22. • **111**. See Francis Williams, *Bevin: Portrait of a Great Englishman* (1952), p. 145. • **112**. Matthew Worley, *Labour Inside the Gate: A History of the British Labour Party Between the Wars* (2005), p. 114. • **113**. Phillips, *General Strike*, p. 281; Farman, *General Strike*, p. 260; Renshaw, *General Strike*, p. 225. • **114**. *The Economist* (20 November 1926). • **115**. Citrine, *Men and Work*, p. 217; Wiliam Camp, *The Glittering Prizes: A Biographical Study of F. E. Smith, First Earl of Birkenhead* (1960), p. 194. • **116**. Citrine, *Men and Work*, p. 218; Farman, *General Strike*, p. 251. • **117**. Mowat, *Britain Between the Wars*, p. 331; Taylor, *English History*, p. 248; Phillips, *General Strike*, p. 287. • **118**. Peter Mathias, *The First Industrial Nation: An Economic*

History of Britain, 1700–1914 (2001), p. 449. • **119**. C. Cross, *Philip Snowden* (1966), p. 221. • **120**. Philip Snowden, *An Autobiography* (1934), p. 730. • **121**. Keith Laybourn, *Philip Snowden: A Biography* (1988), p. 113. • **122**. T. Wilson, *The Downfall of the Liberal Party 1914–35* (1966), pp. 330–4; Roy Jenkins, *Asquith* (1964), p. 514. • **123**. H. H. Asquith, *Memories and Reflections, 1852–1927* (1928), pp. 234–5; cf. also H. H. Asquith, *Speeches by the Earl of Oxford and Asquith* (1927), p. 310. • **124**. Asquith, *Speeches*, p. 310. • **125**. John Campbell, *Lloyd George: The Goat in the Wilderness, 1922–1931* (1977), p. 136. • **126**. Ibid., p. 138. • **127**. Lucy Masterman, *G. F. G. Masters* (1939), p. 61; Campbell, *Goat*, p. 139. • **128**. Asquith, *Memories and Reflections*, p. 236. • **129**. Campbell, *Goat*, p. 136. • **130**. Jones, *Whitehall Diaries*, i, pp. 12–13. • **131**. Francis Stevenson's diary, 15 May 1926, in A. J. P. Taylor, ed., *Lloyd George: A Diary by Frances Stevenson* (1971), pp. 245–6. • **132**. Campbell, *Goat*, p. 137. • **133**. *Manchester Guardian* (21 May 1926); *Morning Post* (21 May 1926); *Westminster Gazette* (21 May 1926). • **134**. Campbell, *Goat*, pp. 143–6. See also Frances Stevenson's diary, 30 May 1926 in A. J. P. Taylor, ed., *My Darling Pussy* (1975), pp. 100–1. • **135**. Skidelsky, *Keynes*, pp. 249–50; Peter Rowland, *Lloyd George* (1975), p. 623. • **136**. 'Financing the Gold Standard and British Politics, 1925–1931', in John Turner, ed., *Businessmen and Politics: Studies of Business Activity in British Politics, 1900–1945* (1984), pp. 105–29. • **137**. Taylor, *English History*, p. 206. • **138**. Ibid., p. 359. For an attempt to defend Thomas see David Howell, '"I Loved My Union and My Country": Jimmy Thomas and the Politics of Railway Trade Unionism', *Twentieth Century British History*, 6 (1995), pp. 145–75. • **139**. Wasserstein, *Samuel*, p. 291; Cole, ed., *Diaries of Beatrice Webb*, p. 121. • **140**. Howell, *MacDonald's Party*, p. 279. • **141**. Citrine, *Men and Work*, p. 236; David Howell, *Respectable Radicals: Studies in the Politics of Railway Trade Unionism* (Aldershot, 1999), pp. 278–81. • **142**. Paul Davies, *A. J. Cook, 1883–1931* (1983), pp. 117–18, 166–7, 194–207. • **143**. Ibid., pp. 146–51; Howell, *MacDonald's Party*, p. 135; Citrine, *Men and Work*, pp. 245–6. Sir Alfred Mond, 1st Baron Melchett (1868–1930) founded ICI in 1926. He served in Lloyd George's postwar coalition government, but in 1926 joined the Conservative Party after finding Lloyd George's proposed land reforms too radical. He was portrayed as Mustapha Bond in Aldous Huxley's *Brave New World* and mentioned in T. S. Eliot's *A Cooking Egg* (1920). See Frank Greenaway, 'Mond family', *ODNB* (Oxford, 2004), 38, pp. 614–19 ; G. M. Bayliss, *The Outsider: Aspects of the Political Career of Alfred Mond, 1st Lord Melchett*, Ph.D. thesis, University of Wales, 1969. • **144**. Howell, *MacDonald's Party*, pp. 135–6, 151–2, 280, 300. • **145**. Citrine, *Men and Work*, p. 210. • **146**. Bell, ed., *Diary of Virginia Woolf*, iii, p. 84. • **147**. *G. K. Chesterton's Weekly* (22 May 1926). • **148**. Perkins, *General Stike*, p. 263. • **149**. Middlemas and Barnes, *Baldwin*, p. 392. • **150**. Martin, *Father Figures*, p. 160; Martin, *British Public*, p. 163. Curiously, Martin's biographer passes over the General Strike in silence: C. H. Rolph, *Kingsley: The Life, Letters and Diaries of Kingsley Martin*

(1973). • **151**. Kirkwood, *My Life of Revolt*, p. 232. • **152**. *Sunday Times* (16 May 1926). • **153**. Cole, ed., *Diaries of Beatrice Webb*, p. 98. • **154**. Morrison, *Autobiography*, p. 113; Jennie Lee, *My Life with Nye* (1980), p. 70 One can see why H. G. Wells lampooned Sidney and Beatrice Webb in *The New Machiavelli* as 'the Baileys' – a pair of bourgeois manipulators of limited intelligence and insight. • **155**. Kirkwood, *My Life of Revolt*, p. 234.

Conclusion: Revolutions

1. Roland Mousnier, *Peasant Uprisings in Seventeenth-Century France, Russia and China* (1970), pp. 305–48. • **2**. Geoffrey Holmes, *Politics, Religion and Society in England, 1679–1742* (1986), p. 258; cf. also W. D. Rubinstein, 'The End of "Old Corruption", 1780–1860', *PP* 101 (1983), pp. 55–86; D. Cannadine, *Lords and Landlords: The Aristocracy and the Towns, 1774–1967* (Leicester, 1980). • **3**. See the discussion in Jeremy Paxman, *The English* (1999), pp. 33–4. • **4**. *Hansard* (13 May 1901). • **5**. Simon Featherstone, *Englishness: Twentieth-Century Popular Culture and the Forming of English* (2009). • **6**. P. A. Sorokin, *Social and Cultural Dynamics*, 4 vols (1941), Appendix. • **7**. Peter Mandler, *The English National Character* (Yale, 2006); cf. also Homayun Sidkey, *Perspectives on Culture* (NY, 2004), pp. 174–8. • **8**. André Maurois, *Les Silences du Colonel Bramble* (1918). • **9**. For the crucial role of sport and gambling in British society see A. Nathan, *Sport and Society* (1958); Geoffrey Gorer, *Exploring English Character* (1955); Ross McKibbin, 'Working Class Gambling in Britain, 1880–1939', *PP* 87 (1979) pp. 147–78 ; Paxman, *English*, pp. 194–201. • **10**. George Orwell, 'The Sporting Spirit', in *Shooting an Elephant and Other Essays* (1950). • **11**. See Roger Mettam and Douglas Johnson, *French History and Society: The Wars of Religion to the Fifth Republic* (1974). • **12**. Richard Besel, '1933: A Failed Counter-Revolution', in E. E. Rice, ed., *Revolution and Counterrevolution* (Oxford, 1991), pp. 129–52. • **13**. Dennis Mack Smith, 'Revolution and Counterrevolution in Modern Italian History', in Rice, ed., *Revolution*, pp. 153–70 (esp. pp. 154, 161, 163). • **14**. Quintin Hoare and Geoffrey Nowell-Smith, eds, *Selections from the Prison Notebooks of Antonio Gramsci* (1998), pp. 125–33, 219–22. For the more general implications of the idea see S. E. Finer, *The Man on Horseback: The Role of the Military in Politics* (1962). • **15**. Philip Thody, *French Caesarism from Napoleon to Charles de Gaulle* (1989). • **16**. Peter Baehr and Melvin Richter, eds, *Dictatorship in History and Theory: Bonapartism, Caesarism and Totalitarianism* (Cambridge, 2004); Alfred Cobban, *Dictatorship: Its History and Theory* (1939). • **17**. Douglas Ostrowski, 'The Mongols and Rus', in Abbott Gleason, ed., *A Companion to Russian History*, (2009), p. 78. • **18**. Leon Trotsky, *Where Is Britain Going?* (1926), p. 127. • **19**. There is a huge literature on all this. The Napoleon–Hitler analogy has proved most popular. See Desmond Seward, *Napoléon and*

Hitler: A Comparative Biography (1988); Claude Ribbe, *Le Crime de Napoléon* (Paris, 2005); Steven Englund, 'Si l'habit ne sied pas . . . la comparison Napoleon–Hitler au debut', *Revue des Deux Mondes* (April 2005), pp. 97–117. For Napoleon–Stalin see A. J. P. Taylor, *From Napoleon to Stalin* (1950), and, more generally, Paul W. Schroeder, *The Transformation of European Politics, 1763–1848* (1996), esp. pp. 392–3. The Napoleon–Stalin comparison is of course implicit in Orwell's *Animal Farm*, as Orwell calls his Stalinist pig Napoleon. For Rousseau–Stalin see Robert Nisbet, *Tradition and Revolt* (1968), and J. L. Talmon, *The Origins of Totalitarian Democracy* (1960). • **20**. Baehr and Richter, *Dictatorship in History and Theory*. • **21**. See especially Mark Hagopian, *The Phenomenon of Revolution* (NY, 1975), pp. 52, 112, 123, 185, 363; Perez Zagorin, 'Theories of Revolution in Contemporary Historiography', *Political Science Quarterly*, 88 (1973), pp. 23–52. • **22**. It is interesting to compare the classic works on the English Civil War by the Marxist Christopher Hill with those of the present-day doyen of Civil War studies, Blair Worden, who does not think the old 'grand theories' even worth a passing mention: Worden, *The English Civil Wars, 1640–1660* (2010). Scholars were unhappy with the Marxist interpretation of the French Revolution even earlier. See Alfred Cobban, *The Social Interpretation of the French Revolution* (1968), where he boldly argued that all social, sociological interpretations of that revolution are either platitudes or a case of trying to fit the facts into an a priori scheme. Ibid., pp. 8–14. • **23**. For a lucid summary see Barrington Moore, *Social Origins of Dictatorship and Democracy* (1966), pp. 111–55; See also Edward L. Ayers, *What Caused the Civil War? Reflections on the South and Southern History* (2005); Michael F. Holt, *The Political Crisis of the 1850s* (1978). • **24**. Brinton, *Anatomy of Revolution*, pp. 130–1 • **25**. Trotsky, *Where Is Britain Going?*, pp. 130–1. • **26**. Carl Sagan, *Dragons of Eden: Speculations on the Evolution of Human Intelligence* (1978), p. 42. • **27**. See the tour d'horizon in my own *Invasion: From the Armada to Hitler* (1987), and, at much greater length, Norman Longmate, *Defending the Island: From Caesar to the Armada* (2001); Norman Longmate, *Island Fortress: the Defence of Britain, 1603–1945* (1991). • **28**. For this aspect of the Armada see T. P. Kilfeather, *Ireland: Graveyard of the Spanish Armada* (1967). • **29**. See John A. Harris, *Without a Trace* (1981); Susan Carey, *The Wave: In Pursuit of the Ocean's Greatest Furies* (2010); Sebastian Junger, *The Perfect Storm* (1997). • **30**. See Hamish Haswell-Smith, *The Scottish Islands* (2004); James Morrisey, *A History of the Fastnet Lighthouse* (2005). • **31**. For the Schrodinger equation see W. J. Moore, *Schrodinger: Life and Thought* (Cambridge, 1992), pp. 219–20. • **32**. François Crouzet, 'The Second Hundred Years War: Some Reflections', *French History*, 10 (1996), pp. 432–50; H. M. Scott, 'The Second Hundred Years War, 1689–1815', *Historical Journal*, 35 (1992), pp. 443–69. • **33**. Wolfe Tone's Journal, 26 December 1796, in T. W. Moody,

R. B. MacDowell and C. J. Woods, *The Writings of Theobald Wolfe Tone, 1763–1798*, vol. 2, *America, France and Bantry Bay* (Oxford, 2002). • **34**. Frank McLynn, *Napoleon: A Biography* (1997), p. 483. • **35**. Barry Cunliffe, *The Extraordinary Voyage of Pytheas the Greek: The Man Who Discovered Britain* (2002). • **36**. This voyage is described in Walter Ford Carter, *No Greater Sacrifice, No Greater Love* (2004); cf. also Ran Levi, 'The Wave that Changed Science', *The Future of Things*, 3 (March 2008); *The Economist* (17 September 2009). • **37**. See Stephen M. Walt, *Revolution and War* (Ithaca, NY, 2006), esp. pp. 18–45; Harvey Starr, 'Revolution and War: Rethinking the Linkage Between Internal and External Conflict', *Political Research Quarterly*, 47 (1994), pp. 481–507. • **38**. Peter Holquist, *Making War, Forging Revolution: Russia's Continuum of Crisis, 1914–1921* (Harvard, 2002). • **39**. Goldstone, *Revolution and Rebellion*, p. 20. • **40**. See, for example, T. K. Rabb, 'The Effect of the Thirty Years War on the German Economy', *Journal of Modern History*, 34 (1962), pp. 40–51. • **41**. M. Morineau, 'Budget de l'étât et gestation des finances royales en France en dix-huitième siècle', *Revue Historique*, 264 (1980), pp. 289–336 (esp. p. 325); R. Harris, 'French Finances and the American War, 1777–1783', *Journal of Modern History*, 58 (1976), pp. 233–58. • **42**. Finer, *Man on Horseback*; Constantine P. Danopoulos and Cynthia Watson, eds, *The Political Role of the Military: An International Handbook* (Westport, CT, 1996). • **43**. See Ezekiel Spanheim, *Relation de la Cour de France* (Paris, 1973). • **44**. Michel Winock, *La Fièvre hexagonale: les grands crises politiques, 1871–1968* (Paris, 1999). • **45**. Particularly significant was the failed right-wing army coup against President De Gaulle in April 1961. See Pierre Abramovici, *Le Putsch des généraux* (Paris, 2011); cf. also Adam Roberts, 'Civil Resistance to Military Coups', *Journal of Peace Research*, 12 (1975), pp. 19–36; Edward Luttwak, *Coup d'Etât: A Practical Handbook* (Harvard, 1969). • **46**. See, for instance, the volume by John J. Johnson, *The Military and Society in Latin America* (Stanford, 1964). • **47**. Carl Watts, 'Killing Kith and Kin: the Viability of British Military Intervention in Rhodesia, 1964–5', *Twentieth Century British History* 16 (2005), pp. 382–416. • **48**. Ian F. W. Beckett, *The Army and the Curragh Incident, 1914* (1986); A. P. Ryan, *Mutiny at the Curragh* (1956). • **49**. A. N. Wilson, *After the Victorians* (2005), p. 106. • **50**. Goldstone, *Revolution and Rebellion*, p. 318. • **51**. Thompson, *The Chartists*, p. 83. • **52**. Trotsky, *Where Is Britain Going?*, pp. 23, 27–8. • **53**. For a full investigation of this see David Vincent, *The Culture of Secrecy, 1832–1898* (Oxford, 1999). • **54**. Ernest Barker, 'Some Constants in the English Character', in Judy Giles and Tim Middleton, eds, *Writing Englishness, 1900–1950* (1995), pp. 55–63. See also, at much greater length, Ernest Barker, *The Character of England* (1942). • **55**. Lewis Namier, *England in the Age of the American Revolution* (1961), pp. 14–15. • **56**. Walter Bagehot, *The English Constitution* (1867: new edition, 1963). • **57**. Ibid., p. 248. • **58**. Tom Nairn, *The*

Enchanted Glass: Britain and its Monarchy (1988), p. 128. • **59**. Ibid., passim. • **60**. See Michael Billig, *Talking of the Royal Family* (1992); Edward Shils and Michael Young, 'The Meaning of the Coronation', *Sociological Review*, 1 (1953), pp. 68–81. • **61**. *Guardian* (27 June 2003). • **62**. Stuart MacIntyre, *A Plebeian Science: Marxism in Britain, 1917–1933* (Cambridge, 1980). • **63**. See Taylor, *English History, 1914–1945*, pp. 162–75. • **64**. See especially the views of Perry Anderson and Tom Nairn as examined by E. P. Thompson in 'The Peculiarities of the English', in *The Poverty of Theory and Other Essays* (1978), pp. 35–91. • **65**. David Hume, *A Treatise on Human Nature*, ed. L. A. Selby-Bigge (Oxford, 1975), Book 1, Part 1, Section 1; cf. 'Custom, then, is the great guide of human life' in Hume, *An Enquiry Concerning Human Understanding*, ed. L. A. Selby-Bigge (Oxford, 1975), Part 1, Section 5. • **66**. Michael Oakeshott, *Rationalism in Politics and Other Essays* (1962), pp. 127, 168. • **67**. J. L. Austin, 'A Plea for Excuses', in J. L. Austin, *Philosophical Essays*, ed. J. O. Urmson and G. S. Warnock (Oxford, 1961), p. 182. • **68**. There have been many critiques of 'ordinary language philosophy' but two of the hardest-hitting and most entertaining are Ernest Gellner, *Words and Things* (1959) and Bryan Magee, *Confessions of a Philosopher* (1998). • **69**. Liah Greenfield, *Nationalism: Five Roads to Modernity* (1992). • **70**. C. H. Williams, *The Making of the Tudor Despotism* (1935); P. Williams, 'A Revolution in Tudor History?', *PP* 25 (1963), pp. 3–8; Joel Hurstfield, 'Was There a Tudor Despotism After All?', *TRHS*, 5th series, 17 (1967), pp. 83–108. • **71**. J. H. Hexter, *Reappraisals in History* (Evanston, Ill. 1961), pp. 133, 144–5. It would be naive, however, to imagine that sheep and thc wool trade always work in a progressive direction. In Spain the migratory flocks of sheep (the *mesta*) and their owners were used by centralising monarchs as a weapon against local elites and landlords: Julius Klein, *The Mesta: A Study in Spanish Economic History* (Harvard, 1920), pp. 351–7. • **72**. C. Tilly, *Coercion, Capital and European States,* AD *990–1992* (Oxford, 1992), pp. 124–32; R. Bremner, *Merchants and Revolution: Commercial Change, Political Conflict and London's Overseas Traders, 1550–1663* (Cambridge, 1993), pp. 713–14. • **73**. Barrington Moore, *Social Origins of Dictatorship and Democracy*, pp. 424–6, 444. • **74**. Ibid., pp. 254–5. • **75**. Ibid., pp. 477–8. • **76**. Thompson, 'Peculiarities of the English'. • **77**. 'Perry Anderson, *English Questions*'. (1992), pp. 15–47 (esp. pp. 20–3). • **78**. Thompson, 'Peculiarities'. • **79**. F. Parkin, 'Working Class Conservatism: A Theory of Political Deviance', *British Journal of Sociology*, 18 (1967), pp. 278–90. • **80**. Ronald Hyam, *Empire and Sexuality: The British Experience* (1991), is the best-known such exposition. • **81**. For full details see Byron Farwell, *Queen Victoria's Little Wars* (1972). • **82**. Trotsky, *Where Is Britain Going?*, pp. 22–3. • **83**. A. W. Ward and G. P. Gooch, eds, *The Cambridge History of British Foreign Policy*, vol. 3, *1866–1919* (1923), pp. 9–10. • **84**. Andrew Thompson, *The Impact of Imperialism on Britain from the Mid-Nineteenth Century* (2005), p. 122;

Ross McKibbin, 'Why Was There No Marxism in Great Britain?' *EHR*, 99 (1984), pp. 297–331 (at pp. 316–17). • **85**. V. I. Lenin, *Imperialism: The Highest Form of Capitalism* (1916), in Lenin, *Collected Works* (Moscow, 1964), 22, p. 281. • **86**. Lenin, *Collected Works*, 13, p. 77. • **87**. Elie Halévy, *England in 1815* (1949), pp. 387–485. The theory was essentially restated and revived in B. Samuel, *The Methodist Doctrine* (1974), esp. pp. 197–8. • **88**. Michael Hill, *A Sociology of Religion* (1973), p. 183. • **89**. Gertrude Himmelfarb, *Victorian Minds* (Gloucester, Mass., 1975), pp. 292–9. • **90**. Gerald W. Olsen, ed., *Religion and Revolution in Early Industrial England: Halévy Thesis and Its Critics* (1990); J. D. Walsh, 'Elie Halévy and the Birth of Methodism', *TRHS*, 5th series, 25 (1975), pp. 1–20. • **91**. Brian W. Gobbett, 'Inevitable Revolution and Methodism in Early Industrial England: Revising the Historiography of the Halévy thesis', *Fides et Historia*, 29 (1997), pp. 28–43; Robert F. Wearmouth, *Methodism and Working Class Movements in England, 1800-1850* (1937). • **92**. J. S. C. de Radius, *Historical Account of Every Sect of the Christian Religion* (1848, republished 2003), pp. 89–90. • **93**. Deborah M. Valenze, *Prophetic Sons and Daughters: Female Preachers and Popular Religion in Industrial England* (1985) – with explicit criticism of the Halévy thesis on pp. 5–11. • **94**. Thompson, *Making of the English Working Class* (1963), pp. 354–70. • **95**. Ibid., p. 393. To an extent Thompson's request was answered in Robert Samuel Moore, *Pitmen, Preachers and Politics: The Effect of Methodism on a Durham Mining Village* (1974), esp. pp. 1–27. • **96**. See, for the mainstream, G. Kitson Clark, *The Making of Victorian England* (Harvard, 1962), p. 22 and, for the Marxist, Victor Kiernan, 'Evangelism and the French Revolution', *PP* 1 (1952), pp. 44–56; George Rudé, *Debate on Europe, 1815–1850* (NY, 1972), p. 132. For a middle-of-the-road position see Alan D. Gilbert, 'Religion and Political Stability in Early Industrial England', in Patrick O'Brien and Roland E. Quinault, eds, *The Industrial Revolution and British Society* (1993), pp. 79–99. • **97**. E. J. Hobsbawm, 'Methodism and the Threat of Revolution in Britain', *History Today*, 1 (1957), pp. 15–24; cf. Hobsbawm, *Labouring Men*, pp. 23–33. • **98**. Hill, *Sociology of Religion*, p. 185. • **99**. H. Clegg, A. Fox and A. F. Thompson, *A History of British Trade Unionism* (Oxford, 1964), pp. 466–70. • **100**. Ross McKibbin, 'Why Was There No Marxism', pp. 297–331. • **101**. Ibid. • **102**. E. P. Thompson, 'The Peculiarities of the English', in R. Miliband and J. Savile, eds, *The Socialist Register* (1965), p. 343. • **103**. McKibbin, 'Why Was There No Marxism', pp. 304–6. • **104**. Gareth Stedman Jones, 'Working Class Culture and Working Class Politics in London, 1870–1900', *Journal of Social History*, 7 (1974), pp. 484–6. • **105**. E. F. Dubin, *The Politics of Democratic Socialism* (1940), p. 235. • **106**. C. F. G. Masterman, *The Condition of England* (1909), pp. 142–3. • **107**. McKibbin, 'Why Was There No Marxism', pp. 317, 322. • **108**. D. McLellan, ed., *Karl Marx, Selected Writings* (Oxford, 1977), pp. 594–5. • **109**. McKibbin, 'Why Was There No Marxism', pp. 330–1. • **110**. Gramsci, *Prison Notebooks*. • **111**. Andrew Thorpe, 'The Only Effective Bulwark against Reaction and Revolution: Labour and the Frustrations of the Extreme Left', in Andrew Thorpe, ed., *The Failure of Extremism in Interwar Britain* (Exeter, 1989), pp. 11–28 (at p. 18). • **112**. Ibid., pp. 27–8. • **113**. See Richard Hefferman, *New Labour and Thatcherism* (2001). • **114**. E. Estorick, *Sir Stafford Cripps: A Biography* (1949), p. 122. • **115**. Arthur Henderson, *The Aim of Labour* (Manchester, 1918), pp. 67–70.

Appendix

1. Clifton B. Kroeber, 'Theory and History of Revolution', *Journal of World History*, 7 (1996), pp. 21–40. • **2**. Alexis de Tocqueville, *The Old Regime and the French Revolution*, trans. Stuart Gilbert (NY, 1955), pp. 176–7. • **3**. Ibid., pp. 195–6. • **4**. For a brief synopsis of Marx's theory it is difficult to improve on L. Kolakowski, *Main Currents of Marxism* (2005), pp. 150–353. • **5**. Karl Marx, *Capital*, Book 1, Ch. 31. • **6**. Peter Boesche, *Tocqueville's Road Map: Methodology, Liberalism, Revolution and Despotism* (MD, 2006), p. 86. My understanding of Tocqueville and his reflections on the French Revolution has also been enhanced by Robert T. Garnett, *Tocqueville Unveiled: The Historian and His Sources for the Old Regime and the Revolution* (Chicago, 2003), and Cheryl Welch, ed., *The Cambridge Companion to Tocqueville* (Cambridge, 2006). • **7**. Jack Goldstone, 'Theories of Revolution: The Third Generation', *World Politics*, 32 (1980), pp. 425–533; John Fortan, 'Theories of Revolution Revisited: Towards a Fourth Generation of Revolutionary Theory', *Annual Review of Political Science*, 4 (2001), pp. 139–87. • **8**. See G. Lebon, *The French Revolution and the Psychology of Revolution* (New Brunswick, 1980). • **9**. Ted Gurr, *Why Men Rebel* (1970), esp. pp. 11, 24–6, 48, 59, 232; Faye Crosby, 'Relative Deprivation Revisited', *American Political Science Review*, 73 (1979), pp. 50–6; Ted Gurr, 'A Causal Model of Civil Strife: A Comparative Analysis Using New Indices', *American Political Science Review*, 62 (1968), pp. 1105–24. • **10**. D. C. Schwartz, *Anger, Violence and Politics* (Chicago, 1973). • **11**. Hannah Arendt, *On Revolution* (NY, 1963), pp. 18–19. 'No revolution was ever made in the name of Christianity prior to the modern age.' Ibid., p. 19. • **12**. James C. Davies, 'Circumstances and Causes of Revolution: A Review', *Journal of Conflict Resolution*, 11 (1987), pp. 247–57; Davies, 'J-Curve of Rising and Declining Satisfactions as a Cause of Revolutions and Rebellions', in Hugh Davies Graham and Ted R. Gurr, eds, *Violence in the Americas: Historical and Comparative Perspectives* (NY, 1969), pp. 671–709. • **13**. Lawrence Stone, 'Theories of Revolution', *World Politics*, 18 (1966), pp. 159–76. • **14**. See, for example, the contrast in the same volume between Richard Bessel, '1933: A Failed Counter-Revolution', in E. E. Rice, ed., *Revolution and Counter-Revolution* (Oxford, 1991), pp. 109–29 (at p. 113) and

Fred Halliday, 'The Third World: 1945 and After', in ibid., pp. 129–52 (at p. 135). • **15**. John Dunn, *Modern Revolutions: An Introduction to the Analysis of a Political Phenomenon* (Cambridge, 1972), pp. 11–12 • **16**. Crane Brinton, *The Anatomy of Revolution* (1953), pp. 42–53, 70. • **17**. Ibid., pp. 38, 54–70. • **18**. Ibid., pp. 101–3. • **19**. Ibid., p. 2. • **20**. See the critique in Torbjohn L. Knutsen and Jennifer L. Bailey, 'Over the Hill? *The Anatomy of Revolution at Fifty*', *Journal of Peace Research*, 26 (1989), pp. 421–431 • **21**. Brinton, *Anatomy of Revolution*, pp. 226–37 • **22**. Edmund Burke, *Reflections on the Revolution in France* (1790), in J. C. Nimmo, ed., *The Works of the Rt Hon. Edmund Burke*, 12 vols (1887), iii, p. 280. • **23**. Chalmers Johnson, *Revolutionary Change* (Boston, 1966), pp. 69–72. • **24**. Ibid., pp. 57, 91. • **25**. Chalmers Johnson, *Revolution and the Social System* (Stanford, 1964), pp. 34–57 • **26**. Ibid. • **27**. Theda Skocpol, *States and Social Revolutions* (Cambridge, 1979), pp. 149–57. • **28**. Ibid., p. 117. • **29**. Ibid., pp. 155–7, 172–3. • **30**. Ibid., pp. 89, 99, 128–37. • **31**. Ibid., pp. 68–74, 78. • **32**. Ibid., pp. 123–4. • **33**. Joel S. Migdal, *Peasants, Politics and Revolutions: Pressures Towards Political and Social Change in the Third World* (Princeton, 1975), p. 216. • **34**. See J. Himmelstein and M. S. Kimmel, 'States and Revolutions: The Implications and Limits of Skocpol's Structural Model', *American Journal of Sociology*, 86 (1981), pp. 1145–54; W. Sewell, 'Ideology and Social Revolutions: Reflections on the French Case', *Journal of Modern History*, 57 (1985), pp. 57–85; cf. also David Parker, ed., *Revolutions and the Revolutionary Tradition in the West* (2000). • **35**. Brinton, *Anatomy of Revolution*, p. 246. • **36**. Regis Debray, *Charles de Gaulle: Futurist of the Nation* (1994), pp. 61–2. • **37**. Kolakowski, *Main Currents of Marxism*, pp. 805–8. • **38**. Jack Goldstone, *Revolution and Rebellion in the Early Modern World* (1991), p. 77. • **39**. Ibid., pp. 37, 45, and esp. pp. 83–117. • **40**. Ibid., pp. 250–68. • **41**. Ibid, p. 477. • **42**. E. A. Wrigley and R. Schofield, *The Population History of England* (Harvard, 1980), pp. 534–5. • **43**. Goldstone, *Revolution and Rebellion*, pp. xxvi, 459–75. • **44**. See, for example, A. S. Cohan, *Theories of Revolution: An Introduction* (NY, 1975); Mark N. Hagopian, *The Phenomenon of Revolution* (1975); Perez Zagorin, 'Theories of Revolution in Contemporary Historiography', *Political Science Quarterly*, 88 (1973), pp. 23–52. • **45**. Respectively, S. N. Eisenstadt, *Revolutions and the Transformation of Societies: A Comparative Study of Civilizations* (NY, 1978); Arendt, *On Revolution*, p. 21. • **46**. R. M. MacIver, *The Modern State* (Oxford, 1966), p. 212. • **47**. Samuel P. Huntingdon, *Political Order in Changing Societies* (1968), pp. 3–5, 32–3, 47–50, 265–76. • **48**. See the summary in Ian R. Christie, *Stress and Stability in Late Eighteenth-Century Britain: Reflections on the British Avoidance of Revolution* (Oxford, 1984), pp. 3–14. • **49**. J. C. D. Clark, 'Revolution in the English Atlantic Empire', in Rice, ed. *Revolution and Counter-Revolution*, pp. 27–93 (at p. 28). • **50**. Charles Tilly, *European Revolutions, 1492–1992* (Oxford, 1995), p. 16. • **51**. James C. Davies, 'J-Curve', in Graham and Gurr, *Violence in the Americas*. Nevertheless, even these waters can be muddied. One influential social scientist described the American Civil War as a *political* revolution (T. S. Kuhn, *The Structure of Scientific Revolution* (Chicago, 1962), p. 93). • **52**. Charles Tilly, 'Changing Forms of Revolution', in Rice, ed., *Revolution and Counter-Revolution*, pp. 1–25 (at p. 3). • **53**. See Paul Preston, *The Triumph of Democracy in Spain* (1981). • **54**. James Defronzo, *Revolutions and Revolutionary Movements* (Boulder, Co., 1991), pp. 171–6. See also Samuel Farber, *The Origins of the Cuban Revolution Reconsidered* (NC, 2006); Marifeli Pérez-Stable, *The Cuban Revolution: Origins, Course and Legacy* (Oxford, 1998). • **55**. Jeff Goodwin, *No Other Way Out: States and Revolutionary Movements, 1945–1991* (Cambridge, 2001), p. 9. • **56**. For the proposition that the 'American Revolution' was not a true revolution see especially M. J. Heale, *The American Revolution* (1986). Skocpol, rightly in my view, takes it for granted that it was not a real revolution. On the non-revolutionary nature of the 'American Revolution' see also Barrington Moore, *Social Origins of Dictatorship and Democracy* (1966). For 1688 as an undistinguished epigone to the 1640s see Lawrence Stone, 'The Results of the English Revolution of the Seventeenth Century', in J. G. A. Pocock, ed., *Three British Revolutions: 1641, 1688, 1776* (Princeton, 1980) pp. 244–62; J. S. Morrill, *The Nature of the English Revolution* (1993). A valiant defence of 1688 as a true revolution is provided by Tim Harris, *Revolution: The Great Crisis of the British Monarchy, 1685–1720* (2006), pp. 512–17. • **57**. Martin Kaufman, ed., *Shays's Rebellion: Selected Essays* (Westfield, Mass., 1987); Leonard L. Richards, *Shays's Rebellion: the American Revolution's Final Battle* (Pennsylvania, 2002). • **58**. Eva Haraszti, *The Chartists* (1978), p. 244. See also C. J. Calhoun, 'Classical Social Theory and the French Revolution of 1848', *Sociological Theory*, 7 (1989), pp. 210–25. • **59**. For theoretical discussions of the Mexican Revolution see W. L. Goldfrank, 'Theories of Revolution and Revolution Without Theory: The Case of Mexico', *Theory and Society*, 7 (1979), pp. 135–65; Dunn, *Modern Revolutions*, pp. 48–69. Noel Parker, *Revolutions and History* (2000), characterises the Mexican Revolution as 'a cross between a late liberal revolution and an early liberation struggle' (p. 34). For a narrative-based tour d'horizon of the Mexican Revolution see my own *Villa and Zapata* (2000). • **60**. See the discussion in Skocpol, *States and Social Revolutions*, p. 303. • **61**. Tilly, 'Changing Forms of Revolution', p. 4.

Index